D1593582

AN ANNOTATED SECONDARY BIBLIOGRAPHY SERIES ON ENGLISH LITERATURE IN TRANSITION

1880-1920

HELMUT E. GERBER

GENERAL EDITOR

W. SOMERSET MAUGHAM

JOSEPH CONRAD

THOMAS HARDY

E. M. FORSTER

JOHN GALSWORTHY

GEORGE GISSING

D. H. LAWRENCE

THE CONTRIBUTORS

Pierre Coustillas
University of Lille

Paul Goetsch
University of Köln

William F. Halloran
University of Wisconsin, Milwaukee

Sidney R. Homan
Boston University

Lewis B. Horne
Colorado College

Robert E. Kuehn
Yale University

J. R. Martin
Faculté des Lettres, Université de Montpellier

W. Jerome Mitchell
University of Georgia

Matti Rissanen
University of Helsinki

Charles Sanders
University of Illinois, Urbana

W. Somerset Maugham

AN ANNOTATED BIBLIOGRAPHY OF WRITINGS ABOUT HIM

COMPILED AND EDITED BY

CHARLES SANDERS

NORTHERN ILLINOIS UNIVERSITY PRESS
DE KALB, ILLINOIS

International Standard Book Number 0-87580-015-7
Library of Congress Catalog Card Number 79-111628
Published by the Northern Illinois University Press, DeKalb, Illinois
Manufactured in the United States of America

Design by John B. Goetz

Preface

The primary purpose of our bibliography is to offer scholars interested in the future assessment of W. Somerset Maugham a *representative* body of the criticism of his works from 1897 through 1968. We have gathered annotations from many countries outside of England and the United States—predominantly from France and Germany—but obviously, these entries cannot pretend to be exhaustive.* Although we have included reviews of stage adaptations by other authors, we have omitted reviews of film adaptations, because, generally speaking, the reviews of plays rendered significant criticism of Maugham's original work, whereas scenario reviews seemed to reveal little, if any, criticism of importance. To avoid unnecessary repetition it seemed advisable to withhold many minor entries of a biographical nature as well as all master's theses and all papers written for undergraduate honors. Dissertations subsequently published as books are annotated according to their final form; those which have been reviewed or have been mentioned in other published studies are briefly annotated here. Newspaper reviews cited by general and individual bibliographies, and as many in addition as we ourselves could unearth, have been annotated; but for comprehensiveness the NEW YORK TIMES and the NEW YORK HERALD TRIBUNE must serve to represent the United States, the TIMES (Lond) to represent England. Newspaper coverage in France, where Maugham obtained perhaps even greater success than in England or America, has been more extensive, and includes generally full citations to COMOEDIA, LE FIGARO (and its various supplements), GRINGOIRE, LE JOURNAL DES DEBATS, LES NOUVELLES LITTERAIRES, and LE TEMPS.**

If the boundaries of our study appear somewhat restrictive, we can confidently say that they encompass a fairly rich area. More than one-half of

*A dozen or more entries, particularly from Japan, have been withheld because of faulty bibliographic information.

**The present bibliography omits many provincial newspapers, to which the reader may refer in W. H. Henry, Jr.'s A FRENCH BIBLIOGRAPHY OF W. SOMERSET MAUGHAM. Charlottesville: The Bibliographical Society of the University of Virginia, 1967.

the entries annotated here have not been listed before in either general or individual bibliographies. When the original masterlist for the study was formed, a check was conducted of the indices of every periodical cited by a general or an individual bibliography; and when indices were either unavailable or unreliable, single issues of these periodicals were checked against the American and English premieres and revivals of Maugham's plays and the American and English publication dates of each of his novels, anthologies, and books of travel and criticism.

Except for solving certain bibliographical problems and correcting some inaccuracies, we have refrained, insofar as it was possible, from rendering personal judgments on the material presented here. Maugham's versatility, his presumably ambivalent feelings toward critics, his longevity, his now legendary *bons mots,* his unusual combination of gravity and frivolity, his personality in general—all have joined to evoke a body of criticism as varied as his career. A genuinely thorough study of Maugham's criticism in any one nation where he found a substantial audience constitutes, to no one's surprise, a study also in the tastes and critical allegiances of several decades; if these allegiances are to be documented adequately, they require, perhaps, several monographs in themselves. In the present study the practice has been to select statements not only pertinent to Maugham's work but revelatory of the tastes and criteria of the critics' and Maugham's age as well; a minimal guide to evaluation is maintained simply by including reviews of all full-length studies of Maugham and by starring comprehensive, detailed reviews and essays.

Conclusions about possible future studies of Maugham have been anticipated over a decade ago by Professor Richard A. Cordell. In the closing passage of his "Somerset Maugham: Lucidity versus Cunning" (ENGLISH FICTION IN TRANSITION, I:3, Fall Special 1958, 30-32), Cordell surveyed the areas of Maugham criticism then unexplored. "What," Cordell asked, "is there to be done by any young scholar who might want to 'work' on Maugham?" He found more than one project to suggest:

> Now that we have the perspective—he [Maugham] wrote his last play a quarter century ago—a careful study of his serious plays could be made (the artificial, or high, comedies have already received much attention), their place in serious modern British drama before 1934 [assessed]. A considerable number of Ph.D. theses in Germany and elsewhere in central Europe are worth examination. Papajewski's book [DIE WELT-, LEBENS-, UND KUNSTANSCHAUUNG WILLIAM SOMERSET MAUGHAMS] should be translated into English. Yet to be done is a careful study of the exact influence on Maugham of his scientific studies and training. Not very much is known about the people whom he was closely associated with before he was eighteen: his parents and

brothers, his clergyman uncle and German wife, the masters, and perhaps schoolmates, at King's School. Knowledge of his friendships and associates at Heidelberg and later in Paris might throw some light on his early creative work. Maugham as a critic of literature and of painting is a subject worthy of examination. A careful survey could be made of the Edwardian theatre and Maugham's position in it alongside Shaw, Pinero, Jones, Barker, Hankin, and the Manchester School. A similar study of the theatre of the nineteen twenties could be made. Maugham's position in the French literary movements since 1920 offers possibilities, for he has been more widely read in France than most popular French writers. Has there been some mutual influence? A fascinating topic would be this rationalist's occasional toying with the mystical: nearly always when he writes of Spain, his strange experiences in India just before the Second World War, his last novel, *Catalina,* and so forth. Perhaps the last word has not been said on certain obvious and often discussed influences—Wilde on his early comedies; the French naturalists on his early novels; Maupassant on his short stories; his wide reading in philosophy; his close association with such artists as Rothenstein, Kelly, and Sutherland; the Heidelberg theatre in 1892, the French theatre at the turn of the century.

The present bibliography reveals these topics still unexhausted. And since, as Maugham has said, "it is thought that has the last word," we hope the studies which Professor Cordell proposed before us may be facilitated now by the representative material gathered in the following pages.

ACKNOWLEDGMENTS

The present bibliography was undertaken in the late winter of 1965. From 1957 until that time ENGLISH FICTION IN TRANSITION (EFT) and ENGLISH LITERATURE IN TRANSITION (ELT) frequently included annotated bibliographical entries on W. Somerset Maugham. These entries—collected in those periodicals under the title "Bibliography, News, and Notes"—were chiefly for works published after 1950, and were at first edited solely by Helmut E. Gerber, later jointly by Gerber and E. S. Lauterbach or Gerber and W. Eugene Davis. The editors received annotations primarily from Pierre Coustillas, Joseph Dunlap, and Marie T. Tate. The following is a summary and a brief description of their work: "Bibliography, News, and Notes," EFT, I, No. 1 (Fall-Winter 1957), 30-32: eighteen bibliographical entries on Maugham, dating from 1950 and after; EFT, I, No. 3 (Fall Special 1958), 38: twelve entries, two of them dating from before 1950; EFT, II, No. 1 (1959), 47: three entries, dating from

1957 and after; EFT, III, No. 1 (1960), 51-52: four entries, dating from 1958-59; EFT, IV, No. 1 (1961), 25: four entries, dating from 1937 to 1960; EFT, IV, No. 2 (1961), 57: three entries, dating from 1960-61; EFT, IV, No. 3 (1961), 51: three entries, dating from 1961; ELT, VI, No. 2 (1963), 108-117: thirty-nine entries, dating from 1953 to 1962; ELT, VI, No. 3 (1963), 166-67: six entries, dating from 1955 to 1963; ELT, VI, No. 4 (1963), 236: five entries, dating from 1954 to 1963; ELT, VII, No. 1 (1964), 32: two entries, dating from 1964; ELT, VIII, No. 2 (1965), 122: three entries, dating from 1963-64. From these one-hundred two entries, I have repeated, almost word-for-word, fifty-five in the present bibliography.

Several other "contributors" to this project remain unacknowledged. Without their assistance, my work could not have been completed as pleasantly as it was, and so I should like to acknowledge them here. Reference libraries from several major universities have given generously of their resources, but I have relied most heavily upon the Reference Department of the Library of the University of Illinois—and in particular, upon the services of Constance Ashmore, T. Edward Ratcliffe, and Richard G. Smith. Especially to Richard Vickers, Personal Assistant to the Editor of the SUNDAY TIMES (Lond), John Seward Fielden, Dean of Business Administration at Boston University, and Klaus W. Jonas, Provost of the University of Pittsburgh, I am indebted for helpful criticisms and answers to my extensive inquiries. In securing translators of the foreign scholarship of Maugham, Professors Maria E. Keen of the University of Illinois and Tauno F. Mustanoja of the University of Helsinki have been of inestimable aid; and for payment of the translators' services—as well as for reproducing the entire manuscript—I am grateful to the Research Funds Committee of the University of Illinois English Department. To Mr. Mário Feiten, Mr. Keneth Kinnamon, and Mrs. Margit Schoenfeld I am indebted for translations from the Portuguese, Spanish, and Hungarian. Finally, the punctual completion of my task would not have been possible without the help of my secretary, Miss Beverly Seward, who shared the responsibility for proofreading at every stage of the way.

CHARLES SANDERS

Contents

PREFACE v

A CHECKLIST OF THE WORKS OF W. SOMERSET MAUGHAM 3

INTRODUCTION 9

THE BIBLIOGRAPHY 14

INDEX OF AUTHORS 383

INDEX OF TITLES OF SECONDARY WORKS 393

INDEX OF PERIODICALS AND NEWSPAPERS 423

INDEX OF FOREIGN LANGUAGES 429

INDEX OF PRIMARY TITLES 431

Note on Entry Style

Titles of Maugham's books and plays appear in italic type; titles of his stories, in roman capitals and lower case with quotation marks. Titles of books and plays by other authors, titles of dramatic adaptations based on Maugham's works, and names of newspapers and periodicals appear in capitals and small capitals. The translations appearing in parentheses are confined to meanings of the phrases; however, it should be noted that the titles of adaptations and translations are seldom literal ones. Comprehensive, detailed reviews and essays are indicated by an asterisk [*].

W. Somerset Maugham

AN ANNOTATED BIBLIOGRAPHY OF WRITINGS ABOUT HIM

A Checklist

OF THE WORKS OF W. SOMERSET MAUGHAM
CITED IN THIS BIBLIOGRAPHY

I. ANTHOLOGIES, AUTOBIOGRAPHY, BOOKS OF TRAVEL, CRITICISM, ESSAYS, ETC.

A. SEPARATE WORKS

The Land of The Blessed Virgin: Sketches and Impressions in Andalusia. [*The Land of The Blessed Virgin*]. Lond., 1905; New York, 1920.

On a Chinese Screen. Lond. and New York, 1922.

The Gentleman in the Parlour: A Record of a Journey from Rangoon to Haiphong. [*The Gentleman in the Parlour*]. Lond. and Garden City, 1930.

Traveller's Library. Garden City, 1933.

Don Fernando: or, Variations on Some Spanish Themes. [*Don Fernando*]. Lond. and Garden City, 1935; revised version, 1950.

The Summing Up. Lond. and Garden City, 1938.

Tellers of Tales. Garden City, 1939.

Books and You. Lond. and Garden City, 1940.

France at War. Lond. and Garden City, 1940.

Strictly Personal. Garden City, 1941; Lond., 1942.

An Introduction to Modern English and American Literature. New York, 1943.

Great Novelists and Their Novels: Essays on the Ten Greatest Novels of the World, and the Men and Women Who Wrote Them. Philadelphia, 1948. The essays were republished as *The Art of Fiction: An Introduction to Ten Novels and Their Authors.* Garden City, 1955; and as *Ten Novels and Their Authors.* Lond., 1954.

A Writer's Notebook. Lond. and Garden City, 1949.

A Choice of Kipling's Prose. Lond., 1952. Published in America as *Maugham's Choice of Kipling's Best*. Garden City, 1953.

The Vagrant Mood. Lond., 1952; Garden City, 1953.

Points of View. Lond., 1958; Garden City, 1959.

Selected Prefaces and Introductions of W. Somerset Maugham. Garden City, 1963; Lond., 1964.

B. Collected Editions

The Partial View. Lond., 1954. Contains *The Summing Up* and *A Writer's Notebook*.

The Travel Books. Lond., 1955. Contains *On a Chinese Screen, The Gentleman in the Parlour, Don Fernando*.

II. DRAMA

A. Separate Works

[First performance dates in England (Lond.) and America (NY) are provided in brackets beside each play, the English first, the American second.]

A Man of Honour. Lond., 1903. [22 Feb 1903; no American production]

The Explorer. Lond. and Chicago, 1912. [13 June 1908; 7 May 1912]

Lady Frederick. Lond. and Chicago, 1912. [26 Oct 1907; 9 Nov 1908]

Mrs. Dot. Lond. and Chicago, 1912. [27 April 1908; 24 Jan 1910]

Jack Straw. Lond. and Chicago, 1912. [26 March 1908; 14 Sept 1908]

Penelope. Lond. and Chicago, 1912. [9 Jan 1909; 13 Dec 1909]

Smith. Lond. and Chicago, 1913. [30 Sept 1909; 5 Sept 1910]

The Tenth Man. Lond. and Chicago, 1913. [24 Feb 1910; 20 March 1929]

Grace (also entitled *Landed Gentry)*. Lond. and Chicago, 1913. [15 Oct 1910; no American production]

The Perfect Gentleman. Unpublished. [27 May 1913; no American production]

The Land of Promise. Lond., 1913; Canada, 1914; N Y, 1922. [26 Feb 1914; 25 Dec 1913]

The Circle. Lond., 1920; N Y, 1921. [3 March 1921; 12 Sept 1921]

The Unknown. Lond. and N Y, 1920. [9 Aug 1920; no American production]

Caesar's Wife. Lond., 1922; N Y, 1923. [27 March 1919; 24 Nov 1919]

East of Suez. Lond. and N Y, 1922. [2 Sept 1922; 21 Sept 1922]

The Camel's Back. Unpublished. [31 Jan 1924; 13 Nov 1923]

Our Betters. Lond., 1923; N Y, 1924 [12 Sept 1923; 12 March 1917]

Caroline (also entitled *The Unattainable)*. Lond., 1923. [8 Feb 1916; 20 Sept 1916]

Love in a Cottage. Unpublished. [26 Jan 1918; no American production]

Home and Beauty (also entitled *Too Many Husbands).* Lond., 1923. [30 Aug 1919; 8 Oct 1919]

Loaves and Fishes. Lond., 1924; N Y, 1926. [24 Feb 1911; no American production)

The Constant Wife. Lond. and N Y, 1927. [6 April 1927; 29 Nov 1926]

The Letter. Lond. and N Y, 1927. [24 Feb 1927; 26 Sept 1927]

The Sacred Flame. N Y, 1928; Lond., 1929. [8 Feb 1929; 19 Nov 1928]

The Breadwinner. Lond., 1930; N Y, 1931. [30 Sept 1930; 22 Sept 1931]

For Services Rendered. Lond., 1932; N Y, 1933 [1 Nov 1932; 12 April 1933]

The Mask and the Face. Unpublished. [No English production; 8 May 1933]

Sheppey. Lond., 1933; Boston, 1949. [14 Sept 1933; 18 April 1944]

The Noble Spaniard. Lond., 1953. [20 March 1909; 20 Sept 1909]

B. Dramatizations by Other Authors, Based on Maugham's Fiction

1. Plays

Rain, by John Colton and Clemence Randolph. N Y, 1923; Lond., 1948. [12 May 1925; 7 Nov 1922]

The Moon and Sixpence, by Edith Ellis. Unpublished. [24 Sept 1925; no American production]

The Painted Veil, by Bartlett Cormack. Unpublished. [19 Sept 1931; no American production]

Theatre (also entitled *Larger Than Life),* by Guy Bolton. N Y, 1942; Lond., 1951. [7 Feb 1950; 12 Nov 1941]

Jane, by S. N. Behrman. N Y, 1952. [29 Jan 1947; 1 Feb 1952]

Before the Party, by Rodney Ackland. Lond., 1950. [26 Oct 1949; no American production]

2. Films

Quartet. [Dramatizations, by R. C. Sherriff, of "The Facts of Life," "The Alien Corn," "The Kite," and "The Colonel's Lady"]. Lond., 1948; Garden City, 1949.

Trio. [Dramatizations, by Maugham, R. C. Sherriff, and Noel Langley, of "The Verger," "Mr. Know-All," and "Sanatorium"]. Lond. and Garden City, 1950.

Encore. [Dramatizations, by T. E. B. Clarke, Arthur Macrae, and Eric Ambler, of "The Ant and the Grasshopper," "Winter Cruise," and Gigolo and Gigolette"]. Lond. and Garden City, 1952.

C. Collected Editions

The Collected Plays. Six Volumes. Lond., 1931-1934. Contents:
Volume I—*Loaves and Fishes, Mrs. Dot, Jack Straw*. 1931.
Volume II—*Penelope, Smith, The Land of Promise*. 1931.
Volume III—*Our Betters, The Unattainable (Caroline), Home and Beauty*. 1932.
Volume IV—*The Circle, The Constant Wife, The Breadwinner*. 1932.
Volume V—*Caesar's Wife, East of Suez, The Sacred Flame*. 1934.
Volume VI—*The Unknown, For Services Rendered, Sheppey*. 1934.

Six Comedies. Garden City, 1937. Contents: *The Unattainable (Caroline), Home and Beauty, The Circle, Our Betters, The Constant Wife, The Breadwinner*.

III. NOVELS

A. Separate Works

Liza of Lambeth. Lond., 1897; N Y, 1921.
The Making of a Saint. Lond. and Boston, 1898.
The Hero. Lond., 1901.
Mrs. Craddock. Lond., 1902; N Y, 1920; revised version, 1928.
The Merry-Go-Round. Lond. and N Y, 1904.
The Bishop's Apron. Lond., 1906.
The Explorer. Lond., 1907; Boston, 1908.
The Magician. Lond., 1908; N Y, 1909.
Of Human Bondage. Lond. and N Y, 1915.
The Moon and Sixpence. Lond. and N Y, 1919.
The Painted Veil. Lond. and N Y, 1925.
Cakes and Ale: Or, The Skeleton in the Cupboard. [*Cakes and Ale*]. Lond. and Garden City, 1930.
The Narrow Corner. Lond. and Garden City, 1932.
Theatre. Lond. and Garden City, 1937.
Christmas Holiday. Lond. and N Y, 1939.
Up at the Villa. Lond. and Garden City, 1941.
The Hour Before the Dawn. Garden City, 1942.
The Razor's Edge. Lond. and Garden City, 1944.
Then and Now. Lond. and Garden City, 1946.
Catalina. Lond. and Garden City, 1948.

B. Collected Edition

Selected Novels. Three Volumes. Lond., 1953. Contents:
Volume I—*Liza of Lambeth, Cakes and Ale, Theatre*.

Volume II—*The Moon and Sixpence, The Narrow Corner, The Painted Veil.*

Volume III—*Christmas Holiday, Up at the Villa, The Razor's Edge.*

IV. SHORT STORIES

A. SEPARATE WORKS

Orientations. Lond., 1899. Contents: "The Punctiliousness of Don Sebastian," "A Bad Example," "De Amicitia," "Faith," "The Choice of Amyntas," "Daisy."

The Trembling of a Leaf: Little Stories of the South Sea Islands. [*The Trembling of a Leaf*]. Lond. and N Y, 1921. Contents: "Mackintosh," "The Fall of Edward Barnard," "Red," "The Pool," "Honolulu," "Rain."

The Casuarina Tree: Six Stories. [*The Casuarina Tree*]. Lond. and N Y, 1926. Contents: "Before the Party," "P. & O.," "The Outstation," "The Force of Circumstance," "The Yellow Streak," "The Letter."

Ashenden: Or, The British Agent. [*Ashenden*]. Lond. and Garden City, 1928. Contents: "A Domiciliary Visit," "Miss King," "The Hairless Mexican," "The Greek," "A Trip to Paris," "Giulia Lazzari," "Gustav," "The Traitor," "Behind the Scenes," "His Excellency," "The Flip of a Coin," "A Chance Acquaintance," "Love and Russian Literature," "Mr. Harrington's Washing."

Six Stories Written in the First Person Singular. [*First Person Singular*]. Lond. and Garden City, 1931. Contents: "The Alien Corn," "The Creative Impulse," "The Human Element," "Jane," "The Round Dozen," "Virtue."

Ah King: Six Stories. [*Ah King*]. Lond. and Garden City, 1933. Contents: "Footprints in the Jungle," "The Door of Opportunity," "The Vessel of Wrath," "The Book-Bag," "The Back of Beyond," "Neil MacAdam."

Cosmopolitans: Very Short Stories. [*Cosmopolitans*]. Lond. and Garden City, 1936. Contents: "Raw Material," "Mayhew," "German Harry," "The Happy Man," "The Dream," "In a Strange Land," "The Luncheon," "Salvatore," "Home," "Mr. Know-All," "The Escape," "A Friend in Need," "The Portrait of a Gentleman," "The End of a Flight," "The Judgment Seat," "The Ant and the Grasshopper," "French Joe," "The Man with the Scar," "The Poet," "Louise," "The Closed Shop," "The Promise," "A String of Beads," "The Bum," "Straight Flush," "The Verger," "The Wash-Tub," "The Social Sense," "The Four Dutchmen."

The Mixture As Before. Lond. and N Y, 1940. Contents: "The Facts of

Life," "Gigolo and Gigolette," "The Lion's Skin," "Lord Mountdrago," "The Lotus Eater," "A Man with a Conscience," "An Official Position," "The Three Fat Women of Antibes," "The Treasure," "The Voice of the Turtle."

Creatures of Circumstance. Lond. and Garden City, 1947. Contents: "The Colonel's Lady," "Flotsam and Jetsam," "Appearance and Reality," "The Mother," "Sanatorium," "A Woman of Fifty," "The Romantic Young Lady," "A Casual Affair," "The Point of Honour," "Winter Cruise," "The Happy Couple," "A Man from Glasgow," "The Unconquered," "Episode," "The Kite."

B. COLLECTED EDITION

Altogether. Collected Stories with a preface by the author and an appreciation by Desmond MacCarthy (also entitled *East and West: The Collected Short Stories of W. Somerset Maugham)*. Lond. and Garden City, 1934.

Introduction

Of the several portraits for which W. Somerset Maugham posed, two—painted nearly four decades apart—stand out in a viewer's memory. The earlier, by Sir Gerald Kelly, entitled *The Jester,* depicts Maugham at thirty-seven, some four years after his astonishing success in the Edwardian commercial theatre. He sits—in a grand armchair, against a turn-of-the-century backdrop of some easy elegance—dressed in high formal fashion, top-hatted and white-gloved, soft, suave, and superficial. The later painting, Graham Sutherland's of 1949, stripped of any title other than the name of its subject, presents a Maugham of seventy-five, one year after he had written his last novel, upon a simple rattan bench, casually dressed, with arms folded, his expression either angry or mimicking anger, his eyes and mouth ambiguously cruel, disdainful, vindictive. There is nothing in the background.

The thirty-eight years which fall between these two portraits contain the bulk of Maugham secondary criticism. They divide almost too neatly into equal halves of success and rejection, partially explaining the transformation of The Jester into the quizzical Old Man with a Razor. Generally speaking, the years 1911 through 1930 witnessed the birth of those works, in almost every genre, for which Maugham was acclaimed: the novels, *Of Human Bondage* (1915) *The Moon and Sixpence* (1919), and *Cakes and Ale* (1930); the plays, *Our Betters* (1917), *Home and Beauty* (1919), and *The Circle* (1921); the short stories, "Red" and "Rain" (1921), "The Outstation" and "The Yellow Streak" (1926); the book of travel, *The Gentleman in the Parlour* (1930). Critics at this time, while never unanimous in their praise of Maugham's work, were nonetheless generous: they might chide his commercial instinct for turning new tricks to camouflage old ones, they might find his latest piece facile, slick, and shallow; but their over-all verdicts were tempered by appreciation for Maugham's epigrammatic verve and repartée, his economy of dialogue, detail, and design, his power to seize and hold his audience's attention. In this period, Maugham's reputation, with its usual highs and lows, gradually spread—

to adopt the self-consciously chosen title of his collected stories—East and West.

The years following the appearance of *Cakes and Ale* and *The Gentleman in the Parlour* are less kind. For while the 1930s purportedly represent, as Maugham's biographers have often said, his "golden period," the secondary criticism sounds, with only a few exceptions, a contrary, long-held brassy note. Thus, for critic Gerald Sykes, after reading *First Person Singular* (1931), Maugham becames one of the "glittering passengers in the grand saloon of that quadruple-screw ship which bore 'The Gentleman from San Francisco' "; and the critic for NATION (NY) senses, in *The Narrow Corner* (1932), that Maugham goes through "his routine bag of tricks like a bored and expert magician, growing increasingly contemptuous of his audience at each performance." Thus the anonymous reviewer for BOOKMAN (Lond) receives *Ah King* (1933) with scorn, finding in the volume's six stories "something incredibly cheap and second-hand that is unpleasantly reminiscent of certain American films woven around the irreconcilability of East and West." Louis Kronenberger (for the NEW YORK TIMES BOOK REVIEW), Malcolm Cowley (in NEW REPUBLIC) and Sylvia Lynd (in the London OBSERVER) greet the collected stories, *Altogether* (1934), with disappointment: the first "looks in vain for . . . the unchallenged reality of *Of Human Bondage*" and, while admitting the variety of Maugham's themes, judges their treatment and effect ruinously the same; the second is irritated by Maugham's smug and insulting tolerance of mankind, and the third characterizes Maugham's *oeuvre* as evincing "only a narrow range of cleverness and knowledge."

The note becomes more ominous with the publication of *Cosmopolitans* in 1936. The total effect of these twenty-nine very short stories, declares Florence Haxton Britten in "Books" (NEW YORK HERALD TRIBUNE), is one of utter "triviality"; and, in the NATION's "Shorter Notices," the reviewer concludes that "far from adding to a reputation already endangered by the existence of so many trifles, this volume sinks it to a new low." With *Theatre* (1937) comes the verdict that will be repeated again and again, in one form or another. This book, according to Caroline Smith in NATION (NY), is third-rate and merely "publicity for a great book [*Of Human Bondage*] which he [Maugham] wrote twenty-two years ago." As E. B. C. Jones sums up in the SPECTATOR (Lond.): Maugham "is often a fascinating raconteur, but never an artist." And so—despite infrequent appreciations to the contrary—it goes with all of Maugham's subsequent works, from *Christmas Holiday* (1939) through *Catalina* (1948): the epigrams have grown stale, the voice and persona raucous, the *données* too patent. The surface may intrigue, but the background is empty.

Maugham's defenders have been at some loss to explain the ugly reversal of his fortunes. To say that older journals of criticism were giving way before the creation of the new, that one generation of reviewers was replaced by another, that Maugham, facing a new audience with new tastes, continued to exercise a worn-out literary mode, is to state a commonplace and, perhaps, a half-truth. Such explanations not only rationalize away Maugham's continually dubious position in letters but also ignore his ability to survive, under similar—indeed, even more dramatic—sets of circumstances, immediately before and after World War I, when long-established publications (like ACADEMY) languished or (like ATHENAEUM) merged with others, when the crumbling majestic certitude of Victorianism was openly challenged by artists and critics alike. Such explanations actually beg the question raised by critics of the thirties and forties, which is one, not so much of method, but of intention, tone, or attitude.

Whatever his method or intention, Maugham's customary attitude is cynical. Desmond MacCarthy, though certainly not the first to describe that attitude, was at least the first to champion it. Indeed, MacCarthy contended (in NEW STATESMAN, 1921) that Maugham's works improved in merit and interest as he continued to write from a cynical point of view, as the works darkened in their skepticism about the depth and permanence of human affection. But Maugham himself was "more than a cynic" (NASH'S-PALL MALL MAGAZINE, 1933); and to understand him as a writer, his audience was directed to observe the narrator of the story, "The Human Element," who, speaking for Maugham, reveals "a very unusual sensibility instantly defended by an unamiable self-protective impulse, which in its turn is corrected by a more just response." In Maugham's treatment of human beings, MacCarthy concluded, the narrator's reactions usually came into play, creating personal, as well as artistic, equipoise.

Yet, judging by their reactions to Maugham's works in the thirties, few critics were as convinced as MacCarthy about any improvement according to cynicism. In the same story MacCarthy cited, they might all too easily detect "an unamiable self-protective impulse," less easily locate "a more just response." Elsewhere they might feel the corrective to come too late or, on arrival, to be as excessive as the initial impulse and so falsify reality. To them, Maugham was (as, say, in *The Narrow Corner)* uncomfortably poised between malevolence and mawkish compensation.

"All he wanted was to die, so long as he could tread a few people under foot, squelch them first: pay them out for being so uninteresting, banal, sheep-like." So Elinor Mordaunt, under the alias A. Riposte, wrote in GIN AND BITTERS (entitled, in England, FULL CIRCLE) of her "hero," Leverson Hurle, a scabrous caricature of Somerset Maugham. Hurle is a churl who sleeps with his employer's wife, Cynthia Stoddard. (Four years earlier he had abandoned Lizzie of Lambeth because she sold herself for ten pounds to buy Leverson a microscope for his scientific studies.) Forced by Mr. Stoddard to marry Cynthia, Hurle, confirmed in the belief that marriage is a bourgeois affair, escapes to the Pacific under the pretext of finishing a book on "a painter's life," a book of no value, "for in it the writer intrudes himself to an extent . . . [that] in the end one knows more about the writer than the painter." Everywhere he goes, Hurle finds himself unwelcome: even America tires of him. His misanthropy dilates; his literary style degenerates. He wants to die. Only Lizzie remains to nurse him—as well as a valet who, on Hurle's deathbed, shaves him to comfort him. Leverson "would have hated even the undertaker to see that contrast of white bristle with the small dark moustache, which had remained so altogether unchanged."

Written one year after Maugham's portrayal of Thomas Hardy, Hugh Walpole, and others in *Cakes and Ale* (and, coincidentally, the same year in which Maugham published "The Human Element" in *First Person Singular),* Mrs. Mordaunt's work is typical of all lampoons with pretensions to satire: its rancor is as narrow as its aim is broad. Still, in its outrageous way, Gin and Bitters foreshadows the gathering critical distrust of Maugham in the 1930s and thereafter, pinpointing those very qualities in his work that irritate all but a few: egotism, disrespect for others, frivolity, misogyny, misanthropy, the imposition of a cynical point of view upon his total perception. Particularly with the six stories of *First Person Singular* Maugham would appear to have picked up Kipling's barrack-room comparison of a cigar and a woman, become intent upon extending and elaborating it with the sangfroid of a weary connoisseur who has seen, tasted, known too much—and would like to forget it. That point of view, to be sure, peppers the works of The Jester (for example, the pastoral interlude of *Liza of Lambeth,* 1897; the aunt of *Mrs. Craddock,* 1902; the title character of *Ashenden,* 1928, to name but a few); in those of the Old Man, it predominates to the exclusion of all other points of view, or such points of view as are allowed to be pitted against it ring hollow, lack conviction.

The "golden period" of the thirties then bears reassessment. In terms of quantity and variety both, it is unquestionably Maugham's most prolific decade; it claims no fewer than three collections of short stories, four novels, four plays, and—significantly—three works of nonfiction (excluding two edited anthologies). But, this period is also that in which Maugham announces his decision to quit the theater, when his fiction, short and long, is received without enthusiasm, more often with contempt. With the single exception of *Cakes and Ale,* Maugham's major achievements belong to the area of expository prose: *The Gentleman in the Parlour, Don Fernando,* and *The Summing Up,* works which satisfied even the most severe of his critics. Autobiography, travel literature, or the longish familiar essay begin to compete with Maugham's interest in fiction, gradually absorb his attention, and become, for him—whether conscious or not—good choices.

During an interview in his late seventies, Maugham was to announce that he had given up the writing of fiction for the essay, a literary genre "no longer in fashion." With Maugham—thin-skinned and witty enough to borrow the title of his next-to-the-last story collection *(The Mixture As Before,* 1940) from a scornful criticism of his preceding collection—one may be sure that the remark was, partially, a rejoinder to the often-repeated criticism that he was a mere storyteller, faddist, or popularizer of ideas. But, by a literary genre "no longer in fashion" Maugham had in mind a particular form from the early nineteenth century: the familiar essay, which he believed to have, in contrast with the majority of twentieth-century essays, few or no propagandistic motives for its existence, to be written with seemingly conversational ease, to be capable of developing any subject that appealed to its author's fancy. A form which invites the introduction and development of opinion—indeed, something not quite a "form," since its unity entirely depends on the author's self-created persona—the essay was amenable to a tone or attitude which, to critics' ways of thinking at least, distorted the reality of character and event in Maugham's fiction.

Maugham's gradual movement toward essay writing is not without some ironies which he, if not his critics, may have perceived. For one, he moved directly against the expressionistic line of modern essayists (like Forster, Orwell, Macdonald, and Mailer) to return to the impressionistic tradition initiated by Lamb and Hazlitt and culminating with Stevenson. For another, his familiar cynical strain became muted as Maugham, freed from constrictions of plot, time or place, struck an easy commerce between Jester and Old Man, alternating their masks, relying solely on voice for their fusion—and for "eminent readability." The titles of his last two essay collections may serve to indicate Maugham's new-found freedom: *The Vagrant Mood* (1952) and *Points of View* (1958).

Of the two, *The Vagrant Mood* is perhaps the better. The six pieces in it range from a genealogy of the petty but pitiful Victorian snob, Augustus Hare (rightfully placed first in the collection), to reflections on the prose style of Edmund Burke (with an understandably sympathetic tribute to Hazlitt), to amusing, if somewhat unflattering, portraits of Arnold Bennett, Henry James, and H. G. Wells. At the center of the collection, and only slightly less admirable than the first-placed "Augustus," is "The Decline and Fall of the Detective Story," perhaps the essay most easily identifiable as issuing from Maugham's fancy. The self-consciously pompous title of the piece, its casual but urbane "armchair" tone, the leisurely paced beginning, the ensuing personal history which seems almost irrelevant, the orderly and careful analysis of the popular detective story plot and its characters, the admiration for a neat story's practitioners, the essay's faintly frivolous conclusion—all are hallmarks of Maugham, dramatist and novelist. For, when he turned from drama and fiction to the essay, Maugham brought to the genre his characteristic craftsmanship.

He brought something else, not to be found before: a relaxation from constraint. In the essay he might indulge his fondness for anecdote, episode, aside, quotation, and allusion. "Augustus" and "The Decline and Fall of the Detective Story" follow and consummate the lines of the travel books and autobiography of the 1930s; they do so without an earlier superficial gloss or a later easy contempt; they require no apology. There, if nowhere in his long works of fiction since 1930 (except for the Elliott Templeton-half of *The Razor's Edge* [1944] and the basic anecdote of *Then and Now* [1946]), one is presented ample proof that "to give in a book . . . a deliberate impression of frivolity, a serious touch is required which a purely frivolous person would be incapable of supplying."

There may indeed be good reason for Maugham's *mimicry* of anger or *ambiguous* look of disdain in Sutherland's portrait.

1897

1 "Books: Some New Novels," Spectator (Lond), LXXIX (13 Nov 1897), 692.

Liza of Lambeth is "relentlessly realistic," although "the squalor of this little book is often positively nauseating."

2 "Fiction," Literature, I (6 Nov 1897), 84.

In *Liza of Lambeth,* M does not write with skill, he does not understand the people about whom he writes, and he does not sympathize with them. The book's one merit is the "complete" and "strong" portrait of Liza, but this is marred by "absolutely unendurable . . . sustained grossness."

3* Filon, Augustin. "Le peuple de Londres et le roman naturaliste" (Londoners and the Naturalist Novel), Le Journal des Debats, 109ème année (27 Oct 1897), 1.

Critical discussion of the English attitude toward "naturalism" with a review of *Liza of Lambeth.* Naturalism is looked at askance by the English, whose natural taste leans rather to works of imagination or comic writings. *Liza* is more daring and brutal than its French counterparts; it is an example of naturalism unalloyed, devoid of romance, exhibiting a harsh, somber reality. The book is well-made, testifies to good craftsmanship, and the quarrel between Liza and Mrs. Blakeston is a praiseworthy scene. The book is moral, turning one way from vice; it is truthful and offers a graphic description of the vulgar and vicious life led by the London rabble: "Liza se perd à dix-huit ans; c'est quatre ans plus tard que la moyenne." [In French.]

4* *"Liza of Lambeth,"* ACADEMY ("Fiction Supplement"), LII (11 Sept 1897), 65.

M's novel is a "deliberate and unashamed mimicry" of Arthur Morrison's work, but it lacks the latter's directness, restraint, and dominating artistic purpose. What should be tragedy, emerges as a "sordid story of vulgar seduction"; and its realism, pursued for its own sake, "sinks into incurable nastiness." The reviewer finished the novel feeling as if he had taken "a mud-bath in all the filth of a London street."

5 "New Novels," ATHENAEUM, No. 3646 (11 Sept 1897), 347.
In *Liza of Lambeth,* M depicts life in Lambeth with "uncompromising fidelity and care" and "in singularly unvarnished language"; the last scene [Liza's dying while her mother and the midwife discuss the merits of rival undertakers] will illustrate that the entire work is "emphatically unpleasing literature."

6* "Novel Notes," BOOKMAN (Lond), XIII (Oct 1897), 23.
"The truth about our slums is a horrid truth, but we do not know it all, and some of the unknown must modify it, no doubt. We are willing to bear the horror, so that our consciences may be roused, our sense of pity awakened; nay, even only to know humanity in some more of its possibilities. But the effect goes when horror is given as a daily food. When a master has once made a black truth real to us, if only the thing would stop there! But the smaller men harp on it again and again *ad nauseam.* Mr. Maughan [*sic*] is not such a very small man, either. He is very clever, and even if he used less bad language his pictures would still be effective. But he has nothing new to tell. . . . [*Liza of Lambeth*] is all very hopeless, and unrelieved by any sense of strong feeling working in the writer. . . . And yet he is clever, and should be heard of again—in other scenes, let us hope."

1898

7* "Books: Recent Novels," SPECTATOR (Lond), LXXXI (6 Aug 1898), 184.

The Making of a Saint has "the colour of life"; the narration is done in "masterly fashion." The return to the hackneyed love-story in the last chapter is "unfortunate" but conventional. "Maugham has written a good novel, and he ought some day to write much better ones."

8* "Historical Romances," ATHENAEUM, No. 3690 (16 July 1898), 95.
The Making of a Saint shows M finding the characteristics of his *Liza of Lambeth* in two ladies of fifteenth-century Forli; his conversations are in a language suitable to nineteenth-century England; his detailed description of atrocities and his lack of delicacy in describing love affairs make the book unpleasant literature, and "its title is unintelligible."

9 Jerrold, Laurence. "Les Livres: Les Lettres anglaises" (Books: English Letters), LA REVUE BLANCHE, XV (15 Feb 1898), 158-59.
Liza of Lambeth is a brave novel, written soberly, with direct and simple action. M's love of his work compels us to love and understand his characters. [In French.]

10* *"The Making of a Saint,"* ACADEMY ("Supplement"), LIV (17 Sept 1898), 270.
M's second novel does not fulfill the expectations of *Liza of Lambeth.* "We discern in the persons of the play an incredible kinship to the Bills and Ducks who swear the cockney oaths and brag the easy amours of the cockney slum." Although "Giulia is more complex and more human," M's treatment of Claudia cannot be approved of, nor can Fra Giuliano's humor be rated "high."

11* "Novel Notes," BOOKMAN (Lond), XIV (Sept 1898), 169; rptd in BOOKMAN (NY), VIII (Nov 1898), 257.
The subject of *The Making of a Saint* "is far removed in time and place from that of *Liza of Lambeth,* but the power which vitalized one is identical with the power that vitalizes the other"; M was successful in the earlier book, because there he wrote of what he had seen; here only of what he had read and imagined.

12 Payne, William Morton. "Recent Fiction," DIAL, XXV (16 Sept 1898), 172.
In *The Making of a Saint,* "there is nothing to indicate the 'making,' in any psychological sense, of 'a saint' out of the swaggering adventurer who tells the story, nothing, in fact, . . . to make it more than an artificial surface chronicle of such incidents as made up the substance of aristocratic life in every Italian state during the age of the despots."

13* "Some Historical Novels," LITERATURE, III (27 Aug 1898), 185-86.
The Making of a Saint is a readable story, excellently told, with exciting incidents well worked up and dialogue neither cumbrous nor flat; but M lacks the "sympathetic imagination" necessary for a good historical novel: "He makes his fifteenth-century Italians do the kind of things

which such people actually did, but he does not succeed in convincing the reader that this was the way they did them."

1899

14 "Novel Notes," BOOKMAN (Lond), XVI (July 1899), 110.
Orientations is "an average book, fairly readable, but with no serious interest or promise about it."

15* *"Orientations,"* ACADEMY, LVII (1 July 1899), 15.
M's third book is better than the "shrill and hysterical" *Liza of Lambeth* or the "rather mediocre" *Making of a Saint,* but the stories do not "differ from each other as widely as [Maugham] would seem to imply": the subjects vary, but the treatment is "practically identical throughout." "A Bad Example" is the best of the collection; the more fantastic tales lack point, "or such point as they have is unoriginal."

16* "Short Stories," ATHENAEUM, No. 3738 (17 June 1899), 751.
Orientations contains M's "best writing," though his "handicraft" is more interesting and original than the subjects of any of his six stories.

1900

17* Findlater, Jane H. "The Slum Movement in Fiction," NATIONAL REVIEW (Lond), XXXV (May 1900), 447-54; rptd in STONES FROM A GLASS WINDOW (Lond: James Nisbet, 1904), pp. 65-88, especially 81-84.
Liza of Lambeth is an example of the rash of "inartistic" pictures of slum-life: "We are spared nothing: the reek of the streets: the effluvia of unwashed humanity; but worse than all these outside things is the hopeless moral atmosphere in which the characters move . . . . Nor does the author seem to write in any spirit of pity, or with any love for the creatures he has made." The book is, hence, "gratuitously brutal."

1901

18 *"The Hero,"* ACADEMY, LXI (13 July 1901), 33-34.
The novel has more cleverness in it than the average reader will see, for it is "mediocrally, if pleasantly written, and the incidents are all extremely quiet and unexciting." The cleverness lies neither in style nor in situations, "but in the unobtrusive success of [the book's] psychology."

19 "New Novels," ATHENAEUM, No. 3848 (27 July 1901), 119.
In *The Hero,* "Mr. Maugham is a little overfond of cynical asides to the reader, after the manner of Thackeray, but he gives here certain proof of his ability as a student of character and of his power to put the result of his study in a convincing manner."

1902

20* Adcock, A. St. John. "Mr. W. S. Maugham's New Novel," BOOKMAN (Lond), XXIII (Dec 1902), 108.
In *Mrs. Craddock,* the portrait of Bertha is "subtle" and "masterly"; the minor characters and episodes are "cleverly drawn," and the social life of the Kentish countryside is "touched in with fidelity. The book as a whole . . . makes a distinct advance on what Mr. Maugham had previously accomplished."

21 "A Novel of the Week: An Imaginative Woman," T. P.'s WEEKLY, I (28 Nov 1902), 75.
Except for the end when Edward breaks his neck and Bertha is aghast at her tranquility over it, *Mrs. Craddock* is "both powerful and true."

22* "The Strong Crude Novel," ACADEMY, LXIII (29 Nov 1902), 577.
The "provincialism" of M's "Epistle Dedicatory" and the italicized aside about English novelists and their heroines, as well as the "ripe lusciousness . . . feeble witticism . . . [and] facile satire" of certain passages in *Mrs. Craddock* are deplorable; yet M has in him "the essentials of a thoroughly sound novelist." The portraits of Edward and Bertha earn genuine respect, despite the book's many obvious faults.

1903

23* [Beerbohm], Max. "A Chaotic Play," SATURDAY REVIEW (Lond), XCV (28 Feb 1903), 261.

"The second act [of *A Man of Honour*] . . . is admirably conceived and written; and the third act is a fine piece of emotional drama. The rest of the play falls to pieces. Mr. Maugham becomes too bitter. . . . A weak and well-meaning young man . . . suddenly . . . becomes a monster. . . . Mr. Maugham should have allowed a few months to elapse between his third and fourth acts. Then we could have all the bitterness that is needed, without any sacrifice to truth."

24* Chambers, E. K. "Mr. Maugham's Irony," ACADEMY, LXIV (28 Feb 1903), 207-8.

A Man of Honour contains passages which drag, its ironical intention might be manifested earlier, and the introduction of the brother-in-law in the last act is bad judgment; but the play is "good honest work, well written, well constructed, and with a point of view of its own."

25 "Drama," ATHENAEUM, No. 3931 (28 Feb 1903), 283.

Beginning as a comedy not unlike CASTE, *A Man of Honour* ends "in a savage sneer at human infirmity." Treated as serious drama, the play is "clever but inadequate"; taken as satire, "it is brilliant, abominable, perverse." M has considerable ability; he needs a "cheerier estimate of humanity."

26* K., H. A. "Plays & Players," SUNDAY SPECIAL (Lond), 1 March 1903, p. 6; rptd by Raymond Mander and Joe Mitchenson, eds, in THEATRICAL COMPANION TO MAUGHAM (Lond: Rockliff, 1955), pp. 24-25 [although Mander and Mitchenson ascribe the review to J. T. Grein].

A Man of Honour "might well be called 'THE SECOND MR. TANQUERAY' "; for just as Pinero's play, a great work in conception and distinction, was the drama of the last decade of the nineteenth century, so M's is of "the first triennium of the twentieth century." M is Pinero's peer, if not his superior, in "supreme simplicity of dialogue and plot."

27 Moy, Thomas W. *"A Man of Honour,"* GRAPHIC, LXVII (28 Feb 1903), 286.

The play belongs to "the new dramatic school, which takes a pleasure in depressing the spirits of the spectator with sordid and gloomy pictures of Society, designed, apparently, to illustrate the comfortless doctrine that life is of necessity a cruel game of cross-purposes, and honour and duty are empty words"; there are, however, "some scenes in which the conflict of human passion is depicted with an uncompromising fidelity and a power which is essentially dramatic."

28* "New Novels," ATHENAEUM, No. 3924 (11 Jan 1903), 44. *Mrs. Craddock* "has a good deal of charmless reality about it. The aunt is a disappointment, for she is announced as quite a character. If Mr. Maugham deserves praise it is for his study of the average man, not the temperamental woman; in this he shows some care and consistency. Mr. Craddock is to us really uninteresting and uninterestingly real."

29 "The Stage Society," TIMES (Lond), 24 Feb 1903, p. 8. *A Man of Honour* is "ugly in subject and . . . dismal in tone." M must be "of the age of all the audacities, he possesses a keen sense of observation, especially for the seamy side of life, and it is inevitable that he should deal with what strikes him most. A man of his manifest ability is bound to become more cheerful by-and-by."

1904

30 "Avenue Theatre," TIMES (Lond), 19 Feb 1904, p. 4. The reviewer still retains the contradictory feelings he experienced when the revived *A Man of Honour* was produced one year before [see "The Stage Society," TIMES (Lond), 24 Feb 1903, p. 8] and so describes the play as "weak-powerful, attractive-repulsive," but awaits "with some eagerness" M's "next serious contribution to the stage."

31* Beerbohm, Max. "An Uncommercial Play," SATURDAY REVIEW (Lond), XCVII (5 March 1904), 207-8.
In the revival of *A Man of Honour,* Jenny Bush is better drawn than Basil Kent; the last act, now revised, is not as effective as the original version; the dialogue is at times "scriptive," then at times "too natural."

32 "Drama," ATHENAEUM, No. 3983 (27 Feb 1904), 282-83. Though M has attempted to remove the blemishes on *A Man of Honour* by repairing the last act, he has not succeeded: "the gloom . . . is scarcely diminished, and the savage satire of humanity remains as pitiless as before."

33 Grein, J. T. *"A Man of Honour,"* SUNDAY TIMES AND SPECIAL (Lond), 21 Feb 1904, p. 7; rptd by Raymond Mander and Joe Mitchenson, eds, in THEATRICAL COMPANION TO MAUGHAM (Lond: Rockliff, 1955), pp. 25-26.

The revision of the play is an improvement over the original version, but some scenes in the third and fourth acts "are too largely spun out."

34 " *'A Man of Honour,'* at the Avenue," ILLUSTRATED LONDON NEWS, CXXIV (27 Feb 1904), 287.

"Now that the author has softened down its cynical ending," the revised play "ranks as the most interesting and observant work our stage has known for many a day."

35* *"The Merry-Go-Round,"* ACADEMY, LXVII (15 Oct 1904), 338.

M sees the social world, his "merry-go-round," as a hospital "with its wards filled to choking with victims of a fantastic passion"; he understands "his patients and their symptoms; he knows the wards of his hospital; he has seen the smoky taper. And there is no dull page, no prosy line, no coarseness, no offence in working out the problem which he has set himself to expound."

36 "New Novels," ATHENAEUM, No. 4018 (29 Oct 1904), 586.

In *The Merry-Go-Round,* the three plots are developed with "considerable power," though joined by the "slightest possible thread of connection." The characterization is remarkable for its "depth and width of range."

37 "The Theatres," GRAPHIC, LXIX (27 Feb 1904), 286.

The revival of *A Man of Honour* is "a work which it is more than worthwhile to go and see, if only for the sake of the second act and its scene between the ill-matched husband and wife."

1905

38 [O'Connor, T. P.] "T. P.'s Bookshelf," T. P.'s WEEKLY, V (3 Feb 1905), 138.

The Land of the Blessed Virgin is "full of the colour which Murillo splashed upon his canvasses."

39 "Spain and the Spanish," ATHENAEUM, No. 4039 (25 March 1905), 366.

The title of *The Land of the Blessed Virgin* raises expectations of legend and folklore, which are not fulfilled; M's love for Spain compensates for his boyish, "gorgeous superlatives."

1906

40 The Baron de B[ook] W[orms]. [Pseudonym for Sir F. C. Burnand]. "Our Booking-Office," PUNCH, CXXX (21 Feb 1906), 144.
The Bishop's Apron, which "for satirical humour and quizzical observation . . . takes a double first," is the best clerical novel since *Barchester Towers.*

41 "New Novels," ATHENAEUM, No. 4093 (7 April 1906), 417.
The Bishop's Apron is a "pleasant satire" with occasion for "much epigram, and several lifelike social sketches."

42* "Novel Notes," BOOKMAN (Lond), XXX (April 1906), 36.
The Bishop's Apron, M's social satire, "is none the less true and biting for being largely clothed in a habit of pleasant and apparently irresponsible flippancy"; the whole book is "an admirable blend of cynical gaiety and broadly farcical comedy." Particularly "jarring" because it is so "mercilessly true" is Winnie's experience with Bertram Railing.

1907

43 Chandler, Frank W. THE LITERATURE OF ROGUERY (Boston: Houghton Mifflin, 1907), p. 495.
Liza of Lambeth is cited as a work of "realism less qualified by sentiment."

44 "Court Theatre: *'Lady Frederick'* by W. Somerset Maugham," TIMES (Lond), 28 Oct 1907, p. 12.
The change between this play and *A Man of Honour* points to a complete transformation in M's identity; this play is "exhilarating entertainment."

45 "Drama," ATHENAEUM, No. 4175 (2 Nov 1907), 560.
In *Lady Frederick,* not all M's "strokes of observation, his sallies of wit, can disguise the fact that there is an element of artificiality running through the scheme of this comedy," though the gaiety of the play and its titular character "conquer . . . prejudices."

46 "Drama," NATION (NY), LXXXV (21 Nov 1907), 478.
The British production of *Lady Frederick* is unlike M's earlier "crudely realistic" *Man of Honour* in that it is "utterly artificial, improbable, and even conventional."

47* "Fiction," TIMES LITERARY SUPPLEMENT (Lond), 19 Dec 1907, p. 390.

In *The Explorer,* the device of the "honorable silence" is annoying and unjustifiable; the novel exhibits a certain "lack of proportion" and "occasional sketchiness." Character development, however, especially of the heroine, is skillful and convincing.

48* Grein, J. T. "Last Night's Premieres," SUNDAY TIMES AND SPECIAL (Lond), 27 Oct 1907, p. 7; rptd by Raymond Mander and Joe Mitchenson, eds, in THEATRICAL COMPANION TO MAUGHAM (Lond: Rockliff, 1955), pp. 55-56.

Lady Frederick is not quite "a lifelike comedy, nor . . . free from the artifice and calculation . . . customary in the days of the 'well-made play.' " M should have set his characters in the 1860s rather than in the present, and perhaps substituted "light verse" dialogue for prose. The play has charm, but M is not, by nature, a comedy writer; he needs "strong situations" and can handle those with originality: only in Lady Frederick's confession of the liaison in Act II does M strike his true vein—the vein of *A Man of Honour.*

49 " *'Lady Frederick,'* at the Court," ILLUSTRATED LONDON NEWS, CXXXI (2 Nov 1907), 634.

"The very fact that the play looks as if it might have been more convincing had the time been set back . . . to the eighteenth century, is the surest proof of its artificiality."

50 " *'Lady Frederick,'* at the Court," TRUTH (Lond), LXII (30 Oct 1907), 1038-39.

The play is "bright, amusing, and admirably acted, and yet it is only a deft shuffling of old material."

51 "The Theatres," GRAPHIC, LXXVI (2 Nov 1907), 610.

Lady Frederick is "not a great play," but is "thoroughly enjoyable."

52* Turner, Reginald. *"Lady Frederick,"* ACADEMY, LXXIII (2 Nov 1907), 96-97.

Some scenes of the play have nothing to do with the main action, and the stage tricks in it have "been served before," but altogether it is a "witty, original and exquisitely-wrought study of a fascinating personality."

1908

53* Beerbohm, Max. "How *Dare* He?" SATURDAY REVIEW (Lond), CV (20 June 1908), 782-83.

The part of Alexander Mackenzie was written expressly for Waller, the leading actor, and the plot does not always correspond to reality. [Tongue-in-cheek review of *The Explorer*.]

54* Beerbohm, Max. *"Jack Straw,"* SATURDAY REVIEW (Lond), CV (4 April 1908), 431-32.

A novelist with M's "subtle talent" should have no traffic with the theater. Public and critics acclaim the play, but "I cannot be quite so enthusiastic." There is "little of sheer invention in the farcical figures and situations. The Parker-Jennings family has been seen many times on stage. "In real life they would, of course, be quite new to us." M "keeps us laughing loudly throughout his play. Such as it is, the thing could not have been better done. But it is far from being the best kind of thing that Maugham can do."

55 "The Bookman Gallery: Mr. William Somerset Maugham," BOOKMAN (Lond), XXXIV (June 1908), 90-91.

M is portrayed as the successful novelist-playwright up to the time when he announces his plans to publish *The Magician.*

56 "Books: Novels," SPECTATOR (Lond), CI (12 Dec 1908), 1002.

In *The Magician,* M "gives a real thrill of horror to his readers" and a "sensation of sickness." A good treatment of the "hackneyed theme of artist life in Paris."

57* C., A. " *'The Explorer,'* at the Lyric Theatre," ACADEMY, LXXIV (20 June 1908), 912.

The play "cannot be conceived of as fruits of maturity," and is, indeed, "by far the least satisfactory of any of . . . [Maugham's] plays." M does not show up as a master of either technique or dialogue, the second act hinges on melodrama, and the ethical problem on which the whole motive is based is "melodramatic in the extreme."

58 [Campbell, Gerald]. "Our Booking-Office," PUNCH, CXXXIV (29 Jan 1908), 90.

The Explorer [novel] is "a Sargent-like portrait of a pioneer as he ought to be. . . . But I should like to know whether *Alec Mackenzie* will buy back *Hamlyn's* Purlieu for his wife when he comes home from the Congo. Mr. Maugham will perhaps add a footnote about it in another edition."

59 [Campbell, Gerald]. "Our Booking-Office," PUNCH, CXXXV (30 Dec 1908), 482.
"In its natural as well as supernatural features the story [of *The Magician*] is gruesomely clever. But for my part I don't care to sup my fill with such horrors. They give me indigestion."

60 "Comedy Theatre: *'Mrs. Dot'* by W. Somerset Maugham," TIMES (Lond), 28 April 1908, p. 10.
"The whole thing is very light, bright, agreeable fooling . . . ."

61* "Drama," ATHENAEUM, No. 4197 (4 April 1908), 426.
In turning from drama of ideas to comedy in *Jack Straw,* M follows Barrie's example. "Taught by experience that, before such inveterate sentimentalists as the majority of English theatre-goers, to treat life in its sterner aspects is to gamble against odds—prompted too, doubtless, by an innate sense of humour—he has devoted himself to comedy." The plot is a modern version of the plot of THE LADY OF LYONS, but in M's play the spirit is farcical; the characters and circumstances, "all possible."

62* "Drama," ATHENAEUM, No. 4201 (2 May 1908), 550.
Mrs. Dot shows a slight falling-off from *Lady Frederick* and *Jack Straw;* "one can see the wire-puller behind the mechanical arrangement of situations. Worse still, he is growing rather stilted in his epigrams, and too fond of tirades."

63* "Drama," ATHENAEUM, No. 4209 (27 June 1908), 799.
The stagecraft in *The Explorer* is "brilliant," the emotional situations possess "strength," the theme is "carefully and cleverly elaborated," the dialogue "bristles with wit"; but the characterization is somewhat "thin," and the play lacks "sincerity."

64 "Drama," NATION (NY), LXXXVII (17 Sept 1908), 270.
Jack Straw contains little to justify the high praise bestowed upon it by the British press. Although the story is entertaining and although stage invention is evident, the mechanism is "slovenly in places" and the dialogue "is by no means brilliant."

65 "Drama," NATION (NY), LXXXVII (12 Nov 1908), 472.
Lady Frederick is "a piece of no particular brilliancy, originality, or purpose—bearing many marks of juvenile imitativeness and inexperience. . . ."

66* Drew at His Best in *'Jack Straw',*" NEW YORK TIMES, 15 Sept 1908, p. 9.
Though a success, the play "is of very light and flimsy texture and rather badly made. What it would seem like in the absence of . . . excellent artists who give it distinction one would rather not imagine." M's particular

weaknesses lie "in an inability to move his characters easily . . . and in a method of exposition that is almost amateurish."

67* Eaton, Walter Prichard. "A Playwright Who Stumbled into Fame," HARPER'S WEEKLY, LII (10 Oct 1908), 32; rptd in THE MAUGHAM ENIGMA, ed by Klaus W. Jonas (N Y: Citadel P, 1954), pp. 101-3.

[This biographical sketch emphasizes M's sudden success in America as well as in England.]

68 "Epilogue," PUNCH, CXXXIV (24 June 1908), 465-66; rptd by Raymond Mander and Joe Mitchenson, eds, in THEATRICAL COMPANION TO MAUGHAM (Lond: Rockliff, 1955), pp. 57-58.

[Mock interview with M at the time he had four plays, *Lady Frederick, Jack Straw, Mrs. Dot,* and *The Explorer,* running concurrently in London.]

69 "Ethel Barrymore in *'Lady Frederick,'* " NEW YORK WORLD, 10 Nov 1908, p. 7.

The play, "in spite of its rather entertaining story, its ready but obvious repartee and its three or four clearly drawn characters, is plainly a theatrical piece, a fabric invented to display the cleverness of its author in the idle art of inventing epigram, rather than to picture life." It is, however, better than *Jack Straw* or *Mrs. Dot* in that it has more "originality and fibre."

70 *"The Explorer,"* ACADEMY, LXXIV (4 Jan 1908), 324.

The "charming flippancy" of *Lady Frederick* is replaced here by a "deep understanding of human nature, and the power of making that understanding 'tell.' " The novel is "solid," in that it is "carefully constructed and conscientiously written."

71 " *'The Explorer,'* at the Lyric," ILLUSTRATED LONDON NEWS, CXXXII (20 June 1908), 916, 918.

The play has brilliance of technique, gripping situations, smart wit, but "a note of insincerity" is detected throughout; the jests, particularly, "seem like fireworks that have been carefully prepared beforehand."

72 " *'The Explorer,'* at the Lyric," TRUTH (Lond), LXIII (17 June 1908), 1517-18.

The play shows the "sober side" of M's "undoubted talent"; the reviewer feels, however, that M's real bent lies "in writing those witty, rather superficial comedies which form such delightful after-dinner entertainments."

73* Grein, J. T. "Last Night's Premieres," SUNDAY TIMES AND SPECIAL (Lond), 14 June 1908, p. 9; rptd by Raymond Mander and Joe Mitchenson, eds, in THEATRICAL COMPANION TO MAUGHAM (Lond: Rockliff, 1955), pp. 45-47.

The story of *The Explorer* is simple, the narrative straightforward, the characterization of major and minor figures "sketched in rapid lines." The comic relief is graceful but not indispensable. Mackenzie's silence in Act III is, perhaps, unconvincing, depending "on the ethical view taken by the audience"; nevertheless, M's stagecraft and sense of proportion are nothing less than "astounding."

74* Grein, J. T. "Premieres of the Week," SUNDAY TIMES AND SPECIAL (Lond), 29 March 1908, p. 4; rptd by Raymond Mander and Joe Mitchenson, eds, in THEATRICAL COMPANION TO MAUGHAM (Lond: Rockliff, 1955), pp. 64-65.

M, like Grant Allen, is versatile and omniscient "in the application of his pen," outdistancing Allen in securing a firm hold on the stage. *Jack Straw* reveals a new feature of M's "chameleonic talent"; for, whereas *Lady Frederick* was pure comedy of fantasy, the new play is "comedy of reality broadened by farcical extravagance." M has *esprit,* a quality revered in French writers and exceedingly rare in the English.

75* Grein, J. T. "Premieres of the Week," SUNDAY TIMES AND SPECIAL (Lond), 3 May 1908, p. 4; rptd by Raymond Mander and Joe Mitchenson, eds, in THEATRICAL COMPANION TO MAUGHAM (Lond: Rockliff, 1955), pp. 61-62.

Mrs. Dot shows that M's imagination is diverse; his sense of humor, keen. He possesses the gift of perfect stagecraft, commanded by "intuition and by careful observation of French methods." Above all, he has delicacy of style and, with "lightning quickness," can "sketch a situation, a phase of life, a characteristic of a coterie."

76* Hamilton, Clayton. "The Drama," FORUM, XL (Oct 1908), 344-45.

"Mr. Maugham has a positive gift for entertainment. He has an easy gay inventiveness; he is capable of assembling a series of amusing situations; and he writes with brilliancy and grace. On the other hand, he appears to possess no decided gift for delineating character, and does not seem to trouble himself about saying anything serious concerning life as it is really lived. In *Jack Straw* he has frankly modelled in the sand. He has written a play that passes in a night, but passes pleasantly."

77* Hamilton, Clayton. "The Drama," FORUM, XL (Dec 1908), 545-46.

Lady Frederick is "on the whole, a better play than *Jack Straw*: but it reveals no abilities on the part of the playwright which were not already evident in the earlier piece. Mr. Maugham is not an author of importance; he has nothing to tell us about life; but he has the pleasing gift of being playful, and the engaging merit of writing with brilliancy and ease."

78 " *'Jack Straw,'* at the Vaudeville," ILLUSTRATED LONDON NEWS, CXXXII (4 April 1908), 508.

The play is "a modernized version of THE LADY OF LYONS," written in a sprightly manner.

79 " *'Jack Straw,'* at the Vaudeville," TRUTH (Lond), LXIII (1 April 1908), 832-33.

The play is "really a delightful farce . . . . It is of the surface surfacey. The dialogue is easy, racy, and full of unexpected turns and twists, and the situations are genuinely amusing."

80 "John Drew as Jack Straw," NEW YORK SUN, 15 Sept 1908, p. 7.

"A new intellect has not arrived on the stage in the person of Mr. Maugham, but a new entertainer has." M's plot in *Jack Straw* is as old as THE LADY OF LYONS, but he has handled it with "fresh and abounding humor."

81* "Lyric Theatre: *'The Explorer'* by William Somerset Maugham," TIMES (Lond), 15 June 1908, p. 12.

If the audience is skeptical about the reality of the hero, that is M's fault: "he seems to have undertaken the delineation of Alexander Mackenzie seriously enough on a conventionally romantic plan and then, as the work progressed, to have found his hero appealing, in defiance of all the dramatic proprieties, to his sense of humour." In heroic drama "there must be no confusion between Alexander the Great and Alexander the Coppersmith."

82 "Merry Light Comedy Is Gay *'Jack Straw,'* " NEW YORK WORLD, 5 Sept 1908, p. 7.

The plot is "as old as Methuselah," but the story is told cleverly, and the dialogue is apt and witty. M has been compared with Clyde Fitch, but he hasn't the latter's skill at plot-making. [Review of the NY premiere of the first of "Mr. J. Somerset Maugham's" *(sic)* comedies.]

83 Metcalfe, [J. S.] "Drama: The Goose that Laid the Golden Eggs," LIFE, LII (24 Sept 1908), 321.

In *Jack Straw,* M is like Clyde Fitch "in that he takes a slender theme and endeavors to make it interesting by its faithfully reproduced fashionable atmosphere, smart lines and mildly laughable situations."

84 Metcalfe, [J. S.] "Drama: Music, Comedy and Newspaper Honesty," LIFE, LII (19 Nov 1908), 558-59.

Lady Frederick is a better play than *Jack Straw,* both in construction and dialogue, though M has appropriated well-known quotations without credit to their originators.

85 "Miss Barrymore in *'Lady Frederick,'* " NEW YORK TIMES, 10 Nov 1908, p. 9.

The play is just deep enough to provide a good night's entertainment.

86 "Miss Barrymore Made Over," NEW YORK SUN, 10 Nov 1908, p. 7.

Lady Frederick is "a delightful comedy, skilfully worked out, full of brilliant, snappy dialogue and well-drawn characters."

87 "Miss Barrymore's *'Lady Frederick'* a Success," NEW YORK HERALD, 10 Nov 1908, p. 12.

M's lines sparkle with comedy, "yet sometimes border on the psychological."

88 "Mr. Drew as a Writer Delights Audience," NEW YORK HERALD, 15 Sept 1908, p. 10.

John Drew will have to divide his popularity with *Jack Straw,* "and that is a compliment, too, to both concerned."

89 " *'Mrs. Dot,'* at the Comedy," ILLUSTRATED LONDON NEWS, CXXXII (2 May 1908), 658.

The play is "a champagne kind of comedy," superficial in ideas and character study, meant simply to amuse, which it does very well.

90 " *'Mrs. Dot,'* at the Comedy," TRUTH (Lond), LXIII (6 May 1908), 1142-43.

Like all M's plays, *Mrs. Dot* is another "delightful after-dinner entertainment."

91 "Music and Drama: *'Jack Straw,'* " NEW YORK EVENING POST, 15 Sept 1908, p. 7.

The play is amusing but of little account so far as literary or dramatic excellence is concerned; its humor is of the "old and obvious sort," and its construction—especially in the first act—is awkward and amateurish.

92* "Music and Drama: *'Lady Frederick,'* " NEW YORK EVENING POST, 10 Nov 1908, p. 9.

The play is neither as new nor as brilliant as published reports might lead one to believe: the plot is ancient, treated without freshness; the wit is too calculated; and the construction is amateurish.

93 "Music, Art and Drama," INDEPENDENT (NY), LXV (12 Nov 1908), 1120.

Jack Straw is "perhaps too thoroly English for American taste." The plot is a mere adventure, and lacks "spontaneous human wit."

94 "Music, Art and Drama," INDEPENDENT (NY), LXV (24 Dec 1908), 1605.

Lady Frederick "contains quick repartée and is wholly adequate as a story." Its success is owing largely to the personality of Ethel Barrymore.

95* "New Novels," ATHENAEUM, No. 4184 (4 Jan 1908), 9. The plot[of *The Explorer*] has not much distinction, the beginning drags, the end is not entirely convincing; but the book is nowhere "tiresome," possesses some "logic" and "shape," and its characterization "draws one on."

96* "New Novels," ATHENAEUM, No. 4232 (5 Dec 1908), 715. In *The Magician,* M plays alternately the parts of the Balzac of PEAU DE CHAGRIN, of the Du Maurier who created Svengali, and of an H. G. Wells "consistently logical in his most fantastic moments." The plot would serve for melodrama; but M brings "successful realism" to his picture, and the lighter parts of his book show "keen humour and observation."

97* "Novel Notes," BOOKMAN (Lond), XXXIII (Feb 1908), 216. The construction of *The Explorer* is not sound, for one believes Fred Allerton to be its central figure only to find Alec Mackenzie usurp his place unexpectedly. The simplicity of style seems "affected," and one tires early of the "epigram-spinning barrister."

98* "Reviews: Novels," SATURDAY REVIEW (Lond), CV (15 Feb 1908), 209.
The Explorer is "interesting as showing how literary perception and instinct may take the place of actual experience." Although lacking firsthand knowledge, M has constructed an "admirable and lifelike" character in Alec Mackenzie and drawn an "accurate and effective" picture of his activities in East Africa. M "feels himself more at home" in the London scenes. The "smart dialogue" would be "effective in a play."

99* "Reviews: Novels," SATURDAY REVIEW (Lond), CVI (26 Dec 1908), 798.
M is castigated for concentrating upon the "obscene side of the Black Art" in *The Magician.* M's central figure is "a very disgusting person." The "horrid 'homunculi'—a medieval idea revived in one of Mr. W. B. Yeats' books with some dignity and reticence—are, in Maugham's hands, merely horrible." The attempt to evoke terror "produces only nausea."

100* "Reviews of New Plays," NEW YORK DRAMATIC MIRROR, LX (26 Sept 1908), 2.
In *Jack Straw* the "not unusual situation has such original turns as to mark the author as a man of considerable imagination as well as fancy. The dialogue has the charm of naturalness without losing brilliancy. It has few epigrams, but it is consistently bright. There is . . . no depth to the play, which aims to be no more than comedy and comes near being farce, but there are qualities that entertain without surfeit. The author shows

weakness in character drawing. The three bounder members of the Jennings family have distinguishing characteristics, but the other people in the play are made in much the same mold, except, of course, Jack Straw."

101 "Reviews of New Plays," NEW YORK DRAMATIC MIRROR, LX (21 Nov 1908), 2.

Lady Frederick "has the same sparkling frothiness as *Jack Straw* . . . . It is chiefly brilliant dialogue without either much heart or much soul. The comedy situations are pleasantly devised and are decidedly amusing."

102 Ruhl, Arthur. "Plays and Players—A Spaniard, a Frenchman, and an Englishman Contribute to Our Entertainment: Happy Mr. Maugham," COLLIER'S, XLII (5 Dec 1908), 22.

In *Lady Frederick,* M has no ideas and nothing to say, but he is in the enviable position of knowing how to give the public what it wants. *Lady Frederick* is no better than *Jack Straw*. "It has graceful sentiment and a suggestion of real feeling, and the witty, reckless Irish heroine is lively and appealing."

103 Ruhl, Arthur. "Plays and Players—Two English and Two American Plays of the Opening Season in New York: Further Petrification of Mr. John Drew," COLLIER'S, XLII (24 Oct 1908), 14.

Jack Straw is "about the shallowest type of entertainment devised by contemporary man. It is a 'society' play, without either the wit or the graceful sentiment which are such plays' only excuse for being."

104* "The Theatres," GRAPHIC, LXXVII (4 April 1908), 479.

Jack Straw "must not be considered too seriously. In truth, though adroit, it is superficial stuff . . . . Perhaps some day a playwright will write a play, and succeed in finding a manager to produce it, in which the differences of class will be shown for what they are, a deep-seated difference of ambition and outlook on life, not a mere trick of speech and a certain knowledge of how to behave in company."

105 "The Theatres," GRAPHIC, LXXVII (2 May 1908), 615.

In *Mrs. Dot,* "the dialogue is crisp, amusing, and epigrammatic, and Mr. Maugham's latest success promises to be also his greatest success."

106* "The Theatrical World," GRAPHIC, LXXVII (20 June 1908), 850.

The Explorer reveals that M, melodramatist, is not in the same rank as M, writer of comedies: the explorer's promise is made, one feels, only for stage purposes, and the resulting unhappiness he spreads because of his promises destroys one's sympathy for him.

107 "The Tragedy of Mr. Maugham's Dramatic Success," CURRENT LITERATURE, XLV (Aug 1908), 202-3.
M is presented to America on the eve of his American stage debut; he is an author who, for a decade, maintained a high literary standard and met with no success, then lowered his standard and found "London at his feet!" [*Liza of Lambeth* is identified, mistakenly, as one of M's plays.]

108* "Vaudeville Theatre: *'Jack Straw'* by W. Somerset Maugham," TIMES (Lond), 27 March 1908, p. 12.
M has added a subtle complication to the formula of the stage impostor deriving from Molière [LES PRECIEUSES RIDICULES] and Marivaux [LE JEU DE L'AMOUR ET DU HASARD]: M makes a man masquerade as himself. "Distinctly diverting entertainment."

109 V[illars], P[aul]. "William Somerset Maugham and His Plays," THEATRE MAGAZINE, VIII (Oct 1908), 278, 280.
M's years as a medical student must have given him a clinical interest in characters, sharpening his powers of observation. M himself is particularly impressed by the smoothness and homogeneity of the American casts who have performed his plays. [Interview.]

110 White, Matthew, Jr. "The Stage," MUNSEY'S MAGAZINE, XL (Nov 1908), 272.
Jack Straw is "thin in texture, and somewhat awkwardly constructed."

1909

111* Archer, William. "The Drama: *'Penelope'* and Popularity," NATION (Lond), IV (16 Jan 1909), 606-7.
Penelope is better than *Mrs. Dot,* the second half of the play better than the first half; still, the whole is "carelessly and unconscientiously written," sacrificing plausibility to momentary comic effects.

112 "At the Theatres," THEATRE MAGAZINE, X (Nov 1909), 137.
M's adaptation of Ernest Grenet-Dancourt's LES GAITES DE VEUVAGE as *The Noble Spaniard* is "clever," but superficial, the actions are at times "unreasonably preposterous," and M does not give the noble Spaniard any real motive for his presumption.

113 B. "Plays of the Week," GRAPHIC, LXXX (9 Oct 1909), 480.
In *Smith,* M has filled in "the interstices with extraordinary cleverness, so that there is not a dull moment, for he views the world with Tom's engaging frankness, and kicks theatrical convention into its well-deserved

gutter. . . . The result of this method is like a breath of Bernard Shaw, only it is all so much more human than he can ever be."

114* Beerbohm, Max. "A Costume Play," SATURDAY REVIEW (Lond), CVI (27 March 1909), 399-400.

The plot of M's adaptation of Ernest Grenet-Dancourt's LES GAITES DE VEUVAGE as *The Noble Spaniard* is thin and hackneyed: "So another shaft is sunk, and another mine worked, to fill up the evening." Of especial merit, however, is "the faithful reconstruction of the manners of a decade so near to us as to make its differences irresistibly touching and amusing." M has "an innate sense for the subtleties of period. . . . The soul of 1850 was more romantic than that of 1860, but its manners were far primmer; and this anomaly, throughout the play, Maugham has preserved with a cunning hand."

115* Beerbohm, Max. "A Parenthesis," SATURDAY REVIEW (Lond), CVII (9 Jan 1909), 39-40.

Beerbohm disagrees with M's statement that it is "most unwise" for dramatists to "take themselves seriously." He prefers plays that are "deliberate attempts to present this or that phase of our various life as it is." Against M's declaration that "to entertain should be the first—perhaps the only—aim of the playwright," Beerbohm finds it "inconceivable" that M regrets his "unwisdom" in writing *A Man of Honour,* which stands on a "far higher level" than his light comedies, even though the latter happen to pay. M should not discourage fellow-artists who, "conscientiously, but unremuneratively, are treading the path to which his own first ambitions led him." Beerbohm suggests that M establish a "jolly little paddocks [experimental theatre] for the colts [serious young dramatists] to kick up their heels in."

116 "Books for Summer Reading," NEW YORK TIMES BOOK REVIEW, 12 June 1909, p. 377.

In *The Explorer* [novel], M follows the "prevailing English fashion of going to Africa for its paraphernalia of adventure."

117* "Comedy Theatre: *'Penelope'* by W. Somerset Maugham," TIMES (Lond), 11 Jan 1909, p. 12.

The play revolves around a commonplace *motif,* but M's "master-stroke of irony" at the end of Act II is a genuine "coup de théâtre," imbuing the *motif* with originality.

118* Comedy Theatre: *'Smith'* by W. Somerset Maugham," TIMES (Lond), 1 Oct 1909, p. 11.

The play is, like M's others, "a curious blend of the fresh and the stale"; the hero is the familiar "backwoodsman" à la Rousseau, and the "social doctrine of babies *v.* bridge" has become one of the commonplaces of the contemporary stage. Only M's wit redeems the play.

119 "Current Fiction," NATION (NY), LXXXVIII (11 March 1909), 255.
M's reputation as a dramatist is not enhanced by either *The Magician* or *The Explorer*; "they show cleverness, but less of a dramatic than of a journalistic sort, quickness to seize the theme of the moment, and facility in turning it to account."

120 "Drama," ATHENAEUM, No. 4238 (16 Jan 1909), 83-84.
Penelope is less artificial than the plays M has previously written; the wit is "less labored," the whole has a "reasonable scheme"; in all, the story "dashes along with a briskness, vivacity, and comic force that are irresistible."

121 "Drama," ATHENAEUM, No. 4248 (27 March 1909), 386.
One can be amused by the "mechanical humours" of M's adaptation of Ernest Grenet-Dancourt's LES GAITES DE VEUVAGE as *The Noble Spaniard,* but may also regret that M has "wasted his talent on material unworthy of it."

122* "Drama," ATHENAEUM, No. 4276 (9 Oct 1909), 435-36.
In *Smith,* M returns to the "seriousness" of *A Man of Honour*. Like Pinero in MID-CHANNEL and Sutro in MAKING OF A GENTLEMAN, M is moved to wrath over the spectacle of the modern woman of fashion who shirks all duties of marriage and maternity; but M has worldly wisdom, and by making his play half satire, half fairy tale, he makes his audience think by allowing it to laugh.

123 "Drama," NATION (NY), LXXXVIII (4 Feb 1909), 122.
The British production of *Penelope* is "in the main a conventional piece, but full of amusing touches and an occasional unexpected turn."

124* "Drama," NATION (NY), LXXXIX (16 Dec 1909), 606.
Penelope is "a very light piece, more nearly allied to farce than comedy. It is like other inventions of the same author, smartly written in places, and it contains some ingenious and amusing situations, but drags occasionally and reveals many signs of haste and carelessness. Of dramatic substance it has little, and such moral as it implies is of doubtful truth or wisdom."

125 "Drama," WORLD TO-DAY, XVII (Nov 1909), 1137.
M's adaptation of Ernest Grenet-Dancourt's LES GAITES DE VEUVAGE as *The Noble Spaniard* is a "Victorian farce": "This is praise, indeed, for the distinction pertains not only to the early Victorian atmosphere disclosed, but also in a measure to the satirical point of view of last-century comedy writers of the Sheridan school."

126 "Drama of the Month," PLAYGOER AND SOCIETY ILLUSTRATED, I (Nov-Dec 1909), 50.

In *Smith,* M has added little to his reputation, although he has sustained it. The brilliance of his dialogue overshadows the improbabilities of plot.

127 "The Drama that Plays," GRAPHIC, LXXIX (16 Jan 1909), 78.

Penelope displays "too much construction and too little spontaneity. . . . It is a French farce without French wit, or, odd as it may sound, French delicacy."

128 "Edeson and Play a Delight," NEW YORK SUN, 21 Sept 1909, p. 7.

M's adaptation of Ernest Grenet-Dancourt's LES GAITES DE VEUVAGE as *The Noble Spaniard,* like its plot, hangs "by a slender thread" when "Mr. Edeson himself is not before the footlights."

129 "*'The Explorer,'* Revived at the Lyric," ILLUSTRATED LONDON NEWS, CXXXIV (29 May 1909), 798.

The play has been thunderously applauded, but even with the changes M has made since its first run [13 June 1908], its plot remains implausible; indeed, the latter half of the play is "a tissue of false sentiments, manufactured pathos, and artificial emotion."

130 "A Feast of Horrors," NEW YORK TIMES BOOK REVIEW, 13 Feb 1909, p. 88.

In *The Magician,* M tells his tale of the weird and terrible with a simple sincerity, matching unhallowed, supernatural practices with the clean, sweet things of common life.

131* Grein, J. T. "Last Night's Premieres," SUNDAY TIMES AND SPECIAL (Lond), 10 Jan 1909, p. 9; rptd by Raymond Mander and Joe Mitchenson, eds, in THEATRICAL COMPANION TO MAUGHAM (Lond: Rockliff, 1955), pp. 68-69.

Penelope, a play "of Parisian grace and English good-nature," is flawed by too much talk and an introduction of superfluous characters. All shortcomings vanish, however, "in the bright sunshine of a sparkling dialogue, a human undercurrent in the action and numberless little episodes and interludes which betray the man of the world as well as the man who knows."

132 Grein, J. T. "Premieres of the Week," SUNDAY TIMES AND SPECIAL (Lond), 3 Oct 1909, p. 4; rptd by Raymond Mander and Joe Mitchenson, eds, in THEATRICAL COMPANION TO MAUGHAM (Lond: Rockliff, 1955), pp. 76, 93.

Smith's subject [a servant's becoming the butt of a coarse person's petty tyranny] is repellent, but the play "makes an excellent evening's entertainment."

133 Hamilton, Clayton. "Imitation and Suggestion in the Drama," FORUM, XLII (Nov 1909), 439.

M's adaptation of Ernest Grenet-Dancourt's LES GAITES DE VEUVAGE as *The Noble Spaniard* is "skillfully planned and cleverly written, and deserves to be remembered as a deft and dashing trifle."

134 "Love and Exploration," NEW YORK TIMES BOOK REVIEW, 27 Feb 1909, p. 117.

In *The Explorer* [novel], M's faculty for character portrayal and his skill in construction are excellent.

135* "Lyric Theatre: *'The Explorer'* by William Somerset Maugham," TIMES (Lond), 20 May 1909, p. 10.

The revived play is no more "than clever hack-work. . . . There is a dose of Kiplingism in it, and a dose of stage-Mayfair 'smartness,' and a dose, an overdose, of that worn-out and wearisome theatrical convention which requires the hero to be cast off by the heroine because through an impossible and absurd chivalry he will not defend himself against calumny."

136* "Marie Tempest Welcomed," NEW YORK SUN, 14 Dec 1909, p. 7.

In *Penelope,* M's theme is familiar to Americans who know Thompson Buchanan's A WOMAN'S WAY or Barrie's WHAT EVERY WOMAN KNOWS. The third act of M's play alone is better than the preceding two; but the general impression gathered from the whole is that M as yet has little to say, and that he says it agreeably but without distinction.

137 Metcalfe, [J. S.] "Drama: Importations Not Entirely Successful," LIFE, LIV (7 Oct 1909), 476.

In M's adaptation of Ernest Grenet-Dancourt's LES GAITES DE VEUVAGE as *The Noble Spaniard,* "it may be that Mr. Maugham set out to satirize the literary qualities and sentimentality of the middle of the last century, but his effort is a boomerang for himself and his abettors."

138 Metcalfe, [J. S.] "Drama: Mr. Maugham to the Fore Again," LIFE, LIV (23 Dec 1909), 916-17.

Penelope "makes no call on high intelligence and is just the thing to fill in the time between a not too long dinner and an early supper."

139 "Miss Anglin Acts Old Chester Role," NEW YORK WORLD, 21 Sept 1909, p. 7.

[Primarily a plot summary of M's adaptation of Ernest Grenet-Dancourt's LES GAITES DE VEUVAGE as *The Noble Spaniard.*]

140 "Mr. Edeson's New Play Very Well Liked," NEW YORK HERALD, 21 Sept 1909, p. 11.

M's adaptation of Ernest Grenet-Dancourt's LES GAITES DE VEUVAGE as *The Noble Spaniard* "has many bright lines, and a few that do not shine, a few earnest lines and some that cross the border of silliness."

141 "Mr. Maugham's *'Penelope,'* at the Comedy," ILLUSTRATED LONDON NEWS, CXXXIV (16 Jan 1909), 74.
"The scheme is thin, . . . and the treatment is never more than surface-deep; but Mr. Maugham's wit is always sparkling, and his command of technique permits of many delightful ingenuities of situation."

142 "Mrs. Tempest Charming in *'Penelope'* Comedy," NEW YORK HERALD, 14 Dec 1909, p. 8.
"The play is best at both ends. The beginning is promising and the end what London would call 'ripping'. . . . The second act dawdles along a bit, but all is forgiven at the end."

143 "Music and Drama: *'The Noble Spaniard,'*" NEW YORK EVENING POST, 21 Sept 1909, p. 7.
M's adaptation of Ernest Grenet-Dancourt's LES GAITES DE VEUVAGE will succeed only through the efforts of its leading actress, Miss Rose Coghlan.

144 "Music and Drama: *'Penelope,'*" NEW YORK EVENING POST, 14 Dec 1909, p. 9.
The first and third acts are "fairly amusing"; the second is "thin and dull."

145 "New Royalty Theatre: *'The Noble Spaniard,'*" TIMES (Lond), 22 March 1909, p. 10; rptd by Raymond Mander and Joe Mitchenson, eds, in THEATRICAL COMPANION TO MAUGHAM (Lond: Rockliff, 1955), pp. 72-73.
M's adaptation of Ernest Grenet-Dancourt's LES GAITES DE VEUVAGE shows the successful relationships of costume and dialect to character in achieving farcical effects. [Primarily a plot summary.]

146 "*'Noble Spaniard'* an Amusing Farce," NEW YORK TIMES, 21 Sept 1909, p. 9.
M's adaptation of Ernest Grenet-Dancourt's LES GAITES DE VEUVAGE is "charming and amusing in situations and dialogue."

147 "*'The Noble Spaniard,'* at the Royalty," ILLUSTRATED LONDON NEWS, CXXXIV (27 March 1909), 442.
M's adaptation of Ernest Grenet-Dancourt's LES GAITES DE VEUVAGE is "one long frolic of amusing nonsense."

148 "*'The Noble Spaniard,'* at the Royalty," TRUTH (Lond), LXV (24 March 1909), 701-2.
M's adaptation of Ernest Grenet-Dancourt's LES GAITES DE VEUVAGE is

"a deft and gossamer-like tissue of absurdities, ingenious situations, and amusing dialogue, while the early Victorian dresses are sublime."

149 " *'The Noble Spaniard,'* By Somerset Maugham," METROPOLITAN MAGAZINE, XXXI (Dec 1909), [pp. 392-93].

The play will not be popular "because it is so frightfully British." [Illustrations of the American production of M's adaptation of Ernest Grenet-Dancourt's LES GAITES DE VEUVAGE.]

150 " *'Penelope,'* at the Comedy," TRUTH (Lond), LXV (13 Jan 1909), 81.

"This picture of vice denouncing virtue is conceived, written, and played in quite the best comedy spirit."

151 " *'Penelope'* Is Only Mildly Amusing," NEW YORK TIMES, 14 Dec 1909, p. 11.

Barring a clever twist in the second act and a funny scene in the third act, M's play is merely DIVORÇONS in a "new frock."

152 "People and Things Theatrical," PEARSON'S MAGAZINE, XXII (Sept 1909), 369-70.

M's efforts are confined to "putting old wine into new bottles," for his plays are "stale" in plot, and freshened with "wit" and occasional "clever turns" of familiar incidents. In *Penelope* Dr. O'Farrell's "air of injured innocence" after discovering his wife's deceit is the "clever turn" to a familiar incident.

153* "The Plays of the Week," NEW YORK DRAMATIC MIRROR, LXII (25 Dec 1909), 5.

Penelope is "the Cyprienne of DIVORÇONS in new gowns. In itself Mr. Maugham's comedy, while possessed of all the sparkle and go of an extraordinarily brilliant dialogue, betrays a remarkable deficiency of unique complications and is singularly barren of any sort of situations. The theme is no longer novel, especially to New York audiences, who have had it treated in A WOMAN'S WAY, in LOVE WATCHES. . . . "

154 "Reviews of New Plays," NEW YORK DRAMATIC MIRROR, LXII (2 Oct 1909), 7.

In M's adaptation of Ernest Grenet-Dancourt's LES GAITES DE VEUVAGE as *The Noble Spaniard,* "there are farcical situations which could have been better developed. There is room for more and brighter lines. The plot is thin and improbable . . . . A few bits that suggest the French origin of the piece rather offend good taste and had better be dispensed with."

155 Ruyssen, Henri. "Comptes Rendus Critiques: Revue du Théâtre Anglais (août 1907-sept. 1908)" (Critical Reports:

Review of the English Theater), REVUE GERMANIQUE, V (1909), 119-20.

The British premiere of *Lady Frederick* was gay, without pretensions, droll, lightly written, not without spirit; and *Jack Straw,* more of a farce than a comedy.

156 S[eaman], O[wen]. "At the Play," PUNCH, CXXXVI (31 March 1909), 232.

If M's adaptation of Ernest Grenet-Dancourt's LES GAITES DE VEUVAGE as *The Noble Spaniard* hadn't Victorian costumes and Hawtrey on which to depend, there would be little left in M's "pot-boiler . . . . to explain his popularity as a playwright."

157 White, Matthew, Jr. "The Stage," MUNSEY'S MAGAZINE, XL (Jan 1909), 555.

Ethel Barrymore's refusal to make herself sufficiently ugly in the "boudoir episode" of *Lady Frederick* and her faulty accent are both censured.

158 White, Matthew, Jr. "The Stage," MUNSEY'S MAGAZINE, XLI (Sept 1909), 898, 900.

Penelope "is almost exactly similar to A WOMAN'S WAY, but . . . not nearly so clever in handling or dialogue . . . ."

159 White, Matthew, Jr. "The Stage," MUNSEY'S MAGAZINE, XLII (Dec 1909), 439-40, 443.

In M's adaptation of Ernest Grenet-Dancourt's LES GAITES DE VEUVAGE as *The Noble Spaniard,* "although that much harped-on string—mistaken identity—is counted upon to sound the note of fun, Mr. Maugham contrives such new and clever ways of twanging it that we enjoy it all . . . . "

1910

160* Archer, William. "The Drama: *'Grace,'* " NATION (Lond), VIII (22 Oct 1910), 157-58.

M is the "English Clyde Fitch," although his talent is "solider" than Fitch's and he does not rely as much on "mere mechanical trickery." *Grace* has more substance than M's earlier plays have manifested, but it "can take no permanent place in dramatic literature." The social picture is "a shallow caricature," which reacts upon the heroine's character, making it incomprehensible. Moreover, M overlooks the fact that the crux of his problem lay not in Grace, but her husband, Claude, who requires better delineation.

161 "At the Theatres," NEW YORK DRAMATIC MIRROR, LXIV (14 Sept 1910), 11.
Smith is "not a new or an original discussion of social vices"; its success is dependent upon "faultless" and superb acting.

162* B., J. M. "The Battle of the Repertory Theatre with Commercialism," GRAPHIC, LXXXII (22 Oct 1910), 650.
Essentially, M is equipped "to go to the heart of life," although he has usually given the public what it wants. In *Grace,* he makes a compromise between commercial and repertory theater through the character of Helen Vernon, who saves the play.

163 B., J. M. "A Plethora of Plays and Players," GRAPHIC, LXXXI (5 March 1910), 308.
In *The Tenth Man,* M's touch is "insecure, because he will insist on rallying nearly all serious conviction."

164* "Drama," ATHENAEUM, No. 4297 (5 March 1910), 287.
The Tenth Man is worked out according to "an arbitrary plan instead of being developed through the natural interaction of character." But though M has copied Bernstein's trick of depending, for his effects, on a violent personality and violent situations, though he reserves his real drama for the last act, one must admire "the sureness of the technique, the broad, clear strokes of individualization, the crispness of wit, and the appropriateness of the dialogue"; the irony of the catastrophe is "overpowering."

165 "Drama," ATHENAEUM, No. 4330 (22 Oct 1910), 499.
M wants to return from comedy to serious drama, but he has become so accustomed to the material of the former that he can no longer distinguish between the sincere and insincere, and thus *Grace*, for all its effectiveness, is "not wholly convincing."

166 "Drama," NATION (NY), XCI (3 Nov 1910), 425.
The British production of *Grace* is "a piece created for its situations, not at all as an exemplification of life or manners."

167 "Drama of the Month," PLAYGOER AND SOCIETY ILLUSTRATED, III (Nov 1910), 45-46.
"If it were not for the charming personality of Miss Irene Vanbrugh . . . *Grace* would be too chilly for this weather."

168 "Duke of York's Theatre: *'Grace'* by W. S. Maugham," TIMES (Lond), 17 Oct 1910, p. 7.
"Apart from the touches of artificiality in the story and a certain failure to distinguish between Victorian fiction and contemporary fact, . . . an undeniably effective piece of work."

169 Findon, B. W. " *'Grace'* by Somerset Maugham," PLAY PICTORIAL, XVII, No. 100 [n. d., but probably late 1910], 2-4.
M follows in the footsteps of Dumas *fils* in presenting good dialogue and excellent sketches of character.

170 "Globe Theatre: *'The Tenth Man'* by W. Somerset Maugham," TIMES (Lond), 25 Feb 1910, p. 12.
"It is not one of Mr. Maugham's happiest efforts. The sentimental business is very stale, the financial intrigue a little bewildering, and some of the politics not a little absurd."

171 Goodman, Edward. "The American Dramatic Problem," FORUM, XLIII (Feb 1910), 189-90.
Like Marie Tempest, the actress, M lacks "the fascination of novelty" but possesses "the more valuable attraction of reliability." *Penelope* has nothing startling or gripping, but there is in it always "a delicious gentle flow of unlabored comedy, aided by a pleasant sparkle of as unlabored cleverness of dialogue."

172* " *'Grace,'* at the Duke of York's," ACADEMY, LXXIX (12 Nov 1910), 470-71.
M is a very "clever," rather than a very "able," writer. He takes his landed gentry "from the comic papers," and his notion of them is "both archaic and ultramodern, and always ignorant"; for all that, M works his story with a sense of the theater and of dramatic effect. Despite the fact that the characters are "unreal," that the story is "insincere and plashy," that there is nothing "of observation of truth in the play from beginning to end," it holds attention through its witty, sometimes cheap, dialogue.

173 " *'Grace,'* at the Duke of York's," ILLUSTRATED LONDON NEWS, CXXXVII (22 Oct 1910), 626.
"The craftsmanship is sound, there is an abundance of epigram, and there are many telling scenes; but . . . Mr. Maugham's is a made play, which does not make us forget we are inside the theatre."

174 " *'Grace,'* at the Duke of York's," TRUTH (Lond), LXVIII (19 Oct 1910), 980-81.
The first act is reminiscent of Pinero's HIS HOUSE IN ORDER; the entire play is clever, but leaves one with "a disagreeable feeling" and the impression that about all of M's work "there is too much head and not enough heart."

175* Grein, J. T. "Last Night's Premieres," SUNDAY TIMES AND SPECIAL (Lond), 16 Oct 1910, p. 9; rptd by Raymond Mander and Joe Mitchenson, eds, in THEATRICAL COMPANION TO MAUGHAM (Lond: Rockliff, 1955), pp. 103-4.

In *Grace,* when M forgets his union of business and art, his touch of tragedy "hits home." But, too often, M window-dresses with "interludes of comedy, . . . linguistic pyrotechnics, . . . [and] collateral characterizations" to appeal to the gallery as well as the stables, and muffles the "pathetic note."

176* Grein, J. T. "Premieres of the Week," SUNDAY TIMES AND SPECIAL (Lond), 27 Feb 1910, p. 4; rptd by Raymond Mander and Joe Mitchenson, eds, in THEATRICAL COMPANION TO MAUGHAM (Lond: Rockliff, 1955), pp. 98-99.

M has the gift of the "homme du monde" in *The Tenth Man*; however, he "forges ahead to a certain point, then all of a sudden stops short, drops into banter." Moreover, his play's inspiration owes a good deal to Bernstein's LA RAFOLE and Fabre's LES VENTRES DORES, to name but two. The play is dull and represents M's first dramatic blunder: M "has been on the crest of the wave, and now there seems to be danger ahead!"

177* J., P. "Correspondence: The Bad Habit of Mr. Maugham," SATURDAY REVIEW (Lond), CX (22 Oct 1910), 517.

Critics are complimenting M on his return to serious drama with *Grace.* After his first play, a serious if commercial failure, and then the series of successful farces, M "always intended to come back to good drama in the end." But "an author cannot write a dozen bad plays and still be the man he was." M has "worked his puppets too long" and "lost the trick of handling flesh and blood."

178 Hamilton, Clayton. "The Plays of the Autumn Season," BOOKMAN (NY), XXXII (Dec 1910), 349-50.

In *Smith,* M's theme is close to Sutro's in THE WALLS OF JERICHO, but M gives it "a clever and dainty treatment."

179 "John Drew Here in '*Smith,*'" NEW YORK SUN, 6 Sept 1910, p. 7.

The fabric of the play is thin, especially in the third act which threatens to become tedious; but the polished acting of the company helped the author over his weak places.

180 "John Drew in Guise of a Rural Moralist," NEW YORK WORLD, 6 Sept 1910, p. 7.

M was more assuredly successful when he wrote trifles; he "has at last [in *Smith*] been afflicted with a mission. Once he was content with mere ripples; now he wants to make waves." M's characters are not believable, though some scenes are written well and contain "a generous supply of bright epigrammatic dialogue in its author's familiar vein."

181 Klauber, Adolph. "Where the Play's the Thing," PEARSON'S MAGAZINE, XXIV (Nov 1910), 646.

Smith is the "most satisfying" of M's comedies so far.

182* Malleus. "The Epigoni," SATURDAY REVIEW (Lond), CX (22 Oct 1910), 513-14.

Up to a point, *Grace* "hangs well together, and contains one really vital and admirable scene, that between Grace and her lover in the second act." Then the play lapses into absurdity. The last scene could have been great if "the data on which it rested were not so ridiculous." [Retells plot.]

183 Metcalfe, [J. S.] "Drama: A British Knight Gone Wrong," LIFE, LV (10 Feb 1910), 245.

"Of lightness in writing" *Mrs. Dot* "comes pretty near being that quality raised to the *n*th power"; it "won't let you go to sleep while you are in the theatre and won't keep you awake after you get home."

184 Metcalfe, [J. S.] "Drama: The New Season Getting into Its Stride," LIFE, LVI (15 Sept 1910), 434.

M's addition of a fourth act to *Smith* "only serves to emphasize his gift of spreading dramatic ideas to what might answer the description of the thin edge of nothing whittled down to a fine point"; the play is, in all, "a slightly amusing, perfectly polite, lighter-than-air, very modish comedy."

185 M[ilne, A. A.] "At the Play," PUNCH, CXXXVIII (2 March 1910), 161.

The Tenth Man suffers from M's not having taken the trouble to make the politics in the play "real."

186 Morton, Edward. "*'The Tenth Man'* at the Globe Theatre," PLAYGOER AND SOCIETY ILLUSTRATED, I (March-April 1910), 248, 250.

[A plot summary, with praise for M's ingenuity.]

187 "Mr. Drew at His Best in *'Smith'* at Empire," NEW YORK TIMES, 6 Sept 1910, p. 9.

Although it has "saccharine" moments and unnecessary padding, the play is M's best so far.

188 *"Mrs. Dot,"* DRAMATIST, I (July 1910), 89.

This play is not worth technical analysis; and it is so shallow it cannot be termed either comedy or farce. Conflict is the key to any play's construction, for from conflict comes personality; but, M hardly seems concerned with this principle.

189 "*'Mrs. Dot'* a Thin but Amusing Farce," NEW YORK TIMES, 25 Jan 1910, p. 9.

To call M's play a comedy "is to strain a definition to the breaking point";

definitely, without a good actress, it can only be an "amiable farce." Its characters and situations are familiar, made individual only through M's "pleasant wit."

190 " *'Mrs. Dot.'* By W. S. Maugham," METROPOLITAN MAGAZINE, XXXII (April 1910), 116-17.
[Illustration, with a plot summary and praise of Billie Burke's performance.]

191 "Music and Drama," NATION (NY), XCI (8 Sept 1910), 226.
Smith, "in spite of its assumption of modernity," exhibits a conventional plot with conventional characters. With its occasionally effective satire, some entertaining lines and humorous situations, there is "more suggestion of labor and artifice than of sincere purpose."

192 "Music and the Drama," WORLD TO-DAY, XVIII (Feb 1910), 136.
Penelope is "built with the cynical sangfroid of a citizen of the world."

193 "Music and the Drama," WORLD TO-DAY, XVIII (March 1910), 246.
Mrs. Dot is a successful comedy in America.

194 "Music, Art and Drama," INDEPENDENT (NY), LXIX (10 Nov 1910), 1025.
In *Smith,* "the curtains are exceedingly happy and well timed."

195 "New Plays," THEATRE MAGAZINE, XI (Jan 1910), xii.
Penelope is "inconsequential, unmoral, seldom brilliant, but never stupid." There is an air of reality about it, but the setting is more Ruritania than Mayfair, as the program indicates.

196* Parsons, Chauncey L. "W. Somerset Maugham, Formalist," NEW YORK DRAMATIC MIRROR, LXIV (14 Dec 1910), 6.
M says that prose comedy is the hardest form to handle, yet it is, in a way, easier than farce. Farce has a broad, more universal appeal; comedy is limited by the traits of the particular nationality which is being satirized. The more gentle comedy is, the smaller its appeal. In his own writing, M starts with the theme and then fills in characters and incidents. He belongs to the "problematical school" of playwriting, for like the Victorian novelists he is concerned with political and social issues. Cultured taste, in his view, has now replaced the art of wild imagination. M then comments on American humor, the bad past London season, the intimate and the large theater, and the theatrical public. [Interview.]

197* "The Players," EVERYBODY'S MAGAZINE, XXIII (Dec 1910). 841-42.
"If the prolific W. Somerset Maugham would learn to write plays as well as he writes dialogue, if he could handle situations as well as he does inci-

dents, if his construction were worthy of his ideas and his impish humor, he would produce some wonderfully brilliant comedies. *Smith* . . . is the best of Maugham's plays thus far seen in this country, but—!"

198* "Plays of the Month," THEATRE MAGAZINE, XII (Oct 1910), 98-99.

Smith is more comedy than satire, and its only effective character is the serene and simple maid, Smith. M, unfortunately, avoids any complications whose resolution lies only in conflict; but it is to his credit that he refuses to make the breadwinner sentimental. The play is superior to Taylor's THE UNEQUAL MATCH, but its light treatment of iniquity makes it inferior to THE WALLS OF JERICHO. Smith herself would be impossible as an American girl, who would be more pert.

199* "The Plays of the Week," NEW YORK DRAMATIC MIRROR, LXIII (5 Feb 1910), 6.

Mrs. Dot is "one of those rippling, shallow but peculiarly entertaining comedies for which Mr. Maugham has become popular. As in *Penelope* and *Lady Frederick* he deals with all the superficialities of a fashionable woman's nature, and paints her foibles, her whims, her coquettry and her characteristic talent for intrigue. If you look for anything intrinsically dramatic you will be disappointed. He never shows us a roaring wild beast. He cages the butterfly and gilds the lily. But his color is always delightful. . . . The dialogue fairly crackles with crispness. His personages are all such interesting characters . . . . [M] is charmingly feminine and has a cunning hand in feminine portraiture."

200 "Reenter Miss Billie Burke," NEW YORK SUN, 25 Jan 1910, p. 7.

Mrs. Dot is "a much more entertaining comedy than . . . spineless and amateurish *Penelope*." M's dialogue is "politely witty," but as is the case in his other plays, it bears "little relation to the action."

201 Ruhl, Arthur. "Just Off the Griddle: Strawberry and Other Ices," COLLIER'S, XLIV (12 Feb 1910), 34.

Penelope and *Mrs. Dot,* like all M's plays, are alike in that "they are made of the oldest stage materials in the world, rearranged and restored with a neat felicity and wit until they seem almost fresh and new. Of course they couldn't fail to be popular."

202 Ruhl, Arthur. "Some of the New Plays—Pieces by Americans—and Others—Which Opened the New York Theatrical Season: Mr. Drew's New Play," COLLIER'S, XLVI (8 Oct 1910), 28-29.

Smith has "all the facile, witty quality of [M's] former pieces with a backbone and robustness that the others lacked."

203 S[eaman], O[wen]. "At the Play," PUNCH, CXXXIX (26 Oct 1910), 302.

Grace is "relieved by a good deal of humour not quite of the highest class." The title heroine's character is inconsequential, but the play should increase M's "early reputation on the serious side."

204 " *'Smith.'* By Somerset Maugham," METROPOLITAN MAGAZINE, XXXIII (Nov 1910), 254-55.

M's play contains "nothing new as to plot; in fact, much the same idea was used in THE WALLS OF JERICHO and THE MOLLUSC." [Illustrations.]

205 " *'The Tenth Man,'* at the Globe," ILLUSTRATED LONDON NEWS, CXXXVI (5 March 1910), 352.

M has borrowed from Bernstein by adopting a "strong" man of finance as his hero. "But the Bernstein methods almost impose a certain artificiality of plot, an elaborate working-up to some startling climax, and Mr. Maugham has not been able to avoid this weakness." Still, the play is exceptionally good "in the consummate neatness of its stagecraft, in the smartness and appropriateness of its dialogue, in the splendid effectiveness of its culminating scene."

206 " *'The Tenth Man,'* at the Globe," TRUTH (Lond), LXVII (2 March 1910), 521.

The "play is not of Mr. Maugham's best."

207* "Two Popular Women Stars in New Plays," NEW YORK WORLD, 25 Jan 1910, p. 7.

The story of *Mrs. Dot* "is as thin as a wafer and really the plot of MUCH ADO ABOUT NOTHING in a setting of modern English society."

208 White, Matthew, Jr. "The Stage," MUNSEY'S MAGAZINE, XLII (Feb 1910), 746-47.

Penelope, "though built on an oft-worked theme, wears well."

209 White, Matthew, Jr. "The Stage," MUNSEY'S MAGAZINE, XLIII (April 1910), 123-24.

London and New York disagree on the merits of M's quartet of comedies—*Lady Frederick, Jack Straw, Penelope,* and *Mrs. Dot*—for they were greeted enthusiastically in the West End but cold-shouldered on Broadway; indeed, *Penelope* lasted but four weeks in New York.

210 White, Matthew, Jr. "The Stage," MUNSEY'S MAGAZINE, XLIV (Nov 1910), 280.

Though all of M's works have so far impressed American audiences as "only rather smart drawing-room twaddle," they recognize in *Smith* that "the bright dialogue serves to build up to a real purpose, and that the comedy does more than merely amuse one during the two hours' traffic of the stage."

211 Winter, William. "Shadows of the Stage," HARPER'S WEEKLY, LIV (19 Nov 1910), 13.
Smith can be viewed as a work of art only if it is viewed as a "farce."

1911

212 "Drama," ATHENAEUM, No. 4349 (4 March 1911), 259-60.
Unlike Trollope, whom he is copying, M in *Loaves and Fishes* does not show Canon Spratte "surrounded by worthier colleagues, does not present his clergyman acting like a clergyman." So long as he has been able to raise a laugh, M has not cared about the "means."

213 "Drama," NATION (NY), XCII (16 March 1911), 275.
Loaves and Fishes is "an amusing but inconsiderable work." [Review of the British production.]

214 "Dramatic Gossip," ATHENAEUM, No. 4346 (11 Feb 1911), 172.
Though touched with artificiality, the revived *Grace* is "too good a piece of work to be dismissed with the short run it obtained at the Duke of York's. . . . "

215* " '*Grace,*' at the Duke of York's," ILLUSTRATED LONDON NEWS, CXXXVIII (11 Feb 1911), 186.
"There are many admirable touches of observation as well as of stagecraft in the [revived] piece; it is a strikingly well-made play, and it contains individual scenes that are plangent in their emotional appeal, varied by comedy that is sometimes of Mr. Maugham's very best brand. And yet the sensitive ear cannot be unconscious of a note of artificiality, here muffled perhaps for the most part, yet audible enough when such a character is on the stage as Grace's dowager mother-in-law . . . almost a caricature of Robertson's Marquise in CASTE."

216 " '*Lady Frederick,*' Revived at the Globe," ILLUSTRATED LONDON NEWS, CXXXVIII (3 May 1911), 622.
"Clever but artificial work," the play's success owes as much to Ethel Irving's performance as it does to M's "seemingly" shaping the part of his heroine for her.

217 Leverson, Ada. THE LIMIT. Lond: Grant Richards, 1911.

[Hereford Vaughan, a character in this novel, is a thinly-veiled caricature of M at the time of his first dramatic success. Dark-eyed, handsome, quiet, thirty-four years of age, Hereford has "eleven plays at the same time being performed in London, New York, Berlin, Paris, and every other European city."]

218* "*'Loaves and Fishes,'* at the Duke of York's," ACADEMY, LXXX (4 March 1911), 266-67.

The play is neither satire nor farce, but "extremely bitter and cruel caricature." Its characters are "wildly treated" and "distorted." "In construction as well as in dialogue," the play is altogether "juvenile."

219* "*'Loaves and Fishes,'* at the Duke of York's," ILLUSTRATED LONDON NEWS, CXXXVIII (4 March 1911), 326.

The play's idea was more suited to the novel from which it was taken [*The Bishop's Apron*], and where it was weak to begin with. Canon Spratte "becomes more and more intolerable the longer he appears before the footlights, and what began with being an amusing skit ends by being a most unpleasant abnormality, for the man has neither good-nature nor decency of feeling."

220 "*'Loaves and Fishes,'* at the Duke of York's," TRUTH (Lond), LXIX (1 March 1911), 542.

"I do not know exactly what the play is a satire upon, because it would be monstrously unjust to call it a satire upon the Church, but it is a very entertaining comedy. . . . "

221 M[ilne, A. A.] "At the Play," PUNCH, CXL (8 March 1911), 177-78.

Loaves and Fishes is "truly funny" and implies a moral lesson lacking in most of M's earlier efforts in the theater.

222* "Mr. Maugham's New Play—Production at the Duke of York's Theatre: *'Loaves and Fishes,'*" TIMES (Lond), 25 Feb 1911, p. 8; rptd by Raymond Mander and Joe Mitchenson, eds, in THEATRICAL COMPANION TO MAUGHAM (Lond: Rockliff, 1955), pp. 51-52.

M's Spratte is a clergyman owing much to Trollope, but M's satire is, unfortunately, not as genial or general as Trollope's, and he cannot render the clerical "atmosphere." M's clergyman is really a "worldling," so thinly disguised "a baby could detect" the humbug he is. The audience will laugh at, but not for a moment believe in, him.

223* Ruyssen, Henri. "Revue annuelle: Le Théâtre anglais" (Annual Review: The English Theater), REVUE GERMANIQUE, VII (1911), 67-68.

M, in *Smith,* joins Pinero, Sutro, and Carton, to satirize the egotistical modish lady. *The Tenth Man* proves that M refuses to allow the taste of the public to be superimposed upon his own, and that he is intent upon educating the English public. [Review of the British premieres of *Smith* and *The Tenth Man.*] [In French.]

224 Webber, John E. "Plays of the Season," CANADIAN MAGAZINE, XXXVI (Jan 1911), 281-91, especially 290.

Smith "oscillates between sentimental comedy and pure farce. . . . Maugham's hand is too fine for either."

1912

225 Archer, William. PLAY-MAKING: A MANUAL OF CRAFTSMANSHIP (Boston: Small, Maynard, 1912), pp. 257, 338, 363.

A Man of Honour illustrates the "obligatory scene"; *Grace* illustrates both "conversion" and the "full close."

226 "Drama," ATHENAEUM, No. 4393 (6 Jan 1912), 23.

Among the published versions of *A Man of Honour, Lady Frederick,* and *Jack Straw, Man* is M's near masterpiece; the two comedies must have made enjoyable writing. In dialogue, *Man* is too self-consciously literary; the comedies sometimes exhibit epigrams which lack spontaneity.

227* *"The Explorer,"* NEW YORK DRAMATIC MIRROR, LXVII (15 May 1912), 6.

This play has an ingenious construction, but the actions of its quixotic hero are too unrealistic. Too much happens in the first half of the play, too little in the second. M should have changed George Allerton's character from weak and contemptible to weak and lovable.

228 " *'The Explorer'* at Daly's," NEW YORK TRIBUNE, 8 May 1912, p. 7.

"The play . . . professes to run no deeper than good dramatic situation and keen, clever dialogue will take it."

229 " *'Explorer'* Blazes No Fresh Paths," NEW YORK TIIMES, 8 May 1912, p. 11.

M substitutes "brackish water and tinned beef for English teacup fare," and the result is a placid melodrama. M began with an exceptional idea but did not take it seriously enough.

230 "May Nights at the Play," NEW YORK SUN, 12 May 1912, II:6.

No attempt to make *The Explorer* "contemporary" can hide M's inexpertness with serious drama. While his genius for comedy is "unusual," here his language "more than once fell into the heroic stencil of melodrama."

231* Metcalfe, [J. S.] "Drama: The Season's Curfew Tolling," LIFE, LIX (23 May 1912), 1073.

M's skill in the "serious vein" is small; the comedy scenes of *The Explorer* are its only redeeming qualities. M "commits the grave error of letting his audience condemn his hero as a fool because the gentleman, for no good reason, won't speak the few words which could do no one any harm, and would clear up a painful state of affairs"; but "if the hero did this there would be no play, and it is in letting the audience see this that Mr. Maugham is inexpert."

232 "New Plays," THEATRE MAGAZINE, XV (June 1912), 171-72.

M is better at light plays, and *The Explorer,* a serious play, is only "conventionally theatrical and by no means convincing." A trio of comedy scenes redeems the play somewhat.

233* Pollock, Channing. "Words and Music," GREEN BOOK MAGAZINE, VIII (July 1912), 123.

The Explorer is written with M's "customary touching faith that anything that lasts two hours, and has four acts, some epigrams and a love story, is a play."

234 Ruyssen, Henri. "Revue annuelle: Le Théâtre anglais (1911-1912)" (Annual Review: The English Theater), REVUE GERMANIQUE, VIII (1912), 292.

Spratte, of *Loaves and Fishes,* is not a convincing clergyman, but the play has some very comic situations capable of evoking laughter. [Review of the British production.] [In French.]

235 "Some Plays of the Month Technically Considered," AMERICAN PLAYWRIGHT, I (15 June 1912), 190-92.

An analysis of *The Explorer* reveals that M's theory of playwriting appears to be "that Story is sufficient and that dramatic form is not necessary, that logic is an impertinence, that Cause and Effect are outworn requirements, that Proposition is required for a part of a play and not for the whole of it."

1913

236 "Billie Burke Grown Serious—in Parts," NEW YORK SUN, 26 Dec 1913, p. 8.

The Land of Promise is entertaining but not plausible in its serious scenes; "the admirable second act suffers from an excessive supply of the virago sister-in-law."

237* "The Comedy: *'The Perfect Gentleman,'* an Adaptation by W. Somerset Maugham of Molière's Comedy 'LE BOURGEOIS GENTILHOMME,'" TIMES (Lond), 28 May 1913, p. 9.

"Mr. Maugham has preferred the vocabulary, sometimes even the slang vocabulary, of 1913. The result is rank incongruity, absurdity, vulgarity."

238 Findon, B. W. *"The Land of Promise* by Somerset Maugham," PLAY PICTORIAL, XXIV, No. 144 [n. d., but probably late 1913], 42-43.

It is "a thoughtful and well-written play," dealing "in a very human way with a very human subject."

239 *"The Land of Promise,"* NEW YORK DRAMATIC MIRROR, LXX (31 Dec 1913), 6.

M makes a great change here from the living room to the wilds of Canada. Despite its "antique theme," the play, which seems parallel to THE TAMING OF THE SHREW and THE GREAT DIVIDE, is more profound than the plot alone suggests.

240 "Maugham's Play Pleases at Lyceum," NEW YORK TIMES, 26 Dec 1913, p. 11; rptd by Raymond Mander and Joe Mitchenson, eds, in THEATRICAL COMPANION TO MAUGHAM (Lond: Rockliff, 1955), pp. 111-12.

The Land of Promise has little depth and breadth, but it is a "wholly pleasant thing."

241 "Miss Billie Burke Acts a Farmer's Wife," NEW YORK WORLD, 26 Dec 1913, p. 11.

The Land of Promise, in contrast with William Vaughn Moody's THE GREAT DIVIDE, "merely scratches the surface" of the theme of the influence which opposed natures have on one another.

242 "Miss Billie Burke in Serious Role Does Real Dramatic Work Effectively," NEW YORK HERALD, 26 Dec 1913, p. 10.

There is "overmuch wrangling" in *The Land of Promise,* and it "grows wearisome at times."

243* Stearns, H. E. "An Interesting Playwright," NEW YORK DRAMATIC MIRROR, LXIX (29 Jan 1913), 3, 7.

M's surface impression is that of an "aesthete" with great "refinement and delicacy of manner," but this impression is reversed upon further acquaintance. M believes that if he had not turned playwright, he would have become a philosopher. It is the relativity of the comic perspective, as opposed to the absoluteness of external rules, which attracts him. In serious drama, where comedy is used mainly for comic relief, its purpose ought to be that of pleasing all and serving as an integral part of the drama. [Interview.]

244 *θ*. "At the Play," PUNCH, CXLIV (4 June 1913), 448.

In M's translation of Molière's LE BOURGEOIS GENTILHOMME as *The Perfect Gentleman,* Sir Herbert Tree's buffoonery in the role of M. Jourdain sets the entire play in a "false key."

1914

245 Gibbs, Philip. "The Case of the 'Superfluous Woman,'" GRAPHIC, LXXXIX (7 March 1914), 402.

Reading Constance Lytton's PRISON AND PRISONERS reveals the similarity of its theme to that of *The Land of Promise,* although both works utter a different "moral."

246* Grein, J. T. "The Week's Premieres," SUNDAY TIMES (Lond), 1 March 1914, p. 6; rptd by Raymond Mander and Joe Mitchenson, eds, in THEATRICAL COMPANION TO MAUGHAM (Lond: Rockliff, 1955), pp. 112-13.

In *The Land of Promise,* M's picture of "the Dominion [Canada] in making" is substantially correct, but his picture of Norah and Frank, especially in Acts III and IV, is questionable. "The fourth act is a sacrifice to convention, as the third is exuberance of realism."

247* Hamilton, Clayton. "Building a Play Backward," BOOKMAN (NY), XXXVIII (Feb 1914), 609-10.

The Land of Promise has a dull chronological sequencing of events. M's poorest play, except for *The Explorer,* it should start "at what is now the middle of the second act, and . . . develop a last act which . . . result[s] from an evolution of character instead of from a fabrication of coincidence."

248* *"The Land of Promise,"* DRAMATIST, V (Jan 1914), 419-20.

The play is poor because it lacks technique; nor do we see the motives which bring about the conversion of the heroine from a lover to a hater of ease. The idea itself is excellent, but with no evidence of sound dramatic principle, the play, despite some excellent dialogue, is not a real drama.

249 " *'The Land of Promise,'* at the Duke of York's Theatre," ACADEMY, LXXXVI (7 March 1914), 311-12.
M seeks to treat the "hidden intimacies" of life with sincerity and candor, but the play is not without some periods of disappointment: the reviewer doubts—given the woman and man they first appeared to be—that Norah and Taylor would have acted as they did in the final scene at Prentice. Nevertheless, the play is "at once an engrossing, original and sterling piece of work."

250* " *'Land of Promise,'* at the Duke of York's," ILLUSTRATED LONDON NEWS, CXLIV (7 March 1914), 368.
The play is worth "a dozen average plays," but M "drifts into artificiality, gives us Petruchio and Katherine imbroglio brought up to date, then loads the husband with misfortunes, and so presents both properly subdued for the conventional happy ending."

251 " *'The Land of Promise'*: Mr. Maugham's Play at the Duke of York's," TIMES (Lond), 27 Feb 1914, p. 10.
M may provide the "local colour" of Manitoba, but his characters are as "stuffy" and "stuffed" as the Londoners they deride.

252 Mantle, Burns. "Some Leading Cave Men," MUNSEY'S MAGAZINE, LI (March 1914), 332, 334, 336-37, 340.
The Land of Promise is part of the syndrome of current drama which features heroes that are "rough, rude and primitive."

253 "Maugham Praises Our Playwrights," NEW YORK TIMES, 5 Jan 1914, p. 9.
M lauds American drama for its "freshness of material," its "splendid young actresses," and its not being "hampered by precedent."

254 Metcalfe, [J. S.] "Drama: The Feast that Follows Famine," LIFE, LXIII (8 Jan 1914), 68.
In *The Land of Promise,* "Mr. Maugham seems to have imbibed the spirit of the territory of intense cold and great crops [the Canadian Northwest], and found in it even poetic inspiration."

255 "New Plays," THEATRE MAGAZINE, XIX (Feb 1914), 99-100.
The Land of Promise has a novel atmosphere in Western Canada, but as a play it is "in no wise fantastic." Although M claims there are no principles of dramatic technique, this play proves that he is not much different in his technique from other playwrights.

256 O., S. "Pygmalion at Home and Abroad," ENGLISH REVIEW, XVII (May 1914), 276-78.
In a comparison of Shaw's PYGMALION and M's *The Land of Promise,* M is freer, fresher, less artificial than Shaw.

257* Pollock, Channing. "Bubbles," GREEN BOOK MAGAZINE, XI (March 1914), 414-15.
Acts II and III of *The Land of Promise* are good. "If you arrive at nine o'clock, and go home at a quarter past ten, you will thoroughly enjoy *The Land of Promise."*

258 S[eaman], O[wen]. "At the Play," PUNCH, CXLVI (4 March 1914), 178.
The Land of Promise is satirized for the large number of eating scenes and its title, for M's play, "too, is a thing 'of promise' rather than achievement, if it is to be judged by the text of the Last Act."

259 "Some Plays of the Month Technically Considered," AMERICAN PLAYWRIGHT, III (15 Feb 1914), 39-42.
An analysis of *The Land of Promise* shows that M's dramatic technique and material are conventional; he is a most clever "amateur."

1915

260* "A Compromise," NATION (Lond), XVII (21 April 1915), 684.
Of Human Bondage is a "camp follower" in the army of "modern realists," whose "prophet" was Arnold Bennett and whose "captain" was Compton MacKenzie. Like all heroes of these realists, Philip is "treated biologically, biographically, and photographically." He is a "parochial" figure, revolving within his own orbit, exhibiting the author's own personality; his career is not a synthesis, but a "serial"—he goes "patiently on from one bondage to another, until he is released at last, not by his own cumulative experience, but by the objective personality of his wife, Sally." M differs from the "realists" only in coloring and quality of texture—where they consciously produce "grey effects," M's coloring is "bright and varied."

261 Cooper, Frederic Taber. "Some Novels of the Month," BOOKMAN (NY), XLII (Sept 1915), 104-5.
Under M's magic touch, *Of Human Bondage* "glows and scintillates with colour and movement and life!"

262* Dreiser, Theodore. "As a Realist Sees It," NEW REPUBLIC, V (25 Dec 1915), 202-4; rptd in NEW REPUBLIC ANTHOLOGY: 1915-1935 (NY: Dodge Publishing Co., 1936), pp. 24-30; in THE MAUGHAM ENIGMA, ed by Klaus W. Jonas (NY: Citadel P, 1954), pp. 114-20; and excerpted in NEW REPUBLIC, CXXXI (22 Nov 1954), 58.

Of Human Bondage is "a novel or biography or autobiography or social transcript of the utmost importance." It is unmoral. Despite some "dissonant voices," the novel has been well-received in America, where one would have expected it to be misunderstood; while in England, where one would expect the novel's true merits to be appreciated, it was received contemptuously on moral and social grounds. It is a novel of utmost import, full of brilliant scenes, and it is utterly frank. M is a "great artist."

263 E[dgett], E[dwin] F[rancis]. "The Bondage of a Youth," BOSTON EVENING TRANSCRIPT, 11 Aug 1915, p. 18.

In *Of Human Bondage,* Philip Carey is "an epitome of humankind in all its ranges between the best and the worst"; the book mingles romance and realism exactly as they are mingled in life.

264 "Fiction," ATHENAEUM, No. 4582 (21 Aug 1915), 128.

Of Human Bondage is too long; the hero is so handicapped that he is removed out of the category of the average, and thus the values he accords love, realism, and religion "are so distorted as to have no interest beyond that which belongs to an essentially morbid personality."

265* Gould, Gerald. "New Novels," NEW STATESMAN, V (25 Sept 1915), 594.

If M belongs to a "school" of writers [which Gould doubts], it is to a French one whose method is that of "disguising selectiveness by profusion, of making life conceal art." M's succession of incidents in *Of Human Bondage* is "almost wantonly casual"; his conversations are "often amazingly vivid, but seldom amusing." Throughout the novel one observes "minuteness without realism, passion without romance, variation without variety." M's line is "length without breadth," and in every detail, seemingly diffuse, "there is . . . concentration." The total effect is of strangeness, "but it is on the grand scale, and in some ways beautiful."

266 "The New Books," INDEPENDENT (NY), LXXXIII (23 Aug 1915), 268.

Of Human Bondage is "prolix" and "splits easily into three novels. . . . And its ethics are frankly pagan, even the betrayal of innocence being glossed over. . . . Unhappy childhood always is a bid for sympathy, but little Phillip [*sic*] grows up into an insufferable egotist and cad. One longs, after reading these novels where spineless men and women yield without a struggle to the forces of evil and are overwhelmed by the world, for the ringing shout of the stout apostle, Paul: 'I have fought a good fight . . . I have kept the faith!' or the nobler voice: 'I have overcome the world.' "

267 "The New Books," OUTLOOK (NY), CX (11 Aug 1915), 874.
In *Of Human Bondage,* M follows the tradition of writing an excessively long novel in which the construction can "go hang" and in which there is no "ending, happy or otherwise."

268* "New Novels," TIMES LITERARY SUPPLEMENT (Lond), 12 Aug 1915, p. 269.
In *Of Human Bondage,* M is like Henry Fielding in the long, biographical style he employs and in the resulting philosophy of life he offers, which is more than just a "slice of life." M maintains a good balance between "life and the man," overplays neither biography nor development of personality, and realizes quite naturally Philip's progress into reality and truth. Nonetheless, M's view of life as being the pattern of the Persian carpet falls somewhat short of what a true poet would feel.

269 *"Of Human Bondage,"* NEW YORK TIMES BOOK REVIEW, 1 Aug 1915, p. 278.
The novel is in the tradition of the old "three-part" British writers, the only difference being that it does not possess three actual divisions. It is "careful and conscientious," its characters are "rich and diverse." M's "leisurely method" gives an opportunity for a great quantity of literary pictures.

270 "Our Booking-Office," PUNCH, CXLIX (25 Aug 1915), 179-80.
The characters of Philip's aunt and Miss Price partially redeem *Of Human Bondage,* which is too long, particularly in view of the repugnant characters of Philip and Mildred.

271 Payne, William Morton. "Recent Fiction," DIAL, LIX (16 Sept 1915), 220.
In *Of Human Bondage,* M's "photographic realism" sustains our interest but misses "the broad effects and the large issues of human characterization"; far from being "compellingly great as the publishers would have us believe," the book is "at least a noteworthy piece of creative composition."

272* "Reviews: Man in the Making," SATURDAY REVIEW (Lond), CXX (4 Sept 1915), 233-34.
Of Human Bondage belongs to the "cradle-to-the-grave order of fiction" and marks "a revolt against impressionism, a return to a Pre-Raphaelite love of detail." Although not "padded or discursive," it is abnormally

long and aims at completeness, to show us "man in the making." A "relentless realist," M "keeps well within his powers." Despite its "depressing atmosphere" and "hopelessness," the book is clever. M has broken new ground in his choice of a hero; he wins and holds our interest in an unattractive personality. Philip's path is "almost perversely unfortunate." In presenting his early life, M overemphasizes the "drab and sordid side of things," but Philip "is really alive," a "distinct achievement." M presents "lifelike cameos" of the other characters, with the exception of Miss Price, who is, "perhaps, unforgettable."

273 Roberts, R. Ellis. "The Amorist," BOOKMAN (Lond), XLVIII (Sept 1915), 171-72.
In *Of Human Bondage,* the details of Philip's life at his two schools are felt to be distracting; the Mildred episodes are the best of the book.

274 "Some of the New Fiction: Maugham Returns to the Novel," SPRINGFIELD SUNDAY REPUBLICAN (Mass), 8 Aug 1915, p. 15.
Of Human Bondage is part of the revival of that kind of novel "minutely narrating the development of one character or a group of characters." M's portraits are "clean-cut," his style polished, his material "diverse."

1916

275 Archer, William. "Drama," NATION (NY), CII (30 March 1916), 364-65.
Caroline could have been called THE UNATTAINABLE [as it was to be]; it is a fine comedy that develops its theme "with unflagging gayety, and with great fertility of scenic . . . invention." [A "theatrical letter" from London.]

276 " *'Caroline'* at the New," GRAPHIC, XCIII (12 Feb 1916), 244.
[Review, which primarily summarizes the plot and commends the actors.]

277 " *'Caroline,'* at the New," ILLUSTRATED LONDON NEWS, CXLVIII (19 Feb 1916), 226.
The play is "artificial comedy, full of sparkle and wit"; the characters are to be considered as "marionettes"; their "antics, with the strings of a master of his craft, are superlatively diverting."

278 " *'Caroline'* Opens at Empire Theatre," NEW YORK SUN, 21 Sept 1916, p. 5.
"There is less real humor in the whole play than in a genuine sidewalk conversation of two skillful American vaudeville actors."

279 "Comedy with a Moral: Mr. Maugham's *'Caroline'* at New Theatre," TIMES (Lond), 9 Feb 1916, p. 11.
The first act is on a very high level; M's "one little mistake" was to complicate, "to weave too much pattern" into what was essentially light comedy, its point and charm being "simplicity."

280 De Foe, Louis [V.] "A British Clyde Fitch," GREEN BOOK MAGAZINE, XVI (Nov 1916), 909-16.
[Sketch of M at the time of his initial success in the theatre (1907-1908).]

281 "Drama," ATHENAEUM, No. 4602 (Feb 1916), 96.
In *Caroline,* M's idea is less hackneyed than usual, but he has not made much of it; sufficient point in secondary items, however, reduces the failure in the main theme.

282 Eaton, Walter Prichard. PLAYS AND PLAYERS: LEAVES FROM A CRITIC'S SCRAPBOOK (Cincinnati: Stewart & Kidd, 1916), pp. 165, 330.
M's *Land of Promise* is written in a "well-knit" fashion, and this adds to the audience's entertainment.

283 Grein, J. T. "The Dramatic World," SUNDAY TIMES (Lond), 13 Feb 1916, p. 4; rptd by Raymond Mander and Joe Mitchenson, eds, in THEATRICAL COMPANION TO MAUGHAM (Lond: Rockliff, 1955), pp. 141-42.
M is as "crafty as old Scribe was and he writes ever so much better." *Caroline* is "as light as a feather" and "whimsical, seasoned with vivid dots and crosses of acute observation."

284 Hornblow, Arthur. "Mr. Hornblow Goes to the Play," THEATRE MAGAZINE, XXIV (Nov 1916), 282.
Caroline is "very thin" entertainment, and not at all like the comedies of Wilde or Shaw. In some ways the play resembles LOVE'S LABOUR'S LOST.

285 "Margaret Anglin Acts *'Caroline'* at Empire," NEW YORK WORLD, 21 Sept 1916, p. 9.
The workmanship is "snappy and smooth and invariably excessively polite," but the third act is excessively padded, and the play's philosophical drift is "almost hidden in froth."

286 "Margaret Anglin Charms in *Caroline,*" NEW YORK DRAMATIC MIRROR, LXXVI (30 Sept 1916), 7.
This is an entertaining play, but not overly deep. The characterization is fairly true, although it is marred by some exaggeration; and despite little action, M's witty dialogue, which may be compared with Wilde's, makes a pleasant evening.

287 Metcalfe, [J. S.] "Drama: The Imperishable Theatre and Some Exhibits," LIFE, LXVIII (5 Oct 1916), 581.
In *Caroline,* M gives us another example of his expertness in spreading the butter very, very thin. . . . Properly condensed the comedy might serve as a curtain-raiser."

288 "Miss Margaret Anglin Pleases Anew in Epigrammatic Comedy," NEW YORK HERALD, 21 Sept 1916, p. 6.
Caroline is "talky and somewhat drawn out," but the play "touches the high watermark of psychological realism, lightly expressed in epigrams."

289 "Music and Drama: *'Caroline,'* " NEW YORK EVENING POST, 21 Sept 1916, p. 9.
The play has some passages of "excellent light comedy," together with much that is "frothy, repetitive, and . . . not a little tedious."

290 "New Productions of the Week," NEW YORK DRAMATIC NEWS, LXIII (30 Sept 1916), 2.
Caroline is "brilliant, witty and cynical comedy . . . admirable alike in construction and technique."

291* Pollock, Channing. "Lollypops," GREEN BOOK MAGAZINE, XVI (Dec 1916), 970-71.
Caroline shows M "is the cleverest writer of one-act plays. Most of these he writes in three or four acts—which proves the extent of his cleverness."

292 "Sparkling Comedy Again with Miss Anglin," NEW YORK TIMES, 21 Sept 1916, p. 9.
Caroline sparkles "with the superlative brilliance of Oscar Wilde."

293 T[horp, Joseph]. "At the Play," PUNCH, CL (16 Feb 1916), 126.
The only flaw in *Caroline* is the ambiguity of the last few sentences before the final curtain.

294 W[ent], S[tanley]. "Drama," NATION (NY), CIII (5 Oct 1916), 331.
In *Caroline,* M "hits upon a theme of real interest and some originality," but "displays in his handling of it almost complete indifference to its merits. The two things that most concern him are the mechanics of play construction and the furnishing of a proper amount of the smart flippancy that can often be passed off as wit."

295 White, Matthew, Jr. "The Stage," MUNSEY'S MAGAZINE, LIX (Dec 1916), 495.
Caroline arouses no interest until the middle of the second act.

1917

296 "A Bitter Comedy on Our Expatriates," NEW YORK TIMES, 13 March 1917, p. 9; rptd by Raymond Mander and Joe Mitchenson, eds, in THEATRICAL COMPANION TO MAUGHAM (Lond: Rockliff, 1955), pp. 117-18.

In *Our Betters,* M's attack is bitter. [Mainly plot summary.]

297 Broun, Heywood. "News of the Play World: Somerset Maugham Writes One Scene Far Off Key and Spoils *'Our Betters,'* " NEW YORK TRIBUNE, 13 March 1917, p. 11.

The second act, overtly immoral, "just about ruins what would otherwise be an amusing entertainment."

298 H[ackett], F[rancis]. "After the Play," NEW REPUBLIC, X (17 March 1917), 200.

Our Betters is "an acrid comedy." Because of its banal story, it misses its chance to be "a strong satiric comedy."

299 Hornblow, Arthur. "Mr. Hornblow Goes to the Play," THEATRE MAGAZINE, XXV (May 1917), 277.

Our Betters represents an advance over M's earlier works; despite the fact that it remains "largely talk," it is "vital" and "splendidly acted."

300 "Idle Rich Satirized on Stage," NEW YORK SUN, 13 March 1917, p. 6.

Act II of *Our Betters* is implausible and often more than mildly shocking.

301 *"The Land of Promise,"* GRAPHIC, XCV (17 Feb 1917), 206.

The revived play is "rather a risky experiment, for we have drifted far from the point of view prevailing in pre-war days, women having acquired meantime an infinitely better opinion of themselves in actual practice (as against vague feministic theory); but, notwithstanding that, the play is just as fresh as ever, and is just as much appreciated by the audience, composed more than ever of women. It is very difficult to understand why this should be so, for Mr. Somerset Maugham's view is compulsively physiological, and as primitive as THE TAMING OF THE SHREW."

302 " *'The Land of Promise'*: Revival at the New Theatre," TIMES (Lond), 9 Feb 1917, p. 9.

M's play is "dramatic" enough, but the finale of Act III [the "rape"] oversteps the limits of art, and is revolting.

303 "Maugham Holds Title Hunters Up to Scorn," NEW YORK WORLD, 18 March 1917, p. 9.

In *Our Betters,* M "cuts a very sorry figure" not only as "guide, philosopher and friend but as a playwright." "The play begins, continues and ends with liaisons. Even if it were not one-half as repellent and bitter as it is, the bluntly spoken vulgarity of the end of its second act would be enough to ruin it."

304 Metcalfe, [J. S.] "Drama: An English Slam at Our Title Hunters," LIFE, LXIX (22 March 1917), 486.

Our Betters "does not seem likely to add to the professional reputation or the American popularity of Mr. Maugham."

305 "Music and Drama: *'Our Betters,'*" NEW YORK EVENING POST, 13 March 1917, p. 9.

The play contains little of M's best, much of his very worst. It is riddled with verbosity, triteness, insincerity, and sensationalism.

306 "New Plays of the Week," NEW YORK DRAMATIC NEWS, LXIV (17 March 1917), 6.

Our Betters has an "interesting plot" and "crisp and very often brilliant" dialogue.

307* *"Our Betters,"* NEW YORK DRAMATIC MIRROR, LXXVII (24 March 1917), 7.

Like Wilde, M writes brilliant satire, but his theme here is "morally sordid" and "offensive." Before the play's opening there was a rumor about the bold second act; what the audience saw opening night was a play that gave too much attention to "human decay." The only redeeming feature is its cleverly cynical dialogue.

308* Pollock, Channing. "Drama with a Domestic Finish," GREEN BOOK MAGAZINE, XVII (June 1917), 964-71.

Our Betters "has the wit of Wilde, the clinical cleverness of . . . [Clyde] Fitch, at least one scene that displays the cumulative power of Bernstein." But the play is not "wholesome. Its brilliance . . . is the brilliance of decay. It is hard and cynical and pitiless."

309 W[ent], S[tanley]. "Review of Plays," NATION (NY), CIV (22 March 1917), 350.

Our Betters is "strong meat, so strong indeed as to become at times positively odorous." Neither comedy nor satire, because it is too savage, the play displays only an overstrained point.

310 White, Matthew, Jr. "The Stage," MUNSEY'S MAGAZINE, LX (May 1917), 640.

Our Betters is "shocking, to be sure, but there's a real purpose behind the shock."

1918

311 Archer, William. "Drama," NATION (NY), CVI (4 April 1918), 413-14.
Love in a Cottage is "an agreeable enough little play, but utterly sketchy and lacking substance." [Review of the British production.]

312 "Lively New Plays," GRAPHIC, XCVII (2 Feb 1918), 156.
Love in a Cottage has "an adroit, workmanlike story, which satisfies many conditions of the stage, even to the introduction of fancy costume."

313* *"Love in a Cottage,"* SATURDAY REVIEW (Lond), CXXV (9 Feb 1918), 114-15.
M's making wealth the "villain" of his play "boomerangs" on him, for it is not wealth but poverty that corrupts the "disagreeable unheroic people" surrounding the suitor, the millionaire, and the heroine.

314 " *'Love in a Cottage'*: Miss Marie Lohr's Season at the Globe," TIMES (Lond), 28 Jan 1918, p. 9; rptd by Raymond Mander and Joe Mitchenson, eds, in THEATRICAL COMPANION TO MAUGHAM (Lond: Rockliff, 1955), pp. 146-47.
All the queer actions of the play's characters are induced by the "demoralizing influence" of the setting, Lake Como. [Tongue-in-cheek review.]

315 T[horp, Joseph]. "At the Play," PUNCH, CLIV (6 Feb 1918), 94.
"I cannot think the players believed in their play [*Love in a Cottage*], which should have an excellent run."

1919

316* Anderson, Maxwell. "In Vishnu-Land What Avatar?" DIAL, LXVII (29 Nov 1919), 477-78; rptd in THE MAUGHAM ENIGMA, ed by Klaus W. Jonas (NY: Citadel P, 1954), pp. 129-32.
"Whatever objection may be raised to the philosophy of art involved in the tale [*The Moon and Sixpence*], there is likely to be little but praise for its workmanship and its criticism of life."

317 Archer, William. "Dramatic Performances in London," WEEKLY REVIEW (NY), I (14 June 1919), 110.
In *Caesar's Wife* "Mr. Maugham's psychology is rather superficial, and

the proconsul's ineffable superiority to all human weaknesses becomes at times just a little exasperating. But there are some very well-written scenes. . . ."

318 "At the Play," OBSERVER (Lond), 30 March 1919, p. 9.
"There is not much 'in' the play [*Caesar's Wife*]; and yet there is a great deal in it: a constant light of high comedy and shrewd sense and subtle expression, so that it is all the more entertaining and interesting than we imagined this old story could be made."

319* Baughan, E. A. "Plays and Players: *'Home and Beauty,'*" JOHN O' LONDON'S WEEKLY, I (20 Sept 1919), 696.
The last act is good in itself, but leaves the two husbands, Bill and Frederick, "where they were," and does not develop Victoria's character; the play really ends with Victoria's announcement of a third marriage.

320 "Billie Burke Back; Wins New Laurels," NEW YORK SUN, 25 Nov 1919, p. 9.
In *Caesar's Wife,* M's theme is "sentimental" but not "novel."

321 "Books of the Day," OBSERVER (Lond), 4 May 1919, p. 4.
In *The Moon and Sixpence,* M makes Strickland's greatness appear as plainly as his odiousness, but does not make an effect of the beauty and power of Strickland's work.

322 "Books of the Fortnight," DIAL, LXVII (6 Sept 1919), 222.
The Moon and Sixpence is "a story . . . told with acrid beauty and satiric penetration into the remoter regions of consciousness, . . . probably the most important novel of recent years"; a review will follow [see Maxwell Anderson, "In Vishnu-Land What Avatar?" DIAL, LXVII (29 Nov 1919), 477-78.]

323 Broun, Heywood. "Drama: *'Too Many Husbands,'* by Maugham, Is Seen at the Booth Theatre," NEW YORK TRIBUNE, 9 Oct 1919, p. 11.
The American version of *Home and Beauty* is "smart, thin, and beautifully played. . . . Mr. Maugham begins with a situation which would delight any American farce writer, and then proceeds to develop it in a manner which would shock most of our local practitioners. His interest lies almost wholly in dialogue."

324* Broun, Heywood. "Repressed Emotion Is the Keynote in *'Caesar's Wife,'*" NEW YORK TRIBUNE, 25 Nov 1919, p. 11.
M "presents a certain set of circumstances and then puts before you some figure in whom the conflict is almost completely internal. You see Prometheus and, perhaps, the rock rather vaguely outlined, but you must imagine

the vultures." M's solution to the problem is "not convincing," and his philosophy is "not sound." The play is moving in its moments of intensity, but otherwise slow.

325* *"Caesar's Wife,"* Dramatic Mirror, LXXX (4 Dec 1919), 1861, 1863.

This play is "more sentimental than witty"; but, fortunately, it is not just another "conventional comedy with a melodramatic tinge." M displays here "a natural method to find a philosophic solution" to a problem. The playwright is better at feminine characterizations.

326 " *'Caesar's Wife,'* at the Royalty," Illustrated London News, CLIV (5 April 1919), 498, 500.

M's characters strike one as puppets who, despite whatever thin ice they skirt, will be "helped across discreetly to conventional safety"; but M's art in selecting and rounding off a theme, and his instinct for what is suitable to the stage and developing it easily and plausibly, are admirable qualities.

327 " *'Caesar's Wife,':* Mr. Maugham's New Play at the Royalty," Times (Lond), 28 March 1919, p. 15; rptd by Raymond Mander and Joe Mitchenson, eds, in Theatrical Companion to Maugham (Lond: Rockliff, 1955), pp. 150-51.

Every work of M has "a finish, a neatness, an air of accomplishment," and he can refurbish and "relacquer even the oldest of themes and make it look as good as new."

328 Campbell, Marjorie Prentiss. "And Here Is Genius!" Publishers' Weekly, XCVI (Aug 1919), 746.

The Moon and Sixpence contains "perfection of character work"; if M fumbles in attempting, as narrator, to give too much, the fault is a minor one.

329* C[ollins], J. P. "A Study in Sepia," Bookman (Lond), LVI (June 1919), 116.

In *The Moon and Sixpence,* "Mr. Maugham paints the painter's portrait in masterly words, but we can no more accept Strickland's art than we can his break-away. It is a study of freakishness, told with a caustic cleverness of phrase, and a cold impartiality of outlook that is studied to a hair. As an essay in fiction with a biographic camouflage, it is a masterpiece in its way, but its human interest is thin."

330 Collins, J. P. "W. Somerset Maugham: Playwright and Novelist," Bookman (Lond), LVII (Oct 1919), 12-15.

Mrs. Craddock is M's best book; *Under Human Bondage* [*sic*] is a "kind of megalomania" in which there is no "real vitality." [Sketch of M to 1919.]

331 Craven, H. T. "Tahiti from Melville to Maugham," BOOKMAN (NY), L (Nov 1919), 262-67.
M's *The Moon and Sixpence* is an unfaithful description of Tahiti. [An ironic appreciation.]

332 De Foe, Louis V. "The Stage's December Events: Mr. Maugham Frivols Again, but This Time Not Unpleasantly," NEW YORK WORLD ("Metropolitan Section"), 30 Nov 1919, p. 5.
One who knows M's novels wonders why his plays [e.g., *Caesar's Wife*] are not better than they are. Their plots are artificial and flimsy, enlivened only by witty dialogue.

333 "A Deluge of Drama: The Opening of the Season," GRAPHIC, C (6 Sept 1919), 332.
Home and Beauty "is clever and highly polished—but so metallic, and to certain temperaments so chilling."

334 E[dgett], E[dwin] F[rancis]. "A Notable Study of Decadent Genius," BOSTON EVENING TRANSCRIPT, 30 July 1919, p. 6.
In *The Moon and Sixpence,* M succeeds in making the illusory existence of Strickland actual to the reader.

335 "Fiction," ATHENAEUM, No. 4643 (25 April 1919), 254.
To paint a convincing portrait of genius is difficult enough; M willfully handicaps himself with "improbabilities" [e.g., Strickland is a stock broker until the age of forty, etc.], but these improbabilities cleverly underscore Strickland's "originality," and the result in *The Moon and Sixpence* is "a creation of singular force and impressiveness."

336 Finck, Henry T., and J. Rankin Towse. "In the Field of Music—the Drama: *'Caesar's Wife,'* " NEW YORK EVENING POST, 25 Nov 1919, p. 9.
The dialogue is witty, some bits of characterization are "neat"; but the play is neither exciting nor convincing, nor is its pattern anything but "conventional."

337 Findon, B. W. "*Caesar's Wife* by W. Somerset Maugham," PLAY PICTORIAL, XXXIV, No. 206 [n. d., but probably late 1919], 66-67.
M told his story with "accustomed grace and charm of expression." [Mainly plot summary.]

338 Findon, B. W. "*Home and Beauty* by W. Somerset Maugham," PLAY PICTORIAL, XXXV, No. 213 [n. d., but probably late 1919], 94, 96.
M has "bestowed an amount of verbal ornamentation and dramatic cun-

ning which keep . . . audiences highly entertained during the three acts."

339 "Finds Wife Married to His Best Friend," NEW YORK SUN, 9 Oct 1919, p. 12.

The plot and dialogue of *Too Many Husbands* [American title of *Home and Beauty*] are managed with spontaneity.

340 Firkins, O. W. "Drama," WEEKLY REVIEW (NY), I (20 Dec 1919), 688.

In *Caesar's Wife,* when M attempts to make human nature sublime, he makes it inhuman; Sir Arthur is "reptilian."

341 " *'Home and Beauty,'* at the Playhouse," ILLUSTRATED LONDON NEWS, CLV (6 Sept 1919), 370.

"Not for years has a first act left its audience so convulsed and helpless with laughter . . . . "

342* "*Home and Beauty* at the Playhouse," SATURDAY REVIEW (Lond), CXXVIII (4 Oct 1919), 308-9.

"Everyone knows that Maugham can do better than his plays. He proves it again and again in his novels. . . . Clearly the work of a satirical rogue," *Home and Beauty* has a serious theme, but humors of too elementary a character. As M sinks from the "excellent farce" of the first act to popular entertainment, the play becomes continually less interesting. By introducing popular incidents and fun, M spoiled a satire without winning substantial general applause.

343* " *'Home and Beauty'*: Mr. Maugham's New Farce at the Playhouse," TIMES (Lond), 1 Sept 1919, p. 8.

The play "has style, wit, elegance, and at the same time the sheer fun that all farce should have, but fun of the choicest sort, quiet fun."

344 Hornblow, Arthur. "Mr. Hornblow Goes to the Play," THEATRE MAGAZINE, XXX (Nov 1919), 347-48.

Slight as it is [*Too Many Husbands* (American title of *Home and Beauty*)], with practically no plot, the piece is wholly delightful," relying on dialogue more than on situation.

345* H[uxley, A. L.] "Drama," ATHENAEUM, No. 4665 (26 Sept 1919), 956.

Home and Beauty "is made of . . . solidly comic stuff. There is no unreal complication of incident; the original fantastic premiss granted, the rest follows naturally. The pastiche of life and character is real enough to be very amusing, and the dialogue is genuinely witty."

346 K., R. "Another Stroke of Realism," NEW YORK CALL ("The Call Magazine"), 16 Nov 1919, p. 10.

In *The Moon and Sixpence,* M's attitude toward woman is "superficial," but his character study of Strickland is "intensely interesting."

347 L., R. *"The Moon and Sixpence,"* NEW REPUBLIC, XXI (10 Dec 1919), 57-58.
M describes Strickland's behavior, but does not convince the reader of Strickland's genius. The characters are skillfully, if somewhat coldly, drawn; they have no souls.

348* L[ewisohn], L[udwig]. "Drama," NATION (NY), CIX (25 Oct 1919), 548.
Too Many Husbands [American title of *Home and Beauty*] "castigates with its laughter not only the people on stage, but also those in the audience who expected a conventional fable to arouse the expected emotion and draw toward the falseness of a common conclusion. . . . To disappoint that expectation, to strip the audience as well as the characters of their vain pretenses—such is the true and bracing business of the comic spirit."

349 L[ewisohn], L[udwig]. "Drama," NATION (NY), CIX (20 Dec 1919), 805-6.
M has built in *Caesar's Wife* a "pretty and harmless" play, as many playwrights are presently doing for pretty actresses.

350* M[ansfield], K[atherine]. "Inarticulations," ATHENAEUM, No. 4645 (9 May 1919), 302; rptd in NOVELS AND NOVELISTS, ed by J. Middleton Murry (NY: Alfred A. Knopf, 1930), pp. 19-22.
"If Strickland is a real man and this book [*The Moon and Sixpence*] a sort of guide to his works, it has its values, but if Mr. Maugham is merely pulling our critical leg it will not do. Then, we are not told enough. We must be shown something of the workings of his mind; we must have some comment of his upon what he feels, fuller and more exhaustive than his perpetual: 'Go to hell.' It is simply essential that there should be some quality in him revealed to us that we may love, something that will stop us for ever from crying: 'If you have to be so odious before you can paint bananas—pray leave them unpainted.' "

351 "The Modern Artist," NATION (Lond), XXV (31 May 1919), 274, 276.
In *The Moon and Sixpence,* "Mr. Maugham's object . . . is to make Strickland detestable, an artistic Jonathan Wild, a Heathcliffe with a palette but without his love. What he really makes him is preposterous and grotesque, so far as a spook can be adjectival at all."

352 " *'The Moon and Sixpence'*: Somerset Maugham's Picture of a Ruthless Genius," SPRINGFIELD SUNDAY REPUBLICAN (Mass), 7 Sept 1919, p. 17.

Although the idea of the story is fantastic, the episodes of Strickland's life are described with "convincing naturalness." The reader is left pondering, however, why Strickland's genius did not manifest itself earlier than it did.

353 "Music and Drama: *'Too Many Husbands,'*" NEW YORK EVENING POST, 8 Oct 1919, p. 9.

As a bedroom farce, the play is infinitely superior to most, because it is handled with "much greater dexterity and lightness of touch." [Review of the American production of *Home and Beauty*.]

354* Nathan, George Jean. COMEDIANS ALL (NY: Alfred A. Knopf, 1919), pp. 151-54.

In his plays M "is merely a pretty juggler of pretty words who blithesomely tosses them aloft and lets them fall about him in indiscriminate, pretty little piles that have plenty of cake frosting but little meaning and less humour." [Nathan applies this opinion specifically to *Caroline*.]

355 "The New Books," OUTLOOK (NY), CXXIII (24 Sept 1919), 144.

In *The Moon and Sixpence,* "one is loth to accept as either true or of any particular moment the idea that instinctive and untrained obsession for art expression could transform overnight a dull stockbroker into an unwholesome brute and a sinister genius."

356 "New Novels," TIMES LITERARY SUPPLEMENT (Lond), 24 April 1919, pp. 224-25.

In *The Moon and Sixpence,* M's analysis of Strickland's life is "merciless, yet not uncharitable," and "explains much."

357 "Our Booking-Office," PUNCH, CLVII (7 May 1919), 371.

In *The Moon and Sixpence,* M's portrait of Strickland is unquestionably successful.

358 Reid, [Louis]. *"Too Many Husbands,"* DRAMATIC MIRROR, LXXX (23 Oct 1919), 1654.

The American production of *Home and Beauty* is "typically English in mood and feeling," and the keen satiric thrust at society is as amusing as anything on stage for the last ten years. The character contrast between the mentally alert and the stupid major was especially effective.

359* "Reviews: The Primitive Man," SATURDAY REVIEW (Lond), CXXVII (17 May 1919), 481-82.

The Moon and Sixpence might be classed as a study in psychology rather than a novel: "it is the analysis of the naked soul of the barbarous or natural man." Without "plot, incident, or love," the book asks "how would the primitive man, who acknowledges no obligation to God or man or woman, who accepts no creed or code of ethics, bear himself to his fellows in his passage through life?" M creates a hero who does not care what others say or think of him. If Strickland was such a genius, he would not have suppressed himself until forty. M "exaggerates his effects" and uses too many "Go to hell's." The ending on the South Sea Islands is good, but Strickland "might have tried for the moon, surely, without being a beastly lunatic."

360 "Somerset Maugham and the New Fiction," NATION (NY) CIX (16 Aug 1919), 227-28.

The Moon and Sixpence is less important than *Of Human Bondage,* but displaying M's intellectual virtues no less trenchantly, the book is written with "controlled power, steady vision, and noble lucidity."

361 "Somerset Maugham's Imaginary Portrait of a 'Modern' Genius," CURRENT OPINION, LXV (Sept 1919), 187-88.

In *The Moon and Sixpence,* Strickland seems to combine the traits of Cézanne, Van Gogh, and especially Gauguin; however, he resembles, too, the "misanthropic" poet, Arthur Rimbaud, in his desire for seclusion.

362* "Somerset Maugham's Story of a Genius," NEW YORK TIMES BOOK REVIEW, 3 Aug 1919, pp. 389-90.

Although Strickland dominates *The Moon and Sixpence* and although he is a man unlike and apart from ordinary humanity, "the novel has a remarkable reality, much due to the drawing of the minor characters." The novel is to be praised for the leisurely way the story's atmosphere is built up, for its first-person narration without the usual accompanying omniscience, and for the many digressions which actually strengthen M's hold on the reader.

363 T[horp, Joseph]. "At the Play," PUNCH, CLVII (10 Sept 1919), 238.

A "bishop might sit and laugh through it [*Home and Beauty*] without noticing its entirely deplorable moral tone. . . . A delightful entertainment, and with this sound lesson in it—Beware of marrying Dear Little Things."

364 Wilkinson, Marguerite. "Books for Christmas Gifts," TOUCHSTONE, VI (Dec 1919), 149.

The Moon and Sixpence is "chiefly interesting to three classes of readers—those who are interested in stories of genius because genius is something romantic and apart from their own experience about which it is interesting to speculate, second those who, with sorrow or with joy, believe that the thistle of moral obliquity can bear the figs of art, and third a smaller class of readers who enjoy any shrewd delineation of unusual character in action."

365 Woollcott, Alexander. "The Play," NEW YORK TIMES, 9 Oct 1919, p. 16; rptd by Raymond Mander and Joe Mitchenson, eds,

in THEATRICAL COMPANION TO MAUGHAM (Lond: Rockliff, 1955), pp. 155-57.
Too Many Husbands [American title of *Home and Beauty*] is "fragile, light of touch" and provides an evening of "unalloyed amusement."

366 Woollcott, Alexander. "The Play," NEW YORK TIMES, 25 Nov 1919, p. 9.
In *Caesar's Wife,* M works with familiar materials, but when he reaches the familiar climax, he thwarts the audience's expectation; the play was received "resolutely."

1920

367* Archer, William. "Drama," WEEKLY REVIEW (NY), III (13 Oct 1920), 326-28.
In the British production of *The Unknown,* M is brave to bring theological discussion to the stage, but his daring is not matched by great intellectual power and technical skill. The discussions are "imperfectly dramatized," the fable is "not happily invented," and the dramatic effect of the last act is achieved at the expense of plausibility.

368 Collins, Joseph. "Fictional Biography and Autobiography," IDLING IN ITALY: STUDIES OF LITERATURE AND OF LIFE (NY: Scribner's, 1920), pp. 148-58.
From the standpoint of literary construction, *The Moon and Sixpence* is a "great" book, but "from the standpoint of one who desires in fiction some verisimilitude of life as it is, or as it should be if it were ideal, it is disgusting and nauseous, atavistic in implication, primitive in delineation, bestial in its suggestion, and it tends to undermine faith in the fundamental goodness of human nature. It is radicalism in realism carried to the *n*th degree."

369* Davis, Elmer. "The Growing Puzzle of Mr. Maugham's Hero," NEW YORK TIMES BOOK REVIEW AND MAGAZINE, 8 Aug 1920, pp. 4, 15.
Gauguin's career may have furnished some incidents for *The Moon and Sixpence,* but M was interested in the painter's character no more than Shakespeare was in the real character of Julius Caesar. The spiritual parallel between El Greco and Strickland is much closer than the parallel between Gauguin and Strickland.

370 E[dgett], E[dwin] F[rancis]. "The Devious Ways of Somerset Maugham," BOSTON EVENING TRANSCRIPT, 16 June 1920, p. 6.

Mrs. Craddock is better than *The Explorer* [novel], and is "as individual and original" as *Of Human Bondage* and *The Moon and Sixpence.*

371 E[dgett], E[dwin] F[rancis]. "The Romantic Land of Andalusia," BOSTON EVENING TRANSCRIPT, 4 Aug 1920, p. 6

"If the reader . . . is not anxious to visit Andalusia after reading these pages [*The Land of the Blessed Virgin*] he is impervious to the picturesqueness of the scene and to the rare qualities of Mr. Maugham's style."

372 G[riffith], H[ubert]. "At the Play," OBSERVER (Lond), 15 Aug 1920, p. 7.

In *The Unknown,* M does not solve his religious doubts, nor does he make a very honest attempt to do so. For the most part, the characters talk in clichés, and Sylvia's snatching the wedding ring away from her lover is converted into melodrama because platitudes come from her glibly.

373 Hornblow, Arthur. "Mr. Hornblow Goes to the Play," THEATRE MAGAZINE, XXXI (Jan 1920), 21.

Good acting saves *Caesar's Wife,* which is, otherwise, very much an "arid waste of inconsequential words." There is nothing "new" about the drama.

374* Latham, G. W. "The Refusers of Bondage," CANADIAN BOOKMAN, II (Jan 1920), 47-48.

Of Human Bondage is unlike *The Moon and Sixpence* in that the first novel "is long, discursive, has plenty of time to talk about irrelevant things, and is little bothered with the elaboration of plot"; the second "is not discursive or detailed; it admits hardly any irrelevancies; it concentrates entirely on the exposition of the life and personality of one character." Strickland, unlike Philip, is a "character in revolt" who pursues his clearly defined ambition.

375* Lewis, V. A. "The Drama in England," NEW WORLD (Lond), III (Nov 1920), 571-72.

"It is somewhat difficult to realize what Mr. Maugham is aiming at [in *The Unknown*]. There is practically no plot, the whole thing being a series of discussions as to the belief, or non-belief in the existence of God. Arguments wax and wane, nobody gets convinced, and in the end we are left just where we were in the beginning; what we have heard only serving to strengthen the oft-expressed opinion as to the futility of attempting to elucidate these matters by controversy, added to the danger of discussing them in these somewhat troublesome and difficult times."

376* MacCarthy, Desmond. "Miscellany: Somerset Maugham," NEW STATESMAN, XV (14 Aug 1920), 524-25.

M has an aptitude for carrying out in workmanlike fashion any literary task he sets himself; his success owes more, then, to "tenacity of purpose rather than to originality." Whereas his novels have some "individuality," his plays have little. *Caroline* is the best play he has thus far written. In his best play and in *The Unknown,* M's fundamental idea is cynical, but *The Unknown* fails because the discussions about the nature of life and man's destiny are conducted by people who lack vigor of mind and depth of feeling.

377 "Mr. Maugham at Sea," ATHENAEUM, No. 4712 (20 Aug 1920), 251-52.

In *The Unknown,* M "seems to have just that kind of intimate knowledge of ordinary Christianity that the ordinary Christian has of the religion of Lhasa."

378 "Mr. Maugham's Strange Play," GRAPHIC, CII (14 Aug 1920), 258.

In *The Unknown,* M has entered "the debatable land of exegetics, and yet manages to hold us tensely. It is not a gratuitous excursion, for he says openly what many people are thinking furiously, if inarticulately . . . 'How can an all-powerful and benevolent God permit War?' "

379 N., J. S. "Shorter Notices," FREEMAN, II (27 Oct 1920), 165-66.

In *The Land of the Blessed Virgin,* M, like his eighteenth-century fellow-countryman, Sterne, is more keenly interested in people than in painting, architecture, or scenery.

380 "The New Books," OUTLOOK (NY), CXXV (14 July 1920), 507.

Mrs. Craddock has "some subtlety, but moves rather heavily and joylessly."

381 "Plays Worth Seeing. 'Who Will Forgive God?' Real Life in the Theatre," JOHN O' LONDON'S WEEKLY, III (28 Aug 1920), 584.

The Unknown "brings the breath of life over the footlights." [Mainly plot summary.]

382 Savage, [C.] Courtenay. "The Theatre in Review," FORUM, LXIII (Jan 1920), 115.

Caesar's Wife is "a very inferior English comedy."

383 Savage, C. Courtenay. "The Theatre in Review," FORUM, LXIV (Dec 1920), 624.

Too Many Husbands [American title of *Home and Beauty*] is "another bedroom farce. . . . very funny in spots. . . . "

384* Seldes, Gilbert. "The Theatre," DIAL, LXVIII (March 1920), 407.

Too Many Husbands [American title of *Home and Beauty*] is "far wittier, far more intelligent" than Booth Tarkington's CLARENCE; however, it will fare badly, and CLARENCE will hold on because the latter is "native and unpretentious and simply amusing."

385 "A Shadow Show of Distant Lands," NEW YORK TIMES BOOK REVIEW, 22 Aug 1920, p. 24.

In *The Land of the Blessed Virgin,* "the philosophy of Mr. Maugham is that of the aesthetician . . . ." He writes with the details and the loving touch of the artist.

386* Swinnerton, Frank. "The Drama: *'The Unknown,'* " NATION (Lond), XXVII (21 Aug 1920), 637-38.

"The characters discuss God for three acts, and reach no conclusion about Him," because M, whose success is with light comedy, is "over-serious," yet hasn't the "intellectual energy to provide a conclusion to his subtle little love story." M's Deity is a "small" thing, about whom his fatuous characters mouth "a whole play of platitudes."

387 T[horp, Joseph]. "At the Play," PUNCH (18 Aug 1920), 125.

M's attempt to discuss religion on the stage in *The Unknown* is not well-timed.

388 Turner, W. J. "Drama," LONDON MERCURY, II (Sept 1920), 609-10.

M's *The Unknown* is chiefly remarkable for its "workmanlike competence"; it owes its origin not to a "poetic impulse," but to "mere brain activity," which is not of a very high order.

389 *"The Unknown,"* SATURDAY REVIEW (Lond), CXXX (21 Aug 1920), 153-54.

The play "fails to excite in us any very great interest or attention." M has nothing new to say about religion and fails to say the old things so as to convince us that he felt them "in an unexpected way." The play is handled "too obviously as a thesis"; the characters "are merely vehicles for the development of the controversy." The "inconclusive and uninspired excursion into religion is characteristic of a time [the post-war years] which is unavoidably obsessed with problems with which it has at the moment neither the energy nor the ability to deal convincingly."

390 " *'The Unknown,'* at the Aldwych," ILLUSTRATED LONDON NEWS, CLVII (14 Aug 1920), 266.

M manages to state his problem "cogently enough to interest his audience in the first two acts of his play, despite the fact that he makes all his orthodox persons intone their utterances in a kind of rhapsodical chant, despite the fact that he can give no really fresh turn, or only a Wells-ian turn, to the age-old argument about the existence of evil." His third act "leaves his hearers cold and hostile."

391* " *'The Unknown':* Mr. Maugham's Play at the Aldwych," Times (Lond), 10 Aug 1920, p. 8; rptd by Raymond Mander and Joe Mitchenson, eds, in Theatrical Companion to Maugham (Lond: Rockliff, 1955), pp. 165-67.

Young Wharton does not provide sentimental or intellectual interest enough to offset the tiresomeness of Sylvia Bullough and Rev. Norman Poole. To those interested in the play's theme, the argument will seem "shallow"; to those who are not, the play will seem to lack "drama."

392 White, Matthew, Jr. "The Stage," Munsey's Magazine, LXVIII (Jan 1920), 715.

Billie Burke's performance in *Caesar's Wife* is praiseworthy.

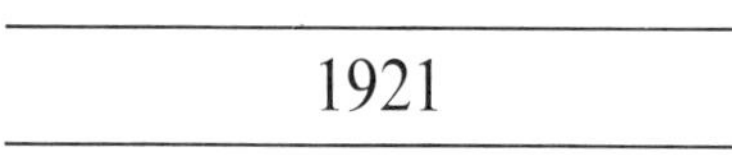

1921

393 Andréades, A. "La saison théâtrale a Londres" (The Theatrical Season in London), Le Figaro, 11 Sept 1921, p. 4.

In the British production of *The Circle,* except for Champion-Cheney, all the characters are convincing. The plot and dialogue are excellent. [In French.]

394 Andrews, Kenneth. "Broadway, Our Literary Signpost," Bookman (NY), LIV (Nov 1921), 232.

"One has always had the impression that Somerset Maugham is a novelist who, now and then, tosses off a play [e.g., *The Circle*] for the fun of it. He has always seemed to turn to the stage for recreation; and he has found it congenial play; he has always had a good time. His comedies have the flash and whir of a good game of tennis on a sunny day."

395 Angell, Hildegarde. "Lesser Maugham," New York Evening Post Literary Review, I (5 March 1921), 3.

Oliver Haddo, the hero of *The Magician,* is comparable to Strickland, a greater character, of *The Moon and Sixpence;* but the book "were better left to obscurity."

396 Archer, William. "Divorce Plays on the London Stage," Weekly Review (NY), IV (14 May 1921), 472-73.

The last part of *The Circle* is not good, but the light comedy scenes preceding it "are nothing less than brilliant."

397* B., L. "Shorter Notices," Freeman, IV (21 Dec 1921), 358.

In *The Trembling of a Leaf,* "unlike a great many present-day writers of fiction," M "has invariably conceived his story before he begins to write it down. Any one of the tales . . . in this collection . . . may be stripped of all the atmosphere and all the literary dress which the storyteller has given it, and it will still remain a recognizable entity—a real and not an imaginary conflict, a real and not a manufactured situation. . . . In actual style, these stories are undistinguished either by brilliant colouring or delicate shading . . . , but they have a cumulative force which brings them close to reality."

398 Benchley, Robert. "Drama: Nature Study," LIFE, LXXVIII (29 Sept 1921), 18.

In *The Circle,* "one delicious situation follows another just as fast as the characters can get on and off the stage."

399 Bettany, Louis. "Mr. Maugham on the White Man's Burden," BOOKMAN (Lond), LXI (Nov 1921), 103.

In *The Trembling of a Leaf,* M's picture of life in the South Seas is "as savage and as gripping as some of the paintings of Goya"; but both Miss Thompson and Dr. Davidson of "Rain" are "too ferocious to be true to type."

400 "Books: Fiction," SPECTATOR (Lond), CXXVII (12 Nov 1921), 638.

In *The Trembling of a Leaf,* M's "Pacific love" themes are hackneyed, but "a certain realistic cynicism prevents them from cloying" and some of his descriptions are "genuinely illuminating." "Mackintosh" and "Rain" are the best of the collection.

401* Boynton, H. W. "The Hapless She," INDEPENDENT (NY), CVII (19 Nov 1921), 193-94.

Liza of Lambeth "is a tale of negative naturalism. Its cockney dialect is laboriously and tiresomely rubbed in. The squalor of its scene and of its people is voluptuously insisted on. Liza is a pathetic, not a shining figure. Her effect falls far short of the pity and terror of the tragic mood, and if she is a symbol of anything, it is of the piteous fatality of the emotion called love. In short, this is an energetic rather than forcible exercise, by a young hand, in the lesser realism of the 'nineties.' "

402 "Briefer Mention," DIAL, LXXI (Oct 1921), 486.

The Land of the Blessed Virgin is "a collection of colour-prints made from emotional snap-shots taken during a siesta in Spain. . . . They are the dead life of Spain—and as remarkable a resurrection as George Moore's more personal miracle in prose."

403 "Briefer Mention," DIAL, LXXI (Dec 1921), 714.

In *Liza of Lambeth,* M "apes the manners of realism, but writes romance."

404 *"The Circle,"* DRAMATIST, XII (Oct 1921), 1079-80.
Although the play contains brilliant dialogue, it is decadent drama. There are no motives for the characters, and the ending is the opposite of what it should have been.

405 " *'The Circle'* at the Haymarket," GRAPHIC, CIII (12 March 1921), 320.
"There isn't a single 'lift' in it, but there are many witty, sardonic lines, and these, together with admirable acting, make it very entertaining."

406 " *'The Circle,'* by Somerset Maugham, at the Haymarket," BOOKMAN (Lond), LX (April 1921), 45.
"The play is worldly and witty, light and entertaining, and leads well up to an easy and laughable curtain."

407 De Foe, Louis V. "Drama," NEW YORK WORLD, 13 Sept 1921, p. 11.
The Circle is "by far the best piece of writing that W. Somerset Maugham has yet done for the stage." Except for Shaw's comedies, it is the "deftest, wisest, most searching and true study that has come out of London since Pinero became content to rest upon the laurels he has well won."

408 Drummond, Curtis. *"The Tenth Man,"* DRAMATIC MIRROR, LXXXIII (23 April 1921), 697.
M has deserted social satire and written here a "tense and interesting melodrama." The play still needs improvements, nevertheless.

409 Edgett, Edwin Francis. "A Visit to the South Sea Islands," BOSTON EVENING TRANSCRIPT, 5 Oct 1921, p. 4.
Each story in *The Trembling of a Leaf* contains enough material for a novel, but M has wisely concentrated it.

410* E[rvine], St. J[ohn]. "At the Play," OBSERVER (Lond), 6 March 1921, p. 11.
"The faults of the play [*The Circle*] are, first, a tendency to lower the plane of the play from comedy to farce; second, a tendency to change from artificial to serious comedy without warning. . . . The third fault is that the cynicism is excessive but not consistently maintained. The fourth fault relates to the character of the wit. All wit has an element of cruelty in it, but great comedy is that in which the cruelty is kept under control. There were occasions when the cruelty got the better of the wit . . . in references to physical defects. A fifth and grave fault was that Arnold's behaviour in the final act, subsequently shown to be insincere, seemed to be perfectly sincere."

411 Field, Louise M. "Latest Works of Fiction," NEW YORK TIMES BOOK REVIEW, 16 Oct 1921, p. 16.
Each of the six stories in *The Trembling of a Leaf* is a combination of realism plus irony and/or sadness, and the collection as a whole is "brilliant, keen, and powerful."

412 Field, Louise M. "Latest Works of Fiction," NEW YORK TIMES BOOK REVIEW, 20 Nov 1921, p. 12.
The American edition of *Liza of Lambeth* has less subtlety and less complexity than M's later works, though no less force or feeling for character. In it, M has shirked nothing of the ugliness of his subject; yet there is a touch of chivalry and of beauty in the underlying love themes.

413 Firkins, O. W. "Drama," WEEKLY REVIEW (NY), V (24 Sept 1921), 275.
The Circle vivifies both M's powers as a playwright and "his infirmities as a teacher." Both Lady Kitty and Champion-Cheney change characters from one act to the next because M "is a farce-writer masquerading as a serious dramatist."

414 G., S. "Shorter Notices," FREEMAN, IV (23 Nov 1921), 262.
"Poor Liza [*Liza of Lambeth*] has been a quarter of a century in a better place, and one seems to hear her whisper gaily to the American reader: 'Not arf.' "

415 Hackett, Francis. *"Liza of Lambeth,"* NEW REPUBLIC, XXVIII (19 Oct 1921), 221-22.
M is sympathetic and sincere in his depiction of "the jungle of Lambeth" and its inhabitants. M's understanding keeps the novel from being tasteless and vile. The ending creates pathos "inwoven with a plain and terrible recognition of the life force that is beyond pathos."

416 Hammond, Percy. "The New Play," NEW YORK TRIBUNE, 13 Sept 1921, p. 8.
The Circle is a good example not only of good play writing but also of "hospitable entertainment."

417 Hornblow, Arthur. "Mr. Hornblow Goes to the Play," THEATRE MAGAZINE, XXXIV (Nov 1921), 316.
Englishmen prove superior to the Americans in writing slick drawing-room comedies, and *The Circle* is a good example. Indeed, it is the best English comedy since Pinero's days. The only major flaw was the "jerky and nervous" characterization that Robert Rendel gave to the young husband.

418 Kaufman, S. Jay. *"The Circle,"* DRAMATIC MIRROR, LXXXIV (17 Sept 1921), 412.

The Selwyns, not M, deserve all the credit for this production, and especially for their handling of the play's ending.

419 L[ewisohn], L[udwig]. "The Beginning," NATION (NY), CXIII (9 Nov 1921), 543-44.

Liza of Lambeth is "definitely dated. But it was a great date [the emergence of naturalism]." The style lacks resonance, but M's vision is "piercing."

420* Lewisohn, Ludwig. "Drama: Somerset Maugham Himself," NATION (NY), CXIII (28 Sept 1921), 356; rptd in THE DRAMA AND THE STAGE (NY: Harcourt, Brace, 1922), pp. 184-87; and in THE MAUGHAM ENIGMA, ed by Klaus W. Jonas (NY: Citadel P, 1954), pp. 104-6.

In *The Circle,* for the first time in drama, M's "intellectual integrity is intact"; he "contacts with reality," for here "conflict and solution are transferred from the superficial compacts and modes of social life into that realm of the reason and of spiritual values in which those modes and compacts are themselves questionable and on trial."

421 " *'Liza of Lambeth'*: A Stark Tragedy by W. S. Maugham," SPRINGFIELD SUNDAY REPUBLICAN (Mass), 20 Nov 1921, p. 11.

The novel is a "miniature," but it is "admirably self-contained" and observes a fine sense of "inner proportions." The defects are a narrow emotional range and air of "businesslike efficiency."

422 Lovett, Robert Morss. "After the Play," NEW REPUBLIC, XXVIII (5 Oct 1921), 161.

The successor to Pinero and Henry Arthur Jones in the modern English comedy of manners, M [in *The Circle*] surpasses his predecessors and "raises his comedy of manners to a drama of characters."

423 McQuilland, Louis. "Somerset Maugham's Tales of the Pacific," JOHN O' LONDON'S WEEKLY, VI (5 Nov 1921), 154.

"The tales [*The Trembling of a Leaf*] are written with a daring that does not give offence"; M's scientific detachment "kills prurience." "Red" exemplifies the texture of M's book; it is "brooding and sardonic."

424* "Miss Lottie Venne Plays Bridge," SATURDAY REVIEW (Lond), CXXXI (12 March 1921), 213-14.

The Circle gives a queer picture of society, but has a serious and original theme. Those who call M a pessimist for presenting this circle of characters are mistaken. The work has truth and logic and a note of hope. When, having seen the ruin of Lord Porteous and Kitty, Edward and Elizabeth decide to challenge Fate and fly, M shows his approval of that action. Edward offers not Romance, but Love; he and Elizabeth are prepared to face pain as well as pleasure. Such is M's thesis, and it is not pessimism but "simple truth."

425* MacCarthy, Desmond. "Drama: *'The Circle,'* " NEW STATESMAN, XVI (19 March 1921), 704-5.

An earlier generalization about *The Unknown* ["Miscellany: Somerset Maugham," NEW STATESMAN, XV (14 Aug 1920), 524-25] that M's fundamental ideas are cynical is borne out in *The Circle.* Moreover, M's work improves in merit and interest as he continues to write from a cynical point of view. *Cynical* means "sceptical with regard to the depth and persistence of human affection." *The Circle* is one of M's best plays, and one of the most cynical. The only objections to the play are these: (1) Lord Porteous is "conventionally drawn and commonplace and uninteresting," and (2) M exhibits an insensitivity to shades of feeling and to language through "vulgar phrases" in the otherwise admirable scene between Elizabeth and Teddy in Act II.

426 "Mr. Maugham in the South Seas: Psychology of White Degeneration Caught in Studies," SPRINGFIELD SUNDAY REPUBLICAN (Mass), 13 Nov 1921, p. 13.

The Trembling of a Leaf is "convincing if not compelling narrative"; "Rain" is the best of the stories.

427 "Mr. Maugham's New Play: *'The Circle'* at the Haymarket," TIMES (Lond), 4 March 1921, p. 10; rptd by Raymond Mander and Joe Mitchenson, eds, in THEATRICAL COMPANION TO MAUGHAM (Lond: Rockliff, 1955), pp. 161-62.

"Mr. Maugham knows how to put a difficult case [Elizabeth's final bolt] in the theatre; none better. Approve ethically, or not, you must approve aesthetically. The orthodox moralist may protest, but he cannot but have enjoyed a very brilliant comedy."

428* Nathan, George Jean. THE THEATRE, THE DRAMA, THE GIRLS (NY: Alfred A. Knopf, 1921), pp. 104-6.

M as a novelist shows constant growth, but as a playwright remains, as he began, "merely an inferior Hubert Henry Davies." *Caesar's Wife* "is a rehash of St. James's Theatre comedy on end: a humourless disposition of marionettes of Grundy, Sutro et Cie upon the eternal triangle checkerboard."

429 "The New Maugham Play at the Haymarket: *'The Circle,'* " ILLUSTRATED LONDON NEWS, CLVIII (12 March 1921), 354.

The brilliancy and honesty of workmanship make one overlook the faults inherent in the play's over-neat and artificial plot.

430 "New Novels," OBSERVER (Lond), 23 Oct 1921, p. 5.

"People who love a pretty story will not love Mr. Maugham's book [*The Trembling of a Leaf*]; but who among us loves a pretty story nowadays, or dares to say so if he does?"

431 "New Novels," TIMES LITERARY SUPPLEMENT (Lond), 13 Oct 1921, p. 663.

In *The Trembling of a Leaf,* every one of M's Pacific natives has something to excite compassion. Most of the stories turn on "the soul of goodness in things evil."

432 Parker, Robert Allerton. "Comedy and Color," ARTS AND DECORATION, XVI (Nov 1921), 19.

The Circle is "written with a sharp pen, dipped in ink that contains too much of acid, and too little of the milk of human kindness."

433* "Reviews: A Comedy of Manners," SATURDAY REVIEW (Lond), CXXXI (18 June 1921), 509.

The Circle was well worth printing, if only as a monument of some of the taste of its time. Contrary to critics who acclaimed the common and dated dialogue when the play was performed, "in *The Circle* we find all Maugham's good qualities—his smartness of dialogue, sense of a situation, and skill at indicating character. But as we have suggested, it also contains that touch of the crude and the common which is nothing less than the germ of corruption and death in any work of art."

434* "Reviews: Fiction," SATURDAY REVIEW (Lond), CXXXII (5 Nov 1921), 540.

In *The Trembling of a Leaf,* "each separate tale is begun by inspiration and completed by artistic perfection." The contrast between "the bitter futile tragedies" and the serene South Sea Island settings is effective: depraved white men drift to the "fairy-tale islands" and "live mainly upon one another's screaming nerves." " 'Rain' is a sheer masterpiece of sardonic horror, beyond criticism." The ending of "Mackintosh" lacks subtlety and truth of character.

435 S[eaman], O[wen]. "At the Play," PUNCH, CLX (9 March 1921), 196.

The beginning of *The Circle* is improbable, its finale futile, but M's wit is "delectable."

436 S[eldes], G[ilbert]. "The Theatre," DIAL, LXXI (Nov 1921), 620.

M began with fine comedy but steadily wrote it "down and down"; perhaps the audience that M knows so well is to blame, but there is no denying the vulgarity of *The Circle*—its conversations, obvious and stupid, totally lack in mental fineness. [Seldes continues to castigate the audience the following month, and makes a casual reference to *The Circle,* DIAL, LXXI (Dec 1921), 724.]

437* Swinnerton, Frank. *"The Circle,"* NATION AND THE ATHENAEUM, XXVIII (19 March 1921), 879-80.

M's new play "is the work of a sentimentalist turned cynic"; the situation is well-prepared and treated with great skill, but "the conflict between . . . sentimentality and . . . cynicism produces a very curious result," making the characterization uncertain and robbing the play of unity. Especially are these qualities manifest in M's handling of Arnold, who must be regarded at one time as a "fussy fool," then as an "injured gentleman."

438 Tarn. "The Theatre: *The Circle,*" SPECTATOR (Lond), CXXVI (26 March 1921), 396.

The play is an "apologia for willfulness." "There is a case for 'free love,' but is there any case for this kind of frigid adultery?"

439 "The Theatre," NEW YORK SUN, 13 Sept 1921, p. 16.

The Circle is M's "most enjoyable comedy."

440* Towse, J. Rankin. "The Play," NEW YORK EVENING POST, 13 Sept 1921, p. 6.

The Circle lacks sincerity and betrays M's tendency to indulge in cynical flippancy; but it is clever, neatly constructed, rich in observation, and shrewd and truthful—if not original—in characterization.

441 Turner, W. J. "Chronicles: Drama," LONDON MERCURY, III (April 1921), 663-64.

The plot of *The Circle* "is handled in a remarkably straight-forward fashion, with an absence of sentimentality or humbug, that could only be called cynical by those who pass by the experience of life in blinkers."

442 Went, Stanley. "The Mature Maugham," NEW YORK EVENING POST LITERARY REVIEW, I (5 Nov 1921), 144.

Liza of Lambeth is "well worth republishing," and *The Trembling of a Leaf* contains "the best work which Mr. Maugham has done"; "Rain" is the best story in the latter book.

443* West, Rebecca. "Notes on Novels," NEW STATESMAN, XVIII (5 Nov 1921), 140, 142.

M's middle name is "certainty": his indomitable character "enables him to make the best and most remunerative use of every grain of talent that he possesses." M's motto from Sainte-Beuve on the flyleaf of *The Trembling of a Leaf* is indicative "of a certain cheap and tiresome attitude towards life, which nearly mars these technically admirable stories." M's cynicism is a cover-up for his lack of any real philosophy; that it is not a real attitude is manifested in the way the philosophy of "The Fall of Edward Barnard" cancels out, or is cancelled out by, the philosophy of "Red," leaving "an impression of nothingness." The volume contains, however, two "more than admirable stories": "Mackintosh" and "Rain."

444 Woollcott, Alexander. "The Play," NEW YORK TIMES, 13 Sept 1921, p. 12.
The Circle is "searching, malicious, and richly entertaining."

1922

445 Abdullah, Achmed. "Under Western Eyes," NEW YORK TRIBUNE, 15 Oct 1922, p. 9.
On a Chinese Screen is written "with a beauty as lucid and exquisite as a vase of Koyao, fifth in rank among the Middle Kingdom's porcelains."

446* Agate, James. "West of Suez," SATURDAY REVIEW (Lond), CXXXIV (9 Sept 1922), 374-75; rptd in AT HALF-PAST EIGHT: ESSAYS OF THE THEATRE (NY: Bernard G. Richards Co, 1923), pp. 212-17; and by Raymond Mander and Joe Mitchenson, eds, in THEATRICAL COMPANION TO MAUGHAM (Lond: Rockliff, 1955), pp. 171-72, 189.
M is "a writer of great distinction," but *East of Suez* is "quite insincere." He "does not say openly and firmly that the trouble with mixed unions between Eurasian women and English men is the English code of morals. For the artist who may not speak truth, there is little discriminating between artificialities." M "hints, and would say if he dare, . . . that the passion of both men is not unreasonable but anti-social, not unlawful but inexpedient. Very few things are immoral which are sincere." M "knows that strange desire will persist, but if there is to be no bother there must be no marriage. He knows, too, that between such outspokenness and the British stage are arrayed all the forces of law and order, the censorship and public opinion, army, navy, and the police. . . . I do not blame the author, but the theatre to which he conforms."

447 Andrews, Kenneth. "Broadway, Our Literary Signpost," BOOKMAN (NY), LVI (Dec 1922), 480.
East of Suez is in M's "earlier manner, which is an awful thing to say about any play."

448 B[enchley], R[obert]. "Drama: French, English, American," LIFE, LXXX (12 Oct 1922), 18.
East of Suez is weakened by the changes in the American version of the play, making it sound as if it were written by Owen Davis.

449 B[enchley], R[obert]. "Drama: Just Dandy," LIFE, LXXX (30 Nov 1922), 18.

In John Colton and Clemence Randolph's dramatization, RAIN, the last scene provides a "powerful thrill."

450 "Books to Buy and Ask For," TIMES (Lond), 8 Aug 1922, p. 9.

What M has done in *On a Chinese Screen* is comparable to what Pierre Loti has done in his work, for M's book "not only gives in a series of word pictures the magnificence and squalor of China, but also more than one penetrating study of the Europeans to whom the strange mysterious country has become a second homeland." [Pre-publication review.]

451* "Briefer Mention," DIAL, LXXII (April 1922), 431.

"Like all pot-boilers, the stories [*The Trembling of a Leaf*] are a rehash of other men's experiences, reactions, and words, with a little of the present compiler stirred in as a binder. In the product, Conrad, Kipling, McFee, the composite magazine story writer and the man who wrote *Of Human Bondage* are equally apparent. . . . The writing, considered even from the standpoint of grammar, is at times absurdly careless; unshepherded pronouns sport about in happy promiscuity through long paragraphs."

452 Broun, Heywood. "The New Plays," NEW YORK WORLD, 23 Sept 1922, p. 11.

East of Suez is "archaic and conventional melodrama," yet "thrilling."

453 Corbin, John. "The Play," NEW YORK TIMES, 8 Nov 1922, p. 18; rptd by Raymond Mander and Joe Mitchenson, eds, in THEATRICAL COMPANION TO MAUGHAM (Lond: Rockliff, 1955), pp. 255-56 [where the criticism is dated 7 Nov 1922].

John Colton and Clemence Randolph's dramatization, RAIN, is "strikingly original in theme, true in characterization, vigorous in drama and richly colored with the magic of the South Seas."

454 "*'East of Suez':* Mr. Maugham's Play at His Majesty's—Peking Up-to-Date," TIMES (Lond), 4 Sept 1922, p. 6.

[Mocking remarks on the attempts at local color in the staging of the play.]

455 E[rvine], St. J[ohn]. *"East of Suez,"* OBSERVER (Lond), 3 Sept 1922, p. 11.

As a study in ethnology, the play is unsatisfactory; as a story well told and skillfully presented, it is excellent.

456 Findon, B. W. "*'East of Suez'* by W. Somerset Maugham,"

PLAY PICTORIAL, XLI, No. 248 [n. d., but probably late 1922], 92.
[Primarily a plot summary.]

457 G[rierson], F[rancis] D. *"East of Suez,"* BOOKMAN (Lond), LXIII (Oct 1922), 53-54.
The production of the play is praiseworthy.

458 "A Group of New Plays," GRAPHIC, CVI (9 Sept 1922), 390.
East of Suez was commendably performed.

459 Hammond, Percy. "The Theaters," NEW YORK TRIBUNE, 22 Sept 1922, p. 8.
East of Suez is "a thick silhouette, composed by Mr. Maugham when presumably, he was in one of his solemn, shallow and mercenary moods. It is a colorful routine fable, related without much ingenuity, though it is in no way a botch."

460 Hammond, Percy. "The Theaters," NEW YORK TRIBUNE, 8 Nov 1922, p. 8.
John Colton and Clemence Randolph's dramatization, RAIN, is "a sight to see."

461 Hornblow, Arthur. "Mr. Hornblow Goes to the Play," THEATRE MAGAZINE, XXXVI (Nov 1922), 299.
There is a good deal of "hard-breathing" and "loud cursing" here, but *East of Suez* remains an "inane and wholly conventional melodrama." In addition, the production itself is second-rate.

462 Lewisohn, Ludwig. "Drama," NATION (NY), CXV (29 Nov 1922), 585-86.
John Colton and Clemence Randolph's dramatization, RAIN, is "morally profound and dramaturgically brilliant."

463* MacCarthy, Desmond. "Drama: *'East of Suez,'*" NEW STATESMAN, XX (7 Oct 1922), 14; rptd in THEATRE (Lond: MacGibbon & Kee, 1954), pp. 131-34.
Daisy is well drawn, but the "most admirable invention in the play is Daisy's grotesque, ever-present nurse." George is a "high-minded, generous English gentleman, who is miserable at having yielded to his passion for his friend's wife"; but M sees deepest into life and character from a cynical point of view, and thus the result of George's handling is "conventional." In the prologue, M's use of the stage's capacity to present realistically a picture of the swarming streets of Pekin is impressive; so is the symbolic tableau of the final act.

464* "Mr. Maugham in China," TIMES LITERARY SUPPLEMENT (Lond), 23 Nov 1922, p. 756.

In *On a Chinese Screen,* although he may expect too much from the merchant-adventurers he tries to sketch, M's creation of a "richness of personality" backs up and fills in any defects in the realism of the material: "it is not a Chinese screen at all, but a very pretty piece of Maughamware, . . . in which the dainty marionettes of his lively imagination, delicate irony, pathos, and whimsical humor play their parts and posture on a scene of which the moving background is partly China and partly the exotically Europeanized Treaty Ports. . . . "

465 "The New Books," NEW YORK EVENING POST LITERARY REVIEW, II (15 July 1922), 810.

The Making of a Saint is "sometimes a little awkward and sometimes a little boring."

466 Overton, Grant. "The Heterogeneous Magic of Maugham," WHEN WINTER COMES TO MAIN STREET (NY: Doran, 1922), pp. 270-85 [biography and bibliography, pp. 286-92]; rptd in AUTHORS OF THE DAY: STUDIES IN CONTEMPORARY LITERATURE (NY: George H. Doran, 1924), pp. 344-56.

[Biographical sketch with a long reference to an unpublished article, "Somerset Maugham in Tahiti," by Hector MacQuarrie, author of TAHITI DAYS.]

467 The Playgoer. " *'East of Suez'* Arrives at the Eltinge Theater," NEW YORK SUN, 22 Sept 1922, p. 16.

The play is "a colorful Chinese melodrama" not quite matching William Archer's success in THE GREEN GODDESS; indeed, it is cold and arouses little sympathy for its leading characters.

468 "The Polite Traveller," OBSERVER (Lond), 3 Dec 1922, p. 4.

In *On a Chinese Screen,* M, like Gautier, has a talent for surfaces, but recognizes there are depths and can often suggest them.

469 R., E. "An Englishman in China," NEW STATESMAN, XX (2 Dec 1922), 274-75.

In *On a Chinese Screen,* M's impressions of China have no suggestion of tedium, but are "transfigured" by his personality; his urbane nature sympathizes with the thought and manner of that ancient civilization.

470 "Recent Books in Brief Review," BOOKMAN (NY), LVI (Dec 1922), 515.

"Some may take exception to the few small pages [of *On a Chinese Screen*] which seem not quite successfully to be trying to be prose poems. Stout-hearted readers will like 'The Vice-Consul,' a striking and horrible thing; everyone, surely, will feel the thrill in 'Romance.' "

471 "The Short Story," Nation and the Athenaeum, XXX (14 Jan 1922), 593-94.
M's seven stories [*The Trembling of a Leaf*] are written in a plain style that conceals a good deal of intensity, and their power is "not only genuine, but controlled and directed"; "Rain" is the best of the group, but "Red" is almost as impressive "on a different plane."

472 Sutton, Graham. "More Maugham," Bookman (Lond), LXII (Sept 1922), 242-43.
Caesar's Wife and *The Land of Promise* exemplify M's general dramatic economy, though neither play is up to the high standard of *The Circle.*

473 Swaffer, Hannen. "Plays & Players," Sunday Times (Lond), (17 Sept 1922), p. 5.
[Review of *East of Suez.*]

474* Tarn. "The Theatre: *'East of Suez,'* " Spectator (Lond), CXXIX (9 Sept 1922), 337.
One feels "shocked indignation" that M could have written anything so "amateurish" after *The Circle.* "Especially striking is the lack of ingenuity in fitting the theme to the fact of theatrical performance." The story is told at "immense length" and with "undeviating crudity," and the play is ruined by a "shallow pretentiousness." "Another piece of work like this and his [M's] reputation as a serious playwright will be gone!"

475 "The Theatres," Times (Lond), 21 Sept 1922, p. 8.
Charles Hawtrey plans to appear in the revival of *Jack Straw. The Circle* has been translated into German and bought for the Berliner Theatre by Director Hollaender.

476 Towse, J. Rankin. " *'East of Suez'* a Maugham Potboiler," New York Evening Post, 22 Sept 1922, p. 7.
The play is "just plain Oriental melodrama of a very common theatrical type."

477 Towse, J. Rankin. " 'Rain' Is Striking but Disappointing," New York Evening Post, 8 Nov 1922, p. 9.
John Colton and Clemence Randolph's dramatization presents a good theme, the first two acts succeed, but the play descends suddenly to melodrama when Sadie is implausibly presented as a repentant Mary Magdalen.

478 Woollcott, Alexander. "The Play," New York Times, 22 Sept 1922, p. 16.

The modifications made in the script for the American production of *East of Suez* are lamentable.

1923

479* Adcock, A. St. John. "William Somerset Maugham," GODS OF MODERN GRUB STREET: IMPRESSIONS OF CONTEMPORARY AUTHORS (NY: Frederick A. Stokes, 1923), pp. 213-19.

Mrs. Craddock is M's "strongest and ablest" novel. [A brief biographical portrait, with emphasis on M's versatility as a novelist and a playwright.]

480* Agate, James. "The Dramatic World," SUNDAY TIMES (Lond), 16 Sept 1923, p. 4; rptd, as *"Our Betters* by Somerset Maugham," in RED-LETTER NIGHTS: A SURVEY OF POST-ELIZABETHAN DRAMA IN ACTUAL PERFORMANCE ON THE LONDON STAGE, 1921-1943 (Lond: J. Cape, 1944), pp. 218-22.

In the "brilliant, heartless" *Our Betters,* M has rewritten one of Henry James' short stories after the manner of Congreve. [M's Elizabeth Saunders is Bessie Alden of "An International Episode" "all over again."] The play is "extraordinarily deft, and its matter is handled with any amount of 'style': neither Sutro, nor Pinero, nor Jones could treat Lady George Grayston with M's "poise"; Barrie, Shaw, Galsworthy, and Bennett could not handle the Duchesse de Surennes well, with M's "icy aloofness." The play would be even better if M had deleted Bessie's American sweetheart and the sentimentalizing Principessa: "these two bring a blurring to the hard lines of the picture, translate us to a world where decency is, and so suggest questions of moral censure."

481 A[nderson], J[ohn]. "*'The Camel's Back'* a Clever Play," NEW YORK EVENING POST, 14 Nov 1923, p. 9.

The play is sprightly, clever, and amusing; but its humor is largely that of plot and situation, which is neither significant nor helpful to the playwright's reputation.

482 Andrews, Kenneth. "Broadway, Our Literary Signpost," BOOKMAN (NY), LVI (Jan 1923), 611-12.

John Colton and Clemence Randolph's dramatization, RAIN, not only reads well but gains "enormous force when it is projected in the playhouse."

483 Benchley, Robert. "Drama: Hautboys and Torches," LIFE, LXXXII (6 Dec 1923), 50.

The Camel's Back "suffers from a bad case of second act. After getting away to one of the best starts in town, it suddenly lies down and rolls over, arising only in the last act to a fairly strong finish."

484* Birrell, Francis. "The Drama: Lunching Out," NATION AND THE ATHENAEUM, XXXIV (3 Nov 1923), 198.
Our Betters is not "comedy," but "satire." Though M did not intend to make his characters as "socially impossible" as they appear, they "can say witty and intelligent things without thereby becoming witty or intelligent themselves. It is all the time Mr. Maugham . . . who is being witty." The play therefore becomes "unlifelike and empty."

485 "Briefer Mention," DIAL, LXXIV (March 1923), 315.
In the published version of *East of Suez,* "Mr. Maugham contrives dramatic situations and then flats them by crude or feeble dialogue, noting however in the stage directions that his character was 'excessively distressed' or 'feels helpless and strangely weak.' "

486 Broun, Heywood. "The New Plays," NEW YORK WORLD, 14 Nov 1923, p. 14.
The first act of *The Camel's Back* is amusing; the second, "profoundly boring"; the third, "mildly diverting."

487 " *'The Camel's Back'* Appears at the Vaudeville Theater," NEW YORK SUN AND GLOBE, 14 Nov 1923, p. 20.
The humor of the play is "more infantile than adult."

488* Chapman, Percy. "L'Art Dramatique aux Etats-Unis" (Dramatic Art in the United States), LE TEMPS, 20 Aug 1923, p. 3.
The greatest success of this season is RAIN, whose study of venality is scarcely different from that in TARTUFFE. The play seeks the hidden motives which our ancestors were ashamed of. [A general survey of the revival in American stagecraft, the influence on it of motion pictures and electricity.] [In French.]

489 "Collected Plays of England's Most Civilized Dramatist," NEW YORK TIMES BOOK REVIEW, 27 May 1923, p. 7.
The Plays of W. Somerset Maugham reveals M as a curious mixture of "reality" and "artificiality." His works "reek of life," but readers perceive his desire to be "civilized to the last nuance," which makes his works occasionally "mannered." M's plays will not add to his literary reputation, "but they can hardly take anything away from it."

490* Corbin, John. "The Play," NEW YORK TIMES, 14 Nov 1923, p. 19.
"That the invention [in *The Camel's Back*] is a good one is simply attested by its antiquity [Shakespeare, Kyd, Juvenal used the same idea]. Mr.

Maugham's use of it is part good. For an act and a half there is much wit and excellent fooling; but the latter half of the second act goes thin to the vanishing point."

491* Dukes, Ashley. THE YOUNGEST DRAMA: STUDIES OF FIFTY DRAMATISTS (Lond: Ernest Benn, 1923), pp. 3, 39-40.

The drama of M has a "peaty flavour," but "it will never cloy the palate"; M has "a resolute intellectual honesty" and the gift "for taking the distant view." "Lightness" suits him best.

492 *"East of Suez,"* DRAMATIST, XIV (Jan 1923), 1140-41.

M seems to think that China is a "good place to bury the brawl of melodramatic mechanism too creaky for home industry." This play, like *The Circle,* is "morally offensive," the "last ditch of degradation;" in addition, the psychology of the characters is "abominably bad."

493 E[rvine], St. J[ohn]. "At the Play," OBSERVER (Lond), 16 Sept 1923, p. 11.

In *Our Betters,* M follows Congreve rather than Sheridan, and Congreve is inferior to Sheridan; one can find little relation to human beings in M's characters.

494* Farjeon, Herbert. "Morality and Mr. Maugham," SATURDAY REVIEW (Lond), CXXXVI (22 Sept 1923), 325-26.

Critics have unfairly levelled unpleasant epithets against *Our Betters.* "Nearly all the plays popularly regarded as cynical are written by romantic sentimentalists in a fit of disgust at the unrepresentative insensibility of their fellow beings." Shaw is an example. *Our Betters* deals with cynical people, but M is not a cynic. The play is an "indictment of those who will not render homage to the goddess of Love." The moral, which the satire carries on its own, is stated too specifically, but it is a fearless play that says something and amuses.

495 Fehr, Bernhard. DIE ENGLISCHE LITERATUR DES 19. UND 20. JAHRHUNDERTS (ENGLISH LITERATURE OF THE 19TH AND 20TH CENTURIES). (Berlin-Neubabelsberg: Akademische Verlagsgesellschaft Athenaion, 1923), pp. 343, 370, 476-78.

[Passing references to M as a dramatist.] [In German.]

496* Field, Louise M. "Maugham's Chinese Sketches," NEW YORK TIMES BOOK REVIEW, 4 Feb 1923, p. 11; rptd in THE MAUGHAM ENIGMA, ed by Klaus W. Jonas (NY: Citadel P, 1954), pp. 191-93.

On a Chinese Screen is "a traveler's notebook, filled with thumbnail sketches of persons, places, and points of view." In general, they convey the impression—with some notable exceptions—of the hardness, narrowness, and self-satisfied lack of understanding of the whites in China.

497 "From Mojave Desert to Siberian Steppe," LITERARY DIGEST INTERNATIONAL BOOK REVIEW, I (Jan 1923), 62-63.
"The bewildering variety, the splendor and the squalor, the virtues and vices, the teeming hordes of China, all pour across these pages [*On a Chinese Screen*] in a succession aglow with color."

498* Gould, Gerald. "New Fiction," SATURDAY REVIEW (Lond), CXXXV (13 Jan 1923), 54.
In *On a Chinese Screen,* M "provides something exceptionally good, with a gesture almost of carelessness. His technical competence . . . has presumably passed into his subconsciousness, and become as effortless as breathing and walking." M's "descriptions are not so much natural as psychological: he reproduces states of mind." By showing in the stories "the effect of China on minds with preconceptions similar to ours," he gives us "the 'feel' of that ancient and alien civilization. . . . If the cold violence of his method suggests cruelty, the philosophy underlying it is kind; for, as he himself says in one of the grimmest and most ironical of his studies, 'the normal is the rarest thing in the world,' and that implies that we should be tolerant of one another's idiosyncrasies."

499 G[rierson], F[rancis] D. *"On a Chinese Screen,"* BOOKMAN (Lond), LXIII (Jan 1923), 208-9.
This collection is as "exquisite as it is refreshing."

500 Hammond, Percy. "The Theaters," NEW YORK TRIBUNE, 14 Nov 1923, p. 14.
The first act is better than the rest of *The Camel's Back,* and on the whole the play is a light, witty, not too elegant trifle.

501 Hines, Jack. "Mr. Maugham on Deck and in the Smoking Room," NEW YORK TIMES BOOK REVIEW, 17 June 1923, p. 7.
[Interview.]

502 Hornblow, Arthur. "Mr. Hornblow Goes to the Play," THEATRE MAGAZINE, XXXVII (Jan 1923), 25.
John Colton and Clemence Randolph's dramatization, RAIN, is much better than M's own poor play, *East of Suez;* in fact, it atones for that earlier failure. Sadie's conversion from harlot to "religionist" is too sudden, but the play itself will interest anyone.

503* Lewisohn, Ludwig. "The Case of Somerset Maugham," NATION (NY), CXVI (3 Jan 1923), 19-20.
M has the style and intelligence to turn out better works than his mechanical plays like *East of Suez,* and the fragmentary *The Moon and Sixpence.* But he contents himself in *On a Chinese Screen* with viewing the pity and beauty of the world as a "pageant. He gives us glimpses of that pageant

rendered in a form as frugal, as precise, as permanent as he can make it. That seems to him the only effort worthy of a serious mind, all other efforts being doomed to busy futility and sordid failure in the end." [General assessment of M's career.]

504 Lewisohn, Ludwig. "Drama," NATION (NY), CXVII (28 Nov 1923), 614-15.

M's execution in the first act of *The Camel's Back* is good, but the play, on the whole, "runs down."

505* MacCarthy, Desmond. "Miscellany—Somerset Maugham: *'Our Betters,'*" NEW STATESMEN, XXI (6 Oct 1923), 738-39; rptd in THEATRE (Lond: MacGibbon & Kee, 1954), pp. 119-24; and by Raymond Mander and Joe Mitchenson, eds, in THEATRICAL COMPANION TO MAUGHAM (Lond: Rockliff, 1955), pp. 118-21.

M's play is only "satire" for those "who attribute to the author their own moral reactions to what he shows them"; it is rather a "sardonically detached comedy," an exposure "in the manner of Maupassant of one luxuriant corner of the social jungle." In the last act M demonstrates his "remarkable power," employing anticlimax "of the first order."

506 Mais, S. P. B. "Somerset Maugham," SOME MODERN AUTHORS (NY: Dodd, Mead & Co, 1923), pp. 115-28, 288-95.

On the basis of *East of Suez* and *The Circle,* and the novels from *The Merry-Go-Round* to *The Moon and Sixpence,* "Maugham ought to be one of the most formative influences of the present day. There is certainly no one who could exert such a healthy restraint on the young writer who fears to face the truth. Maugham, like Adam, is strong enough to be naked and unashamed."

507 "Mr. Maugham in Asia," SPRINGFIELD SUNDAY REPUBLICAN (Mass), 21 Jan 1923, p. 7.

East of Suez has a marvelous "silent" first scene, but the situations of the play are "improbable, though not impossible."

508 "The Opening of the Play Season," GRAPHIC, CVIII (22 Sept 1923), 444.

Our Betters is a "startling production" with "scintillating wit."

509 "*'Our Betters,'* at the Globe," ILLUSTRATED LONDON NEWS, CLXIII (22 Sept 1923), 550.

M's play is comparable to Congreve's comedies of manners, but the two authors differ in that M's characters never bear "any resemblance to genuine human nature"; they have a "cold glitter" about them, but no "human warmth."

510 " *'Our Betters':* Mr. Maugham's Play at the Globe," TIMES (Lond), 13 Sept 1923), p. 8.
Like its heroine, the play is "clever, cynical, and shameless," with the design to amuse more than to convince.

511 "RAIN," DRAMATIST, XIV (April 1923), 1154.
Does John Colton and Clemence Randolph's dramatization succeed because the world is wicked, or because RAIN is a just criticism of the missionary's inefficacy? The play relies too much on prejudice against self-righteousness; drama of its type may lead us to "dramatized atheism."

512 "Reviews: The Golden Age," NATION AND THE ATHENAEUM, XXXII (27 Jan 1923), 650.
On a Chinese Screen presents a praiseworthy picture of China and how the average European or American resident lives there.

513 "Reviews of Books—Life in China: Colorful 'Vignettes,' by W. Somerset Maugham," SPRINGFIELD DAILY REPUBLICAN (Mass), 3 Jan 1923, p. 8.
In *On a Chinese Screen,* whether ten pages or a paragraph, each of the fifty-eight studies "is a finished piece of art, painting with the delicate, sure touch of the perfect craftsman a picture with all the atmosphere and feeling which its subject demands." M's artistic skill is revealed best in the character sketches.

514 S[eaman], O[wen]. "At the Play," PUNCH, CLXV (19 Sept 1923), 282, 284.
"The high comedy, touched with farce, of the last Act went far to redeem the play [*Our Betters*]."

515* Shanks, Edward. "The Drama: *'Our Betters,'* " OUTLOOK (Lond), LII (6 Oct 1923), 271.
M is the "brightest ornament" of Shaftesbury Avenue while he continually gives "Shaftesbury Avenue the last thing one would expect it to endure. No soft sentiment, . . . no happy ending, no conventional view of life."

516 T., G. "The Globe Theatre. *'Our Betters,'* " BOOKMAN (Lond), LXV (Oct 1923), 56.
The play is a bitter satire on "petty and sordid intrigue."

517* Tarn. "The Theatre: *Our Betters,*" SPECTATOR (Lond), CXXXI (22 Sept 1923), 386-87.
"A neat, entertaining and entirely classical piece," much like some of Congreve's and Wycherley's, but not as good. The play is nonetheless "an excellent example of an honored type." M is "consistently shocked by his characters" and "strictly moral." The plot functions merely as a vehicle to

expose the "gilded vice" of the "vulgar and shameless" characters. The play suffers from its theme that all American women marrying Europeans turn bad and that all "such marriages constitute a menace to society."

518 "The Theatre," TIME, II (26 Nov 1923), 14.
"Playwright Maugham herein [*The Camel's Back*] concerned himself with an irresponsible investigation of the regions of the utterly inane. He involved himself in such a feathery swirl of epigram and complication that along in Act II he found that he simply could not make his wits' ends meet. He gave up trying."

519 T[horp, Joseph]. "At the Play," PUNCH, CLXIII (13 Sept 1923), 260.
The pageantry of the production is incongruous with the tragic theme of *East of Suez.*

520 Willoughby, Pearl Vivian. "Modern Dramaturgy: British and American." Unpublished thesis. University of Virginia, 1923. Pp. 12, 15, 23, 36, 68, 133.
In turn-of-the-century drama, action begins to give place to thought or the center of interest "has shifted from deeds to ideas." Several of M's plays exemplify particular shifts.

521* Wilson, B. F. "What I Think of Your Theatre," THEATRE MAGAZINE, XXXVIII (Aug 1923), 27, 60.
M predicts that the United States will have a national theater in about ten years [e.g., about 1933]. One advantage an American dramatist has over the English dramatist is that he can draw on a hundred different races for his material; and New York audiences are more diversified. M likes O'Neill, but dislikes Shaw for his obsession with ideas. In his own work M finds writing the play difficult enough and therefore has little time for rehearsals or rewriting. He does not write while traveling, but collects material, most recently on a nine-month trip to the Far East. M and O'Neill are alike in their efforts to write about man's reaching beyond his environment. [Interview.]

1924

522 Andréades, A. "Le théâtre anglais contemporain" (The Contemporary English Theater), LE FIGARO SUPPLEMENT LITTERAIRE, 22 Nov 1924, p. 2; rptd, partially, in CHRONIQUE DES LETTRES FRANÇAISES, May-June 1925, pp. 391-92.

In the British production of *Our Betters,* M has traveled a long way from the days of *Lady Frederick* and *Mrs. Dot.* His dialogue has finesse, his characters are of a piece. With *The Circle* and *Our Betters* he continues the theatre of Congreve and Vanbrugh. [In French.]

523 Bulloch, J. M. "The Play of the Day, Old and New," GRAPHIC, CIX (9 Feb 1924), 176.

The Camel's Back "not only sentimentalises sentiment, but does so in a disagreeable way. . . . "

524* " *'The Camel's Back':* New Farce at the Playhouse," TIMES (Lond), 1 Feb 1924, p. 8; rptd by Raymond Mander and Joe Mitchenson, eds, in THEATRICAL COMPANION TO MAUGHAM (Lond: Rockliff, 1955), pp. 194-95.

When M "is in the vein, his wit almost rivals Congreve's. On this occasion he is not in the vein, and the only reminder of Congreve we can find is that his hero is named Valentine."

525* Cru, Robert-L. "La Saison Théâtrale à Londres" (The Theater Season in London), LE TEMPS, 15 Sept 1924, p. 2.

M is among the playwrights of the "cynical school": he has specialized in a new genre on the British stage. In *East of Suez,* M showed with rare bluntness the relations between white men and women of other races. In *Our Betters,* this year, he presents a picture of depravity in a shady society composed of American expatriates. Not since the Restoration has there been so keen an analysis of high society's vices; it is, however, a tedious analysis as well, for M's aristocracy is spurious: the vices of the gentlemen of THE WAY OF THE WORLD have a gracefulness that is not found in the sink of iniquity M delights in. [General survey of the British stage for the season.] [In French.]

526 Farrar, John. "To See or Not to See," BOOKMAN (NY), LVIII (Jan 1924), 560.

The American production of *The Camel's Back* failed because "it was not based on an original idea, . . . and [because] it was miscast."

527 "A Maugham Farce at the Playhouse," ILLUSTRATED LONDON NEWS, CLXIV (9 Feb 1924), 246.

To enjoy *The Camel's Back,* one must "emulate, in part, the dramatist's own cynicism, must pardon in his heroine the most extravagant disregard of kindliness, let alone truth, and must not be over-squeamish in other respects." After the first act, "artificiality runs riot, and acting is compelled to be mere virtuosity."

528* Nathan, George Jean. MATERIA CRITICA (NY: Alfred A. Knopf, 1924), p. 91.

M "is a playwright who has never quite realized himself. He has all the qualities that should make him the first polite comedy writer of the present-day English theatre; . . . salt and erudition, taste and dexterity, invention and viewpoint; yet an apparently inborn British conventionality contrives too often to reduce his high talents to the level of that conventionality."

529 Prévost, Marcel. "Pluie" (Rain), LA REVUE DE FRANCE, 4ème année, No. 2 (15 March 1924), 264.

General critical remarks affixed to a translation of "Rain." [In French.]

530 Tarn. "The Theatre: Two Farces," SPECTATOR (Lond), CXXXII (9 Feb 1924), 198.

"Maugham has not wasted one moment of his time inventing a situation," and his characters are all stock figures. Although "insignificant," *The Camel's Back* is not dull, and the dialogue is amusing.

531 Vernon, Frank. THE TWENTIETH-CENTURY THEATRE (Lond, Calcutta, & Sydney: George C. Harrap, 1924), pp. 60-61.

Lyon Phelps' belief that modern dramatic history would be the same if M had never written a play is wrong. M, with Sutro, purged the offensive dialogue of the nineties, and though he is not of the "new movement," he is not insusceptible to the influences of his time, and represents the "chastened" old theater.

532 Wright, Ralph. "Theatre: Sugar and Salt," NEW STATESMAN, XXII (9 Feb 1924), 511.

M has a hard intellectual core to the best of his jokes that leaves them often lastingly satisfactory, but he is the "laziest dramatist in the world," incapable of filling any one play with the best that is in him. He portrays characters admirably, his wit is highly individualized, but his appeal is purely to the intelligence, and one fears for him at the moments of feeling. Luckily these moments are few in *The Camel's Back,* which is "delightfully light, heartless and unbothered by reality."

1925

533* Agate, James. "The Dramatic World," SUNDAY TIMES (Lond), 17 May 1925, p. 6; rptd as RAIN in THE CONTEMPORARY THEATRE, 1925. With an Introduction by C. E. Montague (Lond: Chapman & Hall, 1926), pp. 157-62; and by Raymond Mander and Joe Mitchenson, eds, in THEATRICAL COMPANION TO MAUGHAM (Lond: Rockliff, 1955), pp. 256-58.

John Colton and Clemence Randolph's dramatization, RAIN, shows there was not enough material in M's tale, "Rain," for a full-length play, "but the padding was the very best possible, and . . . the third act was extremely fine."

534* Agate, James. "The Dramatic World," SUNDAY TIMES (Lond), 27 Sept 1925, p. 6; rptd, as THE MOON AND SIXPENCE, in THE CONTEMPORARY THEATRE, 1925. With an Introduction by C. E. Montague (Lond: Chapman & Hall, 1926), pp. 163-67.
Edith Ellis' dramatization of THE MOON AND SIXPENCE has two admirable scenes out of six; the first scene is entirely unnecessary, and the sixth is anti-climactic; the second and third scenes were "full of the right kind of harshness and brutality."

535 Albalat, Antoine. "Revue des livres" (Book Reviews), LE JOURNAL DES DEBATS [POLITIQUES ET LITTERAIRES], 22 Sept 1925, p. 3.
The Trembling of a Leaf stories are amusing, but their inner meaning is sad. [Review of the French translation.] [In French.]

536 Audiat, Pierre. "Les lettres françaises" (French Letters), LA REVUE DE FRANCE, 5ème année, no. 4 (15 July 1925), 395.
In *The Trembling of a Leaf,* M achieves his dramatic effects without a word of commentary or explanation; he is the "Kipling of the Pacific." [Review of the French translation.] [In French.]

537* Aynard, Joseph. *"L'Archipel aux Sirènes" (The Trembling of a Leaf),* LE JOURNAL DES DEBATS [POLITIQUES ET LITTERAIRES], 15 Nov 1925, p. 3; rptd as "Littératures étrangères" (Foreign Literature), JOURNAL DES DEBATS, HEBDOMADAIRE, (20 Nov 1925), pp. 852-64.
Though M is not a descriptive writer, *The Trembling of a Leaf* is a typical example of the new trend in exoticism developing in English letters. Like Farrèze or Boissière, M is interested in studies of colonial psychology rather than in pilgrimages to the enchanted islands idealized for their beauty; the title of his book must be viewed as ironic. The recurring themes of the stories are the influence of the climate on Europeans, the problem of mixed races; but M takes no side in any conflict, as evidenced in "The Fall of Edward Barnard." Neither Zola nor Maupassant could have put more detached realism into the portrait of Davidson in "Rain." [Review of the French translation.] [In French.]

538* Bennett, Arnold. "Drama: RAIN," NEW STATESMAN, XXV (23 May 1925), 164-65.

John Colton and Clemence Randolph have "padded" where no padding was necessary; the first act is too long, the last too short.

539* Birrell, Francis. "The Drama: The Artistic Temperament, New Style," NATION AND THE ATHENAEUM, XXXVIII (3 Oct 1925), 16.

The fault of Edith Ellis' dramatization of THE MOON AND SIXPENCE is not "that it alters the life of Gauguin, but that it spoils it"; the hero has been "considerably brutalized to suit a Fascist generation," and the play is as "romantic about Art" as were, in their own way, TRILBY and VIE DE BOHEME.

540 "Books—Life: Painting the Veil, Mr. Maugham Does Not Gild the Lily," TIME, V (13 April 1925), 12.

In *The Painted Veil,* although the subject matter is sensational and the style undistinguished, M has one rare grace: humility. "He writes sensationalism with an air of having his manner dictated absolutely by his material. His story is as compact as a surgical dressing." [Story summary.]

541 Borel, P. "Un Après-midi avec Somerset Maugham" (An Afternoon with Somerset Maugham), LES NOUVELLES LITTERAIRES, 26 June 1925, p. 5.

[Interview.] [In French.]

542* "Briefer Mention," DIAL, LXXIX (Aug 1925), 173.

In *The Painted Veil,* "the horror of the action recalls the pleasure of the most exciting fairy tales. Yet the thought keeps well enough apace with the plot to lead us to mature reflection. The characters are superficially drawn and the theme is pulled awry by a husband who is a little too bad himself to point a moral for his wife, but barbarous action together with Mr. Maugham's power to employ and entertain our intelligence results in a grown-up midnight tale of terror."

543* Brown, Ivor. "The Theatre: Beauty and the Beast," SATURDAY REVIEW (Lond), CXL (3 Oct 1925), 369-70.

Depicting "the tendency of genius to be morally contemptible," Edith Ellis' dramatization of THE MOON AND SIXPENCE is a satire of "the fanatic of art." The view that "Strickland's egotism, ruthless to the point of sadistic mania, is more than a pardonable quality and has its own nobility" is "sentimental nonsense." M is to be thanked for exposing "the sentimental cant that is often talked about the unruly artist." Since the artist "has a thousand delights denied to others," he is less to be pardoned for bad behavior. However, it is not certain that M intended this interpretation.

544* Brown, Ivor. "The Theatre: Mr. Maugham's New Play," SATURDAY REVIEW (Lond), CXXXIX (16 May 1925), 523-24.

John Colton and Clemence Randolph's dramatization, Rain, is an effective play. Davidson's "raging lust for purity . . . may be understood in the glaring lights of American religiosity. . . . With its harshness and its lack of mercy, with its adventures in the uglier aspects of sexual psychology, it is distinctly a piece for the post-war public. . . . Pornography that is informed with the quality of mercy and with the psychological doctrine of repressions can certainly attract."

545 Cahuet, Albéric. "Les Livres et les écrivains" (Books and Writers), L'Illustration, 83ème année, no. 4311 (17 Oct 1925), 420.

[Brief review of *The Trembling of a Leaf.*] [In French.]

546 Collins, Joseph. "A Woman Who Couldn't Go Straight," Literary Digest International Book Review, III (May 1925), 405-7.

The Painted Veil is "a splendid story, superbly told." [Mainly plot summary.]

547* Cru, Robert-L. "La Saison théâtrale à Londres" (The Theatrical Season in London), Le Temps, 31 Aug 1925, p. 3.

The contemporary British public is superficial, evincing a permanent conflict between two groups of artists: those of the intelligentsia and those of the general masses. The British theater tends to encourage the most shocking situations or abnormal characters as a compensation for the originality which it lacks: such situations are to be found in the works of M. After *East of Suez,* two years ago, those who read *The Painted Veil* will have no difficulty understanding the anti-British movement in the Far East. The public's new craze for South Sea stories united with the popularity of salacious stories should insure M's success on the stage with Rain. Its argument is as old as Jocelyn. M lacks a certain simplicity and even sincerity: he overdoes his effects and strives to astonish and scandalize. [General survey of the current British theater season.] [In French.]

548* Dorsenne, Jean. "Un grand romancier anglais: A propos *L'Archipel aux Sirènes*" (A Great English Novelist: On *The Trembling of a Leaf),* Les Nouvelles Litteraires, 24 Oct 1925, p. 6.

M may be compared to Conrad and R. L. Stevenson, but strikes a note strangely new and original. Unlike facile Americans or idealistic Frenchmen working in the genre of the "exotic," M studies the actual repercussions of the Polynesian climate on the minds of whites. Thus, M's book is an excellent antidote to a romantic work such as Le Mariage de Loti. [Review of the French translation.] [In French.]

549 E[rvine], St. J[ohn]. "The Week's Theatres," OBSERVER (Lond), 27 Sept 1925, p. 11.

In Edith Ellis' dramatization of THE MOON AND SIXPENCE, Strickland is not a convincing character.

550 Farrar, John. "W. Somerset Maugham: Novelist and So Forth," W. SOMERSET MAUGHAM: NOVELIST, ESSAYIST, DRAMATIST, ed by Charles Hanson Towne (NY: George H. Doran [1925]), pp. 5-7.

M is, essentially, a novelist; his short stories are "really tremendously compressed novels" and even his sketches and essays constitute "novels in little."

551 "Fiction: The Way," SPECTATOR (Lond), CXXXIV (23 May 1925), 850-51.

The Painted Veil is trite, pretentious, and insincere. "The exposition is particularly shallow," and neither the passion nor the "nobility of thought" is convincing. M is a "popularizer of ideas."

552 Frierson, William C. L'INFLUENCE DU NATURALISME FRANÇAIS SUR LES ROMANCIERS ANGLAIS DE 1885 A 1900 (THE INFLUENCE OF FRENCH NATURALISM ON ENGLISH NOVELISTS FROM 1885 TO 1900). (Paris: Marcel Girard, 1925), pp. 184-87.

Liza of Lambeth is M's only novel with pretensions to naturalistic realism, more naturalistic than the novels of Arthur Morrison, though the influence on this particular book seems to stem from Dickens, Zola, and Shaw as well as Morrison. [In French.]

553 "Garrick Theatre: RAIN by John Colton and Clemence Randolph," TIMES (Lond), 13 May 1925, p. 14.

The play is "an exciting, sordid, sub-tropically hot little drama."

554* Goodrich, Marcus Aurelius. "After Ten Years *'Of Human Bondage,'*" NEW YORK TIMES BOOK REVIEW, 25 Jan 1925, p. 2; rptd in W. SOMERSET MAUGHAM: NOVELIST, ESSAYIST, DRAMATIST, ed by Charles Hanson Towne (NY: George H. Doran, [1925]), pp. 37-44; excerpted in NEW YORK TIMES BOOK REVIEW, 6 Oct 1946, p. 6

The novel suffered neglect because of the "gaudy critical methods" beginning to come into vogue about the time M started writing; these methods were the "impressionistic" reviews encouraged by critics like Huxley, Firbank, and Hergesheimer. M's novel did not allow for such reviews, because he passed by the opportunity to indulge in poster effects so that he might attain "a vital sweep of living, effulgent, integral color." The reader of *Of Human Bondage* feels he has "seen life, if not defined, at least epically epitomized." [A recounting of the belated literary success story of *Of Human Bondage,* including excerpts from newspaper and magazine reviews written upon the novel's initial publication.]

555 "The Gossip Shop," BOOKMAN (NY), LXI (May 1925), 377-78.
The Painted Veil is "technically perfect, . . . emotionally true, . . . one of the great short novels of our time."

556 "The Gossip Shop," BOOKMAN (NY), LXI (July 1925), 623.
London enthusiastically received the dramatization of RAIN and there was a fracas over *The Painted Veil* [in which persons in China thought they saw themselves portrayed].

557 Griffith, Hubert. "This Week's Theatres," OBSERVER (Lond), 17 May 1925, p. 11.
The third act of John Colton and Clemence Randolph's dramatization, RAIN, needs a scene, "of the very first importance and dramatic weight, between the Paphnutius, Rev. Davidson, and the Thaïs, Sadie Thompson."

558 H., B. P. *"The Painted Veil,"* BOSTON EVENING TRANSCRIPT, 11 April 1925, p. 6.
The novel is "sensational fiction of the 'news-stand' variety"; M's style is particularly bad.

559 H., H. "The Drama: The Tropics at Second Hand," OUTLOOK (Lond), LVI (3 Oct 1925), 229.
In Edith Ellis' dramatization of THE MOON AND SIXPENCE, the island scenes do not sustain the intensity achieved in the earlier London and Montmartre scenes; the play is, in general, "oversentimentalized, often commonplace."

560* J[ennings], R[ichard]. "The Theatre: Nightmare Drama," SPECTATOR (Lond), CXXXIV (30 May 1925), 883-84.
The theatrical season is full of "rather monotonous moral shocks, provided by plays not fit for the elderly" [e.g., John Colton and Clemence Randolph's dramatization, RAIN]. M and others depend upon the "meteorological mechanics" of thunder, lightning, and rain to establish the "required atmosphere of tension," and to symbolize "violent tempers, passionate temperaments, and maniacal obsessions." This "prompts the melodramatic method" and "excludes delicate developments." Davidson's sin and suicide are not altogether believable; the play is "crude but vigorous."

561 Kennedy, P. C. "New Novels," NEW STATESMAN, XXV (9 May 1925), 107.
The end of *The Painted Veil* "is the silliest ever inflicted by a brilliant writer on a brilliant story."

562 "Les Livres: *'L'Archipel aux Sirènes'* " (Books: *The Trembling of a Leaf*), JOURNAL DE GENEVE, 96ème année, no. 189 (13 July 1925), 2.

[Review of the French translation.] [In French.]

563 Lovett, Robert Morss. "Seven Novels," NEW REPUBLIC, XLII (22 April 1925), 243.

The Painted Veil is "a peculiarly sordid and brutal episode . . . , relieved by the art with which it is told." M remains detached except for his description of Kitty Fane's regeneration: here he appears to be looking for an ending.

564* Mann, Dorothea Lawrence. "Somerset Maugham in His Mantle of Mystery," W. SOMERSET MAUGHAM: NOVELIST, ESSAYIST, DRAMATIST, ed by Charles Hanson Towne (NY: George H. Doran, [1925]), pp. 17-36.

Biographically there is a parallel between M and El Greco, especially in the manner in which both artists sought "beauty through the medium of ugliness. Like the figures of El Greco the characters of Maugham have a troubling reality even when they seem out of drawing." [Towne identifies (p. 19) Mann's article as originating from the BOSTON EVENING TRANSCRIPT, and Klaus W. Jonas gives its date of appearance in that newspaper as "Nov 1921" in his BIBLIOGRAPHY OF THE WRITINGS OF W. SOMERSET MAUGHAM, p. 70. The article has not been found in the issues of Nov 1921; although, in Towne's book, it contains a discussion of *The Painted Veil* (published in America in March 1925), the article also does not appear in the TRANSCRIPT from March through July 1925.]

565 " 'THE MOON AND SIXPENCE,' at the New," ILLUSTRATED LONDON NEWS, CLXVII (3 Oct 1925), 654.

In Edith Ellis' dramatization, Strickland "seems too extravagant to be credible."

566* "Mr. Maugham Excels as a Craftsman," NEW YORK TIMES BOOK REVIEW, 22 March 1925, p. 7.

Not only is M a true craftsman, but in *The Painted Veil* "he is also something of a humanist." He knows the smooth art of telling a story, but in past works, with the exception of *Of Human Bondage,* he has relied too heavily on intellect, and is only now learning to use and appeal to the sensibilities. When one has reached the middle of *The Painted Veil,* he feels the novel begin to glow with warmth and sympathy, its characters to become more than artistic creations.

567 "Mr. Maugham's Novel," OBSERVER (Lond), 3 May 1925, p. 4.

In *The Painted Veil,* M's success as a dramatist interferes with his success as a novelist. He twice succumbs to the playwright's temptation of sacrificing "truth" to "brilliancy of effect": when Walter expresses his contempt for Kitty, and when Kitty yields to Charley in spite of her detestation of him.

568 "New Novels," TIMES LITERARY SUPPLEMENT (Lond), 14 May 1925, p. 332.

In *The Painted Veil,* the over-use of sex and adultery as a plot vehicle, and the stilted, unnatural dénouement are objectionable. "Without questioning the morality of his [M's] intention, and while applauding his talent for satire, one may doubt whether it is strictly necessary to the indictment of lust that purely lustful episodes should be described so conscientiously."

569 "New Theatre: 'THE MOON AND SIXPENCE' by Edith Ellis," TIMES (Lond), 25 Sept 1925, p. 10.

The strangeness of the story's facts is implausible in the theater, and the protagonist becomes, "for theatrical purposes, an inhuman monster, or rather, a maniac."

570* "Novels in Brief," NATION AND THE ATHENAEUM, XXXVII (23 May 1925), 246.

In *The Painted Veil,* "the silliness of the main situations only tests Mr. Maugham's skill as a writer and his power of convincing us that we are dealing with the momentous problem of a woman's soul. His lay figures might come to vivid life in a play."

571 Omicron. "From Alpha to Omega," NATION AND THE ATHENAEUM, XXXVII (30 May 1925), 268.

John Colton and Clemence Randolph's dramatization, RAIN, is a quite "passable melodrama," in which the "scales are weighted against religion and virtue with a thoroughness that should appeal to a decadent generation."

572 "Our Booking-Office," PUNCH, CLXVIII (13 May 1925), 530-31.

Despite a feeling that Kitty seems treated like a puppet and her second "fall" sounds a too cynical note, *The Painted Veil* is good, especially in its beginning scene and well-paced suspense.

573 Paterson, Isabel. "A Shelf of Recent Books," BOOKMAN (NY), LXI (May 1925), 346-47.

"There is no flaw in the structure of the story [of *The Painted Veil*], but there is a lack. It does not touch the springs of emotion; but it rivets attention, and compels admiration for the austere excellence of the workmanship. It is an emotional situation scrutinized by the cold light of reason."

574* Paterson, Isabel. "Squaring the Triangle," NEW YORK HERALD TRIBUNE BOOKS, 12 April 1925, p. 5.

In *The Painted Veil,* M looks "upon his puppets with chill, remote contempt"; Kitty and Charles "are depicted as abject and insignificant," and Walter is "equally unattractive." The characters' springs of action "are entirely sensual and selfish." M generally affects the reader, however, with his restraint, except on the final page, where he emerges into "rank sentimentality."

575 Patin, Jacques. "Le Carnet du bouquiniste" (The Notebook of an Antiquarian), LE FIGARO SUPPLEMENT LITTERAIRE, 12 Sept 1925, p. 3.

The Trembling of a Leaf makes you dream and think simultaneously. M suggests rather than states. The best story of the collection is "The Fall of Edward Barnard." [Review of the French translation.] [In French.]

576 "Recent Novels," TRUTH ("Special Literary Supplement") (Lond), XCVII (6 May 1925), ii.

In *The Painted Veil,* "the wronged husband . . . is a dramatic masterpiece"; the book, as a whole, is "an elemental tragedy developed with the ruthless logic of life to its inevitable issue."

577 Régnier, Henri de. "La Vie littéraire" (The Literary Life), LE FIGARO, 15 Sept 1925, p. 4; rptd in LE FIGARO HEBDOMADAIRE, 23 Sept 1925, pp. 4-5.

If the British call M the "Kipling of the Pacific," the French think of him as the British Maupassant. In *The Trembling of a Leaf,* he resembles Loti in choice of subject, but displays more art. [Review of the French translation.] [In French.]

578 Roberts, R. Ellis. "The Coloured Film," BOOKMAN (Lond), LXVIII (July 1925), 222.

In *The Painted Veil,* M fails to analyze Walter ("a man whose character has depth and subtlety and strangeness") competently, and thus the character is "unpersuasive."

579 Royde-Smith, N. G. "The Drama: Spiritual and Spiritualistic," OUTLOOK (Lond), LV (23 May 1925), 345.

M's name should not even appear on the programme for John Colton and Clemence Randolph's second-rate dramatization of RAIN, founded on one of the best of his short stories.

580 Ségur, Nicolas. "La Vie littéraire: Littératures étrangères" (The Literary Life: Foreign Literature), LA REVUE MONDIALE, CLXVI (1 July-15 Aug 1925), 419-20.

The stories of *The Trembling of a Leaf* are original and give evidence of a great talent. [Review of French translation.] [In French.]

581 Souday, Paul. "Les Livres" (Books), LE TEMPS, 9 July 1925, p. 3.
[Brief review of the French translation of *The Trembling of a Leaf.*] [In French.]

582 Sutton, Graham. "W. Somerset Maugham," SOME CONTEMPORARY DRAMATISTS (NY: George H. Doran, 1925), pp. 95-117.
The reason for M's dramatic success is that as a clever man he knows how to cajole "the understanding of the less clever" without boredom or insult. M follows Wilde and is the "playwright's playwright."

583 "Tangled Emotions," SPRINGFIELD SUNDAY REPUBLICAN (Mass), 10 May 1925, p. 7.
In *The Painted Veil,* M tells his story well, though "one would prefer him in another vein."

584 "The Theatres: Dirty Weather at the Garrick," TRUTH (Lond), XCVII (20 May 1925), 922.
John Colton and Clemence Randolph's dramatization, RAIN, is "a striking enough piece of work," but not quite up to the story as M wrote it.

585 "The Theatres: Maugham, MOON AND SIXPENCE," TRUTH (Lond), XCVIII (30 Sept 1925), 597.
"After its transference to the South Seas the play [Edith Ellis' dramatization of THE MOON AND SIXPENCE] goes to pieces."

586 T[horp, Joseph]. "At the Play," PUNCH, CLXVIII (20 May 1925), 555-56.
John Colton and Clemence Randolph's dramatization, RAIN, suggests M must have had a bitter experience with a religious fanatic and desired revenge. The play is "astonishingly moving."

587 Towne, Charles Hanson. "Mr. W. Somerset Maugham at Home," W. SOMERSET MAUGHAM: NOVELIST, ESSAYIST, DRAMATIST, ed by Charles Hanson Towne (NY: George H. Doran, [1925]), pp. 8-12.
M travels widely because his interest in life is profound; he keeps copious notes, and feels nothing is too trivial to chronicle; he is an "acute psychologist" who can draw equally well the "cruel" picture of a Charles Strickland of *The Moon and Sixpence* or the "sympathetic" picture of the Mother Superior in *The Painted Veil.*

588* Towne, Charles Hanson, et al. W. SOMERSET MAUGHAM:

NOVELIST, ESSAYIST, DRAMATIST. With a Note on Novel Writing by Mr. Maugham (NY: George H. Doran, [1925]).
Contents: five articles and reviews by five different writers, a mock exchange of letters between M and a "Francis Van Buren Hale of Boston," and excerpts from various periodical reviews of M's works. The five articles, annotated under individual entries, are in their order: (1) John Farrar, "W Somerset Maugham: Novelist and So Forth," pp. 5-7; (2) Charles Hanson Towne, "Mr. W. Somerset Maugham at Home," 8-12; (3) Carl Van Doren and Mark Van Doren, "W. Somerset Maugham," 13-16; (4) Dorothea Lawrence Mann, "Somerset Maugham in His Mantle of Mystery," 17-36; (5) Marcus Aurelius Goodrich, "After Ten Years *'Of Human Bondage,'*" 37-44. The mock exchange of letters between M and Mrs. Hale is entitled "To a Young Novelist," pp. 45-54, and previously appeared as "Novelist or Bond Salesman," BOOKMAN (NY), LX (Feb 1925), 683-86.

589 Vandérem, Fernand. "Les Lettres et la vie" (Letters and Life), LA REVUE DE FRANCE, 5ème année, no. 4 (15 Aug 1925), 767-68.
In *The Trembling of a Leaf,* M resembles Poe as much as he does R. L. Stevenson and J. Conrad. [Review of French translation.] [In French.]

590* Van Doren, Carl. "Tom Jones and Philip Carey: Heroes of Two Centuries," CENTURY, N. S. LXXXVIII (May 1925), 115-20.
Fielding and M set out to faithfully trace the career of a young man during the troubled years in which he is finding his proper gait and place; their attitudes and their heroes differ, because the two centuries are far apart in mental and moral attitudes. Fielding's legal training and the literary beliefs of his time influenced the general, rich, and panoramic treatment of TOM JONES; M's medical training influenced his study of the "individual" in *Of Human Bondage.* If Philip's strength and problem are unequally matched, the reader must remember that knowledge and doubt have increased since Tom Jones' time. In actuality, Philip and Tom can be found in every generation, the former representing the individual who must make his own pattern out of life, the latter representing one who assembles traits from every quarter and in whose story many persons recognize something which recalls their own.

591 Van Doren, Carl and Mark Van Doren. "Maugham 1874—," AMERICAN AND BRITISH LITERATURE SINCE 1890 (NY: Century, 1925), pp. 205-8; rptd as "W. Somerset Maugham," in W. SOMERSET MAUGHAM: NOVELIST, ESSAYIST, DRAMATIST, ed by Charles Hanson Towne (NY: George H. Doran, [1925]), pp. 13-16.
Of Human Bondage is M's greatest work, *The Moon and Sixpence* his "second best."

592* Waldman, Milton. "Fiction," London Mercury, XII (June 1925), 208-10.

The Painted Veil begins with a scene of "extraordinary dramatic power," but the rest of the book "never attains this level" again. M's detachment from his characters' debaucheries is almost "impudent"; his "sordid thrusters . . . are not as representative of humanity as his bright aloofness would lead one to suspect."

593 Went, Stanley. "Maugham's Latest," Saturday Review of Literature, I (21 March 1925), 611.

With its skillfully compressed beginning, *The Painted Veil* shows unquestionable art, though some readers may have differences of opinion about M's taste in treating his heroine the way he does.

594* Weygandt, Cornelius. A Century of the English Novel (NY: Century, 1925), pp. 168, especially 364-67, 430.

Of Human Bondage brought M a "following," but *The Moon and Sixpence* won him an "audience." M does not distinguish between irony and sarcasm, has not attained to the former, although he is proficient in the latter, "a cheap thing." M is not an accurate observer of life; for instance, in the first scene of *Of Human Bondage,* he "makes the mother ask what is the sex of the child she has borne only after she has sent for her boy of seven [sic] to comfort her in her prostration." The book is important "from the historical standpoint." It exhibits M's greatest weakness: that while he analyzes character powerfully, he cannot pass beyond "to the creation of character." M is a "keen student of humanity but hardly an artist at all."

595 Williams, Harold. Modern English Writers: Being a Study of Imaginative Literature 1890-1914. Third, Revised Edition (Lond: Sidgwick & Jackson, 1925 [1918]), pp. 285-87, 405.

"In wit, art and character-drawing" M is a better dramatist than Arnold Bennett. In his plays up through 1909 he follows Wilde; from 1909 to 1914 he seems influenced by Galsworthy and Shaw.

1926

596* Agate, James. A Short View of the English Stage: 1900-1926 (Lond: Herbert Jenkins, 1926), pp. 21-22, 33, 86-87, 106, 107-13.

M is one of several playwrights to whom "people in search of amusement go as automatically as they drop in to Fortnum and Mason's to buy *pâté de foie gras.*" His technique is flawless, and he was one of the playwrights who "brought about the renaissance of English drama between the years 1900 and 1914." *Our Betters* is a "magnificent piece of satire," although *The Circle* is his best play. M's success has been a curse as well as a blessing, however; for he is responsible "for the flood of dismal and dreary lubricity which at once began to swamp the English stage"—i.e., the works of Noël Coward, Frederick Lonsdale, Michael Arlen, and Sir Patrick Hastings. The latter playwrights have not M's "immense interest in life" but, rather, exhibit only one side of life; to them, the "whole world is composed of vicious babies, . . . and nobody who has grown up is worth writing about."

597 Anderson, John. "The Play," NEW YORK EVENING POST, 30 Nov 1926, p. 18.

The Constant Wife is "deft, clever, and altogether delightful."

598 Benchley, Robert. "Drama: Something Good," LIFE, LXXXVIII (16 Dec 1926), 19.

While far from perfect, *The Constant Wife* "has a great many lines of high comedy and not a few of wisdom."

599* Birrell, Francis. "The Drama: Underdone and Overdone," NATION AND THE ATHENAEUM, XXXIX (26 June 1926), 352-53.

In the revival of *Caroline,* M's phrasing has "the genuine Congrevian ring," his "humours" make an agreeable pattern, and he suggests more than he says; moreover, M makes a genuine comment on existence, "the real moral protest of the comic writer against human fraud." Yet, M does not take trouble, nor has he even "quite made the best of himself . . . ; he will always dine with the best company [but] . . . will through his own fault remain at the lower end of the table."

600 Bourdon, Charles. "Les Romans: *'La Passe Dangereuse'* " (Novels: *The Painted Veil*), LA REVUE DES LECTURES, 14 ème année, no. 6 (15 June 1926), 501-2.

Despite the theme of adultery, the story's expression is "decent"; the heroine is not a simple courtesan: she leaves the dangerous "pass." [Review of the French translation.] [In French.]

601 " *'Caroline':* Revival at the Playhouse," TIMES (Lond), 14 June 1926, p. 12.

"Let us not be lulled by the grateful warmth of good entertainment into supposing that this bubble . . . is anything else than a bubble."

602* Chassé, Charles. "Van Gogh et Gauguin—héros de romans" (Van Gogh and Gauguin—Heroes of Novels), LE MERCURE DE FRANCE, CXC (15 Aug 1926), 5-29, especially 21-29.

There are similarities between Gauguin and M's Strickland in *The Moon and Sixpence*. The work is invaluable not only for its considerable artistic merits but also for its depiction of the painter's psychology. [In French.]

603 " *'The Constant Wife'* Deft and Sparkling," NEW YORK TIMES, 30 Nov 1926, p. 26; rptd by Raymond Mander and Joe Mitchenson, eds, in THEATRICAL COMPANION TO MAUGHAM (Lond: Rockliff, 1955), pp. 202-3 [Mander and Mitchenson ascribe the review to J. Brooks Atkinson].

The part seems to have been written for Ethel Barrymore—and probably was.

604 Dorsenne, Jean. "Les Romans: *'La Passe Dangereuse'* " (Novels: *The Painted Veil*), LES NOUVELLES LITTERAIRES, 14 Aug 1926, p. 3.

M's portrait of Kitty is "unpityingly exact." There is magic in M's art. [Review of the French translation.] [In French.]

605 Dottin, Paul. "Les Lettres étrangères" (Foreign Letters), LA REVUE DE FRANCE, 6ème année, no. 4 (15 Aug 1926), 793-94.

[Brief review of the French translation of *The Trembling of a Leaf*.] [In French.]

606* Dottin, Paul. "Le réalisme de Somerset Maugham" (The Realism of Somerset Maugham), LA REVUE DE FRANCE, 6ème année, no. 3 (1 June 1926), 574-81; rptd as "Le Livre du cholera et de la trahison: *'The Painted Veil'* " (The Book of Cholera and Treachery: *The Painted Veil),* in Dottin's W. SOMERSET MAUGHAM ET SES ROMANS (W. SOMERSET MAUGHAM AND HIS NOVELS) (Paris: Perrin, 1928), pp. 189-212; same as Klaus W. Jonas's translation, "The Realism of Somerset Maugham," THE MAUGHAM ENIGMA, ed by Klaus W. Jonas (NY: Citadel P, 1954), pp. 133-45.

M was hardly more than a name until Mme. Blanchet published her translation of *The Trembling of a Leaf* [*L'Archipel aux Sirènes*] in LA REVUE DE FRANCE. After reading *The Painted Veil,* one can assert that the Victorian novel is dead and that, by reaction, the realistic novel has come into existence. Thanks to his sobriety, his sense of measure, his French-like simplicity, M is the best representative of the contemporary realistic school. No cant; frank description of carnal love. Kitty Lane, like Hardy's heroines, yields to a natural impulse, to the mysterious urge of destiny. The chapter in which she realizes she is pregnant invites comparison with THE BLUE LAGOON by De Vere Stacpoole. Besides, as is shown by the case of Kitty, M is a psychological realist. His frankness borders on brutality and cruelty. Yet M is not insensitive to beauty; nor does he leave upon one an impression of pessimism. In this he is superior to Hardy; his works show a balance between beauty and ugliness, joy and sadness. He is the perfect type of realist after the fashion of Maupassant; yet also in the line of English realism, which originated with Defoe and Richardson. M occupies a high place in contemporary literature, on a par with Kipling, Galsworthy and Bennett. [In French.]

607 Drew, Elizabeth A. THE MODERN NOVEL: SOME ASPECTS OF CONTEMPORARY FICTION (NY: Harcourt, Brace, 1926), pp. 93, 96, especially 98-100, 252.

M is one of the modern writers who studies, especially in *Of Human Bondage,* the "human spirit."

608 "East of Singapore," NEW YORK TIMES BOOK REVIEW, 17 Oct 1926, pp. 6, 8.

The Casuarina Tree consists of "six smoothly constructed, tailor-made short stories, in the conventional pattern and with just that touch of color which is now permitted by London haberdashers." "The Force of Circumstance" is much better than the other five stories; "The Yellow Streak" is the least entertaining, "possibly because it is constructed around an experience the author himself underwent."

609 Edgett, Edwin Francis. "The Divergence of Marshall and Maugham," BOSTON EVENING TRANSCRIPT, 16 Oct 1926, p. 4.

The Casuarina Tree displays M's various skills as they extend from his light, blithesome *Penelope* mood to that of *Of Human Bondage.*

610 "English in the East," SPRINGFIELD SUNDAY UNION AND REPUBLICAN (Mass), 7 Nov 1926, p. 7F.

M's postscript to *The Casuarina Tree* is "most inviting," and all six stories are good; "The Outstation," however, makes "more of an impression" than the others.

611 F[ield], L[ouise] M. "In This Month's Fiction Library," LITERARY DIGEST INTERNATIONAL BOOK REVIEW, IV (Nov 1926), 773.

In *The Casuarina Tree,* "P & O" is the least memorable of the six stories; "The Outstation," the most remarkable.

612 Gabriel, Gilbert W. "The Constant Infidelities," NEW YORK SUN, 30 Nov 1926, p. 30.

In *The Constant Wife,* M has successfully united the "suave frivolity" of his early comedies with the "caustic and combative" qualities of his later plays.

613 Gabriel, Gilbert W. "Physician, Novelist and Playwright," MENTOR, XIV (Dec 1926), 50-51.

[Biographical sketch and general appreciation.]

614 Gould, Gerald. "New Novels," OBSERVER (Lond), 5 Sept 1926, p. 6.
In *The Casuarina Tree,* M presents a dazzling picture from which he omits the human spirit; one reads the stories with excitement, but ends in discontent.

615 Hammond, Percy. "The Theatres," NEW YORK HERALD TRIBUNE, 30 Nov 1926, p. 16.
The Constant Wife is "a first-rate and enjoyable amplification of many adages—ranging from 'what is sauce for a gander is sauce for a goose' to 'a rolling stone gathers no moss.' "

616* Hartley, L. P. "New Fiction," SATURDAY REVIEW (Lond), CXLII (18 Sept 1926), 317.
The stories of *The Casuarina Tree* are distinguished by "great narrative power, an unfailing eye for dramatic effect . . . and a ruthless insight into and insistence upon the ignobler motives." M emphasizes too exclusively "fact and event"; he should attempt "some larger, more impersonal correlation." Although nearly perfect within its limits, M's work is bounded by cynicism. A dead-end is no "substitute for completion"; a writer who "ignores the determination of life to go on weakens the effect of his work."

617* Hartley, L. P. "A Quartet," BOOKMAN (Lond), LXXI (Oct 1926), 51-52.
In presenting character stripped of idealism and in basing motive in selfishness, M "severely limits the appeal of his work [*The Casuarina Tree*] and even involves himself in inconsistency. He writes as a moralist, that is he makes us conscious of the badness of certain actions; but he hardly ever draws a character illustrating that standard of which his men and women so lamentably fall short. His standard appears to be an abstraction; a high-water mark set far above the reach of any tide."

618 "Les Livres: *'La Passe Dangereuse'* " (Books: *The Painted Veil*), JOURNAL DE GENEVE, 97ème année, no. 232 (25 Aug 1926), 2.
[Review of the French translation.] [In French.]

619 Moody, William Vaughn, and Robert Morss Lovett. A HISTORY OF ENGLISH LITERATURE FROM BEOWULF TO 1926 (NY: Charles Scribner's Sons, 1926), p. 470.
Mention of Philip Carey [here spelled 'Cary'] from *Of Human Bondage* as a "close approximation" to Ernest Pontifex of THE WAY OF ALL FLESH.

620 "A Mouse from the Mountain and Other Fiction: *The Casuarina Tree,*" SPECTATOR (Lond), CXXXVII (4 Sept 1926), 350.
The stories are "grimly dramatic yet packed with clear observation and

romance." The best is "The Yellow Streak." All concern the problems of Westerners attempting to "live by laws that are alien." In the study of Warburton ["The Outstation"], M "builds up his plot compactly into a short story which is a model of form and economy."

621* Muir, Edwin, "Fiction," NATION AND THE ATHENAEUM, XL (9 Oct 1926), 30.

The six stories of *The Casuarina Tree* are "well constructed and sincerely wrought," and give "an intelligent criticism of life." "Before the Party" and "The Letter" do not "move quite as intensely as they should, but 'The Outstation' is one of the best stories written in our time," and only less admirable are "The Force of Circumstance" and "The Yellow Streak."

622 "New Books in Brief Review," INDEPENDENT (NY), CXVII (9 Oct 1926), 428.

"There is not a great story" in *The Casuarina Tree,* "but there is not a bad or a sloppy one, either; all are marked with that power to condense personalities and narratives into the salient, vital elements which is the hallmark of the genuine short-story writer."

623 "New Novels," TIMES LITERARY SUPPLEMENT (Lond), 9 Sept 1926, p. 594.

The Casuarina Tree reveals M's deft craftsmanship, tolerant curiosity, detached observation, and intellectual kindliness.

624 "Our Booking-Office," PUNCH, CLXXI (22 Sept 1926), 335-36.

All of the six stories in *The Casuarina Tree* are admirably written; only "The Force of Circumstance" is not interesting.

625 Overton, Grant. "The Somerset Maugham of '*The Casuarina Tree,*'" BOOKMAN (NY), LXIV (Nov 1926), 298, 305.

M is to be praised for his nearly perfect objectivity, for his economy, for writing "visually," for "staging" each of his six stories with exactitude of intention and precision of effect.

626 Paterson, Isabel. "Somewhere East of Suez," NEW YORK HERALD TRIBUNE BOOKS, 3 Oct 1926, p. 5.

In *The Casuarina Tree,* M conveys that "ordinary" people are "capable of powerful and even fatal emotions; he is experimenting, on the whole quite successfully, with a special kind of realism." M is to be praised for not resorting to "romanticizing of externals" but employing the directly opposite method of "severity" and "economy."

627* Phillips, Henry Albert. "In the Shadow of the Casuarina Tree," NEW YORK EVENING POST LITERARY REVIEW, VII (2 Oct 1926), 7.

In *The Casuarina Tree,* M never interposes his presence, yet his presence is a "subtle potentiality"; the whole book is "like a fine Oriental tapestry. The longer one contemplates it, the better one understands it." The best story of the group is "The Letter," although the characterization in "The Outstation" ranks with M's earlier portrait of Sadie Thompson.

628 Régnier, Henri de. "La Vie littéraire" (The Literary Life), LE FIGARO, 6 July 1926, p. 4; rptd in LE FIGARO HEBDOMADAIRE, 14 July 1926, p. 4.

The Painted Veil is an original and powerful story. M's observation, technique, and portrait of Kitty are all excellent. [Review of the French translation.] [In French.]

629* Shanks, Edward. "Fiction," LONDON MERCURY, XIV (Oct 1926), 649-50.

The Casuarina Tree derives from earlier Kipling, though M has his own tract of country [Borneo and the Malay Peninsula] and his own manner; more striking than country or manner is the Kiplingesque "efficiency in the use of this manner": every detail moves toward the general effect of a story, and no "inch" of a story is bare of detail. The characters are as solid and vivid as a story requires.

630 Skinner, R. Dana. "The Play," COMMONWEAL, V (22 Dec 1926), 188.

The Constant Wife "offers the most trite and threadbare of all answers to the 'double standard' problem"; the laughter M provokes "is freighted with halitosis."

631* Souday, Paul. "Les Livres: *'La Passe Dangereuse'* " (Books: *The Painted Veil*), LE TEMPS, 24 June 1926, p. 3.

M should be compared to Loti and Stevenson rather than Maupassant. *The Painted Veil* is not a novel in the exotic impressionistic tradition; only a minority of British writers are sensitive to the lures of exoticism. M deals with British citizens in British surroundings. This is a psychological (not analytical, for everything is shown through action) novel which could as easily be set in London, and even more possibly in Paris. [Review of the French translation.] [In French.]

632* "Theatre," TIME, VIII (13 Dec 1926), 36.

In *The Constant Wife,* "playwright Maugham presents what, a decade or two ago, would have been termed a 'problem play,' done with a modish superciliousness. . . . The dialogue is conscious of its own glitter. The audience is aware that actors settle themselves, preen themselves, for the utterance of shining platitudes, universal conversation in the pseudo-Voltairian manner."

633 Vandérem, Fernand. "Les Lettres et la vie" (Letters and Life), LA REVUE DE FRANCE, 6ème année, no. 5 (1 Sept 1926), 170-76.

The Painted Veil is a beautiful novel by a great novelist. [Review of the French translation.] [In French.]

634 Van Doren, Carl. "The Roving Critic," CENTURY, N. S. XCI (Dec 1926), 254-55.

"Even if the six stories . . . were not intelligent, dexterous, supple, and neat," *The Casuarina Tree* "would be worth buying for the postscript alone" [in which M speaks to readers attempting to identify the living originals of his characters of fiction].

635 Vowinckel, Ernst. DER ENGLISCHE ROMAN DER NEUESTEN ZEIT UND GEGENWART: STILFORMEN UND ENTWICKLUNGSLINIEN (THE CONTEMPORARY ENGLISH NOVEL: GENRES AND DEVELOPMENT) (Berlin: F. A. Herbig, 1926), pp. 81, 82-84.

M stylizes reality in order to inquire into the meaning of life. [Describes contents of *The Painted Veil, Of Human Bondage,* and *The Trembling of a Leaf.*] [In German.]

636* Williams, Blanche Colton. "Short Turns in Divers Places," BOOKMAN (NY), LXIV (Nov 1926), 361-62.

In *The Casuarina Tree,* "moved by the dramatic and even melodramatic event, [M] knows that the most tragic is but a repetition of instances in life and in fiction. He plays, therefore, not to the external climax but away from it" [e.g., in "The Letter" the "real climax" is the ultimate picture of Leslie, not her crime].

637 Woollcott, Alexander. "The Stage," NEW YORK WORLD, 30 Nov 1926, pp. 13-14.

The Constant Wife is a good deal less of a play than *Our Betters* or *The Circle,* but full of "wisdom and cheerfulness and rippling laughter."

638 Young, Stark. "London and Maine," NEW REPUBLIC, XLIX (15 Dec 1926), 108.

The Constant Wife in its treatment of the "single standard" in marriage stumbles between serious attack and glittering comic "flight." The comedy rises only to "witty pretension."

1927

639 Agate, James. "The Dramatic World," SUNDAY TIMES (Lond), 27 Feb 1927, p. 6; rptd by Raymond Mander and Joe Mitchenson eds, in THEATRICAL COMPANION TO MAUGHAM (Lond: Rockliff, 1955), pp. 208-9 [although Mander and Mitchenson cite the review as unsigned in the SUNDAY TIMES].

The Letter is "superb theatre throughout, with the exception of a little bit at the end when the author suddenly switches over to the technique of the film."

640 Atkinson, J. Brooks. "The Play," NEW YORK TIMES, 27 Sept 1927, p. 30.

As well written as M's *The Letter* is, much of its success depends on Katherine Cornell's performance.

641 Bailey, Ralph Sargent. "The Curtain Rises," INDEPENDENT (NY), CXIX (12 Nov 1927), 482.

M of *The Letter* differs from M of *The Circle;* one is somewhat disappointed over losing the author's "wicked humor."

642 Barretto, Larry. "The New Yorker," BOOKMAN (NY), LXIV (Feb 1927), 733.

The crown for writing the wittiest dramatic dialogue should be taken from Frederick Lonsdale and awarded to M. The only flaw in M's *The Constant Wife* is that for the first fifteen minutes it is so clever that the mind grows momentarily dizzy.

643 Bauer, Gérard. "Le Théâtre" (The Theater), LES ANNALES POLITIQUES ET LITTERAIRES, No. 2281 (13 March 1927), 268.

The story, translated into the theater, becomes artificial and unreal. [Review of the French adaptation of John Colton and Clemence Randolph's RAIN.] [In French.]

644* Beauplan, Robert de. "Les Théâtres 'PLUIE' " (Theaters: RAIN), L'ILLUSTRATION, 85ème année, no. 4384 (12 March 1927), 263.

To enjoy the play, one should have a better understanding of Puritanism. To make the equivalent for Frenchmen, the adapters have resorted to Montmartre slang. But it is difficult to imagine a girl from Montmartre feeling the emotions that Sadie experiences in front of Davidson, this mixture of hatred and mystic respect. [In French.]

645* Bellamy, Francis Rufus. "Lights Down," OUTLOOK (NY), CXLVII (12 Oct 1927), 181-82.

The Letter is "cheap and tawdry," lacking in genuineness. "Its dialogue is penned exclusively from the pages of THE COMPLETE WRITER and its heroine is merely a beautiful woman who sends thrills up and down the backs of the audience because she invests with dramatic glamour a commonplace description of an affair with a man. Instead of the local color and exotic detail with which one might have expected Mr. Maugham to invest his play, there is nothing that does not suggest Long Island or New York just as well as the Oriental deep."

646 Benchley, Robert. "Beginning a Sort of Department," BOOKMAN (NY), LXVI (Nov 1927), 267-68.

[Brief censure of *The Letter* (play), but no reasons are offered.]

647 Benchley, Robert. "Drama: Minority Reports," LIFE, XC (13 Oct 1927), 23.

The Letter is "an ordinary piece of dramatic cabinet-making."

648 Berton, Claude. "Les Visages de la comédie: Freudisme" (Aspects of Comedy: Freudianism), LES NOUVELLES LITTERAIRES, 19 March 1927, p. 8.

[Review of the French adaptation of John Colton and Clemence Randolph's dramatization, RAIN.] [In French.]

649 Bidou, Henry. "Notes de la Semaine: Le Pacifique à la mode" (Notes of the Week: The Pacific à la mode), LES ANNALES POLITIQUES ET LITTERAIRES, No. 2281 (13 March 1927), 265.

As a result of the premiere of the French adaptation of John Colton and Clemence Randolph's RAIN many imitations will follow because the Pacific is "the mode." [In French.]

650* Bidou, Henry. "La Semaine dramatique: Théâtre de la Madeleine: 'PLUIE' " (The Week's Drama: Theatre de la Madeleine: RAIN) LE JOURNAL DES DEBATS [POLITIQUES ET LITTERAIRES], 7 March 1927, p. 3.

In the French adaptation of RAIN, the Pacific Ocean has become the suburbs of literature. M's story is a masterpiece of force and tone; the two American adapters have brought it to the stage with considerable damage: to pad out the play, they have added O'Hara, a sailor in love with Sadie, and an inferior mawkish creation mouthing sentimental commonplaces; to enliven the plot, they have introduced an abduction of cinema variety, which is improbable and childish. M's precise swift dialogue is replaced by verbosity. Ironically, Davidson speaks less in the French version, and his zeal becomes merely revolting. [In French.]

651* Birrell, Francis. "The Drama: Thrillers," NATION AND THE ATHENAEUM, XL (5 March 1927), 757.

As a "thriller," M's *The Letter* is good, up to a point: the play abounds in various characters, local color, good dialogue, and omits "sentimental fudge." But M, in dramatizing a good short story, finds himself short of material good enough for three acts, and so Act III "drags lamentably."

652 Borgex, L. "Lettre de Londres: Une oeuvre nouvelle de W. Somerset Maugham" (London Letter—A New Work by W. Somerset Maugham), COMOEDIA, 22 April 1927, p. 5.

In the British production of *The Constant Wife,* the story is that of the sentimental triangle, established in the "Boulevard tradition"; but M seems to have gone out of his way to shock the public. [In French.]

653* "Briefer Mention," DIAL, LXXXII (March 1927), 254.

In *The Casuarina Tree,* the "six tales . . . lack nothing of dramatic competence in the depiction of their violent actions. . . . but the author's sympathies, and consequently the reader's, are only spectacularly engaged." Thus the characters seem "histrionic," simply "parts" to be played, lacking "warmth of presence."

654* Brisson, Pierre. "Chronique Théâtrale: 'PLUIE' " (Theater Chronicle: RAIN), LE TEMPS, 7 March 1927, p. 2.

As a storyteller M's gifts have been strong movement, terseness, a dry and precise vigor. He conjures up things without describing them; his evocations are scanty but stick to the memory: they leave behind them a mirage. But this kind of art is as little dramatic as can be. RAIN in the French adaptation, follows the story but remains rather poor theatre, since the story's value lies competely in indirect narration, and the main action remains wrapped in mystery. There is a constant contrast, in the story, between the precise scenes presented by M and the turbid, secret drama which is be enacted out of sight. This clever process becomes a grave obstacle on the stage, where one is prepared by three acts for a crisis which, when it comes to a head, is suppressed. The play is thus episodic; the characters are merely caricatures; Parisians have no sympathy for Davidson's puritan faith: his sanctifying zeal becomes almost cynical. [In French.]

655* Brisson, Pierre. "Théâtre de la Madeleine: 'PLUIE' " (RAIN), LE TEMPS, 4 March 1927, p. 4.

The French adaptation of RAIN is inferior to the short story; the characters appear wooden on the stage, and Davidson's part remains unintelligible for a French audience. [In French.]

656* Brown, Ivor. "The Theatre: Heartless House," SATURDAY REVIEW (Lond), CXLIII (16 April 1927), 598-99.

M thinks of human beings "almost in terms of metal; so they are forged and so they endure." They are possessed only by desire, men for women and women for men and pearls. Middleton's adventure seems only an affectation, and "there is something dull about casual lechery." *The Constant Wife* is a collection of inhumans and impossible situations. "The dramatist who thus rejects reality must have the substitute." In this case, M was "out of form."

657 Brown, Ivor. "The Theatre: Here Are Tigers," SATURDAY REVIEW (Lond), CXLIII (5 March 1927), 350-51.

M's bleak *The Letter* is told quietly. "A connoisseur of the old-fashioned, full-throated acting might ask on this occasion whether murder could be so trivial. But the tensity is there, if the noise is not, and the counterfeit of the inexpressive Englishman is subtly conceived and sustained." [Mainly plot summary.]

658* Carb, David. "Seen on the Stage," VOGUE, LXIX (1 Feb 1927), 118.

In *The Constant Wife,* M's last scene reverses the usual theatrical values [after earning her "keep," Constance feels free to leave her husband to accompany Bernard Kersal to Italy]; this is also a reversal of the usual social values, and significantly indicative "of the upheaval in moral values of our time."

659* Carb, David. "Seen on the Stage," VOGUE, LXX (15 Nov 1927), 166.

The Letter is "a tense tale containing two weaknesses that may prove fatal. One is that the first act and the last are very much alike — they both hinge on a confession by Mrs. Crosbie, and the confessions themselves are woefully similar in tone. The other weak spot is a whole scene that has no value whatsoever to the play and as drama is nil. The attorney buys the letter — that is all."

660 *"The Constant Wife,"* DRAMATIST, XVIII (April 1927), 1339-40.

M is good with nothing but dialogue; and the financial success of the play rests entirely on its "promiscuous theme." A major flaw is the wife's retaliation against her husband's infidelities only after the desire for vengeance has had time to cool. *The Constant Wife* represents mere storytelling, a vicarious pleasure for a jaded audience of thrill-seekers.

661* Cunliffe, John W. MODERN ENGLISH PLAYRIGHTS: A SHORT HISTORY OF THE ENGLISH DRAMA FROM 1825 (NY & Lond: Harper, 1927), pp. 210-11.

The Circle is more than a "well-made play"; perhaps in the last scene

Porteous changes too suddenly "from mere irascibility to common sense and good feeling, while Champion-Cheny [sic], who has hitherto shown signs of intelligence, unexpectedly develops an almost imbecile self-conceit; but the situation is amusing enough to bear the strain, and Maugham was prudent enough to end on a note of comedy rather than on the moral tone of condemnation for the escaping lovers or the romantic one of condonation of their offence."

662 De Casseres, Benjamin. "Broadway to Date," ARTS AND DECORATION, XXVI (Feb 1927), 57, 84.
The Constant Wife is "full of sophisticated lines, which nowadays anybody can turn out."

663 De Casseres, Benjamin. "Broadway to Date," ARTS AND DECORATION, XXVIII (Dec 1927), 102.
The Letter is "a long, long way from RAIN," and one remembers Katherine Cornell's performance better than he does the plot.

664 Dickinson, Thomas H. AN OUTLINE OF CONTEMPORARY DRAMA (Boston: Houghton Mifflin, 1927), p. 251.
M mentioned along with Herbert Henry Davies as chief among writers of "new English comedy," combining "with a light and even careless method a power of scathing analysis and heartless exposition."

665 Eaton, Walter Prichard. "Playhouse and Plays," NEW YORK HERALD TRIBUNE BOOKS, 6 Nov 1927, p. 22.
The Letter is "second rate stuff," and though M has printed two endings, differing in their technical method, they reach the "same conclusion."

666* E[rvine], St. J[ohn]. "At the Play," OBSERVER (Lond), 27 Feb 1927, p. 15.
"There can be no dispute about the dramatic quality" of *The Letter*. "But Mr. Maugham bored, perhaps, by travelling over the same ground twice, has not maintained the intensity of his play throughout the three acts. He has written dialogue which, in many passages, is far below his quality, and has, in my opinion, made a grave technical error in his final act, where he employs a sort of 'cut-back' from the films to illustrate Leslie's true account of the crime. This 'cut-back' ruinously interrupted the drama of the last act, especially as the hats of Joyce and Withers and Robert Crosbie were allowed to remain in the scene. . . . The technique of the moving-picture and the technique of the theatre are distinct and separate."

667* E[rvine], St. J[ohn]. "The Week's Theatres," OBSERVER (Lond), 10 April 1927, p. 15.
The Constant Wife cannot be judged correctly because a mix-up for first-night seating arrangements made the audience angry and the actors nervous.

668 Farjeon, Herbert. "The London Stage," GRAPHIC, CXV (12 March 1927), 421.

In *The Letter,* Gladys Cooper, M's leading lady, "stands in need of a famous playwright far less than Mr. Maugham in need of a famous actress."

669* Farjeon, Herbert. "The London Stage," GRAPHIC, CXVI (16 April 1927), 123.

In *The Constant Wife,* "the characters not only deliver themselves freely of epigrams: they carry the epigrams, as it were, into practice. The situation on which the curtain descends at the finish is so superciliously unconventional that I doubt whether even the glamour surrounding Miss Fay Compton will entirely blind audiences to the ethical questionability of her stage conduct."

670 Farrar, John. "Anonymously," BOOKMAN (NY), LXVI (Nov 1927), 284-85.

The Letter [play] is "taut, violent drama."

671 "A Fine Maugham Play for Miss Cooper," ILLUSTRATED LONDON NEWS, CLXX (5 March 1927), 418.

The Letter's "technique is scrupulously austere; no time is wasted on the superfluous fireworks of dialogue; its drama marches steadily forward from exciting start to grim finish."

672 Flers, Robert de. "La Semaine dramatique" (The Week's Drama), LE FIGARO, 8 March 1927, p. 1; rptd in LE FIGARO HEBDOMADAIRE, 16 March 1927, pp. 2-3.

[Biographical sketch of M, followed by a plot summary and an examination of the performances of the French adaptation of John Colton and Clemence Randolph's dramatization of RAIN.] [In French.]

673 Fréjaville, Gustave. "Théâtres-Théâtre de la Madeleine: PLUIE" (RAIN), LE JOURNAL DES DEBATS [POLITIQUES ET LITTERAIRES], 4 March 1927, p. 3.

The French adaptation of RAIN is strange to Frenchmen because Davidson's tyranny and fanaticism do not correspond to social realities in Europe so much as they do in America. The play thus succeeds for Parisians only because of Jane Marnac's brilliant performance in the part of Sadie Thompson. [In French.]

674 Gabriel, Gilbert [W.] "Manhattan Aisles," NEW YORK SUN, 27 Sept 1927, p. 18.

The Letter is not M at his best, yet it is "an unusually sharp piece of theater."

675 Graham, Gladys. "Strange Bedfellows," Saturday Review of Literature, III (15 Jan 1927), 514.

The suave, cleverly wrought stories of *The Casuarina Tree* are good reading. M can draw "a delicacy of style across the reddest and rawest of passions."

676 Guyon-Cesbron, Jean. "Les Lettres anglaises" (English Letters), La Revue Hebdomadaire, 36ème année: 5 (May 1927), 238-40.

In this atrociously true and human story [the French translation of *The Painted Veil*], there is not one false note.

677 Hammond, Percy. "The Theaters," New York Herald Tribune, 27 Sept 1927, p. 22.

The Letter is "an orderly melodrama."

678* Holt, Edgar. "Drama: *'The Letter,'*" New Statesman, XXVIII (19 March 1927), 698.

M has proceeded "from the artificial to the superficial"; the whole play lies on the surface, its points made with "pedantic precision," its construction faulty [three scenes — the opening, the one in the Chinese quarter, and the "throw-back" — could be detached advantageously].

679 Hornblow, Arthur. "Mr. Hornblow Goes to the Play," Theatre Magazine, XLV (Feb 1927), 16.

The Constant Wife is a light piece which will not bear close inspection; nor is it M at his "most sophisticated or best."

680 Jennings, Richard. "The Theatre: *The Constant Wife*," Spectator (Lond), CXXXVIII (16 April 1927), 685.

M's "celebrated 'restoration' manner hardly shows at its best." The plot is "a mixture of Ibsen and Congreve." The theme is "old fashioned," resembling Dumas' Françillion of 1893. M's style is "bookish, unnatural." "All the characters are commentators, and the argument overwhelms deliciously daring conversation."

681 Jennings, Richard. "The Theatre: *The Letter,*" Spectator (Lond), CXXXVIII (5 March 1927), 358.

The "inset scene" within the confession scene is perhaps "necessary for suspense," "a doubtful advantage," but it is "a really good entertainment of the detective type, illustrating a 'passionate crime.' "

682 Krutch, Joseph Wood. "Drama," Nation (NY), CXXIV (5 Jan 1927), 20-21.

In *The Constant Wife,* "a sufficient number of the author's epigrams actually come off to make it entertaining."

683 Krutch, Joseph Wood. "Drama," NATION (NY), CXXV (19 Oct 1927), 430-31.

M's *The Letter* does not provide sufficient material for a full-length play.

684 Lalou, René. PANORAMA DE LA LITTERAIRE ANGLAISE CONTEMPORAINE (PANORAMA OF CONTEMPORARY ENGLISH LITERATURE) (Paris: Kra, 1927), pp. 216, 224, 229.

M, a prolific playwright, has probably done his best work in short stories such as "Rain" and "Mackintosh." [In French.]

685 *"The Letter,"* PLAY PICTORIAL, L, No. 302 [n.d., but probably late 1927], 74.

[Primarily a plot summary of the play.]

686 Nichols, Beverley. "W. Somerset Maugham, or Dark and Difficult," ARE THEY THE SAME AT HOME? BEING A SERIES OF BOUQUETS DIFFIDENTLY DISTRIBUTED (Lond: J. Cape, 1927), pp. 240-44.

[Diffuse and subjective portrait of M.]

687 Omicron. "Plays and Pictures," NATION AND THE ATHENAEUM, XLI (16 April 1927), 50.

A capable group of actors and actresses in *The Constant Wife* gives "verisimilitude to artificial dialogue and unnatural dialogue," and assists the viewer in overlooking "the mechanical stupidity of the plot."

688 "The Playhouse: *'The Letter'* by W. Somerset Maugham," TIMES (Lond), 25 Feb 1927, p. 12.

"What a feat of dexterity the whole play is! With what economy and with what understanding of the uses of the stage it is written! It never pauses or falters; not an outline is blurred."

689 "RAIN Produced in Paris," TIMES (Lond) 9 March 1927, p. 12.

The dramatization has been a great success at the Théâtre de la Madeleine, Paris.

690 Recouly, Raymond. "Un romancier dramaturge: *La Lettre* de Somerset Maugham" (A Novelist-Dramatist: *The Letter* by Somerset Maugham), LE FIGARO, 18 Aug 1927, pp. 1-2.

[Review of the British production.]

691* Rey, Etienne. "Théâtre de la Madeleine: 'PLUIE' " (RAIN), COMOEDIA, 4 March 1927, pp. 1-2.

RAIN will be more successful in a Puritan city like New York rather than in Paris. In Davidson, Parisians see a comical hypocrite like Tartuffe. [In French.]

692 Rouveyre, André. "Théâtre: Jane Marnac dans 'PLUIE'" (Theater: Jane Marnac in RAIN), LE MERCURE DE FRANCE, CXCVI (15 May 1927), 145-47.

The French find it hard to comprehend the fanaticism of a Dr. Davidson, but the French adaptation of John Colton and Clemence Randolph's RAIN is one of the better plays of the season. [In French.]

693 Sayler, Oscar M. "The Play of the Week," SATURDAY REVIEW OF LITERATURE, IV (15 Oct 1927), 193-94.

The Letter loses demonic intensity in expanding and diluting the fifty-page narrative of the short story to fit the traditional two-hour stage time. What grips the viewer is the performance of Katherine Cornell.

694 Seldes, Gilbert. "The Theatre," DIAL, LXXXII (Feb 1927), 169.

The Constant Wife is "one of the most negligible plays in years, one in which all the epigrams are machine-turned and the wit heavy-handed."

695 Seldes, Gilbert. "The Theatre," DIAL, LXXXII (June 1927), 533-34.

Despite the unanimous praise of *The Constant Wife* by New York drama critics, the play is "full of strained smartness."

696 Simon, Robert A. "'*The Letter*' in Print," NEW YORK EVENING POST, 15 Oct 1927, III: 15.

M's play is cleverly built, but reading the text proves that K. Cornell's contribution to the play's success is "great."

697* "Six Plays," TIMES LITERARY SUPPLEMENT (Lond), 3 Nov 1927, p. 784.

M is an artist of feeling and perception, who can still make technical brilliance his servant. However, he is not beyond throwing out an occasional light piece of entertainment, "launching a paper boat." In *The Constant Wife* he loads the entertainment with too much cargo when suddenly Constance, who had been made a puppet for nothing more than entertainment, begins to pronounce a solemn conjugal doctrine, and the play sinks under its own weight.

698 Souday, Paul. "Le Mouvement dramatique" (The Drama Movement), LA REVUE DE PARIS, 34ème année, no. 2 (1 April 1927), 677.

Horace de Carbuccia's French translation of John Colton and Clemence Randolph's dramatization, RAIN, would have been better if the translator had gone to M's original text and worked from it. [In French.]

699 Speth, William. "Le Théâtre" (The Theatre), LA REVUE MONDIALE, CLXXVI (15 April 1927), 389-91.
In the French adaptation of John Colton and Clemence Randolph's dramatization, RAIN, the main character seems to be Davidson, but the audience is more interested in Sadie Thompson. [In French.]

700* "Strand Theatre: *'The Constant Wife'* by W. Somerset Maugham," TIMES (Lond), 7 April 1927, p. 14.
One is puzzled "why what began with a few epigrams should end in so strange an admixture of artificial seriousness and artificial gaiety." If the play contained any emotion, "someone might have had the pleasure of being shocked, but it is hard to be shocked by a bowl of goldfish swimming, coldly, but in an elaborate pattern after one another's decorative tails."

701 "Theatre," TIME, X (3 Oct 1927), 40.
"But for the acting of the star [K. Cornell in *The Letter*], the evening would have been unimpressive."

702 "The Theatres: Mr. Maugham's Murder Mystery," TRUTH (Lond), CI (2 March 1927), 413.
The Letter is "honest, ruthless work."

703 "The Theatres: Strange Doings in Harley Street," TRUTH (Lond), CI (13 April 1927), 727.
In *The Constant Wife,* M's "neo-feminist propaganda makes for only mild entertainment."

704 T[horp, Joseph]. "At the Play," PUNCH, CLXXII (13 April 1927), 414-16.
In *The Constant Wife,* M disturbs his witty pattern, especially in Act II, "by prolonging situations beyond their effective climaxes, and more fundamentally, by charging the light fabric . . . with the burden of a serious argument."

705 Vandérem, Fernand. "Les Lettres et la vie" (Letters and Life), LA REVUE DE FRANCE, 7ème année, no. 2 (1 April 1927), 555-56.
[Review of the French translation of John Colton and Clemence Randolph's dramatization, RAIN.] [In French.]

706 Waldman, Milton. "Chronicles: The Drama," LONDON MERCURY, XVI (May 1927), 85.
In *The Constant Wife,* M is "tedious, not for a few moments only here and there, but throughout. His people are banal, his situations trite and his epigrams completely devoid of wit."

707 Woollcott, Alexander. "The Stage," NEW YORK WORLD, 27 Sept 1927, p. 11.
[Noncommittal review of *The Letter*.]

708 Wyatt, Euphemia Van Rensselaer. "The Drama," CATHOLIC WORLD, CXXIV (March 1927), 815-16.
"Although smartly written and neatly constructed," *The Constant Wife*, "in which virtue and honor are reckoned as economic commodities, cannot be said to have a very pleasant flavor."

709* Wyatt, Euphemia Van Rensselaer. "The Drama," CATHOLIC WORLD, CXXVI (Nov 1927), 243-44.
The Letter is "as generous a vehicle for the emotional actress as were the great old dramas of Sardou," except that M's first act begins where Sardou's would have ended, thus requiring, and receiving, formidable stamina from both the playwright and his leading lady.

710 Young, Stark. "Miss Katherine Cornell," NEW REPUBLIC, LII (12 Oct 1927), 207-8.
The Letter has poor dialogue; the characters are merely "engines" of the plot. The play has little suspense and no credibility.

1928

711 Atkinson, J. Brooks. "The Play," NEW YORK TIMES, 20 Nov 1928, p. 28; rptd by Raymond Mander and Joe Mitchenson, eds, in THEATRICAL COMPANION TO MAUGHAM (Lond: Rockliff, 1955), p. 213.
The Sacred Flame is "another of Mr. Maugham's shilling shockers. . . . Papier-mâché is papier-mâché, no matter how skillfully you mold it." The play is riddled with "sentimentalism."

712 Audiat, Pierre. "L'Actualité littéraire" (Current Literature), LA REVUE DE FRANCE, 8ème année, no. 4 (15 Aug 1928), 710-11.
[Brief review of the French translation of *The Moon and Sixpence* and of Paul Dottin's SOMERSET MAUGHAM ET SES ROMANS.] [In French.]

713 Balmforth, Ramsden. "Somerset Maugham's *The Unknown:* The Problem of Agnosticism," THE PROBLEM-PLAY AND ITS INFLUENCE ON MODERN THOUGHT AND LIFE (Lond: George Allen & Unwin, 1928), pp. 108-21.
M's "destructive" criticism should aid many who seek "firm and clear

ground for the foundations of a new faith to see how necessary it is that they should first rid their minds of the false idols and beliefs of the past."

714 Beauplan, Robert de. "Les Théâtres: *'Le Cercle'* " (The Theaters: *The Circle*), L'ILLUSTRATION, 86ème année, no. 4475 (8 Dec 1928), 704.

The French adaptation is excellent and not lacking in savor. [In French.]

715 B[ellamy], F[rancis] R[ufus]. "Lights Down: A Review of the Stage," OUTLOOK (NY), CXLVIII (7 May 1928), 383.

The revived *Our Betters* is set forth with the "utmost suavity, keen, bitter wit, and much exceedingly accurate observation of human nature."

716 Bellamy, Francis R[ufus]. "The Theatre," OUTLOOK (NY), CL (5 Dec 1928), 1275.

The Sacred Flame is "paper and paste throughout."

717 Benchley, Robert. "Drama: Pulmotor Drama," LIFE, XCI (15 March 1928), 19.

The revival of *Our Betters* is "good entertainment."

718 Benchley, Robert. "The Theatre: Less Efficiency, Ladies, Please!", LIFE, XCII (28 Dec 1928), 9.

The third act of *The Sacred Flame* is "tremendously moving."

719* Berton, Claude. "Les Visages de la Comédie-Dramaturgie Européenne: A l'OEuvre-*Le Cercle*" (Aspects of Comedy: European Dramaturgy: At the l'OEuvre: *The Circle*), LES NOUVELLES LITTERAIRES, 1 Dec 1928, p. 11.

In his pungency and luminous pessimism M is akin to the French naturalists. *The Circle* [in its French adaptation] is constructed precisely as Maupassant might have constructed a play, and is a slap in the faces of the Eminent Victorians. Passion, for M, is not a vague neurasthenia, but precise sufferings, a crippling disease. The devouring evil in the play is old age. [In French.]

720 "La bonne référence" (The Good Reference), GRINGOIRE, 7 Dec 1928, p. 9.

Critics and the public agree that the French adaptation of *The Circle* is very good. [In French.]

721 Bordeaux, Henry. "Courrier des lettres" (Courier of Letters), LE FIGARO SUPPLEMENT LITTERAIRE, 20 Oct 1928, p. 4.

[Long discussion of censorship in Belgium, particularly of M's *The Moon and Sixpence* in the Walloon parts of Belgium and Flanders.] [In French.]

722 Bourdon, Charles. "Les Romans: *L'Envoûte*" (Novels: *The*

Moon and Sixpence), LA REVUE DES LECTURES, 16ème année, no. 9 (15 Sept 1928), 1012-14.

The book has scurrilous detail and elaborates the Romantic conception that genius is above God's laws. [Review of the French translation.] [In French.]

723 Brown, John Mason. "The Year's at the Spring," THEATRE ARTS MONTHLY, XII (May 1928), 315-16.

The revived *Our Betters* shows the "tradition of heartlessness which is the admitted core of all high comedy." In *Our Betters* even love is "only one of its most acid jokes." However, the play is not very witty for it uses mere cynicism too often in place of the glittering epigram.

724 C., A. C. "Recent Fiction," NEW REPUBLIC, LIV (18 April 1928), 279.

Ashenden obtains the ideal which Arnold Bennett did not in THE GRAND BABYLON HOTEL. "Nothing is exaggerated. Proportion is observed. Reality is not outraged."

725* Carb, David. "Seen on the Stage," VOGUE, LXXI (15 April 1928), 94-95.

World War I has made America less imitative, more aggressively self-reliant; so the revived *Our Betters* is dated. The comedy "is for the most part a series of duologues, and, thus, a bit jerky." Nevertheless, the play is still "shimmering . . . , witty, penetrating."

726* Cazamian, Louis. "Les Livres" (Books), LA REVUE ANGLO-AMERICAINE, V:2 (Feb 1928), 289-90.

In *The Casuarina Tree,* after Oceania and China, M passes on to the Malay and Archipelago in much the same manner as, and with much the same matter of, *The Trembling of a Leaf*. M shows a greater moral and social detachment than Kipling, a more intransigent capacity for analysis, a more daring power of observation, a deeper intuition. He better expresses the subconsciousness and the enigmas of the ego. M combines naturalism, descriptive lyricism, the teachings of the Russian novel and Freudian psychology. These compact dramatic stories may, however, be too cleverly told, after all. [In French.]

727 Croisset, Francis de. "A la maison de l'OEuvre⸗*Le Cercle* de Somerset Maugham" (At the l'OEuvre: *The Circle* by Somerset Maugham), GRINGOIRE, 30 Nov 1928, p. 8.

The play, in the French adaptation, is in M's best manner—cruel, gay, lyrical, and disenchanted, full of love though without hope. [In French.]

728 Croquet, James de. "Répétitions générales: Au théâtre de l'OEuvre⸗*Le Cercle* (Dress Rehearsals at the l'OEuvre Theater:

The Circle), LE FIGARO, 23 Nov 1928, p. 3; rptd in LE FIGARO HEBDOMADAIRE, 28 Nov 1928, p. 19.

The French actors have stressed the play's pure comedy rather than its irony. [Review of the French adaptation.] [In French.]

729 d'Houville, Gérard. "Chronique dramatique du FIGARO: *Le Cercle*" (Drama Chronicle of Figaro: *The Circle*), LE FIGARO, 26 Nov 1928, p. 2.

The Parisian public has responded better than the British to the depth of observation, the pungency of the dialogue, the great comedy of the situations, and the underlying pathos in the French adaptation. [Review of the French adaptation, in French.]

730 Dottin, Paul. WILLIAM SOMERSET MAUGHAM ET SES ROMANS (WILLIAM SOMERSET MAUGHAM AND HIS NOVELS), (Paris: Perrin, 1928).

A detailed examination of *Liza of Lambeth, Mrs. Craddock, Of Human Bondage, The Moon and Sixpence, The Trembling of a Leaf,* and *The Painted Veil.* [In French.] [See, also, Paul Dottin, "Le réalisme de Somerset Maugham", LA REVUE DE FRANCE, 6ème année, no. 3 (1 June 1926), 574-81.]

731 Enäjärvi, Elsa. "Naamioitten paraati" (Parade of the Masks), VANHA ILOINEN ENGLANTI (MERRY OLD ENGLAND), (Porvoo-Helsinki: WSOY, 1928), pp. 237-38.

The characters of M's plays are drawn almost with mathematical exactitude. He is a passionate lover of intelligence—one could almost say, of calculation. [In Finnish.]

732 Ervine, St. John. "At the Play," OBSERVER (Lond), 23 Dec 1928, p. 7.

In the American production of *The Sacred Flame,* the first act is slow in movement, diffuse in speech; the second act becomes "expeditious," and interest mounts up to the end.

733* Ervine, St. John. "The New Play: Maugham on Mother-Murder," NEW YORK WORLD, 21 Nov 1928, pp. 15, 16.

The Sacred Flame is "melodramatic," but so then are Ibsen's and Shaw's plays, especially if the term designates "wild and unreasonable behavior and speech of men and women in the throes of high love and high hate." The first act is excessively prolix, the final speeches might be shortened, but the entire play is "extraordinarily impressive."

734 Farrar, John. "Anonymously," BOOKMAN (NY), LXVII (April 1928), 294.

Ashenden is a "thriller and magnificent portraiture" at once.

735 "Fiction Notes," BOOKMAN (NY), LXVII (May 1928), xxi. "The story [of *Mrs. Craddock*], in spite of all corrections, remains curiously *démodé*. . . . But once we have accustomed ourselves to a certain primness and stiffness of movement, we recognize the Maugham of today—a little more earnest, a little duller, but the same. The chorus of this disallowed tragedy, in the person of the heroine's spinster aunt, is a delightfully cynical echo. The Victorian Age itself cannot wither a really salty woman."

736 "Fiction Notes," BOOKMAN (NY), LXVII (July 1928), xxiv. "Mr. Maugham cannot quite bring himself to forget human nature even in a pot-boiler, and he has dotted the book [*Ashenden*] with passages reminiscent of his best work."

737 Gould, Gerald. "New Novels," OBSERVER (Lond), 1 April 1928, p. 8.
Ashenden is not M at his best or profoundest, but it has a firmness of texture, and will be hard to put down even though the Russian part, at the end, is weakest of all the book's sections.

738 Grégorio, Paul. "Répétitions Générales: *Le Cercle*" (Dress Rehearsals: *The Circle*), COMOEDIA, 22 Nov 1928, p. 2.
Review of the French adaptation. [In French.]

739 Hammond, Percy. "The Theaters," NEW YORK HERALD TRIBUNE, 20 Nov 1928, p. 22.
The Sacred Flame is "a forbidding tin-type of one of life's most cruel crises. . . . I suspect that the trouble . . . is that it is a confusion of pen, ink and paper, some honest, daring innovations concerning the cosmic urge and a cynical belief that a sow's purse may be manufactured from a silk ear."

740* Hartley, L. P. "New Fiction," SATURDAY REVIEW (Lond), CXLV (14 April 1928), 471-72.
The stories in *Ashenden* "are not simply thrillers nor yet simply studies of character, but something between the two; and the best of them sit comfortably on both stools." In "His Excellence," M tries to "touch the heart," but fails; "may he always strive to curdle the blood."

741 H[umbourg?], P[ierre?]. "La Critique des livres: *L'Envoûte*" (Book Criticism: *The Moon and Sixpence*), LES NOUVELLES LITTERAIRES, 8 Sept 1928, p. 3.
M's style is neat and vivid; his exploration of Strickland's motives through his actions, convincing. [Review of the French translation.] [In French.]

742 Krutch, Joseph Wood. "Drama," NATION (NY), CXXVII (19 Dec 1928), 694.

The Sacred Flame is "a pretty good example of the rather mechanical sort of play which Maugham has got into the habit of giving us."

743* Lefèvre, Frederic. "Une heure avec W. Somerset Maugham, romancier et conteur anglais" (An Hour with W. Somerset Maugham, English Novelist and Short-Story Writer), LES NOUVELLES LITTERAIRES, 7ème année, no. 287 (14 April 1928), pp. 1, 4; rptd in UNE HEURE AVEC . . . VIème Série (Paris: Ernest Flammarion, 1933), pp. 58-70.

A biographical sketch followed by an interview bearing on such subjects as the translations of M's books, the theater and the novel, the French language, M's favorite authors and books (Stendhal, Jules Renard and his JOURNAL, Anatole France and LA VIE LITTERAIRE, Verlaine, the Pléiade Poets, Maupassant and UNE VIE, Proust), foreign writers, M's projects (to write a species of CANDIDE), his methods of work. M thinks his best book is *Of Human Bondage.* [In French.]

744 "Les Livres≠*L'Envoûte* par Somerset Maugham" (Books: *The Moon and Sixpence* by Somerset Maugham), JOURNAL DE GENEVE [NATIONAL POLITIQUE ET LITTERAIRE], 99ème année, no. 220 (21 Aug 1928), 2.

Brief mention of the French translation. [In French.]

745 Lockridge, Richard. "Two Plays out of Money," NEW YORK SUN, 20 Nov 1928, p. 20.

For an act *The Sacred Flame* "flickered in an atmosphere made tremulous by the words breathed into it. Then it glowed with increasing intensity . . . making the way to a play worth seeing—a play too full, perhaps, even of the smooth talk Maugham has written into it; but for all that one having depth and breadth and meaning."

746 Marble, Annie Russell. "Dramatic Novelists: W. Somerset Maugham," A STUDY OF THE MODERN NOVEL, BRITISH AND AMERICAN, SINCE 1900 (NY & Lond: D. Appleton, 1928), pp. 148-52.

[A brief biography, selected bibliography, with a brief appreciation of *Of Human Bondage.*]

747 "Les Meilleurs nouveautés: Paul Dottin≠SOMERSET MAUGHAM ET SES ROMANS" (The Best New Publications: Paul Dottin: SOMERSET MAUGHAM AND HIS NOVELS), LA REVUE DES LECTURES, 16ème année, no. 10 (15 Oct 1928), 1212.

M delights in abominable situations and characters guided by their instincts. [In French.]

748 "Mr. Maugham's Latest," NEW YORK TIMES BOOK REVIEW, 15 April 1928, p. 14.
Ashenden is entertaining, but "forgettable." M tells his tales with "ease and distinction," but a year from now the book will not be on the library shelves that hold *Of Human Bondage.*

749 "New Novels," TIMES LITERARY SUPPLEMENT (Lond), 12 April 1928, p. 270.
Ashenden is "only moderately entertaining." The description is "desultory," the conversation "of no particular interest." The story of Giulia Lazzari and Chandra Lal is one of the best, though even here "the element of excitement is tenuous."

750 "Novel Notes," BOOKMAN (Lond), LXXIV (May 1928), 138. In *Ashenden,* the end seems to "fall off," and the long monologue by the ambassador at X is "rather dull," but M knows what he is talking about, and on the whole the book is "very good."

751 "Other Fiction," TRUTH (Lond), CIII (2 May 1928), 858. In *Ashenden,* "The skill with which the author succeeds throughout in giving you [the impression of actuality], while at the same time investing his record with sustained dramatic interest of the tensest sort, is a notable achievement."

752 "Our Booking-Office," PUNCH, CLXXIV (2 May 1928), 504. In *Ashenden,* "the spy story becomes patently true even if it should happen to be invention."

753 "Les Pièces de Théâtre: *Le Cercle* (*The Circle*), 21 Novembre 1928 (Th. de L'OEuvre)," LA REVUE DES LECTURES, 16ème année, no. 12 (15 Dec 1928), 1406.
The French adaptation is "unhealthy." [In French.]

754 Rey, Etienne. *"Le Cercle"* (*The Circle*), COMOEDIA, 23 Nov 1928, pp. 1-2.
The French adaptation is clever, brisk, and pleasant. According to Rey, M appropriated some of his maxims from Rey's book, REFLEXIONS SUR L'AMOUR (Reflections on Love), into the play. [In French.]

755 Salpeter, Harry. "Of W. Somerset Maugham," NEW YORK WORLD ("Metropolitan Section"), 11 Nov 1928, p. 10.
[Sketch of and interview with M at the time of his arrival in New York for the American premiere of *The Sacred Flame.*]

756 Seldes, Gilbert. "The Theatre," DIAL, LXXXIV (Feb 1928), 166.
The Letter was "trashy" and it failed "to work its melodramatic content for

all it is worth," but the reason for its quick closing in New York is deplorable: "the little remnant of integrity which Mr. Maugham held on to when he refused to compound a crime by being sentimental about it."

757 Seldes, Gilbert. "The Theatre," DIAL, LXXXIV (May 1928), 439.

The revived *Our Betters* was "second best" M initially, but now that its "slashing bitterness" has been changed to "complacent comedy," it lacks importance.

758 Shanks, Edward. "Fiction," LONDON MERCURY, XVIII (May 1928), 98.

Much about *Ashenden* is "inconclusively enigmatic," but there is about the whole work "an atmosphere of truth"; the final episode, with its "ironic and pathetic tragedy of which Maugham is a master," is best.

759 "Shorter Notices," NEW STATESMAN, XXXI (5 May 1928), 134.

In *Ashenden,* the story of "The Hairless Mexican" and its "lurid sequel" are to be taken with several grains of salt, but generally M's "acute social sense and his brightly cynical attitude to life are given full play."

760* Skinner, R. Dana. "The Play," COMMONWEAL, VII (11 April 1928), 1294.

Although *Our Betters* "is by no means a short play, it really contains only enough solid material for a one-act sketch and the conversational padding is hardly brilliant enough to prevent long stretches of boredom between the occasional flashes of fine satirical wit." [Review of the revival.]

761 Souday, Paul. "Les Livres: *L'Envoûte*" (Books: *The Moon and Sixpence*), LE TEMPS, 23 April 1928, p. 3.

M is at once a popular and a "highbrow" writer. His work is completely different from that of symbolists' novels. The book is not a biography of Gauguin in novel form. [Review of the French translation.] [In French.]

762 "Theatre," TIME, XII (3 Dec 1928), 42-43.

"Melodramatic in outline, declamatory in some lines, slow in the first act," *The Sacred Flame* "remains not a profound play, but a sensitive, skillful one."

763 Ward, A. C. TWENTIETH-CENTURY LITERATURE—THE AGE OF INTERROGATION: 1901-1925 (Lond: Methuen, 1928), pp. 102, 103, 211.

M combined the technique of Pinero with the verbal mannerisms of Wilde, and has been able to bridge completely the twenty-five years between Wilde and Noël Coward. *Caesar's Wife* is one of M's "best" plays.

764 Way, Oliver. "Modern Life in Books," GRAPHIC, CXX (7 April 1928), 22.
Ashenden is "the very triumph of realism," for realism invades the stronghold of romance, the Secret Service.

765 Wild, Friedrich. DIE ENGLISCHE LITERATUR DER GEGENWART SEIT 1870: DRAMA UND ROMAN (MODERN ENGLISH LITERATURE SINCE 1870: Drama and Novel) (Wiesbaden: Dioskuren-Verlag, 1928), pp. 70-71, 314, 328-31, 332.
Some of M's early plays betray Ibsen's influence. His later ones are cynical, satirical comedies with farcical elements. M's exotic stories are enriched by symbolic and expressionistic motifs which his early naturalistic fiction does not use. *Of Human Bondage,* thought by some his best work, includes a number of sordid love affairs. [In German.]

766 Wyatt, Euphemia Van Rensselaer. "The Drama," CATHOLIC WORLD, CXXVII (April 1928), 80-81.
"One cannot evince any gratitude for Mr. Maugham's tainted cleverness" in the revival of *Our Betters.*

1929

767 "A l'étalage" (On Display), GRINGOIRE, 24 May 1929, p. 4.
[Brief review of the French translation of *The Casuarina Tree.*] [In French.]

768 Ambrière, Francis. "La Critique des livres: *Le Sortilège Malais*" (Book Criticism: *The Casuarina Tree*), LES NOUVELLES LITTERAIRES, (19 Oct 1929), p. 3.
The French translation is a collection of remarkable stories—not for originality of subject, art of composition, or psychology, but for sheer power to perceive and project a vision. [In French.]

769 Audiat, Pierre. "L'Actualité littéraire" (Current Literature), LA REVUE DE FRANCE, 9ème année, no. 4 (1 July 1929), 120-21.
"The Outstation" is the most distinguished story in the French translation of *The Casuarina Tree.* [In French.]

770* Bauer, Gérard. "Le théâtre" (The Theater), LES ANNALES POLITIQUES ET LITTERAIRES, No. 2325 (1 Jan 1929), 41.
The Circle, adapted by H. de Carbuccia, combines caricature and bitterness. Its interest does not lie in the story, nor in its moral, which has nothing new about it; but in the capacity the English have for attacking conventions without rupturing the tone. M reveals a rare sense of social

burlesque. *The Circle* is full of clever mischievousness, of a cruelty that does not stop halfway. From the comic, the play passes on to a sense of pain. [In French.]

771 Beauplan, Robert de. "Les Théâtres: *La Lettre*" (Theaters: *The Letter*), L'ILLUSTRATION, 87ème année, no. 4521 (26 Oct 1929), 487.

In the French adaptation, the use of the cinematic technique to bind the last scene to the first is clever. [In French.]

772 Belfor, A. "*La Flamme Sacrée* de Somerset Maugham (The Playhouse)" (*The Sacred Flame* by Somerset Maugham [The Playhouse]), LE FIGARO, 28 March 1929, p. 3.

The British production of the play is intense and well-constructed, but not so well written as the author's masterpieces, RAIN and *The Circle*. The subject matter requires a more delicate treatment; the play is too long. [In French.]

773 Béraud, Henri. "Les Sortilèges de Somerset Maugham" (The Magic of Somerset Maugham), GRINGOIRE, 30 Aug 1929, p. 4.

The French translation of *The Casuarina Tree* reveals that M is a man of wide experience; he differs from "trashy" contemporary novelists in that he exhibits no frills and affectations, if he is not preoccupied with "thoughts" and "fine style." His literature is virile. His craftsmanship is masterly. [In French.]

774 Borgex, L. "Lettre de Londres—Un grand succès de Mr. Somerset Maugham" (London Letter—A Great Success by Mr. Somerset Maugham), COMOEDIA, 22 Feb 1929, p. 3.

In the British production of *The Sacred Flame,* M relies less on the spontaneity of his wit than on subject matter for success. [In French.]

775 Bourdon, Charles. "Les Pièces de Théâtre—*'La Lettre'*—18 Octobre 1929 (Athénée)" (Plays: *The Letter*—18 October 1929 [Athénée]), LA REVUE DES LECTURES, 16ème année, no. 11 (15 Nov 1929), 1305-6.

The French adaptation is dramatic and well-built, preserving the atmosphere of the short story. [In French.]

776 Bourdon, Charles. 'Les Romans: *'Le Sortilège Malais'* " (Novels: *The Casuarina Tree*), LA REVUE DES LECTURES, 17ème année, no. 8 (15 Aug 1929), 913.

The French translation is curious enough, yet of a mediocre profit. [In French.]

777* Brown, Ivor. "The Theatre: Old and New Fires," Saturday Review (Lond), CXLVII (16 Feb 1929), 210-11.
M's youthful plays were "mere mannequins to parade the bravery of his wit. . . . Recently he has settled down to narrative drama which is ungarnished by show of epigram and depends simply on good story-telling for its effect." Although *The Sacred Flame* is a problem play, M is concerned with "the art of three-dimensional story-telling" and not "the public agonizing of conscience" over a moral dilemma. Mrs. Tabret, an unconvincing character, is the one weak link of the play.

778 Brown, Ivor. "The Week's Theatres," Observer (Lond), 10 Feb 1929, p. 15.
In tension and economy both, *The Sacred Flame* is excellent, but the tension of the third act is achieved by straining probability, and Mrs. Tabret's character is not altogether convincing.

779* Brûlé, A. "Livres" (Books), La Revue Anglo-Americaine, VI:4 (April 1929), 368.
Review of Paul Dottin's Somerset Maugham et ses Romans. The book is that of a shrewd admirer who writes in good faith and keeps down his enthusiasm. Dottin's criticism bears on the most characteristic works, which are divided into "English novels" and "exotic novels." The painter Strickland in *The Moon and Sixpence* serves as a link between the two categories. *Ashenden,* published probably after Dottin's book, confirms the critic's views.

780 "Butler Davenport Gives Maugham Drama," New York Times, 21 March 1929, p. 29.
In *The Tenth Man,* the dialogue is stilted and rhetorical, the characterization is not "acute," and there is an impression about the whole play that it was cast in a mold early in the author's career.

781 Cordell, Richard A. "William Somerset Maugham," Representative Modern Plays—British and American—From Robertson to O'Neill (NY: Thomas Nelson, 1929), p. 288.
[Biographical and critical introduction to *The Circle.*]

782* Cru, Robert-L. "La Saison Théâtrale à Londres" (Theatrical Season in London), Le Temps, 5 Aug 1929, p. 2.
The British contemporary theater is unusually rich, with M and Galsworthy in reaction against Victorian sentimentality. *The Sacred Flame* is M's most perfect drama, though its subject and analysis have offended proponents of traditional morality. The story is less shocking than Phedre or Oedipus Rex and is treated with as much strength and terseness; it is the greatest play of the year. [In French.]

783 "Dans le métro" (In the Subway), GRINGOIRE, 12 July 1929, p. 2.

Asked about his future plans, M replies: "I shall only wear dark blue waistcoats." [Interview.] [In French.]

784 Deval, Jacques. "A travers les théâtres" (In the Theaters), REVUE DES DEUX MONDES, 99ème année, septième periode (1 Feb 1929), 708.

M has less verve than Shaw, less profundity than Galsworthy, but surpasses both in power of emotion. [Brief review of Horace de Carbuccia's adaptation of *The Circle.*] [In French.]

785 Deval, Jacques. "A travers les théâtres" (In the Theaters) REVUE DES DEUX MONDES, 99ème année, septième periode (1 Dec 1929), 705-7.

[Generally favorable review of Horace de Carbuccia's adaptation of *The Letter.*] [In French.]

786 d'Houville, Gérard. "Chronique des Théâtres de Paris: Th. de l'Athénée: *La Lettre*" (Drama Chronicles of Paris: Athénée Theater: *The Letter*), LE FIGARO, 21 Oct 1929, p. 5.

In the French adaptation of the play, the ending is less satisfactory than the original story's ending. [In French.]

787* Dottin, Paul. "Livres" (Books), LA REVUE ANGLO-AMERICAINE, VI:3 (Feb 1929), 285.

In *Ashenden,* the hero of a series of episodes presents a degraded view of the author: M distinguished himself during World War I, unlike his hero. The book is fictionalized autobiography; but it marks a progress: it is more intense, its realism is more cruel, and its characterization shrewder than in earlier works. The scene of Chandra Lal's suicide and the description of Petrograd are praiseworthy. Future historians will set great store by the book. [In French.]

788 Farjeon, Herbert. "The London Stage," GRAPHIC, CXXIII (23 Feb 1929), 277.

M is a master of his craft; his skill falls short only of the management that conceals management. *The Sacred Flame* is challenging, but beneath it, there is "a desire to pick a quarrel that is not worth picking."

789 Finot, Louis-Jean. "Les Romans et la vie" (Novels and Life), LA REVUE MONDIALE, XCII (1 Aug 1929), 322.

[Brief review of the French translation of *The Painted Veil.*] [In French.]

790 Grein, J. T. "The World of the Theatre," ILLUSTRATED LONDON NEWS, CLXXIV (23 Feb 1929), 318.

The Sacred Flame is M's "finest play since *The Circle.*" [Review of the acting.]

791 Jennings, Richard. "The Theatre: *The Sacred Flame,*" SPECTATOR (Lond), CXLII (16 Feb 1929), 228-29.

Not really the "cynic" he is called, M offers here "poetical garnishing and a touch of sentimentality." Technically the play has the "finest economy of well-calculated effect." Some incidents are "unlikely," but the play is "almost painfully exciting."

792 Kessel, Joseph. "De Singapore à l'Athénée" (From Singapore to the Athénée), GRINGOIRE, 25 Oct 1929, p. 9.

Because of its blunt exposition, inexorable development, and weaving of action and feeling, the French adaptation of *The Letter* connects more immediately than either RAIN or *The Circle,* particularly with French audiences. [In French.]

793 Kutter, Hans. "W. Somerset Maugham—en profil," 1929, ed by N. G. Hahl, Hans Kutter, and Erik Therman (Helsinki: E. N. Tigerstedt, 1929), pp. 24-35.

As a short-story writer, M shows a sense for the dramatic, but he is certainly no playwright. He has written a few real novels and short stories ("Before the Party," "The Outstation," "The Force of Circumstance," "Rain"), but he has not written a single real play. His drama contains too much material which is either self-evident or borrowed goods. The audience is left with a bitter and sour taste in its mouth. M's most lovable book is *On A Chinese Screen.* [In Finnish.]

794 Lemmonier, Léon. "A travers les Théâtres" (In the Theaters), GRANDE REVUE, CXXVIII (Jan 1929), 511-13.

The Circle is a piece with incontestable literary qualities. [Review of the French adaptation, in French.]

795 Lemmonier, Léon. "A travers les Théâtres" (In the Theaters), GRANDE REVUE, CXXXI (Dec 1929), 334-35.

The last act of *The Letter* is banal, of no psychological interest, implausible. [Review of the French adaptation, in French.]

796 Marteaux, Jacques. "Les Spectacles à Paris≠Les Répétitions Generales≠A l'Athénée: *La Lettre* de Somerset Maugham" (Plays in Paris: Dress Rehearsals at the Athénée: *The Letter* by Somerset Maugham), LE JOURNAL DES DEBATS [POLITIQUES ET LITTERAIRES], 21 Oct 1929, p. 4.

The play simply answers the question why Leslie killed Gerald; it is a "thriller" which follows the progress of a letter, and is cleverly constructed. [Review of the French adaptation, in French.]

797 Martin du Gard, Maurice. "Le Théâtre" (The Theater), LES NOUVELLES LITTERAIRES, 26 Oct 1929, p. 12; rptd in CARTE ROUGE: LE THEATRE ET LA VIE, 1929-1930 (Paris: Flammarion, 1930), p. 126.

[Review of the French premiere of *The Letter.*] [In French.]

798 N-to, Olli. "Avioliittokomedia Ruotsalaisessa Teatterissa" (Marriage Comedy at the Swedish Theater), HELSINGIN SANOMAT, 15 Sept 1929, p. 16.

The first act of *The Constant Wife* is boring. The characters are introduced, but nothing happens. In the second act, there is suspense or dramatic tension which approaches tragedy. The wittiness of the dialogue and the amusing psychological observations make the second and third acts most enjoyable. [Review of the Finnish adaptation, in Finnish.]

799 "The Playhouse: *'The Sacred Flame,'* " TIMES (Lond), 9 Feb 1929, p. 8; rptd by Raymond Mander and Joe Mitchenson, eds, in THEATRICAL COMPANION TO MAUGHAM (Lond: Rockliff, 1955), pp. 213-14.

The play lacks "suppleness" and "the final sympathy and pity" of tragedy; but its narrative is "clear and vigorous," its principal characters have "abundant life," its suspense "is maintained without artificial contrivance," and its end "fulfils and justifies what has preceded it."

800 Prévost, Marcel. "Conteurs Etrangères modernes" (Modern Foreign Storytellers), GRINGOIRE, 4 Oct 1929, p. 4.

Many British writers are appreciated in France, but no writer has been so fully "assimilated" as M. [In French.]

801 "Les Répétitions Générales: *La Lettre* à l'Athénée (Dress Rehearsals: *The Letter* at the Athénée), COMOEDIA, 19 Oct 1929, p. 2.

[Review of the French adaptation.] [In French.]

802 Rey, Etienne: *"La Lettre"* (*The Letter*), COMOEDIA, 20 Oct 1929, pp. 1-2.

The play is not first-rate despite its picturesqueness, variety of themes, dramatic formulas. [Review of the French adaptation, in French.]

803* Rouveyre, André. "Théâtre" (Theater), LE MERCURE DE FRANCE, CCIX (1 Jan 1929), 155-58.

M's aim is to depict irresponsible old age in a sarcastic and bitter atmosphere. The repetition of events in the second generation is mechanical and gratuitous; the play is only a game and the parallelism between the two generations the weakest side of it. The end is slightly too forced to carry conviction. [Review of the French adaptation of *The Circle* by H. de Carbuccia.] [In French.]

804 Rouveyre, André. "Théâtre" (Theater), LE MERCURE DE FRANCE, CCXVI (15 Nov 1929), 181-82.

The French adaptation of *The Letter* is not boring but is inferior to RAIN, and, especially, *The Circle.* [In French.]

805 Sée, Edmond. "Les Lettres françaises" (French Letters), LA REVUE DE FRANCE, 9ème année, no. 6 (1 Dec 1929), 563-64.

The French translation of *The Letter* [play] is marvelously constructed and full of surprises. [In French.]

806 Souday, Paul. "Le Mouvement dramatique" (The Drama Movement), LA REVUE DE PARIS, 36ème année, no. 1 (15 Jan 1929), 463-64.

[Brief review of Horace de Carbuccia's adaptation of *The Circle.*] [In French.]

807 Speth, William. "Le Théâtre" (The Theater), LA REVUE MONDIALE, CXCIV (1 Nov 1929), 85.

[Brief review of the French adaptation of *The Letter.*] [In French.]

808 "Théâtres: Comment nait une collaboration?" (Theaters: How Is a Collaboration Begun?), COMOEDIA, 19 Oct 1929, p. 2.

[Article explaining how M and his French adaptor, Carbuccia, came to meet and work together.] [In French.]

809 "Thèâtres: *La Lettre*" (Plays: *The Letter*), LE TEMPS, 20 Oct 1929, p. 4.

The dress rehearsal was successful. [In French.]

810 "The Theatres: Realism Without Rawness," TRUTH (Lond), CV (20 Feb 1929), 334-35.

Long speeches and many turns of phrase endanger the tension of *The Sacred Flame.*

811 T[horp, Joseph]. "At the Play," PUNCH, CLXXVI (20 Feb 1929), 218.

The Sacred Flame is well-made, admirably told, "a problem play with a problem really worth solving."

812 V., H. "Kansallisteatterin englantilainen uutuus" (New English Play at the National Theater), SUOMEN SOSIALIDEMOKRAATTI, 17 Oct 1929, p. 6.

The Constant Wife is compiled with English exhaustiveness. One listens to the dialogue with pleasure, because it has been created with masculine intelligence, by a personality who enjoys his creative work. [Review of the Finnish adaptation, in Finnish.]

813 Vandérem, Fernand. "Les Lettres et la vie" (Letters and Life), LA REVUE DE FRANCE, 9ème année, no. 5 (1 Oct. 1929), 536-40.

In *The Casuarina Tree*, "The Outstation" must be regarded the "pearl" of the collection for its union of drama and comedy. [Review of the French translation, in French.]

1930

814 A., E. "Psykologist kriminaldrama på Kansan Näyttämo" (Psychological Crime Drama at the People's Stage), HUFVUDSTADSBLADET, 3 Oct 1930, p. 7.

The Letter rises to a higher artistic level than thrillers in general because of its intrigue and of the psychological analysis of its characterization. [Review of the Finnish adaptation, in Finnish.]

815 "Books: Beer & Skittles," TIME, XVI (6 Oct 1930), 79.

Cakes and Ale has "workmanlike" qualities. M "does not believe in 'great' books; has never written, will never write one. His habitual bitterness, whether natural or acquired, has become part of his stock-in-trade. He now uses it effectively, usually cloaks it in brusque but polite irony." [Story summary.]

816 "Books: Journeyman," TIME, XV (5 May 1930), 79-80.

"Exotic parts have a kind of fascination for Traveler Maugham, but little glamour. [*The Gentleman in the Parlour*] is consequently better reading than most such records." [Mainly summary of the contents.]

817 "*'The Breadwinner,'* at the Vaudeville," ILLUSTRATED LONDON NEWS, CLXXVII (11 Oct 1930), 636.

The play will not "suit all palates"; it is a "hard, bitter, occasionally overbrutal satire on youth." Provocative and interesting as the play is, its third act is "weak," especially in the two "seductions" of Battle.

818* Brewster, Dorothy and Angus Burrell. "Time Passes," ADVENTURE OR EXPERIENCE: FOUR ESSAYS ON CERTAIN WRITERS AND READERS OF NOVELS (NY: Columbia U P, 1930), pp. 37-75; rptd in MODERN FICTION (NY: Columbia U P, 1934), pp. 84-109.

Of Human Bondage is a "chronicle novel" which draws its themes from Spinoza.

819 Britten, Florence Haxton. "A Gentleman and a Writer," NEW YORK HERALD TRIBUNE BOOKS, 5 Oct 1930, p. 3.
In *Cakes and Ale,* M has "taken his fun where he finds it," and although the novel is not as "sturdy" as *Of Human Bondage* and *The Moon and Sixpence*, "it has wit—and cynical wisdom."

820* Brown, Ivor. "Private Lives," OBSERVER (Lond), 5 Oct 1930, p. 6.
In *Cakes and Ale,* "the study of the affable Kear and of the whole process whereby Driffield is canonized is exquisite in its justice. The style is a model of irony controlled. Mr. Maugham never raises his voice too high, nor brandishes his arm too widely. It is true that he stops too soon. We never know how Kear finally composed the embarrassing muddle of Driffield's life. We are left suddenly in the air; but the air is Alpine in its power to sting and quicken and enchant."

821* Brown, Ivor. "The Week's Theatres," OBSERVER (Lond), 5 Oct 1930, p. 15.
In *The Breadwinner,* M turns the tables on the old story of the turbulent son who will not enter the father's business but writes free verse on a liberal allowance: "the father . . . has the bag and baggage exit." But Charles Battle comes in to the play's first act too late; the young people shout their egotism too loud and too long. *Home and Beauty,* revived, is "one of the wittiest trifles of our time."

822 B[utcher], F[anny]. " *'Cakes and Ale'* Brews Up Book Selling Squall," CHICAGO DAILY TRIBUNE, 25 Oct 1930, p. 10.
"The novel . . . is not . . . one of Mr. Maugham's most brilliant pieces of work. It does not touch *Of Human Bondage*. . . . It has pages of perfectly priceless writing about writing, but it is not a classic."

823* " *'Cakes and Ale'*: Somerset Maugham Satirizes the Literary Career," SPRINGFIELD SUNDAY UNION AND REPUBLICAN (Mass), 5 Oct 1930, p. 7E.
M's satire on two authors is followed by a narrative equivalent to a short story, and the satire and the narrative are not "essentially connected." M's wit is not as "fresh and incisive" as it has been, and he is guilty of some "indelicacies." In sum, his "petulant jest does not come off."

824 Cartier, Maurice. "A l'étalage" (On Display), GRINGOIRE, 14 Nov 1930, p. 4.
Ashenden is different from cheap spy literature in which spies are worldly "tycoons" travelling in state with the indispensable "femme fatale." M's short stories illustrate the despicable hunted lives of informers. [Review of the French translation, in French.]

825 Colton, Arthur. "Travelling with Composure," SATURDAY REVIEW OF LITERATURE, VI (28 June 1930), 1159.

M's *The Gentleman in the Parlour* is agreeable reading; it displays an effortless ease of style and a perfect telling of anecdotes. M notes "that the British Empire is tottering because the ruling Briton has become a sentimentalist."

826 Coxe, Howard. "Veal and Vinegar," NEW REPUBLIC, LXIV (22 Oct 1930), 273-75.

In *Cakes and Ale,* M might have made more of his material. Driffield is a nebulous figure, though Rosie, the barmaid wife, shows M at his best. In the similarity of the temper of the minds behind the novels, *Cakes and Ale* is reminiscent of THE WAY OF ALL FLESH.

827 Dottin, Paul. "Les Lettres étrangères" (Foreign Letters), LA REVUE DE FRANCE, 10ème année, no. 4 (15 July 1930), 365-72.

[Review of *The Gentleman in the Parlour,* primarily summarizing the book's contents.] [In French.]

828 Eaton, Walter Prichard. THE DRAMA IN ENGLISH (NY: Charles Scribner's Sons, 1930), p. 291.

M's *The Circle* along with Galsworthy's SKIN GAME and Shaw's SAINT JOAN are the only examples of worthy drama in the decade before and the decade after World War I.

829* Eppinger, Dóra. W. SOMERSET MAUGHAM: REGÉNY ÉS SHORT-STORY. A Kir. Magy. Pázmány Péter Tudományegyetem Angol Philologiai Intézetének Kiadványai, III. (W. SOMERSET MAUGHAM: NOVEL AND SHORT STORY. The Editions of the Institute for English Philology of the Royal Hungarian Peter Pázmány University, III.) Budapest: Királyi Magyar Egyetemi Nyomda, 1930.

An analysis of M's art and skills shows how they result not—as Paul Dottin would have it in SOMERSET MAUGHAM ET SES ROMANS (1928)—in depth and originality of thought, but in "effective routine." M is not a legitimate literary descendant of Wells, Galsworthy, Bennett, or Conrad; nor is he representative of any one modern literary group. Rather, M incorporates the most popular qualities of various writers and groups of the twentieth century, and effects a compromise between them "for the sake of success." His "English realism" results in a predilection for the narrative and in a recognition of the importance of plot over "psychological romanticism"; it also leads him to a certain "sociological cynicism," which, however, is unlike that of his literary predecessors or contemporaries in that it is not "didactic." The English short story suits his purpose, and the pulse of the short story is to be found in his novels as well. But in all of his works the idea of success is M's calculated guideline. He omits controversial elements and attempts no modern literary experiments which might hinder or damage that success. For example, in his "Eastern" stories, M capitalizes upon a vogue made current by Kipling, but without Kipling's consideration of imperialism. The East becomes more often than not a mere backdrop, evidenced (1) by M's lack of interest in the culture and philosophy peculiar to the East, and (2) by the absence of lyrical expansiveness in his perfunctory topographical descriptions. In *Of Human Bondage,* Philip questions life, but art and philosophy are alien to his compromise with life as a doctor; and his philosophical conclusion is safely half-nihilistic and half-optimistic. In sum, then, M's goal of "success" is demonstrable in his general chronological ordering of events, his calculated avoidance of experiment in plot construction and characterization, in his refusal to pursue philosophical speculation deeply, in his allegiance to life rather than art, in his reluctance to use symbols, and in his plain style. [In Hungarian.]

830* Farjeon, Herbert. "The London Stage," GRAPHIC, CXXX (11 Oct 1930), 73.

"In the thing he hates, Mr. Maugham has rather lost sight of the thing he loves. When Mr. Battle [of *The Breadwinner*], actually possessing in his pocket the means of saving himself, allows himself to be hammered on the Stock Exchange, what is it that gives Mr. Maugham most satisfaction? Is it the idea that Mr. Battle, the breadwinner, will now cut adrift from Golders-Greenery and embark alone on the seas of mystery and adventure? Or is it that Mr. Battle's family will have to go without their *marrons glacés?* Everything points to the latter."

831 Field, Louise M. "Somerset Maugham Comes Back from Mandalay," NEW YORK TIMES BOOK REVIEW, 4 May 1930, p. 6.

The Gentleman in the Parlour is an "exceptionally varied, exceptionally colorful" portrait, "made more entertaining by the author's comments."

832 G., D. F. *"Cakes and Ale,"* BOSTON EVENING TRANSCRIPT, 19 Nov 1930, p. 5.

This is the "season's most effective novel, with satire cleverly tempered by discretion and sincerity admirable because of its restraint."

833 "A Gauguin of Golders Green," TRUTH (Lond), CVIII (8 Oct 1930), 587.

In *The Breadwinner,* M's control slips, notably in the unduly emphasized selfishness of the family in Act I.

834* *"The Gentleman in the Parlour,"* TIMES LITERARY SUPPLEMENT (Lond), 20 March 1930, p. 230.

"While he [M] can recreate the atmosphere of those lonely jungle paths and faraway villages in the hills, he has no less skill in reconstructing those personal encounters that to him are one of the greatest pleasures of travel." Although there is little practical information, the unexpectedness and spontaneity and freshness of the character sketches—such as that of the Buddhist monks watching a game of patience—apparently more than make up for it. "For Maugham sight-seeing has few charms; he prefers impressions to facts. . . ."

835 Gibson, Ashley. "Out of the East," BOOKMAN (Lond), LXXVIII (April 1930), 42.

M banishes his "cynicism" and in *The Gentleman in the Parlour* offers a blend of portraiture, drama, sensitive and piquant comment—all at their best.

836 Gore-Brown, Robert. "The Theatre: Parents' Assistant," SATURDAY REVIEW (Lond), CL (4 Oct 1930), 403.

The story of Charles Battle's rebellion, upon finding his family unbearable, "makes of *The Breadwinner,* otherwise not one of Maugham's best plays, a saga." [Play summarized with approval.]

837 Gorman, Herbert. "Quarterly Reviews," CENTURY, N. S. XCVIII (Spring 1930), 310-12.

The Gentleman in the Parlour is "a sensitive man's adventure and set down as such, and that . . . is the best kind of travel book."

838 H., E. "Dramatists' Novels: Maugham and Van Druten," BOOKMAN (Lond), LXXIX (Nov 1930), 155.

In *Cakes and Ale,* M has drawn Rosie so well she overshadows Driffield.

839 Hansen, Harry. "The First Reader," NEW YORK WORLD, 3 Oct 1930, p. 12.

"We have not had a good, ironic novel such as [*Cakes and Ale*] in a long, long time. The story is slight; the humor is entirely in cynical characterization. . . . It's a book for those to whom the writing, making and reading of books is a world theater. But it involves recognition that some of its best passages are based upon a cruel and cynical attack upon the dead."

840 Howe, Susanne. WILHELM MEISTER AND HIS ENGLISH KINSMEN: APPRENTICES TO LIFE (NY: Columbia U P, 1930), pp. 287-90.

Of Human Bondage is a descendant of the "old apprentice tradition." Philip Carey's ideal of life, his raw confrontation with life, his crises and final reconciliation bear resemblances to Wilhelm Meister's experiences.

841 "In the Far East: Mr. Somerset Maugham's Travels," TIMES (Lond), 11 March 1930, p. 10.

A dramatist, M is more interested in people than facts, and *The Gentle-*

man in the Parlour is valuable for its portraits, scenes, and varied moods.

842* Jennings, Richard. "The Theatre: *The Breadwinner*," SPECTATOR (Lond), CXLV (18 Oct 1930), 525.

"Maugham reminds one, this time, of the lazy schoolboy who shows up a patched copy: so good, in this passage, that one longs to award him top marks as the best of our living writers of comedy; so feebly farcical, in another, that one longs to rap him over the knuckles." Clever "satirical manner (parodying the tragic Strindberg) of reversing judgment upon the troops of wronged women, who have been pitied as slaves to tyrannical man!" "Admirable theme," but too much "padding" and too many " 'unfunny' horrors."

843 "The Leisure Arts," OUTLOOK AND INDEPENDENT, CLVI (12 Nov 1930), 427.

Cakes and Ale "will hardly go onto the shelf beside *Of Human Bondage*."

844* MacCarthy, Desmond. "Two Comedies," NEW STATESMAN, XXXVI (11 Oct 1930), 14-15; rptd as "Somerset Maugham and Noël Coward," in HUMANITIES. Preface by Lord David Cecil (NY: Oxford U P, 1954), pp. 94-98.

Though no Ibsen, M turns "topsy-turvy" the Ibsenite theme of A DOLL'S HOUSE. "It is quite a good idea for a comedy, but *The Breadwinner* is not quite a good play": although the last two acts hold the attention, the first lacks entertaining dialogue, and the four cousins are "deplorably silly and boring."

845* Marchand, Leslie A. "Maugham Paints a Sardonic Portrait," NEW YORK TIMES BOOK REVIEW, 12 Oct 1930, p. 7.

One of the characteristics of M is that he is often "transparently, unblushingly autobiographical." His technique is disconcerting, sometimes devastating in its unmasking of the secret and irrational currents of our lives. In *Cakes and Ale,* he has exposed the skeleton in the cupboard of the Grand Old Man of English Literature, the last of the Victorians. But every other character he has drawn from life. There is something bracing about the sincerity of his style which strips life to the bone, revealing not only cancerous growth, but the healthy flesh as well.

846 Meissner, Paul. "Kulturprobleme des modernen englischen Dramas" (Cultural Problems in the Modern English Drama), ZEITSCHRIFT FÜR FRANZÖSISCHEN UND ENGLISCHEN UNTERRICHT, XXIX (1930), 9-25, especially p. 15.

[Brief mention and high praise of M's *The Sacred Flame* as the story of a mother's love.] [In German.]

847* Mortimer, Raymond. "The Drama: Somerset Maugham," NATION AND THE ATHENAEUM, XLVIII (11 Oct 1930), 45.
M's strength lies in his "wit," which is merely common sense, "the truth about subjects about which it is customary to lie"—particularly as this wit is directed against women's "hypocrisy . . . hardness . . . selfishness . . . and their unfairness." In the revived *Home and Beauty,* M produces a brilliant farce on the foibles of women; in one weak scene of *The Breadwinner,* however, M does not take the trouble to be original and reverts to the motif of the earlier play.

848 "Mr. Maugham as Traveller," NEW STATESMAN, XXXIV (8 March 1930), 712.
In *The Gentleman in the Parlour,* M knows what effects he is capable of producing, and what he intends to do. His descriptions are often "felicitous" and have great "honesty"; particularly are these qualities evident in his account of a journey on horseback through the Shan States and of his brief sojourn at King Tung.

849 N-o, Olli. "Ensi-ilta Kansan Näyttämöllä" (First Night at the People's Stage), HELSINGIN SANOMAT, 3 Oct 1930, p. 7.
The Letter shows that M knows how to make a play: there is plenty of suspense and psychological analysis, though neither is very profound. [Review of the Finnish adaptation, in Finnish.]

850 "New Novels," SATURDAY REVIEW (Lond), CL (4 Oct 1930), 409.
Characterization in *Cakes and Ale* is accurate. M "has the dramatist's eye" and, "with a keen perception of the ironies of existence, indicates the smile and the glance with which personal encounters are handled in real life." The narrator's defect is not "cheap cynicism," but "a sort of defensiveness of spirit, masked behind his irony and reserve." [Plot summary.]

851 "New Novels," TIMES LITERARY SUPPLEMENT (Lond), 2 Oct 1930, p. 778.
In *Cakes and Ale,* the conflict in purpose between Kear and Ashenden is amusing, but the digressions on literature, writing, and writers are unfortunate.

852 Norman, Sylvia. "Reviews: Trio," NATION AND THE ATHENAEUM, XLVI (8 March 1930), 768.
In *The Gentleman in the Parlour,* "Mr. Maugham is the perfect literary traveller. He hates facts, but out of his own complex, mellow artistry he fashions a narrative in which incidents and character sketches are like polished gems on a chain of individual workmanship."

853 "Our Booking-Office," PUNCH, CLXXVIII (2 April 1930), 391.
The Gentleman in the Parlour is a "fascinating record," though "that contentment with incompleteness which gives something of a sub-human air to all Impressionist pictures is present."

854 "Our Booking-Office," PUNCH, CLXXIX (29 Oct 1930), 503.
Cakes and Ale is an "entertaining trifle."

855 P., J-o *"Pyhä Liekki" (The Sacred Flame),* AAMULEHTI, 31 Jan 1930, p. 5.
The greatest weakness in the play's construction is the fictitious position of Mrs. Tabret. The naturalistic treatment proves successful towards the end, but the first act remains a mere exposition. [Review of the Finnish adaptation, in Finnish.]

856* Partridge, Bellamy. "Rare Traveller," NEW YORK HERALD TRIBUNE BOOKS, 20 April 1930, p. 5.
In *The Gentleman in the Parlour,* M is "genial and tolerant"; he omits "useless description," but never overlooks a fellow who "has a story in him." More metaphysically inclined in recent years, M "has put his finger very neatly through some of the tissue-paper arguments on which the West has based its claims to some very considerable mansions in the skies." Never was M more "readable" or so "wholly delightful."

857* Pawlowski, Gaston de. "Mr. Ashenden, Agent Secret" (Mr. Ashenden, Secret Agent), GRINGOIRE, 5 Dec 1930, p. 4.
M is becoming the most "Parisian" British author. If travel tends to make Frenchmen recreate the world in their image, to the British it is simply an enlargement of their knowledge. M is typically British in his decent handling of the scenario of *Ashenden*: he remains aloof from the story, is never involved in the development of the plot. The French live through their books, make no difference between the fictitious world and the world of adventure. M will write a masterpiece when he has nothing "to say" or narrate, when he allows his thoughts to develop themselves in complete freedom. [In French.]

858* Priestley, J. B. "A Letter from England," SATURDAY REVIEW OF LITERATURE, VII (1 Nov 1930), 299.
The Breadwinner is only the beginning of a comedy, not a complete one. The first Mrs. Driffield is "the only real character" in *Cakes and Ale.* Though M discourages readers from identifying Driffield in this novel with Thomas Hardy, he has given Driffield too many factual resemblances to Hardy to make his own simple denial truly convincing. M is undervalued

in England as a novelist perhaps because of his popularity as a playwright.

859 Pritchett, V. S. "The Artist in Travel," CHRISTIAN SCIENCE MONITOR, 26 April 1930, p. 7.

In *The Gentleman in the Parlour,* there is nothing portentous about M's satisfaction with the Eastern world; he sees it as a "comedy of manners and customs, touched here and there with a bit of a problem play or a flare of melodrama; sentimental in no unpleasant sense, but not quite successfully urbane."

860 Pritchett, V. S. "Fiction: Five Established Novelists," LITERARY SUPPLEMENT TO THE SPECTATOR (Lond), CXLV (18 Oct 1930), 554.

Cakes and Ale is written with "coolness and malice." M exposes the "humbug and nonsense" about "established authors" with biting irony. Although M's "trapesings to and fro in his memory of Driffield are decidedly mechanical," the book is still "delightful."

861 R., H. "Domestic Interiors: Three Current Plays," BOOKMAN (Lond), LXXIX (Nov 1930), 154.

In *The Breadwinner,* M's ability to gain our sympathy at the Breadwinner's escape from his children is praiseworthy.

862 Rascoe, Burton. "Among the New Books," ARTS AND DECORATION, XXXIV (Dec 1930), 100, 104.

In *Cakes and Ale,* the portrayal of Rosie as the "Cyprian Venus incarnate" is praiseworthy.

863 S., A. W. "Recent Books: Skeleton in the Cupboard," NEW YORKER, VI (11 Oct 1930), 88.

M's material is good, and *Cakes and Ale* has the "sweep and feeling of an extraordinary work."

864 S., R. *"The Gentleman in the Parlour,"* BOSTON EVENING TRANSCRIPT, 24 May 1930, p. 5.

The observations and the style in which they are written are both excellent.

865 " *'The Sacred Flame'* in Rome," TIMES (Lond), 11 March 1930, p. 14.

The success of M's play in Rome has alarmed the Vatican's OSSERVATORE ROMANO with its "exotic heresies in which life belongs to the weak and amoral."

866 Schneider, Isidor. "Tranquil Journeys," NATION (NY), CXXXI (30 July 1930), 129.

The Gentleman in the Parlour is a depressing, languid and tepid book;

the two fairy tales it includes serve no other purpose than to prove to Mr. M how clever he is.

867 Shipp, Horace. "Mirth and Magic," ENGLISH REVIEW, LI (Nov 1930), 651-52.

In *The Breadwinner,* M's hatred of "wives in general and the younger generation *en masse*" defeats his dramatic purpose.

868 "Shorter Notices," NEW STATESMAN, XXXVI (11 Oct 1930), 28.

In *Cakes and Ale,* M's dexterity does not conceal "the thinness of his theme"; he tells his story with "wit and unfailing intelligence, but never a sign that the problem he is handling has, too, its profundities."

869 T., O. "Kirjeen salaisuus" (Secret of the Letter), UUSI SUOMI, 3 Oct 1930, p. 6.

One good play [*The Constant Wife*] is followed by a disappointment: the Finnish adaptation of *The Letter* leaves the spectator cold. [In Finnish.]

870 T[horp, Joseph]. "At the Play," PUNCH, CLXXIX (15 Oct 1930), 442-43.

In *The Breadwinner,* M "is never quite unserious, and the velvet glove of his flippancy always hides a sharp-pointed nail or two. And the young things have been asking for it."

871 Tomlinson, Kathleen C. "New Novels," NATION AND THE ATHENAEUM, XLVIII (25 Oct 1930), 140.

For all its "cleverness," *Cakes and Ale* "is a confession of lack of creative gift."

872* Van Doren, Mark. "Thomas Hardy Veiled," NATION (NY), CXXXI (29 Oct 1930), 475; rptd in THE MAUGHAM ENIGMA, ed by Klaus W. Jonas (NY: Citadel P, 1954), pp. 146-48.

In *Cakes and Ale,* M has written a true and witty book; "very slight," it abounds with observations and epigrams that are "always clever, always bitter, and frequently wise."

873 "Vaudeville Theatre: *'The Breadwinner,'*" TIMES (Lond), 1 Oct 1930, p. 10; rptd by Raymond Mander and Joe Mitchenson, eds, in THEATRICAL COMPANION TO MAUGHAM (Lond: Rockliff, 1955), pp. 219-20.

M has shown how he might have written Strindberg's THE FATHER.

874* "Wanderer into Many Lands: *The Gentleman in the Parlour,*" LITERARY SUPPLEMENT TO THE SPECTATOR (Lond), CXLIV (22 March 1930), 495.

The book is "good reading and good value." M's attitude toward the Empire is cynical, but "not all his cynicism can conceal his underlying faith." M never "underlines or overemphasizes"; he is interested in people, not in "giving a picture" of the East or in moral precepts. The reader will not find facts, "but his personality will have been enriched by contact with a mind that is both subtle and sensitive," not to mention "amusing."

875* Waugh, Evelyn. "The Books You Read," GRAPHIC, CXXX (11 Oct 1930), 74.

In *Cakes and Ale,* M's "poise" is both a triumph and a limitation; never boring, never clumsy, never shocking, at the same time his compositions never display "those sudden transcendent flashes of passion and beauty which less competent novelists occasionally attain."

876 Way, Oliver. "Modern Life in Books," GRAPHIC, CXXVII (15 March 1930), 426.

In *The Gentleman in the Parlour,* M's true worth rests on his skill as an observer rather than on his ability to create, but his blend of observation and construction will outlive the more "imagined," but less polished, work of some of his contemporaries.

877 Went, Stanley. "To the Life," SATURDAY REVIEW OF LITERATURE, VII (18 Oct 1930), 240.

Whether Edward Driffield was modelled after Thomas Hardy or not makes no difference to a reader's enjoyment of *Cakes and Ale,* for the characters are large and true to life. The book is "a brilliant piece of writing, with a deal of human nature and some acute and iconoclastic literary criticism in it."

1931

878 "Action Against Woman Novelist," TIMES (Lond), 6 Oct 1931, p. 5.

M issues a writ of libel against Mrs. Elinor Mordaunt for her novel, FULL CIRCLE [published in the United States under the title, GIN AND BITTERS, by A. Riposte (1931).] [See entry in this bibliography under Riposte, A.].

879 Atkinson, J. Brooks. "The Play," NEW YORK TIMES, 23 Sept 1931, p. 19.

In *The Breadwinner,* M leaves his theme "where he languidly picked it up"; he is too bored and tired, and merely shuffles about "in the old bag of tricks."

880 Austruy, Henri. "Révue dramatique" (Drama Review), LA NOUVELLE REVUE, Series IV, CXLVI (Nov 1931), 69-70.

[Primarily a plot summary and evaluation of the actors' performances in Horace de Carbuccia's adaptation of *The Sacred Flame*.] [In French.]

881 Bason, Frederick T. A BIBLIOGRAPHY OF THE WRITINGS OF WILLIAM SOMERSET MAUGHAM (Lond: Unicorn P, 1931).
[A bibliography of M's booklength publications up to 1930.]

882 Beauplan, Robert de. "Les Théâtres: *Le Cyclone*" (Theaters: *The Sacred Flame*), L'ILLUSTRATION, 89ème année, no. 4623 (10 Oct 1931), 206.
Pathos and mystery in the French adaptation of *The Sacred Flame* are the same as in THE TRIAL OF MARY DUGAN, although the case which is investigated, with a clever progression, does not pass the family circle. [In French.]

883* Bellessort, André. "Chronique dramatique" (Drama Chronicle), LE JOURNAL DES DEBATS, HEBDOMADAIRE, 1 Oct 1931, pp. 597-98; rptd as "La Semaine dramatique: *Le Cyclone*" (The Week's Drama: *The Sacred Flame*), LE JOURNAL DES DEBATS [POLITIQUES ET LITTERAIRES], 5 Oct 1931, p. 3.
In the French adaptation, the adapter, Carbuccia, softens the harsh British flavor of the original. Mrs. Tabret's confession about her nightly visits to her son is unfair, however, for the play is a detective story, and no element in such a plot must be unknown at the start. [In French.]

884 Benchley, Robert. "The Theatre: Maybe It Was the Heat," NEW YORKER, VII (3 Oct 1931), 34.
In *The Breadwinner,* there are "six or seven good lines repeated over and over again for two and a half hours."

885 Bickley, Francis. "Books to Read," GRAPHIC, CXXXIV (10 Oct 1931), 33.
In *First Person Singular,* the best of the stories is "The Round Dozen."

886* Boissy, Gabriel. "L'interprétation du *Cyclone*" (Interpretation of *The Sacred Flame*), COMOEDIA, 3 Oct 1931, 2.
The staging of the French adaptation was too sumptuous for psychological drama; the interpretation was too solemn. The first act is slow; the second, except for a few lengthy passages, too accelerated. [In French.]

887 "Book Notes," NEW REPUBLIC, LXVII (20 May 1931), 27.
GIN AND BITTERS by A. Riposte has "only spindly legs of its own, and even as a parody it falls pretty flat, the author's knowledge of Mr. Maugham apparently being confined to gossip and the internal evidence of his writings. The sum total is neither malicious enough to be amusing, nor penetrating enough to be of much interest."

888* "Books in Brief," FORUM, LXXXVI (Nov 1931), x.
M's stories may be "hollow, artificial, deficient in genuine emotional force, but one is guaranteed their technical perfection. In [*First Person Singular*], he is at his best when he essays pure and ironic comedy — as in 'The Round Dozen,' 'Jane,' and 'The Creative Impulse.' In his more serious ventures, where the deeper human emotions are involved, he merely makes one nostalgic for better days. What, one wonders, has happened to the man who wrote *Of Human Bondage*? Why should he have traded his heritage for so slick a mess of pottage?"

889 "Books in Brief," NATION (NY), CXXXII (29 April 1931), 484.
GIN AND BITTERS by A. Riposte "loses all its force by being completely infantile in its anger."

890 "Books: Maugham Mauled," TIME, XVII (13 April 1931), 79-80.
The hero of GIN AND BITTERS by A. Riposte is a distorted portrait of M himself. In the novel, M is ridiculed for his unflattering portraits of Thomas Hardy [Edward Driffield] and Hugh Walpole [Alroy Kear] in *Cakes and Ale* and criticized for his unscrupulous use, in his novels, of details from the private lives of his friends and acquaintances.

891 Bourdon, Charles. "Les Pièces de Théâtre: *Le Cyclone*" (Plays: *The Sacred Flame*), LA REVUE DES LECTURES, 19ème année, no. 11 (15 Nov 1931), 1335-37.
[A neutral review of the French adaptation, quoting other critics who condemn the play for its immorality and absurdity.] [In French.]

892 Bourdon, Charles. "Les Romans: *Ashenden*" (Novels: *Ashenden*), LA REVUE DES LECTURES, 19ème année, no. 2 (15 Feb 1931), 166.
The book is a detective story, with little concern about morality. [Review of the French translation, in French.]

893 Brande, Dorothea. "Novels and Short Stories," BOOKMAN (NY), LXXIV (Nov 1931), 336-37.
First Person Singular is generally good, though one notes M's fear of showing emotion and his anxiety for avoiding platitude to such an extent that his situations become "unbelievable."

894* Brisson, Pierre. "Chronique Théâtrale: Théâtre des Ambassadeurs: *Le Cyclone*" (Dramatic Chronicle: Ambassadeurs Theater: *The Sacred Flame*), LE TEMPS, 5 Oct 1931, p. 3.
The play, in the French adaptation, is a story of detection, yet a solemn story used to illustrate a point of conscience. Because it develops on two

planes, one higher than the other, the play "limps" and is disproportionate in its impact; the play switches from the question "Who did it?" to "Why was it done?" and one counteracts the other. If the criminal's name is given at first, there will be no suspense; if it is withheld to the end, the moral case is confined to a last-minute confession by an old woman. M unwisely chose the latter, and his play resulted in a dilatory detective story and a moral drama much too short. [In French.]

895* Britten, Florence Haxton. "Consecrated Butchery," New York Herald Tribune Books, 5 April 1931, p. 6.
Gin and Bitters by A. Riposte is "tentatively" suspected to have been written by Rose Macaulay as a satire on M, which is not so much an attack of fencing "as of consecrated butchery."

896 Britten, Florence Haxton. "Never? Well Hardly Ever," New York Herald Tribune Books, 27 Sept 1931, p. 2.
In *First Person Singular,* M's passionate concern is for human nature, which he views with "delicate, intense disdain," believing that the codes by which men, and especially women, live are "silly in the extreme." "The Alien Corn" and "Jane" are the best of the six stories; only "The Creative Impulse" falls short of being memorable.

897 Butcher, Fanny. " '*Cakes and Ale*' Defended Now by Own Author," Chicago Daily Tribune, 26 Sept 1931, p. 12.
In *First Person Singular,* the brightest of the six stories is "The Creative Impulse."

898 C., R. M. "Books, Books, Books," New Yorker, VII (19 Sept 1931), 68.
First Person Singular is "not profound . . . but written with . . . grace and suavity."

899 Carb, David. "Seen on the Stage," Vogue, LXXVIII (15 Nov 1931), 116.
The Breadwinner "maunders, goes kittenish, resorts to silly and irrelevant ruses, and gets nowhere. The last act should be the first."

900 Cartier, Maurice. "A l'Etalage" (On Display), Gringoire, 4 Dec 1931, p. 4.
[Brief mention of the French translation of *Cakes and Ale,* citing M's original but simple and sophisticated technique.] [In French.]

901 Chatfield-Taylor, Otis. "The Latest Plays," Outlook and Independent, CLIX (7 Oct 1931), 182.
The Breadwinner is a "slender tale," written lazily, but still better than the great majority of successful plays.

902 Chesterton, A. K. "The Bishop Cries 'Immoral,'" ADVENTURES IN DRAMATIC APPRECIATION. With an Introduction by W. B. Kempling (Lond: T. Werner Laurie, [1931]), pp. 29-33.
[A vindication of *The Sacred Flame* against the Bishop of London's charge that the play was "the most immoral play in town."]

903 Cookman, A. V. "London Also Has a New Maugham Play," NEW YORK TIMES, 11 Oct 1931, VIII: 2.
Bartlett Cormack's dramatization of THE PAINTED VEIL is "second-rate . . . because it pretends to be on a much higher plane than it actually is." As it becomes harder to believe in Kitty's spiritual development, it becomes more delightful to listen to Waddington, whose cynical wit is reminiscent of M's.

904 Cru, Robert-L. "La Saison Théâtrale à Londres" (The Theatrical Season in London), LE TEMPS, 27 July 1931, p. 2.
The British stage faces a crisis: there are many licentious plays being produced, and the film industry rivals and influences stagecraft. M's *The Breadwinner* is a reaction against the light immoral plays of young dramatists. [General survey of the theatrical season in England.] [In French.]

905 D., F. "*Le Cyclone* aux Ambassadeurs" (*The Sacred Flame* at the Ambassadeurs), LE TEMPS, 3 Oct 1931, p. 5.
M tries to arouse suspicion about Stella, yet after the first act of the French adaptation everybody whispered the real name of the murderess. This was fun, the fun of children discovering something behind curtains. But it prevented one from speaking about the mother's case, which ought to be the major subject. [In French.]

906 Dangerfield, George. "Fiction," BOOKMAN (NY), LXXIII (May 1931), 320-21.
GIN AND BITTERS by A. Riposte is "a book of straw, and of straw swayed by malice, and by malice to no particular end."

907 David, André. *"Le Cyclone" (The Sacred Flame),* GRINGOIRE, 9 Oct 1931, p. 9.
The French adaptation is swift-moving, building act by act to a final scene whose pathos is not unworthy of Greek tragedies. [In French.]

908 David, André. *"La Lettre" (The Letter),* GRINGOIRE, 13 Feb 1931, p. 9.
[Review of the revival of the French adaptation.]

909 De Casseres, Benjamin. "Broadway to Date," ARTS AND DECORATION, XXXVI (Dec 1931), 68.

The Breadwinner is "all humorous and laughable and shiningly epigrammatic; but it has the real sting in it of great comedy."

910 Delini, Jean. "Les Avant-Premières Avant *Le Cyclone*" (The Pre-opening Performances: Before *The Sacred Flame*), COMOEDIA, 1 Oct 1931, p. 2.

[Review of the French adaptation.] [In French.]

911 Destez, Robert. "Spectacles Echos et propos: Reprise" (Entertainments: News Items and Remarks: Revival) LE FIGARO, 16 Feb 1931, p. 6.

The revival of the French adaptation of *The Letter* is a model play, though not so original as some critics would have us believe and despite the many imitations of its scene-cuttings which have followed. [In French.]

912 d'Houville, Gérard. "Chronique des Théâtres de Paris: Ambassadeurs *Le Cyclone*" (Drama Chronicles of Paris: Ambassadeurs-*The Sacred Flame*), LE FIGARO, 9 Oct 1931, p. 5.

The play is entrancing and "mathematical" and gives evidence of M's sense of vigorous construction, keen pathos, and irony. [Review of the French adaptation, in French.]

913 d'Houville, Gérard. "Chronique des Thèâtres de Paris Athénée Reprise de *La Lettre*" (Drama Chronicle of Paris Athénée Revival of *The Letter*), LE FIGARO, 16 Feb 1931, p. 5.

The revival of the French adaptation has obtained the same success as it did during its first two hundred performances. [In French.]

914 Dilly Tante [Pseudonym for Stanley J. Kunitz]. LIVING AUTHORS: A BOOK OF BIOGRAPHIES (NY: H. W. Wilson, 1931), pp. 257-58.

[Biographical portrait of M up to the time of *Cakes and Ale* (1930).]

915 Dodd, Lee Wilson. "Set of Six," SATURDAY REVIEW OF LITERATURE, VIII (17 Oct 1931), 206.

Among the stories in *First Person Singular* displaying M's customary craftsmanship are two superb pieces—"Jane," a comedy, and "The Alien Corn," a tragedy. The tone of M's writing, however, is "clear, cold, charmless, efficient," and his preface reveals truculent feelings toward critics.

916 Dottin, Paul. LA LITTERATURE ANGLAISE (ENGLISH LITERATURE) (Paris: Armand Colin, 1931), pp. 176, 196.

[Discussions of M's plays, RAIN and *The Letter,* and fiction, *Mrs. Craddock, Of Human Bondage, The Moon and Sixpence, The Trembling of a Leaf, The Painted Veil,* and *Cakes and Ale.*]

917 Dubech, Lucien. "Le Théâtre" (The Theater), LA REVUE UNIVERSELLE, XLVII:15 (1 Nov 1931), 383-84.

The Sacred Flame is a "police drama" with tragic pretensions. When M decides to "hit hard," he should also "hit fairly." [Review of the French adaptation, in French.]

918 "Entertainments: The Theatres," TIMES (Lond), 31 Aug 1931, p. 8.

The four-week festival of M's plays at Croydon will include *The Land of Promise, The Circle, Home and Beauty,* and *The Breadwinner.*

919 Farjeon, Herbert. "The London Stage," GRAPHIC, CXXXIII (3 Oct 1931), 470.

Up to a point, Bartlett Cormack's dramatization of THE PAINTED VEIL "may be recognized as a thoroughly saleable, if not particularly high-quality, article"; but the end lets down, "for we are given a very halting happy ending instead of the touch of bitterness native to Mr. Maugham."

920 *"First Person Singular,"* BOOKMAN (Lond), LXXXI (Nov 1931), 140.

The themes of M's stories are "trivial and even a little threadbare," and the stories themselves need only half the space allowed them. The book's real interest lies in M's "asides" in which he sweeps away "sentimental conventions and pretences."

921 *"First Person Singular,"* NEW REPUBLIC, LXVIII (21 Oct 1931), 280.

The characters appear too insignificant to be real, and the author appears to dislike them.

922 Frantel, Max. "Une Reprise à l'Athénée *La Lettre*" (A Revival at the Athénée: *The Letter*), COMOEDIA, 15 Feb 1931, p. 2.

The revived French adaptation succeeds because of Carbuccia's skilful adaptation of the dialogue.

923 " 'GIN AND BITTERS' Held Up: English Edition Called Off After Friends of Maugham Protest," NEW YORK TIMES, 7 May 1931, p. 26.

Elinor Mordaunt was prevailed upon not to publish her novel [presumably a satire on M] in England after its vogue in the U. S. [See, also, Elinor Mordaunt, "GIN AND BITTERS," NEW YORK TIMES, 14 May 1931, p. 22.]

924 Gould, Gerald. "New Novels," OBSERVER (Lond), 20 Sept 1931, p. 6.

Elinor Mordaunt's FULL CIRCLE [published in the United States as GIN

AND BITTERS by A. Riposte] is "a satire which, if aimed at a living person, would defeat its object rather than its objective."

925 Gould, Gerald. "New Novels," OBSERVER (Lond), 4 Oct 1931, p. 8.

In *First Person Singular,* the stories are not on the same scale or in the same tradition as *Of Human Bondage;* these are "slight . . . almost genial . . . and illustrate the author's quick, direct, rather terrifying competence. He is a master of his craft; and he knows a lot, if sometimes perhaps not quite enough, about human nature."

926 Graham, Gladys. "More Bitters than Gin," SATURDAY REVIEW OF LITERATURE, VII (11 April 1931), 729.

"The author's scathing dislike of the hero, his style of brilliant invective, and his perverse delight in his task make the novel [GIN AND BITTERS by A. Riposte] a most diverting *tour de force.* Here is entertainment not based on froth, amusement not bedded in the obvious."

927 Grégorio, Paul. "Les Répétitions Générales≠Aux Ambassadeurs≠*Le Cyclone*" (Dress Rehearsals: At the Ambassadeurs: *The Sacred Flame*), COMOEDIA, 2 Oct 1931, p. 2.

The play is a pathetic tragedy similar to THE TRIAL OF MARY DUGAN. [Review of the French adaptation, in French.]

928 H., H. "Last Night's Play: 'THE PAINTED VEIL' at the Playhouse," OBSERVER (Lond), 20 Sept 1931, p. 16.

Bartlett Cormack's dramatization "is not a very persuasive story . . . for, although its bones are there, the flesh and blood with which they are clothed seem conventional, rather than individual."

929 Hammond, Percy. "The Theaters," NEW YORK HERALD TRIBUNE, 23 Sept 1931, p. 16.

The Breadwinner is "a feeble contrivance, given to zigzags and deviations."

930 H[orsnell, Horace]. "At the Play," PUNCH, CLXXXI (7 Oct 1931), 386-87.

Bartlett Cormack's dramatization of THE PAINTED VEIL is "ethically speaking . . . not a nice story, nor . . . a very convincing one."

931 Hutchens, John. "Anchors Aweigh: Broadway in Review," THEATRE ARTS MONTHLY, XV (Dec 1931), 990.

The Breadwinner is a poor play because it lacks moral or intellectual conflict, and is nothing but a series of tired epigrams. There is too little drama surrounding the hero, Charles Battle.

932* Jennings, Richard. "The Theatre: *The Circle*," SPECTATOR (Lond), CXLVI (7 March 1931), 344.

Ten years after its first performance *The Circle* is only a little rusty around its moral edges, and that is a remarkable accomplishment for a play that "illustrates contemporary manners in a period of rapid progress." M had "a good start, a little in advance of his age, since he ignores its pseudo-moral prejudices." But "morals having marched on or down," the elopement is no longer "a hopeless plunge out of good society."

933 Krutch, Joseph Wood. "Drama," NATION (NY), CXXXIII (14 Oct 1931), 408.

The Breadwinner is "mostly talk and very far from being Somerset Maugham at his best."

934 Lacretelle, Pierre de. "W. Somerset Maugham, Romancier et Conteur" (W. Somerset Maugham, Novelist and Story-teller), GRINGOIRE, 27 Nov 1931, p. 4.

Cakes and Ale is different from novels of M's typical manner. Familiar characteristics are its light irony, sense of the ridiculous, a cruel indifference to the man's fortunes M enjoys describing. *Cakes and Ale,* however, is a kind of "novelistic comedy," a satire meant to discourage literary biography; the tone is Proustian, as is the time structure. [Review of the French translation, in French.]

935* Lockridge, Richard. " *'The Breadwinner,'* " NEW YORK SUN, 23 Sept 1931, p. 32.

The play is "a suavely malicious comedy, barbed in unexpected places, and . . . perhaps the first offering which gives evidence of having been written by a grownup. It is unfortunate . . . that the grownup can hardly, in this instance, be said to have written a play." The play is really over at the end of Act II.

936* MacAfee, Helen. "The Library of the Quarter: Outstanding Novels," YALE REVIEW, N. S. XX (Winter 1931), viii.

The "situation" of *Cakes and Ale* is its most important feature; although much is told of the three novelists' behavior, "one never gets a complete view of them. As a study of situation without development of character, it might have made an admirable short story."

937 MacCarthy, Desmond. "Two New Plays," NEW STATESMAN AND NATION, N. S. II (26 Sept 1931), 373.

Bartlett Cormack's dramatization of THE PAINTED VEIL is weakest in the development of the theme of "Christian unselfish love" through the nuns; they are "stagey."

938 Marteaux, Jacques. "Les Spectacles de Paris=Les Répétitions Générales=Aux Ambassadeurs=*Le Cyclone*" (The Entertainments of Paris: Dress Rehearsals: At the Ambassadeurs: *The Sacred*

Flame), LE JOURNAL DES DEBATS [POLITIQUES ET LITTERAIRES], 3 Oct 1931, p. 5.

British writers are masters of criminal literature; they are unrivalled in creating "cascades of emotions and suspense." The adapter's problem was treating correctly the characters of M's play, who are terribly British in their frames of mind. [In French.]

939 Mercier, Armand. *"La Lettre" (The Letter),* GRINGOIRE, 21 Aug 1931, p. 9.

[A recounting of the actual incidents on which M based his story and play.] [In French.]

940 Mordaunt, Elinor. " 'GIN AND BITTERS,' " NEW YORK TIMES, 14 May 1931, p. 22.

[Letter to the editor denying the statements in the article, " 'GIN AND BITTERS' Held Up" (NEW YORK TIMES, 7 May 1931, p. 26), claiming Mrs. Mordaunt had been prevailed upon by M's friends not to publish GIN AND BITTERS in England.]

941 Morgan, Louise. "Somerset Maugham," WRITERS AT WORK (Lond: Chatto & Windus, 1931), pp. 53-60.

In an interview, M discusses the nature of a writer as well as his own work and tastes.

942 Moses, Montrose J. "W. Somerset Maugham," DRAMAS OF MODERNISM AND THEIR FORERUNNERS (Boston: Little, Brown, 1931), pp. 413-17.

Critical introduction to *The Circle*. M has no play "to compare in solid worth with his *Of Human Bondage* or *Liza of Lambeth*." His wit aims deep, but his expression "skims the top in constant verve of badinage." In theme, M "smatters of Victorian inheritance," but his irony, scorn, and repartée are "in the Wilde tradition."

943 Moses, Montrose J. "W. Somerset Maugham," REPRESENTATIVE BRITISH PLAYS: VICTORIAN AND MODERN (Boston: D. C. Heath, 1931), pp. 653-56.

[Biographical and critical introduction to *Our Betters*.]

944* "Mr. Maugham Looks On," NEW YORK TIMES BOOK REVIEW, 20 Sept 1931, p. 6.

Not only do the stories of *First Person Singular* contain few of the faults traditionally associated with the first-person narrative technique, but "indeed, the charm of the book derives from the atmosphere of personal communion which the idiom of the first person singular establishes between reader and author." Unfortunately, however, the book as a whole is much too slender in plot and much too inconclusive.

945 "Mr. Maugham Ten Years Ago," NEW STATESMAN AND NATION, XXXVII or N. S. I (7 March 1931), 66.

Although social conditions have changed since the premiere of M's play, and although the characters are "cardboard," no new comedy as good as *The Circle* has "been produced in the ten years since its first appearance."

946 "New Novels," TIMES LITERARY SUPPLEMENT (Lond), 17 Sept 1931, p. 702.

Elinor Mordaunt in her FULL CIRCLE [British title of GIN AND BITTERS by A. Riposte] "is abundantly clever even when she is administering slightly malicious raps here and there in the English literary world. She has humour and insight and an easy and entertaining way of writing."

947* "New Novels," TIMES LITERARY SUPPLEMENT (Lond), 1 Oct 1931, p. 750.

The use of the first person singular in telling the stories of *First Person Singular* renders them both implausible and exaggerated. "In his observation of life, the author's critical, rather cynical, personality gives point and spice to some of his stories; but so far from adding to the naturalism that he might have attained by this personal method, he has, partly through carelessness, destroyed our sense of reality in some instances."

948 "Novels about Novelists," NEW YORK TIMES BOOK REVIEW, 19 April 1931, p. 7.

GIN AND BITTERS by A. Riposte is "a pretentious and mannered work which bears the marks of hurried composition. . . . We feel . . . that Mr. Riposte's identity will have no catastrophic consequences and that his present pseudonymity may well be as salutary as it is mysterious."

949 "THE PAINTED VEIL," TRUTH (Lond), CX (30 Sept 1931), 515.

The happy ending of Bartlett Cormack's dramatization [Kitty's marriage to Waddington] is attributed [wrongly] to M's original work.

950* "The Playhouse: 'THE PAINTED VEIL,'" TIMES (Lond), 21 Sept 1931, p. 10; rptd by Raymond Mander and Joe Mitchenson, eds, in THEATRICAL COMPANION TO MAUGHAM (Lond: Rockliff, 1955), p. 267.

Bartlett Cormack's dramatization "is enacted with more theatrical skill than has gone into its telling. We frequently get the impression that we are skimming a novel, picking out the dialogue and taking for granted the atmosphere which alone makes the dialogue plausible within its own convention."

951 Porché, François. "Le Mouvement dramatique" (Drama

Movement), LA REVUE DE PARIS, 38ème année, no. 5 (15 Oct 1931), 944-45.

Primarily a plot summary of Horace de Carbuccia's adaptation of *The Sacred Flame*. [In French.]

952 Rageot, Gaston. "Le Théâtre: Debuts de saison" (Theater: Openings of the Season), REVUE BLEUE, 69ème année, no. 21 (17 Oct 1931), 645-46.

The Sacred Flame is a play of solid structure and of high human interest. [Review of the French adaptation, in French.]

953 Rey, Etienne. *"Le Cyclone" (The Sacred Flame),* COMOEDIA, 3 Oct 1931, pp. 1-2.

M shows, with this play, that he is no prisoner to a set type of play. *The Sacred Flame,* in the French adaptation, is a terse, rapid drama which, after verging on detective melodrama, reveals its true purpose in the last act. [In French.]

954* Riposte A. (Pseudonym for Mrs. Evelyn May Wiehe (*née* Clowes) Mordaunt; known also by the pseudonym of Elinor (or Elenor) Mordaunt]. GIN AND BITTERS (NY: Farrar, Rhinehart, 1931); published as FULL CIRCLE (Lond: M. Secker, 1931).

In a scene reminiscent of the opening scene of *The Painted Veil,* Leverson Hurle, the hero, awakens, as is his custom, in his employer's wife's bed. Thinking patronizingly of "that poor devil Gissing," Leverson meets Mr. Stoddard, his employer, for breakfast, only to learn that Stoddard knows of the liaison, and is going to dismiss him as well as force him to marry Mrs. Stoddard (Cynthia).

Heading for Lambeth, Leverson thinks of his first book which appeared at the outset of the Boer War and because of the War had bad sales. He recalls his early days of scientific training when he was badly stuck in the middle of his third novel and when he lived in Bloomsbury with Lizzie. She was the "best critic he ever had, ever was to have," for when he read her passages from his book, she replied: "That's all bunkum, folks ain't like that," etc. Four years before, he had parted from Lizzie because she sold herself for ten pounds in order to buy Leverson a microscope for his scientific studies. During those four years his third novel had failed because "he had endeavored to draw upon his imagination, unsupported by fact" [cf. the reviews of *Liza of Lambeth* with those of *The Making of a Saint* and *Orientations*]. He turned to plays, and in the beginning "these showed a lightness of touch"; but finally, in his decadence, he began lambasting his fellow writers, alive and dead [see the reviews, of course, of *Cakes and Ale*].

Confirmed in the belief that marriage is just another bourgeois affair, nevertheless Leverson marries Cynthia Stoddard "to make an honest woman of her." Now more than ever he finds the need to escape, which he does: into the Pacific, with the excuse of finishing a book on "a painter's life." He travels, finishes the book, but it is no good, "for in it the writer intrudes himself to an extent . . . [that] in the end one knows more about the writer than the painter."

A two-year sojourn in Singapore ensues, and here Leverson procures the materials for a book about a "highly placed and powerful seducer," a "too-easily flattered young wife" and her "ineffectual, though talented, husband" [the plot of this book follows too closely the plot of *The Painted Veil* to be further detailed]. The only reason that this book begins, unlike all of Leverson's other books, in "the thick of things" is that Cynthia decided to join him in Singapore and brought with her her dog Chang, who had an immense hatred for Leverson and destroyed the first three chapters of the manuscript.

After the monumental success of this book, and separation from Cynthia, Leverson becomes intoxicated with his general success, yet subject to abysmal fits of depression from which he wants no escape: "All he wanted was to die, so long as he could tread a few people under foot, squelch them, first: pay them out for being so uninteresting, banal, sheep-like." Everywhere he goes now he finds himself an unwelcomed visitor; his last resort is America, but America tires of him. Back in England, he agrees to divorce Cynthia in a scene reminiscent in dialogue of the scene between Lady Kitty and Lord Porteous in Act III of *The Circle.*

After this, Leverson's health deteriorates; he continues to write, but the awkwardness and triteness of his style become more pronounced. He is lonely, but avoids contact with others. Only the faithful Lizzie of Lambeth remains to nurse him. As his last comfort on his dying day he requests his valet to shave him: Leverson "would have hated even the undertaker to see that contrast of white bristle with the small dark moustache, which had remained so altogether unchanged."
[Although the author denies in a foreword any "attempt at the portraiture of any living or once living person," the tone is tongue-in-cheek, and what follows is a "satire" manifestly aimed at M.]

955 Ross, Virgilia Peterson. "The New Books," OUTLOOK AND INDEPENDENT, CLIX (30 Sept 1931), 156.
In *First Person Singular,* M has an "evil eye" and can spot "a particle of soot in your cerebellum." In these stories, except for "The Creative Impulse," you are stung "with a tart, convincing truth."

956 Sawyer, Newell W. "The Comedy of Manners from Sheridan to Maugham: The Study of the Type as a Dramatic Form and as a Social Document." Unpublished thesis. University of Pennsylvania, 1931. Pp. 152, 197, 198, 204, 217, especially 224-28, 238, 239.

Because M failed to move the public with *A Man of Honour,* his first serious attempt in drama, he deliberately turned to light entertainment as a "dramatic huckster." His characters are generally the same in every play; "their persiflage is the froth of wit, not the rare distillment itself."

957 Sée, Edmond. "A travers l'actualité théâtricale" (In the Theater Currently), LA REVUE DE FRANCE, 11èmé année, no. 6 (1 Nov 1931), 187-90.

[Primarily a plot summary of the Paris premiere of *The Sacred Flame.*] [In French.]

958 Shand, John. "Late Irony of Mr. Maugham, with Some Remarks on Edgar Wallace," THEATRE MAGAZINE, LIII (Feb 1931), 30, 56.

The first act of *The Breadwinner* is not especially entertaining. The joke of the play is comparable to that in ARMS AND THE MAN, where people appear ridiculous when measured by the "lunatic" common sense of the hero.

959 Smet, Robert de. "Le Théâtre anglais depuis la guerre" (The English Drama Since the War), LA REVUE DE PARIS, 38ème année, no. 6 (1 Dec 1931), 631.

The hero of *The Breadwinner* is Ibsen's heroine of A DOLL'S HOUSE masculinized; the play is expertly drawn, the dialogue excellent. [In French.]

960 Speth, William. "Le Théâtre" (The Theater), LA REVUE MONDIALE, CCV (15 Oct 1931), 371-72.

The Sacred Flame is a "police piece" turned into art without retarding action and suspense. [Review of the French adaptation, in French.]

961 Strong, L. A. G. "Fiction: The Test that Failed," SPECTATOR (Lond), CXLVII (10 Oct 1931), 468.

First Person Singular supports M's comment that "vulgarity is essential to any writer who aims at more than a partial rendering of life." M is "beautifully detached" and "knows his craft from A to Z," but seems to despise it. He spends too much time satirizing "highbrow writers," but is himself "one of the most subtle craftsmen of our time."

962* Sunne, Richard. "Current Literature: Books in General," NEW STATESMAN AND NATION, N. S. II (24 Oct 1931), 516.

In *First Person Singular,* M's characters are like dolls that he would want, but cannot make, to come alive; through "imaginative timidity" M keeps them "controlled, elegant, mannered, obedient." There is, in this book, thus, "a pitiful competence, a null deftness"; there are no surprises for the reader, but one fears more that there were, in these stories, no surprises for M himself.

963* Sykes, Gerald. "An Author in Evening Dress," NATION (NY), CXXXIII (25 Nov 1931), 576; rptd, in THE MAUGHAM ENIGMA, ed by Klaus W. Jonas (NY: Citadel P, 1954), pp. 177-79.

M is to many minds "a force . . . for the stable of W. R. Hearst" or one of the "glittering passengers in the grand saloon of that quadruple-screw ship which bore 'The Gentleman from San Francisco' . . . ." The stories of *First Person Singular* overlook no clichés and attest to his pseudo-suavity.

964 "Tales by Maugham: *'First Person Singular'* a Collection of Merit," SPRINGFIELD SUNDAY UNION AND REPUBLICAN (Mass), 4 Oct 1931, p. 7E.

M's technique is discursive, but there is nothing superfluous in any one of the six stories.

965 "Theatre," LIFE, XCVIII (9 Oct 1931), 19.

The failure of *The Breadwinner* is due to M's "indifferent material."

966 "Theatre," TIME, XVIII (5 Oct 1931), 24.

The Breadwinner is "simply a bag of parlor tricks performed by dialog."

967 Tucker, S. Marion. "W. Somerset Maugham and His Plays," MODERN AMERICAN AND BRITISH PLAYS (NY & Lond: Harper and Bros., 1931), p. 1.

[Biographical and critical introduction to *The Circle.*]

968* Vernon, Grenville. "Gammon and Spinach," COMMONWEAL, XIII (25 March 1931), 588.

Although the portrait of Alroy Kear is "effective," that of Driffield is not, because while the narrator says he thinks Driffield "overrated," he does not "give the slightest hint as to why the novelist had so impressed the imagination of the world." In *Cakes and Ale,* M has "turned his talents to a meanness of spirit which arouses disgust."

969* Wakefield, Gilbert. "The Theatre: Mr. Maugham's Apology," SATURDAY REVIEW (Lond), CLI (23 March 1931), 459.

Through one of his characters in *The Circle*, M protests that he is neither a humorist nor a cynic, but "merely a very truthful man." "He is no fanatic filled with a burning indignation; the shams and follies of the world are merely facts, amusing facts that require to be stated, rather than denounced. And so he writes about them in the form of comedy." M is mature, self-controlled, responsible. The ruling class and their politics are merely a frame in *The Circle,* a "cynical" romance which makes the point that the younger generation will suffer the same disillusionment as the older. M mercilessly exposes "the life endured by all who sacrifice the comfort and security of dull responsibility for the glamour and illusion of romantic love."

970 Watson, E. Bradlee, and Benfield Pressey. *"The Circle* by W. Somerset Maugham," CONTEMPORARY DRAMA: NINE PLAYS (NY: Charles Scribner's Sons, 1931), pp. 240-41.
[Critical introduction.]

971* Wyatt, Euphemia Van Rensselaer. "The Drama," CATHOLIC WORLD, CXXXIV (Nov 1931), 209.
The idea of *The Breadwinner* is not original; indeed, it is a repetition of Chapter I from *The Moon And Sixpence,* except that the stockbroker in this play has not, as Strickland did in the novel, the excuse of an artistic urge. Having made his decision in Act I, he requires two additional acts merely "to pack his bag. Meanwhile the paradox of paternal indifference is turned and twisted *ad infinitum."*

972 Young, Stark. "French and English," NEW REPUBLIC, LXVIII (7 Oct 1931), 207-9.
Except for a few scenes, *The Breadwinner* "represent[s] the abandonment of that trouble and concern which not only life but the stage has hitherto required."

1932

973* Agate, James. "The Dramatic World," SUNDAY TIMES (Lond), 6 Nov 1932, p. 6; rptd as "Too Bad to Be True," in FIRST NIGHTS (Lond: Ivor Nicholson and Watson, 1934), pp. 124-28; and, as *"For Services Rendered,"* in RED-LETTER NIGHTS: A SURVEY OF POST-ELIZABETHAN DRAMA IN ACTUAL PERFORMANCE ON THE LONDON STAGE, 1921-1943 (Lond: J. Cape, 1944), pp. 223-27.
For Services Rendered shows M "basking in his famous bitterness, apparently unaware that jaundice, like beauty, is in the eye of the beholder." M indicts an entire nation for failure to recompense the renderers of service, but he himself heals no wounds, for he "is too busy being bitter about our lack of pity to find pity of his own." Moreover, M has chosen to depict a set of people who would be "worthless with Peace piping her hardest." Nevertheless, the play offers much to praise: the construction is magnificent,

and the action of the last scene "electrifying"; the dialogue is spare, taut; every character, "complete in itself." If faulty in argument, the play is "a piece of dramatic carpentry of which the English theatre may justly be proud."

974* Armstrong, Anne. "New Novels," SATURDAY REVIEW (Lond), CLIV (26 Nov 1932), 564-65.
The Narrow Corner is "beautifully written . . . in easy, flowing, but never rhetorical style." There is nothing "theatrical" in the dialogue, but the plot is implausible. The principal shortcoming lies in the treatment of women. M realizes man's complexity, "but women to him are all of a piece — 100 per cent uninteresting angels (off stage) or passionate and consuming vamps in the spot light." M's art is incomplete as long as "he does not at least attempt to draw credible women."

975 Arrowsmith, J. E. S. "Fiction," LONDON MERCURY, XXV (Jan 1932), 305.
In *First Person Singular,* M's characters, though not very prepossessing," are "utterly truthfully displayed"; his "vivid and competent writing is a pleasure to read in itself."

976 Bastia, Jean. "Autour de *'Cercle'* " (Around *The Circle*), GRINGOIRE, 30 Dec 1932, p. 9.
[Verse review of the French adaptation of *The Circle.*] [In French.]

977 Bellessort, André. "La Semaine dramatique: *Le Cercle*" (The Dramatic Week: The Circle), LE JOURNAL DES DEBATS [POLITIQUES ET LITTERAIRES], 26 Dec 1932, p. 3; rptd in LE JOURNAL DES DEBATS, HEBDOMADAIRE, 30 Dec 1932, pp. 1124-26.
The dialogue is spare, simple, vivid. M has written more tragic plays but none so bitter. Here he has stirred the "dregs of passion" and shown that a father's example is of little profit to the son. [Review of the revived French adaptation, in French.]

978 Billy, André. "Amours Anglaises" (English Love Affairs), GRINGOIRE, 4 Nov 1932, p. 4.
The "singularity" of the stories in the French translation of *First Person Singular* derives chiefly from their British origin. Samoa, English-style, is, for most Frenchmen characterized by oddness and stubbornness, an inevitable concern for self-respect. [In French.]

979 "Books: East of Suez," TIME, XX (14 Nov 1932), 56.
The Narrow Corner is not another *Of Human Bondage*. "Maugham tells his eventful narrative sparely, almost drably. . . ." [Plot summary.]

980 Bourdon, Charles. "Les Romans=*La Ronde de L'Amour*"

(Novels: *Cakes and Ale*), LA REVUE DES LECTURES, 20ème année, no. 2 (15 Feb 1932), 158-59.

A book of more interest to the British reader. [Review of the French translation.] [In French.]

981 Bourdon, Charles. "Les Romans: '*Amours Singulières*'" (Novels: *First Person Singular*), LA REVUE DES LECTURES, 20ème année, no. 12 (15 Dec 1932), 1410.

M finds no deep meaning to man's destiny. He is constantly pushing himself forward and speaks of literary success with a disgusting vanity. [Review of the French translation.] [In French.]

982 Brande, Dorothea. "Seven Novels of the Month," BOOKMAN (NY), LXXV (Nov 1932), 735.

The Narrow Corner "is recommended to all who like the exotic, fatalistic, more than slightly misogynistic Maugham novel."

983* Britten, Florence Haxton. "A Cynical, Gifted Story Teller," NEW YORK HERALD TRIBUNE BOOKS, 13 Nov 1932, p. 3.

M does not live up to the epigraph to *The Narrow Corner* from Marcus Aurelius "to investigate systematically and truly all that comes under . . . [one's] observation of life." For all the brilliance and fascination of his novels, M has grown "more restricted" in his version of life, "measurably more narrowminded and disillusioned." Yet M remains a "first-rate storyteller," and *The Narrow Corner* "is a neat, vigorously written story of psychological investigation . . . enriched with shrewd characterizations and a definite philosophy of life, approaching the Conradian LORD JIM rather than an Edgar Wallace thriller."

984 Brown, Ivor. "The Week's Theatres," OBSERVER (Lond), 6 Nov 1932, p. 15.

Tragic effect in *For Services Rendered* is marred by "the gratuitous imposition of miseries that have nothing to do with the special case suggested in the title."

985 Brûlé, A. "Livres" (Books), LA REVUE ANGLO-AMERICAINE, IX (Aug 1932), 561-62.

The Moon and Sixpence [Tauchnitz ed.] is one of M's better novels. Gauguin is greater and more impressive than M's Strickland, but M's storytelling can be appreciated for its own merits. [In French.]

986 C., R. M. "Books: South Sea Rogues," NEW YORKER, VIII (12 Nov 1932), 65.

The ending of *The Narrow Corner* is slightly "muddled," but the suavely ironic tone is well sustained.

987 Cartier, Maurice. "A l'Etalage" (On Display), GRINGOIRE, 15 Jan 1932, p. 4.
[Brief mention of the French translation of *The Painted Veil.*] [In French.]

988 Cartier, Maurice. "A l'Etalage" (On Display), GRINGOIRE, 22 Jan 1932, p. 4.
[Brief mention of the French translation of *The Trembling of a Leaf* and Paul Dottin's LA LITTERATURE ANGLAISE.] [In French.]

989 Cartier, Maurice. "A l'Etalage" (On Display), GRINGOIRE, 5 Feb 1932, p. 4.
[Brief mention of the French translation of *The Moon and Sixpence.*] [In French.]

990 Cartier, Maurice. "A l'Etalage" (On Display), GRINGOIRE, 1 April 1932, p. 4.
[Brief mention of the French translation of *The Casuarina Tree.*] [In French.]

991 Cartier, Maurice. "A l'Etalage" (On Display), GRINGOIRE, 21 Oct 1932, p. 4.
[Brief mention of the French translation of *First Person Singular.*] [In French.]

992 Cazamian, M[adeleine]. L. "Livres" (Books), LA REVUE ANGLO-AMERICAINE, IX (Feb 1932), 276-77.
Cakes and Ale is a clever, versatile, fluent narrative with a facile, disenchanted philosophy. The literary circles and the characters are happily defined and satirized with gusto. [In French.]

993 Cloud, Yvonne. "Some New Fiction," BOOKS OF THE MONTH, II (Dec 1932), 20.
Dr. Saunders is an unnecessary character in *The Narrow Corner* and the dramatic moments arrive anticlimactically, without shock. [Tongue-in-cheek review.]

994 D'Amico, Silvio. "Theatro drammatico: *'Colui che guadagna il pane'*" (Drama: *The Breadwinner*), NUOVA ANTOLOGIA, CCLXXXII (1 March 1932), 137-38.
In the Italian translation, the dialogue is alternately dull and lively, but through a moral analysis of the story it is clear that the play takes up a serious issue and then treats it realistically. M is associated more closely with Pinero and Shaw than with European playwrights who also treat social issues. [In Italian.]

995 Daniels, Jonathan. "Aboard the Lugger," SATURDAY REVIEW OF LITERATURE, IX (12 Nov 1932), 237.

The excellence of *The Narrow Corner* derives from the masterful drawing of the three male characters and from the convincing presentation of the background of sea and islands. The ending, however, is a bit too pat, and the portrait of Louise Frith not too successful.

996 d'Houville, Gérard. "Chronique des Théâtres de Paris: Reprise du *Cercle*" (Paris Theater Chronicle: Revival of *The Circle*), LE FIGARO, 26 Dec 1932, p. 5.

[Review of the revival of the French adaptation.] [In French.]

997 Dottin, Paul. "Les Lettres étrangères: Somerset Maugham, romancier satirique" (Foreign Letters: Somerset Maugham, Satirical Novelist), LA REVUE DE FRANCE, 12ème année, no. 2 (1 April 1932), 565-71.

M's success is based on his readers' perceiving behind even the most exaggerated of his characters "universal humanity." [Review-article on M's works, especially *Cakes and Ale*.] [In French.]

998* "Entertainments — The Globe Theatre: *'For Services Rendered,'*" TIMES (Lond), 2 Nov 1932, p. 10; rptd by Raymond Mander and Joe Mitchenson, eds, in THEATRICAL COMPANION TO MAUGHAM (Lond: Rockliff, 1955), p. 240.

"We may wonder if the dramatist has not underrated the healing power of time, but so clearly has he defined the War influence at work in this remote town of today, that while the play is before us we find it more convenient to accept than to analyze them."

999 F., D. C. *"For Services Rendered,"* THEATRE WORLD (Lond), XVIII (Dec 1932), 274.

Although one might find it hard to believe there could be so many cases of post-war unhappiness gathered in one family, the play's construction and writing as well as its dialogue and characterization make M "a playwright for whom the word 'great' is the only possible choice."

1000 Fleming, Peter. "The Theatre: *For Services Rendered,*" SPECTATOR (Lond), CXLIX (11 Nov 1932), 659.

As an "arraignment of the nation's gratitude," the play fails because M "has piled on a good deal of extraneous agony." By blaming everything on "the dogs of war," M weakens his argument. The play "drags" until the third act, when it comes "savagely to life." "Let no one say that this play, however well its temper suits our times, is Maugham's best."

1001 "*'For Services Rendered,'* at the Globe," ILLUSTRATED LONDON NEWS, CLXXXI (12 Nov 1932), 786.

"A gripping piece of work," the characters seem so real that "it is as if the fourth wall of a house has been removed that we may spy upon the family circle."

1002* Gould, Gerald. "New Novels," OBSERVER (Lond), 13 Nov 1932, p. 6.

M "cannot score off us in the old game of the Cynic with the Heart of Gold." *The Narrow Corner* has a "thrilling plot, a captivating descriptive style, a wide and gorgeous range of scene; humour, wit, vivacity and veracity in detail"—but the hero, Dr. Saunders, is "a grandmother in wolf's clothing."

1003* Grein, J. T. "The World of the Theatre," ILLUSTRATED LONDON NEWS, CLXXXI (26 Nov 1932), 854.

Not all the characters in *For Services Rendered* are "victims of the aftermath of war," but actually most of them are "representative of the drab lives that eke out a cloistered, monotonous, hopeless existence in countless provincial cities." M has written plays better in structure, greater in depth and dramatic value.

1004 Jack, Peter M. "Maugham and the Comic Spirit," NEW YORK TIMES BOOK REVIEW, 13 Nov 1932, p. 6.

The Narrow Corner is "far and away the best of the Far East stories of conflicting civilizations and character."

1005 Lang, André. "Le Livre parlé" (The Book Discussed), LES ANNALES POLITIQUES ET LITTERAIRES, No. 2398 (15 Jan 1932), 56-67.

Cakes and Ale is a book in the line of CHARLES DEMAILLY. [In French.]

1006 "Livres et Revues: *Amours Singulières*" (Books and Reviews: *First Person Singular*), JOURNAL DE GENEVE [NATIONAL, POLITIQUE ET LITTERAIRE], No. 296 (29 Oct 1932), 2.

In the French translation, "The Alien Corn" is enjoyable. [In French.]

1007 L[ovett], R[obert] M[orss]. *"The Narrow Corner,"* NEW REPUBLIC, LXXIII (14 Dec 1932), 143.

M "shows himself a virtuoso in embroidering and embellishing an episode until it fills the space of a novel." The novel displays "facile workmanship."

1008 MacCarthy, Desmond. "Miscellany: *'For Services Rendered,'* " NEW STATESMAN AND NATION, N. S. IV (12 Nov 1932), 577-78; rptd in THEATRE (Lond: MacGibbon & Kee, 1954), pp. 134-39.

This is "the best play Maugham has written." [Mainly plot summary.]

1009* Marchand, Leslie A. "The Exoticism of Somerset Maugham," LA REVUE ANGLO-AMERICAINE, IX:4 (April 1932), 314-28;

rptd in THE MAUGHAM ENIGMA, ed by Klaus W. Jonas (NY: Citadel P, 1954), pp. 54-71.

Although M's canon is uneven, one feels in it "something fundamentally sound and of lasting value." A naturalist whose formula rested upon the exploding of conventional thought and action, M found the "exotic background" of the South Seas an ideal source of new material; he learned "that there were just about as many bubbles of pretence and convention to be burst in the outposts as in the same levels of European civilization. . . ." To his new material M brought his customary "clinical aloofness," at once his weakness and strength. Exoticism did not alter M's method, but was rather a "useful medium."

1010 Marteaux, Jacques. "Les Spectacles à Paris: Aux Ambassadeurs: *Le Cercle*" (The Entertainments of Paris: At the Ambassadeurs: *The Circle*), LE JOURNAL DES DEBATS [POLITIQUES ET LITTERAIRES], 24 Dec 1932, p. 4.

The play [the revival of the French adaptation] is a powerful comedy, embroidering upon the old theme that in love affairs, other people's experiences do not help. [In French.]

1011 Moran, Helen. "Fiction - II," LONDON MERCURY, XXVII (Dec 1932), 171.

"A good story, told by a finished craftsman," *The Narrow Corner* is M's best book "since *The Moon and Sixpence.*"

1012 "New Books and Reprints," TIMES LITERARY SUPPLEMENT (Lond), 13 Oct 1932, p. 736.

In "The Book-Bag" (short story to be collected in *Ah King* one year later) M the technician rather than M the artist was at work.

1013 "New Maugham Play Is Hailed in London," NEW YORK TIMES, 2 Nov 1932, p. 23.

For Services Rendered, so unlike M's former plays, has proved a success in London and will likely have even more of a success in America. M has called the play his "swan song," but "London takes this with a grain of salt. . . . "

1014 "New Novels," TIMES (Lond), 8 Nov 1932, p. 19.

In *The Narrow Corner,* M's characters are "round" and his skill in displaying the various facets of a personality have never been "used to more advantage." The book's high moments are "intensified by restraint, mounting surely to tragedy and ending with a smile."

1015* "New Novels," TIMES LITERARY SUPPLEMENT (Lond), 10 Nov 1932, p. 834.

The Narrow Corner is invested with a sense of mystery, but with humor, wit, and tragedy as well. It is "a fine piece of craftsmanship," due especially to M's exact and incisive observation of character. "One of the reasons which have made Maugham so effective an interpreter of character is his knowledge that no human personality is ever wholly black, or white, or yellow, but is built up in layers or streaks."

1016 O'Brien, E. D. "The Theatre," ENGLISH REVIEW, LV (July 1932), 667-69.

The misery in *For Services Rendered* is "a little too thickly spread."

1017 "Our Booking-Office: A Cynical Craftsman," PUNCH, CLXXXIII (30 Nov 1932), 615.

The Narrow Corner shows that M can create live persons, "even if he has no heart."

1018 Playbill. "Off with the Motley," THEATRE WORLD (Lond), XVIII (Oct 1932), 166.

M states that the supply of dramatists is smaller than that of novelists. [Interview.]

1019* Pollock, John. "Theatre," SATURDAY REVIEW (Lond), CLIV (12 Nov 1932), 502-3.

"Of the place to which this astonishing work [*For Services Rendered*] entitles Maugham, no whisper is heard." He is "the first of living dramatists," the best short-story writer since Kipling, and the only contemporary English novelist with a first-rate European reputation. *"For Services Rendered* is unquestionably the biggest play written since Ibsen's heyday," and it is impossible that anyone should call it depressing or cynical. "The driving force lies in no sin committed by any of the protagonists, but in the vanity, blindness, and egoism of the world's governors, subject but to remotest control by individuals, who caused or allowed War . . . to be let loose on the millions in their care." Men gave their all during a time of danger, and the bankruptcy of the War by the Peace is the "reward for service rendered." "The play is one that every Englishman should see with joy for its greatness, and fear at its indictment of our failure, and pride that it is by an author from among ourselves."

1020 "Shorter Notices," NATION (NY), CXXV (7 Dec 1932), 574.

The Narrow Corner is "an old-fashioned melodrama glossed over by smooth craftsmanship that partially conceals its many defects." M seems to go through "his routine of tricks like a bored and expert magician, growing increasingly contemptuous of his audience at each performance."

1021 Strong, L. A. G. "Fiction: *The Narrow Corner,"* SPECTATOR (Lond), CXLIX (11 Nov 1932), 674.

"While in no sense profound, . . . [the play is] a happy example of

Maugham's work." Emotional tension varies greatly. The skillfully drawn doctor unifies the story. Though he does not take part in the story, his "reflections and ironical detachment keep him the central character."

1022 "The Theatres: Unhappy Families," Truth (Lond), CXII (9 Nov 1932), 717-18.

In *For Services Rendered,* M's locating all the woes of man in war is unconvincing.

1023* Thérive, André. "Les Livres: Somerset Maugham: *La Ronde de L'Amour*" (Books: Somerset Maugham: *Cakes and Ale*), Le Temps, 5 May 1932, p. 3.

In this cleverly constructed story M has shown the simplicity, the ease and the natural power of a great storyteller. The character of Rosie is astonishing; nothing expresses better the atrocious mockery of existence than her re-appearance at the end as a prim settled-down matron. [Review of French translation.] [In French.]

1024 T[horp, Joseph]. "At the Play," Punch, CLXXXIII (9 Nov 1932), 526-27.

For Services Rendered is "sensitively-felt and significantly-expressed tragedy."

1025 Torrès, Henry. *"Le Cercle" (The Circle),* Gringoire, 23 Dec 1932, p. 11.

The play [the revival of the French adaptation] is a most suggestive document on contemporary Britain, still protected from realities of the modern age by a barrier of prejudices and still influenced by the higher middle class. [In French.]

1026 "A Touch of Fever," New Statesman and Nation ("Literary Supplement"), N. S. IV (12 Nov 1932), 594.

In spite of occasional carelessness, *The Narrow Corner* is extremely well written; but, M's "natural sentimentality has so long frozen into cynicism that he forgets how much can be done by a little warmth. His characters, except the villains, move stiffly through lack of it."

1933

1027* Agate, James. "An Old Problem Unsolved," Sunday Times (Lond), 17 Sept 1933, p. 4; rptd, as "Mr. Maugham's Last Play," in First Nights (Lond: Ivor Nicholson and Watson, 1934), pp. 197-203; and by Raymond Mander and Joe Mitchenson,

eds, in THEATRICAL COMPANION TO MAUGHAM (Lond: Rockliff, 1955), pp. 248-51.
In *Sheppey,* M has not given enough time and trouble to what, given the subject, "must be a major work." The first act wastes time instead of developing the great theme "faintly hinted," and is riddled with Galsworthian sentimentality. The theme is announced with "full orchestra" in Act II, but M develops it mistakenly in relation to Sheppey's "impossible family." The third act "throws significance overboard by frittering the end away in a death scene which is not more applicable to Sheppey than to Box and Cox." In fine, M has raised a great issue, bungles it, and "fobs us off with minor entertainment."

1028 Armstrong, Anne. "Journeys of the Spirit," SATURDAY REVIEW (Lond), CLVI (23 Sept 1933), 325.
Though not the best, *Ah King* contains "some of the most satisfying short stories. Ostensibly a travel book, but six times Maugham has imagined what might have happened in such and such a district, and six times he has concocted a plot of his own making, shaken it up with persons and places that are real, and six times has, vulgarly speaking, brought it off."

1029 Arrowsmith, J. E. S. "Fiction - I," LONDON MERCURY, XXIX (Nov 1933), 72.
In *Ah King,* "The Door of Opportunity" displays the subtlest character study, but it is difficult to choose "the best of six such good stories."

1030 Audiat, Pierre. "L'Actualité littéraire" (Current Literature), LA REVUE DE FRANCE, 13ème année, no. 1 (15 Jan 1933), 348.
[Brief review of the French translation of *First Person Singular.*] [In French.]

1031 Audiat, Pierre. "L'Actualité littéraire" (Current Literature), LA REVUE DE FRANCE, 13ème année, no. 4 (15 Aug 1933), 721.
[Brief review of the French translation of *The Narrow Corner.*] [In French.]

1032 Beaumont, F. A. "Luck in Authorship," JOHN O' LONDON'S WEEKLY ("Special Autumn Book Number"), XXX (7 Oct 1933), 4, 12.
M confesses that he has never enjoyed writing for the stage and that he turned to it only because novel-writing "did not pay." He also states that young authors have better opportunities than he had when he was young but that "luck" still plays a major part in a writer's success. [Interview, at the time of M's announcement that *Sheppey* would be his last play.]

1033 Benchley, Robert. "The Theatre: *Fin De* Whatever It Is," NEW YORKER, IX (20 May 1933), 30.

M's translation of Luigi Chiarelli's LA MASCHERA E IL VOLTO as *The Mask and the Face* is "terrible."

1034 Benchley, Robert. "The Theatre: Not Much Change," NEW YORKER, IX (22 Nov 1933), 24, 26.

If in *For Services Rendered* M "had stuck to one or two, or even four or five, examples of the havoc that war can bring to one family, he might have made his point with a little less burlesque effect, but when blindness, insanity, sex-starvation, suicide, cashing phony checks, and even cancer in a dear old mother are thrown in one after the other as debits to be answered for by war lords, we begin to feel, as we felt at DANGEROUS CORNER and WE, THE PEOPLE, that if one more disclosure of sin and suffering is piled on, the thing will become ridiculous and somebody is going to laugh."

1035 Benét, William Rose. "Mr. Maugham's Jumping Johnnies," SATURDAY REVIEW OF LITERATURE, X (25 Nov 1933), 296.

An enjoyable volume, *Ah King* must hold at least one superior story, but the high quality of the set makes it difficult to select that one.

1036 Billy, André. "Du Sud-Tunisien au Pacifique" (Of the South-Tunisian in the Pacific), GRINGOIRE, 7 July 1933, p. 4.

The dual construction imparts to the French translation of *The Narrow Corner* a certain waywardness of progression which shocks the logical-minded French reader. [In French.]

1037 "Books in Brief," FORUM, XC (Aug 1933), v.

In *Traveller's Library,* M's personal preferences are "excellent," his notes "pithy, amusing, and freshly flavored. . . . "

1038 "Books: Old Master Maugham," TIME, XXII (13 Nov 1933), 59.

"Somerset Maugham is the fiction editor's Santa Claus. His stories [in *Ah King*] are intelligent but not highbrow, well-made but not wooden, readable but not offensively scandalous."

1039* Bourdon, Charles. "Les Romans: *Le Fugitif*" (Novels: *The Narrow Corner*), LA REVUE DES LECTURES, 21ème année, no. 8 (15 Aug 1933), 928-29.

The characters are all without moral conscience yet hold an indefinable attraction like those of Conrad and Stevenson. Only at the point where Fred confesses to Dr. Saunders is the novel imperiled, for then the story is reduced to one of love and murder. [Review of the French translation, in French.]

1040 Brickell, Herschel. "The Literary Landscape," NORTH AMERICAN REVIEW, CCXXXVI (Aug 1933), 192.

The introduction and notes of *Traveller's Library* are "charming."

1041* Britten, Florence Haxton. "Maugham's Tragic Tales," NEW YORK HERALD TRIBUNE BOOKS, 12 Nov 1933, p. 4.

In *Ah King,* "Back of Beyond" and "The Book-Bag" are "both of them compellingly tragic tales in which one can believe utterly"; "The Vessel of Wrath," . . . [is] "cumbrously humorous extravaganza rather than a serious effort to build a credible short story"; "The Door of Opportunity," . . . "a beautifully turned piece of character and scene building."

1042 Brown, Ivor. "The Week's Theatres," OBSERVER (Lond), 17 Sept 1933, p. 15.

Sheppey "is angry, confused, sometimes too easily sarcastic . . . , often unlikely. . . . But it is unforgettable. Its mistakes are over-ridden by the mordant genius who makes them."

1043 Caldwell, Cy. "To See or Not to See," NEW OUTLOOK, CLXI (May 1933), 46.

"As a comment on war's aftermath," *For Services Rendered* "is true enough to please pacifists, yet never stirring enough to annoy militarists . . . [and] says nothing that already hasn't been said in dozens of tiresome post-war English novels."

1044 Caldwell, Cy. "To See or Not to See," NEW OUTLOOK, CLXI (June 1933), 48.

M's translation of Luigi Chiarelli's LA MASCHERA E IL VOLTO as *The Mask and the Face* is "a sorry thing of shreds and patches."

1045 Carb, David. "Stage," VOGUE, LXXI (15 June 1933), 39, 60.

M's translation of Luigi Chiarelli's LA MASCHERA E IL VOLTO as *The Mask and the Face* "strives tirelessly for scintillant cynicisms, most of them about marriage and the fascinating duplicity of women—a vein fairly well explored long ago."

1046 Cartier, Maurice. "A l'Etalage" (On Display), GRINGOIRE, 22 Sept 1933, p. 4.

[Brief mention of the French translation of *Ashenden.*] [In French.]

1047 Cartier, Maurice. "A l'Etalage" (On Display), GRINGOIRE, 8 Dec 1933, p. 4.

[Brief mention of the French translation of *On A Chinese Screen.*] [In French.]

1048 Croquet, James de. "L'heure qui passe" (The Passing Hour), LE FIGARO, 16 Jan 1933, p. 1.

The revival of the French adaptation of *The Circle* teaches us that lovers are like forty thieves in the ARABIAN NIGHTS who walked in each other's steps to pretend they were only one. [In French.]

1049 Cru, Robert-L. "La Saison Théâtrale à Londres" (The Theatrical Season in London), LE TEMPS, 14 Aug 1933, p. 2.

For Services Rendered is of great dramatic and literary interest; it is said to be M's last play. [In French.]

1050 Dearmer, Geoffrey. "The Decline of Inspiration in Modern Literature," BOOKMAN (Lond), LXXXIV (April 1933), 6-7.

M is an example of the decline of inspiration in modern literature. His best works have the "merits of excellence, but none, except perhaps *The Circle,* of greatness." With the arrival of M, "ethical motives ceased to be preponderant in the drama."

1051 Denison, Merrill. "Season's End: Broadway in Review," THEATRE ARTS MONTHLY, XVII (June 1933), 416-18.

For Services Rendered failed on Broadway because its character development came from the dissecting room, not the stage. Still, its theme is "thought-provoking and stimulating."

1052 Dottin, Paul. ANGLETERRE, NATION CONTINENTALE (ENGLAND, CONTINENTAL NATION) (Paris: Editions Tallandier, 1933), p. 213.

[Brief discussion of *Liza of Lambeth* and *Of Human Bondage.*] [In French.]

1053 Dottin, Paul. "La Littérature anglaise en 1932" (English Literature in 1932), LA REVUE DE FRANCE, 13ème année, no. 5 (15 Sept 1933), 324-25.

In *The Narrow Corner,* as in all other novels by M, one feels that "direct observation" plays the principal part. [In French.]

1054 Dr., H. "Chronique des Livres" (Book Chronicle), JOURNAL DE GENEVE [NATIONAL, POLITIQUE ET LITTERAIRE], No. 341 (14 Dec 1933), 2.

[Brief mention of the French translation of *On a Chinese Screen.*] [In French.]

1055* Eaton, Walter Prichard. "Some Modern Drama," NEW YORK HERALD TRIBUNE BOOKS, 28 May 1933, p. 10.

"Few if any of the characters in the play [*For Services Rendered*] needed a war to disintegrate them. They are not strong people beaten down, but shabby puppets or cheap rotters, about whose fate it is difficult to get in the least excited. This is Maugham at a low level."

1056 Edgar, Pelham. "The Way of Irony and Satire: Maugham, Douglas, Huxley, Lewis," THE ART OF THE NOVEL: FROM 1700 TO THE PRESENT TIME (NY: Macmillan, 1933), pp. 268-76.

M, like Aldous Huxley, is a master of portraits "as savage as those of Pope or Dryden in their most venomous mood." [*The Moon and Sixpence* and *Cakes and Ale* are examined in light of this general statement.]

1057 Ervine, St. John. THE THEATRE IN MY TIME (Lond: Rich & Cowan, 1933), pp. 118-19, 169.

M's plays exemplify the "revolution in the world of entertainment" from the 1880s to the 1930s.

1058 F., D. C. *"Sheppey,"* THEATRE WORLD (Lond), XX (Oct 1933), 170, 172.

The play is "good theatre" in that it sustains interest from start to finish; it is, nevertheless, "curiously uneven, ranging . . . from light comedy to morality and satire, and ending with a symbolical death scene that did little to clarify what had gone before."

1059 Fadiman, Clifton. "Books: A Man of the World and a Man of the Town," NEW YORKER, IX (11 Nov 1933), 65.

The stories of *Ah King* are good, but no one of them is as satisfying as the best in *First Person Singular.* The best of this collection is "The Book-Bag."

1060 G., R. "Bulletin: Ouvrages Reçus" (Bulletin: Books Received), LA REVUE ANGLO-AMERICAINE, XI (Dec 1933), 191.

[Brief noncommittal review of *The Narrow Corner.*] [In French.]

1061 Gould, Gerald. "New Novels," OBSERVER (Lond), 24 Sept 1933, p. 6.

M's *Ah King* is "rich and exciting," but not of his best; one of the difficulties is the repeated use of "the story-within-the-story" convention which puts the main narrative "into a mouth which could never have uttered it."

1062 Grein, J. T. "The World of the Theatre," ILLUSTRATED LONDON NEWS, CLXXXIII (30 Sept 1933), 498.

In the first act of *Sheppey,* M powerfully surmounted the first difficulty—"that of creating a living human being who could fit . . . idealisation"; but unfortunately, "the spirit, the potentiality, and the vision which set the action in motion give place to satire and gall."

1063 Griffith, Hubert. "The Art of the Playwright," OBSERVER (Lond), 10 Sept 1933, p. 9.

[Interview on the eve of the premiere of *Sheppey.*]

1064 Hammond, Percy. "The Theaters," NEW YORK HERALD TRIBUNE, 13 April 1933, p. 14.

The only trouble in *For Services Rendered* is that it is "over-venomous."

1065 Hammond, Percy. "The Theaters," NEW YORK HERALD TRIBUNE, 9 May 1933, p. 10.
M's translation of Luigi Chiarelli's LA MASCHERA E IL VOLTO as *The Mask and the Face* is "a dubious graveyard lark."

1066 Hart-Davis, Rupert. "The Theatre: *Sheppey*," SPECTATOR (Lond), CLI (22 Sept 1933), 369.
M "has so completely mastered his medium that he cannot be dull." Sheppey is drawn with "consummate skill," as a complete character. His family is "portrayed with sharp irony and streaks of savage caricature."

1067* Krutch, Joseph Wood. "Drama," NATION (NY), CXXXVI (3 May 1933), 511-12.
In *For Services Rendered,* "the virtuosity, to be sure, is no less evident than it always is. Maugham exhibits, for example, an almost uncanny skill in conceiving somewhat melodramatic situations which develop naturally into climaxes just at the moment when they are needed to punctuate the orderly development of an idea, and he never allows himself to forget for an instant any of the requirements for a well-made play." This play "has, in addition, a substance and a sincerity conspicuously lacking in the same author's showy arrangements of life east of Suez or adultery as it is practiced among Our Betters."

1068 Krutch, Joseph Wood. "Drama," NATION (NY), CXXVI (24 May 1933), 593-94.
M's translation of Luigi Chiarelli's LA MASCHERA E IL VOLTO as *The Mask and the Face* is a nice combination of "farce" and "charm."

1069 Krutch, Joseph Wood. "But Is It Art?" NATION (NY), CXXXVII (20 Sept 1933), 711.
M's seven brief essays in *Traveller's Library* are excellent in that "they not only stimulate the desire to read but give one the sense of an intimate companionship with another intelligent and enthusiastic reader!"

1070 "Les Livres nouveaux: Littérature étrangère" (New Books: Foreign Literature), REVUE BLEUE, 71ème année, no. 20 (21 Oct 1933), 639.
[Brief review of the French translation of *First Person Singular.*] [In French.]

1071 Lockridge, Richard. "The New Play," NEW YORK SUN, 13 April 1933, p. 22.
For Services Rendered is "lacking in the emotional force and unity which would have jabbed the point home."

1072 Lockridge, Richard. "The New Play," NEW YORK SUN, 9 May 1933, p. 28.

[Unfavorable review of M's translation of L. Chiarelli's LA MASCHERA E IL VOLTO as *The Mask and the Face.*]

1073 Loveman, Amy. "Treasure Trove," SATURDAY REVIEW OF LITERATURE, IX (17 June 1933), 653.

Traveller's Library is a fine anthology, the fruit of careful reading and selection. It includes nothing that is not good—"and that covers Mr. Maugham's own urbane and discriminating comments."

1074 MacAfee, Helen. "The Library of the Quarter: Outstanding Novels," YALE REVIEW, N. S. XXII (Winter 1933), xxii.

In *The Narrow Corner,* M holds no surprises for his readers; his scene is once again "in that Eastern borderland where Europeans and Asiatics mingle to no very good purpose." The novel's one "positive contribution" is the "study of an English doctor with a large practice in a Chinese city, and the manner in which he has built himself into his adopted world."

1075 MacCarthy, Desmond. "Mr. Maugham's New Play," NEW STATESMAN AND NATION, N. S. VI (16 Sept 1933), 325-26; rptd in THEATRE (Lond: MacGibbon & Kee, 1954), pp. 124-28.

In *Sheppey,* M is not "sentimentalizing" the hero.

1076* MacCarthy, Desmond. "William Somerset Maugham: 'The English Maupassant'—An Appreciation," NASH'S-PALL MALL MAGAZINE, XCI (May 1933), 12-15, 66-68; rptd as a pamphlet (Lond: William Heinemann, 1934); in W. S. Maugham, *Altogether* (Lond: Heinemann, 1934) [no pagination]; and in MEMORIES (Lond: MacGibbon and Kee, 1953), pp. 61-68.

Novelists enjoy first-rate prestige when their works "delight the many and satisfy the discriminating few." Although M began "as an author for the few," his name became associated with popular money-making plays so that the development of his reputation has been on the whole "from without inwards." At first, M seemed to have no talent for comedy and he seemed to be "as business-like as a novelist as he is as a playwright. The itch for perfection doesn't trouble him; the adequate will do." But later M's higher qualities became evident; he was a "sincere realist . . . as much a man of the world as he is an artist." M is more than a "cynic": to be put in possession of elements necessary to understanding him as a writer, the reader would do well to observe the narrator of "The Human Element," who, speaking for M himself, reveals "a very unusual sensibility instantly defended by an unamiable self-protective impulse, which in its turn is corrected by a more just response." In M's handling of human beings, usually "these three reactions come into play."

1077* March, Fred T. "Tales of the East by Somerset Maugham," NEW YORK TIMES BOOK REVIEW, 19 Nov 1933, p. 9.
"The stories in *Ah King* are all gently moving psychological narratives beneath the surface of which is a small core of horror or perversity." M is brilliant only in flashes, persuasive only upon occasion, subtle only rarely. But he is a good, intelligent storyteller, with a reservoir of professional cleverness.

1078 Mortier, Alfred. QUINZE ANS DE THEATRE (1917-1932) (FIFTEEN YEARS OF DRAMA [1917-1932]) (Paris: Albert Messein, 1933), pp. 470-71.
The Sacred Flame, as adapted by H. de Carbuccia, is a laborious and puerile play. [In French.]

1079 "Mr. Maugham's Anthology," NEW YORK TIMES BOOK REVIEW, 11 June 1933, p. 8.
In *Traveller's Library,* M "has made a prodigal and excellent collection . . . excellently planned for travelers by steamship or by plane," but appealing to anyone.

1080* Muir, Edwin. "New Novels," LISTENER, X (4 Oct 1933), 519.
M is one of the "most skilful novelists writing today"; he is honest, efficient, and describes life as he sees it, not as he would like to see it. But, one feels that M sees with "one eye and that the clarity of his view of human life has been reached by leaving out an astonishing number of things." The best stories in *Ah King* are "The Door of Opportunity" and "Neil MacAdam."

1081* Muir, Percy H. "William Somerset Maugham: Some Bibliographical Observations," BOOK-COLLECTOR'S QUARTERLY, IX (Jan-March 1933), 72-84; ibid, X (April-June 1933), 19-26
[A criticism of Frederick T. Bason's A BIBLIOGRAPHY OF THE WRITINGS OF W. SOMERSET MAUGHAM (1931), pointing out mistakes and problems.]

1082 "New Novels," TIMES (Lond), 19 Sept 1933, p. 6.
Ah King is stamped with M's literary imprint; no story is unworthy of him, although "The Vessel of Wrath" and "The Book-Bag" seem better than the rest.

1083 "New Novels," TIMES LITERARY SUPPLEMENT (Lond), 21 Sept 1933, p. 628.
In *Ah King,* M is not a great stylist, but an admirable teller of tales with a great power for holding the reader's attention. He possesses a certain inability to appreciate any beauty of character in women, choosing to portray them as weak, hypocritical, and selfish.

1084 "The News-Week in Entertainment," NEWS-WEEK, I (22 April 1933), 28.

For Services Rendered is "penetrating and unflinching, if exaggerated."

1085 "The News-Week in Entertainment," NEWS-WEEK, I (20 May 1933), 30.

M's translation of Luigi Chiarelli's LA MASCHERA E IL VOLTO as *The Mask and the Face* is "dull and pretentious."

1086 N[ichols], L[ewis]. "The Play," NEW YORK TIMES, 13 April 1933, p. 15.

For Services Rendered is a trifle wordy at times, and has incidents which don't further the main action, but as a whole is "good."

1087 N[ichols], L[ewis]. "The Play," NEW YORK TIMES, 9 May 1933, p. 20; rptd by Raymond Mander and Joe Mitchenson, eds, in THEATRICAL COMPANION TO MAUGHAM (Lond: Rockliff, 1955), pp. 244-45.

M's translation of Luigi Chiarelli's LA MASCHERA E IL VOLTO as *The Mask and the Face* "allowed itself the relaxation of a good many titters in place of the more lordly comedy — and quite often it just sat down and rested."

1088 "Our Booking-Office: Malay Scandal," PUNCH, CLXXXV (27 Sept 1933), 362-63.

Ah King is "reminiscent of the gossip of scandalmongers at a village tea-party and very much more unsavoury." The only truly amusing story is "The Vessel of Wrath."

1089* P., G. C. "Theatre," SATURDAY REVIEW (Lond), CLVI (23 Sept 1933), 327-28.

"Maugham is a serious and brilliant writer of plays whose work must have a significance beyond that of the passing moment." *Sheppey* is wrongly charged with bad construction and a refusal to deal seriously with theme and character. An objectionable action, however, is M's "killing off his Christian hairdresser at the end of act three." Of the entrance of the "Grey Lady — who is Death" at the end of the play: "Not even Shakespeare could make a ghost effective," and there is no reason for Sheppey to die. Otherwise, M pursues "his characters along the most natural lines of their development," and he was not dealing "with any tremendous theme to which he ought to have hung closely in some kind of fervour of revivalism." The play is important and interesting, but not among M's best.

1090 Pierhal, Armand. "Les Revues étrangères: William Somerset Maugham" (Foreign Reviews: William Somerset Maugham), LES NOUVELLES LITTERAIRES, 23 Sept 1933, p. 7.

An acknowledged repetition of an article by Mme. Kathleen Bellamy in

LA NACION (Buenos Aires, 20 Aug 1933), tracing the difficulties of M's literary career as a symbol of all writers' difficulties in general. [In French.]

1091 Playbill. "Off with the Motley," THEATRE WORLD (Lond), XX (July 1933), 36-37.

M upholds his belief in the ephemeral nature of drama. [Interview with M after the failure of *For Services Rendered*.]

1092 Plomer, William. "Fiction: *Ah King*," SPECTATOR (Lond), CLI (29 Sept 1933), 420.

M's short stories "are among the best now being written." Though he "seldom explores the depths and intricacies of human nature," he is well-versed in human behavior and has the power of discovering the remarkable in the lives of ordinary people. "The best of these stories, 'Neil MacAdam,' seems to me as good as Maupassant."

1093* Quèry, Suzanne. LA PHILOSOPHIE DE WILLIAM SOMERSET MAUGHAM (THE PHILOSOPHY OF WILLIAM SOMERSET MAUGHAM) (Paris: Les Editions de France, 1933).

[Study of M as a thinker rather than as a novelist analyzing his deep-felt pity and veiled stoicism, his attitude toward men, women in love, environment and its influence.] [In French.]

1094 Sée, Edmond. "Le Théâtre et la vie" (Drama and Life), LA REVUE DE FRANCE, 13ème année, no. 1 (1 Feb 1933), 505-6.

[Brief review of the French translation and revival of *The Circle*.] [In French.]

1095 "*'Sheppey,'* at Wyndham's," ILLUSTRATED LONDON NEWS, CLXXXIII (23 Sept 1933), 484.

This "bitter, discontented play . . . will leave the average playgoer wondering what lesson it is desired to teach, or what particular vice it seeks to flagellate."

1096* Skinner, R. Dana. "The Play," COMMONWEAL, XVII (26 April 1933), 719.

In *For Services Rendered,* M has written "a curiously inept play about a theme that deserves superb and rich treatment." Not only is the tale incredible, but M has "smeared nearly every incident of the play with destructive pessimism and a philosophy of superlative selfishness."

1097 Skinner, R. Dana. "The Play and the Screen," COMMONWEAL, XVIII (26 May 1933), 107.

"All the king's writers and all the king's actors could not make Chiarelli's dull epigrams a play." [Review of M's translation of Luigi Chiarelli's LA MASCHERA E IL VOLTO as *The Mask and the Face*.]

1098 Strowski, Fortunat. LE THEATRE ET NOUS (THE THEATER AND US) (Paris: Les Editions de la Nouvelle Revue Critique, 1933), pp. 29-30, 147-48, 161-62.
[Discussions of the use of props in the French productions of *The Letter,* RAIN, and *The Constant Wife.*] [In French.]

1099 "The Theatre: New Plays in Manhattan," TIME, XXI (24 April 1933), 21.
In *For Services Rendered,* Fay Bainter gave a praiseworthy impersonation of Eva Ardsley—"the one three-dimensional role the piece affords." Few would consider the play "a dramatic milestone."

1100 "Theatre: New Plays in Manhattan," TIME, XXI (15 May 1933), 52.
M's translation of Luigi Chiarelli's LA MASCHERA E IL VOLTO as *The Mask and the Face* is a "handy translation from the Italian."

1101* Thérive, André. "Les Livres" (Books), LE TEMPS, 31 Aug 1933, p. 3.
In *First Person Singular* and *The Narrow Corner*, M is the master of the narrative, of neatness, precision, and the elegant care not to display the deep universal truths born of an attentive observation. He is a good example in France for those who hate snobbery and boredom. All the stories of *First Person Singular* are bound by the common theme of immorality or pretentiousness in society. *The Narrow Corner* is an exotic novel, surpassing Stevenson's short stories or the finest tales of Joseph Conrad. Here M clearly confronts Oriental wisdom and European affectation. [Review of the French translations, in French.]

1102 Walpole, Hugh. "Tendencies of the Modern Novel: I. -England," FORTNIGHTLY REVIEW, N. S. CXXXIV (Oct 1933), 407-15; rptd in TENDENCIES OF THE MODERN NOVEL (Lond: George Allen and Unwin, 1934), pp. 14, 23.
On studying the "vacant chairs" in English letters, M is refused a seat because he used "old methods" and has never attained to the "dignity" of *Of Human Bondage* again.

1103 W[oodruff], D[ouglas]. "At the Play," PUNCH, CLXXXV (27 Sept 1933), 358.
Sheppey is "a simple story and unsatisfactory as a plot." The play is "not the bearer of a message from the New Testament nor . . . a hackneyed contrast between Christian precept and worldly practice, but a comedy of lower middle-class feeling and no more."

1104* Wyatt, Euphemia Van Rensselaer. "The Drama," CATHOLIC WORLD, CXXXVII (May 1933), 208-10.

In *For Services Rendered,* M's thesis is that World War I was responsible for the individual tragedies he shows, but one wonders if the tragedies might not have occurred equally as well under circumstances of peace, and indeed, if the characters themselves could not have thought more of what they had to offer life than of what life had to offer them.

1105 Wyatt, Euphemia Van Rensselaer. "The Drama," Catholic World, CXXXVII (June 1933), 337-38.
M's translation of Luigi Chiarelli's La Maschera e il Volto as *The Mask and the Face* was poorly staged.

1106* "Wyndham's Theatre: *'Sheppey'* by W. Somerset Maugham," Times (Lond), 15 Sept 1933, p. 10.
M takes on a "prodigious subject" but instead of discussing it, he turns in the third act "into a by-path" and takes "a short cut home." Instead of discussing the life of the Gospel or criticizing Sheppey's interpretation, he gives a bitter and brilliant ironic study of the family's self-protective resistance. M has written with fluency, judgment and wit—"with everything indeed, except the supreme devotion that might have exchanged success for a masterpiece."

1107 Young, Stark. "Sur le Lac," New Republic, LXXV (24 May 1933), 46-47.
[Review of M's translation of Luigi Chiarelli's La Maschera e il Volto as *The Mask and the Face.* No discussion of the translation. Production of the play was poorly received.]

1108 Yvon, P. "Livres" (Books), La Revue Anglo-Americaine, X (Feb 1933), 271-72.
First Person Singular contains amusing or tragical stories, but always bitter. [In French.]

1934

1109 Audiat, Pierre. "L'Actualité littéraire" (Current Literature), La Revue de France, 14ème année, no. 4 (15 Aug 1934), 718-19.
In *Ah King,* the stories are not only distinguishable from one another, but their characters are also distinctly realized. [Review of the French translation, in French.]

1110* Bellessort, André. "La Semaine dramatique: Théâtre Sarah Bernhardt: *La Lettre*" (The Dramatic Week: Sarah Bernhardt Theater: *The Letter*), LE JOURNAL DES DEBATS [POLITIQUES ET LITTERAIRES], 10 Sept 1934, p. 3.

Elements of the detective novel neutralize the play's psychological interests; M's real originality is to have evoked Europeans' sensual lives in the colonies, and in doing so, he is more daring than either Kipling or Conrad. The flashback presents a problem: it is a cinematographic trick, used for an unnecessary scene. The stage and the cinema are heterogeneous arts; cinema's province is the art of simultaneity, theater's the art of the concrete and the actual. [Review of the revived French adaptation.] [In French.]

1111 Billy, André. "Femmes dans la Jungle" (Women in the Jungle), GRINGOIRE, 29 June 1934, p. 4.

M is more interested in the crimes committed by respectable people. The French translation of *Ah King* contributes to his reputation as a storyteller and a moralist. [In French.]

1112 "Books: Maugham Shorts," TIME, XXIV (13 Aug 1934), 60.

Especially important in *East and West* is the preface, in which M "gives his views on the art of the short story, pays his respects to the two masters of the trade, Maupassant and Chekhov."

1113 Brûlé, A. "Livres" (Books), LA REVUE ANGLO-AMERICAINE, XII:2 (Dec 1934), 174.

The six short stories of *Ah King* show M at his best; the most remarkable one is "The Book-Bag." [In French.]

1114 Brûlé, A. "*Plays, Volume I* (*Lady Frederick, Mrs. Dot, Jack Straw*), Tauchnitz," LA REVUE ANGLO-AMERICAINE, XI (June 1934), 462.

M's preface is the most interesting part of the book. M's dialogue is dimly reminiscent of Oscar Wilde's, but more vulgar in order to please the public at large. The plays have been performed successfully, have brought M some fame and royalties, but have nothing to do with literature. [In French.]

1115* Brûlé, A. "*Plays, Volume II (Penelope, Smith, The Land of Promise),* Tauchnitz," LA REVUE ANGLO-AMERICAINE, XI (Aug 1934), 552.

M did not give himself much trouble in his plays. He knows the playwright's task admirably and does not expect too much of the reader, building well-made plots with some ideas to sustain them, the psychology more or less false. "Happy are those authors who can write with such virtuosity and be as little self-exacting without being haunted by remorse." [In French.]

1116 Brûlé, A. "*Plays, Volume III (Our Betters, Caroline, Home* *and Beauty),* Tauchnitz," LA REVUE ANGLO-AMERICAINE, XII (Oct 1934), 74.

M himself gives an idea of the value of his plays by saying that he only thought of the "entertainment of the audience," and that "art has nothing to do with the multitude." It is a pity there exists no sanatorium where authors can be cured of realism and commercial art. [In French.]

1117* Brûlé, A. "*Plays, Volume IV (The Circle, The Constant Wife, The Breadwinner),* Tauchnitz," LA REVUE AMERICAINE, XII (Dec 1934), 165.

The Circle is a clever but flimsy production, *The Constant Wife* would suit the *théâtre de boulevards, The Breadwinner* deals with a more important subject: it is a protest against the absurdity of our civilization. However, the subject has already been treated by Wells in MARRIAGE and Aldington in ALL MEN ARE ENEMIES. [In French.]

1118 Cartier, Maurice. "A l'Etalage" (On Display), GRINGOIRE, 15 June 1934, p. 4.

With a mixture of irony, candid observation, drama and secret compassion, M in *Ah King* has infused the short story with a new life. [Review of the French translation, in French.]

1119 Cartier, Maurice. "A l'Etalage" (On Display), GRINGOIRE, 7 Dec 1934, p. 12.

First Person Singular reveals M's careful analysis of English manners. [Review of the French translation, in French.]

1120 Chandler, Frank W., and Richard A. Cordell. "Somerset Maugham," TWENTIETH CENTURY PLAYS (NY: Thomas Nelson and Sons, 1934), pp. 293-94.

[Biographical and critical introduction to *The Breadwinner.*]

1121* Cowley, Malcolm. "Angry Author's Complaint," NEW REPUBLIC, LXXX (22 Aug 1934), 51-52; rptd in THE MAUGHAM ENIGMA, ed by Klaus W. Jonas (NY: Citadel P, 1954), pp. 180-84. 180-84.

Though M is "the best plain story-teller writing in English," his characters in *East and West* are unvaryingly complacent Britons of good family. M shares their prejudices, but does not like them. His smug and insulting tolerance of humankind gives M's stories a quality that may explain why so many readers dislike them.

1122 Cru, Robert-L. "La Saison Théâtrale à Londres" (The Theatrical Season in London), LE TEMPS, 9 July 1934, p. 2.

Sheppey is in the tradition of good comedies of manners. [General survey of the theatrical season in England.] [In French.]

1123 Dorsenne, Jean. "Le Théâtre: *La Lettre*" (The Drama: *The Letter*), GRINGOIRE, 14 Sept 1934, p. 10.

No writer has dared depict the influence of a sensual or oppressive climate not only on the whites as a class but on white women in particular. Leslie's case would be monstrous for metropolitans yet scarcely surprising for colonials. [Review of the revival of the French adaptation.] [In French.]

1124 Dottin, Paul. "La Littérature anglaise en 1933" (English Literature in 1933), LA REVUE DE FRANCE, 14ème année, no. 3 (1 June 1934), 523-24.

In *Ah King,* M is without illusions, and satirizes "Pharisees" only. [In French.]

1125 Dukes, Ashley. "The Scene in Europe," THEATRE ARTS MONTHLY, XVIII (Feb 1934), 101.

Sheppey fails because M reduces an intriguing theme to nothing more than an "ironic reflection on the Christlikeness of a Christian society." The play's short run resulted both from this failure, and from the public's increasing dislike of thesis plays.

1126 "Echos: *La Femme dans la Jungle* de W. Somerset Maugham" (Echos: *Ah King* by Somerset Maugham), JOURNAL DE GENEVE, 29 June 1934, p. 2.

M's reputation is now solidly established; he excels in the long short story of passion in the East. "The Door of Opportunity" is particularly good. [In French.]

1127 "Expert Short Stories," SATURDAY REVIEW OF LITERATURE, XI (11 Aug 1934), 46.

The thirty stories of *East and West* are distinguished by M's flair for characters. He is particularly gifted in presenting "the human being under all the curious warpings that nature and circumstances have lent him." M frequently compares favorably with Kipling.

1128* Greene, Graham. "Books of the Day: Maugham's Short Stories," SPECTATOR (Lond), CLIII (31 Aug 1934), 297; rptd as Part 2 of "Some Notes on Somerset Maugham," COLLECTED ESSAYS (NY: Viking, 1969), pp. 199-202.

The "Preface" to *Altogether* is "a finely written, delightfully 'sensible' essay on the short story." M "represents Maupassant's influence when most English short-story writers of any merit represent Chekhov's." M is "a writer of great dedication" whose occasional banality results from a "rather blasé attitude toward the details of his story." The narrative is something that "has to be got through." Like Maupassant's, M's best stories are anecdotes. Those that fail sprawl into the novel's region. The first-person-singular leads to monotony in a collected volume and shows the limitations of M's interest in his craft. M's defense of popular magazines is criticized because "his good fortune has blinded him to the demands the popular magazine makes on its less famous writers."

1129 Hansen, Agnes Camilla. TWENTIETH CENTURY FORCES IN EUROPEAN FICTION (Chicago: American Library Association, 1934), p. 84.

M was influenced by Bergson, showing "fate as the inevitable result of character, and how the individual's power to shape destiny depended on his own spiritual development."

1130* Hoops, Reinald. DER EINFLUSS DER PSYCHOANALYSE AUF DIE ENGLISCHE LITERATUR (THE INFLUENCE OF PSYCHOANALYSIS ON ENGLISH LITERATURE) (Heidelberg: Carl Winter, 1934), pp. 109-14, 182, 212-15, 217.

M's analysis of character is convincing. With the exception of his short story "Rain" (in which M uses typical dream symbols unobtrusively to anticipate the outcome of the action), his fiction does not show the influence of psychoanalysis. Parts of his novel, *Of Human Bondage,* may, however, be elucidated with the help of psychoanalytical concepts. Perhaps his aversion from the elaborate treatment of sexual questions prevented him from using psychoanalysis in his fiction. In his play, *The Sacred Flame,* important ideas of psychoanalysis are taken for granted. [In German.]

1131* Kronenberger, Louis. "The Story-Telling Art of Mr. Maugham," NEW YORK TIMES BOOK REVIEW, 12 Aug 1934, p. 2.

M can attract, with his gift for storytelling, anyone from the man in the street to the genuine highbrow, yet his sense of values lags behind his artistic abilities. In *East and West,* one looks in vain for the realistic promise of the early novels and the unchallenged reality of *Of Human Bondage.* "His themes are remarkably varied, his locales are diversified, his story-telling is flexible; and yet for all their variety these tales seem altogether alike and produce an altogether like effect. . . . Nowhere has his brilliance served to uncover depth—it has been turned into a kaleidoscope, not into a light."

1132 Lang, André. "Le Livre parlé" (The Book Discussed), LES ANNALES POLITIQUES ET LITTERAIRES, No. 2512 (7 Sept 1934), 282.

In *Ah King,* M makes the reader perceive life "as it is" and smile. [Review of the French translation, in French.]

1133 Leggett, H. W. THE IDEA IN FICTION (Lond: George Allen & Unwin, 1934), pp. 45, 65, 111, 112, 120, 142.

The *tempo* of a novel is differentiated from the *tempo* of a play through an analysis of M's structure in *Penelope. The Narrow Corner* is a novel in which the occasion performs somewhat less than its normal function. A passage from *Ashenden* exemplifies how an author's character is revealed in his style. M is a craftsman in the class of authors like Jane Austen.

1134* Lynd, Sylvia. "Books of the Day," OBSERVER (Lond), 26 Aug 1934, p. 4.

In *The Works of W. Somerset Maugham* [Collected Edition including *Liza of Lambeth, The Painted Veil, Ashenden, Cakes and Ale*] and *Altogether: The Collected Short Stories* [British title of *East and West*], M shows himself to be an animal who defends himself before he is attacked. If he has been treated unsatisfactorily by critics, it is because "he does not fit into ready-made states of soul, and seldom fits into ready-made states of opinion." M's world is as free from flattery as La Rochefoucauld's, as full of "humiliating disasters" as Maupassant's. But M's forte is "theatre" and in his novels and short stories, this quality "falsifies" life in a way it would not in a play. It leads, in the novels, to long speeches, "theatricalities of words." Only *Of Human Bondage* is free of the foregoing flaws, but it is far too long, conveys no emotion to the reader. M, in sum, has "only a narrow range of cleverness and knowledge."

1135 "Miscellany: Somerset Maugham," NEW STATESMAN AND NATION, N. S. VII (6 Jan 1934), 13-14.

[A general assessment of M's career as a playwright and novelist, with a caricature portrait overleaf.]

1136* Mortimer, Raymond. "Re-reading Mr. Maugham," NEW STATESMAN AND NATION, N. S. VIII (25 Aug 1934), 243-44.

In *Altogether: The Collected Stories* [British title of *East and West*], M "does not hit, either instinctively or on reflection, the perfect word to indicate an object"; in his writing there are few clichés, but there is also little vividness. In dialogue, however, M excels; in only a few words his characters reveal their social backgrounds, their pretensions, and the passions they seek to conceal. The stories are therefore excellent for their "suspense." Although M does not possess "a poetic vision of the world," at least he does not pretend to it, and he has always had a literary virtue greater than craftsmanship—"the power to seize and hold the reader's attention."

1137 "Mr. Maugham's Novels," TIMES LITERARY SUPPLEMENT (Lond), 19 July 1934, p. 506.

The Works of W. Somerset Maugham [including *Liza of Lambeth, The Painted Veil, Ashenden,* and *Cakes and Ale*] reveals that "more successfully than almost any novelist of his period, Arnold Bennett excepted," M has "attempted in fiction that rigid precision of form which is essential in another art closer to his heart, the drama."

1138 "Novels for the Library List: Short Story Collections," SATURDAY REVIEW (Lond), CLVIII (22 Sept 1934), 151.
M has selected the stories of *Altogether* [British title of *East and West*] and written a preface which discusses "the relative merits of de Maupassant and Chekhov and also indicates his own methods of composing the short story."

1139 "Our Booking-Office: Drama in Fiction," PUNCH, CLXXXVII (5 Sept 1934), 278-79.
Altogether [British title of *East and West*] suggests that M is not interested in ordinary people, and his stories seem anecdotal, but his climaxes never fail. "The Alien Corn" is among "the best of several perfect works of art."

1140 Pellizzi, Camillo. IL TEATRO INGLESE (THE ENGLISH THEATER) (Milan: Fratelli Treves Editori, 1934), pp. 356-59.
M's variety in theme and intention makes it difficult to classify him in one school of playwrights. [In Italian.]

1141 Sée, Edmond. "A travers l'actualité théâtricale" (In the Theater Currently), LA REVUE DE FRANCE, 14ème année, no. 5 (1 Oct 1934), 572.
[Brief review of the French revival of *The Letter*.] [In French.]

1142* "Shorter Notices," NATION (NY), CXXXVIII (10 Jan 1934), 51.
In *Ah King,* M's method is suave and sleek. "When a story fails as 'The Vessel of Wrath' does, it is the validity of the material which may be questioned and not the way it was handled. 'The Door of Opportunity' succeeds because the balance between character and incident is recorded with a certainty and ease that make the narrative tense and exhilarating. If the author allows himself no feeling, neither does he indulge in the more intellectual sport of cynicism. This prohibits . . . great dramatic qualities or any satire. But Mr. Maugham, with disarming self-confidence in his truly acute powers of observation and in his technical skill, never attempts to produce more than exciting exhibitions of human behavior."

1143 Smet, Robert de. "Le Mouvement dramatique en Angleterre" (The Drama Movement in England), LA REVUE DE PARIS, 41ème année, no. 5 (1 Oct 1934), 700-701.
In *Sheppey,* the conversation with Death is a beautiful scene, but its symbolism is incongruent with the rest of the play's method of construction and presentation. [In French.]

1144 Strowski, Fortunat. "Le Secret de Somerset Maugham" (The Secret of Somerset Maugham), GRINGOIRE, 19 Jan 1934, p. 4.

M is most of all a moralist in the French manner of La Bruyère and La Rochefoucauld. [Critical appreciation.] [In French.]

1145 Thiébaut, Marcel. "Parmi les livres" (Among Books), La Revue de Paris, 41ème année, no. 4 (15 July 1934), 476-77.

In *Ah King,* M's ability is extraordinary, never boring. [Review of the French translation, in French.]

1146 Thiébaut, Marcel. "Parmi les livres: Somerset Maugham" (Among Books), La Revue de Paris, 41ème année, no. 1 (15 Jan 1934), 952-55.

M is a gentleman-writer, walking with hands in pockets, interested in everything but especially his compatriots in foreign lands. [Review of the French translation of *On A Chinese Screen.*] [In French.]

1147 W., F. *"Ah King,"* Bookman (Lond), LXXV (Feb 1934), 461-62.

M's capacity for dialogue fares less well in narrative than it does in drama, and in the stories of the present collection there is "something incredibly cheap and second-hand that is unpleasantly reminiscent of certain American films woven around the irreconcilability of East and West." "Neil MacAdam" is best because it is the most economically told; "The Vessel of Wrath" has an excellent idea, "ruinously overwritten."

1148 Walpole, Hugh. Captain Nicholas: A Modern Comedy. Garden City: Doubleday, Doran, 1934.

The fictive novelist, "Somerset Ball," is often roughly treated by the younger aesthetes because they are exasperated by his slick "shamness." However, Captain Nicholas adds as the last word that Ball's novels are redeemed by a "real sense of terror. . . . He knows what it is to be frightened —unlike all your splendid modern young Siegfrieds who go cynically up the mountain although they know the fire's false. Ball knows the fire's real. He was burnt once." [This novel appears to contain *two* portraits of M, the portrait of Somerset Ball intended, perhaps, to disguise the fact that Captain Nicholas himself represents certain traits of M. Nicholas wanders from place to place with his daughter, Lizzie (cf. Leverson Hurle of Gin and Bitters by A. Riposte), finally settles with a family whose harmony is temporarily disrupted by Nicholas' philosophy that "family life and old-fashioned ideas like fidelity and religion are absurd now," etc.]

1149 Williams, Orlo. "Books New and Old: Realistic Prose Drama," National Review (Lond), CII (May 1934), 676-83.

The hope for new life in the drama is based not in the restoration of verse, but of "poetic intelligence" to dramatic art; the lack of "poetic intelligence" is found, for example, in M's *The Sacred Flame,* in which the tension is sustained not by the moral conflict in any of the characters' hearts, but "the question of the detective drama: 'Who did the deed?' " [Review of Volumes V and VI of *Collected Plays*.]

1935

1150 "Books," NEWS-WEEK, VI (27 July 1935), 39-40.
[Noncommittal survey of *Don Fernando*'s contents.]

1151 "Books: Might-have-been," TIME, XXVI (5 Aug 1935), 60.
Don Fernando is interesting but not a substitute for the novel M wanted to write.

1152 Brenner, Anita. "A Gentleman and His Personality," NATION (NY), CXLI (21 Aug 1935), 221.
M should have entitled *Don Fernando* "Personality: My Own and Some Unlike Mine."

1153* Brown, Ivor. "British Comedy," THEATRE ARTS MONTHLY, XIX (Aug 1935), 585-93.
M started out like Wilde, but his comic style may now best be described as a "plain style." Like Noël Coward, he relies on the actor's projection of his words rather than on the words themselves. His comedy is not like the "light farce" of Shakespeare, Congreve, and Sheridan because it is a "mixture of humor and pathos, realistic, underwritten, matter-of-fact."

1154 Canby, Henry Seidel. "The Soul of Spain," SATURDAY REVIEW OF LITERATURE, XII (27 July 1935), 7.
In *Don Fernando,* a "diary of a cultivated writer's experiences with the soul of Spain," M shows himself not happy with Spanish history, and more lively, though less sound, with Spanish art. M's digressions and aperçus offer some of the most interesting passages of the book.

1155 Cartier, Maurice. "A l'Etalage" (On Display), GRINGOIRE, 31 May 1935, p. 4.
In *The Narrow Corner,* M draws astonishing characters with his customary indulgent lucidity. [Review of the French translation, in French.]

1156 *"Don Fernando,"* KIRKUS, III (15 July 1935), 200.
[Brief appraisal.]

1157* Ervine, St. John. "The Plays of W. Somerset Maugham," LIFE AND LETTERS, XI (March 1935), 640-55; rptd as "Maugham the Playwright," THE WORLD OF SOMERSET MAUGHAM, ed by Klaus W. Jonas (NY: British Book Centre, 1959), pp. 142-62.

In his plays, as in his novels, M "tells a story in a terse and quick and vivid manner," his views more often than not subordinated to the tale. M deplores "wasting time on opinions or extraneous decoration." A great craftsman, a born storyteller, M is a better dramatist than Congreve, and if he took his plays as seriously as he does his novels, he could "become the most notable dramatist of his day." The plays fall into three clearly-marked categories: (1) those light comedies in which M himself scarcely obtrudes a thought *(Lady Frederick)*; (2) those comedies in which the cynicism commonly attributed to M reveals itself, particularly in connection with marriage *(Caesar's Wife, The Circle,* and *The Constant Wife)*; and (3) those plays of "deepening bitterness" *(For Services Rendered* and *Sheppey).* In this last group, particularly in *Sheppey,* one discerns the voice of "that generous-minded and socially-indignant doctor," which was to be found in M's first novel *Liza of Lambeth* and which M will hopefully assert in a future "noble play."

1158 Fadiman, Clifton. "Books: Mr. Maugham's Golden Age," NEW YORKER, XI (20 July 1935), 51-52.

The remarks on El Greco are the "high point" of *Don Fernando,* but the entire book is "beautifully written" and "constantly interesting."

1159* Greene, Graham. "Books of the Day: Spanish Gold," SPECTATOR (Lond), CLIV (21 June 1935), 1076; rptd in THE MAUGHAM ENIGMA, ed by Klaus W. Jonas (NY: Citadel P, 1954), pp. 194-96; and as Part 1 of "Some Notes on Somerset Maugham," COLLECTED ESSAYS (NY: Viking, 1969), pp. 197-99.

Don Fernando marks a change from M's earlier "coloured, violent stories of the popular magazines"; it is his "best book." It may seem "superficially discursive" at times, but M is always working toward the statement of his theme, that the Spanish "excelled in what is greater than art—in man." The theme is portrayed with "the highest kind of justice."

1160 Holliday, Terence. "The Love Story of Mr. Maugham and Spain," NEW YORK HERALD TRIBUNE, 21 July 1935, p. 7.

As a writer M is "professional to the last degree," but as a traveler, reader, observer of painting and architecture, "he has never lost the saving, distinguishing touch of the amateur," and so his impressions in *Don Fernando* are "delightfully alive."

1161 Isaacs, Edith J. R. "Merry Feast of Playgoing: Broadway in Review," THEATRE ARTS MONTHLY, XIX (April 1935), 257.

The revival of John Colton and Clemence Randolph's dramatization, RAIN, is still fresh; it gets the audience's attention despite—perhaps because of—its conventionality. It lives, in effect, by its defects as well as its virtues.

1162 K., V. "Harvinaisen mielenkiintoinen ensi-ilta Kaupungin-teatterissa" (A Particularly Interesting First Night at the Town Theater), KARJALA, 1 Nov 1935, p. 3.
M's way of revealing human misery is too merciless, often without any trace of humor. But there is something in his plays that calls forth serious thinking and self-examination on the part of the audience. [Review of the Finnish adaptation of RAIN.[[In Finnish.]

1163 Linn, James Weber, and Houghton Wells Taylor. A FOREWORD TO FICTION (NY and Lond: D. Appleton-Century, 1935), pp. 67, 69, 73, 77-81, 193 ["The Letter"]; 25, 52, 55-56, 93, 188, 192 [*Of Human Bondage*].
"The Letter" is used to illustrate the structure of a short story, and Philip of *Of Human Bondage* is used to illustrate the "developing" character.

1164 "Maugham Comes Back with Autobiography," NEW YORK TIMES, 9 Nov 1935, p. 13.
M returned to America after nine years absence and brought with him the manuscript of "his autobiography for which he has not yet found a title." M has seen twenty-eight of the thirty plays he wrote, but no film versions of any of his works. He has given up writing plays because "a novelist can have a lot of fun boring people." [Interview.]

1165 Mortimer, Raymond. "Mr. Maugham," NEW STATESMAN AND NATION, N. S. IX (29 June 1935), 966.
Parts of *Don Fernando* "are rather dull, notably seventeen pages, where seven would have been enough, of a Sixteenth Century Dialogue. . . . [The] book is for educated persons, written by one of the most intelligent men alive."

1166 Neuschaeffer, Walter. DOSTOJEWSKIJS EINFLUSS AUF DEN ENGLISCHEN ROMAN (DOSTOEVSKI'S INFLUENCE ON THE ENGLISH NOVEL), Anglistische Forschungen, 81 (Heidelberg: Carl Winter, 1935), pp. 39-42.
The narrator in *The Moon and Sixpence* resembles Vanya in THE INSULTED AND THE INJURED. Dostoevski's influence is evident in *Ashenden,* especially in Chapter VI, which is reminiscent of CRIME AND PUNISHMENT. Ashenden himself occasionally reminds the reader of Raskolnikoff. The last tale in *Ah King* echoes THE BROTHERS KARAMAZOV, Book IV, Chapter 3. On the whole, M views his characters from the outside and does not lay their souls bare as the Russian writer does. [In German.]

1167 "New Novels," TIMES LITERARY SUPPLEMENT (Lond), 27 June 1935, p. 414.
Don Fernando is deep, profound and probing. M sees and understands much

more than any of the previous "reviewers" of Spain and Spanish history. His book is well-researched, well-imagined; but best of all is his happy balance which "strikes between the objective and subjective in an essentially personal and beautifully written book."

1168 Poore, C[harles] G. "Somerset Maugham's Spanish Themes," NEW YORK TIMES BOOK REVIEW, 21 July 1935, p. 2.

Don Fernando is "a diverting and discursive exploration of Spain's Golden Age," in which the best passages are descriptions of the way a hungry and indomitable people lived. Reading it is "like reading all the material someone had gathered for a historical novel, and everything else that had entered his mind as he went along."

1169 Pritchett, V. S. "Somerset Maugham Revisits Spain," CHRISTIAN SCIENCE MONITOR WEEKLY MAGAZINE SECTION, 24 July 1935, p. 12.

M's sentimental and vulgar man-of-the-world attitude appears very little in *Don Fernando,* and his final judgment on Spanish greatness is profound.

1170 Sitwell, Osbert. "The Spain of Somerset Maugham," LONDON MERCURY, XXXII (Sept 1935), 485-86.

M, like Yeats, never rests on his past accomplishments; *Don Fernando* is "intensely original," filled with "illuminating side-shots" (such as the one on Zurbarán).

1171 "Spanish Themes: Mr. Somerset Maugham's New Book," TIMES (Lond), 21 June 1935, p. 10.

With *Don Fernando,* M cannot fail to add to his reputation as dramatist and novelist; his balance between subjectivity and objectivity is "invariably stimulating."

1172* Stein, Aaron. "Books on Our Table: Somerset Maugham Considers Spain and the Golden Age," NEW YORK POST, 27 July 1935, p. 7.

In *Don Fernando,* M's judgments of Spanish literature are not corrupted by his admiration of the Spaniards as men; his portraits are "warm and virile." The entire book "weaves a circular pattern of philosophy, criticism and biography around its central idea until the statement of its conclusion brings sudden and vivid cohesion to the seemingly haphazard graces of the elaborate frame."

1173* Swinnerton, Frank. THE GEORGIAN LITERARY SCENE: A PANORAMA (Lond & Toronto: W. Heinemann, 1935), pp. 14, 178, 185, especially 208-15, 220, 243, 298.

M is a "born novelist and dramatist of the non-heroic type." Realism and melodrama are his domain, but not romance. M's unromantic *Of Human*

Bondage, a chronicle novel, differs from other novels of its kind by virtue of its "simplicity" and its depiction of Philip "without archness, defence, and unnecessary explanation." It resembles, in plot, George Moore's A MODERN LOVER, but, in contrast to Moore, M says precisely what he means, and the reader reads his book effortlessly. [See, also, THE GEORGIAN LITERARY SCENE: 1910-1935 — A PANORAMA. Eighth Edition (Lond: Hutchinson, 1954), pp. 18, 143, 144, 150, especially 167-74.]

1174 Swinnerton, Frank. "New Maugham Book Gossip About Spain," CHICAGO DAILY TRIBUNE, 20 July 1935, p. 6.

Not a novel, not a history, not a book of travel, not a critical essay, *Don Fernando* is "a remarkable personal combination of all these different things."

1175 Taggard, Ernestine K. "Somerset Maugham," SCHOLASTIC, XXVI (9 March 1935), 6, 11.

Of Human Bondage is M's greatest work, *The Moon and Sixpence* his next best. [Conventional biographical sketch.]

1176 "The Theatre: RAIN," TIME, XXV (25 Feb 1935), 56.

In the revival of John Colton and Clemence Randolph's dramatization, Tallulah Bankhead in the role of Sadie Thompson is praiseworthy but her interpretation is less subtle than that of Jeanne Eagels, in the earlier production.

1177 Trend, J. B. "A Workman in His Workshop," OBSERVER (Lond), 7 July 1935, p. 4.

Don Fernando is not only readable, but "important as a contribution to Spanish studies." M's views on Spanish literary history may be shocking, but they are valid.

1178 Vernon, Grenville. "The Play," COMMONWEAL, XXI (1 March 1935), 513.

In the revival of John Colton and Clemence Randolph's dramatization, RAIN, Tallulah Bankhead gives a "magnificent performance."

1179 Walton, Edith H. "The Book Parade," FORUM, XCIV (Sept 1935), iv.

Don Fernando "is almost flawlessly written and . . . flavored with Mr. Maugham's characteristic brand of sophisticated irony."

1180* White, Leigh. "Essays of Defeat," NEW REPUBLIC, LXXXIV (16 Oct 1935), 278-79.

In *Don Fernando,* M displays a "troubling coexistence of genius and banality," a coexistence perhaps attributable to his attempt to deny middle-class virtues while at the same time he accepts them as standards.

1181 Wyatt, Euphemia Van Rensselaer. "The Drama," CATHOLIC WORLD, CXLI (April 1935), 86-87.
The revival of John Colton and Clemence Randolph's dramatization, RAIN, "is not . . . great. . . . It was a sensation and the sensation is flat."

1936

1182* Bellessort, André. "La Semaine dramatique*-Le Pélican*" (The Dramatic Week: *The Breadwinner*), LE JOURNAL DES DEBATS [POLITIQUES ET LITTERAIRES], 21 Dec 1936, p. 2.
In the last twenty years there has been a revolution in British literature. After continually criticizing French morality, the British have burst all shackles weighing upon the individual perhaps more rapidly than in France. Though not one of M's best plays *The Breadwinner* is his most biting social satire; showing that all respect for the family has vanished. Diana's proposal to be Battle's mistress shocked all Paris and should have been omitted in adaptation. [Review of the French adaptation, in French.]

1183 "Books," NEWS-WEEK, VII (22 Feb 1936), 52.
Cosmopolitans is "amusing and salutory."

1184 "Books — Briefly Noted: Fiction," NEW YORKER, XII (22 Feb 1936), 69.
Cosmopolitans is "entertaining trivia. . . . Many [of the stories] would make excellent radio sketches, . . . and all . . . are perfect for reading aloud."

1185 Brisson, Pierre. "Chronique des Spectacles" (Chronicle of Entertainments), LE FIGARO, 20 Dec 1936, p. 5.
The Breadwinner borders on vaudeville. [Review of the French adaptation, in French.]

1186* Britten, Florence Haxton. *"Cosmopolitans,"* NEW YORK HERALD TRIBUNE BOOKS, 23 Feb 1936, p. 10.
"It would be impossible for Mr. Maugham to write a dull story, or an incompetent one. But in this collection of twenty-nine little anecdotes of the wide, wide world and the seven seas he comes as close to going over the edge about twenty-nine times as Charlie Chaplin on roller skates does in 'Modern Times.' His recoveries — like Charlie's — are occasionally superb." The total effect is one of "triviality."

1187 Butcher, Fanny. "Book Business Greets Return of Happy Days," CHICAGO DAILY TRIBUNE, 22 Feb 1936, p. 14.
Cosmopolitans is "not Mr. Maugham at his best."

1188 Cartier, Maurice. "A l'Etalage" (On Display), GRINGOIRE, 3 Jan 1936, p. 4.
[Brief mention of the French translation of *Ah King.*] [In French.]

1189 Cartier, Maurice. "A l'Etalage" (On Display), GRINGOIRE, 10 July 1936, p. 4.
On A Chinese Screen is one of the most picturesque books dealing with the East, employing delicate touches, and revealing satirical observations. [Review of the French translation, in French.]

1190 *"Cosmopolitans,"* KIRKUS, IV (1 Jan 1936), 2.
[Brief appraisal.]

1191 Croisset, Francis de. "*Le Pélican,* pièce féroce et candide" (*The Breadwinner,* a Ferocious and Candid Play), LE FIGARO, 15 Dec 1936, p. 5.
The play, in the French adaptation, is M's most typical, and along with *The Circle,* his most original; it is ruthless and candid, cruel with undertones of tenderness. [In French.]

1192* Croquet, James de. "Dernière heure théâtrale: *Le Pélican ou une Etrange Famille*" (The Latest Theatrical Scene: *The Breadwinner*), LE FIGARO, 16 Dec 1936, p. 3.
The British possess the souls of exiles; they have another motherland, though they don't know where it is. For Battle, it is solitude, but he had no chance ever to land there. In this play we witness the comical side of a tragedy. [Review of the French translation.] [In French.]

1193 D., F. "Les Spectacles⸗*Le Pélican*⸗Aux Ambassadeurs" (Entertainments: *The Breadwinner* at the Ambassadeurs), LE TEMPS, 17 Dec 1936, p. 5.
The French adaptation has been mildly received. M should have delved deeper into his characters; escape and disengagement are now in fashion in England, and knowing Gide's FAMILLE, JE TE HAIS, one expects richer implications resounding more gloomily. [In French.]

1194 "Fiction: Mr. Maugham's Mixture as Before," TIMES (Lond), 31 March 1936, p. 10.
The stories of *Cosmopolitans* "are all very slight and may not add greatly to the author's reputation: but if read 'one or two now and then,' as directed, they will not noticeably diminish it."

1195 Fréjaville, Gustave, "Les Spectacles⸗Répétitions Générales⸗Théâtre aux Ambassadeurs⸗*Le Pélican ou une Etrange Famille*" (Entertainments: Dress Rehearsals: Theatre of the Ambassadeurs:

The Breadwinner), LE JOURNAL DES DEBATS [POLITIQUES ET LITTERAIRES], 17 Dec 1936, p. 4.
Most of the characters in the French adaptation are created with a truth of caricature. The play is vastly different from the insipid milk and water to which French audiences are accustomed. [In French.]

1196* "Good Short Shorts," CHRISTIAN SCIENCE MONITOR WEEKLY MAGAZINE SECTION, 6 May 1936, p. 10.
In *Cosmopolitans,* "if at all, the stories err on the side of completeness, for after reading a dozen the reader begins to feel a little artificiality in the inevitable 'snapper' with which they end. Best are 'The Luncheon,' 'Salvatore' and 'Mr. Know-All.' "

1197* Greene, Graham. "Books of the Day: Short Stories," SPECTATOR (Lond), CLVI (17 April 1936), 718-20.
In *Cosmopolitans,* M is technically competent as ever, but his stories have no "echo of the general life." They are limited to "the liner routes and the leisured quarters." Since he has no "intuitive or empirical knowledge" of the poor, his portraits of them are "picturesque" and unbelievable.

1198 Greene, Graham. JOURNEY WITHOUT MAPS (Garden City, N Y: Doubleday, Doran, 1936), pp. 205 ff.
M's portrait of Mr. Davidson in "Rain" serves as a contrast to Greene's portrait of Dr. Harley, a missionary in Liberia.

1199 Hoffman, Paul. "Bookshelf," ATLANTIC MONTHLY, CLVII (April 1936), n. p.
Cosmopolitans consists of "expanded anecdotes" to be read when the reader "has nothing better to do."

1200 Hutchison, Percy. "Maugham's Short Short-Stories," NEW YORK TIMES BOOK REVIEW, 23 Feb 1936, p. 4.
In *Cosmopolitans,* M brings together "a varied collection that is technically brilliant and rich in entertainment." But he has seldom, if ever, shown himself so caustic, so sardonic, as he appears in certain of these pieces. Granted a general lack of depth, he still possesses the power to entertain.

1201 J-n, H. "Maughamin 'SADE' Koitossa" (Maugham's 'RAIN' at the Koitto), UUSI SUOMI, 4 Feb 1936, p. 7.
The Finnish adaptation is a powerful drama based on a story of human tragedy. M seems to have treated his subject perhaps with too great an emphasis on action, without sufficiently revealing the motives or analyzing the development of his characters. [In Finnish.]

1202 J-n, H. "Maugham-voitto Kanallisteatterissa" (An Excellent

Play by Maugham at the National Theater), Uusi Suomi, 20 Feb 1936, p. 8.

In the Finnish adaptation of *Sheppey,* M creates lifelike characters; the dialogue is truly dramatic and concentrates on the essential. The development of the action is dynamic and effective. [In Finnish.]

1203 L., I. "Voimakas näytelmä Kansanteatterissa" (A Powerful Drama at the People's Theater), Helsingin Sanomat, 3 Feb 1936, p. 3.

Rain contains a sharp criticism of the negative features of religion and missionary work. The construction is skillful and the characterization shows expert knowledge of the psychology of man. [Review of the Finnish adaptation, in Finnish.]

1204 M., P. "Les Livres nouveaux" (New Books), Revue Bleue, 74ème année, no. 7 (4 April 1936), 249.

In *East and West,* M is greater than Kipling in cosmopolitanism. "Rain," "The Fall of Edward Barnard," "The Letter" are singled out for praise. [Review of the French translation, in French.]

1205* MacKay, L. A. "Somerset Maugham," Canadian Forum, XVI (May 1936), 23-24.

Cosmopolitans shows M a master of "pure technique"; the danger is that the technique's "transparency" is merciless when he has little to say. But at its worst it is inoffensive; "and at its best it has an ease and rapidity that make it unsurpassed for presenting a reasonable man's picture of generally unreasonable people."

1206 Martin du Gard, Maurice. "Le Théâtre" (The Theater), Les Nouvelles Litteraires, 26 Dec 1936, p. 10.

The French adaptation of *The Breadwinner* is neither a tragedy nor a comedy, but a satire. [In French.]

1207* M[axence], J[ean]-P[ierre]. "Vient de paraître" (Just Appeared), Gringoire, 3 Jan 1936, p. 4.

In *East and West,* whether M writes a psychological or detective story, it ends usually in violent action: in suicide in "Rain," in tragic misunderstanding in "Red." M resorts to no cheap tricks; his satire is subtle and cruel; his art does not halt at appearances but probes into people's souls. His most admirable features are his skilfulness, his construction, dynamism and cohesion of narrative, a kind of sedate humor and even sometimes poetry. [Review of the French translation, in French.]

1208* McIver, Claude Searcy. William Somerset Maugham: A Study of Technique and Literary Sources. Upper Darby, Pa.: The Author, 6 S. Brighton Avenue, 1936.

M's and Maupassant's method, technique, material, and philosophy are similar. Because M's short stories are artistically superior to the plays, and, with only three or four exceptions, the novels as well, these works provide the best illustrations. Within the range of fiction, and more narrowly that of the story, M and Maupassant are comparable in that (1) both writers are realists in their choice of material and in their handling of it; (2) both writers have drawn freely upon their own experience and that of other people for their material; (3) both writers share a tendency to write stories about people who are outwardly commonplace but whose lives contain a dramatic experience — tragic, pathetic, humorous, or grotesque; (4) for both writers marital infidelity is a stock theme, nearly always treated in a comic or satiric vein. M and Maupassant achieved individual styles, but between them there is a notable resemblance in (1) their use of satire and irony, (2) their sardonic humor, (3) their vividness and verisimilitude, (4) their economy of expression and precision of form.

Though neither M nor Maupassant has expressed any important or original philosophical views, both writers show a marked similarity in their declarations on points relating to life and letters. In the domain of aesthetics both hold the views that (1) lucidity is achieved by simplicity and exactness of expression; (2) that a work of art is to be an accurate, realistic, and convincing interpretation of life as seen through the eyes of the artist; (3) that a realistic work of fiction should be not a chronicle of commonplace incidents but of selected and significant events; (4) that art is of secondary importance in life, that it is a refinement devised by the human mind, a luxury with which men provide themselves only after their physical desires have been satisfied; (5) that propaganda has no place in art. In the domain of ethics and religion both M and Maupassant offer, again, no notably original ideas, but parallel one another in their beliefs (1) that man's passions and instincts are stronger than his reason; (2) that women attach more importance to love than men; (3) that man is utterly alone in life, and that the tragedy in life arises from the fact that he is not in harmony with his fellow-men; (4) that society is stupid and tyrannical. Both men reveal the profound influence of Schopenhauer.

M is unlike Maupassant, however, in that he does not share the Frenchman's fear of death or his preoccupation with sex; moreover, M exhibits more restraint and better taste in the choice of subjects. Finally, M goes beyond Maupassant when he tries to explain why his characters behave as they do. But, these differences do not diminish the many similarities; Maupassant's influence is manifest everywhere in the composition of M's short stories.

1209 "New Books — A Selected List," LONDON MERCURY, XXXIV (May 1936), 85.
The stories of *Cosmopolitans,* "eminently entertaining" and "deftly turned," show their author at his "excellent second best."

1210 "The New Novels: Very Short Stories," TIMES LITERARY SUPPLEMENT (Lond), 4 April 1936, p. 297.
Many of the best stories of *Cosmopolitans* "are written round, rather than towards, their *dénouements*. Some of the best are sketches rather than stories and have no *dénouement* at all."

1211 P., C. B. "Short Stories by Two Britons," BOSTON EVENING TRANSCRIPT, 7 March 1936, p. 2.
The stories of *Cosmopolitans* "suffer from the common malady of anthologies: too extended a sitting with them dims the quality and dulls the mind."

1212 Quennell, Peter. "New Novels," NEW STATESMAN AND NATION, N. S. XI (4 April 1936), 530.
"Extreme brevity" does not well suit M; the stories of *Cosmopolitans* "flick by like houses and gardens seen from a railway carriage: no sooner have they aroused our interest than they vanish for good."

1213 "Shorter Notices," NATION (NY), CXLII (11 March 1936), 328.
"Far from adding to a reputation already endangered by the existence of so many trifles," *Cosmopolitans* "sinks it to a new low."

1214 V., L. "W. Somerset Maugham: *'Pääviotto'* " (W. Somerset Maugham: *Sheppey*), HELSINGIN SANOMAT, 20 Feb 1936, p. 4.
The play does not follow the laws of drama; its merit lies in vigorous dialogue and in keen observation of life and the human mind. [Review of the Finnish adaptation, in Finnish.]

1215 V[illard?], L[éonie?]. "Livres" (Books), LA REVUE ANGLO-AMERICAINE, XIII (Aug 1936), 561-62.
[Brief review of *Don Fernando*.] [In French.]

1216* Villard, Léonie, "Livres" (Books), LA REVUE ANGLO-AMERICAINE, XIII (Oct 1936), 68-70.
Review of volumes V-VI of the Tauchnitz edition of M's *Plays* criticizing the pathetic character of the happy ending and the comparative shallowness of the characters in *Caesar's Wife*. *The Sacred Flame* is of unquestionable value, lifelike and credible. *For Services Rendered* is perhaps the most searching satire in the contemporary theater. *Sheppey* is evidence that M should not abandon the stage and bears promise of a self-renewal. [In French.]

1937

1217 Beauplan, Robert de. "Les Théâtre≠*Le Pélican*" (Plays: *The Breadwinner*), L'ILLUSTRATION, 95ème année, no. 4896 (2 Jan 1937), 25.
[Brief review of the French adaptation.] [In French.]

1218 Bidou, Henry. "Chronique Théâtrale≠Le Sujet de deux pièces anglaises" (Drama Chronicle: The Subject of Two English Plays), LE TEMPS, 4 Jan 1937, p. 2.
The Breadwinner is pervaded by an almost unbearable pessimism softened by M's comic spirit. The play is flawed in that only four of the eight characters in the play actually participate in the action. [Review of the French adaptation, in French.]

1219 "Bibliographie" (Bibliography), ETUDES ANGLAISES, I (Jan 1937), 189.
The 1936 edition of *Cakes and Ale* has a good plot, healthy realism, and easy style. [In French.]

1220 "Bibliographie" (Bibliography), ETUDES ANGLAISES, I (Jan 1937), 189-90.
Cosmopolitans contains dexterous, if mechanical, stories, recalling the manner of O. Henry. [In French.]

1221 "Books," NEWS-WEEK, IX (6 March 1937), 36.
In *Theatre* M gives a penetrating delineation of Julia.

1222 "Books: Actress," TIME, XXIX (15 March 1937), 89.
Theatre is "entertaining" and "well up to [M's] high professional standard." [Much plot summary.]

1223 Bookwright. "Reprints, New Editions," NEW YORK HERALD TRIBUNE BOOKS, 18 April 1937, p. 19.
"As reading [*Six Comedies*], no one of them seems to me better than several of [M's] longish stories."

1224* Bowen, Elizabeth. "A Straight Novel," NEW STATESMAN AND NATION, N. S. XIII (27 March 1937), 525; rptd in COLLECTED IMPRESSIONS (NY: Alfred A. Knopf, 1950), pp. 132-35.
In *Theatre,* M does not employ tricky construction; his style is "neutral, functional, and fully efficient." The novel is "an astringent tragi-comedy" in which M "anatomises emotion without emotion" and "handles without

pity a world where he finds no pity." His "disabused clearness and hardness" may diminish his subject, but M is a "first-rate professional writer."

1225* Brasillach, Robert. *"Servitude Humaine* de Somerset Maugham" (*Of Human Bondage* by Somerset Maugham), Gringoire, 2 July 1937, p. 4.

M has been known to Frenchmen thus far by his plays and his stories of the South Seas; they are surprised to see a short-story writer yielding to the enchantment of the old English novel form. The main character in the novel is neither Philip nor Mildred, but *time*. Like the characters, who either vanish entirely or keep reappearing older and changed, time is vested with a double face, with memory and forgetfulness. The ending is not bitter, for Philip accepts life. [Review of the French translation, in French.]

1226 Brighouse, Harold. "Private Lives," Manchester Guardian, 23 March 1937, p. 7.

In *Theatre* M, like Clemence Dane and Booth Tarkington, has "raised the modern standard of the novel of the theatre." [Mainly plot summary.]

1227 Butcher, Fanny. "Noted English Authors Offer Three New Books," Chicago Daily Tribune, 13 March 1937, p. 2.

Theatre, "like the heroine's whole life, is a superbly brilliant piece of acting. It, also like her life, lacks any true and devastating emotion. Both are masterpieces of théâtre."

1228 C., P. "Le Livre du Jour≠*Servitude Humaine*" (The Book of the Day: *Of Human Bondage*), Journal de Geneve, 2 July 1937, p. 1.

M looks on the world with the moving sincerity of a man who is not there for his pleasure, who knows that others are in the same position; hence his mixture of bitter irony with hearty sympathy, his contempt for humanity and his tenderness for the individual. Very few writers have so successfully united sarcasm with gentleness as M has done in this novel. [Review of the French translation, in French.]

1229 Chack, Paul. "Portrait≠Somerset Maugham," Gringoire, 9 July 1937, p. 5.

M is the most French-minded British writer. His travel books present no easy, colorless exoticism, yet do not reveal his full power. *Of Human Bondage* is his masterpiece. [Biographical sketch.] [In French.]

1230 C[olum], M[ary] M. "The Book Forum," Forum, XCVII (May 1937), iv.

M's portrayal of Julia in *Theatre* is remarkable, but the whole book gives an impression of "emptiness."

1231 Cookman, A. V. "The Theatre," LONDON MERCURY, XXXVI (July 1937), 278.

The initial failure of *The Constant Wife* may be due to the public's taking it too seriously: "but now [the revival] that it has become slightly old-fashioned in point of style it is easier to enjoy as a piece of artificiality."

1232* Cordell, Richard A. W. SOMERSET MAUGHAM. Toronto, NY & Edinburgh: Thomas Nelson and Sons, 1937.

After an introductory biographical chapter treating of M to 1937, Cordell reviews M's achievements as a novelist, dramatist, short-story writer, and critic and traveller. Every novel from *Liza of Lambeth* (1897) to *Theatre* (1937) receives, at the least, a brief summary of its artistic flaws and merits, but fuller treatment is given *Of Human Bondage, The Moon and Sixpence, The Painted Veil, Cakes and Ale,* and *The Narrow Corner.* In similar fashion, Cordell criticizes every play from "Schiffbrüchig" to *Sheppey,* providing in most instances the names of the British theaters in which they were first produced, and premiere dates. M's stories are shown to follow Maupassant's vogue "for the abrupt surprise ending . . . except that [M] substitutes a surprising ethical point of view for the unexpected final incident"; although M's stories "remain tales of incident," their primary focus is on the unaccountability of human nature. M was well-qualified to write good books of travel, for he was a "realist" and indulged "in no bogus enthusiasms." Cordell hazards no final guess about M's future position in English letters, but believes that M achieved notable success in each genre he attempted.

1233 Croquet, James de. "Le Théâtre" (The Theater), LES ANNALES POLITIQUES ET LITTERAIRES, No. 2570 (10 Jan 1937), 8-9.

The Breadwinner, as adapted by F. de Croisset, is a comedy with tragic elements and unity of place and time. [In French.]

1234* Dangerfield, George. "English Ebb, American Flow," SATURDAY REVIEW OF LITERATURE, XV (3 April 1937), 3-4, 26, 28.

The American and the English novel are like two tides, the first advancing, the second receding. The English novel, refusing to look into the future, has begun to show signs of fatigue. One proof of this is the treatment of radicalism in Arthur Calder-Marshall's PIE IN THE SKY compared with that in Steinbeck's IN DUBIOUS BATTLE. M's *Theatre,* "a museum piece," appears simply bourgeois; he lacks a quality that John P. Marquand has, for Marquand "takes nothing for granted, everything is new, even the obvious." The English novel grew unhurriedly; the American continues with a shout [e.g., Daniel Fuchs' LOW COMPANY, John Steinbeck's OF MICE AND MEN].

1235 DeVoto, Bernard. "Master of Two Dimensions," Saturday Review of Literature, XV (6 March 1937), 3.

Theatre is "as fine a specimen of the well-made novel as this generation has seen." However, M is unable to endow his characters with feeling.

1236 Dottin, Paul. "Comptes Rendus Critiques" (Critical Reports), Etudes Anglaises, I (July 1937), 354-55.

Theatre is a novel of M's "better vein," though in perfecting technique M seems increasingly to lose his humanity. Julia is, psychologically, well-realized; the male characters are too repugnant or naive "to live with intensity." [In French.]

1237 Dottin, Paul. "La Littérature anglaise en 1936" (English Literature in 1936), La Revue de France, 17ème année, no. 4 (15 July 1937), 316.

[Brief review of *Cosmopolitans*.] [In French.]

1238* Dottin, Paul. "Claude S. McIver's Somerset Maugham: A Study of Technique and Literary Sources," Etudes Anglaises, I (May 1937), 261-62.

The technical relations between the American short story and *Cosmopolitans* have regrettably not been noted. McIver does not pay enough attention to the plays which were written after 1925; nor does he deal adequately with the influence of Stendhal. [In French.]

1239* Dottin, Paul. Le Theatre de William Somerset Maugham (The Drama of William Somerset Maugham). Paris: Perrin, 1937.

The plays are chronologically grouped as Comedies Pleasant *(Mrs. Dot, Jack Straw, Lady Frederick, Penelope, Smith, The Tenth Man, Landed Gentry, The Land of Promise)*; Comedies Unpleasant *(Our Betters, Home and Beauty, The Unknown, The Circle)*; Exotic Plays *(Caesar's Wife, East of Suez,* Rain, The Painted Veil, *The Explorer, The Letter)*; and Social Revolt *(The Constant Wife, The Breadwinner, The Sacred Flame, For Services Rendered, Sheppey).* M's plays exhibit his sense of pathos in human life, his keen perception of man's distress. M wished to be a great novelist; was only a playwright by necessity. [In French.]

1240 Epardaud, Edmond. "Au Cap Ferrat: Chez Somerset Maugham, romancier et arboriculteur" (At Cap Ferrat: At the Home of Somerset Maugham, Novelist and Pomologist), Les Nouvelles Litteraires, 24 July 1937, p. 8.

[Interview.] [In French.]

1241 F., D. C. *"The Constant Wife,"* Theatre World (Lond), XXVII (June 1937), 261.

The revival is "a welcome event, for the author has no equal in the art of construction, characterisation and dialogue."

1242 Fadiman, Clifton. "Books: A Week Among the English," NEW YORKER, XIII (6 March 1937), 69-70.

Theatre "may be theatrical, but it's a good show."

1243 Flament, Albert. "Cap Ferrat—M. Somerset Maugham" (Cap Ferrat—Mr. Somerset Maugham), LA REVUE DE PARIS, XLIV (5 Oct 1937), 944-49.

[Visit to and interview with M.] [In French.]

1244 "Globe Theatre: *'The Constant Wife,'*" TIMES (Lond), 20 May 1937, p. 14.

M's revived play lacks the "poetry" of life, but it has a story, is entertaining and true, and is written well.

1245 Hoffman, Paul. "Bookshelf," ATLANTIC MONTHLY, CLIX (May 1937), n. p.

Julia Lambert's prototype [*Theatre*] "may be found in any one of the myriad novels, short stories, and plays that have been written about the theatre," and the " 'story' element . . . is scarcely a novel one." The "bright spots" are too few; in the main, the novel is a "pedestrian performance."

1246 Horsnell, Horace. "New Novels," OBSERVER (Lond), 21 March 1937, p. 6.

Theatre is "one of the neatest, if not, perhaps, the deepest, of Mr. Maugham's studies of women in love. It attempts nothing that it does not expertly achieve, and is as readable as it is admirably written."

1247* Hutchison, Percy. "Maugham's Portrait of a Woman," NEW YORK TIMES BOOK REVIEW, 14 March 1937, p. 4.

In *Theatre,* M has produced an expertly fashioned novel, but one which lacks the warmth of human sympathy. It resembles *Of Human Bondage* in that it is the study of the evolution of a human being, but the two subjects of study differ markedly, for the heroine of *Theatre* is assured, beautiful, of radiant personality. Although lacquered in style, and hard in treatment, it appears to reflect accurately something of life.

1248 J-n, H. "Helsingin Kansanteatteri. W. Somerset Maugham: *Pyhä Liekki*" (Helsinki People's Theater. W. Somerset Maugham: *The Sacred Flame*), UUSI SUOMI, 7 Feb 1937, p. 8.

This is not one of M's best plays. The treatment in the Finnish adaptation reveals that M is perhaps too productive; only towards the end of the play is the spectator impressed. [In Finnish.]

1249 Jones, E. B. C. "Fiction: *Theatre,*" SPECTATOR (Lond), CLVIII (26 March 1937), 593.

The novel is "a full-length study of the histrionic temperament." M's style is "undistinguished, sometimes slovenly." "Descent into cliché" conveys the impression of "the writer despising his reader." M lacks "greatness of theme," and his "subject matter is completely earthbound." His object is the detached, humorous description of life, but he is inferior to "his avowed master," Maupassant, in the necessary style and atmosphere. "He is often a fascinating raconteur, but never an artist."

1250 Kivijärvi, Erkki. " '*Pyhä Liekki*' Kansanteaterissa" (The Sacred Flame at the People's Theater), HELSINGIN SANOMAT, 4 Feb 1937, p. 3.

The play in the Finnish adaptation is a proof of the author's unerring sense for the theater. The construction is masterly, and coherent dialogue rolls the action steadily forward. [In Finnish.]

1251 MacKay, L. A. "Intelligent Entertainment," CANADIAN FORUM, XVII (May 1937), 68.

In *Theatre,* M has rediscovered Defoe's trick of "candid plausibility"; one finds himself reading M's books not so much as fiction as if they were biography. The story of this novel is excellent and "intelligent entertainment."

1252 Matthews, T. S. "Three Professionals," NEW REPUBLIC, XC (17 March 1937), 173.

Although *Theatre* holds nothing unusual, M exhibits a professional's skill in telling his story.

1253 McIver, Claude S[earcy]. "William Somerset Maugham," READING AND COLLECTING, I (July 1937), 5-6, 15.

[Biographical sketch with a checklist of M's books, plays and miscellanea. In the sketch McIver wrongly attributes the publication date of "1914" to *The Making of a Saint* (it was 1898)—in his checklist the date for this novel is correct.]

1254 Mérac, Robert. "Nos Soirées: Le Théâtre: *Le Pélican*" (Our Evenings: The Theatre: *The Breadwinner*), GRINGOIRE, 1 Jan 1937, p. 15.

The play in the French adaptation is stimulating in the same bitter vein as RAIN and *The Circle*. [In French.]

1255 "Le Mois Théâtral: Théâtre des Ambassadeurs: *Le Pélican* (The Theatrical Month: Theater of the Ambassadeurs: *The Breadwinner*), LAROUSSE MENSUEL ILLUSTRE, No. 360 (Feb 1937), n. p.

[Plot summary.] [In French.]

1256* Mortimer, Raymond. "Miscellany—Thank Heaven for Mr. Maugham: *'The Constant Wife,'* at the Globe Theatre," NEW STATESMAN AND NATION, N. S. XIII (29 May 1937), 882.
M's beginning is not as deftly machined as is usual with his plays, and the wife is too "superior to everyone else in the play"; but the play has wit and displays a good sense of the theater. Indeed, allowing the wife to expound his views, M writes a better play here than in *The Breadwinner,* and the whole play "shines like a good deed in a naughty world." [Review of the revival.]

1257 "Mr. Somerset Maugham's New Novel," TIMES (Lond), 23 March 1937, p. 10.
In *Theatre,* M's pictures of the theatrical routine are "brilliantly observed and rendered, and once more that unpretentious yet so superbly calculated style adds its own grace to a story as unashamed as it is worldly."

1258 Muller, Herbert J. MODERN FICTION: A STUDY OF VALUES (NY and Lond: Funk & Wagnalls, 1937), pp. 240-43, 289, 290.
Of Human Bondage is found, in some ways, to be superior to THE WAY OF ALL FLESH; mainly, its ideas are better dramatized.

1259 Muret, Maurice. "Un roman de Somerset Maugham" (A Novel by Somerset Maugham), LE JOURNAL DES DEBATS [POLITIQUES ET LITTERAIRES], 3 Oct 1937, p. 4.
Of Human Bondage is a powerful novel, and more than a novel in the hackneyed sense of the word. *Of Human Bondage* emphasizes the gap between the Victorian and modern British novel; it is based on the French model of Flaubert's L'EDUCATION SENTIMENTALE. [Review of the French translation, in French.]

1260 "The New Novels—An Actress' Life and Loves," TIMES LITERARY SUPPLEMENT (Lond), 27 March 1937, p. 239.
Theatre is lively but dry, generating little emotion, but providing plenty of entertainment.

1261 "Other Books: Selected List," LONDON MERCURY, XXXV (April 1937), 648-49.
In *Theatre*, "the story is told fluently and plausibly, the details look like concrete truth, the characters react credibly. . . . "

1262* "Other New Books: Literary," TIMES LITERARY SUPPLEMENT (Lond), 27 Nov 1937, p. 913.
In W. SOMERSET MAUGHAM (1937), Richard A. Cordell "shows little insight into the reasons why Mr. Maugham, notwithstanding that his inventive and emotional range both as a storyteller and a playwright is a narrow one, has so much to teach the aspiring writer of fiction."

1263 "Our Booking-Office: Merely Players," PUNCH, CXCII (7 April 1937), 391-92.

Theatre "needs relieving . . . not so much by greater tenderness to the half-wits it victimises as by some reference to more auspicious possibilities."

1264* P., I. M. "Turns with a Bookworm," NEW YORK HERALD TRIBUNE BOOKS, 11 April 1937, p. 18.

Theatre is "the answer to the perennial request for a good novel, neither more nor less"; its theme of the externalization of a personality is "superficial"; it is "more notable for craftsmanship than content." *Of Human Bondage* is not really "first-class," but "an unusual, interesting, hybrid species of autobiography" written in "commonplace prose," with secondary characters not created, but "merely observed."

1265 Pierhal, Armand. "Un beau roman de Somerset Maugham: Grandeur et Servitude Humaines" (A Great Novel by Somerset Maugham: Human Nobility and Slavery), LES ANNALES POLITIQUES ET LITTERAIRES, No. 2573 (25 Feb 1937), 176-80.

Of Human Bondage is a biographical novel with a strictly narrative method, which rules out digressions whether moral or ideological, as well as descriptions; it belongs to the great tradition of the English novel. The self-effacement of the author increases the credibility of the tale. [In French.]

1266 Pound, Reginald. THEIR MOODS AND MINE (Lond: Chapman & Hall, 1937), p. 262.

[Brief portrait of an unfriendly encounter with M.]

1267* Rageot, Gaston. "Le Théâtre: Deux pièces anglaises et un melodrame française" (The Drama: Two English Plays and a French Melodrama), REVUE BLEUE, 75ème année, no. 1 (2 Jan 1937), 29.

On the basis of the French adaptation of *The Breadwinner,* the trouble with the play is that the author thinks Battle right, while the public thinks him wrong. [In French.]

1268 R[ichard], M[arius]. "Les Lettres et la vie" (Letters and Life), LA REVUE DE FRANCE, 17ème année, no. 5 (15 Oct 1937), 715-20.

Of Human Bondage is a great novel, but not a masterpiece, comparable to Flaubert's L'EDUCATION SENTIMENTALE. [Review of the French translation, in French.]

1269 Richardson, Maurice L. "Mrs. Woolf and Others," BOOKS OF THE MONTH, VII (April 1937), 13.

Theatre is M's worst book in terms of improbable characterization and action. But M's storytelling is so expert "that he could get away with a triangle drama between a charwoman, a crocodile, and a pillar-box."

1270 Rousseaux, André. "La Vie Litteraire" (The Literary Life), LE FIGARO LITTERAIRE, 25 Sept 1937, p. 6.

Of Human Bondage is well-constructed, never boring despite its length. It is charged with human values and mystery as well as a powerful human poetry. [Review of the French translation, in French.]

1271* Schlösser, Anselm. DIE ENGLISCHE LITERATUR IN DEUTSCHLAND VON 1895 BIS 1934 MIT EINER VOLLSTANDIGEN BIBLIOGRAPHIE DER DEUTSCHEN UBERSETZUNGEN UND DER IM DEUTSCHEN SPRACHGEBIET ERSCHIENENEN ENGLISCHEN AUSGABEN (ENGLISH LITERATURE IN GERMANY FROM 1895 TO 1934 WITH A DEFINITIVE BIBLIOGRAPHY OF GERMAN TRANSLATIONS AND ENGLISH EDITIONS APPEARING IN GERMAN LANGUAGE AREAS) (Jena: Walter Biedermann, 1937), pp. 43, 47, 60, 124, 127, 268, 476.

M's plays were popular in Germany before and after World War I, although not all the translations of them actually appeared in print. Most of his novels and tales have been translated. [The translations of M's works published before 1936 are listed.] [In German.]

1272 Sée, Edmond. "Le Théâtre et la vie" (Drama and Life), LA REVUE DE FRANCE, 17ème année, no. 1 (15 Feb 1937), 712.

[Brief review of the Paris premiere of *The Breadwinner*.] [In French.]

1273 Shackleton, Edith. "New Novels," TIME AND TIDE, XVIII (27 March 1937), 410.

"You may not like Julia in *Theatre,* but you will have to believe in her."

1274* Smith, Caroline. "New Novels," NATION (NY), CXLIV (20 March 1937), 332.

Theatre "is put together expertly, in the best theatrical tradition. The lighting is costly, the sets are modern, the direction is of the best, the acting could hardly be improved upon. But the play is third-rate." All of M's recent novels "are excellent publicity for a great book which he wrote twenty-two years ago."

1275* Soskin, William. "Reality on the Stage, Make-Believe in Life," NEW YORK HERALD TRIBUNE BOOKS, 7 March 1937, p. 3.

In *Theatre* M "is fascinated with the problem of essential reality as against the appearance of the universe," and its "sardonic excitement" comes when Julia's "lovely coat of personal enamel cracks." If there are situations in it "too patly negotiated" and if Julia's swift realization requires more deliberate and opaque dramatization, the book is still superb for its "intelligence, adroit comedy, . . . [and] sparkling gallery of people."

1276 *"Theatre,"* KIRKUS, V (1 Feb 1937), 37.
[Brief appraisal.]

1277* Thérive, André. "Les Livres: *Servitude Humaine*" (Books: *Of Human Bondage*), LE TEMPS, 28 Oct 1937, p. 3.
The only failure of this powerful novel in the French translation is its lack of mystery. It was intended to be a psychological novel in the Russian style: Philip could be named Oblomov, a second-rate dull man, lacking moral imagination, though ennobled and made tolerable by the author. The latter is accomplished by dramatizing Philip's unconscious hankering after happiness, his attracting to himself all those who can punish him. [In French.]

1278 Thiébaut, Marcel, "Parmi les livres" (Among Books), LA REVUE DE PARIS, 44ème année, no. 5 (15 Sept 1937), 457-59.
Of Human Bondage ends naturally on a note of optimism as it develops the theme of Philip's "stoic resolve." [Review of the French translation, in French.]

1279* Ward, Richard Heron. WILLIAM SOMERSET MAUGHAM. Lond: Geoffrey Bles, 1937.
On the philosophic basis of Platonic, Christian, and Jungian elements, an artist may be seen as the instrument through which the "collective unconscious" is to be expressed. This "collective unconscious" is rendered at its best through an artist whose subjective inspiration and experience will not prevent objective communication with the "collective unconscious" of his audience. Fortunately for M, he is neither a totally "subjective" nor a totally "objective" writer; he does more than merely observe life, so he is between the two, as evidenced by his compassion and tolerance, devoid of all self-pity. In view of these qualities, "Before the Party" is M's best story, *For Services Rendered* and *Sheppey* (despite the latter's flawed craftsmanship) his best plays, and *Cakes and Ale* his best novel. *Of Human Bondage* is less satisfactory because its conception of reality is too "individual."

1938

1280* Arns, Karl. "Claude Searcy McIver, WILLIAM SOMERSET MAUGHAM," BEIBLATT ZUR ANGLIA, XLIX (1938), 23.
M is the most important short-story writer to work under the influence of Maupassant. McIver discusses this in detail, but perhaps his study was not worth doing, since both M and Maupassant do not attempt a metaphysical interpretation of life, and neglect the meaning of art for life. [In German.]

1281* Beach, Joseph Warren. "[Review of] Claude Searcy McIver, WILLIAM SOMERSET MAUGHAM: A STUDY OF TECHNIQUE AND LITERARY SOURCES," JOURNAL OF ENGLISH AND GERMANIC PHILOLOGY, XXXVII (April 1938), 319.

[Censures McIver for lack of precision and logic, and for not providing sufficient evidence.]

1282* Belgion, Montgomery. "Books of the Quarter," CRITERION, XVII (1938), 748-52.

M's writing is generally without "substance," but this very lack makes the fact of his entertaining his reader all the more "miraculous." [Review of *The Summing Up,* with a general assessment of M's career.]

1283 Benét, Stephen Vincent. "A Self-Taught Trade," SATURDAY REVIEW OF LITERATURE, XVII (16 April 1938), 3-4.

Kipling in SOMETHING OF MYSELF and M in *The Summing Up* discuss the work of becoming a writer and give advice on craftsmanship. An aspiring young writer could learn much from the craftsmanship of *Cakes and Ale* and *The Circle* or from the form of M's short stories. M has never taken human beings for granted; he has, in his fiction, created three living women. His work includes one masterpiece [*Of Human Bondage*], no work that is not professional, and an autobiography of "extreme intellectual honesty."

1284 "Books," NEWSWEEK, XI (28 March 1938), 30.

The Summing Up is "a book of essays on everything, loosely bound by threads of personal history. It's . . . delightful reading."

1285 "Books: Reticent Writer," TIME, XXXI (28 March 1938), 63.

In *The Summing Up,* M gives his readers "a candid appraisal of his own temperament and accomplishments, some shrewd reflections on writing, some commonsense aphorisms, about as few revelations of his personal life as it would be possible for an autobiographer to give." The work is somewhat boring.

1286 Butcher, Fanny. "Maugham Does Own Life Story with Fine Skill," CHICAGO DAILY TRIBUNE, 2 April 1938, p. 14.

The Summing Up is a service not only to the art of writing but to the art of living as well.

1287* Colum, Mary M. "Life and Literature," FORUM, XCIX (May 1938), 278-79.

"In spite of the fact that [in *The Summing Up*] he laments that his brain is not a better instrument, Maugham's great drawback is that he is too intelligent for the rest of his equipment. He can stir the reader's intellect to excitement, but, since *Of Human Bondage,* his writing has given no glow to the heart, no wings to the imagination. He has observed; he has, within limits, felt keenly; he has had his own vision of the world; he has fed his mind with literature and philosophy; but he lost somewhere what nearly everyone has in youth and what very great writers keep a long time—his fire and his wings."

1288 Connolly, Cyril. ENEMIES OF PROMISE (Lond: George Routledge & Sons, 1938), especially pp. 37-38, 85-88, 117-19, 151, 155, 158; Revised Edition (NY: Macmillan, 1948), especially pp. 66-69, 76-77, 79-80, 92-93.

An investigation into the literary situation of 1938 and into what will possibly have happened in ten years' time, with citations of M's opinions and practices.

1289* Cowley, Malcolm. "The Maugham Enigma," NEW REPUBLIC, XCIV (30 March 1938), 227-28; rptd in THE MAUGHAM ENIGMA, ed by Klaus W. Jonas (NY: Citadel P, 1954), pp. 200-4.

Why has M never written another book half so good as *Of Human Bondage?* There are at least two good reasons suggested from a reading of *The Summing Up*: (1) M was obsessed by his past when he wrote *Of Human Bondage* and felt the need to perform public confession and to receive absolution; (2) M's success separated him from those circles that gave him his best subjects—that is, the poor people he knew as a medical student and starving writer. Since 1918 M has been writing about a class from which he is spiritually alienated.

1290 Dottin, Paul. "Comptes Rendus Critiques" (Critical Reports), ETUDES ANGLAISES, II (July-Sept 1938), 318-20.

The Summing Up is written in good faith and with remarkable candor; not an autobiography of the usual type, but a long monologue, well-conducted though without a preconceived plan. [In French.]

1291 Dottin, Paul. "La Littérature anglaise en 1937" (English Literature in 1937), LA REVUE DE FRANCE, 18ème année, no. 3 (15 June 1938), 520-22.

M represents realism at its purest. The theme of *Theatre* is banal, but the author rejuvenates it. [In French.]

1292 Dreiser, Theodore. "Introduction," *Of Human Bondage* (New Haven: Yale U P, 1938), pp. iii-xiv.

Twenty-two years after the first publication the novel "still establishes itself . . . as [the product] of an extremely sensitive, searching and life-loving as well as life-criticising mind." [See Dreiser's review, "As a Realist Sees It," NEW REPUBLIC, V (25 Dec 1915), 202-4.]

1293 Epardaud, Edmond. "Quatre mois aux Indes avec Somerset

Maugham" (Four Months in the Indies with Somerset Maugham), LES NOUVELLES LITTERAIRES, 14 May 1938, p. 4.
[Interview with M, who speaks of his experiences in India and China.] [In French.]

1294 Evans, B. Ifor. "Mr. Maugham Reflects on Life," MANCHESTER GUARDIAN, 11 Jan 1938, p. 5.
Evans believes that M is "one of the most important writers of a contemporary prose that is worthy of Swift," and that *The Summing Up* yields confirmation of his view.

1295 Fadiman, Clifton. "Books: Somerset Maugham Adds It Up," NEW YORKER, XIV (26 March 1938), 66-67.
In *The Summing Up,* on all matters except religion M is "keen, shrewd, and frequently original"; his religious observations are only "commonplaces of skepticism."

1296 Garnett, David. "Current Literature: Books in General," NEW STATESMAN AND NATION, N. S. XV (8 Jan 1938), 50.
The Summing Up is too long and diffuse; significant detail is sandwiched between judgments of much less importance so that one feels that M has told him less than he really has.

1297 Gassner, John. "The Theatre," ONE ACT PLAY MAGAZINE, II (May 1938), 78-79.
The Circle is "not only sufficient unto its own day, but . . . still sufficient. If it is not a great comedy, it still has abiding qualities, for it is founded on a rock. The granite is the idea that every generation makes its own mistakes. . . . " [Review of the revival.]

1298 Geismar, Maxwell. "Not Interested," NATION (NY), CXLVIII (9 April 1938), 420.
The Summing Up, M's "literary will," doesn't alter our judgment of the work of a man who forsook art for artistry, but does add to our appreciation of his harmonious and humble if unpenetrating mind.

1299* Greene, Graham. "Books of the Day: Maugham's Pattern," SPECTATOR (Lond), CLX (14 Jan 1938), 59; rptd as Part 3 of "Some Notes on Somerset Maugham," COLLECTED ESSAYS (NY: Viking, 1969), pp. 202-5.
In *The Summing Up,* M objectively appraises himself and "defines his limitations perfectly." "His life contained material for dramatization and he used it for *fiction.*" M has never bared his soul to the public. His limitations result from his agnosticism: "Rob human beings of their heavenly and their infernal importance and you rob them of their individuality."

With his "contempt for human life, his unhappy honesty," M will be remembered as "the narrator."

1300 Hansen, Harry. "Among the New Books," HARPER'S MAGAZINE, CLXXVI (May 1938), n. p.

The Summing Up is "a frank and honest testament," which should displace half the college texts on writing, "for purposes of debate if not for agreement."

1301 Holliday, Terence. "Man of Letters," SATURDAY REVIEW OF LITERATURE, XVII (26 Oct 1938), 5.

M's account of himself and of his profession in *The Summing Up* is given with those virtues of style he extols—lucidity, simplicity, euphony, and liveliness.

1302 Jack, Peter M. "Somerset Maugham Sums Up," NEW YORK TIMES BOOK REVIEW, 27 March 1938, pp. 2, 19.

The Summing Up is a "brilliant demonstration of what it is to be a writer, without invading the privateness of being a person." M's brain is clear and logical, but neither very subtle nor very powerful.

1303 Johnson, A. Theodore. "Shorter Reviews," SOUTHERN REVIEW, III (Winter 1938), 618-21.

"Though workmanlike and highly competent," *Theatre* will add little to M's reputation as novelist.

1304 Kinninmont, Kenneth. "Up for Judgment," BOOKS OF THE MONTH, VIII (Jan 1938), 5-6.

M does not seek the lime-light, but allows his works to represent him. In *The Summing Up,* he avoids personalia and gives one more reason to admire his work.

1305 Klein, Robert. "A Producer to a Playwright: A Letter to Mr. Somerset Maugham," LONDON MERCURY, XXXVIII (May 1938), 16-26.

[An article in the form of an open letter to M by a producer of M's plays in Germany, disagreeing with M's "bitter" views on the producer-director in *The Summing Up*. Using over half of M's plays, Klein demonstrates the need for the artistic director to deviate sometimes from the playwright's original intention to guarantee theatrical and box office success.]

1306* Krutch, Joseph Wood. "Drama," NATION (NY), CXLVI (30 April 1938), 512-13.

M would be the first to admit that he is not a great dramatist; he does not invent characters, but borrows them from the "dramatic storehouse" and manipulates them like puppets. His virtue is that he gives his characters excellent dialogue, "and if one never believes for a moment that they are really alive, neither does one ever catch them doing or saying anything which is merely stupid or expected." [Review of the revival of *The Circle.*]

1307 "The Listener's Chronicle," LISTENER, XIX (19 Jan 1938), 152.

There is in *The Summing Up* "a defensive note not strictly consistent with its judicial title." M's conclusions may be trite; but "he shares with the Chinese philosophers a faculty for making his serenity exhilarating."

1308 "Maugham Sums Up: Agnostic's Cool Philosophy of Life," SPRINGFIELD SUNDAY UNION AND REPUBLICAN (Mass), 27 March 1938, p. 7E.

M's conclusions in *The Summing Up* exhibit a "calculating clarity of intellect which Voltaire and Swift possessed. Our national [American] temperament of compromise and our instinctive sense that the undiscovered ends of life are best unresolved have made such cool dissection unpopular. . . ."

1309 Maxence, Jean-Pierre. "Les Livres de la Semaine. Somerset Maugham: *Le Magicien*" (Books of the Week. Somerset Maugham: *The Magician*), GRINGOIRE, 1 April 1938, p. 4.

The Magician is, after *Of Human Bondage,* the richest and most interesting of M's works. It is neither pure imagination nor an exercise in style. It reveals great craftsmanship and creative power. [Review of the French translation.] [In French.]

1310* "Mr. Maugham Sums Up: An Artist and His Values," TIMES LITERARY SUPPLEMENT (Lond), 8 Jan 1938, p. 25; abridged in TIMES LITERARY SUPPLEMENT (Lond), 26 March 1938, p. 217.

"As stimulating as good talk," *The Summing Up* is neither a book of recollections nor an autobiography, but a "sorting out" of the author's thoughts on the subjects which have interested him most. Intimacy does not come easily, and there is open contradiction, cynicism, and introspection. But on the positive side, one can list an acute power of observation (fostered by travel and social intercourse), invention, fluency of expression, and an appreciation of literature.

1311 "Mr. Somerset Maugham," NEW YORK TIMES, 14 Feb 1938, p. 16.

[Editorial disagreeing with M's belief that the King James Bible has been a harmful influence on English prose.]

1312* Nathan, George Jean. "Theatre Week: Maugham the Romantic," NEWSWEEK, XI (25 April 1938), 26.

M's plays prove him a skillful writer, an expert in the handling of character, and the possessor of an "independent and richly fertile imagination." The revived *The Circle* proves M not a "cynic" but a "romantic" in that he cheers his young lovers on.

1313 O'Hara, Frank H., and Marguerite H. Bro. A HANDBOOK OF DRAMA (Chicago: Willett, Clark, 1938), pp. 89-95 especially 121, 169, 216.

Full discussion of the methods of characterization (by setting, physical action, personal appearance, by what others say) in *The Circle.*

1314 "Other Books: Selected List," LONDON MERCURY, XXXVII (Feb 1938), 469.

In *The Summing Up,* "the range and liveliness of [M's] ideas and the precision with which he expresses them afford . . . an unusually close view of the mental processes of an industrious, methodical, successful man of letters."

1315 "Our Booking-Office: Review of the Cosmos," PUNCH, CXCIV (19 Jan 1938), 82.

M is to be congratulated for his industry, determination, and his moderation and detachment in speaking of his achievements and beliefs in *The Summing Up.*

1316* Pritchett, V. S. "Living and Writing," FORTNIGHTLY REVIEW, N. S. CXLIII (March 1938), 369-70.

Under its superficial self-possession, *The Summing Up* reveals a curious rootlessness, pathos, and bewilderment, kept in their place by M's "warranted pride in his craft, in the accomplished planning of his career and the candid acceptance of his limitations." M fell short because his indifference led him to be merely a commentator on character, and the field of his comment is very limited; preoccupied with the misleading evidence of convention, "he has confined himself to debunking the conventional view."

1317 P[ritchett], V. S. "Mid-Channel Creature," CHRISTIAN SCIENCE MONITOR WEEKLY MAGAZINE SECTION, 23 March 1938, p. 10.

The Summing Up is "not a book about a happy man or a happy life; it is a book of a man wounded and aloof, who has sought consolation in excelling in his profession. It is an immensely readable book."

1318 Soskin, William. "A Novelist Ponders Life, Death and God," NEW YORK HERALD TRIBUNE BOOKS, 27 March 1938, p. 3.

The value of *The Summing Up* lies not in its "cosmic thoughts and sweeping considerations" but rather "in the graceful, well considered comments on the arts [M] has practiced, the people he has met, the successes and failures he has had."

1319 Squire, Tom. "The Closed Pattern: W. SOMERSET MAUGHAM, by Richard Cordell," THEATRE ARTS MONTHLY, XXII (Feb 1938), 157.

Cordell works well with his subject; even his prose style begins to resemble M's. And he succeeds in showing a purpose, a pattern in M's theatrical career. [Review of Cordell's study (1937).]

1320* Squire, Tom. "Literary Accounting: *The Summing Up*, by W. Somerset Maugham," THEATRE ARTS MONTHLY, XXII (Sept 1938), 695-96.

M's predictions are not always convincing, even though his verdict on Shaw and Ibsen [that they took away the *magic* of theater by infusing plays with too many nondramatic ideas] is sound. The book is, for the most part, frank and honest, but perhaps part of the reason for M's departure from the theater — besides his admitted reason that his work was becoming unfashionable — was his own somewhat unjustified pessimism.

1321 *"The Summing Up,"* KIRKUS, VI (1 Jan 1938), 6.

[Brief appraisal.]

1322 "Theatre: Old Play in Manhattan," TIME, XXXI (2 May 1938), 26.

Seventeen years after the original Broadway production the revival of *The Circle* "still 'played' and still had point." "*The Circle* wears well because it offers no dated problem in morals, but a permanent reflection on human nature."

1323* van der Vat, D. G. *"'The Summing Up,'"* ENGLISH STUDIES, XX (Dec 1938), 269-74.

Particularly in its omission of oppressive self-portraiture and in its maintenance of a detached tone, M's book is superior to others of its kind. M has achieved what is rarer than pure poetry: pure prose. In style, his book "is so uniformly excellent that it is entirely superfluous to hunt for passages to illustrate its perfection."

1324 Vernon, Grenville. "Criticism," COMMONWEAL, XXVIII (6 May 1938), 50.

The most valuable portions of *The Summing Up* are those on the art of the dramatist and the novelist.

1325* Vernon, Grenville. "The Stage and Screen," COMMONWEAL, XXVIII (6 May 1938), 48-49.

The characters in the revived *The Circle* are "real," the dialogue "meaty and informed by wit"; but, one feels the play's "cynicism" is deliberately contrived for dramatic effect, so that the play belongs to the perishable "comedy of manners" rather than to the permanent "high comedy" in which morals and ethical standards are "of all time." While M labels his play a "comedy," it is "more truly a tragedy, the tragedy of the author's soul," which has no trust in itself and so finds life meaningless.

1326 Weeks, Edward. "Bookshelf," ATLANTIC MONTHLY, CLXI (June 1938), n. p.
In *The Summing Up,* M evaluates his success without cynicism and pretentiousness, in an "effortless and beautifully articulate English . . . without even the necessity of taking you into his private life."

1327* West, Rebecca. "Etat des Lettres Anglaises" (The State of English Letters), JOURNAL DE GENEVE, 8 Aug 1938, pp. 1-2.
Of all the writers who prevailed before World War I only Shaw and Wells remain, but they are unproductive. Since the War only one British writer has achieved the fame of those two: M. In his works he considers the British way of life with the nostalgia and the cynicism of a sensible child obliged to leave his happy family for the company of indifferent strangers. Most of his stories are devoted to soldiers, civil servants and sailors met during his travels; his subject matter is the same as Kipling's, and his audience is the general mass, not the intelligentsia. [In French.]

1328 Williams, Orlo. "Books New and Old: A Lone Wolf," NATIONAL REVIEW (Lond), CX (March 1938), 393-98.
The Summing Up contains more description or narrative than reflection; its only persistent unity is M's self.

1329 Wolfe, Humbert. "Books of the Day," OBSERVER (Lond), 9 Jan 1938, p. 4.
In *The Summing Up,* M does not write like Pascal, but in his passionate search for detachment he attains a measure of wisdom and serenity that brings the Frenchman back to mind.

1330 "A Writer's Art: Mr. Maugham Sums Up," TIMES (Lond), 7 Jan 1938, p. 18.
[Primarily a summary of the contents of *The Summing Up* with a tone of approval.]

1331* Wyatt, Euphemia Van Rensselaer. "The Drama," CATHOLIC WORLD, CXLVII (June 1938), 346-47.
M is not superficial, but "he rarely cuts deep enough into life. . . . The pettiness of his world deflects the genius of his pen." The revived *The Circle* is an excellent showcase of his art, however, and "marks the high-water mark of the British school of drawing-room comedy, with the characterization of Pinero to balance the wit of Wilde."

1939

1332* Aldington, Richard. "Somerset Maugham: An Appreciation," SATURDAY REVIEW OF LITERATURE, XX (19 Aug 1939), 3-4, 12; published separately, as W. SOMERSET MAUGHAM: AN APPRECIATION. TOGETHER WITH "SIXTY-FIVE" BY W. SOMERSET MAUGHAM, AND A BIBLIOGRAPHY, AN INDEX OF SHORT STORIES, AND APPRECIATIONS. NY: Doubleday, Doran, 1939.

"Serious critics," unable to account for the popularity of a writer of M's intellect, ability, and fidelity to a personal vision of truth, either ignore or condescend to M as a writer unworthy of "serious consideration." Actually M is successful because he has a knowledge of, and an interest in, people, accompanied by an ability to present them in words; because he knows the arts of successful plotting and skillful narrative; and because he is a man of the world and not of the library.

1333 "Arts Theatre: *'The Constant Wife'* by Somerset Maugham," TIMES (Lond), 11 Sept 1939, p. 6.

Halfway through an "artificial comedy" M decides to change his play into "a rather second-rate problem play." [Review of the revival.]

1334 Becker, May Lamberton. "Books for Young People," NEW YORK HERALD TRIBUNE BOOKS, 12 Nov 1939, p. 11.

In *Princess September and the Nightingale* [from *The Gentleman in the Parlour* originally], illustrated by Richard C. Jones, "The fable is both droll and deep; a child likes the drollery, an adult recognizes the depth. . . . "

1335 Benét, Rosemary Carr. "Some of the Highlights," SATURDAY REVIEW OF LITERATURE, XXI (18 Nov 1939), 22.

Princess September and the Nightingale [from *The Gentleman in the Parlour* originally] is "one of the handsomest books of the season, but in a sophisticated way."

1336 Block, Anita. THE CHANGING WORLD IN PLAYS AND THEATRE (Boston: Little, Brown, 1939), pp. 10, 11, especially 82-95 and 328-33.

M's plays, especially *Constant Wife* and *For Services Rendered,* illustrate (1) the conflict with sexual standards and (2) plays against war in the twentieth-century theater.

1337 "Books," NEWSWEEK, XIV (23 Oct 1939), 41-42.

In *Christmas Holiday,* "one suspects, it was the story, as a story, that primarily interested the author."

1338 "Books—Briefly Noted: General," NEW YORKER, XV (24 June 1939), 72.
In *Tellers of Tales,* M's selection is "good," and his introduction "is full of sense, taste, and easy learning."

1339 "Books—Recent Books: Fiction," TIME, XXXIV (30 Oct 1939), 72.
Christmas Holiday is "melodrama within melodrama, made credible by Maugham's professional slickness."

1340 *"Christmas Holiday,"* KIRKUS, VII (15 July 1939), 262.
[Brief appraisal.]

1341 Colum, Mary M. "Life and Literature," FORUM, CII (Dec 1939), 260-61.
In *Christmas Holiday*, the portrayal of the unseen Robert Berger is "deft"; M's lecture on art seems at first "dragged in, but it manages to reveal the Russianness of Lydia and her difference from the young Englishman who admires the works of art he has been taught to admire."

1342* Connolly, Francis X. "Fiction," COMMONWEAL, XXXI (24 Nov 1939), 121.
What makes the conflict of *Christmas Holiday* "come alive is not the underlying philosophic criticism of society or of the individuals, but Maugham's deft handling of background and melodrama. Despite the improbability of Lydia and Fenimore as characters, they speak, act and live in the atmosphere of realism. The sights and sounds of Paris linger after the unnatural events of the Berger murder have become blurred. One receives the unfortunate impression that Maugham has become so mature that his work has become rotten."

1343 Cordell, Richard A. "The Almost Perfect Anthology," SATURDAY REVIEW OF LITERATURE, XX (24 June 1939), 7.
One can find little fault with M's selection of stories for *Tellers of Tales* and a great deal to admire in his own introduction.

1344 Cordell, Richard A. "Five-Day Adventure," SATURDAY REVIEW OF LITERATURE, XX (21 Oct 1939), 10.
Almost the best of M's novels to date, *Christmas Holiday* has an engrossing story, a clean style, a group of interesting characters, and the impress of the author's view of the universe. M shows an awareness of political, social, and economic problems.

1345 D., M. *"Christmas Holiday,"* SPRINGFIELD SUNDAY UNION AND REPUBLICAN (Mass), 29 Oct 1939, p. 7E.
"The book has high narrative interest but seems rather purposeless."

1346 Dottin, Paul. "La Littérature anglaise en 1938" (English Literature in 1938), LA REVUE DE FRANCE, 19ème année, no. 4 (15 July 1939), 236-37.

The Summing Up is the literary testament of a man of integrity. [In French.]

1347 Fadiman, Clifton. "Books: Recreations of a Dean," NEW YORKER, XV (21 Oct 1939), 75-76.

The "entire melodrama [*Christmas Holiday*], complete with psychological trimmings, is too disproportionately elaborate for such a vacuous ending, particularly when you consider that it's practically impossible to get interested in Charley in any case."

1348* Greene, Graham. "Underworld," LONDON MERCURY, XXXIX (March 1939), 550-51.

Christmas Holiday, ridden with clichés, displays several examples of an "odd ignorance of human feeling"; the story-within-a-story technique is so "maladroitly handled" here that it seems incredible that M could have used it so well in his earlier *Cakes and Ale.*

1349 Jack, Peter M. "Somerset Maugham's New Novel Is One of His Best," NEW YORK TIMES BOOK REVIEW, 22 Oct 1939, p. 6.

"Brilliant as ever, but more timely and thoughtful," *Christmas Holiday* is in M's familiar skillful vein of mixed adventure and ironic comment.

1350 Johnson, Edgar. "Growing Pains," NEW REPUBLIC, CI (8 Nov 1939), 21-22.

In his novel [*Christmas Holiday*] of young manhood, M does not show the artistry of the youthful Prokosch [NIGHT OF THE POOR], or the bitterness of the middle-aged Aldington [REJECTED GUESTS]; but instead, depending upon formula and stereotype for action and character, he shows only indifference.

1351 Jordan, Alice M. "The Booklist," HORN BOOK MAGAZINE, XV (Sept 1939), 297.

[Brief recommendation of *The Princess and the Nightingale* (from *The Gentleman in the Parlour* originally) for "special collections."]

1352 Kruschwitz, Hans. "Beiträge zur Behandlung von Schullektüren. 1. Die Darstellung der englischen Gesellschaft in W. S. Maughams Lustspiel *Jack Straw*" (Contributions on the Handling of School Literature. 1. The Representation of English Society in W. S. Maugham's Play *Jack Straw*), ZEITSCHRIFT FÜR NEUSPRACHLICHEN UNTERRICHT, XXXVIII (1939), 12-16.

Jack Straw is suitable for discussion at high school level since it casts light on the structure of English society and its ideal of the gentleman. [In German.]

1353 Kruschwitz, Hans. "Die Rassenfrage in W. S. Maughams 'The Alien Corn': Beitrag zur Deutung einer Schullektüre" (The Race-Question in W. S. Maugham's "The Alien Corn": A Contribution on Interpreting School Literature), ZEITSCHRIFT FÜR NEUSPRACHLICHEN UNTERRICHT, XXXVIII (1939), 107-10.

M's unbiased account proves the Nazi thesis that racial barriers are natural ones and that the Jews will always remain the alien corn in any country. [In German.]

1354* MacKay, L. A. "Books of the Month," CANADIAN FORUM, XIX (April 1939), 27.

Christmas Holiday at first looks as if it "did not quite know where it was heading for, but with the final chapter the admirable economy and the artful arrangement . . . became clear. The characters, however, do not all ring equally true. In particular, the young man studying to be the perfect professional terrorist, though quite conceivable, and necessary to the spiritual path of the hero, is not thoroughly convincing in himself."

1355* Marriott, Charles. "Books of the Day: Three New Novels," MANCHESTER GUARDIAN, 7 Feb 1939, p. 7.

One is struck by the easy mastery of the material of *Christmas Holiday* in both construction and narration; it is an "episode" that would have delighted Maupassant and that has been explored with a touch reminiscent of James's "squeeze of the orange." One weakness is Charley's account of visiting the Louvre with his parents, which distorts the impression already formed of them.

1356 Mullan, Eunice G. "Recommended Children's Books," LIBRARY JOURNAL, LXIV (15 Sept 1939), 713.

"Its subtleties and humor" make *Princess September and the Nightingale* [from *The Gentleman in the Parlour* originally] "definitely of interest to adults rather than children."

1357 "New Books," CATHOLIC WORLD, CL (Dec 1939), 377.

Princess September and the Nightingale [from *The Gentleman in the Parlour* originally] is delicate in plot and its illustration.

1358* "New Novels," TIMES (Lond), 10 Feb 1939, p. 20.

"If we ignore the fact that few people are so dull as those who insist on relating the story of their lives, we may concede that Mr. Maugham's art is far too accomplished for him to fail altogether, that the narrative [in *Christmas Holiday*] has much of his usual crispness, and that there are several passages in which the novelist of the worldly momentarily retrieves the novel from the status of the novelette." [Review of *Christmas Holiday.*]

1359 "Novels of the Week: In Russian Mood," TIMES LITERARY SUPPLEMENT (Lond), 4 Feb 1939, p. 71.

Christmas Holiday is "deeply interesting, but is it a good novel?" The indirect and fragmentary style of construction is not wholly suited to a work of psychological intimacy, yet the narrative has an "immense and deceptive ease."

1360 "Our Booking-Office: A Young Man in Paris," PUNCH, CXCVI (15 Feb 1939), 194-95.

In *Christmas Holiday,* "each scene . . . is perfectly vivid, each character is living and distinct, and the progress of Charley's disillusionment, quietly told in a beautifully spare, almost hesitant, style, is a profound tragedy."

1361 Owens, Olga. "Jekyl to Hyde," BOSTON EVENING TRANSCRIPT, 21 Oct 1939, p. 1.

The only weakness of *Christmas Holiday* is that there is a "lack of balance between the completely normal Charley and the three who are made foils for him."

1362 *"Princess September and the Nightingale,"* KIRKUS, VII (15 Aug 1939), 341.

[Brief appraisal.]

1363 "Reich and Soviet Sign 10-Year Pact," NEW YORK TIMES, 24 Aug 1939, p. 6.

On 23 Aug 1939 IZVESTIA published a literary article attacking British ruling classes on the basis of the writings of M, J. B. Priestley, and A. J. Cronin. M is said to "preach a lie" about the bourgeois British that he knows to be false.

1364 "Reprints, New Editions," NEW YORK HERALD TRIBUNE BOOKS, 25 June 1939, p. 17.

M's criticism in *Tellers of Tales* is excellent and the variety of the volume itself commendable.

1365 Richardson, Maurice [L]. "Hard, Medium and Soft," BOOKS OF THE MONTH, IX (Feb 1939), 14.

In *Christmas Holiday,* the art snobbery of Charley's parents is funny but labored; Simon is a "tremendous bore."

1366* Savini, Gertrud. DAS WELTBILD IN WILLIAM SOMERSET MAUGHAMS DRAMEN (THE WORLDVIEW IN WILLIAM SOMERSET MAUGHAM'S PLAYS). Erlangen: Junge & Sohn, 1939.

As a dramatist, M wishes to entertain and to reproduce as exactly as possible the manners and customs of the day. His comedies deal with the glittering surface of life in Mayfair, but include criticisms of other strata of society. M likes to portray women without a sense of duty as well as women either enjoying or hating their modern independence. His treatment of love, marriage, religion, and morals reveals the relaxing of moral codes and the general spirit of disillusionment engendered by World War I. M's view of the world is largely negative. However, he often criticizes the upper middle class and depicts personalities who are opposed to the widespread disintegration of values. Therefore some of his plays at least continue to be performed in the Third Reich. [In German.]

1367 Schorer, Mark. "A Hammock Book," BOSTON EVENING TRANSCRIPT, 24 June 1939, p. 1.

In *Tellers of Tales,* M relies on familiar artists, does not go back to the original texts of the stories, and omits too many important writers.

1368 Shawe-Taylor, Desmond. "New Novels," NEW STATESMAN AND NATION, N. S. XVII (11 Feb 1939), 212.

In *Christmas Holiday,* M's inventive and narrative powers are at their best, but the unfolding of Lydia's tragedy is a strain on them. When M changes from indirect to direct narration, interest in Lydia and Charley's relationship flags.

1369 "Shorter Notices," NATION (NY), CXLIX (21 Oct 1939), 448.

In *Christmas Holiday,* "Mr. Maugham is not at his best. . . . "

1370* Soskin, William. "When the Bottom Falls Out of a Man's World," NEW YORK HERALD TRIBUNE BOOKS, 22 Oct 1939, p. 5.

In *Christmas Holiday,* the series of speeches by Simon and Lydia have a didactic tone, "and the argumentation surrounding them suggests that M himself realized that he did not make his ambitious purpose [to dramatize the issue of moral individualism vs. an amoral manipulation of power in the interest of dictatorship] implicit in his story. The novel is saved through "sprightly incident . . . adroit manipulation of people . . . and the excellence of Maugham's satirical thrusts."

1371* Swinnerton, Frank. "New Novels," OBSERVER (Lond), 5 Feb 1939, p. 6.

Christmas Holiday is "very nearly a masterpiece," with the "beautiful simplicity of MANON LESCAUT." However, the book is flawed by the caricaturing of Charley's parents and the long essay on aesthetic criticism.

1372 "Telegrams in Brief," TIMES (Lond), 17 June 1939, p. 11.

The French Minister of Education approves the proposal of the University of Toulouse to confer an honorary degree on M.

1373 "Telegrams in Brief," TIMES (Lond), 3 Aug 1939, p. 11.
M is promoted to Commander of the Legion of Honour in Paris.

1374 *"Tellers of Tales,"* KIRKUS, VII (1 May 1939), 180.
[Brief appraisal.]

1375 *"Tellers of Tales,"* NEW REPUBLIC, CI (Dec 1939) 213.
This is a collection of "fair to excellent reading" for one's Christmas list.

1376 V., L. "Bibliographie" (Bibliography), ETUDES ANGLAISES, III (July-Sept 1939), 334.
In *The Magician,* the novelist has followed the medieval tradition which has it that the artificial creation of life is a sacrilege which requires the connivance of the powers of evil. Oliver Haddo is a sort of modern Gilles de Rais. [In French.]

1377 V-hl, V. "Kaukaisen Idän mystiikkaa Kaupunginteatterin lavalla" (Mysticism of the Far East at the Stage of the Town Theater), KARJALA, 11 Feb 1939, p. 10.
In *East of Suez,* the patterns are on the surface; they lack profundity and greatness. M is a skillful writer, but one would not like to call him a poet. [Review of the Finnish translation, in Finnish.]

1378 van Gelder, Robert. "A Month's Reading in One Book," NEW YORK TIMES BOOK REVIEW, 2 July 1939, p. 6.
Tellers of Tales is a "vast, inclusive selection of the better short stories of a hundred years. . . . " M's taste would seem to be excellent, and his first demand is for entertainment.

1379 W., K. S. "Books: The Children's Harvest," NEW YORKER, XV (25 Nov 1939), 73.
Princess September and the Nightingale [from *The Gentleman in the Parlour* originally] is "neatly told," but the story hasn't "quite the fairy tale quality which takes a child into a make-believe world, and its humor is a sophisticated humor at which children do not laugh."

1380* Waugh, Evelyn. "Books of the Day: The Technician," SPECTATOR (Lond), CLXII (17 Feb 1939), 274; rptd in THE MAUGHAM ENIGMA, ed by Klaus W. Jonas (NY: Citadel P, 1954), pp. 153-55.
In "technical felicity," *Christmas Holiday* is M's best novel; it has characteristic "accuracy, economy and control." "Preposterous" characters and ideas seem "perfectly convincing," but in the last sentence the bottom falls out of the novel. Nothing has really happened to Charley; "he has merely had an instructive and profitable holiday, and will be just the same kind of fellow in future with a slightly wider and wiser outlook."

1381 Weeks, Edward. "Bookshelf," Atlantic Monthly, CLXIV (Dec 1939), n. p.
Christmas Holiday is to be praised for its "keen observations," its "contrast of character," and its "English of almost Gallic precision"; but too much "rhetoric" and "introspection" deprive the narrative of its momentum, and "feeling" is lacking.

1940

1382 Barry, Iris. "Midsummer Nights' Fare," New York Herald Tribune Books, 12 July 1940, p. 4.
In *The Mixture as Before,* M's style communicates exactly what he intended. None of the stories, not even the most heartfelt "Lotus Eater," could be called important; all of them, to a remarkable degree, give the impression of showing the "inside mechanism of human behavior" by a man "expert," but "detached." Altogether, the collection is "perfect midsummer nights' fare."

1383 Bates, H. E. "Books & Life," Books of the Month, X (April 1940), 18.
[Brief review of *Books and You.*]

1384 Bates, H. E. "H. E. Bates Reviews," Books of the Month, X (June 1940), 16-17.
The Mixture as Before is poor in style and characterization.

1385 Benét, William Rose. "English Maupassant," Saturday Review of Literature, XXII (27 July 1940), 6.
"At his best he [M] is an admirable observer; at his worst he is apt to spread on color too lavishly and thicken the dramatic values. But he is one of the few who can deal with sex honestly; and he is both sophisticated and astute." [Review of *The Mixture as Before.*]

1386 "Books—Briefly Noted: General," New Yorker, XVI (30 March 1940), 67.
Books and You contains "entertaining but limited judgments."

1387 "Books—Briefly Noted: General," New Yorker, XVI (4 May 1940), 76.
France at War is a "short, neat propaganda essay. . . . The author knows his subject."

1388 "Books of the Week: New Novels," TIMES (Lond), 8 June 1940, p. 9.
As a description of the contents of *The Mixture as Before,* the title is "not exact. The masterly method of concise and vivid statement is unchanged, but these pieces generally lack the fascinating cynicism remarkable in the early work."

1389 "Books: Recent & Readable," TIME, XXXVI (22 July 1940), 84.
The ten stories in *The Mixture as Before* are told "with an elderly tartness and urbanity for which the author . . . is famed."

1390 Brighouse, Harold. "Books of the Day: New Fiction," MANCHESTER GUARDIAN, 21 June 1940, p. 2.
The Mixture as Before "at lowest valuation is first-rate entertainment."

1391 C., R. J. "Maugham's Mixture," SPRINGFIELD SUNDAY UNION AND REPUBLICAN (Mass), 14 July 1940, p. 7E.
The writing in *The Mixture as Before* seems a little too slick to be first-class.

1392 Dell, Robert. "Billet D'Amour," SATURDAY REVIEW OF LITERATURE, XXII (1 June 1940), 6.
The worst kind of propaganda, *France at War* "reminds one of nothing so much as a goody-goody book written by a pious lady for Sunday school scholars."

1393 Etzkorn, Leo R. "New Book Survey," LIBRARY JOURNAL, LXV (1 March 1940), 209.
Books and You is "written in a highly popular style."

1394 Fadiman, Clifton. "Books: Mr. Maugham's Mixture," NEW YORKER, XVI (13 July 1940), 60-61.
The tales in *The Mixture as Before,* of which "Lord Mountdrago" is the best, are "diverting, ingenious, well-told."

1395* Flanner, Janet. "Behind the Maginot Line," NEW YORK HERALD TRIBUNE BOOKS, 12 May 1940, p. 4.
"Hastily, simply and passionately written by an author who rarely writes hastily or simply but who has always passionately known and loved France," *France at War* is a brochure "of multiple small searing truthful illuminating details concerning precisely what millions of French are doing . . . to keep . . . their Gallic hearts burning at the quite white heat which French history now demands."

1396* Forbes-Boyd, Eric. "Among the New Books," CHRISTIAN SCIENCE MONITOR WEEKLY MAGAZINE SECTION, 27 July 1940, p. 10.
In *The Mixture as Before,* M's "insight has led him to discover chiefly

the weaknesses of human nature, but it has not led him into cynicism. He exhibits his fallible, petty, or worldly creatures . . . with the sole desire that we should grasp their struggles and their essential humanity. His world may not be to everyone's taste, but there is no denying the quality of his art; the clean beauty of the prose would, alone, make the book worth reading."

1397 Forbes-Boyd, Eric. "Those Fabulous Days Before the World War—A London Letter," CHRISTIAN SCIENCE MONITOR WEEKLY MAGAZINE SECTION, 11 May 1940, p. 11.

In *Books and You,* only M's remarks on Dickinson and Emerson are likely to arouse much disagreement.

1398 *"France at War,"* KIRKUS, VIII (1 April 1940), 160.

[Brief appraisal.]

1399 *"France at War,"* SPRINGFIELD SUNDAY UNION AND REPUBLICAN (Mass), 5 May 1940, p. 7E.

[Noncommittal review of M's belief about the French war-effort.]

1400 "The France that Was," CHRISTIAN SCIENCE MONITOR WEEKLY MAGAZINE SECTION, 24 Aug 1940, p. 10.

After the surrender of France, one reads M's eulogy, *France at War,* with frustration.

1401 J., A. W. *"France at War,"* MANCHESTER GUARDIAN, 19 March 1940, p. 3.

[Primarily a summary of the book's contents, emphasizing the one wish of the French that the Germans "may never, under any circumstances, be able to disturb her again. Idealists may not like it, but that is the fact."]

1402 "The Listener's Book Chronicle," LISTENER, XXIII (4 April 1940), 697.

In *Books and You,* M's list of books to be read is, "barring some of the French novels, one that every schoolmaster or mistress would hand to an upper form if he or she wanted to avoid giving the victims of education any pain." M's criticism is "attractively honest."

1403 "Literary: Tour Among Good Books," TIMES LITERARY SUPPLEMENT (Lond), 23 March 1940, p. 148.

In *Books and You,* M's choice "deals only with books about which the world of letters is almost unanimous in agreeing are great and powerful." There is hence little room for criticism of the resulting list. It is significant, however, that M seems to choose his books not from a desire for critical immunity, but from his own surety of taste.

1404 Littell, Robert. "Outstanding Novels," YALE REVIEW, N. S. XXIX (Winter 1940), x.

Christmas Holiday contains "a brilliant idea inexplicably muffed"; its two plots or stories are told with "expertness," but also without "color, with a frigid clarity which seems always about to turn into something else, yet never does."

1405* Littell, Robert. "Outstanding Novels," YALE REVIEW, N. S. XXX (Autumn 1940), x.

M "always gives one the impression of knowing exactly what he is doing. This knowledge somehow seems to be the ceiling which has limited his remarkable talent: none of his characters ever eludes him and flies away from that knowledge on wings of his own." M has an air of "alert weariness," but although he may have lost his zest for life, he has not lost his zest for telling about it; thus the mixture in *The Mixture as Before* has "a cool but by no means unpleasantly bitter taste."

1406 Morehouse, Ward. "Somerset Maugham," STAGE, I (Nov 1940), 48-49.

[Interview, with an emphasis on M's career in the theater.]

1407 Mortimer, Raymond. "Current Literature: Books in General," NEW STATESMAN AND NATION, N. S. XIX (23 March 1940), 402.

[General appreciation of *France at War*.]

1408 "New Books," CATHOLIC WORLD, CL (Feb 1940), 635.

Christmas Holiday "is intended for the entertainment of the highly sophisticate; anyone else may be shocked, or even disgusted."

1409 "New Books," CATHOLIC WORLD, CLI (Sept 1940), 254-55.

In *Books and You,* M's human approach is admirable, but M's wavering between the moral and amoral in certain judgments, as well as his frequent "bromides" are not."

1410* "Novels of the Week: Appeal to an Author," TIMES LITERARY SUPPLEMENT (Lond), 8 June 1940, p. 277.

Apparently the secret of the ten seemingly nothing-less-than-brilliant short stories in *The Mixture as Before* lies in M's craftsmanship, and his scrupulous, passionate observation of life. The stories reveal a deep knowledge of men and women, a meditative candor, an accuracy of statement, an appearance of ease, and a precision of mind, but detachment of touch.

1411 O'Brien, Kate. "Books of the Day: Fiction," SPECTATOR (Lond), CLXIV (7 June 1940), 788.

"The clipped and narrow wisdom" of M's later work in *The Mixture as*

Before is "too narrow and clipped for everlastingness," and his values "are too rigidly diminished by formal cynicism."

1412 "Other New Books," NEWSWEEK, XV (25 March 1940), 38. *Books and You* contains "stimulating essays."

1413 "Other New Books," NEWSWEEK, XVI (15 July 1940), 40. *The Mixture as Before* contains "ten characteristic short stories by a modern master of the medium."

1414* Pritchett, V. S. "Current Literature: Books in General," NEW STATESMAN AND NATION, N. S. XIX (15 June 1940), 750; rptd as *"The Mixture As Before,"* in THE MAUGHAM ENIGMA, ed by Klaus W. Jonas (NY: Citadel P, 1954), pp. 185-90.
In *The Mixture as Before,* M has something in common with Kipling, a good deal with Shaw. He is Kipling "turned inside out, discovering alcohol, beachcombing and middle class sex, where Kipling portrayed the Roman overlord and evoked the secret, savage hierarchy of the jungle." Like Shaw, M has the "trick of turning things upside down"; particularly is this evident in his short stories, and pre-eminently in the present collection. These stories are highly "patterned," have "enormous readability," and carry "one to the most savage height of irony"; but they make no profound impression.

1415 Pruette, Lorine. "How to Like to Read," NEW YORK HERALD TRIBUNE BOOKS, 14 April 1940, p. 21.
"The coolly, distinguished, informal but never intimate essay seems particularly appropriate" to M, and *Books and You* "will prove the modest and delightful prelude to a full volume of criticism."

1416* Rick, K. "Claude Searcy McIver, WILLIAM SOMEREST MAUGHAM; Paul Dottin, LE THEATRE DE SOMERSET MAUGHAM; W. Somerset Maugham, *The Summing Up*," ENGLISCHE STUDIEN, LXXIV (1940-41), 246-48.
McIver overemphasizes Maupassant's influence and overlooks the question of racial mixture so important to the German reader of M. Except for minor blemishes, Dottin's monograph is well written. *The Summing Up* illuminates M's reading; a few of his short stories will outlast the plays and novels. [In German.]

1417 Searles, Ruth. "Startling Reality Pervades New Book," BOSTON EVENING TRANSCRIPT (Books and Special Features), 13 July 1940, p. 1.
In *The Mixture as Before,* M writes with "sterling worth" about worthless people, and has the knack of pleasing everybody.

1418* Spencer, Theodore. "Somerset Maugham," College English, II (Oct 1940), 1-10; rptd as "An Appreciation," in The Maugham Enigma, ed by Klaus W. Jonas (NY: Citadel P, 1954), pp. 72-83.

Because M is not an experimenter, but a traditionalist, modern critics have spurned him. M deserves better, and popular opinion recognizes the fact by disagreeing with the critics. M's four categories (style, drama, fiction, and philosophy) from *The Summing Up* illustrate M's merits.
M's style is economical and efficient, his tone anecdotal; but his studied ease and deftness make one think "that his way of saying a thing is more important to him than what he has to say"; thus, M's prose is "frequently good but [it] never reaches sublimity," and because this is so, it lacks "that final insight which reveals the universal through the particular."

M's career as a novelist falls into two main divisions: (1) from *Liza of Lambeth* to *Of Human Bondage*; and (2) from *Cakes and Ale* [publication date (1930) mistakenly given as 1922] to *Christmas Holiday,* including the short stories. In the first period the best novels are, excluding *Bondage, Liza* and *Mrs. Craddock,* straightforward books in the late nineteenth-century realistic tradition, with two main virtues: natural and convincing dialogue, and firmly and clearly conceived main characters. In the second period the novels manifest a more personal technique and tone: their structure is less tight; they have about them an air of easy freedom, and this is enhanced by M's use of the first person singular point of view.

M uses the first person in all three ways it can be used: to make the story sound as if it actually happened, to give it a particular tone or philosophical atmosphere, and to add a more normal point of view to the peculiarity of the main characters. But the very use of the first person limits M: he reveals his attitude toward life, and that is a mellow version of his earlier discovery of "egoism" as man's sole motivation; thus, "moral struggle" and its attendant grandeur is entirely absent. Even M's *Of Human Bondage* misses greatness, then, by not pressing us urgently "into new areas of awareness," but merely filling out in a moving, efficient, and vivid way "areas of awareness which we already possess."

But M is not to be dismissed entirely because he is excluded from the very top rank of contemporary writers: his honesty, craftsmanship, and gifts for arousing interest and holding attention keep our sensitivities alive and provide examples of "that common basis of value and tradition which must always be the groundwork for writing of the superior kind."

1419 Stearns, Austin. "Mr. Maugham's Advice on What's Worth Reading," New York Times Book Review, 31 March 1940, p. 2.

Books and You provides a sound, conventional, basic guide for young people, and for the multitude of adults still confused by their literary heritage.

1420 Sylvester, Harry. "Books of the Week," COMMONWEAL, XXXII (2 Aug 1940), 313-14.

"None of the stories in this book [*The Mixture as Before*] are great stories and only perhaps two are very good, 'Gigolo and Gigolette' and 'An Official Position.' "

1421 "Topics of the Times," NEW YORK TIMES, 6 Jan 1940, p. 12.

M is wrong in his view that it was Whitman who brought poetry home to the American common man; Longfellow deserved the honor M gives to Whitman. [Editorial.]

1422* van Gelder, Robert. "Mr. Maugham on the Essentials of Writing," NEW YORK TIMES BOOK REVIEW, 24 Nov 1940, p. 2; rptd in WRITERS AND WRITING (NY: Charles Scribner's, 1946), pp. 138-41; and in THE MAUGHAM ENIGMA, ed by Klaus W. Jonas (NY: Citadel P, 1954), pp. 37-40.

M, in an interview, comments on (1) his evacuation from his villa in southern France at the beginning of the Blitzkrieg, (2) the future of the War, and especially of England's RAF, (3) why he has sworn off fiction, taken to writing articles, (4) the process of writing fiction, (5) his habit of traveling the world to find people to write about, (6) the great novelist's constitution, and (7) the advisability of having moral standards.

1423 van Gelder, Robert. "Tales by Maugham," NEW YORK TIMES BOOK REVIEW, 14 July 1940, p. 6.

The Mixture as Before is remarkable for its presentation of characters and basic situations.

1424* Verschoyle, Derek. "Books of the Day: The Best Books in the World," SPECTATOR (Lond), CLXIV (19 April 1940), 562.

In *Books and You,* Stendhal is M's favorite author, with Proust and Tolstoi close seconds. Dickens is "the greatest English novelist," while Jane Austen "gives more real pleasure than anything." M "deals rather summarily with poetry, confessing that he likes anthologies." He unnecessarily excludes living authors. Among American writers, M allows that Melville, Whitman, and Poe were men of genius, but Melville is the only "great and original writer" in America.

1425 Woods, Katherine. "Somerset Maugham on France at War," NEW YORK TIMES BOOK REVIEW, 19 May 1940, p. 6.

France at War attempts to understand the phenomenon of the French, a passionately peace-loving people, now dedicated with grim concentration to war. The message of this book, a message addressed directly to the British public, would seem to be "Sauvez la France!"

1426 "World Affairs: The Spirit of France," TIMES LITERARY SUPPLEMENT (Lond), 23 March 1940, p. 142.

In *France at War,* M looks at the human factor behind the intricacies of political and historical machinery. The warning note offered is not to separate Hitler from the German people; Germany cannot be regarded as a separate entity from her ruler.

1941

1427 Aho, O. "W. S. Maugham in näytelmätekniikasta" (On the Dramatic Technique of W. S. Maugham), VALVOJA-AIKA, XIX (1941), 123-30.

M writes comedies of manners. Their plots are seldom new or original, but M knows how to make old ones interesting or dramatically rewarding. In his problem plays there is a surprising amount of action on the psychological level. M's dialogue and sentence structure are always unambiguous; he aims at extreme simplicity. Sometimes the dialogue is distinctly rhythmical; at times, an unusual word or phrase is chosen for sonority, though never at the cost of clarity in expression. M's comedies are full of reckless satire; he avoids direct characterization: his characters show no development. The plays are intended to entertain; they have entertained for thirty years, many of them are still enjoyable, and will remain so. [In Finnish.]

1428 Atkinson, [J.] Brooks. "The Play," NEW YORK TIMES, 13 Nov 1941, p. 34; rptd by Raymond Mander and Joe Mitchenson, eds, in THEATRICAL COMPANION TO MAUGHAM (Lond: Rockliff, 1955), pp. 276-77.

Guy Bolton's dramatization of THEATRE is a "brilliantly varnished old hackney coach."

1429* Bates, H[erbert]. E[rnest]. THE MODERN SHORT STORY: A CRITICAL SURVEY (Boston: The Writer, 1941), pp. 7, 15, 74, 105, especially 140-46, 222.

In comparison with Conrad, Chekhov, and Maupassant, M suffers. M's stories are "easily available, pleasantly readable," but it is unfortunate that M chose Maupassant as a model rather than keep "more closely to Butler": if he had rejected Maupassant and followed Butler, "we should have been presented with the first full-length English short-story writer worthy of comparison with the best continental figures. Unfortunately Maugham, in spite of an excellent eye, a dispassionate steadiness, a genius for the diagnoses of human frailty, and a cosmopolitan temperament, lacks . . . compassion." This lack gives his work the impression of "cheapness."

1430 "Books," NEWSWEEK, XVII (7 April 1941), 55.
Up at the Villa could have been dictated while M was "talking in his sleep."

1431 "Books—Briefly Noted: Fiction," NEW YORKER, XVII (6 Sept 1941), 63-64.
M's information about the sad state of French morale is interesting, but the rest of the narrative in *Strictly Personal* is "unimportant."

1432 Carbuccia, Horace de. "Adieu à mon ami anglais" (Goodbye, My English Friend), GRINGOIRE, 7 Nov 1941, pp. 1-2; reissued as a pamphlet, Paris: Les éditions de France, 1942.
[Carbuccia, an adaptor of M's plays before World War II, attacks M and the English during the German occupation of France, by giving a translation of M's short story "The Treasure," in which the intimate relations between a worldly man and his chambermaid are described, and by suggesting that the original of the chambermaid was actually M's manservant.] [In French.]

1433 Colt, Alice M. "New Book Survey," LIBRARY JOURNAL, LXVI (1 Sept 1941), 730-31.
In *Strictly Personal,* "the intimacy of the account and the never-failing humor will charm many readers."

1434 Cowley, Malcolm. "Personal Histories," NEW REPUBLIC, CV (15 Sept 1941), 345-46.
M never makes clear the psychological connection between the trivialities of his private world and the tragedies of a collapsing France, both of which he describes. Yet *Strictly Personal* does contribute to our knowledge of the causes of the fall of France.

1435 Dangerfield, George. "Diary of a New Dimension," SATURDAY REVIEW OF LITERATURE, XXIV (13 Sept 1941), 13.
Strictly Personal is a portrait of a personality, carefully written and filled with what some might consider irrelevancies but which are in fact important contributions to the full portrait.

1436 Dennis, Nigel. *"Up at the Villa,"* NEW REPUBLIC, CIV (19 May 1941), 704.
M perverts his talents to make *Up at the Villa* his "worst novel." He no longer shows an ability to construct stories "with an admirable balance between straight narrative and the study of human behavior."

1437 Fadiman, Clifton. "Books: Mixed Bag," NEW YORKER, XVII (5 April 1941), 88.

Up at the Villa is "always diverting, never insulting."

1438 Gibbs, Wolcott. "The Theatre: Murder, Maugham, and Miss George," NEW YORKER, XVII (22 Nov 1941), 39-40.

Guy Bolton's dramatization of THEATRE retains the general outline of the original, but not "its urbane and sardonic spirit."

1439 Grace, William J. "Seeing the War," COMMONWEAL, XXXIV (10 Oct 1941), 594-95.

M's judgments of Gamelin, Daladier, Weygand, Pétain, and Chamberlain in *Strictly Personal* are essentially well taken.

1440* Gunn, Neil M. "On Backgrounds," SCOTS MAGAZINE, XXXIV (March 1941), 437-40.

Using, as an example, M's dissection of the English gentleman from his own "background" illustrates the importance of one's "background" in literary endeavor.

1441* Hauser, Marianne. "A Maugham Story," NEW YORK TIMES BOOK REVIEW, 6 April 1941, p. 7.

Up at the Villa does not hold any surprises except the ones which are always expected in a M story—it is close knit and splendidly built. It has a striking plot, full of both psychological and dramatic potentialities, but it comes off thin and pale, "leading nowhere into human depths but always ending in drawing room talk."

1442 Hillyer, Dorothy. "Mr. Maugham on Men, Women," NEW YORK HERALD TRIBUNE BOOKS, 6 April 1941, p. 2.

In *Up at the Villa,* the dramatic situation springs directly from the characters themselves, and their behavior under tension is in direct accord with all their previous experience. Like Rowley Flint, his hero, M has an instinctive understanding "of the difference between the sexes," and his style is "swift and lucid."

1443 Johnson, Pamela Hansford. "Bread and Circuses," BOOKS OF THE MONTH, XI (June 1941), 18-19.

Up at the Villa is "fascinating and elegant," though M is blinded by affection for his heroine, Mary Panton.

1444 Krutch, Joseph Wood. "Drama," NATION (NY), CLIII (29 Nov 1941), 548.

Guy Bolton's dramatization of THEATRE begins "as half-Maughamish, half-Cowardish" . . . but "degenerates into a sentimental and stagey backstage comedy."

1445 Krutch, Joseph Wood. "An Epicurean on Liberty," NATION (NY), CLIII (4 Oct 1941), 311; rptd in THE MAUGHAM ENIGMA, ed by Klaus W. Jonas (NY: Citadel P, 1954), pp. 205-7.
M's moral purpose in writing *Strictly Personal* is praiseworthy.

1446 Littell, Robert. "Outstanding Novels," YALE REVIEW, N. S. XXX (Summer 1941), xiv.
Up at the Villa is "extremely readable, well-planned and empty-hearted."

1447 Loveman, Amy. "Maughamette," SATURDAY REVIEW OF LITERATURE, XXXIV (10 May 1941), 15.
Although the story of *Up at the Villa* is intrinsically incredible, M holds the reader's attention with his consummate craftsmanship.

1448 Marriott, Charles. "Mr. Maugham and Others," MANCHESTER GUARDIAN, 16 May 1941, p. 3.
Up at the Villa is like carved sculpture "in which the subject is realised by the removal of superfluous material."

1449 Monroe, N. Elizabeth. THE NOVEL AND SOCIETY: A CRITICAL STUDY OF THE MODERN NOVEL (Chapel Hill: Universtiy of North Carolina P, 1941), p. 265.
M may think men moved by savage egoism, love a dirty trick played on human beings to achieve continuation of the species, but he must not try to make "his distorted vision representative." Any novelist who submits to nothing but his own view can be a "pernicious influence."

1450* Montague, Clifford M. "William Somerset Maugham—Dramatist," POET LORE, XLVII (Spring 1941), 40-55.
At the beginning of his career, M, like Oscar Wilde, wrote drama about high society, with bright repartée; but M was determined to build his reputation on more solid foundations, and became a "far better and greater dramatist than Wilde." At the outset M "resurrected the dramatic trick of situation," and knowing the weight of women's influence in contemporary drama, he "developed women in his dramas that are epitomes of what most women, in their heart of hearts, wish they were or could become." To these qualities must be added M's knowledge of what his audiences wanted, his craftsmanship, and his "economy of matter." M became, however, increasingly concerned with "serious ideas," and in his last three plays, "out-Ibsenized Ibsen." He became too bluntly cynical for either popular acceptance or popular success, and since 1933 has called himself an "ex-dramatist." Whether M's blunt cynicism contains merit or not, at least he did not compromise "in his use of what he considered important." [Contains a brief bibliography of M's published and unpublished plays as well as his translations of plays, p. 55.]

1451* "Novels of the Week: Tragedy of Error," TIMES LITERARY SUPPLEMENT (Lond), 17 May 1941, p. 237.
M exhibits an inability to make up his mind in the matter of a personal philosophy, an inability which plagues him through all his later work [e.g., *Up at the Villa*], "and seems to provide him with an unfailing creative impulse." In addition to being a storyteller, a manipulator of plot and character, and a professional craftsman, M takes on another dimension: that of the philosopher. His primary philosophical themes are the importance of fortune and of physical attributes (health, charm, privilege), and their complete irrelevance to the more important concepts of evil and suffering, which M generally ignores.

1452 O'Brien, Kate. "Books of the Day: Fiction," SPECTATOR (Lond), CLXVI (16 May 1941), 536.
"In character and substance the book [*Up at the Villa*] is a magazine story by an expert." It is "neat and inessential" and "will keep many women murmuring happily and uneasily, as they race over the easy pages."

1453 O'Hara, John. "Entertainment Week," NEWSWEEK, XVIII (24 Nov 1941), 24.
Guy Bolton's dramatization of THEATRE is "a play for the matinee and taxi crowd."

1454 "Other New Books," NEWSWEEK, XVIII (15 Sept 1941), 62.
Strictly Personal is "not particularly rewarding."

1455 "Our Booking-Office: The Born Story-Teller," PUNCH, CC (18 June 1941), 594.
In *Up at the Villa,* the characters all speak alike, their motives are improbable, and they are not interesting; but the book has that quality—readableness—that makes even quite bad books "well loved."

1456 Owens, Olga. "Novels," BOSTON EVENING TRANSCRIPT, 19 April 1941, V:1.
M's "artful simplicity of style, his masterful handling of character and of the most bizarre drama are qualities that make this [*Up at the Villa*] an arresting book."

1457 Seyd, Felizia. "Maugham's Mosaic of War and Morale—1940," NEW YORK HERALD TRIBUNE BOOKS, 7 Sept 1941, p. 5.
The title of *Strictly Personal* is "misleading," for M has foregone his privileges of employing artistic dramatization and arrangement, "brilliancy of metaphor," and anecdote "to safeguard the truthfulness of his story." Yet, the book remains as "brilliantly his own as any."

1458 *"Strictly Personal,"* KIRKUS, IX (15 July 1941), 326.
[Brief appraisal.]

1459 "The Theater," TIME, XXXVIII (24 Nov 1941), 62.
"A gal familiar to Broadway for a generation, with her hard little face and her soft, flabby hips, THEATRE needs all the expert make-up and massage that Playwrights Bolton & Maugham know how to apply. . . . Even so, it's not very pleasant fun." [Review of Guy Bolton's dramatization.]

1460 "Topics of the Times," NEW YORK TIMES, 4 April 1941, p. 20.
[Editorial criticizing M's views on the fall of France in World War II.]

1461 *"Up at the Villa,"* KIRKUS, IX (1 Feb 1941), 38.
[Brief appraisal.]

1462 van Gelder, Robert. "Mr. Maugham's Wartime Memoir," NEW YORK TIMES BOOK REVIEW, 14 Sept 1941, p. 9.
Strictly Personal is a kind of personal record, illuminated by anecdotes reflecting the general conditions surrounding the fall of France.

1463 Vernon, Grenville. "The Stage and Screen," COMMONWEAL, XXXV (28 Nov 1941), 144.
In Guy Bolton's dramatization of THEATRE, the dialogue is excellent, and the story, though slightly theatrical and old-fashioned, gives actors "a chance to show what they can do."

1464 Watts, Richard, Jr. "The Theaters," NEW YORK HERALD TRIBUNE, 13 Nov 1941, p. 22.
Guy Bolton's dramatization of THEATRE is "the artificial telling of an artificial fable." Its "brittle facility," quiet romantic appeal and polish ensure its popularity and success.

1465 Weeks, Edward. "Bookshelf," ATLANTIC MONTHLY, CLXVII (May 1941), n. p.
Up at the Villa stands "on the border line between a long short story and a vest-pocket novel."

1466 Weeks, Edward. "Bookshelf," ATLANTIC MONTHLY, CLXVIII (Oct 1941), n. p.
The incidents are "charged with irony, shrewd discernment, and pity," and *Strictly Personal* "is by turns nostalgic, castigating, and coolly illuminating."

1467* West, Anthony. "New Novels," NEW STATESMAN AND NATION, N. S. XXI (31 May 1941), 562.
With restraint, M, in *Up at the Villa,* tells an "incredibly melodramatic

anecdote about some particularly unpleasant visitors to Florence"; from a technical point of view it is "brilliant," especially in the way M manages in such short space to represent "three completely different types of male pride . . . exposed to a particularly deadly type of feminine sexual ethics."

1468 Winterich, John. "How This Book Came to Be," *The Moon and Sixpence* (NY: The Heritage Reprints, 1941), pp. 7-14.
"While Charles Strickland would never have been created if Paul Gauguin had never been born, Charles Strickland is no more Paul Gauguin than he is Paul Revere." [General biographical introduction.]

1469 "The World of Books: Why France Fell," SPRINGFIELD DAILY REPUBLICAN (Mass), 10 Sept 1941, p. 10.
Strictly Personal is "personal" in a limited sense only; its interest is much wider in that it presents "the salient facts that have profoundly influenced the course of the war."

1470 Young, Stark. "Stage Traffic," NEW REPUBLIC, CV (8 Dec 1941), 762.
Guy Bolton's dramatization of THEATRE is "full of hokum, tricks and stale situations."

1471* Zabel, Morton Dauwen. "A Cool Hand," NATION (NY), CLII (3 May 1941), 534-36; rptd, with revisions, in CRAFT AND CHARACTER IN MODERN FICTION (NY: Viking P, 1957), pp. 308-12.
Both *Of Human Bondage* and *Cakes and Ale* were followed up by long successions of trivial works; M's drama, on revival, will not stand up. *Up at the Villa,* contrary to what critics say about its not having a "wasted word," is "fictional drivel": *"All the words are wasted!"* [Includes a general assessment of M's career.]

1942

1472 "Close-Ups of Thomas Mann and Somerset Maugham," HOUSE AND GARDEN, LXXXII (Aug 1942), 38-39.
[Photographs with some paragraphs on M's life in South Carolina during World War II.]

1473 Fadiman, Clifton. "Books: Mixed Bag," NEW YORKER, XVIII (20 June 1942), 57.

The Hour Before the Dawn is deftly told, except for a burst of melodrama at the end; the characters, however, are not "absorbing."

1474* Feld, Rose. "Somerset Maugham's War Novel," NEW YORK HERALD TRIBUNE BOOKS, 21 June 1942, p. 4.

The Hour Before the Dawn has "stretches of good writing, spots of original characterization, but . . . goes completely berserk on plot." Particularly, M fails when he writes as though he expects his dénouement [the discovery that Dora Friedberg is a secret agent] to be a surprise.

1475 Frierson, William C. THE ENGLISH NOVEL IN TRANSITION: 1885-1940. Norman: University of Oklahoma P, 1942; rptd (NY: Cooper Square Publishers, 1965), pp. 98-100, 174-77, 197-200.

Of Human Bondage is an example of the "life novel in England" from 1910-1917. [Details M's relationship to the naturalists.]

1476 Gerould, Gordon Hall. THE PATTERNS OF ENGLISH AND AMERICAN FICTION: A HISTORY (Boston: Little, Brown, 1942), p. 437.

M is an explorer of the varying scenes of the Far East and the South Seas in *The Casuarina Tree* and *The Moon and Sixpence*.

1477 Gilder, Rosamond. "Hectic Holiday: Broadway in Review," THEATRE ARTS, XXVI (Jan 1942), 15.

Guy Bolton's dramatization of THEATRE fails to catch M's usual wit.

1478 H., E. "New Shows of the Month: 'RAIN,'" THEATRE WORLD (Lond), XXXVII (Aug 1942), 8.

The revival of John Colton and Clemence Randolph's dramatization was a "memorable" performance.

1479 Haines, Helen E. WHAT'S IN A NOVEL (NY: Columbia U P, 1942), pp. 5, 21, 31, 35.

Of Human Bondage is a "backlog of realism."

1480 *"The Hour Before the Dawn,"* KIRKUS, X (1 May 1942), 202.

[Brief appraisal.]

1481 "In Brief," NATION (NY), CLV (4 July 1942), 18.

"The twilight hour of Mr. Maugham's professional life is dark indeed. His latest novel [*The Hour Before the Dawn*], written with his chin up, his tongue in his cheek, and his eye on Hollywood, lacks the old cynicism, but it lacks, too, the old craftsmanship."

1482 Jack, Peter M. "The New Novels of Fiction," NEW YORK TIMES BOOK REVIEW, 21 June 1942, p. 6.

The Hour Before the Dawn is written with deliberation, without the usual hysteria, dramatics, whimsy, and heroics accompanying accounts of war. "Turning the pages, one feels the relief of integrity."

1483 Jackson, Katherine Gauss. "In Brief," HARPER'S MAGAZINE, CLXXXV (Aug 1942), n. p.

"The mind rebels at accepting from Mr. Maugham so over-simplified a version [*The Hour Before the Dawn*] of THERE'LL ALWAYS BE AN ENGLAND."

1484 Kunitz, Stanley J. and Howard Haycraft (eds) "Maugham, William Somerset," TWENTIETH CENTURY AUTHORS (NY: H. W. Wilson, 1942), pp. 934-36.

M has a habit of depicting living people in his books and so making enemies; he is master of a literary style. [Biographical sketch.]

1485 Littell, Robert. "Outstanding Novels," YALE REVIEW, N. S. XXXII (Autumn 1942), viii.

The Hour Before the Dawn "contains enough twists of plot to supply no end of suspense, but as the events cast their shadows before them, and the people are contrived out of cardboard one doesn't care two pins."

1486 Mortimer, Raymond. "Books in General: The Fall of France," NEW STATESMAN AND NATION, N. S. XXIII (14 March 1942), 179-80.

In *Strictly Personal,* M has carried "too far" his indictment of France's government as the sole agent of its fall to Hitler; but the book has "interest" and is written in a "pellucid" style.

1487 "New Shows of the Month: *'Home and Beauty,'*" THEATRE WORLD (Lond), XXXVII (Dec 1942), 5-6.

Sentiment about collusion in divorce has changed since 1919, but the revived play is still enjoyable.

1488 "Other New Books," NEWSWEEK, XIX (22 June 1942), 71.

Despite its background, the talk in *The Hour Before the Dawn* sounds "pre-war, brittle, and trivial."

1489 "Plays and Pictures: *'Home and Beauty,'* at the Playhouse," NEW STATESMAN AND NATION, N. S. XXIV (21 Nov 1942), 338.

M extracts the fun from the play's situation with the "utmost elegance"; the play has something of the "style" that keeps THE IMPORTANCE OF BEING EARNEST "untarnished." [Review of the revival.]

1490 "Plays and Pictures: 'RAIN,' at the St. Martin's" NEW STATESMAN AND NATION, N. S. XXIV (4 July 1942), 8.

M "could have made an even better job of this play," i.e., John Colton and Clemence Randolph's revived dramatization.

1491* Redfern, James. "The Theatre: *Home and Beauty*," SPECTATOR (Lond), CLXIX (20 Nov 1942), 479.

M's comedy was the product of the last war, so its satire has been blunted by "improvements in our general social behavior." But the main theme, "the portrait of a selfish beauty befooling men," is still valid. M excels at unmasking a callous ruthlessness invested with "totally blinding charm" so as not to be "intolerable on the stage." The characters are "lifted to Maugham's imputed level of intelligence by clever acting." [Review of revival.]

1492 Roberts, R. Ellis. "The Art of Somerset Maugham," SATURDAY REVIEW OF LITERATURE, XXV (27 June 1942), 6.

The Hour Before the Dawn shows M at his best. His characters are "quick, vivid, and idiosyncratic." He portrays exquisitely "the private and domestic tragedies [of the Hendersons] in the light of the great public tragedy of the [Second World] war."

1493 Weeks, Edward. "Bookshelf," ATLANTIC MONTHLY, CLXX (Aug 1942), 101.

Because the characterization "lacks force" and the experiences which the Hendersons live through are "over-familiar," *The Hour Before the Dawn* does not seize "fresh hold upon the imagination."

1494 "The World at War—i: Submit or Starve—France under the Germans," TIMES LITERARY SUPPLEMENT (Lond), 28 Feb 1942, p. 98.

Strictly Personal is "vivid, arresting and nostalgic—and admittedly slight."

1495* Wright, Basil. "The Theatre: 'RAIN,'" SPECTATOR (Lond), CLXIX (3 July 1942), 11.

Despite the fact that a revived John Colton and Clemence Randolph's dramatization "is too grimly and persistently melodramatic," and deficient in "other minor details," it is "definitely the work of a man who understands the needs of the stage and the technique by which those needs can be fulfilled." The first act is "a model of dramatic writing." Horn "achieves, on a diet of sleep and raw alcohol, a misty imitation of the idyllic South Seas life" which isolation and the climate attempt to nullify, and Davidson is a "man on the edge of mania." "The play remains good theatre."

1496 Wyatt, Euphemia Van Rensselaer. "The Drama," CATHOLIC WORLD, CLIV (Jan 1942), 473.

Guy Bolton's dramatization of THEATRE is less coarse than M's novel, "but no less trite."

1943

1497 "Anthologist and Critic," CHRISTIAN SCIENCE MONITOR WEEKLY MAGAZINE SECTION, 3 July 1943, p. 11.

In *Introduction to Modern English and American Literature,* M's introductions are as tasteful and good in judgment as the pieces he reprints.

1498 "Books: Book Notes," TIME, XLI (24 May 1943), 104.

In *Introduction to Modern English and American Literature,* M "steps in from time to time with offhand comments."

1499 "Editor's Choice," COMMONWEAL, XXXVIII (21 May 1943), 126.

M's *Introduction to Modern English and American Literature* is "a book of quality."

1500 Papajewski, Helmut. "Die Weltanschauung William Somerset Maughams" (William Somerset Maugham's Worldview), ANGLIA, LXVII / LXVIII (1943/44), 251-317.

[An early development of some ideas later elaborated in Papajewski's DIE WELT-, LEBENS- UND KUNSTANSCHAUUNG WILLIAM SOMERSET MAUGHAMS (THE WORLD-, LIFE-, AND ARTISTIC VISION OF WILLIAM SOMERSET MAUGHAM), 1952.] [In German.]

1501 Scully, Frank. "Maugham," ROGUES' GALLERY: PROFILES OF MY EMINENT CONTEMPORARIES (Hollywood: Murray & Gee, 1943), pp. 15-36.

At seventy M's "chance to become an all-out . . . honest writer is gone. He, like Hitler, has missed the bus. To the various initials which honor and adorn the various capsule biographies about him, may now be added: R. I. P." [Profile of M.]

1502 Wagenknecht, Edward. CAVALCADE OF THE ENGLISH NOVEL (NY: Henry Holt, 1943), pp. 420, 564-65.

Of Human Bondage belongs to the "school" of Samuel Butler.

1503 Weidman, Jerome. "Introduction," THE W. SOMERSET MAUGHAM SAMPLER (Garden City, NY: Garden City Pub Co., 1943), pp. vii-xxi.

[General appreciation.]

1944

1504 Adams, J. Donald. "Speaking of Books," NEW YORK TIMES BOOK REVIEW, 12 March 1944, p. 2.
Although M has few illusions about himself and knows a good deal about human nature, his works lack warmth because he acts as a "spectator" towards life.

1505 Adams, J. Donald. "Speaking of Books," NEW YORK TIMES BOOK REVIEW, 7 May 1944, p. 2.
John Hersey, in contrast to M, is one who loves humanity and therefore shows greater promise of literary stature.

1506* Agate, James. "Mr. Blakelock Ruins a Play," SUNDAY TIMES (Lond), 29 Oct 1944, p. 2; rptd in THE CONTEMPORARY THEATRE: 1944 AND 1945 (Lond: George C. Harrap, 1946), pp. 126-28.
The Breadwinner is two-thirds "admirable comedy," for the third act relies on farce rather than comedy, M having exhausted his theme. In this revival, Denys Blakelock as Charles Battle is too elegant: he makes the evening and also "ruins it."

1507 Agate, James. "Three Actresses," SUNDAY TIMES (Lond), 25 Nov 1944, p. 2; rptd in THE CONTEMPORARY THEATRE: 1944 AND 1945 (Lond: George C. Harrap, 1946), pp. 238-39.
The revived *The Sacred Flame* is "a powerful play."

1508 Agate, James. "A Word to Mr. Gielgud," SUNDAY TIMES (Lond), 15 Oct 1944, p. 2; rptd in THE CONTEMPORARY THEATRE: 1944 AND 1945 (Lond: George C. Harrap, 1946), pp. 120-22.
The production of the revived *The Circle* was not logically interpreted, because its producer, John Gielgud, "is not by nature a comedian" and for comedy "substitutes a wonderful line of something which is half superciliousness and half moral priggishness."

1509 "Author's £10,000 Gift to His Old School," TIMES (Lond), 24 Oct 1944, p. 6.
M donates £10,000 to King's School, Canterbury, for establishing scholarships.

1510 Barnes, Howard. "The Theaters," NEW YORK HERALD TRIBUNE, 19 April 1944, p. 16.

Sheppey is more of a portrait than a play, and at that a blurred blending of Cockney comedy and religious parable.

1511* Basso, Hamilton. "Profiles: Very Old Party—I," NEW YORKER, XX (30 Dec 1944), 24-28, 30, 32-34; continued in "Profiles: Very Old Party—II," NEW YORKER, XX (6 Jan 1945), 28-32, 34-38.

[Biographical and critical estimate of M up to the eve of his seventy-first birthday.]

1512* Beach, Joseph Warren. "Maugham Considers Mystics," NEW YORK TIMES BOOK REVIEW, 23 April 1944, p. 3.

For all M's uncanny faculty for reducing human motives to the lowest common denominator, "he has long stood for a humanism which cherished the surface values of civilization even when it could not quite recall the ground on which they were based." Out of this belief comes *The Razor's Edge*. However, the Oriental mode of spirituality which M offers as a solution will not be hailed by readers. M's characters and knowledge of manners are his forte.

1513 Binsse, Harry Lorin. "More Books of the Week," COMMONWEAL, XL (28 April 1944), 44.

The degenerative process which began after *Of Human Bondage* has not ceased; the total effect of *The Razor's Edge* is "unbelievably cheap and trifling." Elliott Templeton, and especially his death scene, are the book's only redeeming moments.

1514 "Books—Briefly Noted: Fiction," NEW YORKER, XX (22 April 1944), 81.

In *The Razor's Edge,* "everything is so neatly fitted together, . . . and the author writes with such ease, that the reader is almost lulled into forgetting that Mr. Maugham by even very lax critical standards, has turned out an inferior job—one that suggests that if he keeps on writing with his tongue in his cheek, it may well become permanently stuck there."

1515* "Books. Old Man with a Razor," TIME, XLIII (24 April 1944), 99-100, 102.

The Razor's Edge "deserves to rank after *Of Human Bondage* . . . and *The Moon and Sixpence* . . . as one of [Maugham's] three major novels." *The Razor's Edge* "is the crowning triumph of that utterly dispassionate virtuosity to which he has always aspired—a persuasive as well as an entertaining book, by a man of 70 who is still 'of the earth, earthy,' about a young man who has found a faith."

1516 Butcher, Fanny. "Maugham's Distinctive Qualities Endure," CHICAGO SUNDAY TRIBUNE BOOKS, 23 April 1944, p. 11.

The Razor's Edge is not to be read for a "religious message"; Larry is the least convincing of its characters.

1517* Connolly, Cyril. "The Art of Being Good," NEW STATESMAN AND NATION, N. S. XXVIII (26 Aug 1944), 140; rptd in THE CONDEMNED PLAYGROUND—ESSAYS: 1927-1944 (Lond: Routledge, 1945), pp. 250-54.

The Razor's Edge is M's best novel since *Cakes and Ale,* and as "powerful propaganda for the new faith . . . Vedanta of the West," ranks with Huxley's GREY EMINENCE and Heard's MAN THE MASTER. Mysticism is not new to M; the worldliest of our novelists, he has always been "fascinated by those who renounce the world," as in their different ways *The Moon and Sixpence, Don Fernando,* and *Christmas Holiday* attest. The only major flaw of the novel is that M fails to convince the reader of Larry's "conversion"; M should not "have confined Larry to any known religious system" but "let him have his revelation and then leave it at that." M is to be commended for his masterful self-portrait, his handling of the major characters, and his desire to tell the truth "in a form which releases all the possibilities of his art."

1518 Cowley, Malcolm. "The Devil a Monk Was He," NEW REPUBLIC, CX (1 May 1944), 609.

The Razor's Edge is one of M's weaker novels, memorable chiefly for the portrait of Elliott Templeton.

1519 Feld, Rose. "A Quest for the Absolute," NEW YORK HERALD TRIBUNE WEEKLY BOOK REVIEW, 23 April 1944, p. 19.

In *The Razor's Edge,* M succeeds in making Larry "likable and real," though the discussion of his "finding the Absolute in India is a little on the heavy side."

1520 Gibbs, Wolcott. "The Theatre: The Mixture as Before," NEW YORKER, XX (29 April 1944), 42.

"Conceding his new tendency to deliver spiritual messages, Mr. Maugham [in *Sheppey*] is still a dramatist with both style and technique. . . . "

1521 Gilder, Rosamond. "The Sum of the Season," THEATRE ARTS, XXVIII (June 1944), 335-36.

Sheppey, two acts of good talk, presents a "sardonic proof" of Christ's admonition to give to the poor. But when Death appears as an uninteresting young woman, both the dialogue and the action falter.

1522 Hansen, Harry. "The First Reader," NEW YORK WORLD-TELEGRAM, 20 April 1944, p. 19.

In *The Razor's Edge,* M's delvings into religious philosophy are superficial; his hero makes few changes in the lives of those around him.

1523* "Haymarket Theatre: *'The Circle,'* by W. Somerset Maugham," TIMES (Lond), 12 Oct 1944, p. 6.

The play "is by no means a comedy of manners. The moral implicit in its fun is something very different from the sententious couplets Congreve perfunctorily tagged on to plays which pretended to neither feeling nor morality. . . . [The] 'bold' ending is surely frivolity's not unhopeful and rather wistful salute to sincerity." [Review of the revival.]

1524 Hillyer, Dorothy. "Somerset by Maugham: From Sophisticate to Mystic in New Novel About Americans," BOSTON GLOBE, 3 May 1944, p. 17.

In *The Razor's Edge,* Larry carries the theme; but Elliott Templeton is its "outstanding characterization." The novel presents a strong " 'no' to the forces of materialism."

1525 Krutch, Joseph Wood. "Drama," NATION (NY), CLIX (2 Dec 1944), 698.

In the Mamoulian-Dietz musical version of RAIN as SADIE THOMPSON, "Sadie's story is still a good story and . . . , still holds the attention, still arouses the simple emotions it was intended to arouse." But the music hasn't much character, the entire production lacks integration.

1526 Lalou, René. LA LITTERATURE ANGLAISE, DES ORIGINES A NOS JOURS (ENGLISH LITERATURE, FROM ITS BEGINNINGS TO OUR DAY) (Paris: Presses Universitaires de France, 1944), p. 113.

M, in becoming a master "exoticist" [as in *The Moon and Sixpence*], has also become a realist and a satirist—as later exemplified by works such as *The Casuarina Tree, The Painted Veil,* and *The Narrow Corner.* [In French.]

1527 MacCarthy, Desmond. *"The Circle,"* NEW STATESMAN AND NATION, N. S. XXVIII (28 Oct 1944), 283; rptd in THEATRE (Lond: MacGibbon & Kee, 1954), pp. 129-31.

[Review of the revival repeats the general view (indeed, one identical paragraph) MacCarthy expressed in his earlier review of the play: "Drama: *'The Circle,'* " NEW STATESMAN, XVI (19 March 1921), 704-5.]

1528 Marriott, Charles. "New Novels," MANCHESTER GUARDIAN, 21 July 1944, p. 3.

In cast, setting, and the emotional relationships between the characters, *The Razor's Edge* is reminiscent of Henry James's A LONDON LIFE.

1529 Marshall, Margaret. "Drama," NATION (NY), CLVIII (29 April 1944), 521.
Sheppey is "a collage of warmed-over clichés—of situation, characterization, and dénouement."

1530 Morehouse, Ward. "The New Play," NEW YORK SUN, 19 April 1944, p. 26.
Sheppey is "strange, frequently fascinating and well-acted."

1531 Nathan, George Jean. "*Sheppey:* April 18, 1944," THE 'THEATRE' BOOK OF THE YEAR: 1943-1944 (NY: Alfred A. Knopf, 1944), pp. 302-4.
"One of the talented author's distinctly inferior performances," the play changes moods with little preparation and talks itself "into desuetude" in its middle section.

1532 "New Books," CATHOLIC WORLD, CLIX (June 1944), 284.
The Razor's Edge "may be described as a novel of manners with a dash of mysticism thrown in, for what purpose it is hard to say."

1533 Nichols, Lewis. "The Play," NEW YORK TIMES, 19 April 1944, p. 27.
Sheppey is "quiet and slow, with the aimlessness of a sleep-walker."

1534 Nichols, Wallace B. "Truth and Fantasy," BOOKS OF THE MONTH, XIV (July 1944), 13.
In *The Razor's Edge* the parts are better than the book as a whole. Larry and M seem not to have absorbed the Vedanta philosophy. The death of Elliott Templeton is a scene alone making the book worth reading.

1535 "Novels of the Week: Modern Mystic," TIMES LITERARY SUPPLEMENT (Lond), 15 July 1944, p. 341.
The Razor's Edge is fascinating, but somewhat sentimental. "Its worldliness seems passionately honest, its otherworldliness unreal."

1536* O'Brien, Kate. "Fiction: *The Razor's Edge*," SPECTATOR (Lond), CLXXIII (21 July 1944), 64, 66.
The novel is "solid, skillful, accurately calculated" and provides "food for reflection." M's power of construction is "almost perfect," and he has "precision, tact, irony," and totally lacks pomposity. He strips everything down to the reasonable, and he observes relentlessly. M is too set in technique to develop the potentialities of his themes. Larry is a beautiful symbol, but M does not "hack down to the bones of the man himself."

1537 "Other New Books," NEWSWEEK, XXIII (1 May 1944), 71.
The Razor's Edge is "well-bred and readable as its predecessors."

1538 "Our Booking-Office: A Blunted Edge," PUNCH, CCVII (9 Aug 1944), 126.

In *The Razor's Edge,* M is a "surer chronicler of a snob's progress than a pilgrim's." Larry should have been deleted altogether while M concentrated solely on Elliott Templeton.

1539 Phelan, Kappo. "The Stage and Screen," COMMONWEAL, XL (5 May 1944), 61-62.

Sheppey is "a picture puzzle with a good many pieces missing." M has dodged the issue; his thinking is "superficial."

1540 Phelan, Kappo. "The Stage and Screen," COMMONWEAL, XLI (1 Dec 1944), 174-75.

The Dietz-Mamoulian musical version of RAIN as SADIE THOMPSON is "a sort of million sprawl with none of its parts ever plainly divided, and more, with what loose divisions as are present . . . poorly planned."

1541 Prescott, Orville. "Outstanding Novels," YALE REVIEW, XXXIII (Summer 1944), 765.

In *The Razor's Edge,* M's "malicious caricatures of the international society are slick, amusing, and witty," but Larry "is neither believable as a person nor as a bringer of a message."

1542* Rascoe, Burton. "Theater: Maugham's New Play *Sheppey* Based on Religious Theme," NEW YORK WORLD-TELEGRAM, 19 April 1944, p. 26.

The play is "unsatisfactory theater"; it is slow to the point of tediousness, does not move in a "straight line" dramatically, initiates two themes but comes to no conclusion about either.

1543 *"The Razor's Edge,"* KIRKUS, XII (15 Feb 1944), 77.

[Brief appraisal.]

1544* Redfern, James. "The Theatre: *The Circle* and *The Breadwinner*," SPECTATOR (Lond), CLXXIII (27 Oct 1944), 383.

The Circle "is no more than a smart, effective piece of theatricality and worldly wisdom in which the spontaneity and charm of Yvonne Arnaud effortlessly knocks the author's thesis sky-high." *The Breadwinner* is "a better play." The wife is "the most horrible woman M ever portrayed." [Review of revivals.]

1545 "Reprints and New Editions," NEW YORK HERALD TRIBUNE BOOK REVIEW, 18 June 1944, p. 19.

Mention of the Heritage reprint of *The Moon and Sixpence* and M's letter to John T. Winterich revealing the model of Strickland as Gauguin.

1546 S., L. A. "A Man in Search of Faith," CHRISTIAN SCIENCE MONITOR WEEKLY MAGAZINE SECTION, 13 May 1944, p. 10.
Larry is the least believable character in *The Razor's Edge.*

1547 Smith, Harrison. "The Imperturbable Mr. Maugham," SATURDAY REVIEW OF LITERATURE, XXVII (22 April 1944), 7-8.
In *The Razor's Edge,* M's intention is not at all clear. One hopes that the next work from such a skilled practitioner will be more definite and explicit. [Discussions of Smith's review can be found under "Letters to the Editor," SATURDAY REVIEW OF LITERATURE, XXVII (13 May 1944), 19-20, and XXVII (27 May 1944), 17.]

1548 Spectorsky, A. C. "Maugham's Glass-Smooth and Spectacular Writing Skill," CHICAGO SUN BOOK WEEK, 23 April 1944, p. 4.
M had no burning urge to write *The Razor's Edge*, and so the reader gets "a pleasant, rambling, charming and entertaining book" which he mustn't "examine too closely."

1549 "Theater," NEWSWEEK, XXIII (1 May 1944), 78.
Sheppey is "a confusing parable that talks itself into a fatal relapse."

1550 "Theater: Music in the Rain," NEWSWEEK, XXIV (27 Nov 1944), 100.
The Mamoulian-Dietz musical version of RAIN as SADIE THOMPSON is "neither good straight drama nor orthodox musical."

1551 "The Theater: New Musical Play in Manhattan," TIME, XLIV (27 Nov 1944), 48.
The reviewer observes that the "undistinguished" songs and dances of the Mamoulian-Dietz musical version of RAIN as SADIE THOMPSON detract from the dramatic impact of the story.

1552 "The Theater: New Play in Manhattan," TIME, XLIII (1 May 1944), 58.
Edmund Gwenn's interpretation of the title role is praiseworthy but *Sheppey* itself is not. "The last play which Maugham wrote alone is not too shining a valedictory. The hand that wrote this good-by was a little tired, a little cold."

1553* Trilling, Diana. "Fiction in Review," NATION (NY), CLVIII (6 May 1944), 547.
When M says in *The Razor's Edge* that he is strangely chilled on confronting a genuine emotion, "he reveals the flirtatious nature of his occasional excursions into mysticism as he suggests the reason for the failure of his whole literary career. Mysticism, that is, is bound to be inviting to the person who is afraid of the deep emotions; yet it can never fully win him,

any more than humanity can fully win him. All the characters in Maugham's latest novel inevitably inhabit the non-dimensional universe which is all that is left when the deep emotions have been disavowed."

1554 W., A. "New Shows of the Month: *'The Circle,'*" THEATRE WORLD (Lond), XL (Nov 1944), 9-10.

"The play's strain of irony and regret is not lost in the fun of dialogue and situation." [Review of the revival.]

1555 Weeks, Edward. "Bookshelf," ATLANTIC MONTHLY, CLXXIII (May 1944), 127, 129.

The Razor's Edge contains "a brilliant counterpoint between the urgent quest of youth and the cynical retreat of age, but in the development the tempo slows down as the indoctrination of Larry demands more and more attention."

1556 Wildi, Max. DER ANGELSÄCHSISCHE ROMAN UND DER SCHWEIZER LESER (THE ANGLO SAXON NOVEL AND THE SWISS READER), Kulturschriftenreihe, 5. (Zürich: Artemis-Verlag, 1944), pp. 73-75.

Though belonging to different generations, M, Morgan, and Priestley have one thing in common; their work is an astounding mixture of conscious artistry and soulless virtuosity. While *Of Human Bondage* is one of the few successful naturalistic novels, such short novels as *Christmas Holiday* deal with sensational events in a technically brilliant manner, cynically substituting *kitsch* for art. [In German.]

1557 Willis, Katherine Tappert. "New Books Appraised," LIBRARY JOURNAL, LXIX (15 April 1944), 354.

The Razor's Edge "is a cynical, sophisticated, typical Maugham story and is far from required reading these days when time and paper are precious."

1558* Wyatt, Euphemia Van Rensselaer. "The Drama," CATHOLIC WORLD, CLIX (June 1944), 263.

"When the wife [in *Sheppey*] returns to find Sheppey sitting back with a smile in his chair, she remarks, 'He always was lucky,' which might mean that Sheppey had escaped the doctors or that he had made a sound spiritual investment. On the other hand, if Sheppey had spent his earthly money to good purpose but on the advice of a mythical God, then all he had won was oblivion. Mr. Maugham dodged the issue but he could hardly expect his audience to accept a thesis as bilateral as a presidential platform."

1945

1559 Adams, J. Donald. "Speaking of Books," New York Times Book Review, 25 Nov 1945, p. 2.
Contrary to M's belief, the King James Bible has not been a harmfu influence on English prose.

1560* Armstrong, Petronella. "Lettres Anglaises d'Aujourd'hui Une Question et Deux Réponses" (English Letters Today: A Question and Two Replies), Journal de Geneve, 13-14 Jan 1945, p. 3
M's mysticism in *The Razor's Edge* was foreshadowed in *Don Fernando* Still, the erotic element of his earlier work remains and creates an imbalance. The theme of the "yogi" will be found in M's succeeding works [In French.]

1561 Bason, Fred[erick] T. "Mr. Somerset Maugham," Saturday Book, Fifth Year (Oct 1945), pp. 279-84.
[A subjective portrait of M, emphasizing his humanity; the original manuscript of this article is in the University of Illinois Rare Book Room M Collection, No. 145, Part 2.]

1562 Gielgud, John. "The Haymarket and the New: London Flocks to Repertory," Theatre Arts, XXIX (March 1945) 167-68.
Gielgud, as producer of the revival of *The Circle,* decided to use costumes suggestive of 1912, for the play seems to portray a pre-war [1914] society

1563 Gilder, Rosamond. "Holiday Goods: Broadway in Review," Theatre Arts, XXIX (Jan 1945), 12.
The Mamoulian-Dietz musical version of Rain as Sadie Thompson is plagued by a medley of styles. It can most charitably be described as "an opulent confusion."

1564* Jones, Siriol Hugh. *"The Sacred Flame,"* New Statesman and Nation, N. S. XXX (8 Dec 1945), 387.
The theme of the revived play—the conflict of two notions of duty and of Christian charity—is "a high and dangerous one, and the characters are for the most part too well-bred to stand the strain of being the means of its expression." Technically, the play is a "study in fact and neatness" verbally, "it can be dreadfully heavy."

1565 Nathan, George Jean. "Sadie Thompson: November 16 1944," The 'Theatre' Book of the Year: 1944-1945 (NY Alfred A. Knopf, 1945), pp. 147-55.

In the Mamoulian-Dietz musical version of RAIN as SADIE THOMPSON, the choreography and choral numbers interfered with the play's flow.

1566 Pfeiffer, Karl G. "Maugham—as I Know Him," REDBOOK, LXXXV (May 1945), 40-41, 60-64; rptd in THE MAUGHAM ENIGMA, ed by Klaus W. Jonas (NY: Citadel P, 1954), pp. 21-36.
[Biographical sketch, most of which is repeated in Pfeiffer's W. SOMERSET MAUGHAM: A CANDID PORTRAIT (1959).]

1567 S., T. "W. Somerset Maugham, *'Päävoitto'*" *(Sheppey),* TURUN SANOMAT, 31 Jan 1945, p. 4.
There is much triviality amidst adequate material in the dialogue. M is skillful and competent, but his production lacks life and is easily forgotten. [Review of the revived Finnish adaptation, in Finnish.]

1568* Stokes, Sewell. "W. Somerset Maugham," THEATRE ARTS, XXIX (Feb 1945), 94-100.
M's retirement from playwriting is linked to the rise of domestic drama which drove his witty and sophisticated comedies from the stage. His serious and social plays are departures from the norm. Unlike Chekhov and Shaw, M first turned to the theater because of a desire for success. His notion that the theater is nothing more than a "box of tricks" may well describe his own work; but perhaps the best theater demands a poetry of which M himself was incapable.

1569 Wyatt, Euphemia Van Rensselaer. "The Drama," CATHOLIC WORLD, CLX (Jan 1945), 357.
In the Mamoulian-Dietz musical version of RAIN as SADIE THOMPSON "the story is too dolorous for a musical, the score not good enough for an operetta, and caricaturing the Davidsons for broad comedy in Act I, destroys the dramatic tension for Act II."

1946

1570 Armstrong, Petronella. "Dernier mot" (The Last Word), JOURNAL DE GENEVE, 7-8 July 1946, p. 3.
Then and Now is simple but impeccable in construction. [In French.]

1571 "Books: Maugham on Old Nick," TIME, XLVII (27 May 1946), 102.
Then and Now is "a talky, occasionally witty costume piece about Machia-

velli in love and Borgia in his glory" and it is "an ironical sermon on the unchanging wonders of human nature."

1572* "Books: Maugham's Machiavelli," NEWSWEEK, XXVII (3 June 1946) 92-93.

Far above the "tawdry" M of slick-magazine short stories or the "pretentious" M of *The Razor's Edge, Then and Now* "is a mixture of history, biography, and fiction and the result of reading and study rather than of experience. For this reason Maugham's new novel is lacking in imagination and characterization of which, in the past, he has been so prolific."

1573 Bourin, André. "Le Monde des Livres: *'Vacances de Noel'* " (The World of Books: *Christmas Holiday*), LES NOUVELLES LITTERAIRES, 8 Aug 1946, p. 3.

The French translation reveals no new facet of M's talent, but nevertheless displays the author's usual narrative power, acute psychology, and spareness of effects. [In French.]

1574 Brighouse, Harold. "Books of the Day: New Novels," MANCHESTER GUARDIAN, 17 May 1946, p. 3.

In *Then and Now,* M "marshals confused history into straightforward narrative, mingling with that a Boccaccian episode."

1575* Brown, John Mason. "English Laughter — Past and Present," SATURDAY REVIEW OF LITERATURE, XXIX (23 Nov 1946), 24-26, 28; rptd in SEEING MORE THINGS (NY & Toronto: McGraw-Hill, 1948), pp. 200-208; and in DRAMATIS PERSONAE: A RETROSPECTIVE SHOW (NY: Viking P, 1963), pp. 183-90.

Oscar Wilde, M, and Noël Coward were gifted and sophisticated, and provided through their works a portrait for the future of British manners of a certain type and period. All three chronicle the decline of an old aristocracy and the emergence of a new. This decline is indicated through the rank and privileges the authors give their characters, in their treatment of women, in the attitudes the characters show toward newspapers, and in the esteem with which America is held in the plays.

1576 Butcher, Fanny. "Machiavelli Is Hero in Maugham Novel," CHICAGO SUNDAY TRIBUNE BOOKS, 26 May 1946, pp. 3, 9.

Then and Now is a "skilfully contrived" but "minor work of a major writer."

1577 Chubb, Thomas C. "Maugham's Machiavelli," NEW YORK TIMES BOOK REVIEW, 26 May 1946, p. 4.

Then and Now is a "vivid, sprightly, and convincing story."

1578 Clinton-Braddeley, V. C. "Books of the Day: Fiction," SPECTATOR (Lond), CLXXVI (17 May 1946), 514.

Then and Now is a "first-class example of brilliant dialogue writing." The characterization is so well done "one could almost consider the book as a biographical study." A new side of M, but "it's still Maugham."

1579 Duhamel, Georges, et al. ALMANACH DES LETTRES, 1947 ALMANAC OF LETTERS, 1947) (Paris: Editions de Flore et La Gazette des Lettres, 1946), 172.

[Brief biographical sketch.] [In French.]

1580 Farrelly, John. "The Current Historical Novel," NEW REPUBLIC, CXIV (24 June 1946), 907-10.

In *Then and Now*, M uses the historical novel for purposes of romantic farce.

1581 Gautier, Jean-Jacques. "Dernière minute parisienne=Aux Bouffes-Parisiens *Avant le Derby*" (The Parisian Latest: At the Bouffes-Parisiens: *Home and Beauty*), LE FIGARO, 12 Dec 1946, p. 3.

The French adaptation is a playlet, without pretensions, without any particular flavor. It means to be comical and succeeds in the first act and often during the third, but the middle is rather long. [In French.]

1582 Gibney, Robert. "Then and Now: Somerset Maugham," VOGUE, CVIII (July 1946), 94, 132-34.

Then and Now is "a stumble" and "a talky elaboration of an anecdote. . . ." [General appraisal of M's career]

1583* Gray, James. "Obituary for the Human Race," ON SECOND THOUGHT (Minneapolis: University of Minnesota P; Lond: Geoffrey Cumberlege, 1946), pp. 165-83.

M will be remembered for *Of Human Bondage* and "Rain." Lately, M has developed into an entertainer and merchandiser, and "communication" with his audience has begun to suffer. "In his recent works Maugham has created no memorable characters, dramatized no memorable characters, dramatized no significant crisis satisfactorily. Beginning as a writer of the second order of excellence, he has allowed his facility to degrade him . . . into a work of the third or fourth order. . . . his work is meretricious and shabby."

1584 Hoult, Norah. "Stories and Tracts for the Times," BOOKS OF THE MONTH, XVI (May 1946), 9.

[Brief review of *Then and Now*.]

1585 Humbert, Henriette and Pierre. "Le Sens de la vie chez

William Somerset Maugham" (The Sense of Life at William Somerset Maugham's Home), LA VIE INTELLECTUELLE, XIV (July 1946), 124-49.

M's works cannot be understood unless one is acquainted with his life. M lacks one thing — charm, a commodity supplied by Maurice Baring (who had a different childhood, consequently a different attitude toward life, and converted to Roman Catholicism). [The authors survey M's life and works, based on *Of Human Bondage* and *The Summing Up;* examine M's loss of faith; his lack of illusions about human nature; his attitude toward women; his opinions on death and religion.] [In French.]

1586* Krutch, Joseph Wood. "Machiavellian Philosophy 'Now' and 'Then,'" NEW YORK HERALD TRIBUNE WEEKLY BOOK REVIEW, 2 June 1946, p. 1.

M's conviction that the chief duty of a novelist is to provide entertainment for intelligent people is the result of something more than a merely personal esthetic theory; M cultivates a "jesting-Pilate attitude" toward truth because his early experiences convinced him that he could not accept involvement without intolerable suffering. The esthetic theory has been rationalized to a point which enables him to develop a method expert and consistent. This is especially true of *Then and Now,* which should be read as "the delightful exercise in intelligent irony it is" rather than for its "questionable, facile serious lesson."

1587* "Machiavelli in Romance," TIMES LITERARY SUPPLEMENT (Lond), 18 May 1946, p. 233.

Nothing that M "writes can fail to stimulate interest and admiration, and yet, partly because his is not a deep-rooted historical sense, still more because the mere contemplation of Machiavelli has so obviously kindled the worldliness and cynicism of temper which restrict imagination in Mr. Maugham, this latest volume [*Then and Now*] of his is insubstantial and disappointing." The mind and character of Machiavelli are blurred by the air of contrivance, although all the necessary physical attributes for a good story are there.

1588 Marcel, Gabriel. "Le Théâtre: *Avant le Derby*" (The Drama: *Home and Beauty*), LES NOUVELLES LITTERAIRES, 19 Dec 1946, p. 10.

M has treated the tragical theme of Zola's JACQUES D'AMOUR in a light, cynical manner. [Review of the French adaptation, in French.]

1589 "Maugham Gift to Library," NEW YORK TIMES, 7 April 1946, p. 16.

M will present the original manuscript of *Of Human Bondage* to the Library of Congress. [See, also, "Books — Authors," NEW YORK TIMES, 9 April

1946, p. 25; and Robert van Gelder, "An Interview with Somerset Maugham," NEW YORK TIMES BOOK REVIEW, 21 April 1946, p. 3.]

1590* "Mr. Somerset Maugham," TIMES LITERARY SUPPLEMENT (Lond), 27 April 1946, p. 199.

"There are English authors today who are more indubitably world figures, intellectual forces in public life; but among the novelists and playwrights pure and simple of his generation none has attained a more active eminence or achieved a more lasting success." *Of Human Bondage* marks the death, not of the romantic artist, but of the idealist philosopher. For M, luck alone is the arbiter in human affairs; this value has given rise to a certain agnosticism of thought, to skepticism, and to pragmatism. Yet the seeming materialist still knew the burden of mystery, as it expressed itself in the collision of common sense with the nonrational, and the irruption into fortunate lives of violence, ugliness, and torment. [Article on the occasion of M's presentation of the manuscript of *Of Human Bondage* to the Library of Congress.]

1591 "New Books," CATHOLIC WORLD, CLXIII (Aug 1946), 475.

Then and Now is "highly romantic fiction with a thin biographical vein," giving "a highly distorted impression of sixteenth-century Italy."

1592 North, Sterling. "Maugham's Novel on Machiavelli," CHICAGO SUN BOOK WEEK, 26 May 1946, p. 2.

"Not since *Cakes and Ale* has Maugham's pen been so wickedly sharp or his humor so caustic" as in *Then and Now*.

1593 Paley, Judith. "Les Romans étrangers" (Foreign Novels), PARU, No. 25 (Dec 1946), 45-46.

In *Christmas Holiday,* M's style is perfect, his theme good, but his interpretation destroys the entire work. [Review of the French translation, in French.]

1594* Paul, David. "Maugham and the Two Myths," CORNHILL MAGAZINE, CLXII (Autumn 1946), 143-48; rptd in THE MAUGHAM ENIGMA, ed by Klaus W. Jonas (NY: Citadel P, 1954), pp. 156-63.

M has enough "curiosity" for two or three writers, but it is accompanied by shallow understanding. These qualities are manifested in the "even and unhesitating banality of his style," which never renders an impression "première et complète," but on the contrary "secondary and incomplete." This is to his advantage, however, because his principal gift is for narrative; nevertheless, M will not see himself simply as a narrator, and is, unfortunately, a shaper of "current mythology." In *The Moon and Sixpence* he formed from the facts of Gauguin's life a symbol of the then-modern "artist-outcast," and again in *The Razor's Edge* he embodies the "newest and most modish of myths, that of the Yogi," in Larry, "the new Parsifal." Larry expresses and enforces "the author's sense of disillusionment with the world that ended in 1940"; in M's world there is no longer a place for a Gauguin-Strickland to escape to, only another dimension, "inwards into trance . . . 'of the same order as the mystics have had all over the world through all the centuries' . . . . Its cosmopolitan origins are presumably the final and most compelling reason for its recommendation."

1595* "The Playhouse: *'Our Betters'* by W. Somerset Maugham," Times (Lond), 4 Oct 1946, p. 6.
The revived play "carries satire to the extremity of burlesque, where veracity gives way to rather spiteful fun, and it is the element of spite in the fun that spoils it for us. The topic is no longer alive, and the wit, diverting as some of it remains, just fails to transcend the topicality."

1596 "Plays Moscow Must Not See," Times (Lond), 2 Sept 1946, p. 4.
M's *The Circle* and *Penelope* are labeled by Soviets' Culture and Life as plays spreading "bourgeois reactionary ideology and morality" and attempting to poison Soviet minds.

1597 Potter, Stephen. "Plays: *'For Services Rendered,'* at the New Lindsey," New Statesman and Nation, N. S. XXXII (20 July 1946), 46.
"A huge theme . . . receives frank treatment in a series of emotional situations which are basically insincere." [Review of the revival.]

1598 Potter, Stephen. "Theatre: *'Lady Frederick,'* at the Savoy," New Statesman and Nation, N. S. XXXII (30 Nov 1946), 396.
The production of the revived play is faulty, particularly for the clash of styles "between du Maurier dresses and the dialogue of early advanced Bright Young."

1599 Prescott, Orville. "Outstanding Novels," Yale Review, XXXVI (Autumn 1946), 189.
As an ironic comedy, *Then and Now* "is stale and obvious, with a dénouement which can be foreseen from the start. And, as a study of the morals and politics of the Renaissance, it is both dull and superficial."

1600 Redman, Ben Ray. "In the Days of Machiavelli," Saturday Review of Literature, XXIX (25 May 1946), 9-10.
Then and Now is "highly diverting." M's translating Machiavelli's comedy, Mandragola, into a novel, "and then making the novel serve as an explanation of the play's genesis," is ingenious and delightful.

1601* Ross, Woodburn O. "W. Somerset Maugham: Theme and Variations," College English, VIII (Dec 1946), 113-122; rptd in ENGLISH JOURNAL, XXXVI (May 1947), 219-28; and in THE MAUGHAM ENIGMA, ed by Klaus W. Jonas (NY: Citadel P, 1954), pp. 84-100.

To estimate M's later artistic achievements, one must study his early fiction, notably *The Making of a Saint,* an unsuccessful historical novel, which reveals three formulaic elements significant to most of M's work: (1) that of a woman (Giulia) who appears to be one thing but is actually something quite different; (2) that of a man (Filippo) tormented by a passion he cannot conquer; and (3) the belief that the knowledge of a beloved's true nature does not release a man from his enslavement. These three elements appear in M's next novel, *Mrs. Craddock,* but they are slightly transformed: Edward Craddock and Gerald Vaudrey take the place of Giulia, and Bertha is the transformation of Filippo. The same elements, again slightly transformed, appear in *The Merry-Go-Round, The Explorer,* and *The Magician.*

In the development of these three elements, there is an implication that man's "rational will is not free"; humanity is psychologically in bondage. This implication is, of course, present in M's greatest re-working of his formula, *Of Human Bondage.* The book is not simply a "great promise," but the "fulfillment of a promise" made at the very beginning of M's career. After this novel, M did not "sell himself out"; he had "written himself out." All in all, M's work is restricted both in breadth and depth. His formula was clearly worked out in *Of Human Bondage,* but he never transcended it and never enlarged his view of life.

1602 Routh, H. V. ENGLISH LITERATURE AND IDEAS IN THE TWENTIETH CENTURY: AN INQUIRY INTO PRESENT DIFFICULTIES AND FUTURE PROSPECTS (Lond: Methuen, 1946), pp. 5, 146-53, 168.

M's novels are better than his plays and they demonstrate a "progressive quality." [An appreciation and biography of M up to the publication of *The Razor's Edge.*]

1603 S., F. "New Shows of the Month: *'The Sacred Flame,'* " THEATRE WORLD (Lond), XLII (Jan 1946), 6.

M's theme is as topical today as it was in 1929, and he did not shirk the issue so that his revived play "retains its power to grip."

1604 "Savoy Theatre: *'Lady Frederick'* by W. Somerset Maugham," TIMES (Lond), 22 Nov 1946, p. 6.

In the revival, the dialogue has lost some of its "ease," but M's skill cannot be obscured by the passage of time; the play seems less old-fashioned than *Our Betters.*

1605 Smiles, Sam. *"Our Betters,"* NEW STATESMAN AND NATION, N. S. XXXII (12 Oct 1946), 263.
Except for the *deus ex machina* [the dancing master of the final scene], the revived play is not "dated," particularly since the public can now see the original version which M intended but which the Censor forbade in 1923.

1606 "Somerset Maugham Gift to Congress Library," TIMES (Lond), 8 April 1946, p. 3.
M donated the manuscript of *Of Human Bondage* to the Library of Congress in Washington on 7 April 1946.

1607 *"Then and Now,"* KIRKUS, XIV (15 March 1946), 129.
[Brief appraisal.]

1608 Trilling, Diana. "Fiction in Review," NATION (NY), CLXII (29 June 1946), 790.
Then and Now "alternates between a textbook dryness of historical outline and an embarrassing primitive effort to liven things up."

1609 van Gelder, Robert." An Interview with Somerset Maugham," NEW YORK TIMES BOOK REVIEW, 21 April 1946, p. 3.
M explains that he wrote an initial version [*Of Human Bondage*] entitled "The Artistic Temperament of Stephen Carey" in 1898, but no one would pay £100 for it—fortunately, for M considers the theme to have been "too big for him" at the time of the first writing. M also announces that he is writing his last book. [Interview during the time of M's presentation of the original manuscript of *Of Human Bondage* to the Library of Congress.]

1610 Van Tieghem, Paul. HISTOIRE LITTERAIRE DE L'EUROPE ET DE L'AMERIQUE, DE LA RENAISSANCE A NOS JOURS (LITERARY HISTORY OF EUROPE AND AMERICA, FROM THE RENAISSANCE TO OUR TIME) (Paris: Librairie Armand Colin, 1946), p. 369.
M's plays—such as *A Man of Honour, Lady Frederick,* and *Caesar's Wife* —have been appreciated less for their art and profundity than their workmanship and comic verve. [In French.]

1611 Villette, S. H. "Retour de Somerset Maugham" (The Return of Somerset Maugham), LES NOUVELLES LITTERAIRES, 11 July 1946, pp. 1-2.
[Biography and appreciation, recounting M's recent activities in America, his writing of *The Razor's Edge* and *Then and Now,* and his award of an honorary doctorate from Toulouse.] [In French.]

1612 Volkov, Nicolai. "Somerset Maugham on the Soviet Stage," THEATRE WORLD (Lond), XLII (April 1946), 27.

[A brief and general survey of M's success as a dramatist and novelist in Russia.]

1613 W., A. "Somerset Maugham nous parle de sa pièce *'Avant le Derby'*" (Somerset Maugham Speaks of His Play *Home and Beauty*), LE FIGARO, 10 Dec 1946, p. 4.

[Interview at the time of the premiere of the French adaptation.] [In French.]

1614* Webster, H. T. "Possible Influence of George Gissing's WORKERS IN THE DAWN on Maugham's *Of Human Bondage*," MODERN LANGUAGE REVIEW, VII (Sept 1946), 315.

Gissing's first marriage as dramatized in his first novel might have influenced M's dramatization of Philip and Mildred in *Of Human Bondage*.

1615 Weeks, Edward. "Bookshelf," ATLANTIC MONTHLY, CLXXVII (June 1946), 160, 162.

In *Then and Now,* the two plots "develop simultaneously and with a clarity and mystification delightful to behold," and the dialogue "is unstilted and as lively as if it had been spoken today."

1616* Wilson, Edmund. "Books: Somerset Maugham and an Antidote," NEW YORKER, XXII (8 June 1946), 96-99; rptd as "The Apotheosis of Somerset Maugham," in CLASSICS AND COMMERCIALS (NY: Farrar, Strauss, 1950), pp. 319-26.

M is "second-rate"; his use of language is "banal, has no personal rhythm at all, nor can he create for us a poetic world." The plot of *Then and Now* is "contrived" and requires half of the pages to be introduced.

1947

1617 Adams, J. Donald. "Speaking of Books," NEW YORK TIMES BOOK REVIEW, 19 Jan 1947, p. 2.

[Article expanding M's ideas on "genius" and "talent."]

1618 Ahonen, Olavi. "Syvää viisautta ja vauhdikasta ajanvietettä" (Profound Wisdom and Fast-Moving Entertainment), SUOMEN SOSIALIDEMOKRAATTI, 25 Nov 1947, p. 4.

In *The Razor's Edge* M's animated narration and his keen and profound psychological observation are at their best. There is, in addition, plenty of philosophy of life in the grand style. [Review of Finnish translation.] [In Finnish.]

1619 "Aldwych Theatre: 'JANE,'" TIMES (Lond), 30 Jan 1947, p. 6; rptd by Raymond Mander and Joe Mitchenson, eds, in THEATRICAL COMPANION TO MAUGHAM (Lond: Rockliff, 1955), p. 282.
S. N. Behrman's dramatization "is plainly an artistic outrage [which] supplies three delightful players with three delightful parts . . . . "

1620 "Books—Briefly Noted: Fiction," NEW YORKER, XXIII (2 Aug 1947), 63.
"There aren't many uncontrived situations in *Creatures of Circumstance* and there are even fewer unforeseeable developments, but Mr. Maugham has so deftly hand-polished his patent-leather entertainment that the age of the material hardly shows at all."

1621 "Books: Old Hand, Old Stuff," TIME, L (28 July 1947), 87.
The stories of *Creatures of Circumstance* are for the most part "without significance," but they are "as well made as ever, and as full of Maugham's slick brand of irony." "The Unconquered" is especially praiseworthy.

1622 Bullock, Florence Haxton [Britten]. "Fifteen New Maugham Stories," NEW YORK HERALD TRIBUNE BOOK REVIEW, 27 July 1947, p. 4.
In *Creatures of Circumstance,* "as in life itself, character and circumstance are two-way forces, with the advantage generally on the side of character."

1623 Clark, Barrett H., and George Freedley. A HISTORY OF MODERN DRAMA (NY & Lond: D. Appleton-Century, 1947), pp. 191, 498.
M's "contribution to twentieth-century English drama lies in his realistic description of the manners and morals of his time."

1624 *"Creatures of Circumstance,"* KIRKUS, XV (15 May 1947), 260.
[Brief appraisal.]

1625 Doughty, A. D. K. "The Mixtures Almost as Before: New Short Stories by Maugham," SAN FRANCISCO SUNDAY CHRONICLE ("This Week"), 10 Aug 1947, p. 11.
Of the fifteen stories in *Creatures of Circumstance,* only two are not disappointing—"The Colonel's Lady" and "The Unconquered"—and these two show how M gained his high reputation.

1626 Durham, Willard Higley, and John W. Dodds. "W. Somerset Maugham," BRITISH AND AMERICAN PLAYS: 1830-1945 (NY: Oxford U P, 1947), pp. 341-42.
[General introduction to *The Circle.*]

1627 Farrelly, John. "Fiction Parade," NEW REPUBLIC, CXVII (11 Aug 1947), 30-32.

The stories in *Creatures of Circumstance* are representative of M's work. Most interesting is M's preface in which he complains of "highbrow" criticism.

1628* "Fiction: Variety of People," TIMES LITERARY SUPPLEMENT (Lond), 19 July 1947, p. 361.

M's career has undergone many changes, from a serious novelist of manners and morals to a short-story writer with polish and economy. In *Creatures of Circumstance* he writes "the magazine story, made-to-measure commodities for the popular fiction market." His flair for incident has led not only to a neglect of character, but to a neglect of style, as well, with the resulting number of clichés. "He has thrown away many good ideas by treating them in a purely conventional way."

1629 Fleming, Peter. "Contemporary Arts: The Theatre," SPECTATOR (Lond), CLXXVIII (7 Feb 1947), 173.

S. N. Behrman's dramatization, JANE, "has no possible importance, but it is extremely amusing." Jane is a "farfetched peg on which to hang a plot." The actors make the play.

1630 Frahne, Karl Heinrich. VON CHAUCER BIS SHAW: EINE EINFÜHRUNG IN DIE LITERATUR ENGLANDS (FROM CHAUCER TO SHAW: AN INTRODUCTION TO ENGLISH LITERATURE) (Hamburg: J. P. Toth, 1947), pp. 259-61.

M continues the tradition of English realism. His early fiction contains disillusioning analyses of contemporary life, his later works tentatively explore solutions to the spiritual crisis of our time. [In German.]

1631 Hart, H. W. "New Books Appraised," LIBRARY JOURNAL, LXXII (July 1947), 1034.

Creatures of Circumstance is "lively and lucid . . . in the De Maupassant tradition."

1632 H[umeau], Ed[mond]. "Les Livres Reçus: *Le Fil du Rasoir*" (Books Received: *The Razor's Edge*), ARTS [SPECTACLES, BEAUX-ARTS, LITTERATURE], 22 Aug 1947, p. 2.

The main interest of the novel in the French translation is to present us with flesh and blood characters. [In French.]

1633* K-ki, A. "Estivä ihminen nyt ja 'aikojen alussa' " (Man in Search of Himself Now and 'at the Beginning of Time'), KALTIO, III: 4 (1947), 111-12.

It is difficult to say what is the most attractive feature in *The Razor's Edge*: is it the author's sympathetic attitude towards mankind? his sense of humor, often sharpened into irony? Larry in his untiring search for truth? Elliott in his whole-hearted pursuit of the vanities of life? It is as if the best characteristics of English and French humorous writers were combined in M. [Review of Finnish translation.] [In Finnish.]

1634 [Keown], Eric. "At the Play," PUNCH, CCXII (12 Feb 1947), 176.

S. N. Behrman's dramatization, JANE, remains "palpably a short story, lacking any solid development and leaving exposed the frail ends of an idea which could perhaps have been made convincing only in a literary form."

1635 Lee, Charles. "Mr. Maugham, Still Urbane," NEW YORK TIMES BOOK REVIEW, 27 July 1947, pp. 4, 23.

In *Creatures of Circumstance,* M has good stories to tell and knows how to tell them; his technique has about it "the grace of all finely executed art."

1636 M., H. G. "New Shows of the Month: *'Smith,'*" THEATRE WORLD (Lond), XLIII (Dec 1947), 8-9.

[Tongue-in-cheek review of the revival.]

1637 Manning, Olivia. "Books of the Day: Short Stories," SPECTATOR (Lond), CLXXIX (8 Aug 1947), 186-88.

"Maugham's age and reputation place him above the criticism of the young." His are "commonplace, middle-aged characters with pasts of remarkable passion and violence." M's intent in *Creatures of Circumstance* "must be to entertain."

1638 Marriott, Charles. "Books of the Day: Short Stories," MANCHESTER GUARDIAN, 7 Aug 1947, p. 3.

"Episode" is perhaps the best of the fifteen stories in *Creatures of Circumstance.*

1639 "Maugham Offers Prize," NEW YORK TIMES, 11 April 1947, p. 23.

M will award £500 annually to a promising young author, the money to be used for travel into foreign countries.

1640 Nicoll, Alardyce. BRITISH DRAMA: AN HISTORICAL SURVEY FROM THE BEGINNINGS TO THE PRESENT TIME. Fourth, Revised Edition (Lond: George C. Harrap, 1947 [1925]), pp. 360, 467-69.

No dramatist of the modern age "so completely captured the spirit that animated the Restoration theatre" as did M. His plays are "savage Wycherley."

1641 Olmsted, Nelson. "Collection of Maughan's [sic] Tales," CHICAGO SUN BOOK WEEK, 27 July 1947, p. 3.

No story in *Creatures of Circumstance* approaches in stature or importance M's earlier great stories, but they are all "good."

1642* Paley, Judith. "Les Romans étrangers" (Foreign Novels), PARU, No. 34 (Sept 1947), 49-50.

After creating two unforgettable characters (Larry and Elliott) in *The Razor's Edge,* M deals with numerous other characters as colorless as those in L. Bromfield's novels. The creation of the characters and the enmeshing of them with others is, however, executed harmoniously, and becomes a measure of M's achievement. [Review of French translation.] [In French.]

1643 "People Who Read and Write: No Bets," NEW YORK TIMES BOOK REVIEW, 22 June 1947, p. 3.

M has just completed *Catalina* and has said it will be his last novel. "But it might be just as well not to bet on it. . . . "

1644 Prescott, Orville. "Outstanding Novels," YALE REVIEW, XXXVII (Autumn 1947), 190-91.

Creatures of Circumstance is "professionally adroit and craftily theatrical"; several stories, notably "The Colonel's Lady," are excellent in their wit, cleverness and imagination, "but in half of them Maugham hasn't bothered to write skilfully."

1645* Pritchett, V. S. "Mr. Maugham," NEW STATESMAN AND NATION, N. S. XXXIV (2 Aug 1947), 94-95.

M hasn't Wells' "imagination," nor Chekhov and Maupassant's "taste for familiar landscape"; but he is "the most readable and accomplished English short-story writer of the serious kind alive." Of the "omniscient or directly told" stories in *Creatures of Circumstance,* "Sanatorium" is the best, but for technical virtuosity "Flotsam and Jetsam" is "astonishing."

1646 "Reprints, New Editions," NEW YORK HERALD TRIBUNE BOOK REVIEW, 1 June 1947, p. 12.

[Recommendation of *East and West.*]

1647 S., F. "New Shows of the Month: 'JANE'," THEATRE WORLD (Lond), XLIII (March 1947), 4.

S. N. Behrman's dramatization "is better than no Maugham play at all."

1648 S., F. "New Shows of the Month: *'Lady Frederick,'* " THEATRE WORLD (Lond), XLIII (Jan 1947), 7.

The revived play "has all the elegance and suavity of Oscar Wilde at his best."

1649 S., M. "Kirjallisuutta: nykyaikaisen romaanin edustajia" (Literature: Representatives of the Modern Novel), VAPAA SANA, 2 Nov 1947, p. 5.

The Razor's Edge cannot be called a great work of art because it lacks originality and profundity, though it is amusing in a much more intelligent way than any present-day American novel. [Review of Finnish translation.] [In Finnish.]

1650 Sigaux, Gilbert. "Les traductions" (Translations), ALMANACH DES LETTRES, 1948 (ALMANAC OF LETTERS, 1948), ed by André Maurois, et al. (Paris: Editions de Flore et La Gazette des Lettres, 1947), p. 120.

[Brief mention of the French translation of *The Razor's Edge*.]

1651 Smith, Harrison. "The Mysterious Mr. Maugham," SATURDAY REVIEW OF LITERATURE, XXX (26 July 1947), 10-11.

After the personal revelation of *Of Human Bondage,* M closed off his inner self to observe the human follies about him. A reader knows in advance exactly what kind of stories [e.g., in *Creatures of Circumstance*] he will get from this far-travelling, widely observing author: a "romantic" background, characters of the well-to-do class with their weaknesses exposed, and superb craftsmanship.

1652 Stokes, Sewell. "The English Spotlight: Buried Treasure," THEATRE ARTS, XXXI (March 1947), 30-31.

The revival of *Lady Frederick* recalls the difficulty producers had in finding an actress willing to appear dishevelled, without makeup (as the third act requires) on stage; even Coral Broune, who plays Lady Frederick in the revival, consented to be photographed only as she appears earlier in the play.

1653 Stokes, Sewell. "Reviewers and Reviews," THEATRE ARTS, XXXI (April 1947), 59.

M would have given the characters "lifelike reticence," but in his dramatization, JANE, Behrman gives them only insults. One gets tired of M's cynical characters; perhaps familiarity breeds contempt.

1654 "The Theatre Royal, Stratford: *'The Land of Promise'* by W. Somerset Maugham," TIMES (Lond), 29 Jan 1947, p. 6.

The characters are "acutely observed and boldly and dramatically drawn but without trace of Mr. Maugham's later disillusionment." [Review of the revival.]

1655 Tindall, William York. FORCES IN MODERN BRITISH LITERATURE: 1885-1946 (NY: Alfred A. Knopf, 1947), pp. 74-75, 132-33, 179-80.

M is the most excellent of "commercial artists" and is remarkable for his generation for treating "colonials without arrogance." *Of Human Bondage* is one of "the most depressing masterpieces of English realism."

1656 Vallette, Jacques. "Lettres anglo-saxonnes: le Yogi de Maugham" (Anglo-Saxon Letters: Maugham's Yogi), LE MERCURE DE FRANCE, CCC (1 May 1947), 162-65.

In *The Razor's Edge,* M was well advised to explain his hero as little as possible. Elliott, Isabel and Sophia are "admirable portraits." The message of the story lies in "escapism"—that of Larry, a man whose type is as old as the world, but whose portrayal, under his modern aspects, is welcome and beneficent. [In French.]

1657 Vallette, Jacques. "Livres" (Books), LE MERCURE DE FRANCE, CCCI (1 Dec 1947), 736-37.

Creatures of Circumstance is easy and agreeable, scarcely surprising or profound. [In French.]

1658 Wagenknecht, Edward. "Maugham—Excellent as Usual," CHICAGO SUNDAY TRIBUNE BOOKS, 27 July 1947, pp. 3, 11.

Creatures of Circumstance is "solid, four-square, down to earth, and completely honest. There is no story that is not absorbing reading; there is no dull page; there are precious few characters who refuse to come alive."

1659 Wescott, Glenway. "Somerset Maugham and Posterity," HARPER'S MAGAZINE, CXCV (Oct 1947), 302-11; rptd in THE WINDMILL, III, No. 12 (1948), 36-47; in THE WORLD OF SOMERSET MAUGHAM, ed by Klaus W. Jonas (NY: British Book Centre, 1959), pp. 163-79; and in IMAGES OF TRUTH: REMEMBRANCES AND CRITICISM (NY: Harper & Row, 1962 [1947]), pp. 59-85; the same as "An Introduction to Maugham," THE MAUGHAM READER (Garden City: Doubleday, 1950), pp. vii-xxvi.

Although M himself and critics have done much to discredit his serious reputation, he is likely to enjoy immortality because, unlike greater geniuses of his day who either allied themselves with narrow ideologies or who invented "recondite crossword puzzles," M "has been sagacious and cautious in his handling of themes of the day which grow commonplace or obscure; . . . has been content to write a pure prosaic prose without any remarkable invention of new ways of expressing things; . . . has written a great amount, so as to constitute a distinct Maugham-world into which his readers can enter, of which they can learn the idiom and the implications, each volume helping them to understand the next; and . . . he has discovered and devised story after story worth telling for the story's sake."

1948

1660 Adams, J. Donald. "Speaking of Books," New York Times Book Review, 12 Dec 1948, p. 2.
In *Great Novelists and their Novels,* M, highly skilled in the gentle art of persuasion, has chosen and then abridged ten novels, with the justification for the abridgment being that "even the greatest novels are imperfect and carry with them into posterity no small amount of excess baggage."

1661* Aldridge, John W. "Mr. Maugham's Ten Sheared Candidates," Saturday Review of Literature, XXXI (2 Oct 1948), 23-24.
In *Great Novelists and their Novels,* M approaches the ten great novels as a professional writer and reader, judging them by the standards he has set for his own craft. Through biography he tries to apply the personality to the work and the work to the personality. The best essays are those in which he achieves an effective balance between the two.

1662 Armstrong, Petronella. "Nouveaux Romans Anglais" (New English Novels), Journal de Geneve, 7-8 Nov 1948, p. 3.
[Review of *Catalina.*] [In French.]

1663 B[ickley], F[rancis]. "Our Booking-Office: It Happened in Spain," Punch, CCXV (25 Aug 1948), 178.
Catalina is "a holiday excursion."

1664* Bloomfield, Paul. "Books of the Day: New Novels," Manchester Guardian, 20 Aug 1948, p. 3.
Catalina "might have been written under a Mediterranean sun by a Frenchman, a sceptical deist, a reluctantly renegade Catholic, a member of the Academy." The book is a "trifle," but it is "brilliantly clever and amusing."

1665 "Books—Briefly Noted: Fiction," New Yorker, XXIV (28 Oct 1948), 111.
"What Mr. Maugham had in mind when he thought up this confection [*Catalina*] is not clear, and why, having thought it up, he went ahead and wrote it is still more perplexing."

1666 "Books: Maugham on Miracles," Newsweek, XXXII (8 Nov 1948), 98.
Neither M's best book nor a failure, *Catalina* blends "historical research with a fine, human, and salty understanding of human nature."

1667* "Books: Old Craftsman," Time, LII (1 Nov 1948), 101-2.
Catalina "is no masterpiece; it is merely a disarming little story laid in Spain

during the Inquisition and written in a grave and effortless style modeled on the old chroniclers, and sometimes edging over into a bland and amusing parody of them." However, M's excellent portrait of Bishop Blasco de Valero makes the work almost a first-rate novel.

1668 *"Catalina,"* KIRKUS, XVI (15 June 1948), 290.
[Brief appraisal.]

1669 Cross, Jesse E. "New Books Appraised," LIBRARY JOURNAL, LXXIII (15 Sept 1948), 1270.
Great Novelists and their Novels is "somewhat uneven in quality, interesting as exposing a seasoned writer's own philosophy of novel writing."

1670 Etzkorn, Leo R. "New Books Appraised," LIBRARY JOURNAL, LXXIII (Aug 1948), 1091.
In *Catalina,* "Maugham, with tongue in cheek, writes beautifully, with whimsy, humor and satire."

1671 Farrelly, John. "Success Story," NEW REPUBLIC, CXIX (25 Oct 1948), 25.
Catalina, a "cynical exploitation . . . of Catholic traditions," uses cliché characters and gives peremptory explanations for motive and action.

1672 *"Great Novelists and their Novels,"* KIRKUS, XVI (15 Aug 1948), 420.
[Brief appraisal.]

1673 H-u, T. "Uusi Maugham-suomennos" (A New Maugham Translation), HELSINGIN SANOMAT, 21 Sept 1948, p. 7.
M has taken no great pains in the creation of his plot; the characterization is superficial. Yet, *The Painted Veil* is pleasant to read. [Review of Finnish translation.] [In Finnish.]

1674* Harcourt-Smith, Simon. "New Novels," NEW STATESMAN AND NATION, N. S. XXXVI (11 Sept 1948), 224.
M is fundamentally "a survival of early Edwardian de-bunking, a functionalist among writers, sworn enemy of just such incrustations as overlay the faltering design of *Catalina*. . . . Every one of the lay-figures . . . might have been borrowed from the prop-department of M. G. M. or Universal." M has turned out "a mixture of Charles Kingsley and bad Norman Douglas."

1675 Hoult, Norah. "New Novels," BOOKS OF THE MONTH, XVIII (Oct 1948), 11.
[Tongue-in-cheek review of *Catalina*.]

1676 Jackson, Joseph Henry. "A Bookman's Notebook: Maugham's New One," SAN FRANCISCO CHRONICLE, 8 Nov 1948, p. 14.

Catalina is "a swift, brilliantly colored tale . . . . Maugham is a good observer."

1677 Kare, Kauko. "Viisaudesta pyhään vihaan" (From Wisdom to Pious Wrath), SUOMALAINEN SUOMI, XVI: 1 (1948), 49-51.

M avoids stylistic snobbery, dramatic climaxes, and art for art's sake. Despite its stylistic simplicity and its lack of decorative detail, *The Razor's Edge* is a solid work. Larry and Elliott belong to the group of the best characters M ever created. [Review of Finnish translation.] [In Finnish.]

1678 Kula, Kauko. "Maugham," AAMULEHTI, 15 Sept 1948, p. 4.

The greatest merit of *The Painted Veil* lies in its characterization. M is a wise and objective narrator; he knows how to pose a problem and how to solve it. His message is positive. [Review of Finnish translation.] [In Finnish.]

1679 " 'Last Novel' by Maugham," CHICAGO SUN-TIMES BOOK WEEK, 28 Nov 1948, p. 9X.

M's concoction of saintliness and cynicism [*Catalina*] "is unlikely to please the religious-minded."

1680 Legouis, E[mile] and Louis Cazamian. HISTOIRE DE LA LITTERATURE ANGLAISE (History of English Literature). Revised Ed. (Paris: Librairie Hachette, 1948 [1924]), pp. 1266, 1279, 1291.

[The footnote on p. 1266 of this volume mistakenly places M's novel, *Mrs. Craddock,* among his plays.] [In French.]

1681* "Liza's Jubilee," TIMES LITERARY SUPPLEMENT (Lond), 24 Jan 1948, p. 52.

Fifty years ago M "was neither imaginative enough to envisage squalor in a temperate climate, nor sufficiently realistic to make a plain report." It is hard to glimpse in the fiftieth anniversary reissue of *Liza of Lambeth* either of the genres in which M was later to excel: "the exotic and the ironic."

1682* Marlow, Louis. "Somerset Maugham," WRITERS OF TODAY. Ed by Denys Val Baker. Two Volumes. (Lond: Sidgwick and Jackson, 1946 [Vol. I], 1948 [Vol. II]). II, 37-52.

A Man of Honour is a play which "stamps Maugham as a kinsman of Ibsen more clearly than Shaw is stamped as such by any of his plays." Other works of M are "Ibsenesque" (to cite but a few: *Smith, The Circle, The Moon and Sixpence, The Breadwinner, The Sacred Flame,* and "The Facts of Life") in that they develop the moral that "private judgment . . . is the wisest and best rule of conduct." M is a serious, moral, as well as tragic, writer; he is "afflicted by human weakness" and lacks Oscar Wilde's "consolation of an irresponsible sense of comedy" or Hardy's consolations of "poetry and nature." He is wrong, as are his critics, to judge his work "second-rate." His style, his irony, his sense of tragedy are all "individual."

1683 Match, Richard. "The Golden Age of Spain," NEW YORK HERALD TRIBUNE BOOK REVIEW, 31 Oct 1948, p. 4.

Catalina is "a semi-precious gem . . . but the work of a master lapidary."

1684 "Maugham's Digest of 10 Great Novels," SPRINGFIELD SUNDAY REPUBLICAN (Mass), 10 Oct 1948, p. 8B.

[Noncommittal review, primarily describing the contents, of *Great Novelists and Their Novels.*]

1685 Miles, George. "Books," COMMONWEAL, XLIX (29 Oct 1948), 77.

Catalina is faulty in plot, preposterous in character analysis; its diction is occasionally trite and awkward.

1686* Morris, Alice S. "Mr. Maugham and the Inquisition," NEW YORK TIMES BOOK REVIEW, 7 Nov 1948, p. 6.

The first 154 pages of *Catalina* are skillful, and M's characters, though conventional, are interesting. M's "serio-farcical irony has a wry and dry bouquet." But in the extended finale, credibility of plot and responsibility are progressively jettisoned. Although the book starts with a "substantial ironic comment on totalitarian manners," it ends up "giving them a substantial whack."

1687 Morris, Lloyd. "Useful Art of Skipping," NEW YORK HERALD TRIBUNE BOOK REVIEW, 26 Sept 1948, p. 10.

In *Great Novelists and Their Novels,* M does not reveal "elements and facets and aspects" which we have missed. [A criticism of M's editing of TOM JONES and DAVID COPPERFIELD appears on p. 20 of the same issue.]

1688 Pekkanen, Toivo. "W. Somerset Maugham, *Veitsen Terällä*" (W. Somerset Maugham, *The Razor's Edge*), ARVOSTELEVA LUETTELO SUOMENKIELISESTÄ KIRJALLISUUDESTA, annex to KIRJASTOLEHTI, XLI: 2 (1948), 16.

The Razor's Edge shows that M can, to some extent, compensate for his lack of original genius with great professional skill. The atmosphere is filled with tension; the characterization is expert and even profound. [Review of Finnish translation.] [In Finnish.]

1689* Prescott, Orville. "Books of the Times," NEW YORK TIMES, 26 Oct 1948, p. 29; rptd as *"Catalina,"* in THE MAUGHAM ENIGMA, ed by Klaus W. Jonas (NY: Citadel P, 1954), pp. 164-66.

In quality, *Catalina* approaches *Cakes and Ale* better than the "flabby pot boilers" like *Then and Now, The Hour Before the Dawn,* and *Up at the Villa.* The book is, at once, a fairy tale, a moral parable, and a fantasy.

1690 R., J. N. B. "Maugham's Folly," Desiderata, I (3 Sept 1948), 1-3.

M is not only "a superb craftsman," but "a creative writer of great insight and imagination." M's classics in the novel and the drama are, respectively, *Cakes and Ale* and *The Circle. Catalina* must be called a "romantic frolic" and qualifies its author for "the role of Elder Phenomenon." [Gives a general assessment of M's career.]

1691 Reed, Henry. The Novel Since 1939 (Lond: The British Council by Longmans, Green, 1948 [1946]), pp. 34-35.

M's *The Razor's Edge* in comparison with Huxley's Time Must Have a Stop and Waugh's Brideshead Revisited is "infinitely the best of the three" in construction and style.

1692* Rolo, Charles. "Reader's Choice," Atlantic Monthly, CLXXXII (Nov 1948), 111.

In *Catalina*, "the writing is outrageous in its use of the cliché," and the episodes are "contrived with the patness of slick magazine fiction. . . . The middle is both an end and a new beginning."

1693 "Stirring the Mixture," Times Literary Supplement (Lond), 21 Aug 1948, p. 470.

Catalina is outwardly cynical, yet intrinsically sentimental, a trifle shapeless, and revealing a basic materialism.

1694 "Story and Film," Times Literary Supplement (Lond), 20 Nov 1948, p. 649.

"Don't see the film of Quartet if you have enjoyed the book." The stories ["The Facts of Life," "The Alien Corn," "The Kite," and "The Colonel's Lady"] are mutilated, and Sherriff's introduction is "obstinately and dully dumb."

1695 Strong, L. A. G. "Books of the Day: Fiction," Spectator (Lond), CLXXXI (20 Aug 1948), 250.

M's excursion into mysticism and miracle fails. "Something more than accurate observation is required." "At the risk of seeming to lack humor, I shall forget *Catalina.*"

1696 Sugrue, Thomas. "A Soul Seeking Heaven," Saturday Review of Literature, XXXI (31 Oct 1948), 13-14.

In *Catalina,* M shows again his consummate abilities as a storyteller.

1697 Thompson, Alan Reynolds. THE DRY MOCK: A STUDY OF IRONY IN DRAMA (Berkeley and Los Angeles: University of California P, 1948), pp. 40-42.
[The last scene of *The Circle* is analyzed for its complex use of irony.]

1698 Trewin, J. C. "Elder Statesmen," THE ENGLISH THEATRE. (LIFE AND LEISURE, I.) (Lond: Paul Elek, 1948), pp. 20-28, especially 26-27.
M's greatest plays are *Our Betters, The Circle,* and *For Services Rendered,* although *The Breadwinner, Sheppey, The Letter* and *The Sacred Flame* "revive well."

1699 V-o, S. "Miellyttävä lisä englantilaiseen käännöskirjallisuuteen" (A Pleasant Addition to Translated English Literature), YLIOPPILASLEHTI, 29 Jan 1948, p. 5.
M does not aim at psychological profundity in his characterization, but his observations are so much to the point that the profiles he draws are often extremely truthful. *The Razor's Edge* is clever and amusing — "entertainment" in the best sense of the word. [Review of Finnish translation.] [In Finnish.]

1700 Vallette, Jacques. "Livres" (Books), LE MERCURE DE FRANCE, CCCIV (1 Nov 1948), 545.
One will enjoy reading *Catalina* while he reflects that M has done much better in the past. [In French.]

1701 Weinberger, Caspar. "Prescription for Painless Reading," SAN FRANCISCO SUNDAY CHRONICLE ("This World"), 5 Dec 1948, p. 19.
The essays of *Great Novelists and Their Novels* show "wise and tolerant" understanding of their subjects; the only one which seems original or revolutionary, however, is that on Melville and what happened to him after his marriage.

1702 Wiebe, Hans. "Die Technik der Kurzgeschichten William Somerset Maughams" (The Technique of William Somerset Maugham's Short Stories). Unpublished thesis. Wurzburg, 1948.
Usually, M gives a brief introduction, preparing the theme, then develops one situation dramatically (often through dialogue or indirect speech), and uses a surprise or a sober ending. The ways in which he indicates the emotions of his characters, describes the backgrounds, and uses various kinds of contrast, are commendable. M's style is simple and euphonious. [Wiebe discusses M's narrative techniques under such headings as "the beginning," "the middle," "the end."] [In German.]

1949

1703 Alle, Fritz. "Der Berbrauch der Umschriehenen Zeitformen in Romanen W. Somerset Maugham" (The Use of the Expanded Time Forms in the Novels of W. Somerset Maugham). Unpublished thesis. University of Graz, Austria, 1949.

[M's usage is investigated to arrive at general conclusions about the functions of the expanded form. Two functions are distinguished from each other, the progressive one and the emphatic. Examples are drawn from *Mrs. Craddock, The Moon and Sixpence,* and *The Razor's Edge*. No significant changes in M's usage are said to occur.] [In German.]

1704* Allen, Walter. The English Novel: A Short Critical History (Lond: Phoenix House, 1949), pp. 271, 287, especially 312-14.

M has been content to work within a narrow range of subject and character "without any compensating quality of style. . . . " But in *Liza of Lambeth, Of Human Bondage,* and *Cakes and Ale,* he rises "above the civilized entertainment which has generally been the end he has proposed for himself."

1705* Anhava, Tuomas. "Taitamisen vaiheilta" (About "Know-How"), Suomalainen Suomi, XVIII: 8 (1949), 494-96.

The Moon and Sixpence is not one of M's best novels. Strickland is such an exceptional personality that he resembles a natural phenomenon rather than a human being. The artistic effect of the novel is greatly weakened by the narrator's unsympathetic attitude towards Strickland; because of it, the only feeling the story creates in the reader is surprise. [Review of Finnish translation.] [In Finnish.]

1706 "Arts Theatre: *'Caroline'* by W. Somerset Maugham," Times (Lond), 23 March 1949, p. 7.

The revival shows how seriously M applied himself to providing theatrical entertainment. Omitted from M's collected edition, the play deserves revival. "The acid drop has acid in it."

1707* Auden, W. H. "Notebooks of Somerset Maugham: The Memoranda of His Lifetime Reveal Varied Interests and Unexpected Ideals," New York Times Book Review, 23 Oct 1949, pp. 1, 22.

A Writer's Notebook is neither a series of personal confessions nor a collection of practical tips for the would-be writer, but the condensation of fifteen volumes of notes on "all kinds of thoughts and emotions of a personal nature."

1708 " 'BEFORE THE PARTY,' at St. Martin's," NEW STATESMAN AND NATION, N. S. XXXVIII (5 Nov 1949), 514.
Having exploited M's original anecdote in Act I, Rodney Ackland's dramatization adds a second act that fails because the characters can under no circumstances demand one's sympathy.

1709 Behrman, S. N. "Books: The Notes of a Popular Pessimist," NEW YORKER, XXV (29 Oct 1949), 88, 91-94.
"From his will and from the force of his character, Maugham has created a way of life that has served him, and a long shelf of books. It has been an extraordinary exercise in craftsmanship. Now, as he approaches the end, he manages to endow it, if not with sunshine, at least with suspense." [Review article of *A Writer's Notebook.*]

1710 Benét, William Rose. "Maughamana, 1892-1949," SATURDAY REVIEW OF LITERATURE, XXXII (22 Oct 1949), 16-17.
The variety of material in *A Writer's Notebook* discloses a mind that is skeptical and an interest in people and in life in other countries. Included are observations and jottings that were later used in M's fiction. The book is "a rich fruitcake of good reading."

1711 Bloomfield, Paul. "A Fairly Intimate Journal," MANCHESTER GUARDIAN, 7 Oct 1949, p. 4.
A Writer's Notebook, in selection and style, is both interesting and readable. M has never stopped "courting" life and he has never lost his identity in the courtship.

1712 "Books: Here & There," TIME, LIV (31 Oct 1949), 80.
While there is an occasional lively passage, much of what M has written in *A Writer's Notebook* is uninspired and commonplace.

1713 "Books: The Maugham Story," NEWSWEEK, XXXIV (24 Oct 1949), 93-94.
M's jottings in *A Writer's Notebook* are more fascinating than they would have been if he had consciously kept a journal.

1714 B[risville], J[ean]-C[laude]. "Chronique et Notes de Livres" (Chronicle and Book Notes), LA NEF, No. 52 (March 1949), 112.
[Primarily a plot summary of the French translation of *Then and Now.*] [In French.]

1715 Brown, John Mason. "Ex Libris," SATURDAY REVIEW OF LITERATURE, XXXII (22 April 1949), 30-31.

R. C. Sherriff's scenarios and the techniques of filming QUARTET adapt themselves to M's stories ["The Facts of Life," "The Alien Corn," "The Kite," and "The Colonel's Lady"] to produce a film that accepts intelligence as part of the viewer's make-up.

1716 Burke, Billie, with Cameron Shipp. WITH A FEATHER ON MY NOSE (NY: Appleton-Century-Crofts, 1949), pp. 36, 86, 101, 107-8, 115 ff., 148, 201.
[Reminiscences of Miss Burke's relationships with M during her performances in *Mrs. Dot* and *The Land of Promise.*]

1717 "Canterbury Week: Old Stagers in *'The Circle,'*" TIMES (Lond), 3 Aug 1949, p. 7.
"The light of pure mischief plays upon it [the revived play] continually, and its sheer technical dexterity must be a joy to anyone who cares for such things."

1718 Collette, [Sidonie Gabrielle]. OEUVRES COMPLETES (COMPLETE WORKS). 15 Volumes (Paris: Flammarion, 1949), x, 381-82.
If the third act were as good as the preceding two, F. de Croisset's adaptation of *The Breadwinner* would be excellent. [In French.]

1719 Comden, Betty. "Maugham and the Movies," NEW YORK TIMES BOOK REVIEW, 29 May 1949, pp. 4, 18.
General comments on the changes R. C. Sherriff made in the scenario versions [QUARTET] of four stories ["The Facts of Life," "The Alien Corn," "The Kite," "The Colonel's Lady"] by M.

1720 Cookman, A. V. "W. Somerset Maugham," THE YEAR'S WORK IN THE THEATRE: 1948-1949 (Lond: The British Council by Longmans Green & Co., 1949), pp. 24-29.
M was wise to retire from playwriting when he did. He continued to write Edwardian plays in the Georgian period and, in the early thirties, found himself completely outmoded. Nevertheless, *The Circle* "should . . . keep its place as a classic serious comedy."

1721 Cournos, John. "Books," COMMONWEAL, LI (21 Oct 1949), 49-51.
A Writer's Notebook is "absorbing" for what the book reveals about M.

1722 d'Houville, Gérard. "Lectures romanesques" (Readings in the Novel), LA REVUE [DES DEUX MONDES], II (1 March 1949), 362-63.
[Review of the French translation of *Then and Now.*] [In French.]

1723* Eaton, Walter Prichard. "Maugham in the Process of Becoming," NEW YORK HERALD TRIBUNE BOOK REVIEW, 23 Oct 1949, p. 5.

A Writer's Notebook is M's *"De Senectute.* It is cool, a little hedonistic, and will seem to many self-satisfied. It will also seem to others not a little sad. The man who studied men to make stories of them seems at the end alone with his books."

1724* Fleming, Peter. "Contemporary Arts: The Theatre," SPECTATOR (Lond), CLXXXIII (4 Nov 1949), 601.

Rodney Ackland's dramatization, BEFORE THE PARTY, leaves an "impression of triviality and cheapness." Playwrights have been writing about the upper middle-class for a long time, and "a sort of formula or recipe has been evolved to which, rather than to life, playwrights conceive it their duty to adhere."

1725 Freedley, George. "The Theatre," LIRBARY JOURNAL, LXXIV (15 Oct 1949), 1605.

A Writer's Notebook should be read by any "embryonic playwright, short-story writer, or novelist."

1726 Gilroy, Harry. "How to Write—by Maugham," NEW YORK TIMES MAGAZINE, 23 Jan 1949, pp. 10, 41-42; rptd in THE MAUGHAM ENIGMA, ed by Klaus W. Jonas (NY: Citadel P, 1954), pp. 41-49.

[Interview, in which M gives some advice to beginning writers.]

1727* Gordon, Caroline. "Notes on Chekhov and Maugham," SEWANEE REVIEW, LVII (Summer 1949), 401-10; rptd, in a slightly altered form, in Caroline Gordon and Allen Tate's THE HOUSE OF FICTION (NY: C. Scribner's, 1950), pp. 382-85.

M's critical remarks in his prefaces to his works have set as bad an example for young writers as the works themselves. By contrast with Chekhov, M appears a poor "journalist" who doesn't work hard enough.

1728* Grennan, Margaret R. "New Books," CATHOLIC WORLD, CLVIII (Jan 1949), 331-32.

"Catalina is a clever story. But it pays the price frequently exacted of cleverness. Maugham has enjoyed his joke, and according to our taste we may or may not laugh with him. But in spite of all its brightness, there is little in the book to tempt us to turn to its pages again." In the essays of *Great Novelists,* M "emphasizes with tiresome monotony the erotic experience—or lack of it—of each author in turn," and renders intelligent estimates which are neither original nor profound.

1729 H., V. "Maughamin Gauguin" (Maugham's Gauguin), ETELÄ-SUOMEN SANOMAT, 5 Aug 1949, p. 4.

Although the reader is not convinced of the truthfulness of the description in *The Moon and Sixpence,* M's way of illustrating Gauguin's life and work is certainly intelligent. It is as if Gauguin's art were transformed into words and ideas in this novel. It lashes old, deep-seated conventional attitudes. [Review of the Finnish translation, in Finnish.]

1730 Howe, Susanne. Novels of Empire (NY: Columbia U P, 1949), pp. 6, 8, 60, 101.

M's stories and his novel, *The Explorer*, are part of the literature influenced by the "colonial" motif and its moral and aesthetic implications.

1731 Jackson, Joseph Henry. "A Bookman's Notebook," San Francisco Chronicle, 21 Oct 1949, p. 21.

In *A Writer's Notebook*, M should have omitted all the material from before 1907 [the time of his first dramatic success, *Lady Frederick*] to leave room for "more of the later notebooks . . . in which the larger part of his great audience will find by far the most meat."

1732 Jaffe, Adrian H., and Virgil Scott. Studies in the Short Story (NY: Dryden P, 1949), pp. 345-53, especially 345, 352.

[A brief discussion of the "levels" of character, situation and theme, as well as the symbolism, of "Rain."]

1733 K-la, K. "Prototyyppikö?" (A Prototype?), Lapin Kansa, 22 July 1949, p. 3.

One must ask whether the author does not too often make the impossible possible. He portrays a type, not a human being. But *The Moon and Sixpence* is skillfully compiled and pleasant to read. [Review of the Finnish translation, in Finnish.]

1734 Kajava, Viljo. "Käännösromaaneja" (Translated Novels), Elanto, 8 Oct 1949, p. 11.

The artistic value of *The Moon and Sixpence* suffers greatly from formality and superficiality. Gauguin's portrait is not truthful. [Review of Finnish translation.] [In Finnish.]

1735 Kemp, Robert. "La Vie des Livres: Les Romanesques" (The Life of Books: Novels), Les Nouvelles Litteraires, 17 Feb 1949, p. 2.

Readers in France of the French translation of *Then and Now,* accustomed to M's exoticism in the vein of Kipling or Conrad, must adjust to M, writer of the historical novel. [In French.]

1736* Krutch, Joseph Wood. "A String of Pearls," Nation (NY), CLXIX (3 Dec 1949), 549-50.

A Writer's Notebook gives proof "of how much can be made in fame, in money, in respectable achievement out of rather small but perfectly genuine talents."

1737 Kula, Kauko. "Katsaus alkuvuoden käänöskirjallisuuteen" (Survey of Translated Literature from the Beginning of the Year), AJAN KIRJA, I: 3 (1949), 87-88.

A reader of *The Moon and Sixpence* will feel that M's main purpose has been to get him confused. A cold and sparkling style keeps the reader awake, and the dialogue is most lifelike, but the air of the novel is perhaps too thin and too cool to be breathed for a long time. [Review of Finnish translation.] [In Finnish.]

1738 Kupiainen, Unto. "Kaksi englantilaista kertojaa" (Two English Narrators), KARJALAINEN, 9 Oct 1949, p. 7.

In *The Moon and Sixpence,* with his biting irony, M succeeds in mastering simultaneously the comic and tragic elements. Yet, he is not simply a cool and ironic observer: he sees the layers of life and points out the logical even in the seemingly senseless. [Review of Finnish translation.] [In Finnish.]

1739 Lambert, Florence. "Le Monde des Livres=Romans=*Plus ça Change*" (The World of Books: Novels: *Then and Now*), LES NOUVELLES LITTERAIRES, 24 March 1949, p. 3.

M's picture of the Italian Cinquecento and an important moment in Machiavelli's life is evoked in the French translation with "poetic accuracy." [In French.]

1740* M., H. G. "New Shows of the Month: *'Caroline,'* " THEATRE WORLD (Lond), XLV (May 1949), 6, 8.

"This play is a farcical comedy in a satirical frame. . . . It [the revival] is presented as Edwardian and to that period it seems to belong. Telephones and two-seaters are incongruous in this setting, but in a 1916 setting the play itself might seem a little stale."

1741 M[allett], R[ichard]. "Booking Office," PUNCH, CCXVII (12 Oct 1949), 422.

A Writer's Notebook is better reading for the "general" reader rather than for the "specialist" interested in diaries or notebooks and how their fragments stimulate artists' minds.

1742 Manner, Eeva-Liisa. "Keskustelemme kirjoista" (Talking about Books), TAITEEN MAAILMA, V: 9 (1949), 23.

If M had occasionally quoted Gauguin's words, *The Moon and Sixpence* would be more convincing. M evidently tried hard, but he probably found the subject too difficult for him: that is why the result remains slack and lifeless. [Review of Finnish translation.] [In Finnish.]

1743 "Maugham Accused by Soviet Writers," NEW YORK TIMES, 7 Aug 1949, p. 26.

M is accused by Soviets' LITERARY GAZETTE "as an unsuccessful British spy who has now placed himself himself at the disposal of Wall Street bosses to aid in the 'spiritual disarmament of the masses.' "

1744* Morgan, Charles. "Books of the Day: Maugham's Workshop," SPECTATOR (Lond), CLXXXIII (7 Oct 1949), 468; rptd in THE MAUGHAM ENIGMA, ed by Klaus W. Jonas (NY: Citadel P, 1954), pp. 208-12.

A Writer's Notebook is valuable because it is "not an ideology masquerading as criticism or an autobiography pretending to final wisdom." Notebooks usually interrupt "the even flow" of writing and experience, but M "is an analytical observer, and his notebooks were necessary to him as a storehouse of material for analysis." The notes were not "scribblings," but "preliminarily polished." M is perpetually interested in "the problem of morals," but represses his interest. He has, when dealing with the abstract, a "disconcerting habit of suddenly refusing a fence and swerving into irrelevance." "Passion for metaphysics" conflicts with "determination not to give himself or his characters the benefit of the doubt." His affected "ruthlessness" results from "honorable fears" which "run like a shudder across these pages," but "are among the winds that drive Maugham's powerful ship."

1745 O'Hearn, Walter. "De Senectute: Mr. Maugham Awaits the Ferryman," COMMONWEAL, L (16 Sept 1949), 553-55.

A Writer's Notebook reveals that M, "a minor Bellini of the written word," possessed a meticulous observation of all he wanted to see and a style both "distinguished and lucid." His age has known greater artists, but "no better craftsman." [General appreciation.]

1746* "Pencil and Rubber," TIMES LITERARY SUPPLEMENT (Lond), 14 Oct 1949, p. 659.

A Writer's Notebook, despite its composition of opinion, reflections, impressions, and anecdotes, presents a "remarkably coherent picture." M sees a need for form and "common sense" but is perhaps a trifle tyrannical in insisting on only his own methods to achieve it. His writing is founded on French traditions; he does not feel the traditionally English need for caricature, but rather makes a conventional introduction of the dramatis personae. His fundamental romanticism, springing from an excessive belief in conventions, suddenly reverses itself.

1747 Playfellow. "The Paint and the Powder," TRUTH (Lond), CXLVI (4 Nov 1949), 498.

In Rodney Ackland's dramatization, BEFORE THE PARTY, the action begins as comedy, and the change of key in the second act is "disconcerting."

1748 Pohjanpää, Lauri. "W. Somerset Maugham, *Kuu ja Kupariraha*" (W. Somerset Maugham, *The Moon and Sixpence*), ARVOSTELEVA KIRJALUETTELO, annex to KIRJASTOLEHTI, XLII: 9-10 (1949), 57.

The Moon and Sixpence is told in a lively way, but the almost morbid selfishness and lack of feeling of the main character leaves a bad taste in the mouth. [Review of Finnish translation.] [In Finnish.]

1749 Prescott, Orville. "Outstanding Novels," YALE REVIEW, XXXVIII (Winter 1949), 384.

Catalina is "a delightfully nonsensical fantasy, satire, farce."

1750* Pritchett, V. S. "Books in General," NEW STATESMAN AND NATION, N. S. XXXVIII (8 Oct 1949), 401.

M has always lacked "the transforming passion which is the impulse of creative writing." He has always possessed, however, "integrity as a writer." M's "honesty" has been "a desire to get questions settled and to make time and place for the continuous demands of his talents" so that he is really more "ruthless" than honest, "a practical rather than a seeking moralist." The notes of *A Writer's Notebook* do not add "a new sensation to our lives, or open us to new experience. They suggest, rather the price [M] has paid for his."

1751 "QUARTET," KIRKUS, XVII (15 April 1949), 215.

[Brief appraisal.]

1752 "Reprints, New Editions," NEW YORK HERALD TRIBUNE BOOK REVIEW, 19 June 1949, p. 13.

[Notice and digest of QUARTET, together with R. C. Sherriff's screenplays of the four stories ("The Facts of Life," "The Alien Corn," "The Kite," and "The Colonel's Lady").]

1753 Reynolds, Ernest. MODERN ENGLISH DRAMA: A SURVEY OF THE THEATRE FROM 1900. With a Foreword by Allardyce Nicoll (Lond: George C. Harrap, 1949), pp. 52, 137, 147, 153, 160, 162, especially 167-68, 169, 170.

Our Betters displays M's "trenchant yet exquisitely humorous satire" to great advantage, and is comparable with the theater of Wycherley and Congreve; but *The Circle* is an "even more perfect piece of characterization."

1754 Rhodes, Russell. "Maugham Cinematized," SATURDAY REVIEW OF LITERATURE, XXXII (18 June 1949), 11.

Comparing the original stories with R. C. Sherriff's QUARTET shows that

Sherriff was remarkably faithful to the originals. "The Alien Corn," for which Sherriff changed characters and invented new ones, is the weakest item, although his surprise ending for "The Colonel's Lady" is neatly effected.

1755 Rovere, Richard H. "New Books," HARPER'S MAGAZINE, CXCIX (Nov 1949), 108.

A Writer's Notebook was "pruned . . . ruthlessly to make a book that is continuously satisfying in the familiar, unstirring, civilized Maugham manner."

1756 S., F. "New Shows of the Month: 'BEFORE THE PARTY,'" THEATRE WORLD (Lond), XLV (Dec 1949), 4.

Rodney Ackland's dramatization "carries us as far as the end of Part 1," but is not successful in its continuing act.

1757* S., V. "Nerokas, kurja elämä" (An Ingenious, Miserable Life), UUSI SUOMI, 24 Aug 1949, p. 8.

M's writing is always enjoyable, although it is this time somewhat repetitious and, consequently, slightly boring. The reader is surprised, in the course [of the Finnish translation] of *The Moon and Sixpence,* that Strickland becomes a sympathetic—even admirable—character. As a biographical novel, it is not indisputably successful. Strickland's case would seem to offer material for a psychological treatise rather than for a work of literary art. [In Finnish.]

1758 Schauer Islas, Anita. WILLIAM SOMERSET MAUGHAM. (Mexico, D. F.: National University of Mexico, 1949).

M's basic characteristics as man and thinker are "individualism, will power, realism, sublimation of deficiencies," agnosticism, and moral relativism. His favorite themes are the force of sexual passion, "the eternal contrast between the ideal and reality," and self-realization through the achievement of spiritual liberty. As a writer, M is a disciple of Maupassant, an objectivist who utilizes a precise and often epigrammatic style, emphasizes plot, and regards holding the reader's attention as the prime function of fiction. [In Spanish.]

1759 "St. Martin's Theatre: 'BEFORE THE PARTY' by Rodney Ackland from a Story by W. Somerset Maugham," TIMES (Lond), 27 Oct 1949, p. 7.

The second act "yields Mr. Ackland's obvious but quite entertaining social satire which is shot through with strongish drama."

1760 Starrett, Vincent. "Books Alive," CHICAGO SUNDAY TRIBUNE BOOKS, 20 Nov 1949, p. 2.

M has achieved both recognition and revelation "and still seems a little lonely." [Review of *A Writer's Notebook.*]

1761* Strassenheim, Edmund Strastil. "Die Kunst der Personenbeschreibung in Romanen John Galsworthys, W. Somerset Maughams und Graham Greenes" (The Art of Character Description in the Novels of John Galsworthy, W. Somerset Maugham and Graham Greene). Unpublished thesis. University of Graz, Austria, 1949. Especially pp. 85-155, 230-41.

Despite his interest in painting, M lacks both Galsworthy's and Greene's ability to visualize his persons clearly, and does not often describe their appearance at all, preferring to analyze their feelings. He tends to portray only flat characters, and is often content with reporting, rather than dramatizing, their qualities. He likes to adopt an ironical attitude towards the representatives of bourgeois society. On the whole, his technique of characterization is less modern than Greene's. [In German.]

1762 Thompson, Ralph. "In and Out of Books: Visitor," NEW YORK TIMES BOOK REVIEW, 16 Jan 1949, p. 8.

[Interview on the occasion of M's visit to the United States to celebrate his seventy-fifth birthday.]

1763 Trewin, J. C. "The World of the Theatre," ILLUSTRATED LONDON NEWS, CCXV (19 Nov 1949), 788.

Rodney Ackland's dramatization, BEFORE THE PARTY, is "a well-braced and well-manoeuvred piece."

1764 Tvn, J. "Romaani Gauguinista" (A Novel About Gauguin), AAMULEHTI, 19 Nov 1949, p. 7.

The Moon and Sixpence describes the adventurous life of an artist, but it does not succeed in revealing his struggle and tragedy. [Review of Finnish translation.] [In Finnish.]

1765* V., A. K. "Kertomakirjallisuutta" (Narrative Literature), VALVOJA, LXIX: 7 (1949), 290-91.

In *The Moon and Sixpence,* M has treated the subject in a way that can hardly be regarded as successful. He has made use of features of Gauguin's life but has changed the name and nationality of his main character. He leads the reader's thoughts to a well-known personality but does not accept the responsibility of the historian. Artistically, too, the result is not convincing. The motive of egocentricity is stretched beyond the limits of credibility. M's attempt to describe creative genius is weak and dilettantish. The narration is fluent and provides "piquant" details. [Review of Finnish translation.] [In Finnish.]

1766 Vallette, Jacques. "Livres" (Books), LE MERCURE DE FRANCE, CCCV (1 April 1949), 728.

M's handling of Borgia in [the French translation of] *Then and Now* is cynical; he has written in an elegant, picturesque and entertaining manner. [In French.]

1767 Vallette, Jacques. "Livres" (Books), LE MERCURE DE FRANCE, CCCVII (1 Nov 1949), 532.

Of Human Bondage is strongly autobiographical in flavor, a bit loose in structure, written in simple and efficient prose, demanding to be read at leisure. [Review of the French reissue.] [In French.]

1768 Weeks, Edward. "Bookshelf," ATLANTIC MONTHLY, CLXXXIV (Nov 1949), 86, 88.

A Writer's Notebook is a big and rich book "in which to seek and find."

1769 *"A Writer's Notebook,"* KIRKUS, XVII (15 Aug 1949), 459. [Brief appraisal.]

1950

1770 Alpert, Hollis. "Three from a Very Old Party," SATURDAY REVIEW OF LITERATURE, XXXIII (7 Oct 1950), 50-52.

The cinema displays the M "quality," his excellences and limitations. "The Verger" and "Mr. Know-All" are triumphs, but "Sanatorium," the longest piece in TRIO, is marred by a touch of sentimentality.

1771* Angoff, Charles. "The Library: W. Somerset Maugham," AMERICAN MERCURY, LXX (Jan 1950), 111-17.

A Writer's Notebook explains why the public has been cool to M, and why his standing as a writer is doubtful; it offers few portraits of, or references to, genuinely good men and women (as is the case, also, in M's novels, stories, and plays); and M does not seem disappointed with, but coldly indifferent to, his weak and mean-spirited characters. In sum, M is too frigidly, too inhumanly, detached; his lack of love for humanity has been perceived by readers, and has repelled them.

1772 Anhava, Tuomas. "Mestariteos ja mestarin teos" (A Masterpiece and a Book by a Master), SUOMALAINEN SUOMI, XVIII: 8 (1950), 503-4.

The Narrow Corner is "light literature" of the highest class. It is a maturer work than *The Moon and Sixpence,* characterized by a "dry freshness" typical of M. [Review of Finnish translation.] [In Finnish.]

1773 "Arts Theatre: *'Home and Beauty'* by W. Somerset Maugham," TIMES (Lond), 1 Sept 1950, p. 6.

The revival is "a deliciously clever and absurd affair." [See, also, "St. Martin's Theatre: *'Home and Beauty'* by W. Somerset Maugham," TIMES (Lond), 28 Sept 1950, p. 6.]

1774 Barrett, William. "The Prince of Entertainers," SATURDAY REVIEW OF LITERATURE, XXXIII (21 Oct 1950), 15.

THE MAUGHAM READER suggests that M deserves a new critical estimate. It shows that M is the prince of entertainers and defines "the full scope and figure of the writer." He has outlasted his contemporaries—Wells, Bennett, and Galsworthy. He is "a philosophic novelist" in the Tolstoyan sense "that, being himself deeply concerned with the meaning of life, he examines scrupulously the meaning of the lives he writes about."

1775 "Books—Briefly Noted: Fiction," NEW YORKER, XXVI (14 Oct 1950), 145-46.

THE MAUGHAM READER is "a good, fat collection." Glenway Wescott's introduction "is weakened by the unnecessarily defensive way he discusses M's place in the contemporary literary hierarchy. . . . "

1776* Breit, Harvey. "Talk with Two Writers," NEW YORK TIMES BOOK REVIEW, 19 Nov 1950, p. 39; rptd as "W. Somerset Maugham and Evelyn Waugh," in THE WRITER OBSERVED (Cleveland: World Publishing Co, 1956), pp. 147-49.

M says that even the difficulties of writing are enjoyable, but that he is writing nothing except essays, and for his own satisfaction, at this point in his life. [Interview.]

1777 Brion, Marcel. "Chroniques: Regards sur la littérature anglaise" (News: Glances at English Literature), LA REVUE DE LA MEDITERRANEE, VII: 2 (March-April 1950), 198-99.

A Writer's Notebook is a "passionate" book, the work of a moralist. [In French.]

1778* Brion, Marcel. "Littératures étrangères: Les 'Carnets' de Somerset Maugham" (Foreign Literature: The Notebooks of Somerset Maugham), LA REVUE [DES DEUX MONDES], III (15 Aug 1950), 741-49.

M is a born storyteller, like Maupassant, Kipling, and Chekhov. M's *A Writer's Notebook* helps one understand why that is so: his notes are personal, original, and works of art in themselves. [In French.]

1779 Budé, A. de. "Somerset Maugham par lui-même" (Somerset Maugham by Himself), JOURNAL DE GENEVE, 9-10 July 1950, p. 3.

In the portraits, maxims, and clinical tone of *A Writer's Notebook,* M is the British writer closest to the French classical tradition. [In French.]

1780 Dempsey, David. "In and Out of Books: Maughamania," NEW YORK TIMES BOOK REVIEW, 5 Feb 1950, p. 8.
[Brief description of an exhibit (at House of Books, 2 West 56th Street, NY) of "some three-hundred manuscripts, letters, and memorabilia" of M in honor of his seventy-sixth birthday.]

1781 Dempsey, David. "In and Out of Books: Visitor," NEW YORK TIMES BOOK REVIEW, 1 Oct 1950, p. 8.
M arrived in NY to launch THE MAUGHAM READER, attend the premiere of TRIO, and present the manuscript of *Of Human Bondage* to the Library of Congress.

1782 Engel, Eliane. "La Saison Théâtrale à Londres" (The Theatrical Season in London), JOURNAL DE GENEVE, 2 Nov 1950, p. 3.
The British revival of *Home and Beauty* did not last long. [In French.]

1783 Greenwood, Ormerod. THE PLAYWRIGHT: A STUDY OF FORM, METHOD, AND TRADITION IN THE THEATRE (Lond: Sir Isaac Pitman and Sons, 1950), pp. 3, 164-65, 169.
Passages from *Our Betters* and THE WAY OF THE WORLD demonstrate the persistence of the traditional comedy of manners; a comparison of *Our Betters* with *Home and Beauty* illustrates the farcical elements of the latter.

1784 H., H. "Theatre," CHRISTIAN SCIENCE MONITOR WEEKLY MAGAZINE SECTION, 22 April 1950, p. 5.
In Guy Bolton's dramatization of THEATRE, having to accept Julia's vagaries as "fundamentally agreeable" is like trying to turn "sauer kraut into sugar."

1785 H-ma, V. "Arvosteluja" (Reviews), ETELÄ-SUOMEN SANOMAT, 1 Oct 1950, p. 5.
The Narrow Corner opens fewer vistas than M's previous novels, though it shows the author's skill as a humorist. His analysis of human minds cannot be easily surpassed in literature. In M, enlightened Western world and deep Eastern mysticism are happily combined. [Review of Finnish translation.] [In Finnish.]

1786 Heilman, Robert B. "Comment," MODERN SHORT STORIES (NY: Harcourt, Brace, 1950), pp. 21-22.
[A brief appreciation of "The Facts of Life."]

1787 J-n, H. "Maughamin komedia Kansallisteatterissa" (Maugham's Comedy at the National Theater), UUSI SUOMI, 9 Sept 1950, p. 10.
The Circle is perhaps the most typical example of M's view of life. He analyzes the feelings which upset the normal course of life with the purest artistic pleasure and curiosity. The greatest merit of the play [in the Finnish

adaptation] lies in its sharp and skillfully composed dialogue. [In Finnish.]

1788* Jalkanen, Hugo. "Kauko-Itää Maughamin silmin" (Far East Through Maugham's Eyes), UUSI SUOMI, 8 Nov 1950, p. 9.
In *The Narrow Corner,* M is a follower of Kipling in his description of colonial life. But Kipling's optimism and conquering spirit are changed into a pessimistic and cynically resigned realization of the dissolution of the Empire and of the decline of life. The characters are truthful; M emphasizes their comic features. Because of his medical training, M is able to describe competently human life and the peculiarities of man's psyche. In this respect he shows the way to a new direction in literary art. [Review of Finnish translation.] [In Finnish.]

1789* Jonas, Klaus W. A BIBLIOGRAPHY OF THE WRITINGS OF W. SOMERSET MAUGHAM. South Hadley, Mass.: 1950.
Manuscript locations, a list of lost manuscripts, typescripts at the Library of Congress, a list of works dealing exclusively with M, a list of articles in newspapers and magazines dealing with M, a list of books containing material on the novelist, and other material are given.

1790* Jonas, Klaus W. "More Maughamiana," PAPERS OF THE BIBLIOGRAPHICAL SOCIETY OF AMERICA, XLIV (Fourth Quarter, 1950), 378-90; also published separately as a pamphlet by the Bibliographical Society of America, 1950.
[Supplements Jonas' own A BIBLIOGRAPHY OF THE WRITINGS OF W. SOMERSET MAUGHAM and Stott's MAUGHAMIANA: THE WRITINGS OF W. SOMERSET MAUGHAM (1950), announces a forthcoming M exhibit at Rutgers University, and includes a list of biographical and critical articles and of unpublished dissertations.]

1791 J[ouve], R[aymond]. "Revue des livres: Romans" (Review of Books: Novels), ETUDES, CCLXV (May 1950), 283.
[Brief review of the French translation of *Up at the Villa.*] [In French.]

1792 Keown, Eric. "At the Play," PUNCH, CCXVIII (22 Feb 1950), 217.
LARGER THAN LIFE [British title of Guy Bolton's dramatization of THEATRE] shows that "the stage is a difficult place for a demonstration of its own artificiality."

1793* Kochan, Lionel. "Somerset Maugham," CONTEMPORARY REVIEW, CLXXVII (Feb 1950), 94-98.
Of Human Bondage possesses an unmistakable "immediacy of emotion" which recurs in none of M's later works. Philip Carey is M himself, and the personal aspect has the effect of giving the novel a greater value than anything else he wrote. This is not true, however, in all the other works in which

there are "subjective incorporations of Maugham," because in them, for all his vigorous criticism of people and institutions, he offers no vision of something better and no objective notion of how to achieve "the something better." M was not denied such a vision, but evaded it, as evidenced by the static quality of his work since 1918. Despite his stylistic similarity to the Frenchman, he is *not,* in outlook, "an English Maupassant." "For all of Maupassant's pessimism, fatalism and general disillusionment one cannot escape the note of indignation and outrage that the world should be thus. One will search in vain for such a note in Maugham's work."

1794 Laitinen, Kai. "Tyynen meren äärillä" (By the Pacific), HELSINGIN SANOMAT, 24 Sept 1950, p. 13.

In the Finnish translation, *The Narrow Corner* resembles an adventure story even more than *The Moon and Sixpence* does. M is not only a refined master of style but also a humorist. [In Finnish.]

1795* Laprade, Jacques de. "Chronique littéraire: Lectures" (Literary Chronicle: Readings), ARTS [SPECTACLES, BEAUX-ARTS, LITTERATURE], 3 Feb 1950, p. 2.

The French translation of *Up at the Villa* will not contribute to M's reputation. M is a clever storyteller, and uses humor, sometimes pleasant, sometimes hackneyed. Yet, M appeals to our instincts; he tears off people's masks, though the masks are always the same: those of Victorian taboos about sex. [In French.]

1796 Lebettre, Francis. MEMENTO D'HISTOIRE DES LITTERATURES ANGLAISES ET AMERICAINES (NOTES ON THE HISTORY OF ENGLISH AND AMERICAN LITERATURE) (Paris: Librairie Classique Eugène Belin, 1950), pp. 160-61.

[Brief mention of M's plays, *The Circle, The Unknown, The Breadwinner;* and fiction, *Liza of Lambeth, Of Human Bondage, The Trembling of a Leaf, The Painted Veil, The Casuarina Tree, The Narrow Corner,* and *The Razor's Edge.*] [In French.]

1797 "Library of Congress Gets Maugham Ms," NEW YORK TIMES, 12 Oct 1950, p. 27.

On 11 Oct 1950 M presented "The Artistic Temperament of Stephen Carey," unpublished precursor of *Of Human Bondage,* to the Library of Congress.

1798 "Maugham Asserts Novelist Is Critic," NEW YORK TIMES, 18 Oct 1950, p. 35.

At a private dinner for the National Institute of Arts and Letters, to which M was elected honorary associate, he asserts there is no such thing as a "mere storyteller."

1799 "THE MAUGHAM READER," KIRKUS, XVIII (1 Aug 1950), 434.
[Brief appraisal.]

1800 Millett, Fred B. (ed) "W. Somerset Maugham," CONTEMPORARY BRITISH LITERATURE. Third and Revised Edition of the Work by John M. Manly and Edith Rickert, 1921 (NY: Harcourt, Brace & Co., 1950), pp. 355-57.
[Short biography and bibliography.]

1801 Morley, Christopher. "Gin and Quinine Tonic," NEW YORK TIMES BOOK REVIEW, 8 Oct 1950, pp. 3, 24.
THE MAUGHAM READER reveals M "has the well-bred man's horror of being anyone. . . . Nothing ever interferes with his story line. . . . He never lets us down; and, by deliberate choice, he never cares to lift us up very far."

1802* Parsons, Luke. "Somerset Maugham: An Evaluation," FORTNIGHTLY REVIEW, N. S. CLXVIII (Nov 1950), 344-45.
M's philosophy "provides an inadequate mental climate for the production of great literature." For most of his characters the determining influences are vanity, vice, above all lust, and there is no hope of redemption. But since "no one can live on a nostalgia for mud alone," M's disillusionment is tempered by "sentimentality." For all his mastery of technique and style, his power to spellbind the reader, he is, in his attitude toward and treatment of life, like Gustave Flaubert, of whom Henry James remarked that "he never puts his ear to the door of the soul."

1803 Playfellow. "The Paint and the Powder," TRUTH (Lond), CXLVII (17 Feb 1950), 165.
In LARGER THAN LIFE [British title of Guy Bolton's dramatization of THEATRE], "there being little seasoning of smart lines, the success of the piece, even taking into account its assets of situation, rests largely upon its cast."

1804 Pohjanpää, Lauri. "W. Somerset Maugham, *Ahtaat Asuinsijat*" (W. Somerset Maugham, *The Narrow Corner*), ARVOSTELEVA KIRJALUETTELO, annex to KIRJASTOLEHTI, XLIII: 8 (1950), 47.
The book [in the Finnish translation] provides a reliable description of people and circumstances; it is a sound routine work but not much else. [In Finnish.]

1805 R:suo, A. "Romaani Kauko-Idästä" (A Novel from the Far East), MAASEUDUN TULEVAISUUS, 23 Sept 1950, p. 7.
The Narrow Corner [in the Finnish translation] is a serious novel, though not one of M's best, ending on a pessimistic note. Its most attractive feature is the author's tolerant and broad-minded attitude towards people. [In Finnish.]

1806 S[imiot?], B[ernard?]. *"Il Suffit d'Une Nuit"* (*Up at the Villa*), HOMMES ET MONDES, XI (March 1950), viii.
[Sentence appraisal and approval of the French translation of *Up at the Villa.*] [In French.]

1807 Smith, Harrison. "The Literary Scene: 1919," THEATRE ARTS, XXXIV (Sept 1950), 33-35.
[Brief comment on M.]

1808 "St. Martin's Theatre: *'Home and Beauty'* by W. Somerset Maugham," TIMES (Lond), 28 Sept 1950, p. 6.
The revival has been moved from the Arts Theatre [see "Arts Theatre: *'Home and Beauty'* by W. Somerset Maugham," TIMES (Lond), 1 Sept 1950, p. 6] to the St. Martin's Theatre, and the "period farce" has much "timeless fun in it" and "its neatness is a constant pleasure."

1809* Stott, Raymond Toole (ed). MAUGHAMIANA: THE WRITINGS OF W. SOMERSET MAUGHAM. (Lond: Heinemann, 1950).
Writings about M, including about fifty items for the 1940s, are listed.

1810 T., O. "A New Maugham Collection," SAN FRANCISCO SUNDAY CHRONICLE ("This World"), 22 Oct 1950, p. 21.
THE MAUGHAM READER shows M at his best and at his worst.

1811 T-la, E. "Maughamin *'Ympyra'* Kansallisen ensimmäisenä ensi-iltana" (Maugham's *'The Circle,'* the Season's First Night at the National Theater), SUOMEN SOSIALIDEMOKRAATTI, 9 Sept 1950, p. 6.
The beginning [of the Finnish adaptation] is slow, but the play wakes into life when Lady Kitty enters. The dialogue is skilful, and the development of the situations clever. [In Finnish.]

1812 Thibault, Henri. "Les Romans étrangers" (Foreign Novels), PARU, No. 62 (July 1950), 43.
In [the French translation of] *Up at the Villa,* M's simplicity verges on banality. [In French.]

1813 Tompan Tuomo [Pseudonym]. *"Ahtaat Asuinsijat" (The Narrow Corner),* ETELÄ-SAIMAA, 10 Oct 1950, p. 4.
An adventure story becomes a book of aphorisms. [Review of Finnish translation.] [In Finnish.]

1814 Trewin, J. C. "The World of the Theatre," ILLUSTRATED LONDON NEWS, CCXVI (25 Feb 1950), 296.
In Guy Bolton's dramatization of THEATRE under the British title of LARGER THAN LIFE, "the plot counts for little, but Julia means a lot."

1815 "An Unpublished Maugham Novel: MS. for Library of Congress," TIMES (Lond), 12 Oct 1950, p. 3.
On 11 Oct 1950 M presented to the Library of Congress the manuscript of "The Artistic Temperament of Stephen Carey," an unpublished early novel which included much of the material later used in *Of Human Bondage.* M gave the manuscript on condition that it should never be published.

1816* Vallette, Jacques. "Livres" (Books), LE MERCURE DE FRANCE, CCCVIII (1 Jan 1950), 165.
In *A Writer's Notebook,* M follows Jules Renard's method without Renard's "bile"; M is candid, honest, a spiritual man without illusions. [In French.]

1817 Vallette, Jacques. "Livres" (Books), LE MERCURE DE FRANCE, CCCVIII (1 March 1950), 531.
Of the French translation of *Up at the Villa:* "L'etiquette d'un Quart de Chaume sur une bouteille de muscadet." [In French.]

1818 Vines, Sherard. 100 YEARS OF ENGLISH LITERATURE (Lond: Gerald Duckworth, 1950), pp. 127, 141, 248, 256.
[Passing mention of M in connection with books of travel, the drama, and the novel and short story.]

1951

1819 "A la devanture du libraire" (In the Front Window of the Bookshop), LE FIGARO LITTERAIRE, 24 Nov 1951, p. 8.
The French translation of *Theatre* as LA COMEDIENNE reveals an impressive psychological portrait of Julia. [In French.]

1820 "Arts Theatre: *'Mrs. Dot'* by W. Somerset Maugham," TIMES (Lond), 29 Sept 1951, p. 2.
Judged by M's later standards, the revived piece is "uncommonly tranquil," though some scenes "have the beauty of a classic comic conception."

1821 B., D. B. "Three Maugham Stories Combined," SPRINGFIELD SUNDAY REPUBLICAN (Mass), 14 Jan 1951, p. 19.
In TRIO, "all three stories ["The Verger," "Mr. Know-All," and "Sanatorium"] bear the true Maugham stamp of wit, sophistication and artistry."

1822* Brown, John Mason. "The Comedy that Came Back," SATURDAY REVIEW OF LITERATURE, XXXIV (29 Dec 1951), 18-19.
In the revival of *The Constant Wife,* the world of the play appears, twenty-

five years after its first performance, outmoded: its characters are ladies and gentlemen who prefer avoiding scenes to make them. Yet the play, with its plea for a single morality, is still daring, and the sophistication of the comedy is admirably put across in this first-rate production.

1823 Edman, Irwin. "The Philosopher as Man of Letters," PROCEEDINGS OF THE AMERICAN ACADEMY OF ARTS AND LETTERS AND THE NATIONAL INSTITUTE OF ARTS AND LETTERS. Second Series, No. 1 (NY, 1951), pp. 59-62; rptd in THE MAUGHAM ENIGMA, ed by Klaus W. Jonas (NY: Citadel P, 1954), pp. 50-53.
M's stories are "exercises in humane wisdom, or philosophy at its best." [An address at the dinner of the National Institute of Arts and Letters at the Knickerbocker Club on Tuesday, 17 Oct 1950 before M's address on the occasion of his being made an Honorary Associate of the Institute.]

1824 Freedley, George. "The Theatre," LIBRARY JOURNAL, LXXVI (15 Feb 1951), 330.
TRIO is useful to those interested in the transformation of a short story into a film script.

1825 Gibbs, Wolcott. "The Theatre: Out of the Mothballs," NEW YORKER, XXVII (15 Dec 1951), 72.
In the revival of *The Constant Wife,* M's "pro-woman" conception is "dated, tiresome, and perhaps a little unrealistic."

1826 Green, Julien. JOURNAL, 1946-1950 (Paris: Librairie Plon, 1951), pp. 318, 319-20.
The Summing Up is enchanting in its honesty and good sense. [In French.]

1827 Hudson, Lynton. THE ENGLISH STAGE: 1850-1950 (Lond: George C. Harrap, 1951), pp. 125-27.
[A review of the familiar facts of M's beginnings in the theater.]

1828 Humeau, Edmond. "Courrier des Lettres: Une mort comme une autre" (Courier of Letters: One Death like Another), ARTS [SPECTACLES, BEAUX-ARTS, LITTERATURE], 6 July 1951, p. 2.
[Reflections on the death of Peter Cheney lead Humeau to compare the writer with M, who belongs "to the field of life-insurance."] [In French.]

1829 Kerr, Walter. "The Stage," COMMONWEAL, LV (28 Dec 1951), 299-300.
The revived *The Constant Wife* "survives the loss of its immediate setting in time, and emerges today as a sustained and frequently funny artifice."

1830 "Mere Storytellers," TIMES (Lond), 25 Oct 1951, p. 7.
[Editorial on M's address, "The Writer's Point of View," delivered to the National Book League on 24 Oct 1951, in essential agreement with (and

recapitulating) M's views. (See, also, "Writer's Point of View: Mr. Somerset Maugham on Purpose of Writing," TIMES [Lond], 25 Oct 1951, p. 2; and Cecil Roberts, "The Storyteller's Art," TIMES [Lond], 27 Oct 1951, p. 7.)]

1831* Mustanoja, Tauno F. "W. Somerset Maugham Portrays Henry James," NEUPHILOLOGISCHE MITTEILUNGEN (Helsinki), LII (April 1951), 99-103.

The opening scene of *The Razor's Edge* read against the background of M's essay on Henry James in *Tellers of Tales* reveals that M dramatized James in the character of Elliott Templeton.

1832 "New Boltons Theatre: *'Loaves and Fishes'* by W. Somerset Maugham," TIMES (Lond), 28 March 1951, p. 6.

"It [the revival] seems today merely a cruel and rather laboured farce, though in 1911 the author entitled it a satire. . . . Flashes of the famous caustic wit . . . light the stage from time to time, but the primary joke is always the same joke, and not a good one at that."

1833 Oppel, Horst. "Zwischen Chaos und Erlösung" (Between Chaos and Deliverance), DIE LEBENDEN FREMDSPRACHEN, III (1951), 100-12, especially 103, 104.

In *The Razor's Edge,* M, the consistent empiricist and realist, comes to discuss, almost against his will, metaphysical solutions to the spiritual malaise of our time. [In German.]

1834 Roberts, Cecil. "The Storyteller's Art," TIMES (Lond), 27 Oct 1951, p. 7.

[Letter to the editor in answer to M's address, "The Writer's Point of View," delivered to the National Book League on 24 Oct 1951, agreeing with M, but adding "suspense" as the abiding quality of all good storytelling from Homer onwards. (See, also, "Writer's Point of View: Mr. Somerset Maugham on Purpose of Writing," TIMES [Lond], 25 Oct 1951, p. 2, and "Mere Storytellers," TIMES [Lond.], 25 Oct 1951, p. 7.)]

1835 Ronimus, O-M. "Kirjojen joulu" (Books for Christmas), YLIOPPILASLEHTI, 18 Dec 1951, p. 7.

The Finnish translation of *Theatre* reveals a sweet Christmas story, inoffensive and trivial. [In Finnish.]

1836* Spence, Robert. "Maugham's *'Of Human Bondage'*: The Making of a Masterpiece," LIBRARY CHRONICLE (University of Pennsylvania), XVII (Spring-Summer 1951), 104-14.

Of Human Bondage, acclaimed a classic by 1925, was greeted indifferently in England and America in 1915. Its deserved rise in stature during the decade after its publication is due to the interest aroused by *The Moon and Sixpence* (1919) and the sustained interest of several influential critics.

1837 T-la, E. "Intiimi teatterimaailman kuvaus" (Intimate Description of Theatrical World), SUOMEN SOSIALIDEMOKRAATTII, 12 Dec 1951, p. 7.

In the Finnish translation, *Theatre* is amusing, flavored with irony, and contains an expert analysis of an actress's psyche. [In Finnish.]

1838 "Theater," NEWSWEEK, XXXVIII (17 Dec 1951), 69.

The revival of *The Constant Wife,* "as a modern-age vehicle . . . has limited driving power, but . . . supports more wit and perception than a carload of Broadway's recent tries at comedy."

1839 "The Theater: Old Play in Manhattan," TIME, LVIII (17 Dec 1951), 76.

The revived *The Constant Wife* "still seems very pleasant after 25 years" and M "is Britain's last playwright with Restoration blood in his veins."

1840 "Toto" [Pseudonym]. "Pikkulämmintä" (Hors d'Oeuvres), HELSINGIN SANOMAT, 31 March 1951, p. 8.

In *The Summing Up,* M holds the reader at a distance and tells him only what he thinks is essential. But, one gets a clear impression of the author—a cool and disillusioned observer of himself and of human life. [In Finnish.]

1841* Trewin, J. C. THE THEATRE SINCE 1900. Illustrated from the Raymond Mander and Joe Mitchenson Theatre Collection (Lond: Andrew Dakers, 1951), pp. viii, ix, 28, 31, 77, 95, 132, 142, 153, especially 154-57, 216, 269, 284, 313.

Our Betters and *The Circle* are "two classic plays, fit to stand by Congreve's patterned flourish like frost flowers in glass."

1842 V-jä, O. "Tekiko viisas aviovaimo oikein?" (Did the Constant Wife Do Right?), AAMULEHTI, 16 March 1951, p. 4.

In [the revival of the Finnish adaptation of] *The Constant Wife,* the problem of adultery is not treated on an ethical level; M is satisfied with illustrating it in broad generalizations. He is witty at the expense of his audience and lashes the weaknesses of the older and younger generations with refined and intelligent irony. The dialogue is amusing, and the characterization to the point. [In Finnish.]

1843* Van Patten, Nathan. "Icelandic Translations of Maugham," PAPERS OF THE BIBLIOGRAPHICAL SOCIETY OF AMERICA, XLV (Second Quarter 1951), 158-59.

[A list of eight Icelandic translations of books by M and one contribution to an anthology, supplementing Klaus W. Jonas' "More Maughamiana,"

PAPERS OF THE BIBLIOGRAPHICAL SOCIETY OF AMERICA, XLIV (Fourth Quarter 1950), 378-90.]

1844 Whicher, George F. "Reprints, New Editions," NEW YORK HERALD TRIBUNE BOOK REVIEW, 4 March 1951, p. 20.

TRIO, with its "smartly tailored stories" ["The Verger," "Mr. Know-All," and "Sanatorium"] and their movie scripts by R. C. Sherriff and Noël Langley, is commendable.

1845 "Writer's Point of View: Mr. Somerset Maugham on Purpose of Writing," TIMES (Lond), 25 Oct 1951, p. 2.

M delivered the ninth annual lecture to the National Book League on the evening of 24 Oct 1951. "The Writer's Point of View," the title of his address, emphasized that the writer's job is to entertain, but a work must interest as well as amuse if it is to be entertaining. [See, also, "Mere Story-tellers," TIMES (Lond), 25 Oct 1951, p. 7, and Cecil Roberts, "The Story-teller's Art," TIMES (Lond), 27 Oct 1951, p. 7.]

1846 "Wyndham's Theatre: *'Home and Beauty'* by W. Somerset Maugham," TIMES (Lond), 2 Jan 1951, p. 7.

"Few things . . . could add more savour to a peacetime dinner than the prospect of Mr. Maugham's sparkling wit, vintage 1919, at the end of it." The third act of the revival, "boisterously satirical," is built up to with momentum.

1952

1847* Anhava, Tuomas. "Platoninen idea" (Platonic Idea), SUOMALAINEN SUOMI, XX: 3 (1952), 174-76.

Theatre stands and falls with Julia. Her life is triumphant, but the story, her frame, is not particularly memorable. M's only purpose seems to have been to tell an amusing story in the French style. The types to be found in the theatrical world are observed with an unerring eye; there are also sharp comments on the psychology of acting. [Review of Finnish translation.] [In Finnish.]

1848 Arland, Marcel, et al. "Les Traductions" (Translations), ALMANACH DES LETTRES, 1953 (ALMANAC OF LETTERS, 1953) (Paris: Pierre Horay, Flore, et la Gazette des Lettres, 1952), p. 124.

[Brief mention of the French translation of *Creatures of Circumstance.*] [In French.]

1849 Atkinson, [J.] Brooks. "First Night at the Theatre," NEW YORK TIMES, 2 Feb 1952, p. 10.
The first act of S. N. Behrman's dramatization, JANE, is brilliant; later, the workmanship becomes labored and verbose; but the whole play is written with grace, wit, taste, and intelligence.

1850 Bélanger, Jean. "Comptes Rendus" (Critical Reports), ETUDES ANGLAISES, V (May 1952), 179.
A Writer's Notebook enables the sensitive reader to collaborate with the novelist to a greater extent than usual. [In French.]

1851 Beyer, William H. "The State of the Theatre: The Season Climaxes," SCHOOL AND SOCIETY, LXXV (24 May 1952), 325-26.
[General praise of S. N. Behrman's dramatization JANE, and the revival of *The Constant Wife*.]

1852 Brooks, Cleanth, John Thibaut Purser and Robert Penn Warren. "Discussion," AN APPROACH TO LITERATURE. Third Edition (NY: Appleton-Century Crofts, 1952 [1936]), pp. 690-93.
[An analysis of the comic elements in *The Circle*.]

1853* Brophy, John. SOMERSET MAUGHAM. (Lond, NY, Toronto: Longmans, Green, for The British Council and the National Book League, 1952).
M cannot be classified either by the literary forms he uses or by the kind of reader he engages, because he undertook and was successful in every genre except poetry, and both "highbrows and lowbrows" read his work. M is better identified by his willingness to give the public what it wants, by his professionalism, by his clinical attitude of detached observation.

1854 Budé, A. de. "Kipling vu par Somerset Maugham" (Kipling Viewed by Somerset Maugham), JOURNAL DE GENEVE, 7-8 Dec 1952, pp. 3-4.
Kipling and M's personalities are totally different, and M's preface to *A Choice of Kipling's Prose* lacks enough biographical facts and precision of insight into Kipling's work. [In French.]

1855 Bunting, John J., Jr. "W. Somerset Maugham and the Christian Preacher," RELIGION IN LIFE, XXI (Summer 1952), 401-10.
Christian ministers should read the works of M for their fine style, their insights, and their reflection of the views of "millions of people."

1856 *"Carnet d'un Ecrivain" (A Writer's Notebook)*, DICTIONNAIRE DES OEUVRES DE TOUS LES TEMPS ET DE TOUS PAYS (DICTIONARY OF THE WORKS OF ALL TIMES AND ALL NATIONS). Four Volumes (Paris: S. E. D. E. and V. Bompiani, 1952), vol. I, 330.

In *A Writer's Notebook,* M permits us to see him as vividly as we might see one of his characters in his novels. [In French.]

1857 Charon, Jacques. "Impressions d'Amérique: Panorama new-yorkais" (Impressions of America: New York Panorama), ARTS/SPECTACLES, 22-28 May 1952, p. 4.

The revival of *The Constant Wife* is more ambitious than the melodramatic, cheap I AM A CAMERA or THE MOON IS BLUE. [In French.]

1858 Clurman, Harold. "The Excellent Mediocre," NEW REPUBLIC, CXXVI (7 Jan 1952), 22.

A "tidbit," *The Constant Wife* is "better than tolerable," but the revival strikes a viewer of the fifties as "old-fashioned."

1859 *"The Complete Short Stories,"* KIRKUS, XX (1 Sept 1952), 573.

[Brief appraisal.]

1860 Crowther, Bosley. " 'Old Party' on the Screen," NEW YORK TIMES BOOK REVIEW, 6 July 1952, p. 10.

Most striking in the demonstration of three of M's stories ["The Ant and the Grasshopper," "Winter Cruise," and "Gigolo and Gigolette"] being cinematized as ENCORE "is how the stories have been enlarged, intensified, and even altered for the screen without denaturing Maugham's familiar attitude and style."

1861 Dempsey, David. "New Editions: A Christmas List," NEW YORK TIMES BOOK REVIEW, 7 Dec 1952, p. 42.

The republished *The Complete Stories of W. Somerset Maugham* shows that the type of short story written by M is based on the power of the anecdote.

1862 d'Houville, Gérard. "Lectures romanesques" (Readings in the Novel), LA REVUE [DES DEUX MONDES], V (15 June 1952), 803.

[The French translation of] *Creatures of Circumstance* contains stories persuading one of the author's "powerful gift." [In French.]

1863* Dobrée, Bonamy. "Books of the Week: Kipling Mishandled," SPECTATOR (Lond), CLXXXIX (26 Sept 1952), 401-2.

In *A Choice of Kipling's Prose,* M's selection, good as it is within its limits, "restricts and confines Kipling's performance, and his introductory essay tends to help the process." M did not understand Kipling's "comic stories," so he excluded them, as well as most of Kipling's later works, leaving out "a whole aspect" of Kipling: his "religious apprehension." M's "selection serves as a casual introduction," but "it is not representative by a long chalk."

1864 Eaton, Walter Prichard. "From the Broadway Season," New York Herald Tribune Book Review, 11 May 1952, p. 29.
A dramatized "profile" of M himself, though "witty" and "penetrating," makes S. N. Behrman's dramatization, Jane, "somewhat unbalanced." The story is neither very "plausible" nor very "original," but it is told with masterful high polish.

1865 "Encore," Kirkus, XX (15 April 1952), 267.
[Brief appraisal.]

1866 *"Le Fil du Rasoir"* (*The Razor's Edge*), Dictionnaire des Oeuvres de tous les Temps et de tous les Pays (Dictionary of Works of all Times and all Nations). Four Volumes (Paris: S. E. D. E. and V. Bompiani, 1952), vol. II, 369.
In *The Razor's Edge,* M intended to write a "roman d'apprentissage" of a young modern intellectual. [In French.]

1867 Findlater, Richard. The Unholy Trade (Lond: Victor Gollancz, 1952), pp. 98, 110-12, 115, 126.
A citation to M's *The Summing Up* to distinguish between the dramatist and the playwright as the poet and the journalist of the theater.

1868 Freedley, George. "The Theatre," Library Journal, LXXVII (July 1952), 1208.
S. N. Behrman's dramatization, Jane, is "suitable for community theatres."

1869 Freedley, George. "The Theatre," Library Journal, LXXVII (15 Oct 1952), 1814.
Encore is "recommended for all cinema and theatre collections."

1870 Gibbs, Wolcott. "The Theater: Anesthesia and Euthanasia," New Yorker, XXVIII (18 Oct 1952), 82.
The effect of the revival of *The Sacred Flame* is "rather more soporific than alarming." M's plotting is conventional, his language peppered with "high-class British clichés."

1871 Hawkins, William. "Theater: 'Jane' a Hilarious Cinderella Tale," New York World-Telegram and Sun, 2 Feb 1952, p. 7.
S. N. Behrman's dramatization is "leisurely, pleasantly contrived, and often studded with the most agreeable sort of laugh-provoking lines."

1872 Hewes, Henry. "Broadway Postscript," Saturday Review (NY), XXXV (25 Oct 1952), 28-29.

The revival of *The Sacred Flame* is a first-rate production of a second-rate play.

1873 "High Comedy," NEW YORK HERALD TRIBUNE BOOK REVIEW, 9 Nov 1952, p. 14.

The Constant Wife, "one of Maugham's better plays, in the hallowed tradition of English high comedy," its stiffness owing to "the times, not the author," should be reissued.

1874* Hobson, Harold. VERDICT AT MIDNIGHT: SIXTY YEARS OF DRAMATIC CRITICISM (Lond, NY, & Toronto: Longmans, Green, 1952), pp. 121-23, 125.

[Review of the contemporary reception and criticism of *The Circle.*]

1875 Hogan, William. "A Selection of the New Books," SAN FRANCISCO SUNDAY CHRONICLE ("This World"), 22 June 1952, p. 19.

S. N. Behrman's dramatization, JANE, is "a bright drawing-room comedy."

1876 "Honorary Degrees at Oxford: Encaenia Addresses," TIMES (Lond), 26 June 1952, p. 10.

M received an honorary D. C. L. from Oxford University on 25 June 1952.

1877* Hughes, Riley. "New Novels," CATHOLIC WORLD, CLXXV (Sept 1952), 474.

In ENCORE [three stories and their screenplays: "The Ant and the Grasshopper," "Winter Cruise," and "Gigolo and Gigolette"], "The stories are not among Maugham's best; interestingly enough the screenplay, in every instance, is more subtle and convincing in characterization than the original story."

1878 J., L. "Nainen —näyttelijätär" (Woman—Actress), TURUN YLIOPPILASLEHTI, I (1952), 17.

In [the Finnish translation of] *Theatre,* the characterization is flavored by sharp irony, but it shows, at the same time, understanding of human weaknesses. M's narrative technique is masterly, and his knowledge of the theatrical world and its types is excellent. [In Finnish.]

1879 Kerr, Walter. "The Theaters," NEW YORK HERALD TRIBUNE, 2 Feb 1952, p. 6.

S. N. Behrman's dramatization, JANE, has "epigrammatic wit, sly style, and genial urbanity," but the second act is disastrous after a thin first; some ground is recovered in the third.

1880* Kronenberger, Louis. "Maugham," THE THREAD OF LAUGHTER: CHAPTERS ON ENGLISH STAGE COMEDY FROM JONSON TO MAUGHAM (NY: Alfred A. Knopf, 1952), pp. 289-98.

M brings his audience back to "the truest kind of comedy of manners—the Restoration kind." He has not only Restoration "talent" but Restoration "temperament": that is, he sees life dispassionately, records what he sees, "expurgating nothing, extenuating nothing." [*Our Betters* and *The Circle* are examined in light of the foregoing statements.]

1881 Kula, Kauko. "W. Somerset Maugham, *Catalina*," ARVOSTELEVA KIRJALUETTELO, annex to KIRJASTOLEHTI, XLVII: 5 (1952), 36.
The novel is composed in a rather superficial way. M is very serious, but the novel is not as refined as his best ones. [Review of Finnish translation.] [In Finnish.]

1882 Laitinen, Kai. "Englantilaisia kertojia" (English Narrators), HELSINGIN SANOMAT, 7 June 1952, p. 4.
M excellently describes Julia's course of hesitating development. On the last pages of [the Finnish translation of] *Theatre,* he confesses his love of the theater, which he has all the time picked at. [In Finnish.]

1883 Lalou, René. "Le Monde des Livres≠Récits≠*Rencontres et Hasards*" (The World of Books: Reviews: *Creatures of Circumstance*), LES NOUVELLES LITTERAIRES, 5 June 1952, p. 3.
The theme common to all the stories [in the French translation] of this collection is that the human biped is a curious animal. [In French.]

1884 Lardner, John. "The Theatre: One Girl Overboard, One Survivor," NEW YORKER, XXVII (9 Feb 1952), 56-57.
In S. N. Behrman's dramatization, JANE, under a strong lens, one "will find the silken flow of the writing pieced out here and there with ribbons of dental floss."

1885 Lauras, A. "Revue des livres: romans" (Book Reviews: Novels), ETUDES, CCLXXV (Nov 1952), 285.
[Brief review of the French translation of *Creatures of Circumstance.*] [In French.]

1886 Marshall, Margaret. "Drama," NATION (NY), CLXXV (18 Oct 1952), 365.
The revival of *The Sacred Flame* shows M as "a skillful writer and a competent maker of plays."

1887* Morgan, Charles. "Books for Christmas: Maugham's Essays," SPECTATOR (Lond), CLXXXIX (21 Nov 1952), 686.
The essays in *The Vagrant Mood* are held together by "the strength and interest of the writer's individuality." Several essays show a split between

the mystic and the materialist; M can be either. This split "creates the tension which is Maugham and we must be grateful for it."

1888* Papajewski, Helmut. DIE WELT-, LEBENS- UND KUNSTANSCHAUUNG WILLIAM SOMERSET MAUGHAMS (THE WORLD-, LIFE-, AND ARTISTIC VISION OF WILLIAM SOMERSET MAUGHAM). (Cologne: Universitäts-Verlag, 1952).

Although M does not burden his stories with philosophical learning and commentaries and sets forth the ideas of his characters objectively, it seems possible to describe the assumptions underlying his fiction and manifesting themselves in *The Summing Up* and in his travel books. A sensitive youth, M became interested in philosophy early. The existence of misery and suffering seemed to him irreconcilable with the idea of an omnipotent and benevolent God. The loss of belief is an experience shared by several of his characters who do not possess the religious temperament. M himself tried in vain to base religious beliefs on reason, studied Eastern religions, but remained an agnostic. He denied absolute values but continued to read the German philosophers as well as Bradley, Spinoza, and others. Like Philip in *Of Human Bondage,* however, M came to embrace skepticism with a feeling of relief. Doubting the freedom of will, he suspected conscience as the guardian of the arbitrary rules evolved by society for its own preservation, and sometimes portrayed characters free from the sense of sin, although he himself had to admit that he could not get rid of his own sensitive conscience. He defended himself against the charge of cynicism by pointing out the relativity of good and evil as well as the lack of consistency in man. Consequently, his fiction dwells at length on the contradictions of human nature and occasionally discovers goodness among the wicked. Though a student of Schopenhauer, M did not believe in the ennobling qualities of suffering. On the whole, he accepted life as a meaningless, but interesting pattern. He adopted the detached attitude of the spectator. Life was for him not very different from art — a beautiful pattern. Since his art thus evades life's tragedies, it sometimes seems flat and limited in spite of the fact that it offers a varied spectacle of life.

The patterns treated fairly often by M are the relations between the sexes, social and psychological problems, the relations between youth and age, and life in exotic countries. [These patterns are discussed in detail with reference to recurring motifs and character types in M's writings.] The experience of the Far East led M to the complete acceptance of life he had longed for. In addition, it strengthened his conviction that art is not the only important value in life.

Desiring to live life completely, M feared that the artist would miss life. Nevertheless, he respected the fanatical devotion to his work shown by many a great artist. He considered the process of creation to be an instinctive one, compared its exultation to the experience of the mystic, and termed it a release from the burden of life. He denied the existence of absolute beauty and saw the value of art in its effect of teaching right actions. [His views on the drama and the novel are discussed at length.] [In German.]

1889 "Recent Books: Mr. Maugham's Kipling." TIMES (Lond), 17 Sept 1952, p. 8.
"The true Kiplingite will thank Mr. Maugham for having started many arguments." [Review of *A Choice of Kipling's Prose.*]

1890* "Recent Books: Variable Moods," TIMES (Lond), 29 Oct 1952, p. 8.
M is a man of variable moods, but behind them one of two figures is always discernible: either the disillusioned moralist of Grant Sutherland's late portrait, or the "top-hatted exquisite of Sir Gerald Kelly's early painting." The latter has written the six essays of *The Vagrant Mood.*

1891 Repo, E. S. "Pihvin voitto" (Beefsteak Wins), PARNASSO, II: 2 (1952), 176-77.
The Finnish translation of *Theatre* is good pastime reading, if the novel is no work of art. M's writing is characterized by competent descriptions of amusing situations and extraordinary people, but it lacks the significance and necessity essential to a work of art. M's narrative style makes the novel worth reading; it is lively, ironic, and shamelessly light-hearted. [In Finnish.]

1892 Shrapnel, Norman. "Kipling's Prose," MANCHESTER GUARDIAN, 22 Sept 1952, p. 5.
[Review of *A Choice of Kipling's Prose*, agreeing with M's introductory essay to the volume.]

1893 S[hrapnel], N[orman]. "Mr. Maugham," MANCHESTER GUARDIAN, 28 Nov 1952, p. 9.
In *The Vagrant Mood,* M's remarks on the style of Burke, on Kant's approach to aesthetics, on the achievements of Zurbarán, are less memorable than his own memories of James, Bennett, and Wells.

1894 Squire, Sir John. "Somerset Maugham as Essayist," ILLUSTRATED LONDON NEWS, CCXXI (15 Nov 1952), 802.
In *The Vagrant Mood,* the chapter, "Some Novelists I Have Known," is "flimsy"; but the five other essays are good.

1895* "Tales from Kipling," TIMES LITERARY SUPPLEMENT (Lond), 10 Oct 1952, p. 660.
Unfortunately, in *A Choice of Kipling's Prose,* M offers neither his personal

favorites, nor, alternatively, a sequence illustrating Kipling's development as a writer. Kipling seems to impress M more by his force as a writer than by his personality or what he has to say. Consequently, in his introductory essay, M has not profited to the fullest from the limited biographical sources, and has indeed misgauged and distorted much of his subject's life and values.

1896 "Theater," NEWSWEEK, XXXIX (11 Feb 1952), 82.
S. N. Behrman's dramatization, JANE, is "a superior conversation piece," although it misses being first-rate drawing-room comedy in the best of Behrman's manner.

1897 "The Theater," TIME, LIX (11 Feb 1952), 79.
S. N. Behrman's dramatization, JANE, is "urbane but upsy-downsy drawing room comedy," its three acts suggesting "three sets of tennis."

1898 "The Theater: Old Play in Manhattan," TIME, LX (20 Oct 1952), 56.
The Sacred Flame "is something Maugham ought never to have written." It "is a sort of drawing room problem whodunit, concocted of about equal parts of Wilde, Pinero and Agatha Christie, doused with platitudes, and served up half-cold." [Review of revival.]

1899 Trewin, J. C. A PLAY TO-NIGHT (Lond: Elek Books, 1952), pp. 20-21.
Not content with M's "open ending" to the short story, Rodney Ackland, in his dramatization of BEFORE THE PARTY, carries the story on, only to provide another "open ending." No one "is likely to write for us the next instalment."

1900 "Tribute to Somerset Maugham: An Evening at St. Pancras," TIMES (Lond), 13 March 1952, p. 6.
On 12 March 1952 at St. Pancras Town Hall, "Before the Party" was given a reading, and an act of *Caroline* was performed as a tribute to M.

1901 V-jä, O. "Rakkautta komedian valossa" (Love in Comedy Form), AAMULEHTI, 18 April 1952, p. 5.
M masters dramatic technique and the art of writing dialogue, but *The Circle* is neither profound nor trivial. It contains intelligent, elegant, and cautious satire. [Review of the revived Finnish adaptation, in Finnish.]

1902 Wyatt, Euphemia Van Rensselaer. "Theater," CATHOLIC WORLD, CLXXIV (Feb 1952), 392.
In the revival of *The Constant Wife,* "Mr. Maugham's characters are wittily alive and their reactions, in spite of the wit, are thoroughly human."

1953

1903 Alpert, Hollis. "Dean of the Smoothies," SATURDAY REVIEW (NY), XXXVI (25 April 1953), 21.
A sign of the vitality of M's *The Vagrant Mood* is that M and his work can still excite controversy.

1904 "Arts Theatre: *'The Breadwinner'* by W. Somerset Maugham," TIMES (Lond), 29 Jan 1953, p.5.
"The piece revives extremely well," but M has laid a trap for his critics, for whether or not they agree with M's thesis, they are bound to offend one part or another of the nation.

1905 "Arts Theatre: *'Penelope'* by W. Somerset Maugham," TIMES (Lond), 11 Sept 1953, p. 2.
The modern audience admires the "boldness" of the revived play less than its "neatness."

1906 B., D. B. "Half Dozen Essays by Master Writer," SPRINGFIELD SUNDAY REPUBLICAN (Mass), 3 May 1953, p. 10C.
In *The Vagrant Mood,* M's approach is "oblique"; his essays are "no less compelling than his stories." M respects quality and his work is "eminently readable."

1907 B., D. B. *"Maugham's Choice of Kipling's Best,"* SPRINGFIELD SUNDAY REPUBLICAN (Mass), 27 Sept 1953, p. 6C.
[Review, explaining and upholding M's opinions about Kipling.]

1908 "Books — Briefly Noted: General," NEW YORKER, XXIX (11 April 1953), 138.
The Vagrant Mood provides "on the whole, an enjoyable, if hardly a memorable, evening."

1909 "Books: Kipling Revisited," TIME, LXII (7 Sept 1953), 110, 112.
In *Maugham's Choice of Kipling's Best,* M considers Kipling England's greatest short story writer; "Maugham's selection of 16 tales is made chiefly from Kipling's early works, which Maugham thought were his best."

1910 "Books: Table Talk at 79," TIME, LXI (6 April 1953), 117-18, 120.
In *The Vagrant Mood,* the "Old Party's" writing hand has lost none of its cunning. The essay on Augustus Hare is particularly interesting.

1911 Bourget-Pailleron, Robert. "Revue dramatique" (Drama Review), LA REVUE [DES DEUX MONDES], VI (15 March 1953), 356-57.

The story, "Jane," provides better motivation than S. N. Behrman's JANE. [Review of the French adaptation, in French.]

1912 Brown, Allen B. "W. Somerset Maugham as a Novelist." Unpublished thesis. State University of Iowa, 1953.

M's worth as a novelist is determined by comparing five of his best known novels (*Liza of Lambeth, Of Human Bondage, The Moon and Sixpence, Cakes and Ale,* and *The Razor's Edge*) with eight other novels written about the same times (TESS OF THE D'URBERVILLES, MAGGIE, THE WAY OF ALL FLESH, FORTITUDE, POINT COUNTER POINT, THE CONSTANT NYMPH, PASSAGE TO INDIA, and MAGNIFICENT OBSESSION). M emerges a most able craftsman, with small range in theme, characterization and situation; a realist who desires religion and romance; a writer of the second rank.

1913 C[amp], A[ndré]. "Une semaine dans un fauteuil" (A Week in an Armchair), ARTS/SPECTACLES, 13-19 March 1953, p. 3.

The French adaptation of JANE as DOROTHEE has a slow start and a too lengthy third act. [In French.]

1914 Carrington, C. E. "Out of the Barracks and Bazaars," NEW YORK TIMES BOOK REVIEW, 30 Aug 1953, pp. 1, 20.

In *Maugham's Choice of Kipling's Best,* M's selection of Kipling's prose and his introductory essay will probably be disputed by many Kipling lovers. M's selection — with one exception — is taken from the work done before Kipling's thirty-seventh year; M felt that Kipling's "best stories are those of which the scene is laid in India. . . ."

1915* Cosman, Max. "A Pattern of Doubt," ARIZONA QUARTERLY, IX (Autumn 1953), 246-57.

Whether one studies M's drama, short stories, or novels, he discovers that his characteristic expression is one of "doubt." M's doubt has made him "hollow to himself," and its cause can be found in his biography: in his "physical inheritance . . . his brittle youth . . . his formative manhood." M's parents were both diseased, and his boyhood was threatened by "consumptive leanings," and in manhood he was sent to a sanatorium. The threat of disease produced anxiety and uncertainty, and M's stifling life after his parents' death increased his unsureness. Thus, M came to doubt where others believed.

1916 Dinkins, Paul. "Other New Books," CATHOLIC WORLD, CLXXVIII (Nov 1953), 157.

"We read the essays in this collection [*The Vagrant Mood*] — realizing that the clichés about Maugham have become clichés because of their truth. He *is* highly intelligent, a skilled technician, even a master, of writing insofar as writing is just an art. . . . The product is wonderfully dependable; it rarely disappoints, and almost never surprises."

1917* Farmer, A. J. "Comptes Rendus" (Critical Reports), ETUDES ANGLAISES, VI (Aug 1953), 268.
In *The Vagrant Mood,* at eighty, M is starting a brilliant essayist's career. [The reviewer gives a detailed analysis of the contents of the book and stresses M's admiration for Zurbarán and his dislike of Conan Doyle.] The most original essay is devoted to Augustus Hare, but the last one, "Some Novelists I Have Known" [i.e., Henry James, Arnold Bennett, and H. G. Wells], is likely to be the reader's favorite. [In French.]

1918 Faverty, Frederic E. "Somerset Maugham in a Vagrant Mood," CHICAGO SUNDAY TRIBUNE BOOKS, 12 April 1953, p. 2.
M skillfully blends biography and criticism in the six essays of *The Vagrant Mood.*

1919 Gautier, Jean-Jacques. "Les Spectacles: Au théâtre St. Georges: DOROTHEE par Jean Wall" (Entertainments: At the St. George Theater: DOROTHÉE [JANE] by Jean Wall), LE FIGARO, 7-8 March 1953, p. 6.
The play in the French adaptation is too long; its tone, excessively naive. [In French.]

1920 Gumpert, Martin. "Ten Who Know the Secret of Age," NEW YORK TIMES MAGAZINE, 27 Dec 1953, p. 10.
[Brief biography of M as one of the "grand old men."]

1921 Halsband, Robert. "Storyteller's Choice," SATURDAY REVIEW (NY), XXXVI (10 Oct 1953), 40.
M is well-qualified to choose from Kipling's work. Though he includes popular stories he doesn't like, he explains his reasons in his introduction to *Maugham's Choice of Kipling's Best* "with his customary urbanity, clarity, and . . . persuasiveness."

1922 Hass, Victor P. "Kipling Still Casts His Magic Spell," CHICAGO SUNDAY TRIBUNE Books, 13 Sept 1953, p. 6.
In *Maugham's Choice of Kipling's Best,* M is correct in his assessment of Kipling and his choice of Kipling's best.

1923 H[oche], K[laus]. "Somerset Maugham und Rudyard Kipling," DEUTSCHE RUNDSCHAU, LXXIX (May 1953), 552.
Liza of Lambeth is a mere curiosity. [In German.]

1924 Holland, Vyvyan. "Lettres de Londres" (London Letters), LES NOUVELLES LITTERAIRES, 29 Jan 1953, p. 5.
The best essay in *The Vagrant Mood* is the final one on the novelists M has known, James, Bennett, and Wells. [In French.]

1925 Jackson, Joseph Henry. "Bookman's Notebook: Somerset Maugham's Kipling," SAN FRANCISCO CHRONICLE, 11 Sept 1953, p. 15.
In *Maugham's Choice of Kipling's Best,* M's preface and his selection are "good."

1926 Jackson, Joseph Henry. "Six by Maugham," SAN FRANCISCO CHRONICLE, 27 March 1953, p. 19.
In *The Vagrant Mood,* M conducts a "stimulating and entertaining conversation." "Some Authors I Have Known" is the most readable essay of the collection.

1927* Jonas, Klaus W. "Somerset Maugham und der Ferne Osten" (Somerset Maugham and the Far East). Unpublished thesis. Münster, 1953.
In dealing with the Far East, M continues a tradition reaching back to the eighteenth century. But he also makes use of personal impressions and experiences. Restlessness and curiosity, as well as the belief that in the Far East the mask of culture will fall, caused him to make many trips to the East. In M's opinion, the exotic story should analyze the impact of a foreign environment on the white man temporarily exposed to it. Though M always needs some fact or anecdote to start from, he usually exercises his imagination to transform the factual materials of his stories. Unlike Melville, he is not dependent on secondary sources. [After surveying the settings of the Far Eastern stories and showing that M, though a sober spectator, sometimes discovers romance there, Jonas discusses M's treatment of the Europeans.] M dissects the virtues and failings of the British colonials impartially and is critical of the typical administrator and missionary. He depicts many weak characters who succumb to the powerful influence of milieu and climate, but he also portrays some strong personalities who manage to retain their balance. He stresses the difficulties of racial mixtures and pays attention to the varying attitudes of the natives. Though an agnostic, M takes a sympathetic interest in Eastern religions, especially in their explanations of evil and death. [See, also, Klaus W. Jonas, "Maugham and the East: The Human Condition — Freedom," THE WORLD OF SOMERSET MAUGHAM, ed by Klaus W. Jonas (NY: British Book Centre, 1959), pp. 96-141.] [In German.]

1928 Jonas, Klaus W. "W. Somerset Maugham," ARCHIV FÜR DAS

STUDIUM DER NEUEREN SPRACHEN, CLXXXIX (1953), 326-30; rptd in DIE NEUEREN SPRACHEN, N. S. III (1954), 543-48.

M, the "Dean of English writers," is Britain's last great professional writer and had a steady upward development. M is especially gifted for the short story. [Biographical sketch.] [In German.]

1929 Joost, Nicholas. "The Mellowness of Mr. Maugham," COMMONWEAL, LVIII (24 April 1953), 82-83.

In *The Vagrant Mood,* the essays on Zurbarán and Kant are "weak," but no one could actively dislike M's book because of its "charm and urbanity and ripeness."

1930 Kronenberger, Louis. *"The Circle* by W. Somerset Maugham," CAVALCADE OF COMEDY: 21 BRILLIANT COMEDIES FROM JONSON AND WYCHERLEY TO THURBER AND COWARD (NY: Simon and Schuster, 1953), p. 461.

[Critical introduction.]

1931 Kuner, Mildred C. "The Development of W. Somerset Maugham." Unpublished thesis. Columbia University, 1953.

[See M. C. Kuner, "Maugham and the West: The Human Condition—Bondage," THE WORLD OF SOMERSET MAUGHAM, ed by Klaus W. Jonas (NY: British Book Centre, 1959), pp. 37-95.]

1932 Léaud, F. J. "Comptes Rendus" (Critical Reports), ETUDES ANGLAISES, VI (May 1953), 167.

M's introduction to *Maugham's Choice of Kipling's Best* is rather disappointing; his selection of Kipling's work omits all the pieces written subsequent to 1897. M asserts his preferences but fails to comment upon them. [In French.]

1933* "The Listener's Book Chronicle," LISTENER, XLIX (5 Feb 1953), 232.

The essays in *The Vagrant Mood* are consistent with M's views that literature should give pleasure. Ranging wide in scope and subject matter, the essays are treated in such a seemingly casual manner "that they cannot fail to please . . . ." M's personal acquaintance —or assumed personal acquaintance— with the men discussed adds the "one specialist element" to the otherwise general terms in which the essays are written. The phrases "undemanding," the sentences often "pithy," the viewpoint in these essays is that of "a man of the world"; "Mr. Maugham at his most typical, in fact —one vast shrug-of-the-shoulders in human shape."

1934 Marcel, Gabriel. "Le Théâtre=DOROTHEE" (The Drama: DOROTHEE [JANE]), LES NOUVELLES LITTERAIRES, 26 March 1953, p. 10.

The short story on which the French adaptation of the play is based is not excellent; the play is mediocre. The story was free at least from the sentimental debates of the play's final act. [In French.]

1935 McNaught, Carlson. "Books Reviewed," CANADIAN FORUM, XXXIII (May 1953), 44.
M's introductory essay to *Maugham's Choice of Kipling's Best* is "penetrating."

1936* Morley, Christopher. "The Maugham Seesaw," NEW YORK TIMES BOOK REVIEW, 5 April 1953, p. 5.
In *The Vagrant Mood,* M's "eminent readability" (his talent for mixing the general with the intimate) is enviable—a quality M learned from Hazlitt. M's essays on Burke (relishing M's "shop talk" about style) and Hare (enjoying M's portrayal of nineteenth-century household routine) are praiseworthy. M "seesaws like the Media" in his essays—M's essay on Kant reaching the upper swing, his anecdotes of other authors, the lower.

1937* "New Books in Brief," NATION (NY), CLXXVI (25 April 1953), 351-52.
M is neither sufficiently passionate as a man nor sufficiently concentrated as a writer to be a great novelist, but "he is a superb retailer of anecdotes, reminiscences, and impressions when he merely gives them a slight novelistic touch without making fiction out of them," as in *The Vagrant Mood.*

1938 "Not So Little Women," TIMES (Lond), 28 Jan 1953, p. 7.
[Editorial concerning (and disagreeing with) M's statement that women tire of male authors' idealistic pictures of them.]

1939 Phelps, Robert. *"The Complete Stories of W. Somerset Maugham,"* NEW REPUBLIC, CXXVIII (12 Jan 1953), 23.
M's stories show that he is a good and various observer, though he never allowed himself to take the risks of deep exploration.

1940 Phelps, Robert. "The Waters Wait," NEW REPUBLIC, CXXVIII (27 July 1953), 20.
With reference to *The Vagrant Mood,* M is always reserved. Other writers "risked excess, obeyed compulsion, forgot their dignity." M never has.

1941 Poore, Charles [G]. "Books of the Times," NEW YORK TIMES, 2 April 1953, p. 25.
M's criticisms of James and other novelists are sometimes "shrill" sounding or "acerb," but the essays in *The Vagrant Mood* make "lively reading" in general.

1942 Prescott, Orville. "Books of the Times," NEW YORK TIMES, 31 Aug 1953, p. 15.

M's preface to *Maugham's Choice of Kipling's Best* is "coolly discriminating and judiciously appreciative."

1943* "Recreations of a Novelist," Times Literary Supplement (Lond), 20 Feb 1953, p. 120.

The essays of *The Vagrant Mood* are not "deep," the mood of the volume is "tolerant and urbane," "its manner caustic," and its conclusions "always amusing and often instructive." The essays on detective stories, recent novelists, and Augustus Hare are better than those on Kant, Burke, and Zurbarán. M refuses to lay claim either to scholarship or to literature as he admits that his reading of Burke was due to Hazlitt's enthusiasm for Burke's style. M's evaluation of Hare's writings is debatable. His "deliberate irreverence" toward some novelists he has known seems rather a lack of judgment in the case of his criticism of Henry James—possibly the fault of M's having known James and having disliked his insistence upon being an artist. In "The Decline and Fall of the Detective Story," as well as in "certain astute comments on the writing of contemporary 'serious fiction,' " M is "at his best."

1944 "Reprints and New Editions," New York Herald Tribune Book Review, 18 Jan 1953, p. 14.

[Note recommending *The Complete Short Stories* and their prefaces in which M "shares confidences."]

1945 S., M. "Ylielänyttä rotumystiikkaa" (Hackneyed Racial Mysticism), Uusi Suomi, 9 Feb 1953, p. 4.

M has retained the Kiplingesque attitudes of the British Empire. The revival of the Finnish adaptation of *East of Suez* has an archaic flavor which produces a comical effect. [In Finnish.]

1946 Scott, Nathan A., Jr. "The Relation of Theology to Literary Criticism," Journal of Religion, XXXIII (Oct 1953), 266-77, especially 269-70.

Excepting E. M. Forster, M is "our finest living master of English prose"; but few feel sympathy for his work because they feel about his characters the way Jacques Rivière felt about Stendhal's: "one could never wish for them to be forgiven. . . . In them, humanity is without its wound." In M's work there is an "ultimate note of frivolity."

1947 Simiot, Bernard. "Les Spectacles" (Entertainments), Hommes et Mondes, XXI (May 1953), 281-82.

The French adaptation of Jane as Dorothee is "mediocre" though well-played. [In French.]

1948* Simon, Jean. "Comptes Rendus" (Critical Reports),

ETUDES ANGLAISES, VI (May 1953), 172; same as "Reviews," MODERN LANGUAGE REVIEW, XLVIII (Oct 1953), 465.
Review of Helmut Papajewski's DIE WELT-, LEBENS-, UND KUNSTANSCHAUUNG WILLIAM SOMERSET MAUGHAMS. [Simon traces the fluctuations of M's reputation, noting the current interest in him as shown by new critical works such as Papajewski's. Although Simon doesn't always agree with Papajewski, his work is "well-built" and "conscientious"; Simon's main quarrel is with his seeming lack of sympathy for M.]

1949* Soellner, Rolf. "Book Reviews," JOURNAL OF ENGLISH AND GERMANIC PHILOLOGY, LII (Oct 1953), 592-94.
Analysis of M's philosophy of life and art is difficult because of M's reserve. Papajewski tries to derive it exclusively, therefore, from M's works, though without using all of them. Of the three methods Papajewski uses to arrive at M's philosophy, the first—the study of M's autobiographical works— is perhaps the most valid. The other two —study of comments of the *raisonneurs* in various novels and study of the "repetition of certain ideas"— seem open to objection. Although Papajewski recognizes that M does little moralizing and adds merely "a small accent of evaluation," he often misreads these "accents," as in his interpretation of M's attitude toward Jews, giving the impression that M is anti-Semitic. Evidence from both M's life and his stories refutes this idea. The "best chapter" is that dealing with M's *Kunstanschauung*. Here Papajewski shows "the harmony of M's concept of life and art which lies in the acceptance of the rich and varied pattern of human life." Contrary to Papajewski's criticism on the weakening of M's "tragic attitude," M never strove for the tragic, but for the *comédie humaine*. [Review of Helmut Papajewski's DIE WELT-, LEBENS-, UND KUNSTANSCHAUUNG WILLIAM SOMERSET MAUGHAMS (1952).]

1950 Taylor, Dwight. "Maugham and the Young Idiot," VOGUE, CXXII (1 Sept 1953), 172, 214, 216, 221.
[Account of Taylor's meeting M and Gerald Haxton on board the *Aquitania* in 1922.]

1951 Thiébaut, Marcel. "Le Théâtre à Paris" (The Drama in Paris), JOURNAL DE GENEVE, 29-30 March 1953, p. 3.
[Brief mention of the French adaptation of JANE as DOROTHEE.] [In French].

1952* Trewin, J. C. DRAMATISTS OF TODAY (Lond & NY: Staples P, 1953), pp. 11, 14, especially 37-46, 157, 182, 214.
The Circle is M's greatest play; *East of Suez* is "Oriental spectacle-drama"; *For Services Rendered* is "vinegar-and-verjuice." In *The Breadwinner* M tired of the characters and huddled the play quickly to an end.

1953 U-11, S. *"Suezista Itään" (East of Suez),* HELSINGIN SANOMAT, 10 Feb 1953, p. 8.
This play is one of M's worst. It may have attracted the audience at the beginning of the century; the revival of the Finnish adaptation is a trying experience. [In Finnish.]

1954 *"The Vagrant Mood,"* KIRKUS, XXI (1 March 1953), 170. [Brief appraisal.]

1955 Vallette, Jacques. "Lettres Anglo-Saxonnes" (Anglo-Saxon Letters), LE MERCURE DE FRANCE, CCCXVII (1 Feb 1953), 344.
[Paragraph review of *The Vagrant Mood*, generally enthusiastic about the book's entire contents.] [In French.]

1956* van Druten, John. PLAYWRIGHT AT WORK (NY: Harper and Bros, 1953), pp. 6, 31, 35, 103, 104, 107, 125.
Women characters of *Our Betters* are some "of the best characters" (in terms of dramatic realization) to be found in the drama, but M makes the mistake of including Bessie, "a slight bore" and a "mouthpiece," in the same play.

1957 Walbridge, Earle F. "New Books Appraised," LIBRARY JOURNAL, LXXVIII (1 Sept 1953), 1430.
With reference to *Maugham's Choice of Kipling's Best,* "a less conventional editor might have included 'The House Surgeon' . . . and 'Mrs. Bathurst.' "

1958 Weeks, Edward. "Bookshelf," ATLANTIC MONTHLY, CXCII (Aug 1953), 84.
The Vagrant Mood is "fresh, shrewd, illuminating, witty."

1959 Whicher, George F. "Reprints, New Editions," NEW YORK HERALD TRIBUNE BOOK REVIEW, 8 Nov 1953, p. 17.
The introduction to *Maugham's Choice of Kipling's Best* is "perceptive," the selection commendable.

1960 Winterich, John T. "A Very Old Party Serves a Rich Potpourri of Literary Memories," NEW YORK HERALD TRIBUNE BOOK REVIEW, 5 April 1953, p. 5.
"A compound of admirable and lucid miscellany," *The Vagrant Mood* is a volume whose very variety is part of its charm. The discussions of Zurbarán, Burke, Kant and Hare follow a "sound method": first, "identification"; secondly, "interpretation." Much in these essays is autobiographical, though perhaps presented in a more interesting form than autobiography. "Whatever the method, the product is excellent."

1961* Worsley, T. C. "The Survival of Mr. Maugham," New Statesman and Nation, N. S. XLV (7 Feb 1953), 147-48.
Of all M's plays in Heinemann's reissue of *Collected Plays* in three volumes, *The Circle, Our Betters, The Breadwinner,* and *Sheppey* are "still very capable of amusing"; but their future survival is uncertain. Although witty in the writing, they depend "too much upon theatrical coups," and it may be that "we have lost the secret of reproducing period style." The recent production of *The Breadwinner* verified these opinions: actors and producer could not "establish the style."

1954

1962 Adams, J. Donald. "Speaking of Books," New York Times Book Review, 24 Jan 1954, p. 2.
[Appreciation on the eve of M's eightieth birthday. *The Summing Up* is Adams' favorite of M's works.]

1963* Annan, Noël. "Books in General," New Statesman and Nation, N. S. XLVIII (13 Nov 1954), 61-62.
Although M has set himself up as "a worldly observer older than the rocks on which he sits," he is a "schoolmaster" of the "Pop." His teachings in *Ten Novels and Their Authors* "need to be taken to heart not so much by the critics as by politicians and lawyers," for despite their occasional narrowmindedness and old-fashionedness, M's views are "humane," and should be illuminating to the present Director of Public Prosecutions and the late Home Secretary in their hypocritical fight against "smut."

1964 Barber, Noël. "The New Somerset Maugham," Holiday, XV (Feb 1954), 16, 18-20.
[Sketch of M's routine day at the age of eighty.]

1965 Beecroft, John. "Introduction," Mr. Maugham Himself (Garden City, NY: Doubleday, 1954), pp. ix-x.
[General appreciation.]

1966 Belluc, Roger. "Propos sur le Théâtre" (About the Theater), La Revue de la Mediterranee, XIV:6 (Nov-Dec 1954), 700.
[Review of the French adaptation of Theatre as Adorable Julia.] [In French.]

1967 "The Birthday Honours," Times (Lond), 10 June 1954, p. 4.
M was named Companion of Honour by Queen Elizabeth II. [See, also, "Mr. Somerset Maugham," Times (Lond), 15 July 1954, p. 8.]

1968 Boulton, Marjorie. The Anatomy of Prose (Lond: Routledge & Kegan Paul, 1954), pp. 91-92, 162.
The simplicity of M's style is not achieved at the expense of "individuality."

1969 Bourget-Pailleron, Robert. "Revue dramatique" (Drama Review), La Revue [des deux Mondes], VII (15 Oct 1954), 732-34.
The French dramatization of Theatre as Adorable Julia has charm. [Mainly plot summary.] [In French.]

1970 Brady, Thomas F. "The Eighty Years of Mr. Maugham," New York Times Magazine, 24 Jan 1954, pp. 12, 52-53.
[Interview on the eve of M's eightieth birthday.]

1971 Breit, Harvey. "Repeat Performances Appraised," New York Times Book Review, 5 Dec 1954, p. 55.
[Brief review of Mr. Maugham Himself (1954).]

1972 "The Contractile Vacuole," Times Literary Supplement (Lond), 19 Nov 1954, p. 739.
By concentrating on the novelist rather than upon the novel, M "evidently . . . feels instinctively that a novel is a function of its begetter." "Easily readable," M's *Ten Novels and Their Authors* will be condemned by the critics and welcomed by the public.

1973 Cookman, A. V. "The Prose Drama, "Theatre Programme, ed by J. C. Trewin (Lond: Frederick Muller, 1954), pp. 31-48, especially 43.
T. Rattigan is like M in that both are "born" storytellers.

1974 Cordell, Richard A. "Somerset Maugham at Eighty," College English, XV (Jan 1954), 201-7.
[General appreciation, most of which is repeated in Cordell's Somerset Maugham: A Biographical and Critical Study (1961).]

1975 Darlington, W. A. "Modern Acting," Theatre Programme, ed by J. C. Trewin (Lond: Frederick Muller, 1954), pp. 100-30, especially 114.
With the growing popularity of Ibsen in the 1890s and the partial re-establishment of the drama over the actor, M, like Barrie and Galsworthy, found he "could now write for the theatre without loss of caste."

1976 Deboisge, Gilles. "Les Pièces du mois" (Plays of the Month), France-Illustration, No. 416 (Nov 1954), 102.
[Review of the French adaptation of Theatre as Adorable Julia.] [In French.]

1977* Duesberg, Jacques. "Les 80 ans de W. Somerset Maugham" (W. Somerset Maugham at 80), SYNTHESES (Brussels), VIII (Feb-March 1954), 481-84.

M's works are not likely to become obsolete, for M abstains from making moral judgments: his is no literature of commitment. He has been little written about; there are only two volumes on him. [This statement is obviously wrong, since two studies by Dottin and one by S. Quéry had appeared in France alone before the Second World War.] M has no metaphysics. Critics are puzzled by him: they are content to declare him "competent." His works are to be divided into two parts: (I) The Plays (1903-1933), nearly all of them comedies of manners, brilliant yet superficial satires of the upper classes. M is the successor of Congreve, Wilde and Shaw; but his plays will not live; M himself has said so. The best of them are *Our Betters, The Circle,* and *Home and Beauty*. M had no translator worthy of him. (II) The Works of Fiction: *Cakes and Ale* is M's masterpiece, because it combines the author's shrewdness, discreetness, and indulgence. Unlike Katherine Mansfield, M is a *dynamic* storyteller: a lucid writer, a builder of plots, neat and shorn of the superfluous. His detractors accuse him of being shallow, but he is not so. *Don Fernando* is commendable on account of its simplicity, conciseness, humor and objectivity. [In French.]

1978 Dussane. "Théâtre" (Theater), LE MERCURE DE FRANCE, CCCXXII (1 Nov 1954), 513-14.

The French adaptation of THEATRE as ADORABLE JULIA is humorous without being malicious. [In French.]

1979* Fielden, John Seward. "William Somerset Maugham, the Dramatist." Unpublished thesis. Boston University, 1954.

[See, below, John Seward Fielden, "The Ibsenite Maugham," MODERN DRAMA, IV (Sept 1961), 138-51; " 'Mrs. Beamish' and *The Circle*," BOSTON UNIVERSITY STUDIES IN ENGLISH, II (Summer 1956), 113-23; and "Somerset Maugham on the Purpose of Drama," EDUCATIONAL THEATRE JOURNAL, X (Oct 1958), 218-22 — all based on the thesis.]

1980 Fischer, W[alther]. "Bibliographie" (Bibliography), ARCHIV FÜR DAS STUDIUM DER NEUEREN SPRACHEN (Herrig), CXCI (1954-55), 91-92.

[Lists the contents of the three volumes of *The Selected Novels of W. Somerset Maugham* and labels the various works according to subject matter. Hopes the publisher will also print a collection of M's most important critical work.] [In German.]

1981 Fischer, W[alther]. "Bibliographie" (Bibliography), ARCHIV FÜR DAS STUDIUM DER NEUEREN SPRACHEN (Herrig), CXCI (1954-55), 92-93.

Papajewski reveals the profounder depths in the *seemingly* obvious and simple work of M, especially for German readers. Charles Morgan is M's opposite pole. An index would have been useful for the rich contents of the book. [Review of Helmut Papajewski's DIE WELT-, LEBENS-, UND KUNSTANSCHAUUNG WILLIAM SOMERSET MAUGHAMS.] [In German.]

1982* Gassner, John. MASTERS OF THE DRAMA ([NY:] Dover Publications, by permission of Random House, 1954 [1940]), pp. 325-26.

M could not persuade himself of the need to take drama seriously "in some quarters," and after earlier serious plays, he turned to the writing of farces like *Home and Beauty,* a "1919 variant of the old 'Box and Cox' story . . . ." At the same time, however, M's plays "began to grow sharper and more provocative" (e.g., *Our Betters* and *The Circle*), and he did contribute to the Shavian play-of-ideas tradition in *The Unknown, The Constant Wife, The Breadwinner, For Services Rendered,* and *Sheppey.*

1983 Gautier, Jean-Jacques. "Sur la scène et sur l'écran: Du théâtre du Gymnase: ADORABLE JULIA" (Stage and Screen: At the Theater Gymnase: ADORABLE JULIA), LE FIGARO, 24 Sep 1954, p. 10.

The French adaptation of THEATRE is good vaudeville, a play on players, charming, without pretensions, "stuffed" with witticisms which, most of the time, proceed from the situation. [In French.]

1984 "Gay Eighty," NEW YORK TIMES, 31 Jan 1954, IV:2. [Note comparing M's attitudes in 1938 with those in 1954.]

1985 Guyard, Marius-François. LA GRANDE-BRETAGNE DANS LE ROMAN FRANÇAIS, 1914-1940 (Great Britain in the French Novel, 1914-1940) (Paris: Librairie Marcel Didier, 1954), pp. 43, 88, 94, 96.

[Passing references.]

1986 Hass, Victor P. "Adventure in Good Reading," CHICAGO SUNDAY TRIBUNE BOOKS, 19 Dec 1954, p. 3.

[Review of MR. MAUGHAM HIMSELF.]

1987 Haverstick, John. "Gift Book Miscellany," SATURDAY REVIEW (NY), XXXVII (4 Dec 1954), 31.

MR. MAUGHAM HIMSELF includes some stories, essays, excerpts from *A Writer's Notebook,* and the complete texts of *Of Human Bondage* and *The Summing Up.*

1988* Jonas, Klaus W. (ed) THE MAUGHAM ENIGMA. (NY: Citadel P, 1954).

An anthology containing M's address on April 20, 1946, at the Library of Congress (*"Of Human Bondage* with a Digression on the Art of Fiction," pp. 121-28) and thirty-one reviews, addresses, and appreciations [most of them previously published]. These thirty-one articles, annotated in this bibliography under individual entries, are as follows: Klaus W. Jonas, "Biographical Sketch," pp. 15-20; Karl G. Pfeiffer, "Maugham—as I Know Him," 21-36; Robert van Gelder, "Mr. Maugham on the Essentials of Writing," 37-40; Harry Gilroy, "How to Write —by Maugham," 41-49; Irwin Edman, "The Philosopher as Man of Letters," 50-53; Leslie A. Marchand, "The Exoticism of Somerset Maugham," 54-71; Theodore Spencer, "An Appreciation," 72-83; Woodburn O. Ross, "W. Somerset Maugham: Theme and Variations," 84-100; Walter Prichard Eaton, "A Playwright Who Stumbled into Fame," 101-3; Ludwig Lewisohn, "Somerset Maugham Himself," 104-6; Richard A. Cordell, *"Our Betters,"* 107-10; Richard A. Cordell, *"The Constant Wife,"* 111-13; Theodore Dreiser, "As a Realist Sees It," 114-20; Maxwell Anderson, "In Vishnu-Land What Avatar?" 129-32; Paul Dottin, "The Realism of Somerset Maugham," 133-45; Mark Van Doren, "Thomas Hardy Veiled," 146-48; Richard A. Cordell, *"The Narrow Corner,"* 149-52; Evelyn Waugh, "The Technician," 153-55; David Paul, "Maugham and the Two Myths," 156-63; Orville Prescott, *"Catalina,"* 164-66; Richard A. Cordell, "Somerset Maugham's Short Stories," 167-70; Richard A. Cordell, *"The Trembling of a Leaf,"* 171-76; Gerald Sykes, "An Author in Evening Dress," 177-79; Malcolm Cowley, "Angry Author's Complaint," 180-84; V. S. Pritchett, *"The Mixture as Before,"* 185-90; L. M. Field, "Maugham's Chinese Sketches," 191-93; Graham Greene, "Spanish Gold," 194-96; Richard A. Cordell, *"The Gentleman in the Parlour,"* 197-99; Malcolm Cowley, "The Maugham Enigma," 200-4; Joseph Wood Krutch, "An Epicurean on Liberty," 205-7; Charles Morgan, "Mr. Maugham's Workshop," 208-12.

1989 Jonas, Klaus W. "Biographical Sketch," THE MAUGHAM ENIGMA, ed by Klaus W. Jonas (NY: Citadel P, 1954), pp. 15-20.
[Sketch, most of which is duplicated in Jonas's THE GENTLEMAN FROM CAP FERRAT (1956).]

1990 Kemp, T. C. "The Classic Revival," THEATRE PROGRAMME, ed by J. C. Trewin (Lond: Frederick Muller, 1954), pp. 267-85, especially 279.
Sir John Gielgud has included *The Circle* in his repertory season at the Haymarket in 1944.

1991 Kinnunen, Aarne. "Ensimmainen siirto" (First Move), YLIOPPILASLEHTI, 21 May 1954, p. 6.

Catalina reveals a slightly illogical narrative, even though its climaxes are admirable. [Review of the Finnish translation, in Finnish.]

1992* Krim, Seymour. "Maugham the Artist," COMMONWEAL, LXI (10 Dec 1954), 284-87.

M's honesty about himself, his self-knowledge, is the "foremost" of his gifts. His frank placement of himself—particularly as first person narrator—into his work gains for it the appearance of reality and thus the deception of the reader. M's "acute self-awareness" gained through self-exposure allows him to anticipate and play upon the reactions of his audience. "The Book-Bag" is an example of the "guilelessness" in writing which M has made into an art. His important work is actually "the imaginative acting-out and fulfilling, through the medium of fiction, of the basic emotions common to us all." His fiction is not finally realistic, though making use of realistic "camouflage"; it is "truth to the heart's desire," not "truth to experience" that he records. M has influenced many writers in his handling of "the art of narrative": he can tell a "wonderful story." His faults are (1) his simplification of life to the scale of novel or story, precluding the depth and breadth of scope necessary if he were to "illuminate experience," and (2) his literary style, once direct but later showing a "baldness of expression." His style is "orderly, personal, and gives intimate pleasure" but is also somewhat "easy." Although much of M's work will probably be forgotten—and although M himself is "perhaps only a first-rate 'minor' writer"—he has held and increased his audience through the years, and probably will remain quite "durable."

1993* Krim, Seymour. "Somerset Maugham," COMMONWEAL, LXI (3 Dec 1954), 245-50.

M is a rather ambiguous figure in literature, his work enjoyed by many but looked upon with suspicion—or ignored—by most of "our better critics of this generation." Close to being a master of the art of storytelling, M observes a strict regard for "form." Enjoying popular literature himself and wanting "to be liked," M was able successfully to combine his "pursuit of both the dollar and the muse." With the success of his first book, *Liza of Lambeth,* he gave up medicine and set out to become a "successful London dramatist"—paradoxically enough, by first writing fiction. His youth, spent in France, gives M a "continental attitude," although he hasn't the lavish imagination of Balzac, Dostoevsky and Dreiser in the creation of the diversity of life. Playwriting taught him "economy of writing and pointed presentation," as well as that most important factor, "sure knowledge of his audience." His best known work, *Of Human Bondage,* written as a sort of "purgation," is not typical of M's best work "in either its unrelieved tone, its direct autobiographical source, or its uncharacteristic length." Change of M's attitude over the years is shown by the significant omissions in *The*

Summing Up, closest work to *Of Human Bondage.* After 1915, M began "the second and richest half of his career."

1994 Kula, Kauko. "W. Somerset Maugham, *Catalina,*" ARVOSTELEVA KIRJALUETTELO, annex to KIRJASTOLEHTI, XLVII:5 (1954), 36.

The novel is compiled in a rather superficial way. M is very serious, but [the Finnish translation of] the novel is not as refined as his best ones. [In Finnish.]

1995 L., K. "Maallinen ja taivaallinen rakkaus" (Worldly and Heavenly Love), HELSINGIN SANOMAT, 24 Aug 1954, p. 7.

Catalina [in the Finnish translation] contains the flavor of the old Spanish picaresque novel. It is full of irony and often approximates parody. It is strangely uneven and incoherent, certainly not one of the best of M's novels. [In Finnish.]

1996 L., K. "W. Somerset Maugham 80-vuotias" (W. Somerset Maugham at Eighty), HELSINGIN SANOMAT, 25 Jan 1954, p. 4.

M made his breakthrough as a dramatist. As a short story writer he was the disciple of Maupassant. His style is effortless, concentrated. He is an objective, unimpassioned, unprejudiced observer of life. [Appreciation on M's eightieth birthday.] [In Finnish.]

1997 L., M. "Somerset Maugham ihmeiden ja inkvisition parissa" (Somerset Maugham Amidst Miracles and the Inquisition), KAUPPALEHTI, 15 May 1954, p. 3.

Catalina [in the Finnish translation] contains too much material heaped together, resulting in boredom. The characters are not memorable, and the good points are spoiled by too superficial a treatment. [In Finnish.]

1998 L[emarchand], J[acques]. "ADORABLE JULIA [THEATRE]," LE FIGARO LITTERAIRE, 2 Oct 1954, p. 12.

The French adaptation is spritely vaudeville. [In French.]

1999 Liddell, Robert. SOME PRINCIPLES OF FICTION (Bloomington: Indiana U P, 1954), pp. 52, 55, 64.

[Passing references.]

2000* MacCarthy, Desmond. "Somerset Maugham," THEATRE (Lond: MacGibbon & Kee, 1954), pp. 119-39.

Reprints reviews of *Our Betters,* in "Miscellany: Somerset Maugham: *'Our Betters,'* " NEW STATESMAN, XXI (6 Oct 1923), 738-39; *Sheppey,* in "Mr. Maugham's New Play," NEW STATESMAN AND NATION, N. S. VI (10 Sept 1933), 325-26; *The Circle,* under the same title, in NEW STATESMAN AND NATION, N. S. XXVIII (28 Oct 1944), 283; *East of Suez,* in NEW STATES-

MAN, XX (7 Oct 1922), 14; *For Services Rendered,* in NEW STATESMAN AND NATION, N. S. IV (12 Nov 1932), 577-78.

2001 Mäkelä, S. "Maughamin heikointa" (Maugham's Weakest), SUOMEN SOSIALIDEMOKRAATTI, 12 May 1954, p. 7.

The only rationale for the publication [of the Finnish translation] of *Catalina* is the aspect of novelty. The treatment is superficial and the result remains unconvincing. The only real enjoyment is in the mischievously ironic style. [In Finnish.]

2002 Manninen, Kerttu. "Hyvyyden voitto" (Victory of Goodness), AAMULEHTI, 17 June 1954, p. 8.

Catalina [in the Finnish translation] is a legend told in a cheerful, even mischievous, tone; warmer and more serious than M's earlier works, although not the best, the sharpest, or the most refined novel that M has written. [In Finnish.]

2003 Marcabru, Pierre. "Le Comédien et sa legende: Le secret professionnel" (The Comedian and His Legend: The Professional Secret), ARTS/SPECTACLES, 3-9 Nov 1954, p. 4.

The French adaptation of THEATRE as ADORABLE JULIA elaborates the theme of the comedian stifled by his profession. [In French.]

2004 Marcel, Gabriel. "Le Théâtre: ADORABLE JULIA" (The Drama: ADORABLE JULIA [THEATRE]), LES NOUVELLES LITTERAIRES, 30 Sept 1954, p. 8.

The French adaptation is a play about actors, which owes any success it has to actors. [In French.]

2005 "Maugham Is Cited in Queen's Honors," NEW YORK TIMES, 10 June 1954, p. 33.

M was made Companion of Honour by Queen Elizabeth II on 9 June 1954. [See, also, "Somerset Maugham Honored," NEW YORK TIMES, 15 July 1954, p. 25.]

2006 Middleton, Drew. "Maugham Lives a Role He Wrote; Author, at 80, Becomes Cynosure," NEW YORK TIMES, 26 Jan 1954, p. 25.

[Article describing the way M spent his eightieth birthday.]

2007 "Mr. Maugham," MANCHESTER GUARDIAN, 29 Oct 1954, p. 4.

In *Ten Novels and their Authors,* M's sexual interpretation of WUTHERING HEIGHTS may be disagreeable to his readers.

2008 "MR. MAUGHAM HIMSELF," KIRKUS, XXII (15 Sept 1954), 645.

[Brief appraisal.]

2009 Natan, Alex. "Somerset Maugham, zu seinem 80. Geburstag" (Somerset Maugham on His 80th Birthday), DEUTSCHE RUNDSCHAU, LXXX (Jan 1954), 61-65.

Wide variety is manifest not only in M's work, but in his audience, his style and world view. M's approach is not so much cynical as it is clinical. Medical studies and Schopenhauer and Goethe have all influenced him. [In German.]

2010 P., E. "Juhlittu Maugham" (Maugham Celebrated), PARNASSO, IV:2 (1954), 81.

[An appreciation of M on his eightieth birthday.] [In Finnish.]

2011 Poore, Charles [G]. "Books of the Times," NEW YORK TIMES, 20 Nov 1954, p. 15.

MR. MAUGHAM HIMSELF is an "excellent . . . anthology."

2012* Raymond, John. "Books in General," NEW STATESMAN AND NATION, N. S. XLVII (23 Jan 1954), 101-2.

Klaus Jonas's THE MAUGHAM ENIGMA shows that M, early in life, received the "wound" that Edmund Wilson recognizes as essential "in the make-up of a creative writer." M projected his painful experience so well that, unlike most writers, he became a "master of life." Thus, M, who was once Philip Carey—a raw, unhappy youth—became Ashenden, the worldly, cynical sentimentalist who pulls M "up short of the brick wall, . . . [and] keeps him apart from the men and women of whom he writes." Future critics will not be interested in M because he "is so much *there* in his work, explicit, lucid, unmysterious."

2013 "Recent Books—Authors and Novels: A Personal Choice," TIMES (Lond), 27 Oct 1954, p. 8.

In *Ten Novels and their Authors,* M's list of the ten best novels is "orthodox"; he is more interested in the characters of the novelists themselves than in close consideration of their works.

2014 *"La Ronde de L'Amour" (Cakes and Ale),* DICTIONNAIRE DES OEUVRES DE TOUS LES TEMPS ET DE TOUS LES PAYS (DICTIONARY OF WORKS OF ALL TIMES AND ALL NATIONS). Four Volumes (Paris: S. E. D. E. and V. Bompiani, 1954), IV, 321.

[Plot synopsis of *Cakes and Ale* followed by a judgment that one ought to view the book as a "roman à clef."] [In French.]

2015 S., V. "Romaani 1600-luvun Espanjasta" (A Novel from

Seventeenth-Century Spain), Uusi Suomi, 12 May 1954, p. 15. All through [the Finnish translation of] *Catalina* M remains impartial; only here and there do his skepticism and irony break the surface. His style is matter-of-fact and resembles that of a chronicler. Towards the end, the book becomes more an exposition than a real novel—and the reader falls asleep. [In Finnish.]

2016 S:nen, A. "William Somerset Maugham 80-vuotias" (William Somerset Maugham at Eighty), Turun Sanomat, 24 Jan 1954, p. 7.

M writes in the tradition of Stevenson and Conrad. He has a keen eye for psychological observation. He is a storyteller, painting with a rich variety of colors, and an unprejudiced seeker, but he is not very profound. [Appreciation on M's eightieth birthday.] [In Finnish.]

2017 Schirmer, Walter F. Geschichte der Englischen und Amerikanischen Literatur von den Anfaengen Bis Zur Gegenwart (History of English and American Literature from the Beginnings to the Present). 2 Volumes (Tübingen: Max Niemeyer, 1954), II, 239, 271.

M's plays are very skillfully written but disappointing in content. *The Circle* is his best play; the later plays are marred by his cynical criticism of life. As a novelist M has not lived up to the expectations raised by *Liza of Lambeth* and *Of Human Bondage,* although all his fiction reveals his craftsmanship. [In German.]

2018 Scott, J. D. "Books of the Week: The Maugham Effect," Spectator (Lond), CXCII (29 Jan 1954), 129.

M did not write "poor English." "Conversational ease" is characteristic of M's writing; he achieves simplicity and lucidity in simple sentences. M valued "flow of narrative" above all else. Although not conducive to "suggestion or implication," it becomes, in M's hands, "a work of art." M is "the artist who lives on in the skyscraper of success which he himself has built." [Commemorative piece on M's 80th birthday.]

2019 *"Servitude Humaine" (Of Human Bondage),* Dictionnaire des Oeuvres de Tous les Temps et de Tous les Pays (Dictionary of Works of All Times and of All Nations). Four Volumes (Paris: S. E. D. E. and V. Bompiani, 1954), IV, 397.

The structure of *Of Human Bondage* is remarkable. The style is neuter, but the work as a whole is passionate in its exact and full transcription of "psychological reality." [Plot analysis.] [In French.]

2020 Simiot, Bernard. "Les Spectacles" (Entertainments), Hommes et Mondes, XXV (Oct 1954), 451.

[Brief review of the French adaptation of THEATRE as ADORABLE JULIA.] [In French.]

2021* "Somerset Maugham," TIMES LITERARY SUPPLEMENT (Lond), 22 Jan 1954, p. 57.

What has puzzled critics for years is the remarkable difference between *Of Human Bondage* and the rest of M's work. M used this novel as a means of getting rid of painful and unhappy recollections; it is possible, as M has himself suggested, that success removed him from the society in which he found his best material. To conceal the lack of depth in his portrayal of human nature, M resorts to a "technical brilliance" which—although rendering his works amusing, surprising, and pleasing—yet leaves us with the impression of something lacking: something possessed by other artists "whose less perfect work speaks so hauntingly of a perfection which they suggest yet with all their labour cannot quite reach." Theatrically, M succeeded "at least once." *Our Betters* now seems to have been wasted on an unimportant fragment of society, but *The Circle* should "keep its place as a classic serious comedy." [Appreciation and general assessment of M's career on the eve of his eightieth birthday.]

2022 "Somerset Maugham at 80," NEW YORK TIMES, 25 Jan 1954, p. 18.

[Editorial in honor of M's eightieth birthday.]

2023 "Somerset Maugham 80-vuotias" (Somerset Maugham at Eighty), UUSI SUOMI, 24 Jan 1954, p. 10.

Maupassant and other French writers exercised a great influence on M. His style is easy, close to the spoken word. He is not one of the great masters but nevertheless one of the most outstanding among present-day writers. [Appreciation on M's eightieth birthday.] [In Finnish.]

2024 Squire, Sir John. "Guests at Mr. Somerset Maugham's Party," ILLUSTRATED LONDON NEWS, CCXXV (20 Nov 1954), 896.

In *Ten Novels and Their Authors,* M "takes great trouble to examine what he sees, and his responses to what he sees, and to state the result with the utmost accuracy."

2025 "Stanford Gets Maugham MS," NEW YORK TIMES, 27 Jan 1954, p. 69.

Stanford University was given the original manuscript of *The Trembling of a Leaf*.

2026 Stern, G. B. "Somerset Maugham Comes of Age," JOHN O' LONDON'S WEEKLY, LXIII (22 Jan 1954), 65-66, 68.

[A personal portrait in celebration of M's eightieth birthday.]

2027* Swinnerton, Frank. "Somerset Maugham as a Writer," JOHN O' LONDON'S WEEKLY, LXIII (22 Jan 1954), 76-78; rptd as the first essay, in THE WORLD OF SOMERSET MAUGHAM, ed by Klaus W. Jonas (NY: British Book Centre, 1959), pp. 12-20; the same as "Maugham at Eighty," SATURDAY REVIEW (NY), XXXVII (23 Jan 1954), 13-14, 70-72.

From the beginning of his career until World War II, M found little or no favor from serious critics. Pursuing lucidity and detachment alone, he patronized none of the successive literary vogues of the late nineteenth and twentieth centuries. The popular admiration he finally won in his eighties issues from a generation that was schooled in "fatalism" from the destructive Second World War, a generation that appreciates and needs the lucid and detached qualities which M's canon represents.

2028 T., W. T. "Viisas neitsyt" (Wise Virgin), KARJALA, 21 May 1954, p. 4.

The Finnish translation of *Catalina* contains some excellently drawn characters, some of them fine psychological studies. [In Finnish.]

2029 V., M. *"Kirjava Huntu" (The Painted Veil),* SAVONMAA, 28 Jan 1954, p. 5.

In *The Painted Veil,* M describes the Eastern world in a masterly way. The form of the novel is harmonious, the characterization first-rate. On the other hand, the narration is sluggish and the style monotonous. [Review of Finnish translation.] [In Finnish.]

2030 Walbridge, Earle F. "New Books Appraised," LIBRARY JOURNAL, LXXIX (15 Nov 1954), 2207.

[Brief appraisal of MR. MAUGHAM HIMSELF.]

1955

2031 "American, London and Scottish," TIMES (Lond), 24 Nov 1955, p. 13.

Mrs. Craddock is now included, "with an amusing introduction by the author," in the collected edition of M's works.

2032 "Books in Brief," NEW YORK HERALD TRIBUNE BOOK REVIEW, 12 June 1955, p. 9.

[Short paragraph describing the contents of *The Art of Fiction: An Introduction to Ten Novels and Their Authors.*]

2033 "Briefly Noted," NEW YORKER, XXXI (21 May 1955), 142-43.

In *The Art of Fiction: An Introduction to Ten Novels and Their Authors,* M provides a "clinical scrutiny" of the authors and the "detached mauling" of the novels themselves. Although the volume is "literary mayhem," it holds interest.

2034* Brooks, John. "The New Books," HARPER'S MAGAZINE, CCX (May 1955), 84, 86.

Written as introductions to condensed forms of ten novels, *The Art of Fiction: An Introduction to Ten Novels and Their Authors* contains what might be termed largely "gossip" about the writers' lives, "not so much in relation to their work as to the reader's sensibilities and risibilities." Giving "color, life, and a wonderful narrative force" to these accounts is M's "own lively and distinct feeling about each author." But as "actual criticism" the essays are weak, seeming to put "life before literature." The final chapter is M "at his very best."

2035* Cantwell, Robert. "With a Superior Sense of Reality," NEW YORK TIMES BOOK REVIEW, 24 April 1955, p. 4.

In *The Art of Fiction: An Introduction to Ten Novels and Their Authors,* M's discussion of most of the novels is "sensible, practical, balanced and sometimes unobtrusively acute." Fielding is his standard of a "gentleman born," and most of the other writers' careers are interpreted with an eye on their "social inadequacy." Novelists like Melville and Dostoevsky, "in whom the element of mystery is inescapable," M discusses by comparing them to Fielding's "gentlemanly standard." Though M sees Emily Brontë as a sadist, her book, WUTHERING HEIGHTS, shows power, not lack of self-control. M's "criterion is entertainment"; those qualities which he feels are essential to a good novel are possessed by all of his selections "in abundance."

2036 Cazamian, Madeleine L. LE ROMAN ET LES IDEES EN ANGLETERRE (THE NOVEL AND IDEAS IN ENGLAND). Three Volumes (Paris: Société d'Edition: Les Belles Lettres, 1955 [1935]), II, 222; III, 58.

M's work is uneven, conceived with an eye to success and popularity. Passing mention of *Liza of Lambeth, The Making of a Saint, Mrs. Craddock, The Magician,* and *The Moon and Sixpence.* [In French.]

2037* Dobrinsky, J. "Aspects biographiques de l'oeuvre de Somerset Maugham: l'enfance" (Biographical Aspects in the Work of Somerset Maugham: Childhood), ETUDES ANGLAISES, VIII (Oct-Dec 1955), 299-312.

M's works would benefit by an interpretative biographical study, for such "autobiographical" essays as *The Summing Up* partake less of confession than of literature. They suffer from omissions stemming from the writer's reticence, and reveal to the public a dummy figure ("un personnage plastron") which testifies to the author's desire for immunity from inquisitiveness and his taste for mystification.

In his novels, M lays bare his *affective* memory, under the guise of fiction. This applies especially to *Of Human Bondage,* in which he unburdens his mind by laying the ghost of his past. The fictional aspect of confession, in that it transposes the factual elements of the biography, reveals its *intimate value.* Thus, when relating Philip's infancy in London, M violates the truth, since he himself lived in Paris for the first ten years of his life [1874-1884], but the middle class surroundings are faithfully reproduced; and though he keeps his feelings in check, the emotional significance of this period is made manifest. [Many aspects of M's literary personality can be accounted for by those years spent in France and the fact that French was the language he spoke first as a child.] More than his father's death two years after that of his mother the first bereavement—when he was eight, and the only one mentioned in *Of Human Bondage*—was deeply felt. A legitimate feeling of frustration, along with nostalgia for motherly care, largely accounts for both his hatred (in his works *and* his life) for hard-heartedness or feminine selfishness (Mildred, Mrs. Strickland, Isabel, etc.) and his indulgence to light, but tender-hearted, women like Rosie in *Cakes and Ale.* The cult of "sanctity" which, from *The Painted Veil* (1925) on, is one of his leitmotivs, is not unconnected with this wistful longing. An orphan at ten, M was brought up by his uncle, a Kentish clergyman; his experience, closely akin to Samuel Butler's, and faithfully transcribed in *Of Human Bondage* and *Cakes and Ale,* explains the affinities between the two writers—aggressiveness against the same dogmatic and formalistic excesses together with the quest for a more generous code of morals.

Lastly, M's life at the preparatory school, then at Canterbury King's School, was drawn upon for Philip's childhood. M was not clubfooted like his hero, but he stammered and mispronounced English. Bullied by his schoolfellows and ill-treated by some of his masters, he retired within himself and adopted the attitude of an ironical spectator: he dreamt of an *intellectual and social* revenge and put on an appearance of superior indifference. [In French.]

2038* Doner, Dean. "Spinoza's ETHICS and Maugham," UNIVERSITY OF KANSAS CITY REVIEW, XXI (June 1955), 261-69.

The structure of *Of Human Bondage* is derived from Spinozian concepts. Contrary to most critics beliefs, M substitutes "right action" for the Spinozian "knowledge of God," and shows Philip learning to accept present situations rather than fight them. The novel's final view of life is that it is more than meaningless and requires affirmation and acceptance.

2039 Faverty, Frederic E. "Maugham Dissects Ten Authors," CHICAGO SUNDAY TRIBUNE BOOKS, 8 May 1955, p. 2.
The Art of Fiction: An Introduction to Ten Novels and Their Authors has "verve and readability."

2040 Ford, George H. DICKENS AND HIS READERS: ASPECTS OF NOVEL-CRITICISM SINCE 1836 (Princeton U P for the University of Cincinnati, 1955), pp. 160, 191, 195, 224, 225.
[Primarily general remarks on M in relation to Dickens.]

2041 Green, Julien. JOURNAL, 1950-1954 (Paris: Librairie Plon, 1955), p. 154.
M has a fine spirit, good manners, and is attentive to speakers. M does not think Gide's PORTE ETROITE a good novel because the actions of its characters are insufficiently motivated. [Recounting of Green's visit to M in April 1952.] [In French.]

2042 Heikkilä, Kauko. "Eikä mikään muttu" (Nothing Changes), SATAKUNNAN KANSA, 21 May 1955, p. 6.
Though the style [of the Finnish translation] of *Then and Now* is more attractive than is usual with M's works, the end is a failure: M seems to lose interest after Borgia disappears from his sight. [In Finnish.]

2043 Heikkilä, Kauko. "Kirjailija kirjoittaa kirjailijasta" (An Author on an Author), SATAKUNNAN KANSA, 24 Sept 1955, p. 7.
The construction [of the Finnish translation] of *Cakes and Ale* is masterly. M builds his characters piece by piece until they are viewed from all sides. The style is excellent; the author catches the right tones and atmosphere. [In Finnish.]

2044 K., Y. *"Ei Maistu Elämältä" (Cakes and Ale),* LAPIN LOIMU, II: 4-5 (1955), 24.
Cakes and Ale [in the Finnish translation] is one of M's most outstanding works because of its sharp, though somewhat conventional, satire. It is a specimen of skillful mass production of novels. [In Finnish.]

2045 Korg, Jacob. "Belles-Lettres," NATION (NY), CLXXXI (30 July 1955), 102.
In *The Art of Fiction: An Introduction to Ten Novels and Their Authors,* "Mr. Maugham conducts himself as the canny old broker of literature, giving all the facts clearly and interestingly. His critical evaluations are conservative, and they are offered grudgingly, as though they were tips based on secret information."

2046 L., K. "Politiikan ja lemmen juonet" (Plots of Politics and Love), HELSINGIN SANOMAT, 1 May 1955, p. 17.

M moves in the world of the Italian Renaissance as effortlessly and elegantly as in our own times. The result in [the Finnish translation of] *Then and Now* is a cheerful, lively, and ingenious novel. The character of Machiavelli is convincing. [In Finnish.]

2047 Laitinen, Kai. "Maughamin paras romaani" (Maugham's Best Novel), HELSINGIN SANOMAT, 19 Sept 1950, p. 7.

Cakes and Ale [in the Finnish translation] is M's best novel, a work of art, in its elaboration of every author's tragedy: his solitude and inaccessibility. [In Finnish.]

2048 "The Listener's Book Chronicle," LISTENER, LIII (5 May 1955), 813.

In *The Art of Fiction: An Introduction to Ten Novels and Their Authors,* M "as a critic cuts sharp, but seldom very deep"; therefore, it is the biographical (the "characterizations"), not the critical, parts of his introductions which are the most "valuable." This collection is very readable.

2049 Mander, Raymond and Joe Mitchenson. THE ARTIST AND THE THEATRE: THE STORY OF THE PAINTINGS COLLECTED AND PRESENTED TO THE NATIONAL THEATRE BY W. S. MAUGHAM. With an Introduction by W. S. Maugham. (Melbourne, Lond, & Toronto: William Heinemann, 1955).

[A history and reproduction of the forty-odd oil paintings which M donated to the Trustees of the National Theatre in 1951.]

2050* Mander, Raymond and Joe Mitchenson. THEATRICAL COMPANION TO MAUGHAM: A PICTORIAL RECORD OF THE FIRST PERFORMANCES OF THE PLAYS OF W. SOMERSET MAUGHAM. With an Appreciation of Maugham's Dramatic Works by J. C. Trewin. (Lond: Rockliff, 1955).

This book contains a synopsis of every play, produced or unproduced, that M wrote, and of every play adapted by other writers from his novels and stories. Also included are the exact dates and places of first productions (in England and America), their casts, at least one review of each production, and M's own observations on the productions from letters and *The Summing Up* chiefly. Film versions are also fully documented. Both stage and film versions are amply illustrated. Equally valuable is the nine-part appendix, which painstakingly indexes (1) the plays in the order of their writing, (2) the plays in order of their production, (3) plays adapted by other writers from M's novels and stories, (4) film versions of the plays, (5) film versions of stories and novels by M, (6) first American and New York productions of M's plays and other playwrights' plays from M's novels and short stories, (7) first publications of the plays, English and American, (8) translations and broadcasts, and (9) the names of the characters in M's plays. [See J. C. Trewin's "W. Somerset Maugham: An Appreciation of His Work in the Theatre," 1955.]

2051 Manninen, Kerttu. *"Nytja Ennen" (Then and Now),* AAMULEHTI, 8 May 1955, p. 8.

M is clearly inspired by Machiavelli's personality and way of thought. There is plenty of sparkling wit but little real warmth [in the Finnish translation]. [In Finnish.]

2052 Monod, S. "Comptes Rendus" (Critical Reports), ETUDES ANGLAISES, VIII (April-June 1955), 173-74.

In *The Art of Fiction: An Introduction to Ten Novels and Their Authors,* M concentrates more on the novelists than on their works so that this book could be called more appropriately *Ten Novelists.* It is a lowbrow profession of faith on the art of the novel. [In French.]

2053 "Mr. Maugham Abroad," TIMES LITERARY SUPPLEMENT (Lond), 23 Dec 1955, p. 772.

In *The Travel Books of W. Somerset Maugham* [including *On a Chinese Screen, The Gentleman in the Parlour,* and *Don Fernando*], for the writing and for the spirit of adventure which lies at the back of it, *The Gentleman in the Parlour* "stands out."

2054 P., T. "Mitä libristi lukee—ja mitä myy" (What a Bookseller Reads—and What He Sells), LIBRISTI, XI: 5 (1955), 41-42.

In [the Finnish translation of] *Then and Now,* the total picture remains obscure. The characters are flat and trivial, and the political satire is not particularly sharp. [In Finnish.]

2055 "Presentable Choice," TIMES (Lond), 8 Dec 1955, p. 13.

M "provides a short and characteristically lively preface" to *The Travel Books of W. Somerset Maugham* [including *On a Chinese Screen, The Gentleman in the Parlour,* and *Don Fernando*].

2056 R-suo, A. "Romaani Macchiavellista" (A Novel about Machiavelli), MAASEUDUN TULEVAISUUS, 7 May 1955, p. 13.

M is not at his best, but [the Finnish translation of] *Then and Now* is not totally devoid of attraction and elegance. One can sense a kind of tiredness, a lack of power, and the flavor of routine. [In Finnish.]

2057 S., V. "Macchiavelli elementissään" (Machiavelli in His Element), UUSI SUOMI, 24 April 1955, p. 18.

[The Finnish translation of] *Then and Now* is a real novel, not a biography or a historical treatise, magnificently written and carefully constructed, wise rather than warm. [In Finnish.]

2058 S., V. "Maughamin mainetta" (Maugham's Fame), UUSI SUOMI, 9 Oct 1955, p. 16.

The plot is woven from a variety of materials. M's skill is indisputable, but the Finnish translation of *Cakes and Ale* does not warm the reader, nor does it make a permanent impression. Its art is cool, its wisdom cutting, its life illusionless. [In Finnish.]

2059 "Selected Books," NEW REPUBLIC, CXXXII (16 May 1955), 45.

In *The Art of Fiction: An Introduction to Ten Novels and Their Authors,* M repeats his belief that novelists are storytellers, and deals critically with what he calls the "ten best novels."

2060 Tompan Tuomo [Pseudonym]. "Helsingin horisontista" (Viewed from Helsinki), SAVON SANOMAT, 2 Oct 1955, p. 4.

[Review of the Finnish translation of *Cakes and Ale.*] [In Finnish.]

2061 Tompan Tuomo [Pseudonym]. "Pilkkeitä" (Splinters), ILKKA, 13 April 1955, p. 7.

[Brief review of the Finnish translation of *Then and Now.*] [In Finnish.]

2062 -tonen. "Vanhan parturi-Sheppeyn vaiherikas elämänilta" (The Eventful Evening of Life of Old Barber Sheppey), KALEVA, 26 Feb 1955, p. 6.

In [the revival of the Finnish adaptation of] *Sheppey,* we can see the bad and the good in ourselves. M is an ingenious writer; the problems of his plays concentrate on seeking and finding human happiness. [In Finnish.]

2063* Trewin, J. C. "W. Somerset Maugham: An Appreciation of His Work in the Theatre," THEATRICAL COMPANION TO MAUGHAM, ed by Raymond Mander and Joe Mitchenson (Lond: Rockliff, 1955), pp. 1-16; rptd as "Physician for the Theatre's Ills," THEATRE ARTS, XL (June 1956), 61-63, 94-96.

Although the merit of M's dramatic work of three decades has varied, one quality has remained constant: his ability "to tell a story in terms of the theatre." This narrative power is amply substantiated by the fact that M's dramas come off well under the merciless "X-ray" of radio performances for which there is no visual aid. The plays which will assuredly survive in the future are *The Circle, Our Betters, For Services Rendered, The Constant Wife, Caroline, The Breadwinner,* and possibly *Lady Frederick* and *Smith.* But, in *The Circle* especially are gathered all the qualities which won M's fame: "narrative relish, precision of dialogue, relentless observation of character, wit that is both verbal and visual, and an assured constructive power."

2064 V-m, K. "Elämältä se maistui" (It Savored of Life), KARJALA, 29 Sept 1955, p. 4.
[The Finnish translation of] *Cakes and Ale* reveals M's expert knowledge of the human mind, his elegant narration, and his ability to impress his readers favorably (a quality not without dangers) at their best. The composition is difficult but its realization is faultless. [In Finnish.]

2065 Walbridge, Earle F. "New Books Appraised," LIBRARY JOURNAL, LXXX (1 April 1955), 784.
In *The Art of Fiction: An Introduction to Ten Novels and Their Authors,* M's opinions of Melville's art, Stendhal's amours, and the merits of MADAME BOVARY are "piquant."

2066 "Walpole Salver Sold for £7,800," TIMES (Lond), 8 Dec 1955, p. 12.
M's original autograph manuscript of *The Moon and Sixpence* sold for £2,600 at Sotheby's on 7 Dec 1955; *The Summing Up* fetched £140 (three proofs corrected throughout in M's hand).

2067 Waltari, Satu. "Kaksi kirjailijanrouvaa" (Two Authors' Wives), VIIKKOSANOMAT, No. 45 (1955), 26-27.
Contrasting Rosie and Mrs. Driffield in *Cakes and Ale* shows that M's attitude towards various aspects of life is so tolerant that it becomes irritating. This is the reason why some people consider him a trivial and minor author. *Cakes and Ale* [Finnish translation] is a top achievement of literary witticism and imagination flavored by cynicism. [In Finnish.]

2068* Weales, Gerald. "Mr. Maugham on the Novel," COMMONWEAL, LXII (27 May 1955), 212-14.
M wrote his essays in *The Art of Fiction: An Introduction to Ten Novels and Their Authors* as introductions to abridgements of the ten novels he considered the best ever written; they lack depth, naturally, and so the title of the present collection is misleading, for the few remarks M makes on creativity are "meaningless or . . . so commonplace that they are uninformative."

2069* Wing, Donald G. "The Manuscript of Somerset Maugham's *On a Chinese Screen*," YALE UNIVERSITY LIBRARY GAZETTE, XXIX (Jan 1955), 126.
Yale has just received as a gift from M the manuscript of *On a Chinese Screen,* written after a trip to China and published in 1922. The pages are frequently renumbered showing revision of the order of pages, though only a small part is rewritten. Here are characters in outline who later become familiar as the M family. M also gave Yale the manuscript of *Strictly Personal* in 1942. Yale has proof sheets of other volumes.

1956

2070 Anhava, Tuomas (ed.). MAAILMAN KIRJAT JA KIRJAILIJAT (The Books and Writers of the World) (Helsinki: Otava, 1957), p. 210.

M's plays are skillfully composed, but his knowledge of human nature, his intelligent irony, and his sincere analysis of existence are best revealed in his novels. [In Finnish.]

2071 Assä [Pseudonym]. "Maughamin *'Kirje'* Mikkelin Teatterissa" (Maugham's *The Letter* at the Mikkeli Theater), SAVON SANOMAT, 28 Jan 1956, p. 7.

The plot and its development [in the revival of the Finnish adaptation] are extremely intelligent, but the audience would like to see a more concrete clarification towards the end of the play and a more ingenious final solution. [In Finnish.]

2072 "B. B. C. Television: *'The Letter'* by Somerset Maugham," TIMES (Lond), 3 Dec 1956, p. 5.

The televised production of the play shows that M ends the story at the point of what should have been its most revealing scene [Leslie "discovered" by her husband to be lying]. "For its deftly constructed plot, however compelling attention in such seedy pasteboard figures, *The Letter* is admirable."

2073* Cosman, Max. "Mr. Maugham as Footnote," PACIFIC SPECTATOR, X (Winter 1956), 64-69.

M has been successful because he set out to learn what the public wanted and has given it to them. He adheres to "what is topical, true, but at the same time fundamental." One of the "fundamentals" is love, which M has treated from many different aspects. Another is marriage, his treatment probably influenced by his own unsuccessful marriage. Yet a third is religion, more "moral, sensory, mystical, or personal than doctrinal." Whichever way he swings —to optimism or pessimism— M always returns to the balance of common sense. Popularity does not necessarily mean inferiority. He does well, he is a "professional," in established patterns and thoughts; his weakness lies in the fact that he is no innovator. He is not among first-rate artists because of "an insistent doubt which makes hollow what he writes and how he writes." From his philosophy of entertainment and his "underlying doubt of values" follows his championing of a "limited intellection." His style is "simple, lucid, and euphonious." Some of his stories, a few of his novels, and a play or two may attain permanence. A worker in four genres, one who has given pleasure to many, M deserves at least a "large footnote" in future literary histories.

2074* Dobrinsky, J. "Comptes Rendus" (Critical Reports), ETUDES ANGLAISES, IX (July-Sept 1956), 266-67.

"This novel [the reissue of *Mrs. Craddock*] of desire and disillusion which transposes, with passionate veracity, a painful and early experience of the author, testifies, both in the manner and in the matter, to the influence of the French naturalistic school." The tameness of the plot is atoned for by the brilliance of the dialogue. The revision has failed to weed out all traces of clumsiness and repetitions. A French translation would be welcome. [In French.]

2075* Dobrinsky, J. "Comptes Rendus" (Critical Reports), ETUDES ANGLAISES, IX (Oct-Dec 1956), 366-67.

The reissued *The Magician* is a bewildering shocker written for money. It was meant to exploit the vogue of Huysmans' LA-BAS. Despite the improbability of the plot, one cannot fail to appreciate M's gift for dialogue and his dramatic power. The reviewer is reminded of M's own words: "The greatest authors have written a number of very poor books." [In French.]

2076 Ekholm, Rauno. "Iltojen ratoksi" (Evening Entertainment), SUOMEN SOSIALIDEMOKRAATTI, 1 Aug 1956, p. 7.

[The Finnish translation of] *Creatures of Circumstance* shows M is a skillful storyteller, but his short stories have no permanent value, due to the pleasant monotony with which the author describes most extraordinary events. [In Finnish.]

2077* Farmer, A. J. "Comptes Rendus" (Critical Reports), ETUDES ANGLAISES, IX (Jan-March 1956), 76.

[Review of Klaus W. Jonas' THE MAUGHAM ENIGMA.] M enjoys a spectacular success with the public which is quite out of proportion with his comparative disfavor among the critics. This is what Jonas calls the Maugham Enigma. All the writers represented in this anthology maintain that M is a clever writer, but only a few of them think he can be called an artist. His literary position is insecure. [In French.]

2078 "Fiction," TIMES LITERARY SUPPLEMENT (Lond), 21 Sept 1956, p. 551.

The Magician [reissue] is a "stiffly written tale [which] lacks the genius of a Huysmans on the one hand and the spiritual intensity of a Charles Williams on the other. . . . "

2079* Fielden, John S[eward]. " 'Mrs. Beamish' and *The Circle*,"

BOSTON UNIVERSITY STUDIES IN ENGLISH, II (Summer 1956), 113-23.

A study of M's unpublished comedy, "Mrs. Beamish," reveals a thematic development parallel to that of *The Circle,* and lends credence to the belief that M was not satirizing Kitty and Teddy, but Champion-Cheney and Arnold, in *The Circle*. The ending of the play is *not* anti-romantic; on the contrary, it would support the view that M's title means "that once again romantic love has triumphed . . . over the cold and calculating conventionality of the Champion-Cheneys and the world they represent."

2080 Gould, Jack. "TV: Maugham's *'The Letter'* Revived," NEW YORK TIMES, 16 Oct 1956, p. 67.

[Review of the televised production.]

2081 Jonas, Klaus W. THE GENTLEMAN FROM CAP FERRAT. With a Preface by W. Somerset Maugham. (New Haven: Center of Maugham Studies, 1956); rptd, with minor additions, as the second essay in THE WORLD OF SOMERSET MAUGHAM (NY: British Book Centre, 1958), pp. 21-36.

[A brief biographical sketch of M up to his eighties, emphasizing M's good business sense, friendliness, zest for travel, aristocratic tastes, and sense of humor.]

2082 Laitinen, Kai. "Mainiota Maughamia" (Maugham at His Best), HELSINGIN SANOMAT, 18 Sept 1956, p. 15.

[The Finnish translation of] *Creatures of Circumstance* shows M's narrative technique is more suited to short stories than to novels. The stories show the author's expert knowledge of human nature and his tolerant attitude towards life. [In Finnish.]

2083 "Maugham Novel as Opera," TIMES (Lond), 22 May 1956, p. 12.

M's *Moon and Sixpence* is to become an opera by John Gardiner and Patrick Terry. [See, also, " *'The Moon and Sixpence'* as an Opera," TIMES (Lond), 24 Jan 1957, p. 6; "A Title from 'THE TIMES,' TIMES (Lond), 14 May 1957, p. 3; "The Arts—Sadler's Wells Opera: 'THE MOON AND SIXPENCE,' " TIMES (Lond), 25 May 1957, p. 3; and "Sadler's Wells Theatre: 'THE MOON AND SIXPENCE,' " TIMES (Lond), 4 Oct 1957, p. 3.]

2084 R., V. "Maughamin novelleja" (Maugham's Short Stories), AAMULEHTI, 11 July 1956, p. 7.

Each story in [the Finnish translation of] *Creatures of Circumstance* hides the pearl of an idea or of a valuable psychological observation; yet, as a whole, the stories lack the attraction of an aphorism. They are wise and memorable anecdotes rather than short stories in the ordinary sense of the term. [In Finnish.]

2085 Repo, Ville. "Kirjallisuss ja elämä" (Literature and Life), SUOMALAINEN SUOMI, XXIV: 1 (1956), 48-49.

Cakes and Ale [in the Finnish translation] is an extremely amusing novel. It is a satirical description of the life of an author, but Rosie's feminine, exuberant personality makes it much more human than an ordinary satire generally is. She is the richest and most lifelike of M's female characters. Satire at its best. [In Finnish.]

2086 Rhodes, Anthony. "New Novels," LISTENER, LV (5 Jan 1956), 29.

The reissued *Mrs. Craddock* has "gentleness, clarity, shape" without cynicism. The supposedly "objectionable" passages, though probably shocking to readers in 1902, are not at all shocking to the reader of 1955.

2087 S-o, A. *"Sattuman Satoa" (Creatures of Circumstance),* TYÖKANSAN SANOMAT, 15 June 1956, p. 4.

These short stories [in the Finnish translation] lack the liveliness characteristic of great art. The technique of composition calls to mind some of Ibsen's plays: the conflict and the action have taken place in the past; the curtain rises to show the aftermath. [In Finnish.]

2088* Stott, Raymond Toole. THE WRITINGS OF WILLIAM SOMERSET MAUGHAM: A BIBLIOGRAPHY. (Lond: Rota, 1956).

[Improved and enlarged version of MAUGHAMIANA (1950). Appendix II contains a list of books and articles about M, including about ten items for the 1950s.]

2089 Swinnerton, Frank. BACKGROUND WITH CHORUS: A FOOTNOTE TO CHANGES IN ENGLISH LITERARY FASHION BETWEEN 1901 AND 1917 (Lond: Hutchinson, 1956), pp. 27, 102, 124, 139, 162, 176, 213.

[References to M as novelist and playwright as Swinnerton surveys the pre-World War I literary scene.]

2090 Vallette, Jacques. "Lettres Anglo-Saxonnes" (Anglo-Saxon Letters), LE MERCURE DE FRANCE, CCCXXVI (April 1956), 777.

[Paragraph review of the reissue of *Mrs. Craddock*.] [In French.]

2091 Vallette, Jacques. "Livres" (Books), LE MERCURE DE FRANCE, CCCXXVIII (Dec 1956), 734.

[Paragraph review of the reissue of *The Magician,* recounting how the novel came to be written.] [In French.]

1957

2092 "The Arts —Sadler's Wells Opera: 'THE MOON AND SIXPENCE,' " TIMES (Lond), 25 May 1957, p. 3.

The production of John Gardiner and Patrick Terry's operatic version is poorly integrated: the music conflicts with the dialogue and the tempo of the play itself. [See, also, "Sadler's Wells Theatre: 'THE MOON AND SIXPENCE,' " TIMES (Lond), 4 Oct 1957, p. 3.]

2093* Dobrinsky, J. "Les Debuts de Somerset Maugham au Théâtre: Naissance d'une Vocation et Affirmation d'une Personnalité Littéraire" (The Beginnings of Somerset Maugham in the Theater: Birth of a Vocation and Affirmation of a Literary Personality), ETUDES ANGLAISES, X (Oct-Dec 1957), 310-21.

Turning to the naturalistic drama of Ibsen to restore his self-respect shattered by emotional and intellectual conflicts, M discovered that this outlet was, for him, illusory; he was unable to unite successfully the Ibsenite ideology with his own mode of expression. The neo-Restoration tradition in light Edwardian comedy enabled him to discipline his art and his inspiration, and to attain to a fortune, but not a permanent alliance of the psychological conditions necessary to this balance; a deeply personal theater resulted. Financially secure, certain of his *métier,* yet still experimental and still concerned with the misunderstandings and frustrations caused by the isolation of the individual, M finally achieved catharsis inherent in the idealistic conclusion to *Of Human Bondage*. A new emotional conflict in 1926 caused him to turn to spiritual justification, to problems of old age and death, and away from the theater. [In French.]

2094 Gordon, Caroline. HOW TO READ A NOVEL (NY: Viking P, 1957), pp. 117-18.

M is the foremost exponent of the method of "telling" as opposed to that of "rendering dramatically." He employs "the same narrator, a benevolent, sophisticated, rather languid world traveler, who somewhat resembles Mr. Maugham himself." *Christmas Holiday* in contrast with THE AMBASSADORS proves the foregoing opinions.

2095 Grötz, Alfred."W. Somerset Maughams Erzählung 'The Outstation' " (W. Somerset Maugham's Story "The Outstation"), DIE NEUEREN SPRACHEN, N.S. VI (1957), 367-71.

Compares M's story with Galsworthy's "The Man Who Kept His Form," praises the tight structure of M's work, and analyzes Warburton's illusions as well as the bitterly ironic and satirical ending.

2096 Highet, Gilbert. *"The Magician,"* TALENTS AND GENIUSES: THE PLEASURES OF APPRECIATION (NY: Oxford U P, 1957), pp. 158-64.

Oliver Haddo, the hero of *The Magician,* has a life similar to Aleister Crowley's.

2097 Jensen, Sven Arnold. WILLIAM SOMERSET MAUGHAM: SOME ASPECTS OF THE MAN AND HIS WORK. (Oslo: Oslo U P, 1957).

M's nondramatic writings, beginning with *Of Human Bondage,* evidences M's attitudes toward life, love, and man. Toward life M feels and practices "humorous resignation." Love is, as a rule, unrequited; and "is often nothing but an illusion or a pose." His final attitude toward man has "ended in a spirit of amused tolerance."

2098 K-ki, Atte. "Nuoren miehen kädestä" (From a Young Man's Pen), KALTIO, XIII:5 (1957), 119-20.

M has developed much as a writer since 1902, but many features [in the Finnish translation] of *Mrs. Craddock* are typical of M in his mature days: the witty and outspoken man of the world figures throughout all his works. [In Finnish.]

2099* L., K. "Tunteen kuolema" (Death of Feeling), HELSINGIN SANOMAT, 14 Sept 1957, p. 13.

[The Finnish translation of] *Mrs. Craddock,* in its present form, is a collaboration between the young M and the old M, and this obviously makes it incoherent. Bertha is the favorite of the young author, and Miss Ley the object of the older man's interest. The purpose of the novel remains obscure. [In Finnish.]

2100 L-la, A. "Isä lauloi totuuksia" (Daddy Told a Few Home-Truths), SUOMEN SOSIALIDEMOKRAATTI, 23 March 1957, p. 9.

[The Finnish adaptation of] *The Breadwinner,* though not a masterpiece, yet contains an idea and message of its own. It condemns the violent struggle for position and prosperity, has many a satiric utterance. [In Finnish.]

2101 Lash, Henry. "Tea with Mr. Maugham," LIBRARY JOURNAL, LXXXII (1 Oct 1957), 2317-18.

[Interview.]

2102 Laurilla, A. "Jo nuori Maugham oli ajoittain järkevä" (Even Young Maugham Was Sensible at Times), SUOMEN SOSIALIDEMOKRAATTI, 22 Sept 1957, p. 6.

[The Finnish translation of] *Mrs. Craddock* is a defence of and recommendation for peaceful life. Sometimes one feels that M would have liked to make his novel a description of the tragic fate of a woman, but was prevented by his common sense. [In Finnish.]

2103 "Maugham Wants Letters Burned to Bar Posthumous Publication," NEW YORK TIMES, 13 Nov 1957, pp. 1, 32.

M requests that all of his letters be burned and directs his executors to prevent their publication after his death.

2104 Paavilainen, Matti. "Ironian oppitunti" (Lesson in Irony), YLIOPPILASLEHTI, 13 Sept 1957, p. 8.

[The Finnish translation of] *Mrs. Craddock* reveals a refreshingly unconventional marriage story, though not much more. Its greatest merit lies in the witty dialogue. [In Finnish.]

2105 Palola, Eino. "William Somerset Maugham," HEIDENSTAMISTA UNDSETIIN: SUURTEN KIRJAILIJAIN ELAMÄKERTOJA (FROM HEIDENSTAM TO UNDSET: LIVES OF GREAT AUTHORS) (Porvoo-Helsinki: WSOY, 1957), pp. 380-85.

M is the Maupassant of England. According to English critics, he is a keen observer, a master of form, a refined connoisseur of the world, true to himself and his calling. In other countries, this assessment is not wholeheartedly accepted. There he is regarded as a skilful author whose ideas are not universal but whose satire mercilessly reveals the mental defects of people. [Biographical and appreciative essay.] [In Finnish.]

2106 Pennanen, Eila. "Lyhyitä esittelyjä" (Short Reviews), PARNASSO, VII: 6 (1957), 284-85.

[The Finnish translation shows] *Mrs. Craddock* is a pleasant and amusing book, though one never forgets that it is old and out-of-date. [In Finnish.]

2107 S., A. "Kuritonta sukupolvea englantilaiseen tapaan" ('Undisciplined Generation' in the English Way), MASSEUDUN TULEVAISUUS, 26 March 1957, p. 7.

[The Finnish adaptation of] *The Breadwinner* is as fresh as if it were written yesterday. The plot is not particularly original, but the dialogue is unforced, and there is much sharp psychological observation. [In Finnish.]

2108 S., Am. "Nuorta Maughamia" (By the Young Maugham), UUSI SUOMI, 21 July 1957, p. 11.

[The Finnish translation of] *Mrs. Craddock* shows M had no talent for describing overwhelming passion, but even when taking his faltering first steps on a literary career he could not write an altogether uninteresting book. [In Finnish.]

2109 "Sadler's Wells Theatre: 'THE MOON AND SIXPENCE,'" TIMES (Lond), 4 Oct 1957, p. 3.

Now that everyone is familiar with the score of John Gardiner and Patrick Terry's operatic version, the opera engrosses "attention from first note to last with its strong sense of atmosphere." Still, the play moves slowly, particularly in the last three or four scenes. [See, also, "The Arts —Sadler's Wells Theatre: 'THE MOON AND SIXPENCE,'" TIMES (Lond), 25 May 1957, p. 3.]

2110 "Topics of the Times," NEW YORK TIMES, 4 Dec 1957, p. 38. [Editorial dealing with M's request that his letters be destroyed (see "Maugham Wants Letters Burned," NEW YORK TIMES, 13 Nov 1957, pp. 1, 32) and disagreeing with M's position.]

2111 U-11, S. "Ystävämme Maugham sanoo häijyjä totuuksia" (Our Friend Maugham Tells Home-Truths), HELSINGIN SANOMAT, 22 March 1957, p. 15.

[The Finnish adaptation of] *The Breadwinner* reveals its greatest merit lies in its dialogue. When it is at its best, it equals that written by Shaw. One enjoys the witty and clear-sighted mischievousness of the play, but one would like to find a deeper and more "humane" sense of humor. [In Finnish.]

2112 V-m, K. "Maughamia näyttämöllä" (Maugham on the Stage), UUSI SUOMI, 23 March 1957, p. 14.

[The Finnish adaptation of] *The Breadwinner* has an out-of-date flavor. The final solution is typical of the period between World Wars I and II. [In Finnish.]

1958

2113* Cordell, Richard A. "Somerset Maugham: Lucidity versus Cunning," ENGLISH FICTION IN TRANSITION, I: 3 (Fall Special 1958), 30-32.

Neither "Old" nor "New" critics cared or care for M, so that never before in the long history of literary criticism "has lucidity been so ignored, if not belittled, as a quality of good writing." M's adherents praise his economy, the thrust of his narrative, the lucidity and effectiveness of his style; his numerous detractors deplore his shallow philosophy, sophomoric cynicism, and a simplicity of style that is often puerile. The best works on M are Dottin's two studies —SOMERSET MAUGHAM ET SES ROMANS (1929) and LE THEATRE DE SOMERSET MAUGHAM (1937), Suzanne Query's LA PHILOSOPHIE DE SOMERSET MAUGHAM (1933), and Helmut Papajewski's DIE WELT-, LEBENS-, UND KUNSTANSCHAUUNG WILLIAM SOMER-

SET MAUGHAMS (1952). A number of scholarly projects on M remain to be done. An estimation of M's place in serious British drama before 1934 is essential. Ph.D. theses in Germany and elsewhere in central Europe need examination. The influence of scientific studies and training on M's work is yet uncertain. His early life needs documentation. Studies of M as a critic of literature and of painting are also needed. M's influence in France, his position in the Edwardian theatre, his toying with mysticism are only a few of the subjects not yet fully exhausted.

2114 ENGLISH, XII (Autumn 1958), 122.
R. N. Deb read a paper, entitled "The Short Stories of Somerset Maugham," before the English Association Branch at The University, Allahabad, U. P., India, on 9 Nov 1957. [News note.]

2115 "Essayists Who are Laws unto Themselves," TIMES (Lond), 6 Nov 1958, p. 13.
Points of View shows that M can write on almost anything—"and always he carries his reader along smoothly, comfortably, and with fully justified assurance. There is, after all, nothing quite like a Rolls-Royce at any stage of its existence."

2116* "The Essential Story," TIMES LITERARY SUPPLEMENT (Lond), 14 Nov 1958, p. 657.
In *Points of View,* M is protesting against those who consider storytellers as being of little importance, and reminds us of the importance of the story as a component of the novel. Some novelists have rebelled against the tyranny of story by emphasizing the elements of realism and truth to counter criticism of being fantastic and impossible. But in some few great books there is not only an interest in the sequence of events, but in character, too. Among these books is *Of Human Bondage.*

2117* Fielden, John Seward. "Somerset Maugham on the Purpose of Drama," EDUCATIONAL THEATRE JOURNAL, X (Oct 1958) 218-22.
Critics have been too quick to accept M's statements, in *The Summing Up* and the prefaces to the *Collected Plays,* that the aim of the drama "is not to instruct but to please," to provide an "evening's diversion." They have thus, done M an injustice by dismissing him as "a talented cynic." In his less known works, especially *Don Fernando* (1935), however, he holds that the ultimate goal of art "is an aesthetic emotion that has worth, and it is worthy 'only if it leads to action.' " In his essay on Kant *(The Vagrant Mood,* 1952), M also holds that a work of art should be a diversion *and* that it should affect the soul so that "worthy actions" are produced. The effects are more likely to result from painting, sculpture, poetry, or the poetic drama of the past rather than from the prose play.

2118 Gransden, K. W. "How to Succeed as a Writer," NEW STATESMAN, N. S. LVI (15 Nov 1958), 702.

The few moments in *Points of View* when M removes his mask are preferable; but M's "whole literary personality is a sustained and elaborate pose, a full-dress Edwardian affair," and it is only rarely relaxed.

2119 I., K. J. "Kolmenkymmenen vuoden takaista Maughamia" (A Maugham from Thirty Years Ago), UUSI SUOMI, 4 April 1958, p. 16.

[The Finnish translation shows] *Ashenden* is incoherent, some of its characters too "literary" to be credible. The transformation of forceful experiences to serve artistic purposes has been too difficult a task for M. [In Finnish.]

2120* Jonas, Klaus W. "W. Somerset Maugham Collections in America," JAHRBUCH FÜR AMERIKASTUDIEN, III (1958), 205-13; subsequently issued as Publication No. 2 of the Centre of Maugham Studies (University of Pittsburgh); revised, enlarged, and entered as an appendix, under the title, "A Note on Maugham Collections," THE WORLD OF SOMERSET MAUGHAM, ed by Klaus W. Jonas (NY: British Book Centre, 1959), pp. 180-94.

[Jonas sketches M's relations with William L. Phelps and describes the M collections at Yale, Harvard, Stanford, Princeton, the Library of Congress, the Pierpont Morgan Library, and the New York Public Library as well as some private collections including that of the Center of Maugham Studies in Pittsburgh. Some of M's letters are cited.]

2121 K-la, V. "Vanha hyvä Maugham" (Good Old Maugham), KESKIPOHJANMAA, 29 Oct 1958, p. 2.

[The Finnish translation of] *Of Human Bondage* is curiously attractive; there is excellent and merciless psychological analysis in its masterful construction. Yet, this is not M's most important work; that is *Cakes and Ale.* [In Finish.]

2122* Kermode, Frank. "Eminently Readable," MANCHESTER GUARDIAN, 11 Nov 1958, p. 4.

Points of View is not . . . "valuable as criticism," for it is not easy to see why M praises the Goncourts, and in his essay on Chekhov "he denies us the chance of hearing one prolific story writer on another by confining himself to general praise of Chekhov's constructive power." All the essays, of which the one on Tillotson is most interesting, are "designed to entertain," and they can be read with "remarkable ease."

2123* Kirjamies [Pseudonym]. "Kansainvälistä vakoilua" (International Espionage), ETELÄ-SAIMAA, 18 March 1958, p. 8.

In reading [the Finnish translation of] *Ashenden,* the reader does not feel he is reading a novel. M leads him intelligently and attractively to one direction, but then lets the story end and follows another path. The failure is almost complete. *Ashenden* is one of the worst of M's novels. [In Finnish.]

2124 Kirstinä, Väinö. "Laajamuotoista kertomataidetta" (Narrative Art in Extended Form), KALEVA, 13 Nov 1958, p. 6.
[The Finnish translation of] *Of Human Bondage* suggests that one quarter of the length of the novel would have been sufficient, for the latter part of the book is nothing but a waste of time, paper, and ink. Its greatest merit is its characterization. [In Finnish.]

2125 Konsala, Simo. "Uusi ja vanha menestys" (New and Old Success), SUOMALAINEN SUOMI, XXVI: 2 (1958), 121.
Mrs. Craddock, if it had been written in the mid-nineteenth century, would have placed M by the side of Flaubert in the history of world literature. In the course of the years, however, the book has lost its best flavor, and its setting seems too formal. [Review of Finnish translation.] [In Finnish.]

2126 Kula, Kauko. "Leinosta Franceen: pääsiäisen uutuuskirjoja" (From Leino to Anatole France: New Books for Easter), KAUPPALEHTI, 2 April 1958, p. 16.
[The Finnish translation of] *Ashenden* shows that, despite his great speed, M has time to say some emphatic and profound truths. Like a surgeon, he reveals the essentials beneath the surface. This is not one of M's best books but certainly one of his liveliest and most colorful. [In Finnish.]

2127 "Maugham sodan töissa" (Maugham in Action), HELSINGIN SANOMAT, 15 March 1958, p. 13.
[The Finnish translation of] *Ashenden* reveals plenty of suspense, but the most interesting element is M's way of observing and studying peculiar characters. [In Finnish.]

2128 Miller, Karl. "Books: School of Maugham," SPECTATOR (Lond), CCI (14 Nov 1958), 658.
The essays in *Points of View* are "very lazy and pale" and "full of other men's flowers." M still has a "care for simplicity and the facts of life." When he gives his own literary opinion, he is a good critic and very individual because "he writes it like the person he is." "Aimless," but very "pleasant" book.

2129 "More Suited to Opera: *The Noble Spaniard* on Television," TIMES (Lond), 22 Sept 1958, p. 3.
The televised version of M's adaptation of Ernest Grenet-Dancourt's LES GAITES DE VEUVAGE lends itself to operatic setting better than to television.

2130 "Mr. Maugham Pays Price of Success: Characterless Facility of *Mrs. Dot*," TIMES (Lond), 11 Dec 1958, p. 3.
The text "groans under a load of second-rate epigrams, trivialized situations, and characters labeled as boobies, charmers, and cynics." The televised production of the play was "astonishingly incompetent."

2131 "Mr. Maugham's *Land of Promise*," TIMES (Lond), 21 April 1958, p. 3.
In 1914 M was broaching "a subject which still restricts D. H. Lawrence's most celebrated work to Paris bookstalls." M's characters in the televised version of the play are "strongly realized."

2132 Murch, A. E. THE DEVELOPMENT OF THE DETECTIVE NOVEL (NY: Philosophical Library, 1958), pp. 10, 82, 256.
[References to M's "The Decline and Fall of the Detective Story" (1952) in a study that amplifies M's opinions.]

2133 Petrie, Sir Charles. "A Famous Writer's Outlook," ILLUSTRATED LONDON NEWS, CCXXXIII (22 Nov 1958), 891.
Points of View is "in the great tradition," for all that M's admirers look for is in it; "it must be read as a farewell, not as a literary testament."

2134 R., A. "Onnistunut *Pyhän Liekin* ensi-ilta Mikkelin teatterissa" (Successful First Night of *Sacred Flame* at the Mikkeli Theater), SAVON SANOMAT, 2 March 1958, p. 6.
The construction [of the Finnish adaptation] is skillful; the suspense increases up to the final climax. The spectator would not like to accept the final solution, but the iron logic of the course of events makes it plausible. [In Finnish.]

2135 "Royal Society of Literature," TIMES (Lond), 18 July 1958, p. 12.
M has been elected a vice-president of the Royal Society of Literature.

2136 Santavuori, Martti. "Vakoilusta vielä kerran" (Espionage Again), AAMULEHTI, 1 May 1958, p. 8.
[The Finnish translation of] *Ashenden* contains a fine collection of types. There is a great speed all the time; the reader is hurried here, there, and everywhere. The fault is less serious than it might have been because of the intelligent and witty writing. [In Finnish.]

2137 Stanford University Library. A COMPREHENSIVE EXHIBITION OF THE WRITINGS OF W. SOMERSET MAUGHAM (May 25-August 1, 1958).
[A catalogue compiled by J. Terry Bender, with a preface by W. Somerset Maugham. A group of fifteen dissertations, critical works, bibliographies,

and articles is not listed. The catalogue is based largely on Stott's 1956 bibliography, but it lists a few items not found in Stott's work.]

2138* Tiusanen, Timo. "Lääkärin kahle" (A Physician's Bondage), HELSINGIN SANOMAT, 8 Oct 1958, p. 16.

Of Human Bondage [in the Finnish translation] is not one of M's best novels. There is excellent irony and satire, but the sheer length of the story makes the reader feel bored. Many of the characters lose their interest once their human weaknesses are mercilessly brought into daylight. It seems that M obtains the best results in the short story form. Nevertheless, *Bondage* is a remarkable novel: it reveals the conventionalism, hypocrisy, and social injustices of the Victorian era. [In Finnish.]

2139* Trewin, J. C. THE GAY TWENTIES: A DECADE OF THE THEATRE. Pictures by Raymond Mander and Joe Mitchenson. Foreword by Noël Coward (Lond: Macdonald, 1958), pp. 10, 16, 25, 39, 53, 63, 74, 82, 97, 99, 100, 117.

[Photographs, descriptions, and general criticisms of M's major plays in the 1920's.]

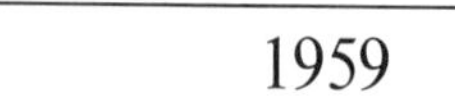

1959

2140 Beavan, John. "Maugham: A 'Free Man' at 85," NEW YORK TIMES MAGAZINE, 25 Jan 1959, pp. 14, 34-35, 37.

[Interview with M on the eve of his eighty-fifth birthday.]

2141 "Books—Briefly Noted: General," NEW YORKER, XXXV (25 April 1959), 172.

Points of View is "not, perhaps, a brilliant turn, but it is full of sharp and nourishing good sense."

2142 "Books—Just Out: 'Last' Essays of a Master," NEWSWEEK, LIII (27 April 1959), 116-17.

M's prose in *Points of View* remains "lucid, precise, urbane, with touches here and there of both acid and affection."

2143 "Books: The Latest Last One," TIME, LXXIII (27 April 1959), 94.

"Few professional writers can honestly say that they do not envy [M's] easy style, his civilized yarner's gift that makes current fiction seem drearily plodding." M succeeds because he talks "mostly about people and not too much about his advertised subject." The essays in *Points of View* are "as bland a job of literary borrowing and cool transformation as has been seen in some time."

2144* Cordell, Richard A. "The Theatre of Somerset Maugham," MODERN DRAMA, I (Feb 1959), 211-17.

M shrewdly stopped writing plays in 1933, when he saw that his approach was becoming "unfashionable," although "he has never been hostile to the new drama." Despite his introduction to the drama of the naturalists in Heidelberg during the 'nineties, he never wrote their kind of "idea-social plays." Although he has said that he wrote plays chiefly for financial success, "he has written only as he pleases and what he pleases —with two exceptions." M's "indifference, sometimes contempt, for popular mores and views" is illustrated with brief comments on many plays written between 1909 and 1933; but M is not to be considered wholly "callously cynical." Not "one of the fifteen plays [written before 1915] has any marked distinction," but some of his later plays are likely to survive, especially *The Circle, Our Betters,* and *The Constant Wife.*

2145 D., A. B. "Uutta Maughamia" (A New Maugham), PÄIVÄN SANOMAT, 30 Dec 1959, p. 4.

The stories [in the Finnish translation] of *The Trembling of a Leaf* are written with a master's pen; they are delicious, but, at the same time, easily digestible. "Rain" belongs to the group of best short stories ever written. [In Finnish.]

2146 Davies, Horton. A MIRROR OF THE MINISTRY IN MODERN NOVELS (NY: Oxford U P, 1959), pp. 113-22.

[Surveys M's rough treatment of Dr. Davidson in "Rain" and Reverend Carey in *Of Human Bondage.*]

2147 Dickie, Francis. "From Forest Fire to France: Somerset Maugham and His Moorish Mansion," AMERICAN BOOK COLLECTOR, X:7 (March 1959), 7, 9, 11, 13.

[Interview.]

2148 Dobrinsky, J. "Comptes Rendus" (Critical Reports), ETUDES ANGLAISES, XII (April-June 1959), 175-76.

[Brief review of *Points of View.*]

2149 "Good Cast in *For Services Rendered,*" TIMES (Lond), 8 July 1959, p. 8.

In the televised production (adaptation by Francis Crowdy), "the passion of the play is evident, and in parts still effective . . . . But it all remains surprisingly remote —a task of historical reconstruction rather than a live experience. Perhaps we have lived through too much since."

2150 Gordon, John D. "New in the Berg Collection: 1957-1958," BULLETIN OF THE NEW YORK PUBLIC LIBRARY, LXIII (March 1959), 134-47.

M is represented in the Berg Collection by the film play of *The Razor's Edge.*

2151 Hogan, William. "Maugham Presents His 'Last' Published Work," SAN FRANCISCO SUNDAY CHRONICLE ("Panorama"), 20 April 1959, p. 35.

[General praise of *Points of View.*]

2152* Jonas, Klaus W. "The Center of Maugham Studies," STECHERT-HAFNER BOOK NEWS, XIII (5 Jan 1959), 53-55.

Discusses the history and purpose of the Center of Maugham Studies [located at the time this article appeared at the University of Pittsburgh; but Professor Jonas has informed the editor of the present bibliography that most of his material is now located at the University of Texas]. "The present collection of the Center appears to be the strongest and most comprehensive one in the field of criticism. Maugham's own works are represented in over three-hundred volumes, about fifty of them autograph copies; there are over a hundred photographs, several original manuscripts, some of them still unpublished; typescripts with corrections and additions in the author's own hand; unpublished doctoral dissertations from various European countries . . . ; and finally, hundreds of newspaper and periodical articles, all of them fully catalogued."

2153* Jonas, Klaus W. "Maugham and the East: The Human Condition—Freedom," THE WORLD OF SOMERSET MAUGHAM, ed by Klaus W. Jonas (NY: British Book Centre, 1959), pp. 96-141.

Because the Far East is the setting of a good deal of M's work [four novels, two travel books, two plays, three collections of short stories], it is appropriate to consider (1) why M turned to the Far East, (2) what he was looking for, and (3) how his experiences proved useful to him.

M's interest in the Far East stemmed from childhood reading of works by Melville and Loti; it was fortified by his later search for material to write about Gauguin, and by a general "restlessness for the unknown," evidenced in the semiautobiographical cravings of Frank Hurrell in *The Merry-Go-Round* and of Philip Carey in *Of Human Bondage.* To these motivations must be added M's periodic dissatisfaction with himself and his feeling that by travel he did not bring back from a journey "quite the same self" that he took. Above all, however, one must remember M's constant interest in man unmasked and unadorned, his belief that civilization made for "an apparent sameness" in people, his hope that in the Far East he would see Englishmen out of their natural element, and perhaps "gain an insight into the contradictory motivations in man." Whatever his reasons, M's character was changed; in *The Summing Up* he stated that through his travels he had learned "tolerance."

M observed that English society in the Far East represented a "micro-England": the women exclude themselves from all foreign influence, stressing their superiority over the natives, frowning on white men who mix with natives or half-caste girls; all Europeans appreciate the few visible ties binding them to their old laws; clubs are the centers of their society; the men have come either for reasons of health, or to find peace, or to make money enough to live comfortably in England on their return; the women have come, generally, because of a desperate desire to marry, and having no luck at home, have seized upon a man from the colonies on furlough in England. Of all the Europeans in the Far East, M mainly satirizes the government officials whose private and official lives are kept separate and whose greatest ability must be "to get along pleasantly with others"; he is also hard on Protestant missionaries. As far as the evil influence of Eastern climate and environment was concerned, M found as many who survived and triumphed over it as he did many who weakened and failed. Relations between white man and Eurasian, especially mixed marriages, are generally doomed to failure: the gap between white and colored, M thinks, is not bridged, but only made more prominent. [See, also, Klaus W. Jonas. SOMERSET MAUGHAM UND DER FERNE OSTEN. Münster, 1953.]

2154 Jonas, Klaus W. "W. Somerset Maugham: An Appreciation," BOOKS ABROAD, XXXIII (Winter 1959), 20-23.

"In his dramatic works one senses the proximity of Oscar Wilde; the epic works vacillate between Naturalism and Impressionism; the exotic hue recalls the names of Joseph Conrad, Stevenson, and Kipling; the disintegration of the novel form as well as the cultivation of the short story parallel with the tendency of the youngest writers."

2155* Jonas, Klaus W. (ed) THE WORLD OF SOMERSET MAUGHAM. (NY: British Book Centre, 1959).

[An anthology, including a preface by M and six essays "intended as a companion piece to THE MAUGHAM ENIGMA" (also edited [1954] by Jonas). Contents: Frank Swinnerton, "Somerset Maugham as a Writer," pp. 12-20; Klaus W. Jonas, "The Gentleman from Cap Ferrat," 21-36; M. C. Kuner, "Maugham and the West—The Human Condition: Bondage," 37-95; Klaus W. Jonas, "Maugham and the East—The Human Condition: Freedom," 96-141; St. John Ervine, "Maugham the Playwright," 142-62; Glenway Wescott, "Maugham and Posterity," 163-79. The appendix ("A Note on Maugham Collections") and five of these essays (Kuner's excepted) received earlier publications of some kind; annotations and information concerning their earlier publication are located in this bibliography under individual entries.]

2156 Kare, Kauko. "Kronikoita" (Chronicles), SUOMALAINEN SUOMI, XXVII: 4 (1959), 247-48.

[The Finnish translation of] *Of Human Bondage* exhibits sharp observation of detail. Some characters are excellently drawn. Despite its many fine qualities, the novel is somewhat shoddy and oversentimental. [In Finnish.]

2157 Kilcoyne, Francis P. "Other New Books," CATHOLIC WORLD, CLXXXIX (July 1959), 329-30.

"Candor compels the opinion that the volume [*Points of View*] is entertaining, informative, but not as valuable as *The Summing Up* and *A Writer's Notebook.*"

2158 Kivinen, Greta. "Vanha ja viisas William Somerset Maugham" (Wise Old William Somerset Maugham), SUOMEN KUVALEHTI, XLIII (1959), 18-19.

M is an eminent twentieth-century representative of the English storytelling tradition. He is an acknowledged dramatist who knows how to captivate both his audience and his readers. Publishers are willing to pay huge sums for every word he writes because he does not write a single unnecessary word. Sometimes with mild benevolence, sometimes with biting satire, M reveals both the good and bad in man. [In Finnish.]

2159 Krutch, Joseph Wood. "In Human Bondage to Books," SATURDAY REVIEW (NY), XLII (25 April 1959), 13.

As a reader and critic M is interested in other writers' works, and his interest is readily communicated to his reader. The four essays comprising *Points of View* give the reader a notion of M's convictions, attitudes, tastes, and preferences.

2160* Kuner, M. C. "Maugham and the West: The Human Condition—Bondage," THE WORLD OF SOMERSET MAUGHAM, ed by Klaus W. Jonas (NY: British Book Centre, 1959), pp. 37-95.

In his novels M deals largely with the "leisure" class, which provides an atmosphere conducive to his gift for satire. The setting for M's novels is, in contrast to his short stories, Europe; "man occupies the centre of the stage, while landscape is a decor to physical or intellectual activity." Through all of M's novels run three "leitmotifs": unrequited love developed as a tragedy destructive to its participants, the discrepancy between appearance and reality, nonconformity in battle against a disapproving world. M's heroines, pleasant and unpleasant, fall into two categories: the unpleasant either "combine a sedate manner with a Strindbergian frenzy to dominate" a man or inflict pain on one man because they "are so blinded by the overpowering urge they feel for other men that all sense of decency or responsibility is obliterated"; the pleasant heroines are either "good-tempered girls of easy virtue who bring comfort and understanding to the men they love," or they "can be friends as well as lovers." M's men incline "towards greater passivity than the women," and however battered they may be by emotional upheavals, "they remain dependable and loyal" to the women who neglect them. M's few "rakes" are foils to the majority of his faithful males, and create havoc "rather from a careless sensuality than a consuming hunger." Outside the action of M's heroines, pleasant and unpleasant, and his heroes, there stands a "disillusioned raisonneur" in almost every novel, commenting "on the follies of humanity and the insignificance of life." All of M's novels, including the unpublished forerunner of *Of Human Bondage* ["The Artistic Temperament of Stephen Carey"], demonstrate that M was "a romantic who would believe" but also "a realist who must doubt" and that his novels over fifty years move from "the impatient anger of youth to the gracious serenity of age."

2161 L., E. "Maugham Etelämerellä" (Maugham on the South Sea), AAMULEHTI, 29 Dec 1959, p. 8.

Some of the stories [in the Finnish translation] of *The Trembling of a Leaf* are hopelessly melodramatic, and the collection has no great literary value. M seems to believe in the mysterious enchantment of the South Sea. [In Finnish.]

2162 Lanoire, Maurice. LES LORGNETTES DU ROMAN ANGLAIS (THE OPERA-GLASSES OF THE ENGLISH NOVEL) (Paris: Librairie Plon, 1959), pp. 72-76, 92-95, 135-38.

[Quotations from *Of Human Bondage* to depict Anglican clergymen, English public schools, and workers in a department store.] [In French.]

2163 Leautaud, Paul. JOURNAL LITTERAIRE (LITERARY JOURNAL). 18 Volumes (Paris: Mercure de France), Vol. VII, 1959, 55. (Vol. XVI, 1964), 100.

[Reference to M's stories, "The Fall of Edward Barnard" and "The Unconquered."] [In French.]

2164 Manninen, Kerttu. *"Elämän Kahle" (Of Human Bondage),* AAMULEHTI, 4 March 1959, p. 8.

The novel [in the Finnish translation] is more open and human than others by M; he had not yet assumed his invulnerable mask of the cool, cynical observer. The book lacks coherence, however. [In Finnish.]

2165 "Maugham Keeps Book Secret," NEW YORK TIMES, 10 Nov 1959, p. 9.

In Tokyo, M discloses that he has written a book to be published after his death.

2166 "Note of Weariness in *Sheppey*: Mr. Maugham's Farewell to the Theatre," TIMES (Lond), 13 May 1959, p. 5.

The televised production of the play reveals the play is a "period piece," and shows signs of the author's weariness.

2167 P-n, E. "Ruotsalaisen teaaterin komediauutuus" (New Comedy at the Swedish Theatre), UUSI AURA, 14 Nov 1959, p. 8.

[The Finnish adaptation of] THEATRE is a typical society comedy: there is no profound analysis, though the play rises above the level of farce. [In Finnish.]

2168 Pennanen, Eila. "Persialainen matto" (Persian Rug), PARNASSO, IX: 2 (1959), 134-35.

In [the Finnish translation of] *Of Human Bondage,* some minor characters are excellently drawn. The novel is long and its structure is loose; it is less coherent than *Cakes and Ale,* but possesses a personal touch the latter lacks. It has been said that M here unmasks himself. But what is revealed behind the mask? Is it only a new mask, or the face, distorted in a sentimental smile of a man looking in a mirror? [In Finnish.]

2169 Pennanen, Esko. "Vanhan mestarin jäähyväiset: William Somerset Maugham 85-vuotispäivänä" (An Old Master's Farewell: On the Eighty-Fifth Anniversary of William Somerset Maugham), UUSI SUOMI, 25 Jan 1959, p. 15.

In *Points of View,* it seems as if life had given M more human warmth and understanding than is usual. He is not satisfied with conventional attitudes, but he is an objective observer who neither condemns nor praises. [In Finnish.]

2170 Pfeiffer, Karl G. "Mr. Maugham's Valedictory," NEW YORK HERALD TRIBUNE BOOK REVIEW, 31 May 1959, p. 8.

Points of View is better than *The Vagrant Mood* "chiefly because it devotes more space to a discussion of writers and Maugham's special qualification as a critic is his insight into the working of the writer's mind during the act of creation."

2171 Pfeiffer, Karl G. W. SOMERSET MAUGHAM: A CANDID PORTRAIT. With an Introduction by Jerome Weidman. (NY: W. W. Norton, 1959).

During a conversation in Beverly Hills (1941), M hinted that Pfeiffer might write the "authoritative work" on him after his death. Ten years later, however, M announced he wanted no biography, so the present book purports to be a "sketch" of M's life, though it "has something to say of his writing, especially in regard to the use he made of his own personality in drawing his characters." [Pfeiffer's sketch is chronologically ordered, combining well-known biographical facts with well-known critical views of M's achievements in all the genres he attempted. No new observations are offered.]

2172 *"Points of View,"* KIRKUS, XXVII (15 Feb 1959), 170-71.
[Brief appraisal.]

2173 Poore, Charles [G]. "Books of the Times," NEW YORK TIMES, 23 April 1959, p. 29.
[Generally high praise of *Points of View*.]

2174 Rolo, Charles. "Reader's Choice," ATLANTIC MONTHLY, CCIII (May 1959), 94-95.
No piece in *Points of View* represents M at his best, though he still retains the power to capture the reader's interest with any subject he chooses to develop.

2175 Viswanath, G. V. "The Novels of Somerset Maugham," QUEST (Bombay), No. 23 (Oct-Nov 1959), 50-52.
Critics have not taken M seriously, while the public has made him a legendary figure. M lays bare the unpleasant truth beneath human pretension and feels it will always be so. His novels and stories are cynical and sophisticated to conceal a more savage disillusionment with human nature. He uses the lowest view of life as a protection. Therefore, M's stories hardly rise above the nature of their themes. His readers feel that they have "seen through" everything. M's treatment of each theme is marred by reducing it to "a level of preconceived superficiality." His failure to achieve depth in *The Razor's Edge* and *Of Human Bondage* results in sentimentality. His writing is lucid, but he had no complex experience to describe that would demand a more complex prose.

2176 Walbridge, Earle F. "New Books Appraised," LIBRARY JOURNAL, LXXXIV (1 April 1959), 1134.
Points of View is "a good, characteristic collection."

1960

2177 Abraham, Pierre. "Le Théâtre" (Theater), EUROPE, 38ème année, nos. 379-80 (Nov-Dec 1960), 278.
The French adaptation, by Pol Quentin, of *The Constant Wife* as *Con-*

stance is a comedy "du boulevard," if of Victorian Piccadilly rather than of today. [In French.]

2178 " *'The Alien Corn'* on Television," TIMES (Lond), 18 March 1960, p. 4.

M's tale is "complex . . . with more sentiment than usual mixed with . . . acute and malicious social observation."

2179 "The Arts: The Conflict of *Caroline,*" TIMES (Lond), 18 May 1960, p. 18.

In the televised production of the play, M's wit carries the action along; the play is solidly built.

2180 "The Arts—Feuillere in Maugham: *The Constant Wife,*" TIMES (Lond), 2 Dec 1960, p. 20.

In his French adaptation, Pol Quentin has pared away the social implications: "although the water may be more shallow, the sparkle is still there."

2181 Bason, Fred[erick T.] THE LAST BASSOON, edited and introduced by Noël Coward (London: Max Parrish, 1960), pp. 8, 34-35, 36, 88, 102, 132.

[Some short comments on, and recollections of, M.]

2182 Bouvard, Philippe. "Dernière minute: Soir de Fête pour *Constance*" (The Latest: An Evening of Festivity for *The Constant Wife*), LE FIGARO, 19 Oct 1960, p. 20.

[Review of the French adaptation.] [In French.]

2183 Brown, Allen B. "Substance and Shadow: The Originals of the Characters in *Cakes and Ale,*" PAPERS OF THE MICHIGAN ACADEMY OF SCIENCE, ARTS, AND LETTERS, XLV (1960), 439-46.

On 12 Nov 1951, M revealed the actual "identities" of the characters in *Cakes and Ale:* the counterparts of the Barton Traffords were the Sidney Colvins; Alroy Kear was Hugh Walpole; Allgood Newton was Sir Edmund Gosse; Jasper Gibbons was Stephen Phillips. M would not admit that Driffield was Thomas Hardy, nor divulge on whom Rosie was modeled, but the latter must originate from the prototype of Mildred in *Of Human Bondage.*

2184 Cody, Richard. "Secret Service Fiction," GRADUATE STUDENT OF ENGLISH, III (Summer 1960), 6-12.

Goebbels condemned *Ashenden,* which is a dreary book, but has, curiously enough, proved to be "the most influential secret service thriller of the 'twenties' "; it anticipates Eric Ambler and Graham Greene.

2185 "Comedy in Classical Tradition: TV Production of *Penelope,*" TIMES (Lond), 7 Oct 1960, p. 4.

The adaptation by Gerald Savory shows M's comedies provide links with social comedies of three hundred years ago; while his plays offer no supremely brilliant wit and no comic transfiguration of the everyday, they "are made with elegant efficiency and win every available laugh with ease."

2186 "*The Constant Wife:* Webber-Douglas School," TIMES (Lond), 22 July 1960, p. 16.
[Generally favorable review of a performance of the play.]

2187 Dussane. "Théâtre" (Theater), LE MERCURE DE FRANCE, CCCXL (Oct 1960), 681-82.
The revival of the French adaptation of *The Constant Wife* as *Constance* is notable for recalling the London "boulevard" of 1910. [In French.]

2188 Gautier, Jean-Jacques. "La Critique dramatique: Au théâtre Sarah Bernhardt: *Constance*" (Dramatic Report: At the Sarah Bernhardt Theater: *The Constant Wife*), LE FIGARO, 21 Oct 1960, p. 22.
The play [in the French adaptation] is badly constructed; characters enter and exit without rhyme or reason. The animation is forced; the chatter, superficial. [In French.]

2189 Hanoteau, Guillaume and Bernard Giquel. "Paris cette semaine" (Paris This Week), PARIS-MATCH, No. 603 (29 Oct 1960), 91.
The French revival of *The Constant Wife* shows the play is "dated" and requires especially good acting to succeed now. [In French.]

2190 Hunt, Albert. "Realism and Intelligence," ENCORE, VII:3 (May-June 1960), 12-17.
"True realism" demands and combines an "empirical outlook" with a "shaping intelligence." The work of M and Rattigan [presumably because it lacks the "shaping intelligence"] is contrived; the work of Arthur Miller and Arnold Wesker is not.

2191 Kajava, Viljo. "Lumotut haaksirikkoiset" (Enchanted Castaways), SUOMEN SOSIALIDEMOKRAATTI, 19 Jan 1960, p. 7.
In [the Finnish translation of] *The Trembling of a Leaf,* M's cool irony cuts deep, particularly when he describes people whose shiny surface conceals final collapse and ruin. The book attracts mainly those people who are looking for suspense and unexpected turns. [In Finnish.]

2192 Korry, Edward M. "A Visit with Somerset Maugham," LOOK, XXIV (5 Jan 1960), 48-50, 53.
[Interview with M on the eve of his eighty-sixth birthday.]

2193* Koskenniemi, V. A. "Novellitaidetta" (Short Story Art), UUSI SUOMI, 20 March 1960, p. 7.

[The Finnish translation of] *The Trembling of a Leaf* shows M is one of the great short story writers of the early twentieth century. His satire, which lashes conventionalism, bureaucracy, and intolerance, calls to mind Maupassant and Chekhov, but his colorful landscapes give evidence of intensive experience of nature which cannot be found in the two other writers. His narrative technique is of high standard, and it is supported by profound knowledge of the human mind. [In Finnish.]

2194 Kula, Kauko. "Viikon kirjat" (Books of the Week), KAUPPALEHTI, 18 Jan 1960, p. 8.

[The Finnish translation shows] *Up at the Villa* is surprisingly light weight. The novel has no particular value, but it is not altogether uninteresting. In any case, it shows M's ability to create a story, his sharp psychological observation, and his technical skill. [In Finnish.]

2195 Langner, Lawrence. THE PLAY'S THE THING (NY: G. P. Putnam's Sons, 1960), pp. 30, 180.

M cited as one of several novelists who wrote with "the greatest ease, and with but little training for the theatre." *The Circle* is the "highest example" of "drawing room comedy."

2196 Lemarchand, Jacques. "*'Constance',* de Somerset Maugham" (*The Constant Wife* by Somerset Maugham), LE FIGARO LITTERAIRE, 29 Oct 1960, p. 16.

The French adaptation is well produced. [In French.]

2197 Marcabru, Pierre. "Les Pièces de la Semaine: *Constance* ou l'Illusion d'une Pièce" (Plays of the Week: *The Constant Wife* or the Illusion of a Play), ARTS/SPECTACLES, 26 Oct-1 Nov 1960, p. 5.

In the French adaptation, richness does not extend beyond the costumes and vain appearances. The text is mediocre, borrowed from M, who stole it from Wilde. The latter at least possessed a covert and deft cruelty, a malicious insolence, a kind of secret impatience in his unconcern; there are no such things in M's play: he contents himself with painting expressionless faces. The characters are always dangling: they have no will, no purpose in life; at their exit, they are waiting behind the scenes to make another entry. [In French.]

2198 Marcel, Gabriel. "Un rôle sur mesure: *Constance*" (A Role Made to Measure: *The Constant Wife*), LES NOUVELLES LITTERAIRES, 3 Nov 1960, p. 10.

In the French adaptation, the first act is poor; the second, more animate;

the third, the best. Still the play is antiquated and bad theater. [In French.]

2199 "Maugham Predicts World Use of English Within 3 Centuries," NEW YORK TIMES, 25 Jan 1960, p. 29.

In Bangkok, on the eve of his eighty-sixth birthday, M tells the American press he hopes for stronger ties between the U. S. and Great Britain and he believes that a variety of English will become the universal language in three centuries.

2200 Maulnier, Thierry. "Le Théâtre: Monstres sacrés" (Drama: Divine Monsters), LA REVUE DE PARIS, 67ème année, no. 2 (Nov 1960), 161-62.

[Review of Pol Quentin's adaptation of *The Constant Wife* as CONSTANCE.] [In French.]

2201 "Miss Diane Cilento as Sadie Thompson," TIMES (Lond), 19 Dec 1960, p. 12.

In the televised production of John Colton and Clemence Randolph's dramatization, RAIN, "the producer . . . has clearly seen that the old theatrical warhorse still has life in it, and, . . . can still carry its audience off at a canter."

2202* *"Our Betters,"* TIMES (Lond), 8 Feb 1960, p. 14.

The televised production shows M has "narrative skill, cast-iron technique, and remarkable fluency of dialogue," but the play "did not grip as older plays by Galsworthy and Shaw have done." The object of satire is sour; the plot needs time to develop, but the intermittent wit of the dialogue is less than the play really needs.

2203 Paasilinna, Erno. "Sattuma korjaa satoa" (It's Left to Chance), SUOMALAINEN SUOMI, XXVIII: 6 (1960), 377-78.

The short stories in [the Finnish translation of] *The Trembling of a Leaf* do not offer sufficient materials for serious analysis. M repeats himself; he makes use of a fluent style and slack humor for literary speculation. [In Finnish.]

2204 Stevenson, Lionel. THE ENGLISH NOVEL: A PANORAMA (Boston: Houghton Mifflin, 1960), pp. 438, 468, 532.

M's *Liza of Lambeth* is an example of the type of novel that anatomized society from 1895 to 1915; in *Of Human Bondage* M turned with the younger writers to examine what "goes on within the individual."

2205* Tiusanen, Timo. "Maugham Etelämerellä" (Maugham on the South Sea), HELSINGIN SANOMAT, 30 Jan 1960, p. 11.

The stories in [the Finnish translation of] *The Trembling of a Leaf* are technically superb, but they show the author's lack of an individual view of life.

He has nothing original to say: that is why he must try to seek out extraordinary characters. The secret of his fame is that he nourishes people's curiosity. [In Finnish.]

2206 "Topics," NEW YORK TIMES, 3 Feb 1960, p. 32.
[Editorial agreeing with and expanding M's views on English becoming the universal language in three centuries. (See, also, "Maugham Predicts World Use of English Within 3 Centuries," NEW YORK TIMES, 25 Jan 1960, p. 29).]

2207 Zhantiyeva, D. " 'Some Points of View' and 'Summing-Ups': The Aesthetic Views and Creative Path of Somerset Maugham," INOSTRANNAJA LITERATURA, No. 2 (Feb 1960), 185-92.
M's aesthetic views reflect the influence of the pessimistic philosophy prevailing at the end of the nineteenth and the beginning of the twentieth centuries, and the theory that art is not called upon to educate, but should merely serve as a means of entertainment. M's philosophy of life and his aesthetic view had a negative influence on his work. His most outstanding work is *Of Human Bondage;* it gives a true-to-life picture of his hero.

1961

2208* Amis, Kingsley. "Mr. Maugham's Notions," SPECTATOR (Lond), CCVII (7 July 1961), 23-24.
Richard A. Cordell's SOMERSET MAUGHAM: A BIOGRAPHICAL AND CRITICAL STUDY (1961) repeats M's opinions and those of his fans. M's "notions about life and art" are "meagre," since he has a "too easily satisfied curiosity" about people and places. He can write both "gimcrack" stuff and "wild forays into imagery." Passion, except as a word, is "usually absent" from his fiction. Yet the "construction" and "timing" of *Cakes and Ale* make it superior to Huxley's EYELESS IN GAZA. *Of Human Bondage,* "direct and literal," is M's best, although after three-quarters it loses coherence. It shows that one barrier, itself an injustice—e. g., Philip's club foot—will lead to other injustices—e. g., Philip's troubles for and with Mildred. M's notion that a writer is a teller of tales only, and so, free, contrasts with "the agents of bondage who haunt" his fictional world. Part of his work, including *The Summing Up,* presents no narrow world. M "has found" a place in English literature.

2209 "Authors Awarded New Honour," TIMES (Lond), 11 May 1961, p. 9.

M was named Companion of Literature by the Royal Society of Literature.

2210* Cordell, Richard A. SOMERSET MAUGHAM: A BIOGRAPHICAL AND CRITICAL STUDY. (Lond: W. Heinemann; Bloomington, Indiana UP, 1961). [Second ed, 1969] [Publication announced].

Contrary to popular belief, M is only "enigmatic in the same way that all men are imperfectly known. . . . The core of his philosophy is found in the writings of wise men in all ages," and indeed, his dictum, "Our business is right living," might be considered a sentence-summary of Emerson's "Self-Reliance." Of M's twenty novels, the three autobiographical novels—*Of Human Bondage, The Moon and Sixpence, Cakes and Ale*—are his best; of the remaining novels, six "have enough merit to interest a discriminating reader today": *Liza of Lambeth, Mrs. Craddock, The Painted Veil, The Narrow Corner, The Razor's Edge,* and *Catalina.*

[Cordell's second book differs from his first less in scope than in organization. Chapters I and II, from the earlier study (treating of M's life in general, and his novels), are revised and extended to include M's activities through his middle-eighties as well as criticisms of his final works from 1937 to 1959. Except for a consideration of two short-story collections after 1937, Cordell's study of M as a short-story writer remains fundamentally unaltered; similarly, Cordell's consideration of M as a dramatist, though shorter in this second book, reveals no change in attitude; the chapter on non-fiction briefly considers M's last works in this area after 1937. In his final chapter Cordell differentiates between the critics sympathetic and unsympathetic to M, and succinctly states the viewpoints of both sides.]

2211 Daruwalla, Bejan. "Somerset Maugham as a Teller of Tales," MODERN REVIEW (Calcutta), CIX (Jan 1961), 55-58.

M's judgment upon his own work as lacking human warmth is too harsh; in his short stories we have "the conscious artist at his brilliant best."

2212* Fielden, John Seward. "The Ibsenite Maugham," MODERN DRAMA, IV (Sept 1961), 138-51.

M is "taken so lightly by dramatic historians and critics" because he contributed no startling technique, he treated life superficially and "never grappled . . . with social problems in a serious way." M is, indeed, "to a surprising extent an Ibsenite," and "over half his plays are in varying degrees problem plays." M has not usually written to please the critics or public, but has often written against the grain; when he wrote for the larger public it was in part to win that public over to his serious plays. M's plays dealing with social problems may be divided into three categories: (1) those in "which the problem is only incidental to the purpose of the play and present only to give rise to a dramatic situation that M wished to exploit" [*The Tenth Man, Grace, Caesar's Wife, East of Suez,* and *The Sacred Flame*]; (2) those in which "M is making an attack . . . on specific vices or foibles of society" [*A Man of Honour, Loaves and Fishes, The Land of Promise, The Unknown, For Services Rendered,* and *Sheppey*]; (3) those "which blend the problem play with the comedy of manners" and for which he will be chiefly remembered [*Smith, Loaves and Fishes, Our Betters, The Circle, The Constant Wife,* and *The Breadwinner*].

2213 G., H. G. "Gjorde Constance rätt?" (Did Constance Do Right?), HUFVUDSTADSBLADET, 2 Dec 1961, p. 8.

The revival of the Finnish adaptation of *The Constant Wife* proves the years have not ruined the play; it is enjoyable even today. The posing of the problem at the end of the play sounds, however, old-fashioned. The dialogue is elegantly polished. [In Finnish.]

2214 Grebanier, Bernard. PLAYWRITING (NY: Thomas Y Crowell, 1961), pp. 288, 289.

For Services Rendered is a play "between comedy and tragedy."

2215* Kendall, Lyle H., Jr. "The First Edition of *The Moon and Sixpence*," PAPERS OF THE BIBLIOGRAPHICAL SOCIETY OF AMERICA, LV (Third Quarter 1961), 242-43.

An "examination of two copies [of *The Moon and Sixpence*] in the W. L. Lewis Collection of rare books and manuscripts at Texas Christian University demonstrates the existence of Stott's conjectural fourth issue." [The "fourth issue" is described and compared (principally its advertisements) with the third issue described by Stott in his 1956 bibliography of M's writings.] "The advertisements in this copy agree with those in Stott's third issue, as far as they are described. . . . "

2216 Lehtola, Erkka. "Tyylikäs ja hillitty komedia" (Elegant and Refined Comedy), AAMULEHTI, 1 Sept 1961, p. 10.

[The Finnish adaptation of] JANE shows M often aims at more profound description than his talent allows. His ambitious wish to penetrate under the surface sometimes results in heaviness which ruins the total effect. There are many moments of pure comedy in JANE, but the moments of quasi-philosophy restrain the free flow of action. [In Finnish.]

2217 Lyons, Leonard. "Maugham-by-the-Sea," SATURDAY REVIEW (NY), XLIV (14 Oct 1961), 44-47, 73-74.

[Interview, describing M's homes, his work and reading habits, his "rejuvenation shots," his bridge partners and guests and acquaintances.]

2218 "Maugham to Endow Writers' Aid Fund," NEW YORK TIMES, 10 Oct 1961, pp. 1, 9.

M, in London, is to leave an endowment to Writers' Aid Fund.

2219 "Mr. Somerset Maugham's Library for School," TIMES (Lond), 30 March 1961, p. 6.
M is to bequeath his library of five thousand books to King's School, Canterbury, and will pay the cost of a new building to house them.

2220 "Mr. W. S. Maugham Honoured," TIMES (Lond), 1 June 1961, p. 12.
M was made honorary Senator of Heidelberg University (Germany) on 31 May 1961.

2221 "News in Brief," TIMES (Lond), 10 Nov 1961, p. 6.
M has accepted the presidency of the Guild of Travel Writers.

2222 Simões, João Gaspar. "Somerset Maugham, Dramaturgo" (Somerset Maugham, Dramatist), QUATRO ESTUDOS (Four Studies). (Cadernos de Cultura, 130) (Rio: Ministério da Educaço e Cultura, Serviço de Documentação, [1961]), pp. 93-120.
M's cynicism is not an intellectual pose camouflaging an impetuous and romantic temperament; it is a "natural gift," enabling him to view and depict life as entertainment for others obliged to attend too closely to life's cruelties and injustices. Unfortunately, M, adept at the telling of an entertaining anecdote suitable to his cynical attitude, rejected his anecdotal method in his last plays—notably in *Sheppey*—so that his cynicism became unpalatable to theater audiences. [In Portuguese.]

2223 "Topics," NEW YORK TIMES, 30 Oct 1961, p. 28.
[Editorial reflecting on awards and grants for young writers, occasioned by M's recent endowment to the Writers' Aid Fund. (See, also, "Maugham to Endow Writers' Aid Fund," NEW YORK TIMES, 10 Oct 1961, pp. 1, 9).]

2224 Weales, Gerald. RELIGION IN MODERN ENGLISH DRAMA (Philadelphia: University of Pennsylvania, 1961), pp. 17, especially 19-21, 279, 280.
In *Sheppey,* M was, like Galsworthy, "gingerly approaching the serious theme of the fool as Christ." In *The Unknown,* M made "the most detailed examination of loss of faith" in the post-World War I era; he is, however, "the legitimate successor of the Jones [Henry Arthur] who insisted that religion in the theater be a device and not a dogma."

2225* Williams, Raymond. "The Figure in the Rug," NEW STATESMAN, N. S. LXII (7 July 1961), 20-21.
In Richard A. Cordell's SOMERSET MAUGHAM: A BIOGRAPHICAL AND CRITICAL STUDY (1961), the chapter summarizing M criticism is "the most interesting for it shows that Maugham has not been thoroughly analyzed: it is not enough to say that he is a 'formula-writer.' " Critically, Cordell's book is "wholly unsatisfactory"; informatively, it is "welcome."

2226 Zeeman, Dorothea. "Von Me. Bovary zum Chapman Report" (From Madame Bovary to the Chapman Report), KULTUR, IX: 166 (Aug 1961), 8.

[Record of the author's conversation with Irving Wallace, who expressed his literary allegiance to M (and Camus and Hemingway).] [In German.]

1962

2227 Arpiainen, Leila. "Hilkka Helinä viehätti juhlametamorfoosissaan" (Hilkka Helinä Enchanting in Her Celebration Metamorphosis), HELSINGIN SANOMAT, 12 Dec 1962, p. 16.

M's talent as a writer of society comedies is generally acknowledged. In [the revival of the Finnish adaptation of] JANE, the actors are brought together and separated just as cleverly as is necessary for the purposes of a three-act comedy. [In Finnish.]

2228 Boothby, Lord [Robert John Graham]. "The Maugham 'Legend,'" MY YESTERDAY, YOUR TOMORROW (Lond: Hutchinson, 1962), pp. 224-28.

Contrary to the opinion of intellectuals who denounce him, M is a great storyteller, born with a dramatic instinct that makes what he writes readable; in the East he "nudges your elbow at every turn." M's insight into human nature is keener than any other living writer's. His philosophy is one of toleration, sense and sensibility. Because he writes not to instruct but to please, a disparaging "legend" has grown around him.

2229 Cierpal, Leo Joseph. "Degeneration and the Religion of Beauty: A Traditional Pattern in Coleridge's 'The Rime of the Ancient Mariner,' Pater's 'The Renaissance,' Maugham's *Of Human Bondage,* and Joyce's ULYSSES." Unpublished thesis, Wayne State University, 1962.

Philip Carey, of *Of Human Bondage,* transcends the "religion of beauty," freeing himself of sado-masochism and finding some freedom in "an embodiment of a neo-pagan earth mother."

2230 del Monte, Alberto. BREVE STORIA DEL ROMANZO POLIZIESCO (SHORT STORIES OF POLICE ADVENTURES), (Bari: Laterza & Figli, 1962), p. 169.

M's *Ashenden* influenced the "spy story" of the 1930's. [In Italian.]

2231 Land, Myrick. "The 'Ridiculous' Mr. Walpole Endures Agonies at the Hands of Mr. Maugham," THE FINE ART OF LITER-

ARY MAYHEM: A LIVELY ACCOUNT OF FAMOUS WRITERS AND THEIR FEUDS (NY: Holt, Rinehart and Winston, 1962), pp. 161-79.

[An account of M's portraying Walpole as Alroy Kear in *Cakes and Ale* and of Elinor Mordaunt's portraying M as Leverson Hurle in GIN AND BITTERS.]

2232 Maulnier, Thierry. "Le Théâtre" (Theater), LA REVUE DE PARIS, 69ème année (April 1962), 135.

Marc-Gilbert Sauvageon's adaptation of THEATRE as ADORABLE JULIA is agreeable and well constructed, with a satiric verve free of malice. [In French.]

2233* O'Connor, William Van. "Two Types of 'Heroes' in Post-War Fiction," PUBLICATIONS OF THE MODERN LANGUAGE ASSOCIATION, LXXVII (March 1962), 168-74.

M's *Of Human Bondage* is one of the novels stemming from the convention established by Huysmans' A REBOURS, Wilde's THE PORTRAIT OF DORIAN GRAY, and Butler's THE WAY OF ALL FLESH—all of which reflect "the artist's sense that he had turned away from an insensitive world, and that the latter rejected him." But the protagonist of the turn-of-the-century novel—the sensitive esthete pursuing art in isolation—was supplanted after World War II by a new hero—the oaf, the opportunist, responsible only to some need in himself.

2234* Romberg, Bertil. STUDIES IN THE NARRATIVE TECHNIQUE OF THE FIRST-PERSON NOVEL (Stockholm, Göteborg, Uppsala: Almqvist and Wikscll, 1962), pp. 9, 67, 68-69, 77, 78, 330, 331.

E. T. A. Hoffmann's technique of pretending to be nothing more than the editor of someone else's manuscript [as in LEBENSANSICHTEN DES KATERS MURR or DIE ELIXIERE DES TEUFELS] strikingly parallels M's technique of the first person narrator.

2235* Zlobina, Maya. "The Surprises in Somerset Maugham," SOVIET REVIEW, No. 3 (June 1962), 3-9.

M has said he "has tried to remain dispassionate and objective" in his work, interested in men only "insofar as they furnish material" for his writing, but he repudiates himself; although guided by the "bourgeois" ideal in his own life, his work shows "hatred and contempt for the bourgeois." The motif of the contradiction between appearance and reality runs through all of the seemingly different stories in *Rain and Other Stories* [Russian translation], compiled and edited by M. Lorye. In "Rain," a "powerful" story, this motif is found in M's idea that "religious fanaticism is merely an expression of perverted sexual urges." He shows that misery and suffering only degrade man instead of ennobling him. Fanaticism is "a cruel and devastating passion" which M the rationalist realizes brings man closer to the level of the beast. This theme of passion M returns to again and again, but religious fanaticism is far "more dangerous," for it hides behind "a mask of lofty and noble ideals." Even among the admired aristocrats M discovers no "true values" which might be seriously opposed to the bourgeois. Warburton in "The Outstation" is as brutal as the lower class Cooper, though even more repellent because of his civilized manner—his "coldbloodedness." Skeptical though he is, M has his illusion of a far-off haven for the individual. An inexhaustible traveler, M loved Tahiti—not so much for its exotic beauty, but for the freedom it allowed the individual and thus the happiness derived from this "free self-expression of the personality." This theme of man's break with society is reiterated in *The Moon and Sixpence,* "The Fall of Edward Barnard," and in "The Creative Impulse." Although denying that he judges his fellow creatures, M does indeed judge them, at times intolerantly and cruelly. His best work cannot keep from generalizations on the whole of society. The artist there overcomes the man and M is thus "better than his reputation."

1963

2236 Amur, G. S. THE CONCEPT OF COMEDY: A RE-STATEMENT (Dharwar, India: Karnatak University, 1963), pp. 36, 38, 123, 131, 141, 151.

[Primarily citations from M's criticism, used to endorse Amur's anatomy of comic effect.]

2237 Boling, Kay. "New Books Appraised," LIBRARY JOURNAL, LXXXVIII (15 Nov 1963), 4376.

Selected Prefaces and Introductions of W. Somerset Maugham contains "crystal-clear thoughts."

2238* Brander, L[aurence]. SOMERSET MAUGHAM: A GUIDE. (Edinburgh & Lond: Oliver & Boyd; NY: Barnes & Noble, 1963).

M, both humble and proud, satisfied his own two criteria for artistic immortality: (1) he produced an *oeuvre,* and (2) his work was read and known by contemporaries. A "cosmopolitan," absorbed by the problem of power in human societies, interested in travel, philosophy, criticism and painting, he lived his life so that he could consciously achieve a pattern; but the pattern "has meaning only as a design for a life of creative writing." His strongest qualities were ambition, perseverance, energy, common sense; his talent was for comedy, "easy and natural," sometimes sardonic, sometimes with a "hard edge of Gallic wit to it." But M has never been satisfied to be merely a comic writer, and *Of Human Bondage,* the last plays and novels, the travel books, the personal and critical writing are all "serious." Indeed, in most of M's works, and throughout his career, one discerns an almost patterned movement from "comedy" to "seriousness." *The Merry-Go-Round,* although a period piece occasionally exhibiting "gorgeous prose" of the aesthetes of the nineties, was M's first full-scale experiment in writing about London, gave prototypes for his later characters and situations, and revealed the embryo of M's serious belief that pain does not refine man but brutalizes him, that it engenders "a score of petty vices . . . but not a single virtue." In *Of Human Bondage* M made his fullest statement about life's meaninglessness, and from his belief in this as well as from his belief that "achievement cannot matter but is necessary in the nature of things," he fashioned a pattern for himself with "stoic resolve." To M, man confronts an irrational world with an heroic courage in which there is "a beauty greater than the world of art." Man strives "because of an instinct for self-assertion," and satisfaction of that instinct "counterbalances all the pains and hardships that confront men. It makes life worth living."

2239 Brooks, Cleanth, and Robert B. Heilman. *"The Circle* by Somerset Maugham," UNDERSTANDING DRAMA: TWELVE PLAYS (NY: Holt, Rinehart and Winston, 1963 [1948]), pp. 12-15 [Appendix A].

[Analysis of M's intentions in *The Circle.*]

2240 "Cloak Without Dagger," TIMES LITERARY SUPPLEMENT (Lond), 8 Feb 1963, p. 92.

In *Ashenden,* M's basis for the characterization of "the Spy" is related to that of Dreighton's THE IPCRESS FILE, that of Ambler's in THE ABILITY TO KILL, and to the kind of international spy conceived in our era. R, the ruthless Military Intelligence Boss, is the real triumph of the *Ashenden* series.

2241* Colburn, William E. "Dr. Maugham's Prescription for Success," EMORY UNIVERSITY QUARTERLY, XIX (Spring 1963), 14-21.

Liza of Lambeth is an example of turn-of-the-century naturalism. The inconsistency of tone is damaging to its effect; particularly is this evident in the section known as "The Idyll of Corydon and Phyllis." The novel is not, contrary to what M has suggested, good as a model for beginners; before he prescribes, the physician should heal himself.

2242 Davies, H. M. P. "The King's School, Canterbury: The Hugh

Walpole Collection: The Somerset Maugham Library," ETUDES ANGLAISES, XVI (Jan-March 1963), 59-62.

The M material in King's School Library includes manuscripts of *Liza of Lambeth* and of *Catalina;* M's personal library of about five thousand books —the working library of a writer. A number of these books have M's marginal comments and personal inscriptions from their authors.

2243 Dietrich, Margret. DAS MODERNE DRAMA: STRÖMUNGEN, GESTALTEN, MOTIVE (MODERN DRAMA: MOVEMENTS, FORMS, THEMES) (Stuttgart: Alfred Kröner, 1963), pp. 71, 77-78, 79, 677.

[Brief, general remarks on M's writing to make money, his relation to the tradition of the English comedy of manners.] [In German.]

2244* Dobrinsky, J. "Comptes Rendus" (Critical Reports), ETUDES ANGLAISES, XVI (July-Sept 1963), 298.

In L. Brander's SOMERSET MAUGHAM: A GUIDE, too much space is allotted *The Unknown, A Man of Honour, Mrs. Craddock.* The portrait of M we obtain from the book hardly differs from the mask the author made for himself; M's personality is more complex than Brander would lead us to believe. [In French.]

2245 Hawkins, Barbara M. "*'Bondage'*: Filming the Straight Story," JOURNAL AND COURIER (Lafayette, Ind), 25 May 1963, pp. 4, 8.

Richard Cordell, biographer of M, after Fulbright lectures at Montpellier and Toulouse, spent five days at Ardmore Studios on the Seven Arts Film Company set of *Of Human Bondage,* with Kim Novak and Laurence Harvey in the leading roles. The film, Cordell is reported as observing, "is adhering to the straight story." In newspaper and taped radio interviews, Cordell was asked if he knew the identity of Mildred; he thinks he does but insists, as in his biographical study, that "whether Mildred is drawn from life is of little import . . . . She is a completely realized human being, unforgettable . . . . "

2246 J:la, O. "Maughamin 'Sade' [RAIN] Kaupunginteatterissa" (Maugham's RAIN at the Rauma Town Theater), TURIN SANOMAT, 10 Nov 1963, p. 20.

The movement of the play [in the Finnish adaptation] is rather slow, and the dialogue is not particularly witty, but its message reaches the audience even today. [In Finnish.]

2247 Jacque, Valentina. "Soviet Critics on Modern English Writing," SOVIET REVIEW, No. 4 (1963), 163-68.

[Summary remarks to prove the "objectivity" of Russian critics on M's work.]

2248 Poore, Charles [G]. "Books of the Times: The Curtain Speeches of Somerset Maugham," NEW YORK TIMES BOOK REVIEW, 5 Oct 1963, p. 23.
Selected Prefaces and Introductions of W. Somerset Maugham shows M's writings to be "rich in frosted disenchantment," in a laughter which generally has a cutting edge.

2249 Reyer, Georges. "Le Match de la vie: Le Roman noir d'un héritage" (The Match's Life: The Black Novel of a Heritage), PARIS-MATCH, No. 731 (13 April 1963), 6, 10, 14, 19, 26.
[Review of M's life as he approached his ninetieth birthday.] [In French.]

2250 Stewart, J. I. M. EIGHT MODERN WRITERS (Oxford: Clarendon P, 1963), pp. 13, especially 245, 263.
M's "professionalism" contrasts with Galsworthy's "amateurism." "It is a professionalism guarded by a Gallic sense of the dignity of letters, but at the same time allowing for a large complaisance in the following of public taste."

2251 Swinnerton, Frank. FIGURES IN THE FOREGROUND: LITERARY REMINISCENCES 1917-40 (Lond: Hutchinson, 1963), pp. 31-36 ("Sophisticated Caveman"), 89-94 ("Maugham and Walpole").
[The first passage recounts M's hard luck in acquiring fame and fortune until the publication of *Cakes and Ale,* the second describes Walpole's sensation upon reading *Cakes and Ale* and Swinnerton's meeting M.]

1964

2252* Allen, Walter. "Summing Up Somerset Maugham at 90," NEW YORK TIMES BOOK REVIEW, 19 Jan 1964, pp. 1, 24.
M is more than a mere teller of tales or a mere entertainer. He is the last survivor of an age that had not divorced the idea of entertainment from the idea of art. M fared poorly in England because Naturalism "never caught on" there, and M began as a Naturalist and has remained one in some essential respects. But M's poor reception is abetted, also, by his sometimes appearing so knowing, so unsurprised, and so worldly that he seems to be condescending or to be writing a "formula" plot for "mere mortals." M lacks an interest in human motives, but from that very lack spring his greatest triumphs: *Liza of Lambeth, Of Human Bondage, Cakes and Ale,* and the Elliott Templeton-half of *The Razor's Edge.* "The more outrageous the specimen confronting him, the greater Maugham's success." Before the incalculability, the absurdity of human behavior M's admi-

ration warms, and the specimen is enhanced by M's satiric response. In view of these beliefs, M's best plays are *The Circle, The Constant Wife,* and *The Breadwinner.* M is neither a small nor a limited writer.

2253 Belloc, Elizabeth. "The Stories of Somerset Maugham," MONTH, CCXVIII (July-Aug 1964), 67-72.

M is a great storyteller with a "plot mind" and a gift for concentration on the significant, but he misses greatness because he lacks "faith" and a strong "ethical sense." A sardonic cruelty haunts his soul.

2254 Dolch, Martin. "Somerset Maugham," INSIGHT II: ANALYSES OF MODERN BRITISH LITERATURE, ed by John V. Hagopian and Martin Dolch (Frankfurt: Hirschgraben-Verlag, 1964), pp. 251-59.

In "The Outstation" M "gradually develops an ironic involution of the usual British-American sympathy for the underdog by first presenting Cooper as an apparently favourable contrast to the stuffy and snobbish Mr. Warburton and then slowly revealing that he is, in fact, far more contemptible." The dialogues are praiseworthy, the commentaries of the omniscient narrator are not.

2255 Fricker, Robert. DAS MODERNE ENGLISCHE DRAMA (MODERN ENGLISH DRAMA), (Göttingen: Vandenhoeck & Ruprecht, 1964), pp. 11, 15, 29-30, 32, 52, 54, 68, 78.

M combines the Wildean comedy of manners with the social drama and thus creates a new kind of problem comedy characterized by its bitter satire and its entertaining qualities. *Our Betters, The Circle, The Breadwinner,* and *The Constant Wife* are his best plays. [In German.]

2256 Gautier, Jean-Jacques. "La Critique de J. J. Gautier-Théâtre Montparnasse-Gaston Baty-*Caroline*" (The Criticism of J. J. Gautier: Theatre-Montparnasse-Gaston Baty: *Caroline*), LE FIGARO, 23 Jan 1964, p. 18.

The French adaptation is a comedy of a forgotten genre, tame, sweetish, dragging along with giggles and outmoded pauses in the alleys of a discolored convention. There is only one good scene, and that is in the beginning when the lovers, given the opportunity, decide not to marry. [In French.]

2257 "Indestructible Maugham—Ashcroft Theatre: *Home and Beauty*," TIMES (Lond), 28 Jan 1964, p. 13.

"How many other writers can sustain a situation, bring to it more twists than was ever found in the longest corkscrew and yet maintain the elegance of its dialogue?" [Review of revival.]

2258 Lemarchand, Jacques. "Le théâtre" (Theater), LE FIGARO LITTERAIRE, 30 Jan-5 Feb 1964, p. 22.

Caroline [in the French adaptation] is a mediocre piece. [In French.]

2259 Lenehan, William T. "Techniques and Themes in early English and American Naturalistic Novels." Unpublished thesis, University of Oklahoma, 1964.

In *Liza of Lambeth* M was seeking techniques to criticize traditional morality.

2260 Leslie, Seymour. THE JEROME COMPLEXION (Lond: John Murray, 1964), pp. 105, 145, 175.

The composer, Delius, who knew Gauguin in Paris, laughed at M's rearrangement of the true story in *The Moon and Sixpence.*

2261 M[arcel], G[abriel]. "Sourires, Larmes, Rires-*Caroline*" (Smiles, Tears, Laughter: *Caroline*), LES NOUVELLES LITTERAIRES, 6 Feb 1964, p. 12.

In the French adaptation, the parts of the well-thinking friends who are eager to see Caroline married have been heavily overacted; M wanted them to be comical, not burlesque. [In French.]

2262 Middleton, Drew. "Maugham at 90: The Summing Up," NEW YORK TIMES, 25 Jan 1964, p. 20.

[Interview on the eve of M's ninetieth birthday.]

2263* "Plain Man's Taste," TIMES LITERARY SUPPLEMENT (Lond), 2 July 1964, p. 566.

When all the material in *Selected Prefaces and Introductions of W. Somerset Maugham* is gathered, it is striking that this writer, who has often insisted on his unlikeness to most other people . . . , expresses a commonsensical Plain Man approach to literature." The defects he attributes to Maupassant ("had some commonness in his nature") and James ("was defeated by a peculiar triviality of soul") are in reality his own defects.

2264 "Quick Guide to New Reading," TIMES (Lond), 18 June 1964, p. 17.

[Brief description of *Selected Prefaces and Introductions of W. Somerset Maugham.*]

2265 Seidlin, Rosemarie. "Somerset Maugham: *On a Chinese Screen*," DIE NEUEREN SPRACHEN, XIII:12 (Dec 1964), 573-81.

M's sophisticated style creates "atmosphere" with a few words, expresses subtle emotional inflections, remains "objective," yet gives moral judgments. These qualities are particularly well-illustrated in the vignette, "The Taipan." [In German.]

1965

2266 "Après une lente agonie l'écrivain Somerset Maugham est mort" (After a Slow Agony Writer Somerset Maugham Is Dead), L'HUMANITÉ, 17 Dec 1965, p. 10.
[Obituary.] [In French.]

2267 "Au passage" (In Passing), ARTS, SPECTACLES, 22-28 Dec 1965, p. 10.
[Obituary.] [In French.]

2268 "Better than Most," NEWSWEEK, LXVI (27 Dec 1965), 32.
[Obituary and appreciation.]

2269 Burgess, Anthony. "W. Somerset Maugham: 1874-1965," LISTENER, LXXIV (23 Dec 1965), 1033.
[Obituary and appreciation.]

2270 Eteläpää, Heikki. "*Caroline* jää saavuttamattomaksi" (*Caroline* Remains Out of Reach), UUSI SUOMI, 24 March 1965, p. 17.
In the Finnish adaptation, the dialogue is easy but boring. The atmosphere is out-of-date and distant. [In Finnish.]

2271 "Flat Dialogue in Far from Boring Comedy —Savoy Theatre: *The Circle*," TIMES (Lond), 15 June 1965, p. 15.
The revived play presents a contradiction between its "extremely careful construction and its hack dialogue."

2272 Gilroy, Harry. "Posthumous Publication Barred by Maugham, Executor Reports," NEW YORK TIMES, 16 Dec 1965, p. 50.
Alexander S. Frere, M's literary executor, reports that M burned all of his notebooks and works in progress five years prior to his death, and that M forbade all posthumous publications.

2273 Kk. "Matt komedi på Intimi" (Tired Comedy at the 'Intimate Theater'), HUFVUDSTADSBLADET, 25 March 1965, p. 8.
The Finnish adaptation of *Caroline* shows the material is worn out; the author is absent-minded. The play is amusing in some places, though not sufficiently so to guarantee a pleasant theatrical experience. [In Finnish.]

2274 Knecht, Jean. "Somerset Maugham, un maître de l'humour élégant et du cynicisme léger" (Somerset Maugham, a Master of Elegant Humor and Light Cynicism), LE MONDE, 17 Dec 1965, p. 12.
[Obituary and appreciation.] [In French.]

2275 Lacretelle, Jacques de. "La dernière escale de Somerset Maugham" (The Last Port of Somerset Maugham), LE FIGARO LITTERAIRE, 23 Dec 1965, pp. 1, 16.
[Obituary and appreciation.] [In French.]

2276 Las Vergnas, Raymond. "Le long voyage de Somerset Maugham" (The Long Voyage of Somerset Maugham), LES NOUVELLES LITTERAIRES, 23 Dec 1965, p. 3.
[Obituary and appreciation.] [In French.]

2277 Menard, Wilmon. THE TWO WORLDS OF SOMERSET MAUGHAM. (Los Angeles: Sherbourne P, 1965).
The two worlds of M are the French Riviera and the South Pacific; in a conversation, M discussed his voyages to Hawaii and Samoa to gather material which resulted in *The Moon and Sixpence, The Trembling of a Leaf,* and *The Painted Veil.* M reminisces about the sexual ethics of the South Pacific; his reading of Stevenson, Rupert Brooke, and Loti; Gauguin and the events surrounding the writing of the stories in *The Trembling of a Leaf,* especially "Miss Thompson" (or "Rain").

2278 Middleton, Drew. "Always True to Himself," NEW YORK TIMES, 16 Dec 1965, p. 50.
[Obituary and appreciation.]

2279 "Mort de Somerset Maugham" (The Death of Somerset Maugham), LE FIGARO, 17 Dec 1965, pp. 1, 21.
[Obituary and appreciation.] [In French.]

2280 "Mr. Somerset Maugham: The Most Assured Writer of His Time," TIMES (Lond), 17 Dec 1965, p. 17.
[Obituary and appreciation.]

2281 Neuveglise, Paule. "Mort cette nuit à 91 ans, sur la Côte d'Azur. Somerset Maugham est peut-être devenu écrivain qu'il était bégue" (Dead This Evening at 91, on the Côte d'Azur. Somerset Maugham Became an Author Perhaps Because He Was a Stammerer), FRANCE-SOIR, 17 Dec 1965, p. 5.
[Obituary and appreciation.] [In French.]

2282 Newell, J. P. "Mr. Somerset Maugham," TIMES (Lond), 24 Dec 1965, p. 10.
[Obituary and appreciation.]

2283 Niiniluoto, Marja. "Maughamin pitkä päivä päättynyt" (Maugham's Long Day at an End), HELSINGIN SANOMAT, 17 Dec 1965, p. 22.
As a short-story writer, M followed the tradition of Maupassant. His

characters are, in a way, static; they show hardly any development. He was accused of triviality and lack of power, but his best novels and short stories reach a high standard in their vitality, clarity and sharp observation. [Obituary and appreciation.] [In Finnish.]

2284 "Notes and Comments," NEW YORKER, XLI (25 Dec 1965), 17.
[Obituary.]

2285 "Obituary Notes," PUBLISHERS' WEEKLY, CLXXXVIII (27 Dec 1965), 74, 76.
[Obituary.]

2286 Quoodle. "Spectator's Notebook: The Great Storyteller," SPECTATOR (Lond), CCXV (24 Dec 1965), 834.
[Obituary and appreciation.]

2287 "The Reporter's Notes: W. Somerset Maugham," REPORTER, XXXIII (30 Dec 1965), 13.
[Obituary and appreciation.]

2288 Reyer, Georges. "Les derniers mots du gentleman du Cap Ferrat: 'Je meurs quéri!' " (The Last Words from the Gentleman of Cap Ferrat: 'I die healed!'), PARIS-MATCH, 25 Dec 1965, pp. 80-81.
[Obituary and appreciation.] [In French.]

2289 Roos, Vappu. SUURI MAAILMANKIRJALLISUUS (GREAT WORLD LITERATURE) (Porvoo-Helsinki: WSOY, 1965), pp. 420-21.
M has dominated English prose writing for half a century. His weightiest productions were composed between the two World Wars. In the course of the years he has moved from a rebel more and more to a best-seller writer, announcing that the author's primary task is to entertain his readers. His short stories are probably the most valuable part of his work. [In Finnish.]

2290 "Une Rue Somerset-Maugham à Saint-Jean-Cap-Ferrat" (A Somerset-Maugham Street in Saint-Jean-Cap-Ferrat), LE FIGARO, 18-19 Dec 1965, p. 9.
[The mayor names a street after M.] [In French.]

2291 "Somerset Maugham," NEW YORK TIMES, 17 Dec 1965, p. 38.
[Obituary and appreciation.]

2292 "Somerset Maugham Burnt Books," TIMES (Lond), 17 Dec 1965, p. 12.

M instructed his literary executor, Alexander S. Frere, that no unpublished writing of his should be printed after his death. M is said to have burned his notebooks and works in progress about five years prior to his death.

2293 "Somerset Maugham est mort" (Somerset Maugham Is Dead), LA CROIX, 17 Dec 1965, p. 2.
[Obituary.] [In French.]

2294 "Somerset Maugham Is Dead at 91," NEW YORK TIMES, 16 Dec 1965, pp. 1, 50.
[Obituary.]

2295 "Somerset Maugham kuollut" (Somerset Maugham Is Dead), UUSI SUOMI, 17 Dec 1965, p. 16.
M was not praised by critics or by his colleagues. But he did not feed his readers with false dreams as so many writers of light literature do. He offered them the ingredients of reality. His novels, short stories, and plays have greatly contributed to the better understanding of the European "spirit of the time" in the 1930s. [Obituary and appreciation.] [In Finnish.]

2296 Taivalkoski, Jussi. "William Somerset Maughamin tarina" (The Story of William Somerset Maugham), PÄIVÄN SANOMAT, 16 Dec 1965, p. 5.
M's works show excellent knowledge of the human mind, intelligent irony, and an understanding of life. His plays are carefully constructed, the characters skilfully chosen. [Obituary and appreciation.] [In Finnish.]

2297 Vartia, Annikki. "Maughamko kiltti?" (Is Maugham Really Nice?), KAUPPALEHTI, 24 March 1965, p. 9.
In the Finnish adaptation of *Caroline,* the dialogue is witty, the humor intelligent, but the play lacks the solid construction of *The Circle.* [In Finnish.]

2298 "W. Somerset Maugham (1874-1965)," TIME, LXXXVI (24 Dec 1965), 58.
[Obituary and appreciation.]

1966

2299 [Allsop, Kenneth]. "K A Remembers a Meeting with S M Enjoying the Truce of Old Age," BOOKS AND BOOKMEN, X (May 1966), 18, 55.
[Interview with M just after his ninetieth birthday.]

2300 Altman, Wilfred. "Somerset Maugham: An Appreciation," CONTEMPORARY REVIEW, CCVIII (Feb 1966), 99-104.
[Conventional biographical portrait.]

2301 Amory, Cleveland. "First of the Month," SATURDAY REVIEW (NY), XLIX (8 Jan 1966), 13, 89.
[Obituary and appreciation.]

2302 Behrman, S. N. "Maugham, Playwright," NEW YORK TIMES, 2 Jan 1966, II: 1, 3.
[Reviews well-known facts of M's career in the theater, and expresses agreement with M that *Our Betters* and *The Circle* will survive.]

2303 "Books: Willie's Last Chapters," TIME, LXXXVII (20 May 1966), 126.
[Review of Robin Maugham's SOMERSET AND ALL THE MAUGHAMS.] "It may be a disservice to one of the world's best storytellers to revive those last ungraceful chapters of his life, but it helps to give his readers perspective."

2304 Brown, Ivor. "William, Half a Conqueror," DRAMA, LXXXI (Summer 1966), 25-26.
[Obituary and appreciation.]

2305 Clinton, Farley. "Men and Letters: Maugham's Bondage," NATIONAL REVIEW (NY), XVIII (22 Feb 1966), 174-76.
[Obituary and appreciation.]

2306 Cuff, Sergeant. "Criminal Record," SATURDAY REVIEW (NY), XLIX (25 June 1966), 31.
The reissue shows *Ashenden* to be "a classic . . . in a highly restricted field."

2307 Davenport, G[uy]. "Somerset Maugham, RIP," NATIONAL REVIEW (NY), XVIII (11 Jan 1966), 16.
[Obituary and appreciation.]

2308 French, Philip. "The Stammerer as Hero," ENCOUNTER, XXVII (November 1966), 67-75.
When M died in 1965, there were a number of works which depicted stammerers as heroes, the defect indicating integrity "in an otherwise glib world." In actuality, however, stammerers lack the control necessary for great art.

2309 Fricker, Robert. DER MODERNE ENGLISCHE ROMAN (THE

MODERN ENGLISH NOVEL.) Second, revised edition (Göttingen: Vandenhoeck & Ruprecht, 1966), p. 195.

M is briefly mentioned as a traditional painter of society.

2310 Goren, Charles. "Maugham Never Forgot the Day I Trumped His Ace," SPORTS ILLUSTRATED, XXIV (17 Jan 1966), 50-51.

[Biographical reminiscences.]

2311 Hänninen, H. "Keskinkertaista komediaa Kaupunginteatterissa" (Mediocre Comedy at the Town Theater), ETELA-SAIMAA, 29 Oct 1966, p. 5.

[The Finnish adaptation of] JANE is a not very amusing, indeed boring, play; it leaves the present-day audience cold. [In Finnish.]

2312 Heywood, C. "Somerset Maugham's Debt to MADAME BOVARY and Miss Braddon's THE DOCTOR'S WIFE," ETUDES ANGLAISES, XIX (Jan-March 1966), 64-69.

Miss Braddon's THE DOCTOR'S WIFE (1864), an adaptation of MADAME BOVARY, was influential upon M in making a similar adaptation from Flaubert in *Mrs. Craddock, The Painted Veil,* and *The Razor's Edge.*

2313 Kanin, Garson. "Remembering Mr. Maugham," NEW YORK TIMES, 4 Sept 1966, II & X: 1, 3.

[Pre-publication excerpts from Kanin's book (1966) of the same title.]

2314 Kanin, Garson. "Remembering Mr. Maugham," VOGUE, CXLVIII (15 Aug 1966), 86-87, 133-34, 136.

[Pre-publication excerpts from Kanin's book (1966) of the same title.]

2315 Kanin, Garson. REMEMBERING MR. MAUGHAM. With a Foreword by Noël Coward. (NY: Atheneum, 1966).

[An account of Kanin's dealings with M for over twenty years, with emphasis on M's relations to the legitimate theater, television, the movies, and various personalities connected with these fields.]

2316 Las Vergnas, Raymond. "Somerset Maugham," LA REVUE [DES DEUX MONDES], 15 Jan 1966, pp. 171-80.

[A biographical essay recounting M's beginnings as an orphan, medical student, dramatist and novelist.] [In French.]

2317 Lehmann, John. "Books and the Arts: A Very Old Party," NEW REPUBLIC, CLIV (8 Jan 1966), 23-24.

[Obituary and appreciation.]

2318 Maugham, Robin. "My Uncle Willie," SATURDAY EVENING POST, CCXXXIX (29 Jan 1966), 79-81.

[Pre-publication excerpt from Robin Maugham's SOMERSET AND ALL THE MAUGHAMS (1966).]

2319 Maugham, Robin. SOMERSET AND ALL THE MAUGHAMS. (NY: New American Library, 1966).

[A study of the ancestors and immediate family of M, intended to illuminate M's complex personality.]

2320* Moskovit, Leonard. "Maugham's 'Outstation': A Single, Serious Effect," UNIVERSITY OF COLORADO STUDIES [Series in Language and Literature], No. 10 (Feb 1966), 107-14.

The term "competent" accurately describes the quality of most of M's short stories but does injustice to the art of his best one, "The Outstation," which puts into practice E. A. Poe's advice to invent incidents to produce a certain unique or single effect. In "The Outstation"—specifically in Warburton—"we see moral self-corruption where it need not have been, and mourn." Fact, development, and treatment work together to produce a serious, powerful effect. To require "some organizing metaphysical statement" from the story is like requiring "that a beautiful and intelligent woman should also be a philosopher."

2321 Naik, M. K. W. SOMERSET MAUGHAM (Norman: University of Oklahoma P, 1966).

M was well-equipped for literary success, but left only "slender baggage" because of his deep-seated conflict between "cynicism" and "humanitarianism." M's cynicism, barring him from a comprehensive artistic vision, was fostered by his orphaned childhood and unfortunate adolescence, his extensive travels, his French origins and affinities. It was manifest in his early works, but became predominant in *The Moon and Sixpence* and subsequent works, most of which employ a detached, amused, ironical first-person narrator representing M and the triumph of his narrow cynical side. Only *Cakes and Ale* among his novels, the short stories, and the travel books display M's cynicism mitigated by and in perfect balance with the broader "humanitarian" view.

2322 Nichols, Beverley. A CASE OF HUMAN BONDAGE. (Lond: Secker & Warburg, 1966).

[A biographical account centering around the events at Le Touquet, emphasizing Gerald Haxton's corrupt hold on M, and attempting to exonerate Syrie Maugham of the character M ascribed to her in "Looking Back."]

2323 Nichols, Beverley. "The Twisted Marriage of Somerset Maugham," LOOK, XXX (18 Oct 1966), 33-37.

[Adaptation from Nichols' book, A CASE OF HUMAN BONDAGE.]

2324* Pollock, John. "Somerset Maugham and His Work," QUARTERLY REVIEW, CCCIV (Oct 1966), 365-78.

In the future, M, both as a novelist and a playwright, will "be set among writers at the top of the first class," a claim supported by an analysis of M's two approaches to creating character in his major plays and novels: either (1) by taking the outer psychological values of a real person and turning them into an imaginary portrait by embodying them in incidents with little or no relation to the model's actual life, or (2) by taking the fundamental values and placing them into fictitious persons who had no relation to his models.

2325* Raven, Simon. "Books: Uncle Willie," SPECTATOR (Lond), CCXVI (8 April 1966), 439-40.

The essential aim of Robin Maugham's SOMERSET AND ALL THE MAUGHAMS is to cash in before anyone else can on the author's uncle Willie. . . . It is not what Lord Maugham puts in that bothers one but what he hasn't" —especially, M's "authority" as a personality that emerged from what he wrote.

2326* Raymond, John. "Abominable Ancestors," PUNCH, CCL (27 April 1966), 633.

[Review of Robin Maugham's SOMERSET AND ALL THE MAUGHAMS.] The reader will willingly exchange "a long stretch of this ancestral paper-chase" for a more extended treatment of the author's father. Robin Maugham should also have more fully portrayed M's "extraordinary professional vanity."

2327 Smith, Harrison. "In the Great Tradition: Maugham the Master Craftsman," SATURDAY REVIEW (NY), XCIX (15 Jan 1966), 25.

[Obituary and appreciation.]

2328 S[mith], W[illiam] G. "Why Maugham Was Miserable," BOOKS AND BOOKMEN, XI (Feb 1966), 22.

[Obituary and appreciation.]

2329 Stavén, Pauli. "Arvaa kuka nai kenet. Yllättävä kälyni yllätti katsojiaan Lappeenrannan kaupunginteatterissa" (Guess Who Marries Whom. Surprises at Lappeenranta Town Theater), SAIMAN SANOMAT, 29 Oct 1966, p. 6.

[The Finnish adaptation of] JANE is a play built upon witty and amusing episodes of conversation. The author's humor is biting but basically neither cynical or ironic. There are no weighty ideas: the play is a game of "guess who marries whom." [In Finnish.]

2330 Weintraub, Stanley. "An Old Acquaintance," SATURDAY REVIEW (NY), XLIX (9 July 1966), 23-29.
Robin Maugham's SOMERSET AND ALL THE MAUGHAMS is "more quarry than biography or critique. Through it Maugham's major novels are seen even more clearly than before as a reflection of his early life."

2331 Whittington-Egan, Richard. "Biography," BOOKS AND BOOKMEN, XI (May 1966), 27.
Robin Maugham's SOMERSET AND ALL THE MAUGHAMS asserts that M portrayed himself in Driffield of *Cakes and Ale:* "It is a fiction with all the sadness of truth."

2332* Whittington-Egan, Richard. "Biography," BOOKS AND BOOKMEN, XI (Aug 1966), 31.
Beverley Nichols in A CASE OF HUMAN BONDAGE perhaps "does not realise how cruel *his* [i.e., in contrast to M's of Syrie Maugham in "Looking Back"] portrayal appears. Perhaps the butterfly is surprised by the sting in his own tail."

2333 Willey, Margaret. "Somerset Maugham, 1874-1965," ENGLISH, XVI (Spring 1966), 1.
[Obituary and appreciation.]

1967

2334 Burt, Forrest D. "A New Methodology for Psychological Criticism of Literature: A Case Study for William Somerset Maugham." Unpublished thesis, Texas Technological College, 1967.

2335 Gerber, Helmut E. "W. Somerset Maugham," THE ENGLISH SHORT STORY IN TRANSITION: 1880-1920 (NY: Pegasus, 1967), pp. 425-26, 510-11.
[Biographical sketch and introduction, with a bibliography.]

2336 Goetsch, Paul. DIE ROMANKONZEPTION IN ENGLAND: 1880-1910 (THE CONCEPTION OF THE NOVEL IN ENGLAND: 1880-1910), (Heidelberg: Carl Winter, 1967), pp. 15, 132, 248, 449.
[Passing references.] [In German.]

2337* Henry, William H., Jr. A FRENCH BIBLIOGRAPHY OF W. SOMERSET MAUGHAM. (Charlottesville: The Bibliographical Society of the University of Virginia, 1967).
[A list of M's works published in France; his contributions to French peri-

odicals; and the Swiss, Belgian, and French criticism of his books, plays, and films.]

2338* Heywood, C. "Two Printed Texts of Somerset Maugham's *Mrs. Craddock*," ENGLISH LANGUAGE NOTES, V (Sept 1967), 39-46.

An examination of the textual variants between the first edition (1902) and the Collected Edition (1937) versions of *Mrs. Craddock* shows that M's restorations concerning Bertha's emotional life add a new dimension in the mutuality of a physical attraction between Bertha and Gerald Vaudrey.

2339 Kujala, Antti. "Novellisti Maugham" (Maugham as a Short Story Writer), TURUN SANOMAT, 2 June 1967, p. 20.

Cosmopolitans [in the Finnish translation], though not M's best stories, is yet likable for their method of telling. [In Finnish.]

2340 Meltti, Raimo. "Lorveja ja lortteja" (Idlers and Loafers), PAIVAN SANOMAT, 28 May 1967, p. 9.

Cosmopolitans [in the Finnish translation] is out of date. [In Finnish.]

2341 Menard, Wilmon. "Maugham's Pacific," SATURDAY REVIEW (NY), L (11 March 1967), 77-78, 80.

[A recounting of M's travels in the Pacific, similar in content to passages in Menard's book, THE TWO WORLDS OF SOMERSET MAUGHAM (1965).]

2342 Paavilainen, Matti. "Elegantit harharetket" (Elegant Odyssey), HELSINGIN SANOMAT, 1 Oct 1967, p. 19.

The stories in *Cosmopolitans* [in the Finnish translation] are old-fashioned. M, as an author, is an Englishman and a gentleman; even today, he deserves the title of master entertainer. [In Finnish.]

2343 Pitkänen, Risto. "Kirjallisuutta kaikki" (It Is All Literature), UUSI SUOMI, 11 June 1967, p. 13.

Cosmopolitans [in the Finnish translation] shows that M's cynicism loses its edge through excessive mechanical refinement. [In Finnish.]

2344 R-suo, A. "Kiehtovia kertomuksia" (Enchanting Stories), MAASEUDUN TULEVAISUUS, 24 Aug 1967, p. 7.

Cosmopolitans [in the Finnish translation] is not great art though full of attraction. [In Finnish.]

2345 Rees, Leslie. "Remembrance of Things Past: (15) A Meeting with Somerset Maugham," MEANJIN QUARTERLY, XXVI (Dec 1967), 452-56.

[Recounting of the author's meeting M at the time of the premiere of *Sheppey.*]

2346 Standop, Ewald, and Edgar Mertner. ENGLISCHE LITERATURGESCHICHTE (ENGLISH LITERARY HISTORY) (Heidelberg: Quelle & Meyer, 1967), pp. 560, 587-88, 621, 641.

M is a follower of French naturalism and a skeptic. *Cakes and Ale* is the best of his later novels; his plays are inferior to his fiction, his comedies of manners better than his problem plays. [In German.]

2347* Taylor, John Russell. THE RISE AND FALL OF THE WELL-MADE PLAY (Lond: Methuen; & N Y: Hill and Wang, 1967), pp. 9, 91, 92-109, 110, 120, 124, 127, 128-29, 131, 133, 137, 138, 140, 163, 164.

With Pinero, the well-made play reached its zenith and began thereafter to decline; but ironically, M "managed to win back a certain area" for it by writing comedies that contrasted sharply with the serious works of Ibsen and Shaw: M succeeded initially because comedies were not thought to require great weight. His gradual failure to please audiences arose from his becoming "readier" to write "non-comic" plays while being unable to "reconcile the disciplines and requirements of the well-made play with the desire to write with high seriousness about the problems of real life which gave an audience the illusion that it was seeing real life unmanipulated by a puppeteer, however masterly." M, like Pinero, dealt best with "the clear-cut and precisely defined." Thus, his best plays are *Our Betters, The Circle, The Constant Wife; Caesar's Wife* is a "real if qualified success"; *East of Suez,* "the silliest play Maugham wrote," and *The Unknown,* a "complete failure."

2348 Vuorio, Hannu. "Kootut anekdootit" (Collected Anecdotes), KANSAN UUTISET, 28 May 1967, p. 7.

[Review of the Finnish translation of *Cosmopolitans.*] [In Finnish.]

1968

2349* Barnes, Ronald Edgar. THE DRAMATIC COMEDY OF WILLIAM SOMERSET MAUGHAM. (The Hague and Paris: Mouton, 1968).

M's drama shows a consistent concern with the inadequacy of society's moral structure. His pre–World War I plays employ a marriage contract symbolic of society, and reflecting the stable Edwardian age; in contrast, the post-War plays conclude with broken contracts, manifesting the social disintegration attending the War. Thereafter, M turned to colonial themes, the colonial representing the fresh thought of a newly developed society unencumbered by tradition.

2350* Harris, Wendell V. "Molly's 'Yes': The Transvaluation of Sex in Modern Fiction," TEXAS STUDIES IN LITERATURE AND LANGUAGE, X (Spring 1968), 107-18, especially 111-12.

Modern fiction is characterized by two prevalent themes: "the repudiation of a large portion of the world's values and the discovery of the importance of physical love." Philip Carey's rejection, in *Of Human Bondage,* "of the established values . . . of society occurs in a sequence which so nearly coincides with the historical chronology of nineteenth- and twentieth-century man's disillusionment as to be almost allegorical"; i. e., Philip first renounces his religious convictions and anticipation of a career at Oxford, then the aesthetic stance of Hayward, next commerce, last his faith in man's power to exercise his will rationally. His salvation is achieved through the physical love of Sally Athelny.

2351 L-la, A. "Elävältä se kirja maistui" (That Book Savored of Life), SUOMEN SOSIALIDEMOKRAATTI, 18 Sept 1968, p. 8.

The Finnish translation of *Cakes and Ale* shows that fluent narration runs smoothly from one time into another. There is plenty of satire in the plot and in the characterization. [In Finnish.]

2352 Menard, Wilmon. "Somerset Maugham and Paul Gauguin," MICHIGAN QUARTERLY REVIEW, VII (Fall 1968), 227-32.

[Discussion of M's reasons for visiting Tahiti in 1917 and his interest in Gauguin; closely similar to sections of Menard's THE TWO WORLDS OF SOMERSET MAUGHAM (1965).]

2353 Menard, Wilmon. "Somerset Maugham in Hollywood," MICHIGAN QUARTERLY REVIEW, VII (Summer 1968), 207-10.

[A recounting of M's associations with Hollywood, especially during the production of *The Razor's Edge.*]

2354 Salerno, Henry F. "William Somerset Maugham [1874-1965]," ENGLISH DRAMA IN TRANSITION: 1880-1920 (NY: Pegasus, 1968), pp. 463-66.

[Biographical and critical introduction to *Our Betters,* comparing and contrasting M's techniques with those of Wycherley and Congreve.]

2355 Sanders, Charles, and R. R. Rice. "W. Somerset Maugham," AT LENGTH (Glenview, Ill: Scott, Foresman, 1968), pp. 281-82.

[Brief introduction to the essay "The Decline and Fall of the Detective Story," suggesting the goals of M as a novelist and a dramatist are evident in his essays, too.]

Index

AUTHORS

Included here are authors of articles and books on Maugham, editors and compilers of works in which criticism on Maugham appears. Editors and translators are identified parenthetically: (ed), (trans). Numbers after each name refer to the item(s) in the bibliography where the name occurs.

A., E.: 814
Abdullah, Achmed: 445
Abraham, Pierre: 2177
Adams, J. Donald: 1504, 1505, 1559, 1617, 1660, 1962
Adcock, A. St. John: 20, 479
Agate, James: 446, 480, 533, 534, 596, 639, 973, 1027, 1506, 1507, 1508
Aho, O.: 1427
Ahonen, Olavi: 1618
Albalat, Antoine: 535
Aldington, Richard: 1332
Aldridge, John W.: 1661
Alle, Fritz: 1703
Allen, Walter: 1704, 2252
Allsop, Kenneth: 2299
Alpert, Hollis: 1770, 1903
Altman, Wilfred: 2300
Ambrière, Francis: 768
Amis, Kingsley: 2208
Amory, Cleveland: 2301
Amur, G. S.: 2236
Anderson, John: 481, 597
Anderson, Maxwell: 316, 1988
Andréades, A.: 393, 522
Andrews, Kenneth: 394, 447, 482
Angell, Hildegarde: 395
Angoff, Charles: 1771
Anhava, Tuomas: 1705, 1772, 1847; (ed): 2070
Annan, Noël: 1963
Archer, William: 111, 160, 225, 275, 311, 317, 367, 396
Arland, Marcel: 1848
Armstrong, Anne: 974, 1028
Armstrong, Petronella: 1560, 1570, 1662
Arns, Karl: 1280
Arpiainen, Leila: 2227
Arrowsmith, J. E. S.: 975, 1029
Assä [Pseudonym]: 2071
Atkinson, J. Brooks: 640, 711, 879, 1428, 1849
Auden, W. H.: 1707
Audiat, Pierre: 536, 712, 769, 1030, 1031, 1109
Austruy, Henri: 880
Aynard, Joseph: 537
B.: 113
B., D. B.: 1821, 1906, 1907
B., J. M.: 162, 163
B., L.: 397
Bailey, Ralph Sargent: 641
Balmforth, Ramsden: 713
Barber, Noël: 1964
Barnes, Howard: 1510
Barnes, Ronald Edgar: 2349
Baron de Book Worms, The [Pseudonym]: See Burnand, Sir F. C.
Barrett, William: 1774
Barretto, Larry: 642
Barry, Iris: 1382
Bason, Frederick T.: 881, 1561, 2181
Basso, Hamilton: 1511
Bastia, Jean: 976
Bates: H. E.: 1383, 1384, 1429
Bauer, Gérard: 643, 770
Baughan, E. A.: 319
Beach, Joseph Warren: 1281, 1512
Beaumont, F. A.: 1032
Beauplan, Robert de: 644, 714, 771, 882, 1217
Beavan, John: 2140
Becker, May Lamberton: 1334
Beecroft, John: 1965

Beerbohm, Max: 23, 31, 53, 54, 114, 115
Behrman, S. N.: 1709, 2302
Bélanger, Jean: 1850
Belfor, A.: 772
Belgion, Montgomery: 1282
Bellamy, Francis Rufus: 645, 715, 716
Bellessort, André: 883, 977, 1110, 1182
Belloc, Elizabeth: 2253
Belluc, Roger: 1966
Benchley, Robert: 398, 448, 449, 483, 598, 646, 647, 717, 718, 884, 1033, 1034
Benét, Rosemary Carr: 1335
Benét, Stephen Vincent, 1283
Benét, William Rose: 1035, 1385, 1710
Bennett, Arnold: 538
Béraud, Henri: 773
Berton, Claude: 648, 719
Bettany, Louis: 399
Beyer, William H.: 1851
Bickley, Francis: 885, 1663
BiDou (or Bidou), Henry: 649, 650, 1218
Billy, André: 978, 1036, 1111
Binsse, Harry Lorin: 1513
Birrell, Francis: 484, 539, 599, 651
Block, Anita: 1336
Bloomfield, Paul: 1664, 1711
Boissy, Gabriel: 886
Boling, Kay: 2237
Bookwright [Pseudonym]: 1223
Boothby, Lord [Robert John Graham]: 2228
Bordeaux, Henry: 721
Borel, P.: 541
Borgex, L.: 652, 774
Boulton, Marjorie: 1968
Bourdon, Charles: 600, 722, 775, 776, 891, 892, 980, 981, 1039
Bourget-Pailleron, Robert: 1911, 1969
Bourin, André: 1573
Bouvard, Philippe: 2182
Bowen, Elizabeth: 1224
Boynton, H. W.: 401
Brady, Thomas F.: 1970
Brande, Dorothea: 893, 982
Brander, Laurence: 2238
Brasillach, Robert: 1225
Breit, Harvey: 1776, 1971
Brenner, Anita: 1152
Brewster, Dorothy: 818
Brickell, Herschel: 1040
Brighouse, Harold: 1226, 1390, 1574
Brion, Marcel: 1777, 1778
Brisson, Pierre: 654, 655, 894, 1185
Brisville, Jean-Claude: 1714
Britten [later, Bullock], Florence Haxton: 819, 895, 896, 983, 1041, 1186, 1622
Bro, Marguerite H.: 1313
Brooks, Cleanth: 1852, 2239
Brooks, John: 2034
Brophy, John: 1853
Broun, Heywood: 297, 323, 324, 452, 486
Brown, Allen B.: 1912, 2183
Brown, Ivor: 543, 544, 656, 657, 777, 778, 820, 821, 984, 1042, 1153, 2304
Brown, John Mason: 723, 1575, 1715, 1822
Brûlé, A.: 779, 985, 1113, 1114, 1115, 1116, 1117
Budé, A. de: 1779, 1854
Bulloch, J. M.: 523
Bullock, Florence Haxton: See Britten, Florence Haxton
Bunting, John J., Jr.: 1855
Burgess, Anthony: 2269
Burke, Billie: 1716
Burnand, Sir F. C.: 40
Burrell, Angus: 818
Burt, Forrest D.: 2334
Butcher, Fanny: 822, 897, 1187, 1227, 1286, 1516, 1576
C., A.: 57
C., A. C.: 724
C., P.: 1228
C., R. J.: 1391
C., R. M.: 898, 986
Cahuét, Alberic: 545
Caldwell, Cy: 1043, 1044
Camp, André: 1913
Campbell, Gerald: 58, 59
Campbell, Marjorie Prentiss: 328
Canby, Henry Seidel: 1154
Cantwell, Robert: 2035
Carb, David: 658, 659, 725, 899, 1045
Carbuccia, Horace de: 1432
Carrington, C. E.: 1914
Cartier, Maurice: 824, 900, 987, 988, 989, 990, 991, 1046, 1047, 1118, 1119, 1155, 1188, 1189
Cazamian, Louis: 726, 1680
Cazamian, Madeleine L.: 992, 2036
Chack, Paul: 1229
Chambers, E. K.: 24
Chandler, Frank W.: 43, 1120
Chapman, Percy: 488
Charon, Jacques: 1857
Chassé, Charles: 602
Chatfield-Taylor, Otis: 901
Chesterton, A. K.: 902
Chubb, Thomas C.: 1577
Cierpal, Leo Joseph: 2229
Clark, Barrett H.: 1623
Clinton, Farley: 2305
Clinton-Braddeley, V. C.: 1578
Cloud, Yvonne: 993
Clurman, Harold: 1858
Cody, Richard: 2184
Colburn, William E.: 2241
Collette, Sidonie Gabriel: 1718
Collins, J. P.: 329, 330
Collins, Joseph: 368, 546

Colt, Alice M.: 1433
Colton, Arthur: 825
Colum, Mary M.: 1230, 1287, 1341
Comden, Betty: 1719
Connolly, Cyril: 1288, 1517
Connolly, Francis X.: 1342
Cookman, A. V.: 903, 1231, 1720, 1973
Cooper, Frederic Taber: 261
Corbin, John: 453, 490
Cordell, Richard A.: 781, 1120, 1232, 1343, 1344, 1974, 1988, 2113, 2144, 2210
Cosman, Max: 1915, 2073
Cournos, John: 1721
Coward, Noël: 2181
Cowley, Malcolm: 1121, 1289, 1434, 1518, 1988
Coxe, Howard: 826
Craven, H. T.: 331
Croisset, Francis de: 727, 1191
Croquet, James de: 728, 1048, 1192, 1233
Cross, Jesse E.: 1669
Crowther, Bosley: 1860
Cru, Robert-L.: 525, 547, 782, 904, 1049, 1122
Cuff, Sergeant: 2306
Cunliffe, John W.: 661
D., A. B.: 2145
D., F.: 905, 1193
D., M.: 1345
D'Amico, Silvio: 994
Dangerfield, George: 906, 1234, 1435
Daniels, Jonathan: 995
Darlington, W. A.: 1975
Daruwalla, Bejan: 2211
Davenport, Guy: 2307
David, André: 907, 908
Davies, H. M. P.: 2242
Davies, Horton, 2146
Davis, Elmer: 369
Dearmer, Geoffrey: 1050
Deboisge, Gilles: 1976
De Casseres, Benjamin: 662, 663, 909
De Foe, Louis V.: 280, 332, 407
Delini, Jean: 910
Dell, Robert: 1392
del Monte, Alberto: 2230
Dempsey, David: 1780, 1781, 1861
Denison, Merrill: 1051
Dennis, Nigel: 1436
Destez, Robert: 911
Deval, Jacques: 784, 785
DeVoto, Bernard: 1235
d'Houville, Gérard: 729, 786, 912, 913, 996, 1722, 1862
Dickie, Francis: 2147
Dickinson, Thomas H.: 664
Dietrich, Margaret: 2243
Dilly Tante [Pseudonym for Stanley J. Kunitz]: 914
Dinkins, Paul: 1916
Dobree, Bonamy: 1863
Dobrinsky, J.: 2037, 2074, 2075, 2093, 2148, 2244
Dodd, Lee Wilson: 915
Dodds, John W.: 1626
Dolch, Martin: 2254
Doner, Dean: 2038
Dorsenne, Jean: 548, 604, 1123
Dottin, Paul: 605, 606, 730, 787, 827, 916, 997, 1052, 1053, 1124, 1236, 1237, 1238, 1239, 1290, 1291, 1346, 1988
Doughty, A. D. K.: 1625
Dr., H.: 1054
Dreiser, Theodore: 262, 1292, 1988
Drew, Elizabeth: 607
Drummond, Curtis: 408
Dubech, Lucien: 917
Duesberg, Jacques: 1977
Duhamel, Georges: 1579
Dukes, Ashley: 491, 1125
Durham, Willard Higley: 1626
Dussane [Pseudonym]: 1978, 2187
Eaton, Walter Prichard: 67, 282, 665, 828, 1055, 1723, 1864, 1988
Edgar, Pelham: 1056
Edgett, Edwin Francis: 263, 334, 370, 371, 409, 609
Edman, Irwin: 1823, 1988
Ekholm, Rauno: 2076
Enäjärvi, Elsa: 731
Engel, Eliane: 1782
Epardaud, Edmond: 1240, 1293
Eppinger, Dóra: 829
Ervine, St. John: 410, 455, 493, 549, 666, 667, 732, 733, 1057, 1157, 2155
Eteläpää, Heikki: 2270
Etzkorn, Leo R.: 1393, 1670
Evans, B. Ifor: 1294
F., D. C.: 999, 1058, 1241
Fadiman, Clifton: 1059, 1158, 1242, 1295, 1347, 1394, 1437, 1473
Farjeon, Herbert: 494, 668, 669, 788, 830, 919
Farmer, A. J.: 1917, 2077
Farrar, John: 526, 550, 588, 670, 734
Farrelly, John: 1580, 1627, 1671
Faverty, Frederic E.: 1918, 2039
Fehr, Bernhard: 495
Feld, Rose: 1474, 1519
Field, Louise M.: 411, 412, 496, 611, 831, 1988
Fielden, John Seward: 1979, 2079, 2117, 2212
Filon, Augustin: 3
Finck, Henry T.: 336
Findlater, Jane H.: 17
Findlater, Richard: 1867
Findon, B. W.: 169, 337, 338, 456

Finot, Louis-Jean: 789
Firkins, O. W.: 340, 413
Fischer, Walther: 1980, 1981
Flament, Albert: 1243
Flanner, Janet: 1395
Fleming, Peter: 1000, 1629, 1724
Flers, Robert de: 672
Forbes-Boyd, Eric: 1396, 1397
Ford, George H.: 2040
Frahne, Karl Heinrich: 1630
Frantel, Max: 922
Freedley, George: 1623, 1725, 1824, 1868, 1869
Fréjaville, Gustave: 673, 1195
French, Philip: 2308
Fricker, Robert: 2255, 2309
Frierson, William C.: 552, 1475
G., D. F.: 832
G., H. G.: 2213
G., R.: 1060
G., S.: 414
Gabriel, Gilbert W.: 612, 613, 674
Garnett, David: 1296
Gassner, John: 1297
Gautier, Jean-Jacques: 1581, 1919, 1983, 2188, 2256
Geismar, Maxwell: 1298
Gerber, Helmut E.: 2335
Gerould, Gordon Hall: 1476
Gibbs, Philip: 245
Gibbs, Wolcott: 1438, 1520, 1825, 1870
Gibney, Robert: 1582
Gibson, Ashley: 835
Gielgud, John: 1562
Gilder, Rosamond: 1477, 1521, 1563
Gilroy, Harry: 1726, 1988, 2272
Giquel, Bernard: 2189
Goetsch, Paul: 2336
Goodman, Edward: 171
Goodrich, Marcus Aurelius: 554, 588
Gordon, Caroline: 1727, 2094
Gordon, John D.: 2150
Gore-Brown, Robert: 836
Goren, Charles: 2310
Gorman, Herbert: 837
Gould, Gerald: 265, 498, 614, 737, 924, 925, 1002, 1061
Gould, Jack: 2080
Grace, William J.: 1439
Graham, Gladys: 675, 926
Graham, Robert John: See Lord Boothby
Gransden, K. W.: 2118
Gray, James: 1583
Grebanier, Bernard: 2214
Green, Julien: 1826, 2041
Greene, Graham, 1128, 1159, 1197, 1198, 1299, 1348, 1988
Greenwood, Ormerod: 1783
Grégorio, Paul: 738, 927
Grein, J. T.: 33, 48, 73, 74, 75, 131, 132, 175, 176, 246, 283, 790, 1003, 1062
Grennan, Margaret R.: 1728
Grierson, Francis D.: 457, 499
Griffith, Hubert: 372, 557, 1063
Grötz, Alfred: 2095
Gumpert, Martin: 1920
Gunn, Neil M.: 1440
Guyard, Marius-François: 1985
Guybon-Cesbron, Jean: 676
H., B. P.: 558
H., E.: 838 [Bookman (Lond)]
H., E.: 1478 [Theatre World (Lond)]
H., H.: 559 [Outlook (Lond)]
H., H.: 928 [Observer (Lond)]
H., H.: 1748 [Christian Science Monitor Weekly Magazine Section]
H., V.: 1729
H-ma, V.: 1785
H-u, T.: 1673
Hackett, Francis: 298, 415
Hagopian, John V. (ed): 2254
Hahl, N. G. (ed): 793
Haines, Helen E.: 1479
Halsband, Robert: 1921
Hamilton, Clayton: 76, 77, 133, 178, 247, 416
Hammond, Percy: 459, 460, 500, 615, 677, 739, 929, 1064, 1065
Hänninen, H.: 2311
Hanoteau, Guillaume: 2189
Hansen, Agnes Camilla: 1129
Hansen, Harry: 839, 1300, 1522
Harcourt-Smith, Simon: 1674
Harris, Wendell V.: 2350
Hart, H. W.: 1631
Hart-Davis, Rupert: 1066
Hartley, L. P.: 616, 617, 740
Hass, Victor P.: 1922, 1986
Hauser, Marianne: 1441
Haverstick, John: 1987
Hawkins, Barbara M.: 2245
Hawkins, William: 1871
Haycraft, Howard (ed): 1484
Heikkilä, Kauko: 2042, 2043
Heilman, Robert B.: 1786, 2239
Henry, William H., Jr.: 2337
Hewes, Henry: 1872
Heywood, C.: 2312, 2338
Highet, Gilbert: 2096
Hillyer, Dorothy: 1442, 1524
Hines, Jack: 501
Hobson, Harold: 1874
Hoche, Klaus: 1923
Hoffman, Paul: 1199, 1245
Hogan, William: 1875, 2151
Holland, Vyvyan: 1924
Holliday, Terence: 1160, 1301
Holt, Edgar: 678

Hoops, Reinald: 1130
Hornblow, Arthur: 284, 299, 344, 373, 417, 461, 502, 679
Horsnell, Horace: 930, 1246
Hoult, Norah: 1584, 1675
Howe, Susanne: 840, 1730
Hudson, Lynton: 1827
Hughes, Riley: 1877
Humbert, Henriette: 1585
Humbert, Pierre: 1585
Humbourg, Pierre: 741
Humeau, Edmond: 1632, 1828
Hunt, Albert: 2190
Hutchens, John: 931
Hutchison, Percy: 1200, 1247
Huxley, A. L.: 345
I., K. J.: 2119
Isaacs, Edith J. R.: 1161
J., A. W., 1401
J., L.: 1878
J., P.: 177
J:la, O.: 2246
J-n, H.: 1201, 1202, 1248, 1787
Jack, Peter M.: 1004, 1302, 1349, 1482
Jackson, Joseph Henry: 1676, 1731, 1925, 1926
Jackson, Katherine Gauss: 1483
Jacque, Valentina: 2247
Jaffe, Adrian H.: 1732
Jalkanen, Hugo: 1788
Jennings, Richard: 560, 680, 791, 842, 932
Jensen, Sven Arnold: 2097
Jerrold, Laurence: 9
Johnson, A. Theodore: 1303
Johnson, Edgar: 1350
Johnson, Pamela Hansford: 1443
Jonas, Klaus W.: 1927, 1928, 1989, 2081, 2120, 2152, 2153, 2154; (ed): 67, 262, 316, 420, 496, 606, 872, 963, 1009, 1121, 1157, 1159, 1289, 1380, 1414, 1418, 1422, 1445, 1566, 1594, 1601, 1659, 1689, 1726, 1744, 1789, 1790, 1823, 1988, 2027, 2155, 2160; (trans): 606
Jones, E. B. C.: 1249
Jones, Hugh Siriol: 1564
Joost, Nicholas: 1929
Jordan, Alice M.: 1351
Jouve, Raymond: 1791
K., H. A.: 26
K., R.: 346
K., V.: 1162
K., Y.: 2044
Kk.: 2273
K-ki, A.: 1633, 2098
K-la, K.: 1733
K-la, V.: 2121
Kajava, Viljo: 1734, 2191
Kanin, Garson: 2313, 2314, 2315
Kare, Kauko: 1677
Kaufman, S. Jay: 418
Kemp, Robert: 1735
Kemp, T. C.: 1990
Kendall, Lyle H., Jr.: 2215
Kennedy, P. C.: 561
Keown, Eric: 1634, 1792
Kermode, Frank: 2122
Kerr, Walter: 1829, 1879
Kessel, Joseph: 792
Kilcoyne, Francis P.: 2157
Kinninmont, Kenneth: 1304
Kinnunen, Aarne: 1991
Kirjamies [Pseudonym]: 2123
Kirstinä, Väinö: 2124
Kivijärvi, Erkki: 1250
Kivinen, Greta: 2158
Klauber, Adolph: 181
Klein, Robert: 1305
Knecht, Jean: 2274
Kochan, Lionel: 1793
Konsala, Simo: 2125
Korg, Jacob: 2045
Korry, Edward M.: 2192
Koskenniemi, V. A.: 2193
Krim, Seymour: 1992, 1993
Kronenberger, Louis: 1131, 1880, 1930
Kruschwitz, Hans: 1352, 1353
Krutch, Joseph Wood: 682, 683, 742, 933, 1067, 1068, 1069, 1306, 1444, 1445, 1525, 1586, 1736, 1988, 2159
Kujala, Antti: 2339
Kula, Kauko: 1678, 1737, 1881, 1994, 2126, 2194
Kuner, Mildred C.: 1931, 2155, 2160
Kunitz, Stanley J.: 914; (ed): 1484
Kupiainen, Unto: 1738
Kutter, Hans: 793
L., E.: 2161
L., I.: 1203
L., K.: 1995, 1996, 2046, 2099
L., M.: 1997
L., R.: 347
L-la, A.: 2100, 2351
Lacretelle, Jacques de: 2275
Lacretelle, Pierre de: 934
Laitinen, Kai: 1794, 1882, 2047, 2082
Lalou, René: 684, 1526, 1883
Lambert, Florence: 1739
Land, Myrick: 2231
Lang, André: 1005, 1132
Langner, Lawrence: 2195
Lanoire, Maurice: 2162
Laprade, Jacques de: 1795
Lardner, John: 1884
Lash, Henry: 2101
Las Vergnas, Raymond: 2276, 2316
Latham, G. W.: 374
Lauras, A.: 1885
Laurilla, A.: 2102

Léaud, F. J.: 1932
Leautaud, Paul: 2163
Lebettre, Francis: 1796
Lee, Charles: 1635
Lefèvre, Frederic: 743
Leggett, H. W.: 1133
Legouis, Emile: 1680
Lehmann, John: 2317
Lehtola, Erkka: 2216
Lemarchand, Jacques: 1998, 2196, 2258
Lemmonier, Léon: 794, 795
Lenehan, William T.: 2259
Leslie, Seymour: 2260
Leverson, Ada: 217
Lewis, V. A.: 375
Lewisohn, Ludwig: 348, 349, 419, 420, 462, 503, 504, 1988
Liddell, Robert: 1999
Linn, James Weber: 1163
Littell, Robert: 1404, 1405, 1446, 1485
Lockridge, Richard: 745, 935, 1071, 1072
Loveman, Amy: 1073, 1447
Lovett, Robert Morss: 422, 563, 619, 1007
Lynd, Sylvia: 1134
Lyons, Leonard: 2217
M., H. G.: 1636, 1740
M., P.: 1204
MacAfee, Helen: 936, 1074
MacCarthy, Desmond: 376, 425, 463, 505, 844, 937, 1008, 1075, 1076, 1527, 2000
MacKay, L. A.: 1205, 1251, 1354
Mais, S. P. B.: 506
Mäkelä, S.: 2001
Mallet, Richard: 1741
Malleus [Pseudonym]: 182
Mander, Raymond (ed): 26, 33, 48, 68, 73, 74, 75, 131, 132, 145, 175, 176, 222, 240, 246, 283, 296, 314, 327, 365, 391, 427, 446, 453, 505, 524, 533, 603, 639, 711, 799, 873, 950, 998, 1027, 1087, 1428, 1619, 2049, 2050, 2063
Manly, John M. (ed): 1800
Mann, Dorothea Lawrence: 564, 588
Manner, Eeva-Liisa: 1742
Manninen, Kerttu: 2002, 2051, 2164
Manning, Olivia: 1637
Mansfield, Katherine: 350
Mantle: Burns: 252
Marble, Annie Russell: 746
Marcabru, Pierre: 2003, 2197
Marcel, Gabriel: 1588, 1934, 2004, 2198, 2261
March, Fred T.: 1077
Marchand, Leslie: 845, 1009, 1988
Marlow, Louis: 1682
Marriott, Charles: 1355, 1448, 1528, 1638
Marshall, Margaret: 1529, 1886
Marteaux, Jacques: 796, 938, 1010
Martin du Gard, Maurice: 797, 1206
Match, Richard: 1683
Matthews, T. S.: 1252
Maugham, Robin: 2318, 2319
Maulnier, Thierry: 2200, 2232
Maurois, André (ed): 1650
Maxence, Jean-Pierre: 1207, 1309
McIver, Claude Searcy: 1208, 1253
McNaught, Carlson: 1935
McQuilland, Louis: 423
Meissner, Paul: 846
Meltti, Raimo: 2340
Menard, Wilmon: 2277, 2341, 2352, 2353
Mérac, Robert: 1254
Mercier, Armand: 939
Mertner, Edgar: 2346
Metcalfe, J. S.: 83, 84, 137, 138, 183, 184, 231, 254, 287, 304
Middleton, Drew: 2006, 2262, 2278
Miles, George: 1685
Miller, Karl: 2128
Millett, Fred B. (ed): 1800
Milne, A. A.: 185, 221
Mitchenson, Joe (ed): 26, 33, 48, 68, 73, 74, 75, 131, 132, 145, 175, 176, 222, 240, 246, 283, 296, 314, 327, 365, 391, 427, 446, 453, 505, 524, 533, 603, 639, 711, 799, 873, 950, 998, 1027, 1087, 1428, 1619, 2049, 2050, 2063
Monod, S.: 2052
Monroe, N. Elizabeth: 1449
Montague, Clifford M.: 1450
Moody, William Vaughn: 619
Moran, Helen: 1011
Mordaunt, Elinor (or Elenor) [Pseudonym for Mrs. Evelyn Mordaunt]
Mordaunt, Evelyn: 940, 954
Morehouse, Ward: 1406, 1530
Morgan, Charles: 1744, 1887, 1988
Morgan, Louis: 941
Morley, Christopher: 1801, 1936
Morris, Alice S.: 1686
Morris, Lloyd: 1687
Mortier, Alfred: 1078
Mortimer, Raymond: 847, 1136, 1165, 1256, 1407, 1486
Morton, Edward: 186
Moses, Montrose: 942, 943
Moskovit, Leonard: 2320
Moy, Thomas W.: 27
Muir, Edwin: 621, 1080
Muir, Percy H.: 1081
Mullan, Eunice G.: 1356
Muller, Herbert J.: 1258
Murch, A. E.: 2132
Muret, Maurice: 1259
Murry, J. Middleton (ed): 350
Mustanoja, Tauno F.: 1831
N., J. S.: 379
N-o (or N-to), Olli: 798, 849

Naik, M. K. W.: 2321
Natan, Alex: 2009
Nathan, George Jean: 354, 428, 528, 1312, 1531, 1565
Neuschaeffer, Walter: 1166
Neuveglise, Paule: 2281
Newell, J. P.: 2282
Nichols, Beverley: 686, 2322, 2323
Nichols, Lewis: 1086, 1087, 1533
Nichols, Wallace B.: 1534
Nicoll, Alardyce: 1640
Niiniluoto, Marja: 2283
Norman, Sylvia: 852
North, Sterling: 1592
O., S.: 256
O'Brien, E. D.: 1016
O'Brien, Kate: 1411, 1452, 1536
O'Connor, T. P.: 38
O'Connor, William Van: 2233
O'Hara, Frank H.: 1313
O'Hara, John: 1453
O'Hearn, Walter: 1745
Olmsted, Nelson: 1641
Omicron [Pseudonym]: 571, 687
Oppel, Horst: 1833
Overton, Grant: 466, 625
Owens, Olga: 1361, 1456
P., C. B.: 1211
P., E.: 2010
P., G. C.: 1089
P., I. M.: 1264
P., J-o: 855
P., T.: 2054
P-n, E.: 2167
Paasilinna, Erno: 2203
Paavilainen, Matti: 2104, 2342
Paley, Judith, 1593, 1642
Palola, Eino: 2105
Papajewski, Helmut: 1500, 1888
Parker, Robert Allerton: 432
Parsons, Chauncey L.: 196
Parsons, Luke: 1802
Partridge, Bellamy: 856
Paterson, Isabel: 573, 626
Patin, Jacques: 575
Paul, David: 1594, 1988
Pawlowski, Gaston de: 857
Payne, William Morton: 12, 271
Pekkanen, Toivo: 1688
Pellizzi, Camillo: 1140
Pennanen, Eila: 2106, 2168
Pennanen, Esko: 2169
Petrie, Sir Charles: 2133
Pfeiffer, Karl G.: 1566, 1988, 2170, 2171
Phelan, Kappo: 1539, 1540
Phelps, Robert: 1939
Phillips, Henry Albert: 627
Pierhal, Armand: 1090, 1265
Pitkänen, Risto: 2343
Playbill [Pseudonym]: 1018, 1091
Playfellow [Pseudonym]: 1747, 1803
Playgoer, The [Pseudonym]: 467
Plomer, William: 1092
Pohjanpää, Lauri: 1748, 1804
Pollock, Channing: 233, 257, 291, 308
Pollock, John: 1019, 2324
Poore, Charles G.: 1168, 1941, 2011, 2173, 2248
Porché, François: 951
Potter, Stephen: 1597, 1598
Pound, Reginald: 1266
Prescott, Orville: 1541, 1599, 1644, 1689, 1749, 1942, 1988
Pressey, Benfield: 970
Prévost, Marcel: 529, 800
Priestley, J. B.: 858
Pritchett, V. S.: 859, 860, 1169, 1316, 1317, 1414, 1645, 1750, 1988
Pruette, Lorine: 1415
Purser, John Thibault: 1852
Quennell, Peter: 1212
Quéry, Suzanne: 1093
Quoodle [Pseudonym]: 2286
R., A.: 2134
R., H.: 861
R., J. N. B.: 1690
R., V.: 2084
R:suo (or R-suo), A.: 1805, 2056, 2344
Rageot, Gaston: 952, 1267
Rascoe, Burton: 862, 1542
Raven, Simon: 2325
Raymond, John: 2012, 2326
Recouly, Raymond: 690
Redfern, James: 1491, 1544
Redman, Ben Ray: 1600
Reed, Henry: 1691
Rees, Leslie: 2345
Régnier, Henri de: 577, 628
Reid, Lewis: 358
Repo, E. S.: 1891
Repo, Ville: 2085
Rey, Etienne: 691, 754, 802, 953
Reyer, Georges: 2249, 2288
Reynolds, Ernest: 1753
Rhodes, Anthony: 2086
Rhodes, Russell: 1754
Rice, R. R.: 2355
Richard, Marius: 1268
Richardson, Maurice L.: 1269, 1365
Rick, K.: 1416
Rickert, Edith (ed): 1800
Riposte, A. [Pseudonym for Mrs. Evelyn Mordaunt]
Roberts, Cecil: 1834
Roberts, R. Ellis: 273, 578, 1492
Rolo, Charles: 1692, 2174
Romberg, Bertil: 2234
Ronimus, O-M: 1835

Roos, Vappu: 2289
Ross, Virgilia Peterson: 955
Ross, Woodburn O.: 1601, 1988
Rousseaux, André: 1270
Routh, H. V.: 1602
Rouveyre, André: 692, 803, 804
Rovere, Richard H.: 1755
Royde-Smith, N. G.: 579
Ruhl, Arthur: 102, 103, 201, 202
Ruyssen, Henri: 155, 223, 234
S., A.: 2107
S., A. W.: 863
S., Am.: 2108
S., F.: 1603, 1647, 1648, 1756
S., L. A.: 1546
S., M.: 1649 [VAPAA SANA]
S., M.: 1945 [UUSI SUOMI]
S., R.: 864
S., T.: 1567
S., V.: 1757, 2015, 2057, 2058
S:nen, A.: 2016
S-o, A.: 2087
Salerno, Henry F.: 2354
Salpeter, Harry: 755
Sanders, Charles: 2355
Santavuori, Martti: 2136
Savage, C. Courtenay: 382, 383
Savini, Gertrud: 1366
Sawyer, Newell W.: 956
Sayler, Oscar M.: 693
Schauer Islas, Anita: 1758
Schirmer, Walter F.: 2017
Schlösser, Anselm: 1271
Schneider, Isidor: 866
Schorer, Mark: 1367
Scott, J. D.: 2018
Scott, Nathan A., Jr.: 1946
Scott, Virgil: 1732
Scully, Frank: 1501
Seaman, Owen: 156, 203, 258, 435, 514
Searles, Ruth: 1417
Sée, Edmond: 805, 957, 1094, 1141, 1272
Ségur, Nicolas: 580
Seidlin, Rosemarie: 2265
Seldes, Gilbert: 384, 436, 694, 695, 756, 757
Seyd, Felizia: 1457
Shackleton, Edith: 1273
Shand, John: 958
Shanks, Edward: 515, 629, 758
Shawe-Taylor, Desmond: 1368
Shipp, Horace: 867
Shrapnel, Norman: 1892, 1893
Sigaux, Gilbert: 1650
Simiot, Bernard: 1806, 1947, 2020
Simoes, Joao Gaspar: 2222
Simon, Jean: 1948
Simon, Robert A.: 696
Sitwell, Osbert: 1170
Skinner, R. Dana: 630, 760, 1096, 1097
Smet, Robert de: 959, 1143
Smiles, Sam: 1605
Smith, Caroline: 1274
Smith, Harrison: 1547, 1651, 1807, 2327
Smith, William G.: 2328
Soellner, Rolf: 1949
Soskin, William: 1275, 1318, 1370
Souday, Paul: 581, 631, 698, 761, 806
Spectorsky, A. C.: 1548
Spence, Robert: 1836
Spencer, Theodore: 1418, 1988
Speth, William: 699, 807, 960
Squire, Sir John: 1894, 2024
Squire, Tom: 1319, 1320
Standop, Ewald: 2346
Starrett, Vincent: 1760
Stavén, Pauli: 2329
Stearns, Austin: 1419
Stearns, H. E.: 243
Stein, Aaron: 1172
Stern, G. B.: 2026
Stevenson, Lionel: 2204
Stewart, J. I. M.: 2250
Stokes, Sewall: 1568, 1652, 1653
Stott, Raymond Toole (ed): 1809, 2088
Strassenheim, Edmund Strastil: 1761
Strong, L. A. G.: 961, 1021, 1695
Strowski, Fortunat: 1098, 1144
Sugrue, Thomas: 1696
Sunne, Richard: 962
Sutton, Graham: 472, 582
Swaffer, Hannen: 473
Swinnerton, Frank: 386, 437, 1173, 1174, 1371, 2027, 2089, 2155, 2251
Sykes, Gerald: 963, 1988
Sylvester, Harry: 1420
T., G.: 516
T., O.: 869 [UUSI SUOMI]
T., O.: 1810 [SAN FRANCISCO SUNDAY CHRONICLE]
T., W. T.: 2028
T-la, E.: 1811, 1837
Taggard, Ernestine K.: 1175
Taivalkoski, Jussi: 2296
Tarn [Pseudonym]: 438
Tate, Allen: 1727
Taylor, Dwight: 1950
Taylor, Houghton Wells: 1163
Taylor, John Russell: 2347
Thérive, André: 1023, 1101, 1277
Therman, Erik (ed): 793
θ [Pseudonym]: 244
Thibault, Henri: 1812
Thiébaut, Marcel: 1145, 1146, 1278, 1951
Thompson, Alan Reynolds: 1697
Thompson, Ralph: 1762
Thorp, Joseph: 293, 315, 363, 387, 519, 586, 704, 811, 870, 1025

Tindall, William York: 1655
Tiusanen, Timo: 2138, 2205
Tomlinson, Kathleen C.: 871
Tompan Tuomo [Pseudonym]: 1813, 2060, 2061
-tonen: 2062
Torrès, Henry: 1025
"Toto" [Pseudonym]: 1840
Towne, Charles Hanson: 587; (ed): 550, 554, 564, 587, 588, 591
Towse, J. Rankin: 336, 440, 476, 477
Trend, J. B.: 1177
Trewin, J. C.: 1698, 1763, 1814, 1841, 1899, 1952, 1973, 1975, 1990, 2063, 2139
Trilling, Diana: 1553, 1608
Tucker, S. Marion: 967
Turner, Reginald: 52
Turner, W. J.: 388, 441
Tvn, J.: 1764
U-11, S.: 1953, 2111
V., A. K.: 1765
V., H.: 812
V., L.: 1214 [HELSINGIN SANOMAT]
V., L.: 1376 [ETUDES ANGLAISES]
V., M.: 2029
V-hl, V.: 1377
V-jä, O.: 1842, 1901
V-m, K.: 2064, 2112
V-o, S.: 1699
Val Baker, Denys (ed): 1682
Vallette, Jacques: 1656, 1657, 1700, 1766, 1767, 1816, 1817, 1955, 2091
Vandérem, Fernand: 589, 633, 705, 813
van der Vat, D. G.: 1323
Van Doren, Carl: 588, 590, 634; (ed): 591
Van Doren, Mark: 588, 872, 1988; (ed): 591
van Druten, John: 1956
van Gelder, Robert: 1378, 1422, 1423, 1462, 1609, 1988
Van Patten, Nathan: 1843
Van Tieghem, Paul: 1609
Vartia, Annikki: 2297
Vernon, Frank: 532
Vernon, Grenville: 968, 1178, 1324, 1325, 1463
Verschoyle, Derek: 1424
Villard, Léonie: 1215, 1216
Villars, Paul: 109
Villette, S. H.: 1611
Vines, Sherard: 1818
Viswanath, G. V.: 2175
Volkov, Nicolai: 1612
Vowinckel, Ernst: 635
Vuorio, Hannu: 2348
W., A.: 1554 [THEATRE WORLD (Lond)]
W., A.: 1613 [LE FIGARO]
W., F.: 1147
W., K. S.: 1379
Wagenknecht, Edward: 1502, 1658
Wakefield, Gilbert: 969
Walbridge, Earle F.: 1957, 2030, 2065, 2176
Waldman, Milton: 592, 706
Walpole, Hugh: 1102, 1148
Waltari, Satu: 2067
Walton, Edith H.: 1179
Ward, A. C.: 763
Ward, Richard Heron: 1279
Warren, Robert Penn: 1852
Watson, E. Bradlee: 970
Watts, Richard, Jr.: 1464
Waugh, Evelyn: 875, 1380, 1988
Way, Oliver: 764, 876
Weales, Gerald: 2068, 2224
Webber, John E.: 224
Webster, H. T.: 1614
Weeks, Edward: 1326, 1381, 1465, 1466, 1493, 1555, 1615, 1768, 1958
Weidman, Jerome: 1503
Weinberger, Caspar: 1701
Weintraub, Stanley: 2330
Went, Stanley: 294, 309, 442, 593, 877
Wescott, Glenway: 1659, 2155
West, Anthony: 1467
West, Rebecca: 443, 1327
Weygandt, Cornelius: 594
Whicher, George F.: 1844, 1959
White, Leigh: 1180
White, Matthew, Jr.: 110, 157, 158, 208, 209, 210, 295, 310, 392
Whittington-Egan, Richard: 2331, 2332
Wiebe, Hans: 1702
Wild, Friedrich: 765
Wildi, Max: 1556
Wilkinson, Marguerite: 364
Willey, Margaret: 2333
Williams, Blanche Colton: 636
Williams, Harold: 595
Williams, Orlo: 1149, 1328
Williams, Raymond: 2225
Willis, Katherine Tappert: 1557
Willoughby, Pearl Vivian: 520
Wilson, B. F.: 521
Wilson, Edmund: 1616
Wing, Donald G.: 2069
Winter, William: 211
Winterich, John: 1468, 1960
Wolfe, Humbert: 1329
Woodruff, Douglas: 1103
Woods, Katherine: 1425
Woollcott, Alexander: 365, 366, 444, 478, 637, 707
Worsley, T. C.: 1961
Wright, Basil: 1495
Wright, Ralph: 532

Wyatt, Euphemia Rensselaer: 708, 709, 766, 971, 1104, 1105, 1181, 1331, 1496, 1558, 1569, 1902
Young, Stark: 638, 710, 972, 1107, 1470
Yvon, P.: 1108
Zabel, Morton Dauwen: 1471
Zeeman, Dorothea: 2226
Zhantiyeva, D.: 2207
Zlobina, Maya: 2235

Index

TITLES OF SECONDARY WORKS

Titles of articles in periodicals and chapters in books are in quotation marks; book titles are in upper case; translations of article titles originally appearing in a foreign language are in parentheses, without quotation marks, and in lower case; translations of book titles originally appearing in a foreign language are in parentheses and in upper case. Numbers after each title refer to the item in the bibliography where the title appears.

"A la devanture du libraire": 1819
"A l'étalage": 767, 824, 900
"A l'Etalage": 987, 988, 989, 990, 991, 1046, 1047, 1118, 1119, 1155, 1188, 1189
"A la maison de l'OEuvre *Le Cercle* de Somerset Maugham": 727
"A travers l'actualité théâtricale": 957, 1141
"A travers les théâtres": 784, 785
"A travers les Théâtres": 794, 795
"Aboard the Lugger": 995
"Abominable Ancestors": 2326
(About "Know-How"): 1705
(About the Theater): 1966
"Action Against Woman Novelist": 878
"L'Actualité littéraire": 712, 769, 1030, 1031, 1109
"Adieu à mon ami anglais": 1432
"ADORABLE JULIA": 1998
(Adventure in Good Reading): 1986
ADVENTURE OR EXPERIENCE: FOUR ESSAYS ON CERTAIN WRITERS AND READERS OF NOVELS: 818
ADVENTURES IN DRAMATIC APPRECIATION: 902
"After the Play": 298, 422
(After a Slow Agony Writer Somerset Maugham Is Dead): 2266
"After Ten Years *'Of Human Bondage'* ": 554
(An Afternoon with Somerset Maugham): 541
"Ah King": 1147
"Ahtaat Asuinsijat": 1813
"Aldwych Theatre: 'JANE' ": 1619
" *'The Alien Corn'* on Television": 2178
(ALMANAC OF LETTERS, 1947): 1579
(ALMANAC OF LETTERS, 1948): 1650
(ALMANAC OF LETTERS, 1953): 1848
ALMANACH DES LETTRES, 1947: 1579
ALMANACH DES LETTRES, 1948: 1650
ALMANACH DES LETTRES, 1953: 1848
"The Almost Perfect Anthology": 1343
"Always True to Himself": 2278
AMERICAN AND BRITISH LITERATURE SINCE 1890: 591
"The American Dramatic Problem": 171
"American, London and Scottish": 2031
(Among Books): 1145, 1146, 1278
"Among the New Books": 862, 1300, 1396
"The Amorist": 273
"Amours Anglaises": 978
THE ANATOMY OF PROSE: 1968
"Anchors Aweigh: Broadway in Review": 931
"And Here Is Genius!": 328
DER ANGELSÄCHSISCHE ROMAN UND DER SCHWEIZER LESER: 1556
ANGLETERRE, NATION CONTINENTALE: 1052
(Anglo-Saxon Letters): 1955, 2090
(Anglo-Saxon Letters: Maugham's Yogi): 1656
(THE ANGLO-SAXON NOVEL AND THE SWISS READER): 1556
"Angry Author's Complaint": 1121
(Annual Review: The English Theater): 223, 234
"Anonymously": 670, 734
"Another Stroke of Realism": 346
"Anthologist and Critic": 1497
"The Apotheosis of Somerset Maugham": 1616

"An Appreciation": 1418
AN APPROACH TO LITERATURE: 1852
"Après une lente agonie l'écrivain Somerset Maugham est mort": 2266
"Un Après-midi avec Somerset Maugham": 541
"L'Archipel aux Sirènes": 537
ARE THEY THE SAME AT HOME? BEING A SERIES OF BOUQUETS DIFFIDENTLY DISTRIBUTED: 686
(Around *The Circle*): 976
"L'Art Dramatique aux Etats-Unis": 488
"The Art of Being Good": 1517
(The Art of Character Description in the Novels of John Galsworthy, W. Somerset Maugham and Graham Green): 1761
THE ART OF THE NOVEL: FROM 1700 TO THE PRESENT TIME: 1056
"The Art of the Playwright": 1063
"The Art of Somerset Maugham": 1492
THE ARTIST AND THE THEATRE: THE STORY OF THE PAINTINGS COLLECTED AND PRESENTED TO THE NATIONAL THEATRE BY W. S. MAUGHAM: 2049
"The Artist in Travel": 859
"The Arts: The Conflict of *Caroline*": 2179
"The Arts—Feuillere in Maugham: *The Constant Wife*": 2180
"The Arts—Sadler's Wells Opera: THE MOON AND SIXPENCE": 2092
"Arts Theatre: *'The Breadwinner'* by W. Somerset Maugham": 1904
"Arts Theatre: *'Caroline'* by W. Somerset Maugham": 1706
"Arts Theatre: *'The Constant Wife'* by Somerset Maugham": 1333
"Arts Theatre: *'Home and Beauty'* by W. Somerset Maugham": 1773
"Arts Theatre: *'Mrs. Dot'* by W. Somerset Maugham": 1820
"Arts Theatre: *'Penelope'* by W. Somerset Maugham": 1905
"Arva kuka nai kenet. Yllättä kälyni yllätti katsojiaan Lappeenrannan Kaupunginteatterissa": 2329
"Arvosteluja": 1785
"As a Realist Sees It": 262
"Aspects biographiques de l'oeuvre de Somerset Maugham: l'enfance": 2037
(Aspects of Comedy⸗European Dramaturgy: At l'OEuvre⸗*The Circle*): 719
(Aspects of Comedy: Freudianism): 648
(At Cap Ferrat: At the Home of Somerset Maugham, Novelist and Pomologist):1240
AT HALF-PAST EIGHT: ESSAYS OF THE THEATRE: 446
AT LENGTH: 2355
(At l'OEuvre: *The Circle* by Somerset Maugham): 727
"At the Play": 156, 185, 203, 221, 244, 258, 293, 315, 318, 363, 372, 387, 410, 435, 493, 514, 519, 586, 666, 704, 732, 811, 870, 930, 1024, 1103, 1634, 1792
"At the Theatres": 112, 161
"Au Cap Ferrat: Chez Somerset Maugham, romancier et arboriculteur": 1240
"Au passage": 2267
"An Author in Evening Dress": 963
(An Author on an Author): 2043
"Author's £10,000 Gift to His Old School": 1509
"Authors Awarded New Honour": 2209
AUTHORS OF THE DAY: STUDIES IN CONTEMPORARY LITERATURE: 466
"Autour de *'Cercle'* ": 976
"Les Avants-Premières⸗Avant *Le Cyclone*": 910
"Avenue Theatre": 30
"Avioliittokomedia Ruotsalaisessa Teatterissa": 798
"B. B. C. Television: *'The Letter'* by Somerset Maugham": 2072
BACKGROUND WITH CHORUS: A FOOTNOTE TO CHANGES IN ENGLISH LITERARY FASHION BETWEEN 1901 AND 1917: 2089
"The Battle of the Repertory Theatre with Commercialism": 162
"Un beau roman de Somerset Maugham: Grandeur et Servitude Humaines": 1265
(Beefsteak Wins): 1891
" 'BEFORE THE PARTY,' at St. Martin's": 1708
"The Beginning": 419
"Beginning a Sort of Department": 646
(The Beginnings of Somerset Maugham in the Theater: Birth of a Vocation and Affirmation of a Literary Personality): 2093
"Behind the Maginot Line": 1395
"Beiträge zur Behandlung von Schullektüren. 1. Die Darstellung der Englischen Gesellschaft in W. S. Maughams Lustspiel *Jack Straw*": 1352
"Belles Lettres": 2045
"Der Berbrauch der Umschriehenen Zeitformen in Romanen W. Somerset Maugham": 1703
(The Best New Productions: Paul Dottin: SOMERSET MAUGHAM AND HIS NOVELS): 747
"Better than Most": 2268
(Between Chaos and Deliverance): 1833
"Bibliographie": 1219, 1220, 1376, 1980, 1981
(Bibliography): 1219, 1220, 1376, 1980, 1981
A BIBLIOGRAPHY OF THE WRITINGS OF W. SOMERSET MAUGHAM: 1789

A BIBLIOGRAPHY OF THE WRITINGS OF WILLIAM SOMERSET MAUGHAM: 881
"Billet D'Amour": 1392
"Billie Burke Back; Wins New Laurels": 320
"Billie Burke Grown Serious—in Parts": 236
(Biographical Aspects in the Work of Somerset Maugham: Childhood): 2037
"Biographical Sketch": 1989
"Biography": 2331, 2332
"The Birthday Honours": 1967
"The Bishop Cries 'Immoral' ": 902
"A Bitter Comedy on Our Expatriates": 296
" *'Bondage'*: Filming the Straight Story": 2245
"The Bondage of a Youth": 263
"La bonne référence": 720
"Book Business Greets Return of Happy Days": 1187
(Book Chronicle): 1054
(Book Criticism: *The Casuarina Tree*): 768
(Book Criticism: *The Moon and Sixpence*): 741
(The Book Discussed): 1005, 1132
"The Book Forum": 1230
"Book Notes": 887
(The Book of Cholera and Treachery: *'The Painted Veil'*): 606
(The Book of the Day: *Of Human Bondage*): 1228
"The Book Parade": 1179
"Book Reviews": 1949
(Book Reviews: Novels): 1885
"Booking Office": 1741
"The Booklist": 1351
"The Bookman Gallery: Mr. William Somerset Maugham": 55
"A Bookman's Notebook": 1731
"A Bookman's Notebook: Maugham's New One": 1676
"Bookman's Notebook: Somerset Maugham's Kipling": 1925
(Books): 581, 779, 787, 985, 992, 1101, 1108, 1113, 1215, 1216, 1657, 1700, 1767, 1768, 1816, 1817, 2091
"Books": 1150, 1183, 1221, 1284, 1337, 1430, 1685, 1721
"Books: Actress": 1222
"Books Alive": 1760
"Books and the Arts: A Very Old Party": 2317
"Books & Life": 1383
(Books and Reviews: *First Person Singular*): 1006
(Books and Writers): 545
(THE BOOKS AND WRITERS OF THE WORLD): 2070
"Books: Beer & Skittles": 815
"Books: Book Notes": 1498
"Books, Books, Books": 898
"Books—Briefly Noted: Fiction": 1184, 1431, 1514, 1620, 1665, 1775
"Books—Briefly Noted: General": 1338, 1386, 1387, 1908, 2141
"Books: The Children's Harvest": 1379
"Books: East of Suez": 979
(Books: English Letters): 9
"Books: Fiction": 400
(Books for Christmas): 1835
"Books for Christmas Gifts": 364
"Books for Christmas: Maugham's Essays": 1887
"Books for Summer Reading": 116
"Books for Young People": 1334
"Books: Here & There": 1712
"Books in Brief": 888, 889, 1037, 2032
"Books in General": 1750, 1963, 2012
"Books in General: The Fall of France": 1486
"Books: Journeyman": 816
"Books—Just Out: 'Last' Essays of a Master": 2142
"Books: Kipling Revisited": 1909
"Books: The Latest Last One": 2143
"Books—Life: Painting the Veil, Mr. Maugham Does Not Gild the Lily": 540
"Books: A Man of the World and a Man of the Town": 1059
"Books: Maugham Mauled": 890
"Books: Maugham on Miracles": 1666
"Books: Maugham on Old Nick": 1571
"Books: Maugham Shorts": 1112
"Books: Maugham's Machiavelli": 1572
"Books: Might-have-been": 1151
"Books: Mixed Bag": 1437, 1473
(Books: *The Moon and Sixpence*): 761
(Books: *The Moon and Sixpence* by Somerset Maugham): 744
"Books: Mr. Maugham's Golden Age": 1158
"Books: Mr. Maugham's Mixture": 1394
"Books New and Old: A Lone Wolf": 1328
"Books New and Old: Realistic Prose Drama": 1149
"Books: The Notes of a Popular Pessimist": 1709
"Books: Novels": 56
"Books of the Day": 321, 1134, 1329
"Books of the Day: The Best Books in the World": 1424
"Books of the Day: Fiction": 1411, 1452, 1578, 1695
"Books of the Day: Maugham's Pattern"; 1299
"Books of the Day: Maugham's Short Stories": 1128
"Books of the Day: Maugham's Workshop": 1744
"Books of the Day: New Fiction": 1390

"Books of the Day: New Novels": 1574, 1664
"Books of the Day: Short Stories": 1197, 1637, 1638
"Books of the Day: Spanish Gold": 1159
"Books of the Day: The Technician": 1380
"Books of the Day: Three New Novels": 1355
"Books of the Fortnight": 322
(Books: *Of Human Bondage*): 1277
"Books of the Month": 1354
"Books of the Quarter": 1282
"Books of the Time: The Curtain Speeches of Somerset Maugham": 2248
"Books of the Times": 1689, 1941, 1942, 2011, 2173
(Books of the Week): 2194
"Books of the Week": 1420
"Books of the Week: Kipling Mishandled": 1863
"Books of the Week: The Maugham Effect": 2018
"Books of the Week: New Novels": 1388
(Books of the Week. Somerset Maugham: *The Magician*): 1309
"Books: Old Craftsman": 1667
"Books: Old Hand, Old Stuff": 1621
"Books: Old Man with a Razor": 1515
"Books: Old Master Maugham": 1038
"Books on Our Table: Somerset Maugham Considers Spain and the Golden Age": 1172
(Books: *The Painted Veil*): 618, 631
(Books Received: *The Razor's Edge*): 1632
"Books: Recent & Readable": 1389
"Books—Recent Books: Fiction": 1339
"Books: Recent Novels": 7
"Books: Recreations of a Dean": 1347
"Books: Reticent Writer": 1285
"Books Reviewed": 1935
"Books: School of Maugham": 2128
"Books: Some New Novels": 1
"Books: Somerset Maugham Adds It Up": 1295
"Books: Somerset Maugham and an Antidote": 1616
(Books: Somerset Maugham: *Cakes and Ale*): 1023
"Books: South Sea Rogues": 986
"Books: Table Talk at 79": 1910
"Books to Buy and Ask For": 450
"Books to Read": 885
(Books: *The Trembling of a Leaf*): 562
"Books: Uncle Willie": 2325
"Books: A Week Among the English": 1242
"Books: Willie's Last Chapters": 2303
"The Books You Read": 875
"Bookshelf": 1199, 1245, 1326, 1381, 1465, 1466, 1493, 1555, 1615, 1769, 1958
"Bread and Circuses": 1443
"*'The Breadwinner'*": 935
"*'The Breadwinner,'* at the Vaudeville": 817
(*The Breadwinner,* a Ferocious and Candid Play): 1191
BREVE STORIA DEL ROMANZO POLIZIESCO: 2230
"Briefer Mention": 402, 403, 451, 485, 542, 653
"Briefly Noted": 2033
BRITISH AND AMERICAN PLAYS: 1830-1945: 1626
"A British Clyde Fitch": 280
"British Comedy": 1153
BRITISH DRAMA: AN HISTORICAL SURVEY FROM THE BEGINNINGS TO THE PRESENT TIME: 1640
"Broadway, Our Literary Signpost": 394, 447, 482
"Broadway Postscript": 1872
"Broadway to Date": 662, 663, 909
"Bubbles": 257
"Building a Play Backwards": 247
(Bulletin: Books Received): 1060
"Bulletin: Ouvrages Reçus": 1060
"But Is It Art?": 1069
"Butler Davenport Gives Maugham Drama": 780
(By the Pacific): 1794
(By the Young Maugham): 2108
"*Caesar's Wife*": 325
"*'Caesar's Wife,'* at the Royalty": 326
"*'Caesar's Wife'*: Mr. Maugham's New Play at the Royalty": 327
"*Caesar's Wife* by W. Somerset Maugham": 337
(*Cakes and Ale*): 2014, 2044
"*Cakes and Ale*": 832
"*'Cakes and Ale'* Brews Up Book Selling Squall": 822
"*'Cakes and Ale'* Defended Now by Own Author": 897
"*'Cakes and Ale'*: Somerset Maugham Satirizes the Literary Career": 823
"*'The Camel's Back'* Appears at the Vaudeville Theater": 487
"*'The Camel's Back'* a Clever Play": 481
"*'The Camel's Back'*: New Farce at the Playhouse": 524
"Canterbury Week: Old Stagers in *'The Circle'*": 1717
"Cap Ferrat—M. Somerset Maugham": 1243
(Cap Ferrat—Mr. Somerset Maugham): 1243
CAPTAIN NICHOLAS: A MODERN COMEDY: 1148
"Le Carnet du bouquiniste": 575
"*Carnet d'un Ecrivain*": 1856

" *'Caroline'* at the New": 276
" *'Caroline,'* at the New": 277
"*Caroline* jää saavutta mattomaksi": 2270
" *'Caroline'* Opens at Empire Theatre": 278
(*Caroline* Remains Out of Reach): 2270
" *'Caroline'*: Revival at the Playhouse": 601
CARTE ROUGE: LE THEATRE ET LA VIE: 797
A CASE OF HUMAN BONDAGE: 2322
"The Case of Somerset Maugham": 503
"The Case of the 'Superfluous Woman' ": 245
"*Catalina*": 1668, 1689
CAVALCADE OF COMEDY: 21 BRILLIANT COMEDIES FROM JONSON AND WYCHERLEY TO THURBER AND COWARD: 1930
CAVALCADE OF THE ENGLISH NOVEL: 1502
"The Center of Maugham Studies": 2152
A CENTURY OF THE ENGLISH NOVEL: 594
"*Le Cercle*": 754, 1025
THE CHANGING WORLD IN PLAYS AND THEATRE: 1336
"A Chaotic Play": 23
"*Christmas Holiday*": 1340, 1345
(Chronicle and Book Notes): 1714
(Chronicle of Entertainments): 1185
(Chronicles): 2156
"Chronicles: Drama": 441
"Chronicles: The Drama": 706
"Chronique des livres": 1054
"Chronique des Spectacles": 1185
"Chronique des Théâtres de Paris: Ambassadeurs⸗*Le Cyclone*": 912
"Chronique des Théâtres de Paris⸗Athénée⸗Reprise de *La Lettre*": 913
"Chronique des Théâtres de Paris: Reprise du *Cercle*": 996
"Chronique des Théâtres de Paris: Th. de l'Athénée: *La Lettre*": 786
"Chronique dramatique": 883
"Chronique dramatique du FIGARO⸗*Le Cercle*": 729
"Chronique et Notes de Livres": 1714
"Chronique littéraire⸗Lectures": 1795
"Chronique Théâtrale⸗PLUIE": 654
"Chronique Théâtrale⸗Le Sujet de deux pièces anglaises": 1218
"Chronique Théâtrale: Théâtre des Ambassadeurs: *Le Cyclone*": 894
"Chroniques: Regards sur la littérature anglaise": 1777
(*The Circle*): 754, 1025
"*The Circle*," 404, 418, 437, 1527
" *'The Circle'* at the Haymarket": 405
"*The Circle* by Somerset Maugham": 2239
" *'The Circle'*, by Somerset Maugham, at the Haymarket": 406
"*The Circle* by W. Somerset Maugham": 970, 1930
"The Classic Revival": 1990
CLASSICS AND COMMERCIALS: 1616
"Claude Searcy McIver, WILLIAM SOMERSET MAUGHAM": 1280
"Claude Searcy McIver, WILLIAM SOMERSET MAUGHAM; Paul Dottin, LE THEATRE DE SOMERSET MAUGHAM; W. Somerset Maugham, *The Summing Up*": 1416
"Claude S. McIver's SOMERSET MAUGHAM: A STUDY OF TECHNIQUES AND LITERARY SOURCES": 1238
"Cloak Without Dagger": 2240
"The Closed Pattern: W. SOMERSET MAUGHAM, by Richard Cordell": 1319
"Close-Ups of Thomas Mann and Somerset Maugham": 1472
(Collected Anecdotes): 2348
COLLECTED ESSAYS: 1128, 1159, 1299
COLLECTED IMPRESSIONS: 1224
"Collected Plays of England's Most Civilized Dramatist": 489
"Collections of Maughan's [sic] Tales": 1641
"The Coloured Film": 578
(The Comedian and His Legend: The Professional Secret): 2003
COMEDIANS ALL: 354
"Le Comédien et sa legende: Le secret professionnel": 2003
"Comedy and Color": 432
"Comedy in Classical Tradition: TV Production of *Penelope*": 2185
"The Comedy of Manners from Sheridan to Maugham: The Study of the Type as a Dramatic Form and as a Social Document": 956
"The Comedy: *'The Perfect Gentleman,'* an Adaptation by W. Somerset Maugham of Molière's 'LE BOURGEOIS GENTILHOMME' ": 237
"The Comedy that Came Back": 1822
"Comedy Theatre: *'Mrs. Dot'* by W. Somerset Maugham": 60
"Comedy Theatre: *'Penelope'* by W. Somerset Maugham": 117
"Comedy Theatre: *'Smith'* by W. Somerset Maugham": 118
"Comedy with a Moral: Mr. Maugham's *'Caroline'* at the New Theatre": 279
"Comment": 1786
"*The Complete Short Stories*": 1859
"*The Complete Stories of W. Somerset Maugham*": 1939
(COMPLETE WORKS): 1718
A COMPREHENSIVE EXHIBITION OF THE WRITINGS OF W. SOMERSET MAUGHAM: 2137
"A Compromise": 260

"Comptes Rendus": 1850, 1917, 1932, 1948, 2052, 2074, 2075, 2077, 2148, 2244
"Comptes Rendus Critiques": 1236, 1290
"Comptes Rendus Critiques: Revue du Théâtre Anglais (août 1907-sept. 1908)": 155
THE CONCEPT OF COMEDY: A RE-STATEMENT: 2236
(THE CONCEPTION OF THE NOVEL IN ENGLAND: 1880-1910): 2336
THE CONDEMNED PLAYGROUND—ESSAYS: 1927-1944: 1517
"Consecrated Butchery": 895
" *'Constance,'* de Somerset Maugham": 2196
"The Constant Fidelities": 612
"*The Constant Wife*": 620, 1241
(*The Constant Wife* by Somerset Maugham): 2196
" *'The Constant Wife'* Deft and Sparkling": 603
"*The Constant Wife*: Webber-Douglas School": 2186
"Contemporary Arts: The Theatre": 1629, 1724
CONTEMPORARY BRITISH LITERATURE: 1800
CONTEMPORARY DRAMA: NINE PLAYS: 970
(THE CONTEMPORARY ENGLISH NOVEL: GENRES AND DEVELOPMENT): 635
(The Contemporary English Theater): 522
THE CONTEMPORARY THEATRE, 1925: 533, 534
THE CONTEMPORARY THEATRE: 1944 AND 1945: 1506, 1507, 1508
"Conteurs Etrangères modernes": 800
"The Contractile Vacuole": 1972
(Contributions on the Handling of School Literature. 1. The Representation of English Society in W. S. Maugham's Play *Jack Straw*): 1352
"A Cool Hand": 1471
"Correspondence: The Bad Habit of Mr. Maugham": 177
"*Cosmopolitans*": 1186, 1190
"A Costume Play": 114
(Courier of Letters): 721
(Courier of Letters: One Death like Another): 1828
"Courrier des lettres": 721
"Courrier des Lettres: Une morte comme une autre": 1828
"Court Theatre: *'Lady Frederick'* by W. Somerset Maugham": 44
CRAFT AND CHARACTER IN MODERN FICTION: 1471
(*Creatures of Circumstance*): 2087
"*Creatures of Circumstance*": 1624
"Criminal Record": 2306
(Critical Reports): 1236, 1290, 1850, 1917, 1932, 1948, 2052, 2074, 2075, 2077, 2148, 2244
(Critical Reports: Review of the English Theater): 155
"Criticism": 1324
(The Criticism of J. J. Gautier: Theatre Montparnasse: Gaston Baty: *Caroline*): 2256
"La Critique de J. J. Gautier-Théâtre Montparnasse-Gaston Baty-*Caroline*": 2256
"La Critique des livres: *L'Envoûte*": 741
"La Critique des livres: *Le Sortilège Malais*": 768
"La Critique dramatique: Au théâtre Sarah Bernhardt: *Constance*": 2188
(Cultural Problems in Modern English Drama): 846
"Current Fiction": 119
"The Current Historical Novel": 1580
(Current Literature): 712, 769, 1030, 1031, 1109
"Current Literature: Books in General": 962, 1296, 1407, 1414
"The Curtain Rises": 641
"*Le Cyclone*": 907, 953
"*Le Cyclone* aux Ambassadeurs": 905
"A Cynical, Gifted Story Teller": 983
(Daddy Told a Few Home-Truths): 2100
"Dans le metro": 783
"De Senectute: Mr. Maugham Awaits the Ferryman": 1745
"De Singapore à l'Athénée": 792
(Dead This Evening at 91, on the Côte d'Azur. Somerset Maugham Became an Author Perhaps Because He Was a Stammerer): 2281
"Dean of the Smoothies": 1903
(Death of Feeling): 2099
(The Death of Somerset Maugham): 2279
"Les Debuts de Somerset Maugham au Théâtre: Naissance d'une Vocation et Affirmation d'une Personnalité Littéraire": 2093
"The Decline of Inspiration in Modern Literature": 1050
"Degeneration and the Religion of Beauty: A Traditional Pattern in Coleridge's 'The Rime of the Ancient Mariner,' Pater's THE RENAISSANCE, Maugham's *Of Human Bondage*, and Joyce's ULYSSES": 2229
"A Deluge of Drama: The Opening of the Season": 333
"Dernier mot": 1570
"Dernière heure théâtral: *Le Pélican ou une Etrange Famille*": 1192
"La dernière escale de Somerset Maugham": 2275

"Dernière minute parisienne-Aux Bouffes-Parisiens: *Avant Le Derby*": 1581
"Dernière minute: Soir de Fête pour *Constance*": 2182
"Les derniers mots du gentleman du Cap Ferrat: 'Je meurs quéri!": 2288
THE DEVELOPMENT OF THE DETECTIVE NOVEL: 2132
"The Development of W. Somerset Maugham": 1931
"The Devil a Monk Was He": 1518
"The Devious Ways of Somerset Maugham": 370
"Diary of a New Dimension": 1435
DICKENS AND HIS READERS: ASPECTS OF NOVEL-CRITICISM SINCE 1836: 2040
(Did Constance Do Right?): 2213
(Did the Constant Wife Do Right?): 1842
"Discussion": 1852
"The Divergence of Marshall and Maugham": 609
"Divorce Plays on the London Stage": 396
"Domestic Interiors: Three Current Plays": 861
"*Don Fernando*": 1156
(DOSTOEVSKI'S INFLUENCE ON THE ENGLISH NOVEL): 1166
DOSTOJEWSKIJS EINFLUSS AUF DEN ENGLISCHEN ROMAN: 1166
"Dr. Maugham's Prescription for Success": 2241
"Drama": 25, 32, 45, 46, 61, 63, 64, 65, 120, 121, 122, 123, 124, 125, 165, 166, 212, 213, 226, 275, 281, 294, 311, 340, 345, 348, 349, 367, 388, 407, 413, 462, 504, 682, 683, 742, 933, 1067, 1068, 1306, 1444, 1525, 1529, 1886
"The Drama": 76, 77, 708, 709, 766, 971, 1104, 1105, 1181, 1331, 1496, 1558, 1569
(The Drama≠ADORABLE JULIA): 2004
(Drama and Life): 1094, 1272
THE DRAMA AND THE STAGE: 420
"The Drama: The Artistic Temperament, New Style": 539
(Drama: *'The Breadwinner'*): 994
"Drama: A British Knight Gone Wrong": 183
(Drama Chronicle): 883
(Drama Chronicle of FIGARO: *The Circle*): 729
(Drama Chronicle: The Subject of Two English Plays): 1218
(Drama Chronicles of Paris: Ambassadeurs≠ *The Sacred Flame*): 912
(Drama Chronicles of Paris: Athénée: Revival of *The Letter*): 913
(Drama Chronicles of Paris: Athénée Theatre: *The Letter*): 786
"Drama: *'The Circle'* ": 425
(Drama: Divine Monsters): 2200
(The Drama≠DOROTHEE): 1934
"Drama: *'East of Suez'* ": 463
'Drama: An English Slam at Our Title Hunters": 304
"Drama: The Feast that Follows Famine": 254
"Drama: French, English, American": 448
"Drama: The Goose that Laid the Golden Eggs": 83
"The Drama: *'Grace'* ": 160
"Drama: Hautboys and Torches": 483
(The Drama: *Home and Beauty*): 1588
"Drama: The Imperishable Theatre and Some Exhibits": 287
"Drama: Importations Not Entirely Successful": 137
"The Drama in England": 375
THE DRAMA IN ENGLISH: 828
(The Drama in Paris): 1951
"Drama: Just Dandy": 449
"Drama: *The Letter*": 678
(The Drama: *The Letter*): 1123
"The Drama: Lunching Out": 484
"Drama: Minority Reports": 647
(The Drama Movement): 698, 806, 951
(The Drama Movement in England): 1143
"Drama: Mr. Maugham to the Fore Again": 138
"Drama: Music, Comedy and Newspaper Honesty": 84
"Drama: Nature Study": 398
"Drama: The New Season Getting into Its Stride": 184
"Drama of the Month": 126, 167
(THE DRAMA OF WILLIAM SOMERSET MAUGHAM): 1239
"The Drama: *'Our Betters'* ": 515
"The Drama: *'Penelope'* and Popularity": 111
"Drama: Pulmotor Drama": 717
"Drama: RAIN": 538
(Drama Review): 880, 1911, 1969
"Drama: The Season's Curfew Tolling": 231
"The Drama: Somerset Maugham": 847
"Drama: Somerset Maugham Himself": 420
"Drama: Something Good": 598
"The Drama: Spirit and Spiritualistic": 579
"The Drama that Plays": 127
"The Drama: Thrillers": 651
"Drama: *'Too Many Husbands,'* by Maugham, Is Seen at the Booth Theatre": 323
"The Drama: The Tropics at Second Hand": 559
(The Drama: Two English Plays and a French Melodrama): 1267
"The Drama: Underdone and Overdone": 599

"The Drama: *'The Unknown'* ": 386
"Drama with a Domestic Finish": 308
DRAMAS OF MODERNISM AND THEIR FORERUNNERS: 942
(Dramatic Art in the United States): 488
(Dramatic Chronicle: Ambassadeurs Theatre: *The Sacred Flame*): 894
THE DRAMATIC COMEDY OF WILLIAM SOMERSET MAUGHAM: 2349
"Dramatic Gossip": 214
"Dramatic Novelists: W. Somerset Maugham": 746
"Dramatic Performances in London": 317
(Dramatic Report: At the Sarah Bernhardt Theatre: *The Constant Wife*): 2188
(The Dramatic Week: *The Breadwinner*): 1182
(The Dramatic Week: *The Circle*): 977
(The Dramatic Week: Sarah Bernhardt Theatre: *The Letter*): 1110
"The Dramatic World": 283, 480, 533, 534, 639, 973
DRAMATIS PERSONAE: A RETROSPECTIVE SHOW: 1575
DRAMATISTS OF TODAY: 1952
"Dramatists' Novels: Maugham and Van Druten": 838
(Dress Rehearsals At the Ambassadeurs: *The Sacred Flame*): 927
(Dress Rehearsals: At l'OEuvre Theatre: *The Circle*): 728
(Dress Rehearsals: *The Circle*): 738
(Dress Rehearsals: *The Letter* at the Athénée): 801
"Drew at His Best in *'Jack Straw'* ": 66
THE DRY MOCK: A STUDY OF IRONY IN DRAMA: 1697
"Du Sud-Tunisien au Pacific": 1036
"Duke of York's Theatre: *'Grace'* by W. S. Maugham": 168
"East of Singapore": 608
(*East of Suez*): 1953
"*East of Suez*": 455, 457, 492
" *'East of Suez'* Arrives at the Eltinge Theater": 467
"*East of Suez* by W. Somerset Maugham": 456
" *'East of Suez'* a Maugham Potboiler": 476
" *'East of Suez'*: Mr. Maugham's Play at His Majesty's—Peking Up-to-Date": 454
(Echos: *Ah King* by W. Somerset Maugham): 1126
"Echos: *La Femme dans la Jungle* de W. Somerset Maugham": 1126
"Edeson and Play a Delight": 128
"Editor's Choice": 1499
"*Ei Maistu Elämältä*": 2044
EIGHT MODERN WRITERS: 2250
"The Eighty Years of Mr. Maugham": 1970
"Les 80 ans de W. Somerset Maugham": 1977
"Eikä mikkään muttu": 2042
DER EINFLUSS DER PSYCHOANALYSE AUF DER ENGLISCHE LITERATUR: 1130
"Elämältä se maistui": 2064
"*Elämän Kahle*": 2164
"Elävältä se kirja maistui": 2351
"Elder Statesmen": 1698
(Elegant and Refined Comedy): 2216
(Elegant Odyssey): 2342
"Elegantit Larharetket": 2342
"Eminently Readable": 2122
(Enchanted Castaways): 2191
(Enchanting Stories): 2344
"ENCORE": 1865
ENEMIES OF PROMISE: 1288
(ENGLAND, CONTINENTAL NATION): 1052
"Englantilaisia ketojia": 1882
DIE ENGLISCHE LITERATUR DER GEGENWART SEIT 1870: DRAMA UND ROMAN: 765
DIE ENGLISCHE LITERATUR DES 19. UND 20. JAHRHUNDERTS: 495
DIE ENGLISCHE LITERATUR IN DEUTSCHLAND VON 1895 BIS 1934 MIT EINER VOLLSTÄNDIGEN BIBLIOGRAPHIE DER DEUTSCHEN UBERSETZUNGEN UND DER IM DEUTSCHEN SPRACHGEBIET ERSCHIENENEN ENGLISCHEN AUSGABEN: 1271
ENGLISCHE LITERATURGESCHICHTE: 2346
DIE ENGLISCHE ROMAN DER NEUESTEN ZEIT UND GEGENWART: STILFORMEN UND ENTWICKLUNGSLINIEN: 635
ENGLISH DRAMA IN TRANSITION: 1880-1920: 2354
(English Drama Since the War): 959
"English Ebb, American Flow": 1234
"English in the East": 610
"English Laughter—Past and Present": 1575
(English Letters): 676
(English Letters Today: A Question and Two Replies): 1560
(ENGLISH LITERARY HISTORY): 2346
(ENGLISH LITERATURE): 916
ENGLISH LITERATURE AND IDEAS IN THE TWENTIETH CENTURY: AN INQUIRY INTO PRESENT DIFFICULTIES AND FUTURE PROSPECTS: 1602
(ENGLISH LITERATURE, FROM ITS BEGINNINGS TO OUR DAY): 1526
(ENGLISH LITERATURE IN GERMANY FROM 1895 TO 1934 WITH A DEFINITIVE BIBLIOGRAPHY OF GERMAN TRANSLATIONS AND ENGLISH EDITIONS APPEARING IN GERMAN LANGUAGE AREAS): 1271
(English Literature in 1932): 1053
(English Literature in 1933): 1124
(English Literature in 1936): 1237

(English Literature in 1937): 1291
(English Literature in 1938): 1346
(ENGLISH LITERATURE OF THE 19TH AND 20TH CENTURY): 495
(English Love Affairs): 978
"English Maupassant": 1385
(English Narrators): 1882
(THE ENGLISH NOVEL): 2309
THE ENGLISH NOVEL IN TRANSITION: 1475
THE ENGLISH NOVEL: A PANORAMA: 2204
THE ENGLISH NOVEL: A SHORT CRITICAL HISTORY: 1704
THE ENGLISH SHORT STORY IN TRANSITION: 1880-1920: 2335
"The English Spotlight: Buried Treasure": 1652
THE ENGLISH STAGE: 1850-1950: 1827
THE ENGLISH THEATRE: 1698
(THE ENGLISH THEATER): 1140
"An Englishman in China": 469
"Ensi-ilta Kansan Näyttämöllä": 849
"Ensimmainen siirto": 1991
"Entertainment Week": 1453
(Entertainments): 1947, 2020
(Entertainments: At the St. Georges Theatre: JANE by Jean Wall): 1919
(Entertainments: *The Breadwinner* At the Ambassadeurs): 1193
(Entertainments: Dress Rehearsals: Theatre of the Ambassadeurs: *The Breadwinner*): 1195
"Entertainments—The Globe Theatre: *'For Services Rendered'* ": 998
(Entertainments: New Items and Remarks: Revival): 911
(The Entertainments of Paris: At the Ambassadeurs: *The Circle*): 1010
(The Entertainments of Paris: Dress Rehearsals At the Ambassadeurs: *The Sacred Flame*): 938
"Entertainments: The Theatres": 918
"An Epicurean on Liberty": 1445
"The Epigoni": 182
"Epilogue": 68
(Espionage Again): 2136
"Essayists Who Are Laws unto Themselves": 2115
"Essays of Defeat": 1180
"The Essential Story": 2116
"Estivä ihminen nyt ja 'aikojen alussa' ": 1633
"Etat des Lettres Anglaises": 1327
"Ethel Barrymore in *'Lady Frederick'* ": 69
(Even Young Maugham Was Sensible at Times): 2102
(Evening Entertainment): 2076
(The Eventful Evening of Life of Old Barber Sheppey): 2062
"Ex Libris": 1715
"The Excellent Mediocre": 1858
(An Excellent Play by Maugham at the National Theatre): 1202
"The Exoticism of Somerset Maugham": 1009
"Expert Short Stories": 1127
"*The Explorer*": 70, 227
" *'The Explorer' at Daly's*": 228
" *'The Explorer,'* at the Lyric": 71, 72
" *'The Explorer,'* at the Lyric Theatre": 57
" *'Explorer'* Blazes No Fresh Paths": 229
" *'The Explorer,'* Revived at the Lyric": 129
"A Fairly Intimate Journal": 1711
"A Famous Writer's Outlook": 2133
"A Feast of Horrors": 130
"Femmes dans la Jungle": 1111
"Fiction": 2, 47, 264, 335, 592, 621, 629, 906, 975, 1342, 2078
"Fiction: *Ah King*": 1092
"Fiction: Five Established Novelists": 860
"Fiction in Review": 1553, 1608
"Fiction: Mr. Maugham's Mixture as Before": 1194
"Fiction: *The Narrow Corner*": 1021
"Fiction Notes": 735, 736
"Fiction—I": 1029
"Fiction Parade": 1627
"Fiction: *The Razor's Edge*": 1536
"Fiction: The Test that Failed": 961
"Fiction: *Theatre*": 1249
"Fiction—II": 1011
"Fiction: Variety of People": 1628
"Fiction: The Way": 551
"Fictional Biography and Autobiography": 368
"Fifteen New Maugham Stories": 1622
"The Figure in the Rug": 2225
FIGURES IN THE FOREGROUND: LITERARY REMINISCENCES 1917-40: 2251
"*Le Fil du Rasoir*": 1866
"Finds Wife Married to His Best Friend": 339
THE FINE ART OF LITERARY MAYHEM: A LIVELY ACCOUNT OF FAMOUS WRITERS AND THEIR FEUDS: 2231
"A Fine Maugham Play for Miss Cooper": 671
"The First Edition of *The Moon and Sixpence*": 2215
(First Move): 1991
(First Night at the People's Stage): 849
"First Night at the Theatre": 1849
FIRST NIGHTS: 973, 1027
"First of the Month": 2301
"*First Person Singular*": 920, 921
"The First Reader": 839, 1522
"Five-Day Adventure": 1344
"*La Flamme Sacrée* de Somerset Maugham (The Playhouse)": 772

"Flat Dialogue in Far from Boring Comedy —Savoy Theatre: *The Circle*": 2271
"*For Services Rendered*": 999
" '*For Services Rendered,*' at the Globe": 1001
FORCES IN MODERN BRITISH LITERATURE: 1885-1946: 1655
(Foreign Letters): 605, 827
(Foreign Letters: Somerset Maugham, Satirical Novelist): 997
(Foreign Literature): 537
(Foreign Literature: The 'Notebooks' of Somerset Maugham): 1778
(Foreign Novels): 1593, 1642, 1812
(Foreign Reviews: William Somerset Maugham): 1090
A FOREWORD TO FICTION: 1163
(Four Months in the Indies with Somerset Maugham): 1293
(FOUR STUDIES): 2222
"*France at War*": 1398, 1399, 1401
"The France that Was": 1400
"French and English": 972
A FRENCH BIBLIOGRAPHY OF W. SOMERSET MAUGHAM: 2337
(French Letters): 536, 805
"From Alpha to Omega": 571
"From the Broadway Season": 1864
(FROM CHAUCER TO SHAW: AN INTRODUCTION TO ENGLISH LITERATURE): 1630
"From Forest Fire to France: Somerset Maugham and His Moorish Mansion": 2147
(FROM HEIDENSTAM TO UNDSET: LIVES OF GREAT AUTHORS): 2105
(From Leino to Anatole France: New Books for Easter): 2126
(From Madame Bovary to the Chapman Report): 2226
"From Mojave Desert to Siberian Steppe": 497
(From Singapore to the Athénée): 792
(From Wisdom to Pious Wrath): 1677
(From a Young Man's Pen): 2098
FULL CIRCLE: 954
"Gammon and Spinach": 968
"Garrick Theatre: RAIN by John Colton and Clemence Randolph": 553
"A Gauguin of Golders Green": 833
"Gay Eighty": 1984
THE GAY TWENTIES: A DECADE OF THE THEATRE: 2139
"A Gentleman and His Personality": 1152
"A Gentleman and a Writer": 819
THE GENTLEMAN FROM CAP FERRAT: 2081
"*The Gentleman in the Parlour*": 834, 864
THE GEORGIAN LITERARY SCENE: A PANORAMA: 1173
GESCHICHTE DER ENGLISCHEN UND AMERIKANISCHEN LITERATUR VON DEN ANFAENGEN BIS ZUR GEGENWART: 2017
"Gift Book Miscellany": 1987
GIN AND BITTERS: 954
" 'GIN AND BITTERS' ": 940
" 'GIN AND BITTERS' Held Up: English Action Called Off After Friends of Maugham Protest": 923
"Gin and Quinine Tonic": 1801
"Gjorde Constance ratt?": 2213
"Globe Theatre: '*The Constant Wife*' ": 1244
"The Globe Theatre: '*Our Betters*' ": 516
"Globe Theatre: 'The Tenth Man' by W. Somerset Maugham": 170
GODS OF MODERN GRUB STREET: IMPRESSIONS OF CONTEMPORARY AUTHORS: 479
"The Golden Age of Spain": 1683
"Good Cast in *For Services Rendered*": 2149
(Good Old Maugham): 2121
(The Good Reference): 720
"Good Short Shorts": 1196
(Goodbye, My English Friend): 1432
"The Gossip Shop": 555, 556
" '*Grace,*' at the Duke of York's": 172, 173, 174, 215
" '*Grace*' by Somerset Maugham": 169
"Un grand romancier anglais: A propos *L'Archipel aux Sirènes*": 548
LA GRANDE-BRETAGNE DANS LE ROMAN FRANÇAIS, 1914-1940: 1985
(GREAT BRITAIN IN THE FRENCH NOVEL, 1914-1940): 1985
(A Great English Novelist: On *The Trembling of a Leaf*): 548
(A Great Novel by Somerset Maugham: Human Nobility and Slavery): 1265
"*Great Novelists and Their Novels*": 1672
(GREAT WORLD LITERATURE): 2289
"A Group of New Plays": 458
"Growing Pains": 1350
"The Growing Puzzle of Mr. Maugham's Hero": 369
(Guess Who Marries Whom. Surprises at Lappeenranta Town Theater): 2329
"Guests at Mr. Somerset Maugham's Party": 2024
"H. E. Bates Reviews": 1384
(Hackneyed Racial Mysticism): 1945
"Half Dozen Essays by Master Writer": 1906
"A Hammock Book": 1367
A HANDBOOK OF DRAMA: 1313
"The Hapless She": 401
"Hard, Medium and Soft": 1365
"Harvinaisen mielenkiintoinen ensi-ilta Kaupunginteatterissa": 1162

"The Haymarket and the New: London Flocks to Repertory": 1562
"Haymarket Theatre: *'The Circle,'* by W. Somerset Maugham": 1523
"Hectic Holiday: Broadway in Review": 1477
HEIDENSTAMISTA UNDSETIIN: SUURTEN KIRJAILIJAIN ELÄMÄKERTOJA: 2105
"Helsingin horisontista": 2060
"Helsingin Kansanteatteri. W. Somerset Maugham: *Pyhä Liekki*": 1248
(Helsinki People's Theater. W. Somerset Maugham: *The Sacred Flame*): 1248
"*The Hero*": 18
"The Heterogeneous Magic of Maugham": 466
"L'heure qui passe": 1048
UNE HEURE AVEC . . . : 743
"Une heure avec W. Somerset Maugham, romancier et conteur anglais": 743
"High Comedy": 1873
(Hilkka Helinä Enchanting in Her Celebration Metamorphosis): 2227
"Hilkka Helinä viehätti juhlametamorfoosissaan": 2227
HISTOIRE DE LA LITTERATURE ANGLAISE: 1680
HISTOIRE LITTERAIRE DE L'EUROPE ET DE L'AMERIQUE, DE LA RENAISSANCE A NOS JOURS: 1610
"Historical Romances": 8
(HISTORY OF ENGLISH AND AMERICAN LITERATURE FROM THE BEGINNINGS TO THE PRESENT): 2017
(HISTORY OF ENGLISH LITERATURE): 1680
A HISTORY OF ENGLISH LITERATURE FROM BEOWULF TO 1926: 619
A HISTORY OF MODERN DRAMA: 1623
"Holiday Goods: Broadway in Review": 1563
"*Home and Beauty* at the Playhouse": 342
" *'Home and Beauty,'* at the Playhouse": 341
" *'Home and Beauty'*: Mr. Maugham's New Farce at the Playhouse": 343
"*Home and Beauty* by W. Somerset Maugham": 338
"Honorary Degrees at Oxford: Encaenia Addresses": 1876
(Hors d'Oeuvres): 1840
"*The Hour Before the Dawn*": 1480
(AN HOUR WITH . . .): 743
(An Hour with W. Somerset Maugham, English Novelist and Short-Story Writer): 743
THE HOUSE OF FICTION: 1727
"How *Dare* He?": 53
"How This Book Came to Be": 1468
"How to Like to Read": 1415
HOW TO READ A NOVEL: 2094
"How to Succeed as a Writer": 2118
"How to Write—by Maugham": 1726
HUMANITIES: 844
"Hyvyyden voitto": 2002
"The Ibsenite Maugham": 2212
"Icelandic Translations of Maugham": 1843
THE IDEA IN FICTION: 1133
"Idle Rich Satirized on Stage": 300
(Idlers and Loafers): 2340
IDLING IN ITALY: STUDIES OF LITERATURE AND OF LIFE: 368
"*Il Suffit d'Une Nuit*": 1806
"Iltojen ratoksi": 2076
IMAGES OF TRUTH: REMEMBRANCES AND CRITICISM: 1659
"Imitation and Suggestion in the Drama": 133
"The Imperturbable Mr. Maugham": 1547
"Impressions d'Amérique: Panorama newyorkais": 1857
(Impressions of America: New York Panorama): 1857
"In and Out of Books: Maughamania": 1780
"In and Out of Books: Visitor": 1762, 1781
"In Brief": 1481, 1483
"In the Days of Machiavelli": 1600
"In the Far East: Mr. Somerset Maugham's Travels": 841
"In the Field of Music—the Drama: *'Caesar's Wife'* ": 336
(In the Front Window of the Bookshop): 1819
"In the Great Tradition: Maugham the Master Craftsman": 2327
"In Human Bondage to Books": 2159
(In Passing): 2267
"In the Shadow of the Casuarina Tree": 627
(In the Subway): 783
(In the Theater Currently): 957, 1141
(In the Theaters): 784, 785
"In This Month's Fiction Library": 611
"In Vishnu-Land What Avatar?": 316
"Inarticulations": 350
"Indestructible Maugham—Ashcroft Theatre: *Home and Beauty*": 2257
L'INFLUENCE DU NATURALISME FRANÇAISE SUR LES ROMANCIERS ANGLAIS DE 1885 A 1900: 552
(THE INFLUENCE OF FRENCH NATURALISM ON ENGLISH NOVELISTS FROM 1885 TO 1900): 552
(THE INFLUENCE OF PSYCHOANALYSIS ON ENGLISH LITERATURE): 1130
(An Ingenious, Miserable Life): 1757
INSIGHT II: ANALYSES OF MODERN BRITISH LITERATURE: 2254
"Intelligent Entertainment": 1251
"An Interesting Playwright": 243

(International Espionage): 2123
"L'interprétation du *Cyclone*": 886
(Interpretation of *The Sacred Flame*): 886
"An Interview with Somerset Maugham": 1609
"Intiimi teatterimaailman kuvaus": 1837
(Intimate Description of the Theatrical World): 1837
"Introduction": 1292, 1503, 1965
"An Introduction to Maugham": 1659
"Ironian oppitunti": 2104
(Is Maugham Really Nice?): 2297
"Isä lauloi totuuksia": 2100
(It Is All Literature): 2343
(It Savored of Life): 2064
(It's Left to Chance): 2203
"*Jack Straw*": 54
" *'Jack Straw,'* at the Vaudeville": 78, 79
"Jekyl to Hyde": 1361
THE JEROME COMPLEXION: 2260
"Jo nuori Maugham oli ajoittain järkevä": 2102
"John Drew as Jack Straw": 80
"John Drew Here in *'Smith'* ": 179
"John Drew in Guise of a Rural Moralist": 180
JOURNAL LITTERAIRE: 2163
JOURNAL, 1946-1950: 1826
JOURNAL, 1950-1954: 2041
JOURNEY WITHOUT MAPS: 1198
"Journeys of the Spirit": 1028
"Juhlittu Maugham": 2010
(Just Appeared): 1207
"Just Off the Griddle: Strawberry and Other Ices": 201
"K A Remembers a Meeting with S M Enjoying the Truce of Old Age": 2299
"Käännösromaaneja": 1734
"Kaksi englantilaista kertojaa": 1738
"Kaksi kirjailijanrouvaa": 2067
"Kansainvälistä vakoilua": 2123
"Kansallisteatterin englantilainen vutuus": 812
"Katsaus alkuvuoden käänoskirjallisuuteen": 1737
"Kaukaisen Idän mystiikkaa Kaupunginteatterin lavalla": 1377
"Kauko-Itää Maughamin silmin": 1788
"Kertomakirjallisuutta": 1765
"Keskinkertaista komediaa Kaupunginteatterissa": 2311
"Keskustelemme kirjoista": 1742
"Kiehtovia kertomuksia": 2344
"The King's School, Canterbury: The Hugh Walpole Collection: The Somerset Maugham Library": 2242
"Kipling Still Casts His Magic Spell": 1922
(Kipling Viewed by Somerset Maugham): 1854
"Kipling vu par Somerset Maugham": 1854
"Kipling's Prose": 1892
"Kirjailija kirjoittaa kirjailijasta": 2043
"Kirjallisuss ja elämä": 2085
"Kirjallisuutta kaikki": 2343
"Kirjallisuutta: nykyaisen romaanin edustajia": 1649
"*Kirjava Huntu*": 2029
"Kirjeen salaisuus": 869
"Kirjojen joulu": 1835
"Kolmenkymmenen vuoden takaista Maughamia": 2119
"Kootut anekdootit": 2348
"Kronikoita": 2156
"Kulturprobleme des modernen englischen Dramas": 846
'Die Kunst der Personenbeschreibung in Romanen John Galsworthys, W. Somerset Maughams und Graham Greenes": 1761
"Kuritonta sukupolvea englantilaiseen tapaan": 2107
"Laajamuotoista kertomataidetta": 2124
"Lääkärin kahle": 2138
"*Lady Frederick*": 52
" *'Lady Frederick,'* at the Court": 49, 50
" *'Lady Frederick,'* Revived at the Globe": 216
"*The Land of Promise*": 239, 248, 301
" *'Land of Promise,'* at the Duke of York's": 250
" *'The Land of Promise,'* at the Duke of York's Theatre": 249
"*The Land of Promise* by Somerset Maugham": 238
" *'The Land of Promise'*: Mr. Maugham's Play at the Duke of York's": 251
" *'The Land of Promise'*: Revival at the New Theatre": 302
THE LAST BASSOON: 2181
"Last Night's Play: 'THE PAINTED VEIL' at the Playhouse": 928
"Last Night's Premieres": 48, 73, 131 ,175
" 'Last Novel' by Maugham": 1679
(The Last Port of Somerset Maugham): 2275
(The Last Word): 1570
(The Last Words from the Gentleman of Cap Ferrat: 'I die healed!'): 2288
"Late Irony of Mr. Maugham, with Some Remarks on Edgar Wallace": 958
(The Latest: An Evening of Festivity for *The Constant Wife*): 2182
"The Latest Plays": 901
(The Latest Theatrical Scene: *The Breadwinner*): 1192
"Latest Works of Fiction": 411, 412
"Lectures romanesques": 1722, 1862
"Leinosta Franceen: pääsiäisen uutuuskirjoja": 2126

"The Leisure Arts": 843
"Lesser Maugham": 395
(Lesson in Irony): 2104
(*The Letter*): 802, 908, 939
"*The Letter*": 685
"A Letter from England": 858
" '*The Letter*' in Print": 696
(Letters and Life): 589, 633, 705, 813, 1268
"*La Lettre*": 802, 908, 939
"Lettre de Londres⸗Un grand succès de Mr. Somerset Maugham": 774
"Lettre de Londres⸗Une oeuvre nouvelle de W. Somerset Maugham": 652
"Les Lettres anglaises": 676
"Lettres Anglaises d'Aujourd'hui: Une Question et Deux Réponses": 1560
"Lettres Anglo-Saxonnes": 1955, 2090
"Lettres anglo-saxonnes: le Yogi de Maugham": 1656
"Lettres de Londres": 1924
"Les Lettres et la vie": 589, 633, 705, 813, 1268
"Les Lettres étrangères": 605, 827
"Les Lettres étrangères: Somerset Maugham, romancier satirique": 997
"Les lettres françaises": 536, 805
"Library of Congress Gets Maugham Ms": 1797
"The Library of the Quarter: Outstanding Novels": 936, 1074
"The Library: W. Somerset Maugham": 1771
"Life and Literature": 1287, 1341
(The Life of Books: Novels): 1735
"Lights Down": 645
"Lights Down: A Review of the Stage": 715
The Limit: 217
"The Listener's Book Chronicle": 1402, 1933, 2048
"The Listener's Chronicle": 1307
"Literary Accounting: *The Summing Up*, by W. Somerset Maugham": 1320
(Literary Chronicle: Readings): 1795
(Literary History of Europe and America, from the Renaissance to our Time): 1610
(Literary Journal): 2163
"The Literary Landscape": 1040
(The Literary Life): 577, 628, 1270
(The Literary Life: Foreign Literature): 580
"The Literary Scene: 1919": 1807
"Literary: Tour Among Good Books": 1403
(Literature and Life): 2085
The Literature of Roguery: 43
(Literature: Representations of the Modern Novel): 1649
La Litterature Anglaise: 916
La Litterature Anglaise, des Origines a nos Jours: 1526
"La Littérature anglaise en 1932": 1053
"La Littérature anglaise en 1933": 1124
"La Littérature anglaise en 1936": 1237
"La Littérature anglaise en 1937": 1291
"La Littérature anglaise en 1938": 1346
"Littératures étrangères": 537
"Littératures étrangères: Les 'Carnets' de Somerset Maugham": 1778
"Lively New Plays": 312
"Living and Writing": 1316
Living Authors: A Book of Biographies: 914
"Le Livre du cholera et de la trahison: '*The Painted Veil*' ": 606
"Le Livre du Jour⸗*Servitude Humaine*": 1228
"Le Livre parlé": 1005, 1132
"Livres": 779, 787, 985, 992, 1108, 1113, 1215, 1216, 1657, 1700, 1768, 1769, 1816, 1817, 2091
"Les Livres": 581, 726, 1101
"Les Livres: '*L'Archipel aux Sirènes*' ": 562
"Les Livres de la Semaine. Somerset Maugham: *Le Magicien*": 1309
"Les Livres: *L'Envoûte*": 761
"Les Livres⸗*L'Envoûte* par Somerset Maugham": 744
"Les Livres et les écrivains": 545
"Livres et Revues: *Amours Singulières*": 1006
"Les Livres: Les Lettres anglaises": 9
"Les Livres nouveaux": 1204
"Les Livres nouveaux: Littérature étrangère": 1070
"Les Livres: *La Passe Dangereuse*": 618, 631
"Les Livres Reçus: *Le Fil du Rasoir*": 1632
"Les Livres: *Servitude Humaine*": 1277
"Les Livres: Somerset Maugham⸗*La Ronde de L'Amour*": 1023
"*Liza of Lambeth*": 4, 415
" '*Liza of Lambeth*': A Stark Tragedy by W. S. Maugham": 421
"Liza's Jubilee": 1681
" '*Loaves and Fishes,*' at the Duke of York's": 218, 219, 220,
"Lollypops": 291
"London and Maine": 638
"London Also Has a New Maugham Play": 903
(London Letter: A Great Success by Mr. Somerset Maugham): 774
(London Letter: A New Work by W. Somerset Maugham): 652
(London Letters): 1924
"The London Stage": 668, 669, 788, 830, 919

(Londoners and the Naturalist Novel): 3
"Le long voyage de Somerset Maugham": 2276
(The Long Voyage of Somerset Maugham): 2276
Les Lorgnettes du Roman Anglais: 2162
"Lorveja ja lortteja": 2340
"Love and Exploration": 134
(Love in Comedy Form): 1901
"*Love in a Cottage*": 313
"*'Love in a Cottage'*: Miss Marie Lohr's Season at the Globe": 314
"The Love Story of Mr. Maugham and Spain": 1160
"Luck in Authorship": 1032
"Lumotut haaksirikkoiset": 2191
"Lyhyitä esittelyjä": 2106
"Lyric Theatre: *'The Explorer'* by William Somerset Maugham": 81, 135
Maailman Kirjat ja Kirjailijat: 2070
"Maallinen ja taivaallinen rakkaus": 1995
"Macchiavelli elementissään": 2057
(Machiavelli in His Element): 2057
"Machiavelli in Romance": 1587
"Machiavelli Is Hero in Maugham Novel": 1576
"Machiavellian Philosophy 'Now' and 'Then' ": 1586
(The Magic of Somerset Maugham): 773
"*The Magician*": 2096
"*The Making of a Saint*": 10
"A Man in Search of Faith": 1546
(Man in Search of Himself Now and 'at the Beginning of Time'): 1633
"*A Man of Honour*": 27, 33
" *'A Man of Honour,'* at the Avenue": 34
"Man of Letters": 1301
"Manhattan Aisles": 674
"The Manuscript of Somerset Maugham's *On a Chinese Screen*": 2069
"Margaret Anglin Acts *'Caroline'* at Empire": 285
"Margaret Anglin Charms in *Caroline*": 286
"Marie Tempest Welcomed": 136
(Marriage Comedy at the Swedish Theater): 798
"Master of Two Dimensions": 1235
(A Masterpiece and a Book by a Master): 1772
Masters of the Drama: 1982
"Le Match de la vie: Le Roman noir d'un héritage": 2249
(The Match's Life: The Black Novel of a Heritage): 2249
Materia Critica: 528
"Matt komedi på Intimi": 2273
"The Mature Maugham": 442
"Maugham": 1501, 1678, 1880
"Maugham Accused by Soviet Writers": 1743
"Maugham and the Comic Spirit": 1004
"Maugham and the East: The Human Condition—Freedom": 2153
"Maugham and the Movies": 1719
"Maugham and the Two Myths": 1594
"Maugham and the West: The Human Condition—Bondage": 2160
"Maugham and the Young Idiot": 1950
"Maugham the Artist": 1992
"Maugham—as I Know Him": 1566
(Maugham as a Short Story Writer): 2339
"Maugham Asserts Novelist Is Critic": 1798
"Maugham at Eighty": 2027
(Maugham at His Best): 2082
"Maugham at 90: The Summing Up": 2262
(Maugham Celebrated): 2010
"Maugham Cinematized": 1754
"Maugham Comes Back with Autobiography": 1164
"Maugham Considers Mystics": 1512
"Maugham Dissects Ten Authors": 2039
"Maugham Does Own Life Story with Fine Skill": 1286
"Maugham 1874—": 591
"The Maugham Enigma": 1289
The Maugham Enigma: 67, 262, 316, 420, 495, 606, 872, 963, 1009, 1121, 1159, 1289, 1380, 1414, 1418, 1422, 1445, 1566, 1594, 1601, 1689, 1726, 1744, 1823, 1988, 1989
"Maugham Etelämerellä": 2161, 2205
"Maugham—Excellent as Usual": 1658
"A Maugham Farce at the Playhouse": 527
"Maugham: A 'Free Man' at 85": 2140
(A Maugham from Thirty Years Ago): 2119
"Maugham Gift to Library": 1589
"Maugham Holds Title Hunters Up to Scorn": 303
(Maugham in Action): 2127
"Maugham in the Process of Becoming": 1723
"Maugham Is Cited in Queen's Honors": 2005
"Maugham Keeps Book Secret": 2165
"The Maugham 'Legend' ": 2228
"Maugham Lives a Role He Wrote; Author, at 80, Becomes Cynosure": 2006
"Maugham Never Forgot the Day I Trumped His Ace": 2310
"Maugham Novel as Opera": 2083
"Maugham Offers Prize": 1639
(Maugham on the South Sea): 2161, 2205
(Maugham on the Stage): 2112
"Maugham Paints a Sardonic Portrait": 845
"Maugham, Playwright": 2302
"Maugham the Playwright": 1157

"Maugham Praises Our Playwrights": 253
"Maugham Predicts World Use of English Within 3 Centuries": 2199
"Maugham Presents His 'Last' Published Work": 2151
"The Maugham Reader": 1799
"The Maugham Seesaw": 1936
"Maugham soda töissa": 2127
"A Maugham Story": 1441
"Maugham Sums Up: Agnostic's Cool Philosophy of Life": 1308
"Maugham to Endow Writers' Aid Fund": 2218
"Maugham Wants Letters Burned to Bar Posthumous Publication": 2103
"Maugham, William Somerset": 1484
"Maughamana, 1892-1949": 1710
"Maugham-by-the-Sea": 2217
"Maughamette": 1447
"Maughamia näyttämöllä": 2112
Maughamiana: The Writings of W. Somerset Maugham: 1809
"Maughamin Gauguin": 1729
"Maughamin *'Kirje'* Mikkelin Teatterissa": 2071
"Maughamin komedia Kansallisteaterissa": 1787
"Maughamin Leikointa": 2001
"Maughamin mainetta": 2058
"Maughamin novelleja": 2084
"Maughamin paras romaani": 2047
"Maughamin pitkä päivä päättynyt": 2283
"Maughamin 'Sade' Kaupunginteatterissa": 2246
"Maughamin 'Sade' Koitossa": 1201
"Maughamin *'Ympra'* Kansallisen ensimmäisenä ensi-iltana": 1811
"Maughamko kiltti?": 2297
(Maugham's Best Novel): 2047
"Maugham's Chinese Sketches": 496
"*Maugham's Choice of Kipling's Best*": 1907
(Maugham's *The Circle* the Season's First Night at the National Theater): 1811
(Maugham's Comedy at the National Theater): 1787
"Maugham's Digest of 10 Great Novels": 1684
"Maugham's Distinctive Qualities Endure": 1516
(Maugham's Fame): 2058
"Maugham's Folly": 1690
(Maugham's Gauguin): 1729
"Maugham's Glass-Smooth and Spectacular Writing Skill": 1548
"Maugham's Latest": 593
(Maugham's *The Letter* at the Mikkeli Theater): 2071
(Maugham's Long Day at an End): 2283
"Maugham's Machiavelli": 1577
"Maugham's Mixture": 1391
"Maugham's Mosaic of War and Morale": 1457
"Maugham's Novel on Machiavelli": 1592
"Maugham's *'Of Human Bondage'*: The Making of a Masterpiece": 1836
"Maugham's 'Outstation': A Single, Serious Effect": 2320
"Maugham's Pacific": 2341
"Maugham's Play Pleases at Lyceum": 240
"Maugham's Portrait of a Woman": 1247
(Maugham's 'Rain' at the Koitto): 1201
(Maugham's 'Rain' at the Rauma Town Theater): 2246
"Maugham's Short Short-Stories": 1200
(Maugham's Short Stories): 2084
"Maugham's Tragic Tales": 1041
(Maugham's Weakest): 2001
"Maugham-voitto Kanallisteatterissa": 1202
"May Nights at the Play": 230
(Mediocre Comedy at the Town Theater): 2311
"Les Meilleurs nouveautés: Paul Dottin: Somerset Maugham et ses Romans": 747
"The Mellowness of Mr. Maugham": 1929
Memento d'Histoire des Litteratures Anglaises et Americaines: 1796
Memories: 1076
"Men and Letters: Maugham's Bondage": 2305
"Mere Storytellers": 1830
"Merry Feast of Playgoing: Broadway in Review": 1161
"Merry Light Comedy Is Gay *'Jack Straw'* ": 82
(Merry Old England): 731
"*The Merry-Go-Round*": 35
"Mestariteos ja mestarin teos": 1772
"Mid-Channel Creature": 1317
"Midsummer Nights' Fare": 1382
"Miellyttävä lisa englantilaiseen käännöskirjallisuuteen": 1699
A Mirror of the Ministry in Modern Novels: 2146
"Mirth and Magic": 867
"Miscellany: *'For Services Rendered'* ": 1008
"Miscellany: Somerset Maugham": 376, 1135
"Miscellany—Somerset Maugham: *'Our Betters'* ": 505
"Miscellany—Thank Heaven for Mr. Maugham: *'The Constant Wife,'* at the Globe Theatre": 1256
"Miss Anglin Acts Old Chester Role": 139
"Miss Barrymore in *'Lady Frederick'* ": 85
"Miss Barrymore Made Over": 86
"Miss Barrymore's *'Lady Frederick'* a Success": 87

"Miss Billie Burke Acts a Farmer's Wife": 241
"Miss Billie Burke in Serious Role Does Real Dramatic Work": 242
"Miss Diane Cilento as Sadie Thompson": 2201
"Miss Katherine Cornell": 710
"Miss Lottie Venne Plays Bridge": 424
"Miss Margaret Anglin Pleases Anew in Epigrammatic Comedy": 288
"Mitä libristi lukee—ja mitä myy": 2054
"*The Mixture as Before*": 1414
"The Mixtures Almost as Before: New Short Stories by Maugham": 1625
"Modern Acting": 1975
"The Modern Artist": 351
(MODERN DRAMA: MOVEMENTS, FORMS, THEMES): 2243
"Modern Dramaturgy: British and American": 520
(MODERN ENGLISH DRAMA): 2255
MODERN ENGLISH DRAMA: A SURVEY OF THE THEATRE FROM 1900: 1753
(MODERN ENGLISH LITERATURE SINCE 1870: DRAMA AND THE NOVEL): 765
MODERN ENGLISH PLAYWRIGHTS: A SHORT HISTORY OF THE ENGLISH DRAMA FROM 1825: 661
MODERN ENGLISH WRITERS: BEING A STUDY OF IMAGINATIVE LITERATURE 1890-1914: 595
MODERN FICTION: 818
MODERN FICTION: A STUDY OF VALUES: 1258
(Modern Foreign Storytellers): 800
"Modern Life in Books": 764, 876
THE MODERN NOVEL: SOME ASPECTS OF CONTEMPORARY FICTION: 607
MODERN SHORT STORIES: 1786
THE MODERN SHORT STORY: A CRITICAL SURVEY: 1429
DAS MODERNE ENGLISCHE DRAMA: 2255
DER MODERNE ENGLISCHE ROMAN: 2309
DAS MODERNEN DRAMA: STRÖMUNGEN, GESTALTEN, MOTIVE: 2243
"Le Mois Théâtral: Théâtre des Ambassadeurs*Le Pélican*": 1255
"Molly's 'Yes': The Transvaluation of Sex in Modern Fiction": 2350
"Le Monde des Livres-Récits-*Rencontres et Hasards*": 1883
"Le Monde des Livres-Romans-*Plus ça Change*": 1739
"Le Monde des Livres: *'Vacances de Noël'*": 1573
'A Month's Reading in One Book": 1378
"*The Moon and Sixpence*": 347
"THE MOON AND SIXPENCE": 534
" 'THE MOON AND SIXPENCE,' at the New": 565
" *'The Moon and Sixpence'*: Somerset Maugham's Picture of a Ruthless Genius": 352
"Morality and Mr. Maugham": 494
"More Bitters than Gin": 926
"More Books of the Week": 1513
"More Maugham": 472
"More Maughamiana": 1790
"More Suited to Opera: *The Noble Spaniard* on Television": 2129
"Mort cette nuit à 91 ans, sur la Côte d'Azur. Somerset Maugham est peut-être devenu écrivain qu'il était bégue": 2281
"Mort de Somerset Maugham": 2279
"A Mouse from the Mountain and Other Fiction: *The Casuarina Tree*": 620
"Le Mouvement dramatique": 698, 806, 951
"Le Mouvement dramatique en Angleterre": 1143
"Mr. Ashenden, Agent Secret": 857
(Mr. Ashenden, Secret Agent): 857
"Mr. Blakelock Ruins a Play": 1506
"Mr. Drew as a Writer Delights Audience": 88
"Mr. Drew at His Best in *'Smith'* at Empire": 187
"Mr. Edeson's New Play Very Well Liked": 140
"Mr. Hornblow Goes to the Play": 284, 299, 344, 373, 417, 461, 502, 679
"Mr. Maugham": 1165, 1645, 1893, 2007
"Mr. Maugham Abroad": 2053
"Mr. Maugham and the Inquisition": 1686
"Mr. Maugham and Others": 1448
"Mr. Maugham as Footnote": 2073
"Mr. Maugham as Traveller": 848
"Mr. Maugham at Sea": 377
"Mr. Maugham Excels as a Craftsman": 566
"Mr. Maugham in Asia": 507
"Mr. Maugham in China": 464
"Mr. Maugham in the South Seas: Psychology of White Degeneration Caught in Studies": 426
"Mr. Maugham Looks On": 944
"Mr. Maugham on Deck and in the Smoking Room": 501
"Mr. Maugham on the Essentials of Writing": 1422
"Mr. Maugham on Men, Women": 1442
"Mr. Maugham on the Novel": 2068
"Mr. Maugham on the White Man's Burden": 399
"Mr. Maugham Pays Price of Success: Characterless Facility of *Mrs. Dot*": 2130
"Mr. Maugham Reflects on Life": 1294
"Mr. Maugham, Still Urbane": 1635

"Mr. Maugham Sums Up: An Artist and His Values": 1310
"Mr. Maugham Ten Years Ago": 945
"Mr. Maugham's Advice on What's Worth Reading": 1419
"Mr. Maugham's Anthology": 1079
"Mr. Maugham's Irony": 24
"Mr. Maugham's Jumping Johnnies": 1035
"Mr. Maugham's *Land of Promise*": 2131
"Mr. Maugham's Latest": 748
"Mr. Maugham's New Play": 1075
"Mr. Maugham's New Play: *'The Circle'* at the Haymarket": 427
"Mr. Maugham's New Play—Production at the Duke of York's Theatre: *'Loaves and Fishes'* ": 222
"Mr. Maugham's Notions": 2208
"Mr. Maugham's Novel": 567
"Mr. Maugham's Novels": 1137
"Mr. Maugham's *'Penelope,'* at the Comedy": 141
"Mr. Maugham's Strange Play": 378
"Mr. Maugham's Ten Sheared Candidates": 1661
"Mr. Maugham's Valedictory": 2170
"Mr. Maugham's Wartime Memoir": 1462
"Mr. Somerset Maugham": 1311, 1561, 1590, 2282
"Mr. Somerset Maugham: The Most Assured Writer of His Time": 2280
"Mr. Somerset Maugham's Library for School": 2219
"Mr. Somerset Maugham's New Novel": 1257
"Mr. W. S. Maugham Honoured": 2220
"Mr. W. S. Maugham's New Novel": 20
"Mr. W. Somerset Maugham at Home": 587
" 'Mrs. Beamish' and *The Circle*": 2079
"*Mrs. Dot*": 188
" *'Mrs. Dot,'* at the Comedy": 89, 90
" *'Mrs. Dot.'* By W. S. Maugham": 190
" *'Mrs. Dot'* a Thin but Amusing Farce": 189
"Mrs. Tempest Charming in *'Penelope'* Comedy": 142
"Mrs. Woolf and Others": 1269
"Music and Drama": 191
"Music and the Drama": 192, 193
"Music and Drama: *'Caroline'* ": 289
"Music and Drama: *'Jack Straw'* ": 91
"Music and Drama: *'Lady Frederick'* ": 92
"Music and Drama: *'The Noble Spaniard'* ": 143
"Music and Drama: *'Our Betters'* ": 305
"Music and Drama: *'Penelope'* ": 144
"Music and Drama: *'Too Many Husbands'* ": 353
"Music, Art and Drama": 93, 94, 194
"My Uncle Willie": 2318
MY YESTERDAY, YOUR TOMORROW: 2228
"The Mysterious Mr. Maugham": 1651
(Mysticism of the Far East at the Stage of the Town Theater): 1377
"Naamioitten paraati": 731
"Nainen—näyttelijätär": 1878
(Narrative Art in Extended Form): 2124
(Narrative Literature): 1765
"*The Narrow Corner*": 1007
(*The Narrow Corner*): 1813
"Nerokas, kurja elämä": 1757
"Never? Well Hardly Ever": 896
(New and Old Success): 2125
"New Boltons Theatre: *'Loaves and Fishes'* by W. Somerset Maugham": 1832
"New Book Survey": 1393, 1433
(New Books): 1204
"New Books": 1357, 1408, 1409, 1532, 1591, 1728, 1755
"The New Books": 266, 267, 355, 380, 465, 955, 2034
"New Books and Reprints": 1012
"New Books Appraised": 1557, 1631, 1669, 1670, 1957, 2030, 2065, 2176, 2237
(New Books: Foreign Literature): 1070
"New Books in Brief": 1937
"New Books in Brief Review": 622
"New Books—A Selected List": 1209
(New Comedy at the Swedish Theater): 2167
"New Editions: A Christmas List": 1861
(New English Novels): 1662
(New English Play at the National Theater): 812
"New Fiction": 498, 616, 740
"New in the Berg Collection: 1957-1958": 2150
(A New Maugham): 2145
"New Maugham Book Gossip About Spain": 1174
"A New Maugham Collection": 1810
"The New Maugham Play at the Haymarket: *'The Circle'* ": 429
"New Maugham Play Is Hailed in London": 1013
(A New Maugham Translation): 1673
"A New Methodology for Psychological Criticism of Literature: A Case Study for William Somerset Maugham": 2334
"New Novels": 5, 19, 28, 36, 41, 95, 96, 265, 268, 356, 430, 431, 561, 568, 614, 623, 737, 749, 850, 851, 871, 924, 925, 946, 947, 974, 1002, 1014, 1015, 1061, 1080, 1082, 1083, 1167, 1212, 1246, 1273, 1274, 1358, 1368, 1371, 1467, 1528, 1674, 1675, 1877, 2086
"The New Novels—An Actress' Life and Loves": 1260
"The New Novels of Fiction": 1482
"The New Novels: Very Short Stories": 1210

"The New Play": 416, 1071, 1072, 1530
"The New Play: Maugham on Mother-Murder": 733
"New Plays": 195, 232, 255
"The New Plays": 452, 486
"New Plays of the Week": 306
"New Productions of the Week": 290
"New Royalty Theatre: *'The Noble Spaniard'* ": 145
"New Shows of the Month: 'BEFORE THE PARTY' ": 1756
"New Shows of the Month: *'Caroline'* ": 1740
"New Shows of the Month: *'The Circle'* ": 1554
"New Shows of the Month: *'Home and Beauty'* ": 1487
"New Shows of the Month: 'JANE' ": 1647
"New Shows of the Month: *Lady Frederick'* ": 1648
"New Shows of the Month: 'RAIN' ": 1478
"New Shows of the Month: *'The Sacred Flame'* ": 1603
"New Shows of the Month: *'Smith'* ": 1636
"The New Somerset Maugham": 1964
"New Theatre: 'THE MOON AND SIXPENCE' by Edith Ellis": 569
"The New Yorker": 642
(News: Glances at English Literature): 1777
"News in Brief": 2221
"News of the Play World: Somerset Maugham Writes One Scene Far Off Key and Spoils *'Our Betters'* ": 297
"The News-Week in Entertainment": 1084, 1085
1929: 793
" *'Noble Spaniard'* an Amusing Farce": 146
" *'The Noble Spaniard,'* at the Royalty": 147, 148
" *'The Noble Spaniard,'* By Somerset Maugham": 149
"Nos Soirées=Le Théâtre=*Le Pélican*": 1254
"Not Interested": 1298
"Not So Little Women": 1938
"A Notable Study of Decadent Genius": 334
"Note of Weariness in *Sheppey*: Mr. Maugham's Farewell to the Theatre": 2166
"A Note on Maugham Collections": 2120
(The Notebook of an Antiquarian): 575
"Notebooks of Somerset Maugham: The Memoranda of His Lifetime Reveal Varied Interests and Unexpected Ideals": 1707
"Noted English Authors Offer Three New Books": 1227
"Notes and Comments": 2284
"Notes de la Semaine: Le Pacifique à la mode": 649
(Notes of the Week: The Pacific à la mode): 649
"Notes on Chekhov and Maugham": 1727
(NOTES ON THE HISTORY OF ENGLISH AND AMERICAN LITERATURE): 1796
"Notes on Novels": 443
(Nothing Changes): 2042
"Nouveaux Romans Anglais": 1662
(A Novel About Gauguin): 1764
(A Novel aboout Machiavelli): 2056
(THE NOVEL AND IDEAS IN ENGLAND): 2036
THE NOVEL AND SOCIETY: A CRITICAL STUDY OF THE MODERN NOVEL: 1449
(A Novel by Somerset Maugham): 1259
(A Novel from the Far East): 1805
(A Novel from Seventeenth-Century Spain): 2015
"Novel Notes": 6, 11, 14, 42, 97, 750
"A Novel of the Week: An Imaginative Woman": 21
THE NOVEL SINCE 1939: 1691
"A Novelist Ponders Life, Death and God": 1318
(A Novelist-Dramatist: *The Letter* by Somerset Maugham): 690
"Novellisti Maugham": 2339
"Novellitaidetta": 2193
"Novels": 1456
"Novels about Novelists": 948
(Novels and Life): 789
NOVELS AND NOVELISTS: 350
"Novels and Short Stories": 893
(Novels: *Ashenden*): 892
(Novels: *Cakes and Ale*): 980
(Novels: *The Casuarina Tree*): 776
(Novels: *First Person Singular*): 981
"Novels for the Library List: Short Story Collections": 1138
"Novels in Brief": 570
(Novels: *The Moon and Sixpence*): 722
(Novels: *The Narrow Corner*): 1039
NOVELS OF EMPIRE: 1730
"The Novels of Somerset Maugham": 2175
"Novels of the Week: Appeal to an Author": 1410
"Novels of the Week: In Russian Mood": 1359
"Novels of the Week: Modern Mystic": 1535
"Novels of the Week: Tragedy of Error": 1451
(Novels: *The Painted Veil*): 600, 604
"Nuoren miehen kädestä": 2098
"Nuorta Maughamia": 2108
"*Nyt ja Ennen*": 2051
"Obituary for the Human Race": 1583
"Obituary Notes": 2285
OEUVRES COMPLETES: 1718
"*Of Human Bondage*": 269
(*Of Human Bondage*): 2019, 2164

(*Of Human Bondage* by Somerset Maugham): 1225
(Of the South-Tunisian in the Pacific): 1036
"Of W. Somerset Maugham": 755
"Off with the Motley": 1018, 1091
"An Old Acquaintance": 2330
(An Old Master's Farewell: On the Eighty-Fifth Anniversary of William Somerset Maugham): 2169
" 'Old Party' on the Screen": 1860
"An Old Problem Unsolved": 1027
"On Backgrounds": 1440
"*On a Chinese Screen*": 499
(On Display): 767, 824, 900, 987, 988, 989, 990, 991, 1046, 1047, 1118, 1119, 1155, 1188, 1189
(On the Dramatic Technique of W. S. Maugham): 1427
ON SECOND THOUGHT: 1583
100 YEARS OF ENGLISH LITERATURE: 1818
"Onnistunut *Pyhän Liekin* ensi-ilta Mikkelin teatterissa": 2134
"The Opening of the Play Season": 508
(THE OPERA-GLASSES OF THE ENGLISH NOVEL): 2162
"*Orientations*": 15
"Other Books: Selected List": 1261, 1314
"Other Fiction": 751
"Other New Books": 1412, 1413, 1454, 1488, 1537, 1916, 2157
"Other New Books: Literary": 262
"*Our Betters*": 307, 1605, 2202
" *'Our Betters,'* at the Globe": 509
"*Our Betters* by Somerset Maugham": 480
" *'Our Betters'*: Mr. Maugham's Play at the Globe": 510
"Our Booking-Office": 40, 58, 59, 270, 357, 572, 624, 752, 853, 854
"Our Booking-Office: A Blunted Edge": 1538
"Our Booking-Office: The Born Story-Teller": 1455
"Our Booking-Office: A Cynical Craftsman": 1017
"Our Booking-Office: Drama in Fiction": 1139
"Our Booking-Office: It Happened in Spain": 1663
"Our Booking-Office: Malay Scandal": 1088
"Our Booking-Office: Merely Players": 1263
"Our Booking-Office: Review of the Cosmos": 1315
"Our Booking-Office: A Young Man in Paris": 1360
(Our Evenings: The Theater: *The Breadwinner*): 1254
(Our Friend Maugham Tells Home-Truths): 2111
"Out of the Barracks and Bazaars": 1914
"Out of the East": 835
AN OUTLINE OF CONTEMPORARY DRAMA: 664
"Outstanding Novels": 1404, 1405, 1446, 1485, 1541, 1599, 1644, 1749
"The Paint and the Powder": 1747, 1803
"*The Painted Veil*": 558
"THE PAINTED VEIL": 949
(*The Painted Veil*): 2029
PANORAMA DE LA LITTERATURE ANGLAISE CONTEMPORAINE: 684
(PANORAMA OF CONTEMPORARY ENGLISH LITERATURE): 684
(Parade of the Masks): 731
"A Parenthesis": 115
"Paris cette semaine": 2189
(Paris Theater Chronicle: Revival of *The Circle*): 996
(Paris This Week): 2189
(The Parisian Latest⸗At the Bouffes-Parisians: *Home and Beauty*): 1581
"Parmi les livres": 1145, 1278
"Parmi les livres: Somerset Maugham": 1146
(A Particularly Interesting First Night at the Town Theater): 1162
(The Passing Hour): 1048
"A Pattern of Doubt": 1915
THE PATTERNS OF ENGLISH AND AMERICAN FICTION: 1476
"*Le Pélican,* pièce féroce et candide": 1191
"Pencil and Rubber": 1746
" *'Penelope,'* at the Comedy": 150
" *'Penelope'* Is Only Mildly Amusing": 151
"People and Things Theatrical": 152
"People Who Read and Write": 1643
"Persialainen matto": 2168
(Persian Rug): 2168
"Personal Histories": 1434
"Le peuple de Londres et le roman naturaliste": 3
"The Philosopher as Man of Letters": 1823
LA PHILOSOPHIE DE WILLIAM SOMERSET MAUGHAM: 1093
(THE PHILOSOPHY OF WILLIAM SOMERSET MAUGHAM): 1093
"Physician for the Theatre's Ills": 2063
"Physician, Novelist and Playwright": 613
(A Physician's Bondage): 2138
"Les Pièces de la Semaine: *Constance* ou l'Illusion d'une Pièce": 2197
"Les Pièces de Théâtre⸗*Le Cercle*⸗21 Novembre 1928 (Th. de L'OEuvre)": 753
"Les Pièces de Théâtre⸗*Le Cyclone*": 891
"Les Pièces de Théâtre⸗*La Lettre*⸗18 Octobre 1929 (Athénée)": 775
"Les Pieces du mois": 1976
"Pihvin voitto": 1891
"Pikkulämmintä": 1840

"Pilkkeitä": 2061
"Plain Man's Taste": 2263
(Platonic Idea): 1847
"Platoninen idea": 1847
"The Play": 365, 366, 440, 444, 453, 478, 490, 597, 630, 640, 711, 760, 879, 1086, 1087, 1096, 1178, 1428, 1533
"The Play and the Screen": 1097
"The Play of the Day, Old and New": 523
"The Play of the Week": 693
A PLAY TO-NIGHT: 1899
"The Players": 197
"Playhouse and Plays": 665
"The Playhouse: *'The Letter'* by W. Somerset Maugham": 688
"The Playhouse: *'Our Betters'* by W. Somerset Maugham": 1595
"The Playhouse: 'THE PAINTED VEIL' ": 950
"The Playhouse: *'The Sacred Flame'* ": 799
PLAY-MAKING: A MANUAL OF CRAFTSMANSHIP: 225
THE PLAY'S THE THING: 2195
"Plays and Pictures": 687
"Plays and Pictures: *'Home and Beauty,'* at the Playhouse": 1489
"Plays and Pictures: 'RAIN,' at the St. Martin's": 1490
"Plays & Players": 26, 473
"Plays and Players: *'Home and Beauty'* ": 319
PLAYS AND PLAYERS: LEAVES FROM A CRITIC'S SCRAPBOOK: 282
"Plays and Players—A Spaniard, a Frenchman, and an Englishman Contribute to Our Entertainment: Happy Mr. Maugham": 102
"Plays and Players—Two English and Two American Plays of the Opening Season in New York: Further Petrification of Mr. John Drew": 103
(Plays: *The Breadwinner*): 1217
(Plays: *The Circle* 21 November 1928 [L'OEuvre Theatre]): 753
"Plays: *'For Services Rendered,'* at the New Lindsay": 1597
(Plays in Paris: Dress Rehearsals At the Athénée: *The Letter* by Somerset Maugham): 796
(Plays: *The Letter*): 809
(Plays: *The Letter* 18 October 1929 [Athénée]): 775
"Plays Moscow Must Not See": 1596
"The Plays of the Autumn Season": 178
"Plays of the Month": 198
(Plays of the Month): 1976
"Plays of the Season": 224
"The Plays of Somerset Maugham": 1157
"Plays of the Week": 113
"The Plays of the Week": 153, 199
(Plays of the Week: *The Constant Wife* or the Illusion of a Play): 2197
(Plays: *The Sacred Flame*): 891
"*Plays, Volume I (Lady Frederick, Mrs. Dot, Jack Straw)*, Tauchnitz": 1114
"*Plays, Volume II (Penelope, Smith, The Land of Promise)*, Tauchnitz": 1115
"*Plays, Volume III (Our Betters, Caroline, Home and Beauty)*, Tauchnitz": 1116
"*Plays, Volume IV (The Circle, The Constant Wife, The Breadwinner)*, Tauchnitz": 1117
"Plays Worth Seeing. 'Who Will Forgive God?' Real Life in the Theatre": 381
PLAYWRIGHT AT WORK: 1596
THE PLAYWRIGHT: A STUDY OF FORM, METHOD, AND TRADITION IN THE THEATRE: 1783
"A Playwright Who Stumbled into Fame": 67
PLAYWRITING: 2214
"A Plethora of Plays and Players": 163
(Plots of Politics and Love): 2046
"Pluie": 529
"*Points of View*": 2172
"The Polite Traveller": 468
"Politiikan ja lemmen juonet": 2046
"Portrait-Somerset Maugham": 1229
"Possible Influence of George Gissing's WORKERS IN THE DAWN on Maugham's *Of Human Bondage*": 1614
"Posthumous Publication Barred by Maugham, Executor Reports": 2272
(A Powerful Drama at the People's Theater): 1203
"Premieres of the Week": 74, 75, 132, 176
(The Pre-opening Performances: Before *The Sacred Flame*): 910
"Prescription for Painless Reading": 1701
"Presentable Choice": 2055
"The Prince of Entertainers": 1774
"*Princess September and the Nightingale*": 1362
"Private Lives": 820, 1226
THE PROBLEM-PLAY AND ITS INFLUENCE ON MODERN THOUGHT AND LIFE: 713
"A Producer to a Playwright: A Letter to Mr. Somerset Maugham": 1305
"Profiles: Very Old Party—I": 1511
"Profiles: Very Old Party—II": 1511
(Profound Wisdom and Fast-Moving Entertainment): 1618
"Propos sur le Théâtre": 1966
"The Prose Drama": 1973
(A Prototype?): 1733
"Prototyyppikö?": 1733
(Psychological Criminal Drama at the People's Stage): 814

"Psykologist kriminaldrama på Kansan Näyttämo": 814
"Pygmalion at Home and Abroad": 256
"Pyhä Liekki": 855
" *'Pyhä Liekki'* Kansanteatterissa": 1250
"Quarterly Reviews": 837
"QUARTET": 1751
"A Quartet": 617
"Quatre mois aux Indes avec Somerset Maugham": 1293
QUATRO ESTUDOS: 2222
"A Quest for the Absolute": 1519
"Quick Guide to New Reading": 2264
QUINZE ANS DE THEATRE (1917-1932): 1078
(The Race-Question in W. S. Maugham's "The Alien Corn": A Contribution on Interpreting School Literature): 1353
(RAIN): 655, 673, 691
"RAIN": 511
("Rain"): 529
" 'RAIN' Is Striking but Disappointing": 477
"RAIN Produced in Paris": 689
"Rakkautta komedian valossa": 1901
"Rare Traveller": 856
"Die Rassenfrage in W. S. Maughams 'The Alien Corn': Beitrag zur Deutung einer Schullektüre": 1353
"The Razor's Edge": 1543
(*The Razor's Edge*): 1866
"Reader's Choice": 1692, 2174
(Readings in the Novel): 1722, 1862
"Realism and Intelligence": 2190
"The Realism of Somerset Maugham": 606
(The Realism of Somerset Maugham): 606
"Le réalisme de Somerset Maugham": 606
"Reality on the Stage, Make-Believe in Life": 1275
"Recent Books—Authors and Novels: A Personal Choice": 2013
"Recent Books in Brief Review": 470
"Recent Books: Mr. Maugham's Kipling": 1889
"Recent Books: Skeleton in the Cupboard": 863
"Recent Books: Variable Moods": 1890
"Recent Fiction": 12, 271, 724
"Recent Novels": 576
"Recommended Children's Books": 1356
"Recreations of a Novelist": 1943
RED-LETTER NIGHTS: A SURVEY OF POST-ELIZABETHAN DRAMA IN ACTUAL PERFORMANCE ON THE LONDON STAGE: 480, 973
"Reenter Miss Billie Burke": 200
"The Refusers of Bondage": 374
"Reich and Soviet Sign 10-Year Pact": 1363
"The Relation of Theology to Literary Criticism": 1946
RELIGION IN MODERN ENGLISH DRAMA: 2224
"Remembering Mr. Maugham": 2313, 2314
REMEMBERING MR. MAUGHAM: 2315
"Remembrance of Things Past: (15) A Meeting with Somerset Maugham": 2345
"Repeat Performances Appraised": 1971
"Répétitions générales: Au théâtre de l'OEuvre*Le Cercle*": 728
"Les Répétitions Générales Aux Ambassadeurs *Le Cyclone*": 927
"Répétitions Générales *Le Cercle*": 738
"Les Répétitions Générales *La Lettre* à l'Athénée": 801
"The Reporter's Notes: W. Somerset Maugham": 2287
REPRESENTATIVE BRITISH PLAYS: VICTORIAN AND MODERN: 943
REPRESENTATIVE MODERN PLAYS—BRITISH AND AMERICAN—FROM ROBERTSON TO O'NEILL: 781
"Repressed Emotion Is the Keynote in *'Caesar's Wife'* ": 324
"Reprints and New Editions": 1545, 1945
"Reprints, New Editions": 1223, 1364, 1646, 1752, 1844, 1959
"Une Reprise à l'Athénée *La Lettre*": 922
"Re-reading Mr. Maugham": 1136
"Retour de Somerset Maugham": 1611
(The Return of Somerset Maugham): 1611
(Review of Books): 535
(Review of Books: Novels): 1791
"[Review of] Claude Searcy McIver,, WILLIAM SOMERSET MAUGHAM: A STUDY OF TECHNIQUE AND LITERARY SOURCES": 1281
"Reviewers and Reviews": 1653
(Reviews): 1785
"Reviews": 1948
"Reviews: A Comedy of Manners": 433
"Reviews: Fiction": 434
"Reviews: The Golden Age": 512
"Reviews: Man in the Making": 272
"Reviews: Novels": 98, 99
"Reviews of Books—Life in China: Colorful 'Vignettes,' by W. Somerset Maugham": 513
"Reviews of New Plays": 100, 101, 154
"Reviews of Plays": 309
"Reviews: The Primitive Man": 359
"Reviews: Trio": 852
(A Revival at the Athénée: *The Letter*): 922
"Revue annuelle: Le Théâtre anglais": 223
"Revue annuelle: Le Théâtre anglais (1911-1912)": 234
"Revue des livres": 535
"Revue des livres: romans": 1885
"Revue des livres: Romans": 1791
"Revue dramatique": 880, 1911, 1969

"Les Revues étrangères: William Somerset Maugham": 1090
"The 'Ridiculous' Mr. Walpole Endures Agonies at the Hands of Mr. Maugham": 2231
THE RISE AND FALL OF THE WELL-MADE PLAY: 2347
ROGUES' GALLERY: PROFILES OF MY EMINENT CONTEMPORARIES: 1501
(A Role Made to Measure: *The Constant Wife*): 2198
"Un role sur mesure: *Constance*": 2198
"Romaani Gauguinista": 1764
"Romaani Kauko-Idästä": 1805
"Romaani Macchiavellista": 2056
"Romaani 1600-luvun Espanjasta": 2015
"Un roman de Somerset Maugham": 1259
LE ROMAN ET LES IDEES EN ANGLETERRE: 2036
"Un romancier dramaturge: *La Lettre* de Somerset Maugham": 690
DIE ROMANKONZEPTION IN ENGLAND: 1880-1910: 2336
"Les Romans: *'Amours Singulières'* ": 981
"Les Romans: *Ashenden*": 892
"Les Romans: *L'Envoûte*": 722
"Les Romans et la vie": 789
"Les Romans étrangers": 1593, 1642, 1812
"Les Romans: *Le Fugitif*": 1039
"Les Romans: *'La Passe Dangereuse'* ": 600, 604
"Les Romans: *La Ronde de L'Amour*": 980
"Les Romans: *'Le Sortilège Malais'* ": 776
"The Romantic Land of Andalusia": 371
"*La Ronde de L'Amour*": 2014
"The Roving Critic": 634
"Royal Society of Literature": 2135
"Une Rue Somerset-Maugham à Saint-Jean-Cap-Ferrat": 2290
"Ruotsalaisen teaaterin komediauutuus": 2167
(*The Sacred Flame*): 855, 907, 953
"*The Sacred Flame*": 1564
(*The Sacred Flame* at the Ambassadeurs): 905
(*The Sacred Flame* at the People's Theater): 1250
(*The Sacred Flame* by Somerset Maugham [The Playhouse]): 772
" *'The Sacred Flame'* in Rome": 865
"SADIE THOMPSON: November 16, 1944": 1565
"Sadler's Wells Theatre: 'THE MOON AND SIXPENCE' ": 2109
"La saison théâtrale à Londres": 393
"La Saison Théâtrale à Londres": 525, 547, 782, 904, 1049, 1122, 1782
"Sattuma korjaa satoa": 2203
"*Sattuman Satoa*": 2087
"Savoy Theatre: 'Lady Frederick' by W. Somerset Maugham": 1604
"The Scene in Europe": 1125
"Season's End: Broadway in Review": 1051
"Le Secret de Somerset Maugham": 1144
(Secret of the Letter): 869
(The Secret of Somerset Maugham): 1144
"Secret Service Fiction": 2184
SEEING MORE THINGS: 1575
"Seeing the War": 1439
"Seen on the Stage": 658, 659, 725, 899
"Selected Books": 2059
"A Selection of the New Books": 1875
"A Self-Taught Trade": 1283
"Une semaine dans un fauteuil": 1913
"La Semaine dramatique": 672
"La Semaine dramatique: *Le Cercle*": 977
"La Semaine dramatique: *Le Cyclone*": 883
"La Semaine dramatique ∙ *Le Pélican*": 1182
"La Semaine dramatique ∙ Théâtre de la Madeleine ∙ PLUIE": 650
"La Semaine dramatique ∙ Théâtre Sarah Bernhardt ∙ *La Lettre*": 1110
"Le Sens de la vie chez William Somerset Maugham": 1585
(The Sense of Life at William Somerset Maugham's Home): 1585
"*Servitude Humaine*": 2019
"*Servitude Humaine* de Somerset Maugham": 1225
"Set of Six": 915
"Seven Novels": 563
"Seven Novels of the Month": 982
"A Shadow Show of Distant Lands": 385
"Shadows of the Stage": 211
"A Shelf of Recent Books": 573
(*Sheppey*): 1567
"*Sheppey*": 1058
"*Sheppey*: April 18, 1944": 1531
" *'Sheppey,'* at Wyndham's": 1095
(Short Reviews): 2106
"Short Stories": 16
"Short Stories by Two Britons": 1211
(SHORT STORIES OF POLICE ADVENTURES): 2230
"The Short Story": 471
(Short Story Art): 2193
"Short Turns in Divers Places": 636
A SHORT VIEW OF THE ENGLISH STAGE: 1900-1926: 596
"Shorter Notices": 379, 397, 414, 759, 868, 1020, 1142, 1213, 1369
"Shorter Reviews": 1303
"Six by Maugham": 1926
"Six Plays": 697
"The Slum Movement in Fiction": 17
(Smiles, Tears, Laughter: *Caroline*): 2261
" *'Smith.'* By Somerset Maugham": 204
SOME CONTEMPORARY DRAMATISTS: 582

"Some Historical Novels": 13
"Some Leading Cave Men": 252
SOME MODERN AUTHORS: 506
"Some Modern Drama": 1055
"Some New Fiction": 993
"Some Notes on Somerset Maugham": 1128, 1159, 1299
"Some Novels of the Month": 261
"Some of the Highlights": 1335
"Some of the New Fiction: Maugham Returns to the Novel": 274
"Some of the New Plays—Pieces by Americans—and Others—Which Opened the New York Theatrical Season: Mr. Drew's New Play": 202
"Some Plays of the Month Technically Considered": 235, 259
" 'Some Points of View' and 'Summing-Ups': The Aesthetic Views and Creative Path of Somerset Maugham": 2207
SOME PRINCIPLES OF FICTION: 1999
SOMERSET AND ALL THE MAUGHAMS: 2319
"Somerset by Maugham: From Sophisticate to Mystic in New Novel About Americans": 1524
"Somerset Maugham": 506, 941, 1120, 1175, 1205, 1406, 1418, 1682, 1793, 1993, 2000, 2021, 2254, 2291, 2316
SOMERSET MAUGHAM: 1853
(Somerset Maugham Amidst Miracles and the Inquisition): 1997
(Somerset Maugham and the Far East): 1927
"Somerset Maugham and His Work": 2324
"Somerset Maugham and the New Fiction": 360
"Somerset Maugham and Noël Coward": 844
"Somerset Maugham and Paul Gauguin": 2352
"Somerset Maugham and Posterity": 1659
"Somerset Maugham: An Appreciation": 1332, 2300
"Somerset Maugham as Essayist": 1894
"Somerset Maugham as a Teller of Tales": 2211
"Somerset Maugham as a Writer": 2027
(Somerset Maugham at Eighty): 2023
"Somerset Maugham at Eighty": 1974
"Somerset Maugham at 80": 2022
SOMERSET MAUGHAM: A BIOGRAPHICAL AND CRITICAL STUDY: 2210
"Somerset Maugham Burnt Books": 2292
"Somerset Maugham Comes Back from Mandalay": 831
"Somerset Maugham Comes of Age": 2026
(Somerset Maugham, Dramatist): 2222
"Somerset Maugham, Dramaturgo": 2222
"Somerset Maugham, 1874-1965": 2333
"Somerset Maugham 80-vuotias": 2023
"Somerset Maugham est mort": 2293
"Somerset Maugham: An Evaluation": 1802
"Somerset Maugham Gift to Congress Library": 1606
SOMERSET MAUGHAM: A GUIDE: 2238
"Somerset Maugham ihmeiden ja inkvisition parissa": 1997
"Somerset Maugham in His Mantle of Mystery": 564
"Somerset Maugham in Hollywood": 2353
"Somerset Maugham in a Vagrant Mood": 1918
(Somerset Maugham is Dead): 2293, 2295
"Somerset Maugham Is Dead at 91": 2294
"Somerset Maugham kuollut": 2295
"Somerset Maugham: Lucidity versus Cunning": 2113
"Somerset Maugham, un maître de l'humour élégant et du cynicisme léger": 2274
(Somerset Maugham, a Master of Elegant Humor and Light Cynicism): 2274
"Somerset Maugham nous parle de sa pièce *'Avant le Derby'* ": 1613
"The Somerset Maugham of *'The Casuarina Tree'* ": 625
"Somerset Maugham: *On a Chinese Screen*": 2265
"Somerset Maugham on France at War": 1425
(Somerset Maugham on His 80th Birthday): 2009
"Somerset Maugham on the Purpose of Drama": 2117
"Somerset Maugham on the Soviet Stage": 1612
"Somerset Maugham par lui-même": 1779
"Somerset Maugham, RIP": 2307
"Somerset Maugham Revisits Spain": 1169
(Somerset Maugham Speaks of His Play *Home and Beauty*): 1613
(A Somerset-Maugham Street in Saint-Jean-Cap-Ferrat): 2290
"Somerset Maugham Sums Up": 1302
"Somerset Maugham und der Ferne Osten": 1927
"Somerset Maugham und Rudyard Kipling": 1923
"Somerset Maugham, zu 80. Geburstag": 2009
"Somerset Maugham's Debt to MADAME BOVARY and Miss Braddon's THE DOCTOR'S WIFE": 2312
"Somerset Maugham's Imaginary Portrait of a 'Modern' Genius": 361
"Somerset Maugham's New Novel Is One of His Best": 1349
"Somerset Maugham's Spanish Themes": 1168

"Somerset Maugham's Story of a Genius": 362
"Somerset Maugham's Tales of the Pacific": 423
"Somerset Maugham's *The Unknown*: The Problem of Agnosticism": 713
"Somerset Maugham's War Novel": 1474
"Somewhere East of Suez": 626
"Les Sortilèges de Somerset Maugham": 773
"The Soul of Spain": 1154
"A Soul Seeking Heaven": 1696
"Sourires, Larmes, Rires⸗*Caroline*": 2261
"Soviet Critics on Modern English Writing": 2247
"Spain and the Spanish": 39
"The Spain of Somerset Maugham": 1170
"Spanish Themes: Mr. Somerset Maugham's New Book": 1171
"Sparkling Comedy Again with Miss Anglin": 292
"Speaking of Books": 1504, 1505, 1559, 1617, 1660, 1962
"Les Spectacles": 1947, 2020
"Les Spectacles à Paris⸗Aux Ambassadeurs⸗*Le Cercle*": 1010
"Les Spectacles à Paris⸗Les Répétitions Générales⸗A l'Athénée: *La Lettre* de Somerset Maugham": 796
"Les Spectacles⸗Au théâtre St. Georges: DOROTHEE par Jean Wall": 1919
"Les Spectacles de Paris⸗Les Répétitions Générales⸗Aux Ambassadeurs⸗*Le Cyclone*": 938
"Spectacles⸗Echos et propos: Reprise": 911
"Les Spectacles⸗Répétitions Générales⸗Théâtre aux Ambassadeurs⸗*Le Pélican ou une Etrange Famille*": 1195
"Les Spectacles⸗*Le Pélican*⸗Aux Ambassadeurs": 1193
"Spectator's Notebook: The Great Storyteller": 2286
"Spinoza's ETHICS and Maugham": 2038
(Splinters): 2061
"Squaring the Triangle": 574
"St. Martin's Theatre: 'BEFORE THE PARTY' by Rodney Ackland from a Story by W. Somerset Maugham": 1759
"St. Martin's Theatre: *'Home and Beauty'* by W. Somerset Maugham": 1808
"Stage": 1045
"The Stage": 110, 157, 158, 159, 208, 209, 210, 295, 310, 392, 637, 707, 1829
"The Stage and Screen": 1325, 1463, 1539, 1540
(Stage and Screen: At the Theatre Gymnase: ADORABLE JULIA): 1983
"The Stage Society": 29
"Stage Traffic": 1470
"The Stage's December Events: Mr. Maugham Frivols Again, but This Time Not Unpleasantly": 332
"The Stammerer as Hero": 2308
"Stanford Gets Maugham MS": 2025
"Startling Reality Pervades New Book": 1417
(The State of English Letters): 1327
"The State of the Theatre: The Season Climaxes": 1851
"Stirring the Mixture": 1693
STONES FROM A GLASS WINDOW: 17
"Stories and Tracts for the Times": 1584
"The Stories of Somerset Maugham": 2253
"Story and Film": 1694
(The Story of William Somerset Maugham): 2296
"The Storyteller's Art": 1834
"Storyteller's Choice": 1921
"The Story-Telling Art of Mr. Maugham": 1131
"A Straight Novel": 1224
"Strand Theatre: *'The Constant Wife'* by W. Somerset Maugham": 700
"Strange Bedfellows": 675
"*Strictly Personal*": 1458
"A String of Pearls": 1736
"The Strong Crude Novel": 22
STUDIES IN THE NARRATIVE TECHNIQUE OF THE FIRST-PERSON NOVEL: 2234
STUDIES IN THE SHORT STORY: 1732
"A Study in Sepia": 329
A STUDY OF THE MODERN NOVEL, BRITISH AND AMERICAN, SINCE 1900: 746
"Substance and Shadow: The Originals of the Characters in *Cakes and Ale*": 2183
"Success Story": 1671
(Successful First Night of *Sacred Flame* at the Mikkeli Theater): 2134
"*Suezista Itään*": 1953
"The Sum of the Season": 1521
"*The Summing Up*": 1321, 1323
"Summing Up Somerset Maugham at 90": 2252
"Sur le Lac": 1107
"Sur la scène et sur l'écran: Du théâtre du Gymnase: ADORABLE JULIA": 1983
"The Surprises in Somerset Maugham": 2235
(Survey of Translated Literature from the Beginning of the Year): 1737
"The Survival of Mr. Maugham": 1961
SUURI MAAILMANKIRJALLISUUS: 2289
"Syvää viisautta ja vauhdikasta ajanvietetta": 1618
"T. P.'s Bookshelf": 38
"TV: Maugham's *'The Letter'* Revived": 2080
"Tahiti from Melville to Maugham": 331
"Taitamisen vaiheilta": 1705

TALENTS AND GENIUSES: THE PLEASURES OF APPRECIATION: 2096
"Tales by Maugham": 1423
"Tales by Maugham: *'First Person Singular'* a Collection of Merit": 964
"Tales from Kipling": 1895
"Tales of the East by Somerset Maugham": 1077
"Talk with Two Writers": 1776
(Talking about Books): 1742
"Tangled Emotions": 583
"Tea with Mr. Maugham": 2101
IL TEATRO INGLESE: 1140
"Die Technik der Kurzegeschichten William Somerset Maughams": 1702
(The Technique of William Somerset Maugham's Short Stories): 1702
"Techniques and Themes in Early English and American Naturalistic Novels": 2259
"Tekikö viisas aviovaimo oikein?": 1842
"Telegrams in Brief": 1372, 1373
"*Tellers of Tales*": 1374, 1375
"Ten Who Know the Secret of Age": 1920
TENDENCIES OF THE MODERN NOVEL: 1102
"Tendencies of the Modern Novel: I.—England": 1102
"*The Tenth Man*": 408
"*'The Tenth Man,'* at the Globe": 205, 206
"*'The Tenth Man'* at the Globe Theatre": 186
(That Book Savored of Life): 2351
"Theater": 1549, 1784, 1838, 1896, 1902
"The Theater": 1897
"The Theater: Anesthesia and Euthanasia": 1870
(Theater Chronicle: RAIN): 654
"Theater: 'JANE' a Hilarious Cinderella Tale": 1871
(Theater: Jane Marnac in 'RAIN'): 692
"Theater: Maugham's New Play *Sheppey* Based on Religious Theme": 1542
"Theater: Music in the Rain": 1550
"The Theater: New Musical Play in Manhattan": 1551
"The Theater: New Play in Manhattan": 1552
"The Theater: Old Play in Manhattan": 1839, 1898
"The Theaters": 459, 460, 500, 677, 739, 929, 1064, 1065, 1464, 1510, 1879
"Theatre": 1276
THEATRE: 463, 505, 1008, 1075, 1527, 2000
"Theatre": 632, 701, 762, 965, 966, 1019, 1089
"The Theatre": 384, 436, 439, 518, 694, 695, 716, 756, 757, 960, 1016, 1231, 1297, 1459, 1725, 1824, 1868, 1869
"Théâtre": 803, 804, 1978, 2187
"Le Théâtre": 770, 2258
"Le Théâtre": 643, 699, 797, 807, 917, 960, 1206, 1233, 2177, 2232
"Le Théâtre à Paris": 1951
"Le Théâtre: ADORABLE JULIA": 2004
(THE THEATER AND US): 1098
"Le théâtre anglais contemporain": 522
"Le Théâtre anglais depuis la guerre": 959
"Le Théâtre: *Avant Le Derby*": 1588
"The Theatre: Beauty and the Beast": 543
THE 'THEATRE' BOOK OF THE YEAR: 1943-1944: 1531
THE 'THEATRE' BOOK OF THE YEAR: 1944-1945: 1565
"The Theatre: *The Breadwinner*": 842
"The Theatre: *The Circle*": 438, 932
"The Theatre: *The Circle* and *The Breadwinner*": 1544
"The Theatre: *The Constant Wife*": 680
"Théâtre de la Madeleine-PLUIE": 655, 691
LE THEATRE DE WILLIAM SOMERSET MAUGHAM: 1239
"Le Théâtre· Débuts de saison": 952
"Le Théâtre: Deux pièces anglaises et un melodrame française": 1267
"Le Théâtre: DOROTHEE": 1934
THE THEATRE, THE DRAMA, THE GIRLS: 428
"The Theatre: *'East of Suez'* ": 474
LE THEATRE ET NOUS: 1098
"Le Théâtre et la vie": 1094, 1272
"The Theatre: *Fin De* Whatever It is": 1033
"The Theatre: *For Services Rendered*": 1000
"The Theatre: Heartless House": 656
"The Theatre: Here Are Tigers": 657
"The Theatre: *Home and Beauty*": 1491
THE THEATRE IN MY TIME: 1057
"The Theatre in Review": 382, 383
"Théâtre: Jane Marnac dans 'PLUIE' ": 692
"Theatre: *'Lady Frederick,'* at the Savoy": 1598
"The Theatre: Less Efficiency, Ladies, Please!": 718
"The Theatre: *The Letter*": 681
"Le Théâtre: *La Lettre*": 1123
"The Theatre: Maybe It Was the Heat": 884
"The Theatre: The Mixture as Before": 1520
"Le Théâtre: Monstres sacrés": 220
"The Theatre: Mr. Maugham's Apology": 969
"The Theatre: Mr. Maugham's New Play": 544
"The Theatre: Murder, Maugham, and Miss George": 1438
"Theatre: New Plays in Manhattan": 1100
"The Theatre: New Plays in Manhattan": 1099
"The Theatre: Nightmare Drama": 560
"The Theatre: Not Much Change": 1034

"The Theatre of Somerset Maugham": 2144
"The Theatre: Old and New Fires": 777
"Theatre: Old Play in Manhattan": 1322
"The Theatre: One Girl Overboard, One Survivor": 1884
(Theater: Opening of the Season): 952
"The Theatre: *Our Betters*": 517
"The Theatre: Out of the Mothballs": 1825
"The Theatre: Parents' Assistant": 836
THEATRE PROGRAMME: 1973, 1975, 1990
"The Theatre: RAIN": 1176
"The Theatre: 'RAIN' ": 1495
"The Theatre Royal, Stratford: *'The Land of Promise'* by W. Somerset Maugham": 1654
"The Theatre: *The Sacred Flame*": 791
"The Theatre: *Sheppey*": 1066
THE THEATRE SINCE 1900: 1841
"Theatre: Sugar and Salt": 532
"The Theatre: Two Farces": 530
"Theatre Week: Maugham the Romantic": 1312
"The Theatres": 37, 51, 104, 105, 475, 615
"Les Théâtres: *Le Cercle*": 714
(The Theaters: *The Circle*): 714
"Théâtres-Comment nait une collaboration?": 808
"Les Théâtres-*Le Cyclone*": 882
"The Theatres: Dirty Weather at the Garrick": 584
(Theaters: How Is a Collaboration Begun?): 808
(The Theaters: *The Letter*): 771
"Théâtres: *La Lettre*": 809
"Les Théâtres: *La Lettre*": 771
"The Theatres: Maugham, MOON AND SIXPENCE": 585
"The Theatres: Mr. Maugham's Murder Mystery": 702
"Les Théâtres-*Le Pélican*": 1217
"Les Théâtres-PLUIE": 644
(The Theaters: RAIN): 644
"The Theatres: Realism Without Rawness": 810
(Theaters: *The Sacred Flame*): 882
"The Theatres: Strange Doings in Harley Street": 703
"Théâtres: Théâtre de la Madeleine: PLUIE": 673
"The Theatres: Unhappy Families": 1022
THEATRICAL COMPANION TO MAUGHAM: 26, 33, 48, 68, 73, 74, 75, 131, 132, 145, 175, 176, 222, 240, 246, 283, 296, 314, 327, 365, 391, 446, 453, 505, 524, 603, 639, 711, 799, 950, 998, 1027, 1087, 1428, 1619, 2050, 2063
(The Theatrical Month: Theatre of the Ambassadeurs: *The Breadwinner*): 1255
(The Theatrical Season in London): 393, 525, 547, 782, 904, 1049, 1122, 1782
"The Theatrical World": 106
"Theatro drammatico: *'Colui che guadagna il pane'* ": 994
THEIR MOODS AND MINE: 1266
(Then and Now): 2051
"Then and Now": 1607
"Then and Now: Somerset Maugham": 1582
"This Week's Theatres": 557
"Thomas Hardy Veiled": 872
"Those Fabulous Days Before the World War—A London Letter": 1397
THE THREAD OF LAUGHTER: CHAPTERS ON ENGLISH STAGE COMEDY FROM JONSON TO MAUGHAM: 1880
"Three Actresses": 1507
"Three from a Very Old Party": 1770
"Three Maugham Stories Combined": 1821
"Three Professionals": 1252
"Time Passes": 818
(Tired Comedy at the 'Intimate Theater'): 2273
"To the Life": 877
"To See or Not to See": 526, 1043, 1044
"Tom Jones and Philip Carey: Heroes of Two Centuries": 590
"Too Bad to Be True": 973
"Too Many Husbands": 358
"Topics": 2206, 2223
"Topics of the Times": 1421, 1460, 2110
"A Touch of Fever": 1026
"Les traductions": 1650
"Les Traductions": 1848
"The Tragedy of Mr. Maugham's Dramatic Success": 107
"Tranquil Journeys": 866
(Translated Novels): 1734
(Translations): 1650, 1848
"Travelling with Composure": 825
"Treasure Trove": 1073
(The Trembling of a Leaf): 537
"Tribute to Somerset Maugham: An Evening at St. Pancras": 1900
"Truth and Fantasy": 1534
"Tunteen kuolema": 2099
"Turns with a Bookworm": 1264
TWENTIETH CENTURY FORCES IN EUROPEAN FICTION: 1129
TWENTIETH-CENTURY LITERATURE — THE AGE OF INTERROGATION: 1901-1925: 763
TWENTIETH CENTURY PLAYS: 1120
THE TWENTIETH-CENTURY THEATRE: 531
"The Twisted Marriage of Somerset Maugham": 2323
(Two Authors' Wives): 2067
"Two Comedies": 844
(Two English Narrators): 1738
"Two New Plays": 937

"Two Plays Out of Money": 745
"Two Popular Women Stars in New Plays": 207
"Two Printed Texts of Somerset Maugham's *Mrs. Craddock*": 2338
"Two Types of 'Heroes' in Post-War Fiction": 2233
THE TWO WORLDS OF SOMERSET MAUGHAM: 2277.
"Tyylikäs ja hillitty komedia": 2216
"Tyynen meren "äärillä": 1794
"An Uncommercial Play": 31
"Under Western Eyes": 445
UNDERSTANDING DRAMA: TWELVE PLAYS: 2239
"Underworld": 1348
('Undisciplined Generation' in the English Way): 2107
THE UNHOLY TRADE: 1867
"The Unknown": 389
" *'The Unknown,'* at the Aldwych": 390
" *'The Unknown'*: Mr. Maugham's Play at the Aldwych": 391
"An Unpublished Maugham Novel: MS. for Library of Congress": 1815
(Up at the Villa): 1806
"Up at the Villa": 1436, 1461
"Up for Judgment": 1304
(The Use of the Expanded Time Forms in the Novels of W. Somerset Maugham): 1703
"Useful Art of Skipping": 1687
"Uusi ja vanha menestys": 2125
"Uusi Maugham-suomennos": 1673
"Uutta Maughamia": 2145
"The Vagrant Mood": 1954
"Vakoilusta vielä kerran": 2136
(Van Gogh and Gauguin—Heroes of Novels): 602
"Van Gogh et Gauguin—héros de romans": 602
VANHA ILOINEN ENGLANTI: 731
"Vanha ja viisas William Somerset Maugham": 2158
"Vanha Lyvä Maugham": 2121
"Vanhan mestarin jäähy väiset: William Somerset Maugham 85-vuotispäivänä": 2169
"Vanhan parturi-Sheppeyn vaiherikas elämäniltä": 2062
"Vaudeville Theatre: *'The Breadwinner'* ": 873
"Vaudeville Theatre: *'Jack Straw'* by W. Somerset Maugham": 108
"Veal and Vinegar": 826
VERDICT AT MIDNIGHT: SIXTY YEARS OF DRAMATIC CRITICISM: 1874
"A Very Old Party Serves a Rich Potpourri of Literary Memories": 1960
(Victory of Goodness): 2002
"La Vie des Livres: Les Romanesques": 1735
"La Vie littéraire": 577, 628
"La Vie Littéraire": 1270
"La Vie littéraire: Littératures étrangères": 580
"Vient de paraître": 1207
(Viewed from Helsinki): 2060
"Viikon kirjat": 2194
"Viisas neitsyt": 2028
"Viisaudesta pyhään vihaan": 1677
"Les Visages de la Comédie-Dramaturgie Européenne: A l'OEuvre-*Le Cercle*": 719
"Les Visages de la comédie: Freudisme": 648
"A Visit to the South Sea Islands": 409
(A Visit with Somerset Maugham): 2192
"Voimakas näytelmä Kansanteatterissa": 1203
VON CHAUCER BIS SHAW: EINE EINFÜHRUNG IN DIE LITERATUR ENGLANDS: 1630
"Von Me. Bovary zum Chapman Report": 2266
"W. S. Maugham in näytelmätekniikasta": 1427
"W. Somerset Maugham": 582, 942, 943, 1568, 1626, 1720, 1880, 1928, 2335, 2355
W. SOMERSET MAUGHAM: 1232, 2321
"W. Somerset Maugham, *Ahtaat Asuinsijat*": 1804
"W. Somerset Maugham and the Christian Preacher": 1855
"W. Somerset Maugham and Evelyn Waugh": 1776
"W. Somerset Maugham: An Appreciation": 2154
"W. Somerset Maugham: An Appreciation of His Work in the Theatre": 2063
W. SOMERSET MAUGHAM: AN APPRECIATION TOGETHER WITH "SIXTY-FIVE" BY W. SOMERSET MAUGHAM, AND A BIBLIOGRAPHY, AN INDEX OF SHORT STORIES, AND APPRECIATIONS: 1332
"W. Somerset Maugham as a Novelist": 1912
(W. Somerset Maugham at Eighty): 1996
(W. Somerset Maugham at 80): 1977
W. SOMERSET MAUGHAM: A CANDID PORTRAIT: 2171
"W. Somerset Maugham, *Catalina*": 1881, 1994
"W. Somerset Maugham Collections in America": 2120
"W. Somerset Maugham: 1874-1965": 2269
"W. Somerset Maugham (1874-1965): 2298
"W. Somerset Maugham 80-vuotias": 1996
"W. Somerset Maugham—in Profile": 793
"W. Somerset Maugham, Formalist": 196

"W. Somerset Maugham, *Kuu ja Kupariraha*": 1748
(W. Somerset Maugham, *The Moon and Sixpence*): 1748
(W. Somerset Maugham, *The Narrow Corner*): 1804
(W. Somerset Maugham: Novel and Short Story): 829
W. Somerset Maugham: Novelist, Essayist, Dramatist: 550, 554, 564, 587, 588, 591
"W. Somerset Maugham: Novelist and So Forth": 550
(W. Somerset Maugham, Novelist and Storyteller): 934
"W. Somerset Maugham, or Dark and Difficult": 686
"W. Somerset Maugham: *'Pääviotto'* ": 1214
"W. Somerset Maugham: *'Pääviotto'* ": 1567
"W. Somerset Maugham: Playwright and Novelist": 330
"W. Somerset Maugham Portrays Henry James": 1831
(W. Somerset Maugham, *The Razor's Edge*): 1688
W. Somerset Maugham: Regény és Short-Story: 829
"W. Somerset Maugham, Romancier et Conteur": 934
"W. Somerset Maugham: Theme and Variations": 1601
"W. Somerset Maugham, *Veitsen Terällä*": 1688
"W. Somerset Maughams Erzählung 'The Outstation' ": 2095
(W. Somerset Maugham's Story 'The Outstation'): 2095
"Walpole Salver Sold for £7,800": 2066
"Wanderer into Many Lands: *The Gentleman in the Parlour*": 874
"The Waters Wait": 1940
"The Way of Irony and Satire: Maugham, Douglas, Huxley, Lewis": 1056
(The Week's Drama): 672
(The Week's Drama: *The Sacred Flame*): 883
(The Week's Drama: Theatre de la Madeleine: Rain): 650
"The Week's Premieres": 246
"The Week's Theatres": 549, 667, 778, 821, 984, 1042
Die Welt-, Lebens-, und Kunstanschauung William Somerset Maughams: 1888
"Die Weltanschauung William Somerset Maughams": 1500
Das Weltbild in William Somerset Maughams Dramen: 1366
"West of Suez": 446
(What a Bookseller Reads—and What He Sells): 2054
"What I Think of Your Theatre": 521
What's in a Novel: 1479
"When the Bottom Falls Out of a Man's World": 1370
When Winter Comes to Main Street: 466
"Where the Play's the Thing": 181
"Why Maugham Was Miserable": 2328
Wilhelm Meister and His English Kinsmen: Apprentices to Life: 840
"William, Half a Conqueror": 2304
"William Somerset Maugham": 479, 781, 1253, 2105
William Somerset Maugham: 1279, 1758
(William Somerset Maugham and his Novels): 606, 730
"William Somerset Maugham and His Plays": 109
(William Somerset Maugham at Eighty): 2016
"William Somerset Maugham—Dramatist": 1450
"William Somerset Maugham, the Dramatist": 1979
"William Somerset Maugham [1874-1965]": 2354
"William Somerset Maugham 80-vuotias": 2016
"William Somerset Maugham: 'The English Maupassant'—An Appreciation": 1076
William Somerset Maugham et ses Romans: 606, 730
William Somerset Maugham: Some Aspects of the Man and his Work: 2097
"William Somerset Maugham: Some Bibliographical Observations": 1081
William Somerset Maugham: A Study of Technique and Literary Sources: 1208
"William Somerset Maughamin tarina": 2296
(William Somerset Maugham's Worldview): 1500
(Wise Old William Somerset Maugham): 2158
(Wise Virgin): 2028
With a Feather on my Nose: 1716
"With a Superior Sense of Reality": 2035
(Woman—Actress): 1878
"A Woman Who Couldn't Go Straight": 546
(Women in the Jungle): 1111
"A Word to Mr. Gielgud": 1508
"Words and Music": 233
"A Workman in His Workshop": 1177
"World Affairs: The Spirit of France": 1426
"The World at War—i. Submit or Starve—France under the Germans": 1494

(The World-, Life-, and Artistic Vision of William Somerset Maugham): 1888
(The World of Books: *Christmas Holiday*): 1573
(The World of Books: Novels: *Then and Now*): 1739
(The World of Books: Reviews: *Creatures of Circumstance*): 1883
"The World of Books: Why France Fell": 1469
The World of Somerset Maugham: 1157, 1659, 2027, 2081, 2120, 2153, 2155, 2160
"The World of the Theatre": 790, 1003, 1062, 1763, 1814
(Worldly and Heavenly Love): 1995
(The Worldview in William Somerset Maugham's Plays): 1366
The Writer Observed: 1776
"A Writer's Art: Mr. Maugham Sums Up": 1330
(A Writer's Notebook): 1856
"Writer's Point of View: Mr. Somerset Maugham on Purpose of Writing": 1845
Writers and Writing: 1422
Writers at Work: 941
Writers of Today: 1682
The Writings of William Somerset Maugham: A Bibliography: 2088
"Wyndham's Theatre: *'Home and Beauty'* by W. Somerset Maugham": 1846
"Wyndham's Theatre: *'Sheppey'* by W. Somerset Maugham": 1106
"The Year's at the Spring": 723
The Year's Work in the Theatre; 1948-1949: 1720
"Ylielänyttä rotumystiikkaa": 1945
The Youngest Drama: Studies of Fifty Dramatists: 491
"Ystävämme Maugham sanoo häijyjä totuuksia": 2111
"Zwischen Chaos und Erlösung": 1833

Index

PERIODICALS AND NEWSPAPERS

Included here are periodicals and newspapers for which entries occur in the bibliography. Numbers after each title refer to the number(s) of the item in the bibliography where the title appears.

AAMULEHTI: 855, 1678, 1764, 1842, 1901, 2002, 2051, 2084, 2136, 2161, 2164, 2216
ACADEMY: 4, 10, 15, 18, 22, 24, 35, 52, 57, 70, 172, 218, 249
AJAN KIRJA: 1737
AMERICAN BOOK COLLECTOR: 2147
AMERICAN MERCURY: 1771
AMERICAN PLAYWRIGHT: 235, 259
ANGLIA: 1500
LES ANNALES POLITIQUES ET LITTERAIRES: 643, 649, 770, 1005, 1132, 1233, 1265
ARCHIV FÜR DAS STUDIUM DER NEUEREN SPRACHEN: 1928, 1980, 1981
ARIZONA QUARTERLY: 1915
ARTS: 1632, 1795, 1828
ARTS AND DECORATION: 432, 662, 663, 862, 909
ARTS/SPECTACLES: 1857, 1913, 2003, 2197, 2267
ARVOSTELEVA KIRJALUETTELO: 1748, 1804, 1881, 1994
ARVOSTELEVA LUETTELO SUOMENKIELISESTÄ KIRJALLISUUDESTA: 1688.
ATHENAEUM: 5, 8, 16, 19, 25, 28, 32, 36, 41, 45, 61, 62, 63, 95, 96, 120, 121, 122, 164, 165, 212, 214, 226, 264, 281, 335, 345, 350, 377
ATLANTIC MONTHLY: 1199, 1245, 1326, 1381, 1465, 1466, 1493, 1555, 1615, 1692, 1768, 1958, 2174
BEIBLATT ZUR ANGLIA: 1280
BOOK-COLLECTOR'S QUARTERLY: 1081
BOOKMAN (Lond): 6, 11, 14, 20, 42, 55, 97, 273, 329, 330, 399, 406, 457, 472, 499, 516, 578, 617, 750, 835, 838, 861, 920, 1050, 1147
BOOKMAN (NY): 11, 178, 247, 261, 331, 394, 447, 470, 482, 526, 555, 556, 573, 625, 636, 642, 646, 670, 734, 736, 893, 906, 982
BOOKS ABROAD: 2154
BOOKS AND BOOKMEN: 2299, 2328, 2331, 2332
BOOKS OF THE MONTH: 993, 1269, 1304, 1365, 1383, 1384, 1443, 1534, 1584, 1675
BOSTON EVENING TRANSCRIPT: 263, 334, 370, 371, 409, 558, 609, 832, 864, 1211, 1361, 1367, 1417, 1456
BOSTON GLOBE: 1524
BOSTON UNIVERSITY STUDIES IN ENGLISH: 2079
BULLETIN OF THE NEW YORK PUBLIC LIBRARY: 2150
CANADIAN BOOKMAN: 374
CANADIAN FORUM: 1205, 1251, 1354, 1935
CANADIAN MAGAZINE: 224
CATHOLIC WORLD: 709, 766, 971, 1104, 1105, 1181, 1331, 1357, 1408, 1409, 1496, 1532, 1558, 1569, 1591, 1728, 1877, 1902, 1916, 2157
CENTURY: 590, 634, 837
CHICAGO DAILY TRIBUNE: 822, 897, 1174, 1187, 1227, 1286
CHICAGO SUN BOOK WEEK: 1548, 1592, 1641
CHICAGO SUNDAY TRIBUNE BOOKS: 1516, 1576, 1658, 1760, 1918, 1922, 1986, 2039
CHICAGO SUN-TIMES BOOK WEEK: 1679
CHRISTIAN SCIENCE MONITOR: 859
CHRISTIAN SCIENCE MONITOR WEEKLY MAGAZINE SECTION: 1169, 1196, 1317, 1396, 1397, 1400, 1497, 1546, 1784
CHRONIQUE DES LETTRES: 522

College English: 1418, 1601, 1974
Collier's: 102, 103, 201, 202
Commonweal: 630, 760, 968, 1096, 1097, 1178, 1324, 1325, 1342, 1420, 1439, 1463, 1499, 1513, 1539, 1540, 1685, 1721, 1745, 1829, 1929, 1992, 1993, 2068
Comoedia: 652, 691, 738, 754, 774, 801, 802, 808, 886, 910, 922, 927, 953
Contemporary Review: 1793, 2300
Cornhill Magazine: 1594
Criterion: 1282
La Croix: 2293
Current Literature: 107
Current Opinion: 361
Desiderata: 1690
Deutsche Rundschau: 1923, 2009
Dial: 12, 271, 316, 322, 384, 402, 403, 436, 451, 485, 542, 653, 694, 695, 756, 757
Drama: 2304
Dramatic Mirror: 325, 358, 408, 418
Dramatist: 188, 248, 404, 492, 511, 660
Educational Theatre Journal: 2117
Elanto: 1734
Emory University Quarterly: 2241
Encore: 2190
Encounter: 2308
Englische Studien: 1416
English: 2114, 2333
English Fiction in Transition: 2113
English Journal: 1601
English Language Notes: 2338
English Review: 256, 867, 1016
English Studies: 1323
Etelä-Saimaa: 1813, 2123, 2311
Etelä-Suomen Sanomat: 1729, 1785
Etudes: 1791, 1885
Etudes Anglaises: 1219, 1220, 1236, 1238, 1290, 1376, 1850, 1917, 1932, 1948, 2037, 2052, 2074, 2075, 2077, 2093, 2148, 2242, 2244, 2312
Europe: 2177
Everybody's Magazine: 197
Le Figaro: 393, 577, 628, 672, 690, 728, 729, 772, 786, 911, 912, 913, 996, 1048, 1185, 1191, 1192, 1581, 1613, 1919, 1983, 2182, 2188, 2256, 2279, 2290
Le Figaro Hebdomadaire: 577, 628, 672, 728
Le Figaro Litteraire: 1270, 1819, 1998, 2196, 2258, 2275
Le Figaro Supplement Litteraire: 522, 575, 721
Fortnightly Review: 1102, 1316, 1802
Forum: 76, 77, 133, 171, 382, 383, 888, 1037, 1179, 1230, 1287, 1341
France-Illustration: 1976
France-Soir: 2281
Freeman: 379, 397, 414
Graduate Student of English: 2184
Grande Review: 794, 795
Graphic: 27, 37, 51, 104, 105, 106, 113, 127, 162, 163, 245, 276, 301, 312, 333, 378, 405, 458, 508, 523, 668, 669, 764, 788, 830, 875, 876, 885, 919
Green Book Magazine: 233, 257, 280, 291, 308.
Gringoire: 720, 727, 767, 773, 783, 792, 800, 824, 857, 900, 907, 908, 934, 939, 976, 978, 987, 988, 989, 990, 991, 1025, 1036, 1046, 1047, 1111, 1118, 1119, 1123, 1144, 1155, 1188, 1189, 1207, 1225, 1229, 1254, 1309, 1432
Harper's Magazine: 1300, 1483, 1659, 1755, 2034
Harper's Weekly: 67, 211
Helsingin Sanomat: 798, 849, 1203, 1214, 1250, 1673, 1794, 1840, 1882, 1953, 1995, 1996, 2046, 2047, 2082, 2099, 2111, 2127, 2138, 2205, 2227, 2283, 2342
Holiday: 1964
Hommes et Mondes: 1806, 1947, 2020
Horn Book Magazine: 1351
House and Garden: 1472
Hufvudstadsbladet: 814, 2213, 2273
L'Humanite: 2266
Ilkka: 2061
Illustrated London News: 34, 49, 71, 78, 89, 129, 141, 147, 173, 205, 215, 216, 219, 250, 277, 326, 341, 390, 429, 509, 527, 565, 671, 790, 817, 1001, 1003, 1062, 1095, 1763, 1814, 1894, 2024, 2133
L'Illustration: 545, 644, 714, 771, 882, 1217
Independent (NY): 93, 94, 194, 266, 401, 622, 641
Inostrannaja Literatura: 2207
Jahrbuch für Amerikastudien: 2120
John O'London's Weekly: 319, 381, 423, 1032, 2026, 2027
Journal and Courier: 2245
Journal de Geneve: 562, 618, 744, 1006, 1054, 1126, 1228, 1327, 1560, 1570, 1662, 1779, 1782, 1854, 1951
Le Journal des Debats: 3, 535, 537, 650, 673, 796, 883, 938, 977, 1010, 1110, 1182, 1195, 1259
Journal des Debats, Hebdomadaire: 537, 883
Journal of English and Germanic Philology: 1281, 1949
Journal of Religion: 1946
Kaleva: 2062, 2124
Kaltio: 1633, 2098
Kansan Uutiset: 2348

KARJALA: 1162, 1377, 2028, 2064
KARJALAINEN: 1738
KAUPPALEHTI: 1997, 2126, 2194, 2297
KESKIPOHJANMAA: 2121
KIRJASTOLEHTI: 1688, 1748, 1804, 1881, 1994
KIRKUS: 1156, 1190, 1276, 1321, 1340, 1362, 1374, 1398, 1458, 1461, 1480, 1543, 1607, 1624, 1668, 1672, 1751, 1769, 1799, 1859, 1865, 1954, 2008, 2172
KULTUR: 2226
LAPIN KANSA: 1733
LAPIN LOIMU: 2044
LAROUSSE MENSUEL ILLUSTRE: 1255
DIE LEBENDEN FREMDSPRACHEN: 1833
LIBRARY CHRONICLE: 1836
LIBRARY JOURNAL: 1356, 1393, 1433, 1557, 1631, 1669, 1670, 1725, 1824, 1868, 1869, 1957, 2030, 2065, 2101, 2176, 2237
LIBRISTI: 2054
LIFE: 83, 84, 137, 138, 183, 184, 231, 254, 287, 304, 398, 448, 449, 483, 598, 647, 717, 718, 965
LIFE AND LETTERS: 1157
LISTENER: 1080, 1307, 1402, 1933, 2048, 2086, 2269
LITERARY DIGEST INTERNATIONAL BOOK REVIEW: 497, 546, 611
LITERARY SUPPLEMENT TO THE SPECTATOR: 860, 874
LITERATURE: 2, 13
LONDON MERCURY: 388, 441, 592, 629, 758, 975, 1011, 1029, 1170, 1209, 1231, 1261, 1305, 1314, 1348
LOOK: 2192, 2323
MAASEUDUN TULEVAISUUS: 1805, 2056, 2107, 2344
MANCHESTER GUARDIAN: 1226, 1294, 1355, 1390, 1401, 1448, 1528, 1574, 1638, 1664, 1711, 1892, 1893, 2007, 2122
MEANJIN QUARTERLY: 2345
MENTOR: 613
LE MERCURE DE FRANCE: 602, 692, 803, 804, 1656, 1657, 1700, 1766, 1767, 1816, 1817, 1955, 1978, 2090, 2091, 2187
METROPOLITAN MAGAZINE: 149, 190, 204
MICHIGAN QUARTERLY REVIEW: 2352, 2353
MODERN DRAMA: 2144, 2212
MODERN LANGUAGE REVIEW: 1614, 1948
MODERN REVIEW: 2211
LE MONDE: 2274
MONTH: 2253
MUNSEY'S MAGAZINE: 110, 157, 158, 159, 208, 209, 210, 252, 295, 310, 392
NASH'S-PALL MALL MAGAZINE: 1076
NATION (Lond): 111, 160, 260, 351, 386
NATION (NY): 46, 64, 65, 119, 123, 124, 166, 191, 213, 275, 294, 309, 311, 348, 349, 360, 419, 420, 462, 504, 505, 682, 683, 742, 866, 872, 889, 933, 963, 1020, 1067, 1068, 1069, 1142, 1152, 1213, 1274, 1298, 1306, 1369, 1444, 1445, 1471, 1481, 1525, 1529, 1553, 1608, 1736, 1886, 1937, 2045
NATION AND THE ATHENAEUM: 437, 471, 484, 512, 539, 570, 571, 599, 621, 651, 687, 847, 852, 871
NATIONAL REVIEW (Lond): 17, 1149, 1328
NATIONAL REVIEW (NY): 2305, 2307
LA NEF: 1714
DIE NEUEREN SPRACHEN: 1928, 2095, 2265
NEUPHILOLOGISCHE MITTEILUNGEN: 1831
NEW OUTLOOK: 1043, 1044
NEW REPUBLIC: 262, 298, 347, 415, 422, 563, 638, 710, 724, 826, 887, 921, 972, 1007, 1107, 1121, 1180, 1252, 1289, 1350, 1375, 1434, 1436, 1470, 1518, 1580, 1627, 1671, 1858, 1939, 1940, 2059, 2317
NEW STATESMAN: 265, 376, 425, 443, 463, 469, 505, 532, 538, 561, 678, 759, 844, 848, 868
NEW STATESMAN (New Series): 2118, 2225
NEW STATESMAN AND NATION: 937, 945, 962, 1008, 1026, 1075, 1135, 1136, 1165, 1212, 1224, 1256, 1296, 1368, 1407, 1414, 1467, 1486, 1489, 1490, 1517, 1527, 1564, 1597, 1598, 1605, 1645, 1674, 1708, 1750, 1961, 1963, 2012
NEW WORLD (Lond): 375
NEW YORK CALL: 346
NEW YORK DRAMATIC MIRROR: 100, 101, 153, 154, 161, 196, 199, 227, 239, 243, 286
NEW YORK DRAMATIC NEWS: 209, 306
NEW YORK EVENING POST: 91, 92, 143, 144, 289, 305, 336, 353, 440, 476, 477, 481, 597, 696
NEW YORK EVENING POST LITERARY REVIEW: 395, 442, 465, 627
NEW YORK HERALD: 87, 88, 140, 142, 242, 288
NEW YORK HERALD TRIBUNE: 615, 677, 739, 929, 1064, 1065, 1160, 1464, 1510, 1879
NEW YORK HERALD TRIBUNE BOOK REVIEW: 1545, 1622, 1646, 1683, 1687, 1723, 1752, 1844, 1864, 1873, 1944, 1959, 1960, 2032, 2170
NEW YORK HERALD TRIBUNE BOOKS: 574, 626, 665, 819, 856, 895, 896, 983, 1041, 1055, 1186, 1223, 1264, 1275, 1318, 1334, 1364, 1370, 1382, 1395, 1415, 1442, 1457, 1477

New York Herald Tribune Weekly Book Review: 1519, 1586
New York Post: 1172
New York Sun: 80, 86, 128, 136, 179, 200, 230, 236, 277, 300, 320, 339, 439, 467, 612, 674, 745, 935, 1071, 1072, 1530
New York Sun and Globe: 487
New York Times: 66, 85, 146, 151, 187, 189, 229, 240, 253, 292, 365, 366, 444, 453, 478, 490, 603, 640, 711, 780, 879, 903, 923, 940, 1013, 1086, 1087, 1164, 1311, 1363, 1421, 1428, 1460, 1533, 1589, 1639, 1689, 1743, 1797, 1798, 1849, 1941, 1942, 1984, 2005, 2006, 2011, 2022, 2025, 2080, 2103, 2110, 2165, 2173, 2199, 2206, 2218, 2223, 2262, 2272, 2278, 2291, 2294, 2302, 2313
New York Times Book Review: 116, 130, 134, 269, 362, 385, 411, 412, 489, 496, 501, 554, 566, 608, 748, 831, 845, 944, 948, 1004, 1077, 1079, 1131, 1168, 1200, 1247, 1302, 1349, 1378, 1419, 1422, 1423, 1425, 1441, 1462, 1482, 1504, 1505, 1512, 1559, 1577, 1609, 1617, 1635, 1643, 1660, 1686, 1707, 1719, 1762, 1776, 1780, 1781, 1801, 1860, 1861, 1914, 1936, 1962, 1971, 2035, 2248, 2252
New York Times Book Review and Magazine: 369
New York Times Magazine: 1726, 1920, 1970, 2140
New York Tribune: 228, 297, 323, 324, 416, 445, 459, 460, 500
New York World: 69, 82, 139, 180, 207, 241, 285, 303, 332, 407, 452, 486, 637, 707, 733, 755, 839
New York World-Telegram: 1522, 1542
New York World-Telegram and Sun: 1871
New Yorker: 863, 884, 898, 986, 1033, 1034, 1059, 1158, 1184, 1242, 1295, 1338, 1347, 1379, 1386, 1387, 1394, 1431, 1437, 1438, 1473, 1511, 1514, 1520, 1616, 1620, 1665, 1709, 1775, 1825, 1870, 1884, 1908, 2033, 2141, 2284
News-Week [or Newsweek]: 1084, 1085, 1150, 1183, 1221, 1284, 1312, 1337, 1412, 1413, 1430, 1453, 1454, 1488, 1537, 1549, 1550, 1572, 1666, 1713, 1838, 1896, 2142, 2268
North American Review: 1040
La Nouvelle Revue: 880
Les Nouvelles Litteraires: 541, 548, 604, 648, 719, 741, 743, 768, 797, 1090, 1206, 1240, 1293, 1573, 1588, 1611, 1735, 1739, 1883, 1924, 1934, 2004, 2198, 2261, 2276
Nuova Antologia: 994
Observer (Lond): 318, 321, 372, 410, 430, 455, 468, 493, 549, 557, 567, 614, 666, 667, 732, 737, 778, 820, 821, 924, 925, 928, 984, 1002, 1042, 1061, 1063, 1134, 1177, 1246, 1329, 1371
One Act Play Magazine: 1297
Outlook (Lond): 515, 560, 579
Outlook (NY): 267, 355, 380, 645, 715, 716
Outlook and Independent: 843, 901, 955
Pacific Spectator: 2073
Paivan Sanomat: 2145, 2296, 2340
Papers of the Bibliographical Society of America: 1790, 1843, 2215
Papers of the Michigan Academy of Science, Arts, and Letters: 2183
Paris-Match: 2189, 2249, 2288
Parnasso: 1891, 2010, 2106, 2168
Paru: 1593, 1642, 1812
Pearson's Magazine: 152, 181
Play Pictorial: 169, 238, 337, 338, 456, 685
Playgoer and Society Illustrated: 126, 167, 186
Poet Lore: 1450
Publications of the Modern Language Association: 2233
Publisher's Weekly: 328, 2285
Punch: 40, 58, 59, 68, 156, 185, 203, 221, 244, 258, 270, 293, 315, 357, 363, 387, 435, 514, 519, 572, 624, 704, 752, 811, 853, 854, 870, 930, 1017, 1024, 1088, 1103, 1139, 1263, 1315, 1360, 1455, 1538, 1634, 1663, 1741, 1792, 2326
Quarterly Review: 2324
Quest: 2175
Reading and Collecting: 1253
Redbook: 1566
Religion in Life: 1855
Reporter: 2287
La Revue Anglo-Americaine: 726, 729, 787, 985, 992, 1009, 1060, 1108, 1113, 1114, 1115, 1116, 1117, 1215, 1216
La Revue Blanche: 9
Revue Bleue: 952, 1070, 1204, 1267
La Revue de France: 529, 536, 589, 605, 606, 633, 705, 712, 769, 805, 813, 827, 957, 997, 1030, 1031, 1094, 1109, 1124, 1141, 1237, 1268, 1272, 1291, 1346
La Revue de la Mediterranee: 1777, 1966
La Revue de Paris: 698, 806, 951, 959, 1143, 1145, 1146, 1243, 1278, 2200, 2232
Revue des Deux Mondes: 784, 785, 1722, 1778, 1862, 1911, 1969, 2316

LA REVUE DES LECTURES: 600, 722, 747, 753, 775, 776, 891, 892, 980, 981, 1039
REVUE GERMANIQUE: 155, 223, 234
LA REVUE HEBDOMADAIRE: 676
LA REVUE MONDIALE: 580, 699, 789, 807, 960
LA REVUE UNIVERSELLE: 917
SAIMAN SANOMAT: 2329
SAN FRANCISCO CHRONICLE: 1676, 1731, 1925, 1926
SAN FRANCISCO SUNDAY CHRONICLE: 1625, 1701, 1810, 1875, 2151
SATAKUNNAN KANSA: 2042, 2043
SATURDAY BOOK: 1561
SATURDAY EVENING POST: 2318
SATURDAY REVIEW (Lond): 23, 31, 53, 54, 98, 99, 114, 115, 177, 182, 272, 313, 342, 359, 389, 424, 433, 434, 446, 494, 498, 543, 544, 616, 656, 657, 740, 777, 836, 850, 969, 974, 1019, 1028, 1089, 1138
SATURDAY REVIEW (NY): 1872, 1903, 1921, 1987, 2027, 2159, 2217, 2301, 2306, 2327, 2330, 2341
SATURDAY REVIEW OF LITERATURE: 593, 675, 693, 825, 858, 872, 915, 926, 995, 1035, 1073, 1127, 1154, 1234, 1235, 1283, 1301, 1332, 1335, 1343, 1344, 1385, 1392, 1435, 1447, 1492, 1547, 1575, 1600, 1651, 1661, 1696, 1710, 1715, 1754, 1770, 1774, 1822
SAVOMAA: 2029
SAVON SANOMAT: 2060, 2071, 2134
SCHOLASTIC: 1175
SCHOOL AND SOCIETY: 1851
SCOTS MAGAZINE: 1440
SEWANEE REVIEW: 1727
SOUTHERN REVIEW: 1303
SOVIET REVIEW: 2235, 2247
SPECTATOR (Lond): 1, 7, 56, 400, 438, 474, 517, 530, 551, 560, 620, 680, 681, 791, 842, 932, 961, 1000, 1021, 1066, 1092, 1128, 1159, 1197, 1249, 1299, 1380, 1411, 1424, 1452, 1491, 1495, 1536, 1544, 1578, 1629, 1637, 1695, 1724, 1744, 1863, 1887, 2018, 2128, 2208, 2286, 2325
SPORTS ILLUSTRATED: 2310
SPRINGFIELD DAILY REPUBLICAN (Mass): 1469
SPRINGFIELD SUNDAY REPUBLICAN (Mass): 274, 352, 421, 426, 507, 513, 583, 1308, 1684, 1821, 1906, 1907
SPRINGFIELD SUNDAY UNION AND REPUBLICAN (Mass): 610, 823, 964, 1345, 1391, 1399
STAGE: 1406
STECHERT-HAFNER BOOK NEWS: 2152
SUNDAY SPECIAL (Lond): 26
SUNDAY TIMES (Lond): 283, 473, 480, 533, 534, 639, 973, 1027, 1506, 1507, 1508
SUNDAY TIMES AND SPECIAL (Lond): 33, 48, 73, 74, 75, 131, 132, 175, 176, 246
SUOMALAINEN SUOMI: 1677, 1705, 1772, 1847, 2085, 2125, 2156, 2203
SUOMEN KUVALEHTI: 2158
SUOMEN SOSIALIDEMOKRATTI: 812, 1618, 1811, 1837, 2001, 2076, 2100, 2102, 2191, 2351
SYNTHESES: 1977
T. P.'S WEEKLY: 21
TAITEEN MAAILMA: 1742
LE TEMPS: 488, 525, 547, 581, 631, 654, 655, 761, 782, 809, 894, 904, 905, 1023, 1049, 1101, 1122, 1193, 1218, 1277
TEXAS STUDIES IN LITERATURE AND LANGUAGE: 2350
THEATRE ARTS: 1477, 1521, 1562, 1563, 1568, 1652, 1653, 1807, 2063
THEATRE ARTS MONTHLY: 723, 931, 1051, 1125, 1153, 1161, 1319, 1320
THEATRE MAGAZINE: 109, 112, 195, 198, 232, 255, 284, 299, 344, 373, 417, 461, 502, 521, 679, 958
THEATRE WORLD (Lond): 999, 1018, 1058, 1091, 1241, 1477, 1487, 1554, 1603, 1612, 1636, 1647, 1648, 1740, 1756
TIME: 518, 540, 632, 701, 762, 815, 816, 890, 966, 979, 1038, 1099, 1100, 1112, 1151, 1176, 1222, 1285, 1322, 1339, 1389, 1459, 1498, 1515, 1551, 1552, 1571, 1621, 1667, 1712, 1839, 1897, 1898, 1909, 1910, 2143, 2298, 2303
TIME AND TIDE: 1273
TIMES (Lond): 29, 30, 38, 44, 60, 81, 108, 117, 118, 135, 145, 168, 170, 222, 237, 251, 279, 302, 314, 327, 343, 391, 427, 450, 454, 475, 510, 524, 553, 569, 601, 688, 689, 700, 799, 841, 865, 873, 878, 918, 950, 998, 1014, 1082, 1106, 1171, 1194, 1244, 1257, 1330, 1333, 1358, 1372, 1373, 1388, 1509, 1523, 1595, 1596, 1604, 1606, 1619, 1654, 1706, 1717, 1759, 1773, 1808, 1815, 1820, 1830, 1832, 1834, 1845, 1846, 1876, 1889, 1890, 1900, 1904, 1905, 1938, 1967, 2013, 2031, 2055, 2066, 2072, 2083, 2092, 2109, 2115, 2129, 2130, 2131, 2135, 2149, 2166, 2178, 2179, 2180, 2185, 2186, 2201, 2202, 2209, 2219, 2220, 2221, 2257, 2264, 2271, 2280, 2282, 2292

Times Literary Supplement (Lond): 47, 268, 356, 431, 464, 568, 623, 697, 749, 834, 851, 946, 947, 1012, 1015, 1083, 1137, 1167, 1210, 1260, 1262, 1310, 1359, 1403, 1410, 1426, 1451, 1494, 1535, 1587, 1590, 1628, 1681, 1693, 1694, 1746, 1895, 1943, 1972, 2021, 2053, 2078, 2116, 2240, 2263

Touchstone: 364

Truth (Lond): 50, 72, 79, 90, 148, 150, 174, 206, 220, 576, 584, 585, 702, 703, 751, 810, 833, 949, 1022, 1747, 1803

Turun Sanomat: 1567, 2016, 2246, 2339

Työkansan Sanomat: 2087

University of Colorado Studies: 2320

University of Kansas City Review: 2038

Uusi Aura: 2167

Uusi Suomi: 869, 1201, 1202, 1248, 1757, 1787, 1788, 1945, 2015, 2023, 2057, 2058, 2108, 2112, 2119, 2169, 2193, 2270, 2295, 2343

Valvoja: 1765

Valvoja-Aika: 1427

Vapaa Sana: 1649

La Vie Intellectuelle: 1585

Viikkosanomat: 2067

Vogue: 658, 659, 725, 899, 1045, 1582, 1950, 2314

Weekly Review (NY): 317, 340, 367, 396, 413

The Windmill: 1659

World To-Day: 125, 192, 193

Yale Review: 936, 1074, 1404, 1405, 1446, 1485, 1541, 1599, 1644, 1749

Yale University Library Gazette: 2069

Ylioppilaslehti: 1699, 1835, 1878, 1991, 2104

Zeitschrift für Französischen und Englischen Unterricht: 846

Zeitschrift für Neusprachlichen Unterricht: 1352, 1353

Index

FOREIGN LANGUAGES

Included here are the languages in which articles and books listed in the bibliography originally appeared. Numbers under each language refer to items in the bibliography where the foreign-language title is given. English language items are not listed.

Finnish: 731, 793, 798, 812, 814, 849, 855, 869, 1162, 1201, 1202, 1203, 1214, 1248, 1250, 1377, 1427, 1567, 1618, 1633, 1649, 1673, 1677, 1678, 1688, 1699, 1705, 1729, 1733, 1734, 1736, 1738, 1742, 1748, 1757, 1764, 1765, 1772, 1785, 1787, 1788, 1794, 1804, 1805, 1811, 1813, 1835, 1837, 1840, 1842, 1847, 1878, 1881, 1882, 1891, 1901, 1945, 1953, 1991, 1994, 1995, 1996, 1997, 2001, 2002, 2010, 2015, 2016, 2023, 2028, 2029, 2042, 2043, 2044, 2046, 2047, 2051, 2054, 2056, 2057, 2058, 2060, 2061, 2062, 2064, 2067, 2070, 2071, 2076, 2082, 2084, 2085, 2087, 2098, 2099, 2100, 2102, 2104, 2105, 2106, 2107, 2108, 2111, 2112, 2119, 2121, 2123, 2124, 2125, 2126, 2127, 2134, 2136, 2138, 2145, 2156, 2158, 2161, 2164, 2167, 2168, 2169, 2191, 2193, 2194, 2203, 2205, 2213, 2216, 2227, 2246, 2270, 2273, 2283, 2289, 2295, 2296, 2297, 2311, 2329, 2340, 2342, 2344, 2348, 2351

French, 3, 9, 155, 223, 234, 393, 488, 522, 525, 529, 535, 536, 537, 541, 545, 547, 548, 552, 562, 575, 577, 580, 581, 589, 600, 602, 604, 605, 606, 618, 628, 631, 633, 643, 644, 648, 649, 650, 652, 654, 655, 672, 673, 676, 684, 690, 691, 692, 698, 699, 705, 712, 714, 719, 720, 721, 722, 726, 727, 728, 729, 730, 738, 741, 743, 744, 747, 753, 754, 761, 767, 768, 769, 770, 771, 772, 773, 774, 775, 776, 779, 782, 783, 784, 785, 786, 787, 789, 792, 794, 795, 796, 797, 800, 801, 802, 803, 804, 805, 806, 807, 808, 809, 813, 824, 827, 857, 880, 882, 883, 886, 891, 892, 894, 900, 904, 905, 907, 908, 910, 911, 912, 913, 916, 917, 922, 927, 934, 938, 939, 951, 952, 953, 957, 959, 960, 976, 977, 978, 980, 981, 985, 987, 988, 989, 990, 991, 992, 996, 997, 1005, 1006, 1010, 1023, 1025, 1030, 1031, 1036, 1039, 1046, 1047, 1048, 1049, 1052, 1053, 1054, 1060, 1070, 1078, 1090, 1093, 1094, 1098, 1101, 1108, 1109, 1110, 1111, 1113, 1114, 1115, 1116, 1117, 1118, 1119, 1122, 1123, 1124, 1126, 1132, 1141, 1143, 1144, 1145, 1146, 1155, 1182, 1185, 1188, 1189, 1191, 1192, 1193, 1195, 1204, 1206, 1207, 1215, 1216, 1217, 1218, 1219, 1220, 1225, 1228, 1229, 1233, 1236, 1237, 1238, 1239, 1240, 1243, 1254, 1255, 1259, 1265, 1267, 1268, 1270, 1272, 1277, 1278, 1290, 1291, 1293, 1309, 1327, 1346, 1376, 1432, 1526, 1560, 1570, 1573, 1579, 1581, 1585, 1588, 1593, 1610, 1611, 1632, 1642, 1650, 1656, 1657, 1662, 1680, 1700, 1714, 1718, 1722, 1735, 1739, 1766, 1767, 1777, 1778, 1779, 1782, 1791, 1795, 1796, 1806, 1812, 1816, 1817, 1819, 1826, 1828, 1848, 1850, 1854, 1856, 1857, 1862, 1866, 1883, 1885, 1911, 1913, 1917, 1919, 1932, 1934, 1947, 1951, 1955, 1966, 1969, 1976, 1977, 1978, 1983, 1985, 1998, 2003, 2004, 2014, 2019, 2020, 2036, 2037, 2041, 2052, 2074, 2075, 2077, 2090, 2091, 2093, 2148, 2162, 2163, 2177, 2182, 2187, 2188, 2189, 2196, 2197, 2198, 2200, 2232, 2244, 2249, 2256, 2258, 2261, 2266, 2267, 2274,

2275, 2276, 2279, 2281, 2288, 2290, 2293, 2316
German: 495, 635, 765, 846, 1130, 1166, 1271, 1280, 1352, 1353, 1366, 1416, 1500, 1556, 1630, 1702, 1703, 1761, 1833, 1888, 1923, 1927, 1928, 1980, 1981, 2009, 2017, 2095, 2226, 2243, 2255, 2265, 2309, 2336, 2346
Hungarian: 829
Italian: 994, 1140, 2230
Portuguese: 2222
Spanish: 1758

Index

PRIMARY TITLES

Included here are all titles by Maugham which occur in titles of articles or books or in the abstracts. References to foreign-language translations of Maugham titles are also listed. Numbers after each title refer to the item in the bibliography where the title appears.

ADORABLE JULIA [THEATRE; play]: 1966, 1969, 1976, 1978, 1983, 1998, 2003, 2004, 2020, 2232

Ah King: 1028, 1029, 1035, 1038, 1041, 1059, 1061, 1077, 1080, 1082, 1083, 1088, 1092, 1109, 1111, 1113, 1118, 1124, 1126, 1142, 1145, 1147, 1188

Ahtaat Asuinsijat [*The Narrow Corner*]: 1804, 1813

"The Alien Corn": 896, 915, 1353, 1694, 1715, 1719, 1752, 1754

THE ALIEN CORN (television adaptation): 2178

Altogether: See *East and West*

Amours singulières [*First Person Singular*]: 981, 991, 1006

"The Ant and the Grasshopper": 1860, 1877

L'Archipel aux sirènes [*The Trembling of a Leaf*]: 537, 548, 562, 606

The Art of Fiction: An Introduction to Ten Novels and Their Authors: See *Ten Novels and Their Authors*

"The Artistic Temperament of Stephen Carey": 1609, 1797, 1815, 2160

Ashenden: 724, 734, 736, 737, 740, 748, 749, 750, 751, 752, 758, 759, 764, 779, 787, 824, 857, 892, 1046, 1133, 2119, 2123, 2126, 2127, 2136, 2184, 2230, 2240, 2306

Avant le derby [*Home and Beauty*]: 1581, 1588, 1613

"The Back of Beyond": 1041

"Before the Party" [story]: 621, 793, 1279, 1900

BEFORE THE PARTY [play]: 1708, 1724, 1747, 1756, 1759, 1763, 1899

The Bishop's Apron: 40, 41, 42

"The Book-Bag": 1012, 1041, 1059, 1082, 1113

Books and You: 1383, 1386, 1393, 1397, 1402, 1403, 1409, 1412, 1415, 1419, 1424

The Breadwinner: 817, 821, 830, 833, 836, 842, 844, 847, 858, 861, 867, 870, 873, 879, 884, 899, 901, 904, 909, 918, 929, 931, 933, 935, 958, 959, 965, 966, 971, 972, 994, 1117, 1120, 1182, 1185, 1191, 1192, 1193, 1195, 1206, 1217, 1218, 1239, 1254, 1255, 1256, 1269, 1272, 1506, 1682, 1698, 1718, 1796, 1904, 1952, 1961, 1982, 2063, 2100, 2107, 2111, 2112, 2212, 2252, 2255

Caesar's Wife: 317, 318, 320, 324, 325, 326, 327, 332, 336, 337, 340, 349, 366, 373, 382, 392, 428, 472, 763, 1157, 1216, 1239, 1610, 2212, 2347

Cakes and Ale: 815, 819, 820, 822, 823, 826, 832, 838, 839, 843, 845, 850, 851, 854, 860, 862, 863, 868, 871, 872, 875, 877, 890, 900, 914, 916, 934, 936, 954, 968, 980, 992, 1005, 1023, 1056, 1219, 1232, 1279, 1283, 1348, 1418, 1471, 1517, 1592, 1689, 1690, 1704, 1912, 1977, 2014, 2037, 2043, 2044, 2047, 2058, 2060, 2064, 2067, 2085, 2168, 2183, 2208, 2210, 2231, 2251, 2252, 2321, 2331, 2346, 2351

The Camel's Back: 481, 483, 486, 487, 490, 500, 502, 504, 518, 523, 524, 526, 527, 530, 532

Carnet d'un écrivain [*A Writer's Notebook*]: 1856

Caroline: 275, 276, 277, 278, 279, 281, 283, 284, 285, 286, 287, 288, 289, 290, 291, 292, 293, 294, 295, 354, 376, 599, 601,

1116, 1706, 1740, 1900, 2063, 2179, 2256, 2258, 2261, 2270, 2273, 2297

The Casuarina Tree: 608, 609, 610, 611, 614, 616, 617, 621, 623, 624, 625, 626, 627, 629, 634, 636, 653, 675, 726, 767, 768, 769, 773, 776, 813, 990, 1476, 1526, 1796

Catalina: 1643, 1662, 1663, 1664, 1665, 1666, 1667, 1668, 1670, 1671, 1674, 1675, 1676, 1679, 1683, 1686, 1689, 1690, 1692, 1693, 1696, 1700, 1728, 1749, 1881, 1988, 1991, 1994, 1995, 1997, 2001, 2002, 2015, 2028, 2210, 2242

Le Cercle [*The Circle*]: 714, 719, 727, 728, 729, 738, 754, 976, 977, 996, 1010, 1025

A Choice of Kipling's Prose: 1854, 1863, 1889, 1892, 1895, 1907, 1909, 1914, 1921, 1922, 1925, 1932, 1935, 1936, 1937, 1942, 1957, 1959

Christmas Holiday: 1337, 1339, 1340, 1341, 1342, 1344, 1345, 1347, 1348, 1349, 1350, 1354, 1355, 1358, 1359, 1360, 1361, 1365, 1368, 1369, 1370, 1371, 1380, 1381, 1404, 1408, 1418, 1517, 1556, 1573, 1593, 2094

The Circle: 393, 394, 396, 398, 399, 404, 405, 406, 407, 410, 413, 416, 417, 418, 420, 422, 424, 425, 429, 432, 433, 435, 436, 437, 438, 439, 440, 441, 444, 472, 475, 492, 506, 522, 596, 637, 641, 661, 719, 720, 727, 728, 729, 738, 753, 754, 770, 772, 781, 784, 792, 794, 803, 804, 806, 828, 918, 932, 942, 946, 954, 967, 969, 970, 976, 977, 996, 1010, 1025, 1048, 1050, 1094, 1117, 1157, 1239, 1254, 1283, 1297, 1306, 1312, 1313, 1325, 1331, 1508, 1523, 1527, 1544, 1562, 1596, 1626, 1682, 1690, 1697, 1698, 1717, 1720, 1753, 1787, 1796, 1811, 1841, 1852, 1874, 1880, 1901, 1952, 1961, 1977, 1979, 1982, 1990, 2000, 2017, 2021, 2063, 2079, 2144, 2195, 2212, 2239, 2252, 2255, 2271, 2302, 2347

"The Colonel's Lady": 1625, 1644, 1694, 1715, 1719, 1752, 1754

Colui che guadagna il pane [*The Breadwinner*]: 994

La Comédienne [*Theatre;* novel]: 1819

The Complete Short Stories: See *The Complete Short Stories of W. Somerset Maugham*

The Complete Short Stories of W. Somerset Maugham: 1859, 1861, 1939, 1944

Constance [*The Constant Wife*]: 2177, 2182, 2187, 2188, 2196, 2197, 2198

The Constant Wife: 597, 598, 603, 612, 615, 630, 632, 637, 652, 656, 658, 660, 662, 667, 669, 679, 680, 682, 687, 694, 695, 697, 700, 703, 704, 706, 708, 798, 812, 869, 1098, 1117, 1157, 1231, 1239, 1241, 1244, 1256, 1333, 1336, 1822, 1825, 1838, 1839, 1842, 1851, 1858, 1873, 1902, 1982, 1988, 2063, 2144, 2177, 2180, 2182, 2186, 2187, 2188, 2189, 2196, 2197, 2198, 2200, 2212, 2213, 2252, 2255, 2347

Cosmopolitans: 1183, 1184, 1186, 1187, 1190, 1194, 1196, 1197, 1199, 1200, 1205, 1210, 1211, 1212, 1213, 1220, 1237, 1238, 2339, 2340, 2342, 2343, 2344, 2348

"The Creative Impulse": 888, 896, 897, 2235

Creatures of Circumstance: 1620, 1621, 1622, 1624, 1627, 1628, 1631, 1635, 1637, 1638, 1641, 1644, 1645, 1651, 1657, 1658, 1848, 1862, 1883, 1885, 2076, 2082, 2084, 2087

"The Decline and Fall of the Detective Story": 1943, 2132, 2355

Don Fernando: 1150, 1151, 1152, 1154, 1156, 1158, 1159, 1160, 1165, 1167, 1168, 1169, 1170, 1171, 1172, 1174, 1177, 1179, 1180, 1215, 1517, 1977, 2053, 2055, 2117

"The Door of Opportunity": 1029, 1080, 1126, 1142

Dorothee [Jane; play]: 1913, 1919, 1934, 1947, 1951

East and West: 1112, 1121, 1127, 1128, 1131, 1134, 1136, 1138, 1139, 1204, 1207, 1646

East of Suez: 446, 447, 448, 452, 454, 455, 456, 457, 458, 459, 461, 463, 467, 473, 474, 476, 478, 485, 492, 503, 506, 507, 519, 525, 547, 1239, 1377, 1945, 1952, 1953, 2000, 2212, 2347

Ei Maistu Elämältä [*Cakes and Ale*]: 2044

Elämän Kahle [*Of Human Bondage*]: 2164

Encore: 1860, 1865, 1877

L'Envoûte [*The Moon and Sixpence*]: 722, 741, 744, 761

"Episode": 1638

The Explorer [novel]: 47, 58, 94, 116, 119, 134, 370, 1601, 1730

The Explorer [play]: 53, 57, 63, 68, 70, 71, 72, 73, 81, 95, 97, 98, 106, 129, 135, 227, 228, 229, 230, 231, 232, 235, 1239

"The Facts of Life": 1682, 1694, 1715, 1719, 1752, 1786

"The Fall of Edward Barnard": 443, 537, 575, 1204, 2163, 2235

La Femme dans la jungle [*Ah King*]: 1126

Le Fil du rasoir [*The Razor's Edge*]: 1632, 1866
First Person Singular: 885, 888, 893, 896, 897, 898, 915, 920, 921, 925, 944, 947, 955, 961, 962, 963, 964, 975, 978, 981, 1006, 1030, 1070, 1101, 1108, 1119
"Flotsam and Jetsam": 1645
For Services Rendered: 973, 984, 998, 999, 1000, 1001, 1003, 1008, 1016, 1019, 1022, 1024, 1034, 1043, 1049, 1051, 1055, 1064, 1067, 1071, 1084, 1086, 1091, 1096, 1099, 1104, 1157, 1216, 1239, 1279, 1336, 1597, 1698, 1952, 1982, 2000, 2063, 2149, 2212, 2214
"The Force of Circumstance": 608, 621, 624, 793
France at War: 1387, 1392, 1395, 1398, 1399, 1400, 1401, 1407, 1425, 1426
Le Fugitif [*The Narrow Corner*]: 1039
The Gentleman in the Parlour: 816, 825, 827, 831, 834, 835, 837, 841, 848, 852, 853, 856, 859, 864, 866, 874, 876, 1334, 1335, 1351, 1356, 1357, 1379, 1988, 2053, 2055
"Gigolo and Gigolette": 1420, 1860, 1877
Grace: 160, 162, 165, 166, 167, 168, 169, 172, 173, 174, 175, 177, 203, 214, 215, 1239, 2212
Great Novelists and Their Novels: 1660, 1661, 1669, 1672, 1684, 1687, 1701
"The Hairless Mexican": 759
The Hero: 18, 19
"His Excellency": 740
Home and Beauty: 319, 323, 333, 338, 339, 341, 342, 343, 344, 345, 348, 353, 358, 363, 365, 383, 384, 821, 847, 918, 1116, 1239, 1487, 1489, 1491, 1581, 1588, 1613, 1773, 1782, 1783, 1808, 1846, 1977, 2257
The Hour Before the Dawn: 1473, 1474, 1481, 1482, 1485, 1488, 1492, 1493, 1689
"The Human Element": 1076
Il suffit d'une nuit [*Up at the Villa*]: 1806
Introduction to Modern English and American Literature: 1497, 1498, 1499
Jack Straw: 54, 61, 62, 64, 66, 68, 69, 74, 76, 77, 78, 79, 80, 82, 83, 84, 88, 91, 93, 100, 101, 102, 103, 104, 108, 110, 155, 209, 226, 475, 1114, 1239, 1352
"Jane" [story]: 888, 896, 915
Jane [play]: 1619, 1629, 1634, 1647, 1653, 1849, 1851, 1864, 1868, 1871, 1875, 1879, 1884, 1896, 1897, 1911, 1913, 1934, 1947, 1951, 2216, 2227, 2311, 2329
Kirjava Huntu [*The Painted Veil*]: 2029
Kirje [*The Letter*; play]: 2071
"The Kite": 1694, 1715, 1719, 1752
Kuu ja Kupariraha [*The Moon and Sixpence*]: 1748
Lady Frederick: 44, 45, 46, 48, 49, 50, 51, 52, 62, 65, 68, 69, 70, 74, 77, 84, 85, 86, 87, 92, 94, 101, 102, 155, 157, 199, 209, 216, 226, 522, 1114, 1157, 1239, 1598, 1604, 1652, 2063
The Land of the Blessed Virgin: 38, 39, 371, 379, 385, 402
The Land of Promise: 236, 238, 239, 240, 241, 242, 246, 247, 248, 249, 250, 251, 252, 254, 255, 256, 257, 258, 259, 282, 301, 302, 472, 918, 1115, 1239, 1654, 1716, 2131, 2212
Landed Gentry: See *Grace*
Larger than Life: See Theatre [play]
"The Letter" [story]: 621, 627, 636, 792, 1163, 1204
The Letter [play]: 639, 640, 641, 645, 646, 647, 651, 657, 659, 663, 665, 666, 668, 670, 671, 674, 677, 678, 681, 683, 688, 690, 693, 696, 701, 702, 707, 709, 710, 756, 771, 775, 785, 786, 795, 796, 797, 801, 802, 804, 805, 807, 809, 814, 849, 869, 908, 911, 913, 916, 922, 939, 1098, 1110, 1123, 1141, 1239, 1698, 2071, 2072, 2080
La Lettre [*The Letter*; play]: 771, 775, 786, 796, 801, 802, 809, 908, 913, 922, 939, 1110, 1123
Liza of Lambeth: 1, 2, 3, 4, 5, 6, 8, 9, 10, 11, 15, 17, 43, 107, 401, 403, 412, 414, 415, 419, 421, 442, 552, 730, 942, 954, 1052, 1157, 1232, 1418, 1681, 1704, 1796, 1912, 1923, 1993, 2017, 2036, 2204, 2210, 2241, 2242, 2252, 2259
Loaves and Fishes: 212, 213, 218, 219, 220, 221, 222, 234, 1832, 2212
"Looking Back": 2322
"Lord Mountdrago": 1394
"The Lotus Eater": 1382
Love in a Cottage: 311, 312, 313, 314, 315
"The Luncheon": 1196
"Mackintosh": 434, 443, 684
The Magician: 55, 56, 59, 96, 99, 119, 130, 395, 1309, 1376, 1601, 2036, 2075, 2078, 2091, 2096
Le Magicien [*The Magician*]: 1309
The Making of a Saint: 7, 8, 10, 11, 12, 13, 15, 465, 954, 1253, 1601, 2036
A Man of Honour: 23, 24, 25, 26, 27, 29, 30, 31, 32, 33, 34, 37, 44, 46, 115, 122, 225, 226, 956, 1610, 1682, 2212, 2244
The Mask and the Face: 1033, 1044, 1045, 1065, 1068, 1072, 1085, 1087, 1097, 1100, 1105, 1107
The Maugham Reader: 1774, 1775, 1781, 1799, 1801, 1810

Maugham's Choice of Kipling's Best: See *A Choice of Kipling's Prose*
The Merry-Go-Round: 35, 36, 506, 1601, 2153, 2238
The Mixture as Before: 1382, 1384, 1385, 1388, 1389, 1390, 1391, 1394, 1396, 1405, 1410, 1411, 1413, 1414, 1417, 1420, 1423, 1988
The Moon and Sixpence [novel]: 316, 321, 322, 328, 329, 331, 334, 335, 346, 347, 350, 351, 352, 355, 356, 357, 359, 360, 361, 362, 364, 368, 369, 370, 374, 395, 503, 506, 587, 591, 594, 602, 712, 721, 722, 730, 741, 744, 761, 779, 819, 916, 971, 985, 989, 1011, 1056, 1166, 1232, 1476, 1515, 1517, 1545, 1594, 1682, 1705, 1729, 1733, 1734, 1737, 1738, 1742, 1748, 1757, 1764, 1765, 1772, 1794, 1836, 1912, 2036, 2066, 2083, 2210, 2215, 2235, 2260, 2277, 2321
The Moon and Sixpence [opera]: 2083, 2092, 2109
The Moon and Sixpence [play]: 534, 539, 543, 549, 559, 565, 569, 585
"Mr. Know-All": 1196, 1770, 1821, 1844
Mr. Maugham Himself: 1965, 1971, 1986, 1987, 2011, 2030
"Mrs. Beamish": 1979, 2079
Mrs. Craddock: 20, 21, 22, 28, 330, 370, 380, 479, 730, 735, 916, 1418, 1601, 1680, 2031, 2036, 2074, 2086, 2090, 2098, 2099, 2102, 2104, 2106, 2108, 2125, 2210, 2244, 2312, 2338
Mrs. Dot: 60, 62, 68, 69, 75, 89, 90, 105, 183, 188, 189, 190, 193, 199, 200, 201, 207, 209, 522, 1114, 1239, 1716, 1820, 2130
The Narrow Corner: 974, 979, 982, 983, 986, 993, 995, 1002, 1004, 1007, 1011, 1014, 1015, 1017, 1020, 1021, 1026, 1031, 1036, 1039, 1053, 1060, 1074, 1101, 1133, 1155, 1232, 1526, 1772, 1785, 1788, 1794, 1796, 1804, 1805, 1813, 1988, 2210
"Neil MacAdam": 1080, 1092, 1147
The Noble Spaniard: 112, 114, 121, 125, 128, 133, 137, 139, 140, 143, 145, 146, 147, 148, 149, 154, 156, 159, 2129
Nyt ja Ennen [*Then and Now*]: 2051
Of Human Bondage: 260, 261, 262, 263, 264, 265, 266, 267, 268, 269, 270, 271, 272, 273, 274, 330, 370, 451, 554, 566, 588, 590, 591, 594, 607, 609, 619, 730, 743, 746, 748, 818, 819, 822, 829, 840, 888, 916, 925, 942, 979, 1052, 1102, 1130, 1131, 1163, 1173, 1175, 1225, 1228, 1229, 1232, 1247, 1258, 1259, 1264, 1265, 1267, 1277, 1278, 1279, 1283, 1287, 1289, 1292, 1309, 1418, 1471, 1475, 1479, 1502, 1513, 1515, 1556, 1583, 1585, 1589, 1590, 1601, 1606, 1609, 1614, 1651, 1655, 1704, 1767, 1781, 1793, 1796, 1797, 1815, 1836, 1888, 1912, 1987, 1988, 1993, 2017, 2019, 2021, 2037, 2038, 2093, 2097, 2116, 2121, 2124, 2138, 2146, 2153, 2156, 2160, 2162, 2164, 2175, 2183, 2204, 2207, 2208, 2210, 2229, 2233, 2238, 2245, 2252, 2350
"An Official Position": 1420
On a Chinese Screen: 445, 450, 464, 468, 469, 470, 496, 497, 498, 499, 503, 512, 513, 793, 1047, 1054, 1146, 1189, 2053, 2055, 2069, 2265
Orientations: 14, 15, 16, 954
Our Betters: 296, 297, 298, 299, 300, 303, 304, 305, 306, 307, 308, 309, 310, 480, 484, 493, 494, 505, 508, 509, 510, 514, 515, 516, 517, 522, 525, 596, 637, 715, 717, 723, 725, 757, 760, 766, 943, 1116, 1239, 1595, 1605, 1698, 1753, 1783, 1841, 1880, 1956, 1961, 1977, 1982, 1988, 2021, 2063, 2144, 2202, 2212, 2255, 2302, 2347, 2354
"The Outstation": 610, 611, 620, 621, 627, 769, 793, 813, 2095, 2235, 2254, 2320
"P & O": 611
Pääviotto [*Sheppey*]: 1214, 1567
The Painted Veil [novel]: 540, 542, 546, 547, 551, 554, 556, 558, 561, 563, 564, 566, 567, 568, 570, 572, 573, 574, 578, 583, 587, 592, 593, 600, 604, 606, 618, 628, 631, 633, 676, 730, 789, 954, 987, 1232, 1526, 1673, 1678, 1796, 2029, 2037, 2210, 2277, 2312
The Painted Veil [play]: 903, 919, 928, 930, 937, 949, 950, 1239
La Passe Dangereuse [*The Painted Veil*]: 600, 604, 618, 631
Le Pélican [*The Breadwinner*]: 1182, 1191, 1192, 1193, 1195, 1217, 1254, 1255
Penelope: 111, 117, 120, 123, 124, 127, 131, 136, 138, 141, 142, 144, 150, 151, 152, 153, 158, 171, 192, 195, 200, 201, 208, 209, 609, 1115, 1133, 1239, 1596, 1905, 2185
The Perfect Gentleman: 237, 243
The Plays of W. Somerset Maugham: 489
"Pluie" ["Rain"; story]: 529
Pluie [Rain; play]; 644, 650, 654, 655, 673, 691, 692, 792, 916, 1178, 1181
Plus ça change [*Then and Now*]: 1739
Points of View: 2115, 2116, 2118, 2122, 2128, 2133, 2141, 2142, 2143, 2148, 2151, 2157, 2159, 2169, 2170, 2172, 2173, 2174, 2176
Princess September and the Nightingale: 1334, 1335, 1351, 1356, 1357, 1362, 1379

Pyhä Liekki [*The Sacred Flame*]: 855, 1248, 1250, 2134
QUARTET: 1694, 1715, 1719, 1751, 1752, 1754
"Rain" [story]: 399, 426, 434, 442, 443, 471, 537, 684, 793, 1130, 1198, 1204, 1583, 1732, 2145, 2146, 2150, 2235, 2277
RAIN [play]: 449, 453, 460, 462, 477, 482, 488, 502, 511, 533, 538, 544, 547, 553, 556, 557, 560, 571, 579, 584, 586, 643, 644, 648, 649, 650, 654, 655, 672, 673, 689, 691, 692, 698, 699, 705, 772, 804, 1098, 1161, 1162, 1176, 1201, 1203, 1239, 1254, 1478, 1490, 1495, 1525, 1540, 1550, 1551, 1563, 1565, 1569, 2201, 2246
The Razor's Edge: 1512, 1513, 1514, 1515, 1516, 1517, 1518, 1519, 1522, 1524, 1528, 1532, 1534, 1535, 1536, 1537, 1538, 1541, 1546, 1547, 1548, 1553, 1555, 1560, 1572, 1594, 1602, 1611, 1618, 1632, 1633, 1642, 1649, 1650, 1656, 1677, 1688, 1691, 1699, 1796, 1831, 1833, 1866, 1912, 2175, 2210, 2252, 2312, 2353
"Red": 423, 443, 471
Rencontres et hasards [*Creatures of Circumstance*]: 1883
"Romance": 470
La Ronde de l'amour [*Cakes and Ale*]: 980, 1023, 2014
"The Round Dozen": 888
The Sacred Flame: 711, 716, 718, 732, 733, 739, 742, 745, 755, 762, 774, 777, 778, 782, 788, 790, 791, 799, 810, 811, 846, 865, 880, 882, 883, 886, 891, 894, 902, 905, 907, 910, 912, 917, 927, 938, 951, 952, 953, 957, 960, 1078, 1130, 1149, 1216, 1239, 1248, 1250, 1507, 1564, 1603, 1682, 1698, 1870, 1872, 1886, 1898, 2134, 2212
SADE [RAIN; play]: 1201, 2246
SADIE THOMPSON [musical comedy]: 1525, 1540, 1550, 1551, 1563, 1565, 1569
"Salvatore": 1196
"Sanatorium": 1645, 1770, 1821, 1844
Sattuman Satoa [*Creatures of Circumstance*]: 2087
"Schiffbrüchig": 1232
The Selected Novels of W. Somerset Maugham: 1980
Selected Prefaces and Introductions of W. Somerset Maugham: 2237, 2248, 2263, 2264
Servitude humaine [*Of Human Bondage*]: 1225, 1228, 2019
Sheppey: 1027, 1032, 1042, 1058, 1062, 1063, 1066, 1075, 1089, 1095, 1103, 1106, 1122, 1125, 1143, 1157, 1202, 1216, 1232, 1239, 1279, 1510, 1520, 1521, 1529, 1530, 1531, 1539, 1542, 1549, 1552, 1558, 1698, 1961, 1982, 2000, 2166, 2212, 2222, 2224, 2345
Six Comedies: 1223
Smith: 113, 118, 122, 126, 132, 161, 178, 179, 180, 181, 182, 184, 187, 191, 194, 197, 198, 202, 204, 210, 211, 223, 224, 1115, 1239, 1636, 1682, 2063, 2212
"Some Novelists I Have Known": 1894, 1917, 1926
Le Sortilège malais [*The Casuarina Tree*]: 768, 776
Strictly Personal: 1431, 1433, 1434, 1435, 1439, 1445, 1454, 1457, 1458, 1462, 1466, 1469, 1486, 1494
Suezista Itään [*East of Suez*]: 1953
The Summing Up: 1283, 1284, 1285, 1286, 1287, 1289, 1290, 1294, 1295, 1296, 1298, 1299, 1300, 1301, 1302, 1304, 1305, 1307, 1308, 1310, 1314, 1315, 1316, 1317, 1318, 1320, 1321, 1323, 1324, 1326, 1328, 1329, 1330, 1346, 1416, 1418, 1585, 1826, 1840, 1867, 1888, 1962, 1987, 2037, 2050, 2066, 2117, 2153, 2157, 2208
"The Taipan": 2265
Tellers of Tales: 1338, 1343, 1364, 1367, 1374, 1375, 1378, 1831
Ten Novels and Their Authors: 1963, 1972, 2007, 2013, 2024, 2032, 2033, 2034, 2035, 2039, 2045, 2048, 2052, 2059, 2065, 2068
The Tenth Man: 163, 164, 170, 176, 185, 186, 205, 206, 223, 408, 780, 1239, 2212
Theatre [novel]: 1221, 1222, 1224, 1226, 1227, 1230, 1232, 1234, 1235, 1236, 1242, 1245, 1246, 1247, 1249, 1252, 1257, 1260, 1261, 1263, 1264, 1269, 1273, 1274, 1275, 1276, 1291, 1303, 1819, 1835, 1837, 1847, 1878, 1882, 1891
THEATRE [play]: 1428, 1438, 1444, 1453, 1459, 1463, 1470, 1477, 1496, 1784, 1792, 1803, 1814, 1966, 1969, 1976, 1978, 1983, 1998, 2003, 2004, 2020, 2167, 2232
Then and Now: 1570, 1571, 1572, 1574, 1576, 1577, 1578, 1579, 1582, 1584, 1586, 1587, 1591, 1592, 1599, 1600, 1607, 1608, 1611, 1615, 1616, 1689, 1714, 1722, 1735, 1739, 1766, 2042, 2046, 2051, 2054, 2056, 2057, 2061
Too Many Husbands: See *Home and Beauty*
The Travel Books of W. Somerset Maugham: 2053, 2055
Traveller's Library: 1037, 1040, 1069, 1073, 1079

"The Treasure": 1432
The Trembling of a Leaf: 397, 409, 411, 423, 426, 430, 431, 434, 442, 443, 451, 471, 535, 536, 537, 545, 548, 562, 575, 577, 580, 581, 589, 605, 606, 726, 730, 916, 988, 1796, 1988, 2025, 2145, 2161, 2191, 2193, 2203, 2205, 2277
TRIO: 1770, 1781, 1821, 1824, 1844
The Unattainable: See *Caroline*
"The Unconquered": 1621, 1625, 2163
The Unknown: 367, 372, 375, 376, 377, 378, 381, 386, 387, 388, 389, 390, 391, 425, 713, 1239, 1796, 1982, 2212, 2224, 2244, 2347
Up at the Villa: 1430, 1436, 1437, 1441, 1442, 1443, 1446, 1447, 1448, 1451, 1452, 1455, 1456, 1461, 1465, 1467, 1471, 1689, 1791, 1795, 1806, 1812, 1817, 2194
Vacances de Noël [*Christmas Holiday*]: 1573
The Vagrant Mood: 1887, 1890, 1893, 1894, 1903, 1906, 1908, 1910, 1916, 1917, 1918, 1924, 1926, 1929, 1933, 1940, 1941, 1943, 1954, 1955, 1958, 1960, 2117, 2170
Veitsen Terällä [*The Razor's Edge*]: 1688
"The Verger": 1770, 1821, 1844
"The Vessel of Wrath": 1082, 1088, 1147
"The Vice-Consul": 470
"Winter Cruise": 1860, 1877
The Works of W. Somerset Maugham: 1134, 1137
A Writer's Notebook: 1707, 1709, 1710, 1711, 1712, 1713, 1721, 1723, 1725, 1731, 1736, 1741, 1744, 1745, 1746, 1750, 1755, 1760, 1768, 1769, 1771, 1777, 1778, 1779, 1816, 1850, 1856, 1987, 2157
"The Yellow Streak": 608, 620, 621
Ympra [*The Circle*]: 1811